PRENTICE HALL MANAGEMENT SERIES

Bowin/Harvey: Human Resource Management: An Experiential Approach 2/e
Caproni: The Practical Coach: Management Skills for Everyday Life 1/e
Carrell/Heavrin: Labor Relations and Collective Bargaining 6/e
Coulter: Strategic Management in Action 2/e
Coutler: Entrepreneurship in Action 1/e
Daniels/Radebaugh: International Business 9/e
David: Strategic Management: Concepts and Cases 8/e
David: Cases in Strategic Management 8/e
David: Concepts in Strategic Management 8/e
Dessler: Management: Leading People and Organizations in the 21st Century 2/e
DiBella: Learning Practices: Assessment and Action for Organizational Improvement (OD Series)
Ghemawat: Strategy and the Business Landscape: Core Concepts 1/e
Gomez–Mejia/Balkin/Cardy: Managing Human Resources 3/e
Greer: Strategic Human Resource Management 2/e
Harvey/Brown: Experiential Approach to Organization Development 6/e
Hersey/Blanchard/Johnson: Management of Organizational Behavior: Leading Human Resources 8/e
Howell/Costley: Understanding Behaviors for Effective Leadership 1/e
Hunger/Wheelen: Essentials of Strategic Management 2/e
Hunsaker: Training in Managerial Skills 1/e
Jones: Organizational Theory 3/e
Mische: Strategic Renewal: Becoming a High-Performance Organization 1/e
Martocchio: Strategic Compensation 2/e
Narayanan: Managing Technology and Innovation for Competitive Advantage 1/e
Osland/Kolb/Rubin: The Organizational Behavior Reader 7/e
Osland/Kolb/Rubin: Organizational Behavior: An Experiential Approach 7/e
Robbins: Organizational Behavior 9/e
Robbins/DeCenzo: Fundamentals of Management 3/e
Sanyal: International Management 1/e
Sloane/Whitney: Labor Relations 10/e
Thompson: The Mind and Heart of the Negotiator 2/e
Tompkins: Cases in Management and Organizational Behavior Vol. I 1/e
Wexley/Latham: Developing and Training Human Resources in Organizations 3/e

Other Books of Interest

de Kluyver: Strategic Thinking: An Executive Perspective
Ghemawat: Strategy and the Business Landscape 1/e
Minztberg/Quinn: Readings in The Strategy Process 3/e
Wheelen/Hunger: Strategic Management and Business Policy 7/e

MANAGING TECHNOLOGY AND INNOVATION
FOR COMPETITIVE ADVANTAGE

MANAGING TECHNOLOGY AND INNOVATION FOR COMPETITIVE ADVANTAGE

❖   ❖   ❖

V. K. NARAYANAN

UNIVERSITY OF KANSAS

UPPER SADDLE RIVER, NEW JERSEY

Narayanan, V. K.
    Managing technology and innovation for competitive advantage / V. K. Narayanan.
    p. cm.
  ISBN 0-13-030506-5
    1. Technology—Management. I. Title.
  T49.5 N35 2000
  658.5—dc21   00-025288

VP/Editorial Director: James C. Boyd
Executive Editor: David Shafer
Managing Editor: Jennifer Glennon
Editorial Assistant: Kimberly Marsden
Assistant Editor: Michele Foresta
Executive Marketing Manager: Michael Campbell
Permissions Coordinator: Suzanne Grappi
Media Project Manager: Michele Faranda
Director of Production: Michael Weinstein
Manager, Production: Gail Steier de Acevedo
Production Coordinator: Kelly Warsak
Manufacturing Buyer: Natacha St. Hill Moore
Associate Director, Manufacturing: Vincent Scelta
Cover Design: Bruce Kenselaar
Full Service Composition: BookMasters, Inc.

10 9 8 7 6 5 4 3
ISBN 0-13-030506-5

To my great uncle and aunt, who saw me through my difficult years

BRIEF CONTENTS

Chapter 1   Introduction   1

PART I   THEORETICAL FOUNDATIONS   19

Chapter 2   Technological Environment   21
Chapter 3   Process of Technological Change: Innovation   59
Chapter 4   Process of Technology Change: Diffusion   95
Chapter 5   Technology and Competition   119
Chapter 6   Process Innovation, Value Chains, and Organization   157

PART II   TECHNOLOGY STRATEGY: BASICS   195

Chapter 7   Technology Intelligence   197
Chapter 8   Technology Strategy: Overview   236
Chapter 9   Technology Strategy: Collaborative Mode   266

PART III   DOMAINS OF TECHNOLOGY STRATEGY   303

Chapter 10   Appropriation of Technology   305
Chapter 11   Deployment in New Products   335
Chapter 12   Deployment of Technology in the Value Chain   376

PART IV   ROLE OF GENERAL MANAGEMENT   417

Chapter 13   Organizing for Innovation   419
Chapter 14   Intellectual Property Strategy   441
Chapter 15   Project Valuation and Financing   460

CONTENTS

Preface   xvii

CHAPTER 1   Introduction   1

Technology: Definition and Characteristics   5
  Levels of Development   6
  Technology as Socially Constructed   6

Management of Technology   7

Two Complementary Perspectives in Management   9
  Market-Based Views   9
  Resource-Based Views   10

Key Concepts   10
  Firm as a Value Chain   11
  Industries as Competitive Domains   12
  Forms of Technological Change   12
  Value Creation and Competitive Advantage   14

Major Themes in the Book   14
  Generic Applicability   14
  Interfacing Technology and Market Factors   14
  The Influence of Globalization   15
  Simultaneity of Competition and Collaboration   15
  Speed in Problem Solving   15
  Make or Buy   15
  Systemic View of Management   15
  Role of Learning   16
  Co-existence of High Tech and High Touch   16

Plan of the Book   16
  Chapter Layout   17
  How to Read the Book   18

PART I   THEORETICAL FOUNDATIONS   19

CHAPTER 2   Technological Environment   21

Environment and Technological Environment   23
  Levels of Environment   23
  Technological Environment   26

Actors in the Technological Environment   27
  Types of Actors   27
  Innovation Networks   29
  Cross-National Differences Among Networks   34

Changes in the Technological Environment   36
   Induced Changes   36
   Autonomous Changes   40

Major Current Developments in the Technological Environment   43
   Globalization   43
   Time Compression   47
   Technology Integration   50

Managerial Implications   56

Chapter Summary   57

CHAPTER 3   Process of Technology Change: Innovation   59

Overview of the Dynamics of Technological Change   63
   Firm Level   63
   Technology Level   64
   Implications for the Management of Technology   65

What Is Innovation?   67
   Definition   67
   Components of Innovation   68

Innovation Dynamics at the Firm Level   69
   Drivers of Innovation   69
   Process of Innovation   70
   Types of Innovation Outputs   72

Technology Evolution   75
   S-curve of Technology Evolution   76
   Technology Progression   80
   Levels of Technology Development   80
   Technology Change Agents   81
   Evolutionary Characteristics of Technological Change   81
   Uncertainty and Technological Insularity   83

Characteristics of Innovative Firms   85
   Organization Structure   87
   Resources   88
   Openness to External Information   88
   Informal Communication   88

Influence of Environmental Trends on Innovation   91

Managerial Implications   92

Chapter Summary   92

CHAPTER 4   Process of Technology Change: Diffusion   95

What Is Diffusion?   96

Dynamics of Diffusion   98
   S-curve Diffusion   99
   Reinvention   100
   Mechanisms of Diffusion   103

A Model of Innovation Adoption   104
  Shifting Characteristics of Adopters over Time   106
  Relative Importance of Decision Stage   107

Factors That Drive the Process of Diffusion   109
  Attributes of an Innovation   109
  Community Effects and Network Externalities   110
  Characteristics of the Population   114

Influence of Environmental Trends on Diffusion   116

Managerial Implications   116

Chapter Summary   117

CHAPTER 5   Technology and Competition   119
  Competitive Domains   121

Competitive Consequences of Technological Change   123
  Creation of New Products   123
  Changes in Value Chain   124
  Changes in Value Constellation   125
  Competitive Rivalry   127

Technological Characteristics of Competitive Domains   129
  Technological Opportunity   129
  Appropriability   129
  Resource Requirements   130
  Collateral Assets   132
  Institutional Milieu   132
  Speed   132

Dynamics of Change in Competitive Domains   133
  The Technology Emergence Phase   134
  Incremental Change Phase   142

A Framework for the Analysis of Technology Emergence   149

Influence of Environmental Trends on Competition   152

Managerial Implications   153

Chapter Summary   154

CHAPTER 6   Process Innovation, Value Chains, and Organization   157

Drivers of Change in Value Chain   160
  Process Innovation and Value Chain   160
  Drivers of Change   162

Modes of Value Chain Configuration   164
  Craft Production   164
  Mass Production   165
  Lean Production   169
  Mass Customization   170
  Differences Among the Four Modes of Value Chain Configuration   176

Value Chain Configuration and Organizational Characteristics   178
  Organizational Structure   *178*
  Organizational Process   *183*
  The Role of the Manager   *184*

Design of Work and Careers   185
  Design of Work   *185*
  Careers in Organizations   *187*

Influence of Environmental Trends   191

Managerial Implications   192

Chapter Summary   193

PART II   TECHNOLOGY STRATEGY: BASICS   195

CHAPTER 7   Technology Intelligence   197

Technology Intelligence   201
  Signals of New Technology   *201*
  What Is Technology Intelligence?   *201*
  Importance of Technology Intelligence   *202*
  Levels of Technology Intelligence   *204*
  External Versus Internal Technology Intelligence   *205*

Mapping Technology Environment   206
  Steps Involved in Mapping the Technology Environment   *207*
  Macro-Level Environment   *209*
  Industry-Level Environment   *210*

Mechanisms for Data Collection   213
  Challenges of Data Collection   *213*
  Organizational Arrangements for Gathering Data   *216*
  Key Principles for Data Collection   *220*
  The Role of the Technical Library   *220*

Analytic Tools   220
  Tools for Forecasting   *221*
  Assessment Tools   *230*

Managing Environmental Analysis in Organizations   231
  Herring Model   *232*
  Evaluation of Intelligence Gathering Activities   *233*

Contemporary Challenges in Mapping the Technology Environment   233

Managerial Implications   234

Chapter Summary   235

CHAPTER 8   Technology Strategy: Overview   236

Technology-Business Connection   239
  The Domains of Technology Choices   *239*
  Linkage Between Technology Choices and Competitive Advantage   *245*

Technology Strategy: Definition   249
  Technology Strategy and the Domains of Technology Choices   *251*
  The Role of the Chief Technology Officer   *251*

The Key Principles Underlying Technology Strategy   251
Objectives   251
Drivers   252
Decision Criteria   254

Technology Strategy Types   254
Appropriateness of Technology Strategy Types   256
Diversified Firms   256

A Framework for Formulating Technology Strategy   258
Strategic Diagnosis   258
Formulation of Technology Strategy   261
Crafting an Implementation Approach   262
Execution   263

Chapter Summary   263

CHAPTER 9   Technology Strategy: Collaborative Mode   266

Collaborative Arrangements: Definition and Trends   269
R&D Alliances   269
Marketing Alliances   269
Outsourcing Arrangements   270
Collaboration Between Small and Large Firms   271

Reasons for Collaborative Arrangements   271
Strategic   273
Operational   276

Collaborative Arrangements in Domains of Technology Strategy   278
Appropriation of Technology   278
Deployment of Technology in New Products   283
Deployment of Technology in the Value Chain   285
Marketing of Technology   288

Risks of Collaborative Activity   289
Intellectual Property Right Risk   289
Competitive Risk   290
Organizational Risk   291

Influence of Environmental Trends   295
R&D Collaboration in Japan and Europe   296
Global Technology Alliances   296

Managerial Implications   299
The Form of Collaborative Arrangement   299
Execution   300

Chapter Summary   301

PART III   DOMAINS OF TECHNOLOGY STRATEGY   303

CHAPTER 10   Appropriation of Technology   305

Evolution of Technology Appropriation Principles   309
Industrial R&D   309
From First to Third Generation   309

Third Generation Approach for the Appropriation of Technology   315
   The Concept of Project Portfolio   315
   Key Principles   316
   Process Involved in Arriving at the Portfolio of Technology
      Appropriation Projects   320

External Sourcing of Technological Capability   322
   Choice of External Sourcing Versus In-house Development   323
   Sources of External Technology   325
   Importing Technological Capabilities from External Sources   326

Productivity of In-House R&D   326
   Benchmarking   327
   Deployment of Quality Principles   328

The Influence of Environmental Trends   329
   Globalization of R&D   329

Managerial Implications   332

Chapter Summary   333

CHAPTER 11   Deployment in New Products   335

New Products: Definitions   340
   Types of New Products   340
   The Concept of Product Family   341

Means of Technology Infusion into Products   342
   Bundling   342
   Disruptive Technologies   345

Product Development: Principles and Process   347
   Strategic Context   347
   Technology Leadership Versus Followership   349
   Timing of New Product Launch   352
   Product Development Process   353

Approaches to Speeding Product Development   356
   Internal Organizational Mechanisms   358
   External Organizational Mechanisms   364
   Internal Technology Approaches   368
   External Technology   369

Influence of Environmental Trends   372
   Globalization of New Product Development   372

Chapter Summary   373

CHAPTER 12   Deployment of Technology in the Value Chain   376

Principles of Technology Deployment in the Value Chain   381
   Environmental Context   381
   Firm-Related Factors   383
   Decision Criteria   387
   Process   389

A Framework for Technology Alternatives in the Value Chain   389
    Computer-Integrated Manufacturing (CIM)   *391*
    Total Quality Management   *394*
    Socio-Technical Systems   *397*
    Re-engineering   *399*
    Outsourcing   *400*
    Buyer-Supplier Relationships and Supply Tiers   *401*
    Turnkey Projects   *402*

Implementation of Value Chain Reconfiguration   404
    Reinvention   *405*
    Mutual Adaptation   *405*
    J-curve of Implementation   *405*

Influence of Environmental Trends on Value Chains   407
    Globalization of Value Chains   *408*

Chapter Summary   414

PART IV   ROLE OF GENERAL MANAGEMENT   417

CHAPTER 13   Organizing for Innovation   419

Organizational Mechanisms for Innovation   421
    Different Characteristics of Organization Designs for Innovation   *421*
    Contemporary Mechanisms of Organizing for Innovation   *425*

Principles and Process of Organizing   430
    The Choice of Organizational Mechanism   *430*
    Managing Linkages   *433*

Characteristics of Continuously Innovative Organizations   435

Role of Leadership   438

Chapter Summary   439

CHAPTER 14   Intellectual Property Strategy   441

Intellectual Property   444

Generic Mechanisms for Intellectual Property Protection   445
    Product-Market Actions   *446*
    Continual Innovation   *447*

U.S. Intellectual Property System   448
    The U.S. Patent System   *448*
    The U.S. Copyright System   *450*
    Trade Secret Protection   *451*
    Trademark Protection   *452*

The Challenges of Globalization   454
    Patent Protection   *455*
    Copyright   *457*
    Trademarks   *457*
    Gray Markets   *457*

Managerial Implications   458

Chapter Summary   458

CHAPTER 15   Project Valuation and Financing   460

Project Valuation   463

  Project Life Cycle   463
  Project Valuation   466
  Option Pricing Models   469

Intellectual Capital   475

Financing   478

  Fundamental Challenges in Financing   478
  Sources of Financing   479
  Financing a Start-Up   480
  Financial Projects in Large Firms   483

Market Signaling   484

Influence of Environmental Trends   485

Managerial Implications   486

  Project Level   486
  Chief Technology Officer   486

Chapter Summary   488

Index   491

This book originated from my experiences at the University of Kansas after nearly a decade of delivering a coherent *strategic* view of technology management. The first time I taught a course on technology—in 1985 to a group of MBA and doctoral students—many of my colleagues viewed the course as a one-time offering that served to satisfy my interests rather than fulfill any function useful to managers. However, the situation began to change during the 1990s; partly because of the push by AACSB and partly because of the interest among engineers and managers who were enrolled in the evening MBA program. The course became a stable elective in the KU MBA program.

From a pedagogical point of view, the course offered three major challenges. First, the field was evolving, and there were numerous approaches to dealing with the content of technology. Some viewed it as operations; others as new product development; and still others as IT, R&D, or innovation. In my view, a strategic view of technology was lacking in these approaches. Second, my own research on technology intelligence, large scale high technology programs such as the space station, valuation of technology and fast cycle projects has left me profoundly dissatisfied with the state of development of the literature on technology and strategy. Third, others such as Burgelman and Richard Rosenbloom were arguing for a strategic view and had developed anthologies to argue their point. Although I learned a lot from their works, my students were without an integrated view of technology, which they repeatedly noted in the comments they provided at the end of the course. This book was crafted to deliver an integrated strategic view of technology.

I have emphasized five major themes throughout the book. First, I have taken the position that technology and innovation are value drivers and that management decisions should be anchored in the fundamental objective of creating competitive advantage. The advantage may come from innovation and imitation and will depend on both market factors and firm resources. Second, I have emphasized an open systems view of management and have underscored the role of environment in management decisions. Indeed, three environmental trends—globalization, time compression, and technology integration—are emphasized throughout the book. Third, I speak to the general manager and, therefore, the big picture is emphasized over the details of any specific approach. Fourth, I have underscored the importance of organizational learning—through scanning, by doing, reflecting, and analyzing—as a critical process in the management of technology. Finally, there is bootstrapping between theory and practice. I believe that concepts are useful to managers and have not shied away from presenting them. All these themes reflect the point of view I elaborated in earlier works: *Macroenvironmental Analysis* (with Liam Fahey) and *Organization Theory: A Strategic Approach* (with Raghu Nath); they have resonated well with my experienced students on whom I tested much of the material presented in the book.

I owe an intellectual debt to three scholars, who have contributed to my thinking about technology over the years. Although my interest in technology dates back to my (engineering) undergraduate student days, it was Professor Sam Doctors who, during my doctoral program at the University of Pittsburgh, made me aware of the management of technology as an academic field of inquiry. While at Pitt, I also had the opportunity to learn about futurism and strategy from William R. King and innovation from Dennis Slevin; their courses incorporated a heavy dose of issues dealing with management of technology.

There are numerous individuals who helped me shape this manuscript. First, Dave Bodde, then at Mid-West Research Institute, but currently at the University of Missouri at Kansas City, first crystallized for me the challenges of the three major environmental drivers—globalization, time compression, and technology integration; I have used these drivers as one of the anchors of the book. Second, the ideas of technology environment and intelligence gathering presented here are an outgrowth of the work done with Liam Fahey, who not only commented upon many of the chapters, but also acted as a cheerleader during the period when the manuscript took shape. Third, Dean Schroeder (Valparaiso University) infected me with his enthusiasm, gave copious but challenging comments to many of the chapters, and indeed was an effective coach throughout the writing of the book. Fourth, I benefited from the comments of Jay Paap and Jan Herring, who generously gave their ideas to the chapter on environmental intelligence, and George Pinches, who critiqued an earlier version of the chapter on financing. Finally, two of my former doctoral students—Pol Hermann (now at Iowa State University) and Dick Firth (currently at the Rochester Institute of Technology)—helped me with many of the boxes in the book, an immense task indeed. Further, Dick not only critiqued but also tested many of the chapters in his classes.

In addition, the following reviewers gave me extensive comments on earlier drafts of several chapters:

Ramesh Sharda (Oklahoma State University)
Dudley Dewhirst (University of Tennessee)
Linda Salchenberger (Loyola University)
Robert Mason (Case Western Reserve University)
Jon Beard (University of Richmond)
Fariborz Partovi (Drexel University)
Rebecca Henderson (MIT)
Dennis M. Anderson (Bentley College)

I gratefully acknowledge their help, but note that the responsibility for any errors is completely mine.

Writing a monograph of this kind is at times frustrating and always lonely. The task was made enjoyable by the two individuals in my life: my wife Sunanda, who despite her own career, made sure I finished the book; and my son Shriram whose childlike questions about this enterprise served as the best motivator for completing the monograph.

Supplemental Material

There is an accompanying Instructor's Manual available on a CD-ROM. In addition there is a Prentice Hall Companion Web site featuring an interactive and exciting online Student Study Guide. Students can access multiple-choice, true/false, and Internet-based essay questions that accompany each chapter in the text. Objective questions are scored online, and incorrect answers are keyed to the text for student review. For more information, contact your local sales representative. (www.prenhall/narayanan)

INTRODUCTION

What is a chief technology officer? It's not a chief scientist. You may remember them: senior, professorial-like, seldom communicating directly with engineers. They gave their companies prestige, came up with lots of new ideas, and usually stayed away from the nuts and bolts of product design.

That's no longer true at Sprint, where Marty Kaplan takes a leading role in innovation and project management. "Boundaries should not exist between a technology and its end result," he says. "My job is to help my company follow certain synergies of design and architecture that create seamless networks. How successful I am determines how well I guide the future direction of Sprint and its European partners."

It's been through Kaplan's efforts in guiding deployment of wave-length division multiplexing (WDM) throughout the Sprint network that the carrier has been able to increase its backbone capacity by four, eight, and 16 times—without replacing equipment and investing in capital expenditure outlay. Kaplan's solution to Sprint's network congestion problem, and the unique, problem-solving process he engineered, earned him the recognition of *America's Network* technologist of the year in 1998.

Marty Kaplan is the senior vice president and chief technology officer (CTO) for Sprint Corp. (Overland Park, Kansas). He joined the company 25 years ago when things like fast-packet switching and synchronous optical networks (Sonet) were unknown. Now, he guides these and other new technologies through an extensive evolution, transforming them into services for millions of subscribers. Kaplan chairs a group that plans the shape of Sprint's global backbone. "I forecast where the network nodes will be, which suppliers build them, and which specifications they follow," he says. "Only by understanding how a technology can launch a new business direction can any individual provide effective leadership and judge the impact of technology on cost-competitiveness. A CTO must be not only an agent of change, but also an educator who can explain the purpose of change.

"Dealing with issues that transition narrow and broadband networks requires an understanding of what we are looking for in such transitions," he continues. "*Leadership* is needed in all the disciplines. You ask yourself, What should I be doing in a particular situation? How should I get ready? How can

I leverage my resources? What products should I look at? The problem with ATM [asynchronous transfer mode] in the early days was that it was driven more by its basic technology than by the needs of the marketplace. This led to a kind of lead/lag effect that confused our vision of what it was capable of really doing for end users."

Much of Kaplan's success at Sprint is his ability to see his role as something that can pay big dividends for the whole organization. One of his responsibilities is in the company's capital program. "I look at our investment in technology as a way of influencing our future," he says. "I constantly urge my engineers to analyze their influence on revenue generation, cost reduction, and cost avoidance. The business case must relate revenue potential to the underlying cost structure; this enables us to forecast what may happen early in the development cycle. The danger is that my organization should not view itself just as a cost center; therefore, I try to grow it in terms of *value*. I find out who, because of their work discipline, can contribute at the highest level, and then I unleash the resources to back them up."

Kaplan views this as a communication process. If enough information flows into a technology, it creates a sense of what it will ultimately produce. "Our job isn't done until we put a product into service and see it working smoothly," he explains. "That's the true distinction between today's CTO and yesterday's chief scientist." A great idea, Kaplan says, will fail if it's not supported all the way down the line. Thus, Kaplan takes responsibility not only for the idea, but also for the planning, integration, engineering, implementation, and testing processes. "The only way I can measure my job is by answering a simple question: Did the customer benefit? That lets everyone work toward a common goal," he says.

"Sprint's 1997 long-distance capital expenditure of roughly $1.3 billion needs a lot of hands-on control," Kaplan says, "so I chair what we call 'technical walk-through.' The originator of the investment presents his or her case to the finance group and everyone else who's involved. All the disciplines are represented—systems development, operations, marketing, and so forth. We ask the originator, What are you doing? How are you doing it? And why in this particular way?"

Sprint has a three-year network evolution plan that Kaplan personally communicated throughout the company, including the board of directors. "We have a five-year capital program. I must know where the forecast came from and what it was based on. I try to make sure that everybody builds to the same set of expectations. This way, they understand what the capital balance looks like, what we are doing, and why we are doing it. Most of our capital programs are signed off during a one-hour technical walk-through. Only the really big ones go to the chairman or the board for final approval," he explains.

Kaplan's responsibilities are similar to those of a small business owner. In rapidly growing companies, these individuals are powerhouses of knowledge who gather the support staff around them and paint a vivid picture of the organization's future. They know what they are and what they are doing, and they instill their philosophy in their colleagues by telling them where the company is headed, what the product is, and what it means to their customers. Usually, these companies reach their full potential only a short time after start-up.

Filling a similar role in a giant corporation such as Sprint requires a tremendous amount of cooperation. "To get this level of support, I use a collaborative network consisting of 'skull' sessions that last two to three hours," Kaplan explains. "When there's a technology topic I want to explore, I get a dozen of the best minds in Sprint around a table. I listen, I moderate, I participate. Technical people who disagree are impassioned in their stances, so my job as CTO is to rationalize their differences. I have to know if these are semantics or if there are real issues to be resolved. If they're real, I must understand [their implications] and guide everyone in a single direction without getting into a win-lose situation. My rule is usually to say, 'Hey—maybe we're all really talking about the same thing.' Technology confrontation is fine, so long as it doesn't inhibit getting things done."

For example, Kaplan brought in people from all over the company to create a new set of dynamics when debating Internet protocol (IP) and ATM applications. "By urging them to support their convictions, I was able to reach a better and a faster answer," he says.

The major challenge of the telecommunications industry, according to Kaplan, is "to move from the Old World to the New World, and make the transition as painless as possible. Our customers are the ones who control capability, so we have to give them what they want when they want it.

"Looking at Sprint's network a year or two down the road, I see total integration of services," he asserts. "We'll have the ability to set up dynamic bandwidth as we need it, when we need it, for any service we need."

This has far-reaching implications for large carriers. "Once you have that ability in place, your cost structure is different," Kaplan says. "When you sell a single service over a single network, that's a high-cost situation. It's not until I can run many applications over a common infrastructure that my cost equation balances. Until now, the industry's main role has been to connect specific protocol subscribers anywhere in the network," he continues. "Now, I must allow them to have video collaboration, content hosting, local caching, and a dozen other things. In essence, I equip them with the capability to use any media distribution at any bandwidth they need."

Thus, the challenge is no longer basic technology—it's layering services on solutions previously developed. "If I were to summarize it in one word, it would be *integration*—integration of technology, integration of services and integration of applications," Kaplan says. "We're finally getting to a point where you can take some things as a given. For example, I have a Sonet layer, which is a transport layer that works continuously, provides a service consistency, and has all the bandwidth I'll ever need."[1]

As described in the preceding vignette, the chief technology officer of Sprint considers his job not as one of development of technology but as one of creating value and acting as an agent of change within the firm. Indeed, in many large corporations, a significant shift is underway in the role and functions of the chief technology officers, and technology managers, in general. Although many of them may have risen through the scientific and engineering ranks of corporations, they are increasingly viewed as individuals who help corporations create value through the development of technology and its deployment in products and processes. In this book, we will deal with the significant challenges of managing technology and describe the role and functions of the chief technology officer.

The shift in the role and functions of the chief technology officer reflects the fact that firms are paying increasing attention to the value implications of technology. This renewed interest in technology is triggered by two reasons.

First, and perhaps the most obvious, technology has been in the forefront of change during the last several decades, bringing new products, transforming our way of life, and changing the rules of the marketplace. Consider, for example, the speed of transportation. It is only during this century that we have witnessed the emergence of automobiles and airplanes as modes of transportation for the average consumer, increasing their access to other regions, nations, and faraway places, in general. Consider also how our lifestyles have changed during this century as a result of newer forms of communication mode: telephone, television, and the Internet. Finally, consider the number of new firms that have come into existence as the result of new advances in technology. Microsoft, currently one of the largest firms in terms of market capitalization, is less than three decades old.

A second, perhaps less obvious, reason for the increased attention to the management of technology is the fact that technology accounts for a large share of the productivity gains during this century. Consider the following question: How can it be that we are wealthier today than we were 100 years ago? The question is puzzling because, if you add up all the things that we own, it is clear that the underlying quantity of raw material has not changed over time; however, the total population has increased significantly. To put the point in extreme form, the total physical mass here on earth is the same as it always has been, but now we must divide that mass among a much larger number of people. So how could it be that we have more total wealth per person than we have ever had before? There is only one explanation for this increase in wealth: We took this raw material that was available to us and rearranged it in a way that made it more valuable. This process of rearrangement and the knowledge that lies underneath it—things that are typically classified as intangible assets in a firm or technology, as we will define it—contributes to the wealth of nations.[2]

During the 1950s, a number of economists reached a remarkable conclusion: The major share of the productivity growth of the U.S. economy could not be accounted for by conventionally measured capital and labor inputs; productivity growth must therefore be due to some form of technological progress. In a classic investigation in this area, Robert Solow estimated that only 12.5 percent of the growth of output per hour of labor can be attributed to the increased use of capital; the remaining 87.5 percent was due to technical change.[3]

The twin facts—the role of technology in the development of new products and processes, and its contribution to productivity enhancement—have not gone unnoticed by firms. In the wake of the information technology revolution and the advent of the Internet, there is currently a growing optimism that quantum leaps in productivity are possible by the effective management of technology. A large number of new products are being developed and marketed as a result of the information revolution. As a consequence, the roles of the chief technology officer and the technology management function within corporations have assumed greater importance in the conduct of many corporations.

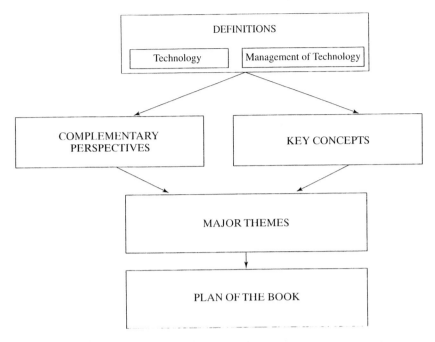

FIGURE 1.1 CHAPTER OVERVIEW

This book is about management of technology: the major principles that underpin the management of technology, the activities involved in technology management, and the general role and functions of technology management. This introductory chapter summarizes the major themes that run through exposition of the technology management function in this book.

Figure 1.1 presents the chapter overview. First, we will define technology and identify some of its unique characteristics. Second, we will outline what we mean by the management of technology. Third, we will sketch the two complementary perspectives that underlie our discussion of the management of technology. Fourth, we will summarize the key concepts that we expect the reader to know, as they read the ensuing chapters. Fifth, we will enumerate the central themes that pervade our exposition of the management technology. Finally, we will outline the plan of the book and conclude with some suggestions on how to read the book.

TECHNOLOGY: DEFINITION AND CHARACTERISTICS

Webster's dictionary defines technology in several ways:

1. The branch of knowledge that deals with industrial arts, applied science, or engineering;
2. The terminology of an art or science; or

3. A technological process, invention, method, or the like and some of the ways in which a social group provides themselves with the material objects of their civilization.

Thus, the word *technology* has a number of meanings, varying from "product" to the various disciplines of science and engineering.

Embedded in the definition is the notion of knowledge. As we noted earlier, the key to economic progress has been the advance in knowledge created by human beings over the centuries. In other words, knowledge lies at the heart of economic progress. We will anchor our definition of technology in knowledge.

Indeed, we will weave two sets of ideas into our concept of knowledge. First, knowledge or technology development spans several levels; second, the development is the outcome of a process of social construction.

LEVELS OF DEVELOPMENT

Technology development is the result of several levels of activity. Broadly, we can identify three levels:

1. Individuals develop ideas, theories, or perspectives that are known only to them or their colleagues or the groups to which they belong. This tacit knowledge may be derived from their experiences, experimentation, or imagination.
2. The second level consists of tacit knowledge that is verified and codified through a scientific process of experimentation. In the process of verification, some of the tacit knowledge will be found to be valid, some will be discarded as superstition, and some may await further attempts at verification. In the process of codification, the tacit knowledge is formalized and put into a language that can be communicated and understood by others. So, as a result of scientific verification and codification, the knowledge becomes available to a large number of people.
3. Finally, there is a level of development where the knowledge is put to use—physically embodied in products, services, or procedures.

So, our definition of technology focuses on knowledge at three levels: tacit, codified and verified, and physically embodied end products and processes. Figure 1.2 illustrates these levels.

TECHNOLOGY AS SOCIALLY CONSTRUCTED

Technology development at all levels is a process of social construction: The development is the outcome of human beings actively making choices, individually and collectively. Four characteristics of technology will be emphasized throughout the book:

1. Opportunity. Technology development takes place when human beings perceive an opportunity for improvement due to either intrinsic or economic reasons. The act of perceiving is the triggering event for technology development; it is truly a human activity.

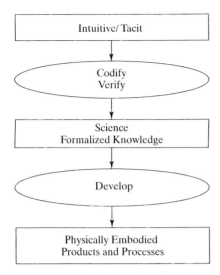

FIGURE 1.2 LEVELS OF
KNOWLEDGE

2. Appropriability: In many cases, where the technology development is due to economic motives, individuals will pursue development only to the extent that there is a reasonable assurance that the fruits of their labor will flow back to the developers.
3. Transferability. Technology or knowledge transfer is not smooth; knowledge is sticky. When human beings communicate, there is no perfect correspondence between the message that the sender intends and the one understood by the receiver.
4. Resources. Technology development consumes resources. The most obvious resources involved are money, time, and people. In addition, other resources—collateral assets—may be needed to exploit a technology opportunity.

In summary, we will view technology as the outcome of a socially constructed process of knowledge development and utilization.

MANAGEMENT OF TECHNOLOGY

In many ways, management of technology is not a new field. The beginnings of technology management can be traced to the 1950s, when R&D management ideas were developed; this was a period characterized by plentiful resources to R&D. During the 1960s and 1970s, there was interest in understanding innovation. However, as we entered the last quarter of the twentieth century, the impact of global competition was keenly felt, and the U.S. economy went through a wrenching period of restructuring. Consequently, there was renewed attention to technology. The current renditions of management of technology reflect the altered views on technology in light of the new realities. See Figure 1.3 for a bird's-eye view of this evolution.

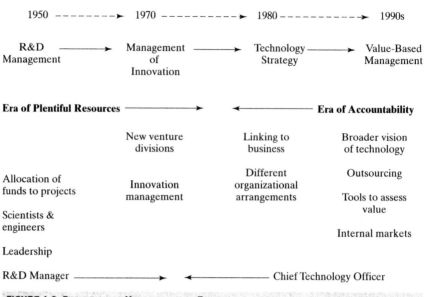

FIGURE 1.3 EVOLUTION OF MANAGEMENT OF TECHNOLOGY

In 1987, the National Research Council defined management of technology in the following way:

> Management of technology links engineering, science, and management disciplines to plan, to develop, and to implement technological capabilities to shape and accomplish the *strategic and operational* goals of an organization.

The three important ideas incorporated in the preceding definition are worthy of repetition:

1. The emphasis in the management of technology is to accomplish the goals of an organization. We will view value creation for investors as the primary goal of technology management in corporations.
2. Technology management focuses on the development of technological capability and its implementation or deployment in products and processes.
3. Technology management within corporations is linked to other management activities such as marketing or manufacturing.

For simplicity, we will redefine the management of technology:

> *Management of technology* focuses on the principles of strategy and organization involved in technology choices, guided by the purpose of creating value for investors.

The definition of management of technology may thus be portrayed in Figure 1.4.

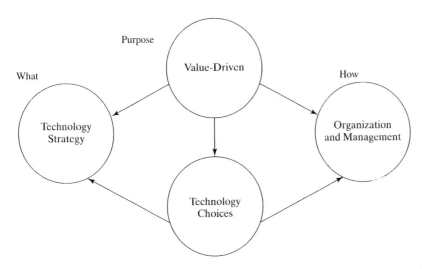

FIGURE 1.4 MANAGEMENT OF TECHNOLOGY

TWO COMPLEMENTARY PERSPECTIVES IN MANAGEMENT

All approaches to management, including the management of technology, start with some statement of a firm's identity and purpose. The answer to the question What is our business? has been provided by two complementary perspectives: market based and resource based.

MARKET-BASED VIEWS

Traditionally, business firms are defined by the markets they serve: Who are our customers? Which of their needs are we seeking to serve? During the 1970s and the 1980s, most management literature and practice were concentrated on the industry environment of the firm, its competitive positioning relative to rivals, and how it satisfied its customers. This perspective came to be known as the market-based perspective.

The market-based perspective prescribed that firms should define their markets broadly rather than narrowly. In a classic illustration of market-based perspective, Ted Levitt chose the example of railroads: Railroads should have perceived themselves to be in the transportation business and not the railroad business. But broadening the target market is of little value if the company cannot easily develop the capabilities required for serving customer requirements on a broad basis. Although railroad companies have entered into airlines, shipping, and trucking, their performance in these markets has been patchy.[4] Perhaps the resources and capabilities of the railroad companies are better suited to real estate development, pipelines, or oil and gas exploration businesses, where

TABLE 1.1   Market-Based and Resource-Based Views

Dimension	Market Based	Resource Based
Drivers of strategy	Customers and competitors	Unique resources
Derivatives	Resources	Market opportunities
Strategy profile	Positional	Core competencies
Appropriate contexts	Mature markets	Dynamic markets

several of them have prospered. Thus, market-based perspective tends to underplay the role of the internal capabilities of the firm.

RESOURCE-BASED VIEWS

In recent years, resource-based views of the firm have developed as a complementary perspective to the market-based approaches. When the external environment is in a state of flux, the firm itself, in terms of its bundle of resources and capabilities, may be a much more stable basis on which to define its identity. In general, the greater the rate of change in a firm's external environment, the more likely internal resources and capabilities will provide a particular foundation for long-term decision making.

The differences between the two approaches are summarized in Table 1.1.

So, what do these perspectives indicate for management of technology? As we noted in our definition, technology management focuses on both developing capabilities and deploying them in various markets. Thus, for our purposes, the management of technology embraces both perspectives: resource based and market based. Indeed, one of the major themes of the book is that both the development of technological capabilities and their deployment in products and processes constitute the central functions of technology management.

KEY CONCEPTS

In our exposition of the management of technology, we will view firms as *open systems:* sets of interrelated activities that interface with the environment. Thus, a firm is viewed as a whole, and any activity that a firm does is meaningful only to the extent that it contributes something to the whole function of the firm. Further, the firm interfaces with the environment at multiple fronts—customers, competitors, government, labor markets, suppliers, and so on. Modern management theories accept the open-systems view of organizations as a given and therefore argue that the effectiveness of each firm is dependent on how it successfully interfaces with the environment. To develop ideas about the management of technology within an open-systems view, we will employ four major concepts: (1) the firm as a value chain, (2) industries as competitive domains, (3) forms of technological change, and (4) value creation and competitive advantage.

FIRM AS A VALUE CHAIN

To describe the firm as a set of interrelated activities, we will employ the term *value chain*. Every firm is a collection of activities performed to design, produce, market, develop, and support its product. All these activities can be represented by using a value chain, shown in Figure 1.5. A firm's value chain and the way it performs individual activities are a reflection of its history, its decision making, and its approach to implementing its decisions and the underlying economics of the activities themselves.

Identifying value activities requires the isolation of activities that are technologically and strategically distinct. Broadly, value chains consist of two sets of activities: primary and secondary activities.

Primary activities are those involved in taking the raw materials and developing the products and services for the customers. The five generic sets of primary activities are inbound logistics, operations, marketing, outbound logistics, and service.

Support activities can be divided into four generic categories: procurement, technology development, human resources management, and firm infrastructure.

Though firms in the same industry may have similar value chains, the value chains of competitors often differ. What do the various activities captured by the value chain of a firm enable it to accomplish? First of all, the value chains help the firm deliver products and services to its customers. To the extent that the products and services are superior to those of the competitors in terms of satisfying the customer's need (i.e., the products and services deliver value to the customer), a firm is likely to be successful. From the customer's point of view, the value delivered by a firm depends on the superiority of its products or service relative to the price paid by the customer. The value appropriated by the firm, on the other hand, depends on the value created by the customers, but in relationship to the firm's cost structure. Value chains provide one

FIGURE 1.5 VALUE CHAIN OF A TYPICAL FIRM

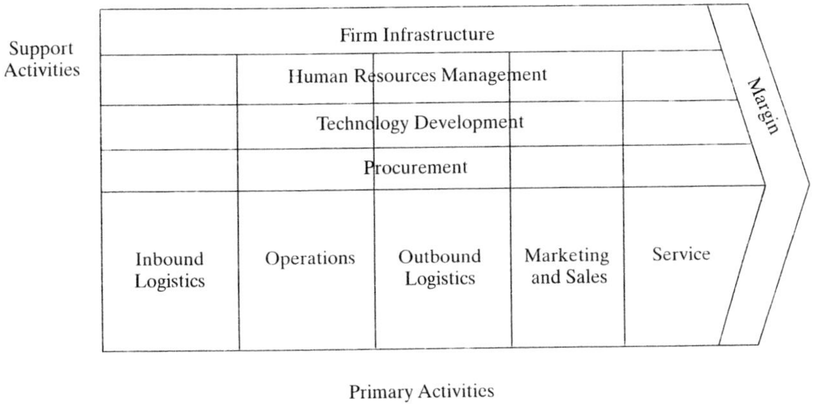

Primary Activities

Source: Adapted with the permission of The Free Press, a Division of Simon & Schuster, Inc., from *Competitive Advantage: Creating and Sustaining Superior Performance* by Michael E. Porter. Copyright © 1985, 1998 by Michael E. Porter.

mechanism by which to capture the cost structure of the firm. The value appropriated by the firm is the basis on which to judge whether the firm creates value for the investors. To be sure, the value appropriated should exceed the opportunity cost of capital.

INDUSTRIES AS COMPETITIVE DOMAINS

An industry represents a group of firms that offer similar products or services to customers. They are domains in which the incumbent firms compete—or simply, competitive domains. Typically, the value appropriation by a firm depends on the attractiveness of its industry. Industries dominated by different types of key competitive resources seem to vary systematically in terms of size, stability, and sources of the profit differences within them.

One classification system distinguishes industries by grouping key competitive resources into three categories: (1) capacity, (2) customers, and (3) knowledge.

> In capacity-driven industries, physical capital investments seem to be relatively large in relation to cost or value added. The steel industry is a good example. Competition takes place mostly on price; expenditures for R&D are quite limited. More generally, capacity-driven industries are likely to be mature, commoditized, and fragmented. The pace of productivity improvement is particularly modest, forcing most companies to focus on incremental refinements or production processes. In general, they register low profitability.

> In customer-driven industries, investments in brands or customer relations generally account for a large part of the cost or value added. The beer industry in the United States is a good example. The brewers compete across a number of functions including product formulation, manufacturing, logistics, pricing, and nonprice aspects of marketing. These initiatives yield only temporary advantages, advantages that can be easily imitated by competitors. More generally, customer-driven industries tend to be less mature, commoditized, and fragmented than capacity-driven industries; they also exhibit more rivalry and higher average profitability.

> In knowledge-driven industries, investments in R&D tend to account for a large part of the cost or value added. The pharmaceutical industry is a good example. It is investment intensive along a number of dimensions, including marketing, but its most striking characteristic is its very high R&D investment rate. As one might expect, pharmaceutical competitors, such as Merck, that have outperformed the industry averages appear to have been superior at innovation, particularly in terms of their ability to introduce unique drugs for common diseases.[5]

Table 1.2 shows examples of industries in each of the three categories.

FORMS OF TECHNOLOGICAL CHANGE

It is useful to distinguish between two types of technological change: process and product.

Process technology pertains to the techniques of producing and marketing goods and services. Process technology also includes work methods, equipment, distribution, and logistics. Thus, it is embedded in a firm's value chain. For example, Henry Ford's idea of assembly line manufacturing and the Japanese management concept of quality

TABLE 1.2   Classification of Industries

Capacity Driven	*Customer Driven*	*Knowledge Driven*
Food processing	Food products	Electrical equipment
Textiles	Consumer chemical products	Specialty chemicals
Basic metals	Household durables	Transport equipment
Stone, clay products	Glass, ceramic products	Scientific equipment
Basic chemicals		Software
Pulp and paper		

Source: From David J. Collis, "The Resource-Based View of the Firm and the Importance of Factor Markets," Harvard University Graduate School of Business Administration, Working Paper, 1993. Reprinted by permission.

circles are examples of process technologies in the automobile industry. Process technology changes are designed to produce and market goods and services faster, more efficiently, or in greater volume. In a university, technological changes represent changes in techniques for teaching courses and, in recent years, have ranged from the traditional lecture format to multimedia presentations and self-based learning methods. As a further example, many supermarket chains have adopted laser scanning checkout systems, which represent a change in the delivery process of a grocery store. Similarly, many firms trading in stocks have introduced artificial intelligence routines based on neural networks; this represents a change in the process of selecting stocks to buy and sell.

Product technology, on the other hand, refers to the elements of technology embodied in the goods and services of a firm. For example, gasoline and electric cars represent different product technologies in the automobile industry. Changes in product technology could range from minor refinements (e.g., different styles of an automobile) to entirely new products (e.g., Wankel automobile engines). Changes in product technology add new features or provide superior substitutes for existing products.

Thus, process technology refers to the way an organization conducts its business, whereas product technology refers to the output of an organization. It should be noted, however, that the *distinction between process and product technology depends on the nature of the firm.* What is often a product technology for one firm may very well be a process technology for another firm. Thus, laser scanning checkout systems represent a process change for the many supermarkets that have adopted these systems; but, they also represent product technology changes for the manufacturers that produce them.

The distinction between product and process technology is important for three reasons:

1. Relative to changes in products, process technology changes are much less visible in the marketplace. Such changes are much more difficult to detect either by a firm's customers or by its competitors. This means that a firm can better conceal some process improvements from the competitors.

2. Both process and product technology changes have ramifications for the economic performance of the firm. In many cases, process technology changes make it feasible for the firm to reduce its cost or cycle time and improve the quality of its products. Japanese firms have often been credited with continual improvement in process technology; this has led to lower costs and higher product quality.

3. Process and product technologies have different consequences for a firm. Product technology helps firms compete for customers; changes in product technology help firms to radically redefine their product/market scope. Process technology changes modify the way a firm conducts its business. Thus, changes in process technology may bring about changes in the organization, including its human resources practices, logistics, and marketing functions.

So, both process and product technologies are important for the ultimate success of a firm. Indeed, in addition to developing technological capabilities, the deployment of capabilities in products and processes is central to the value creation by firms.

VALUE CREATION AND COMPETITIVE ADVANTAGE

When two or more firms compete in the same market, the firm that possesses a competitive advantage over its rival returns a consistently higher rate of profit, or has the *potential* to earn a consistently higher rate of profit. *Competitive advantage* is the ability of the firm to outperform rivals on profitability. Competitive advantage depends on how a firm is able to create for its customers value that exceeds the firm's cost of creating a product. Value is what the customers are willing to pay, and superior value stems from offering lower prices than competitors or from providing unique benefits. From our perspective, *competitive advantage is the key to long-term value creation*. Thus, we will consider competitive advantage to be the major objective behind management of technology decisions.

MAJOR THEMES IN THE BOOK

Nine major themes run through our discussion of the management of technology: generic applicability; interfacing technology and market factors; the influence of globalization; simultaneity of competition and collaboration; speed in problem solving; make or buy; systemic view of management; the role of learning; and co-existence of high tech and high touch.

GENERIC APPLICABILITY

Technology management lies at the heart of *all* firms, be they high technology or not; therefore, it is generically applicable to the management of firms. Although in the technology management area the successes of high-technology firms get a lot of media attention, technology has played and will continue to play a major role in the success of other firms, even service industries. For example, the advent of program trading and applications of neural networks have transformed the financial sector. In our discussion, we will weave examples from the service sector where possible to highlight the generic applicability of technology management.

INTERFACING TECHNOLOGY AND MARKET FACTORS

A major theme emphasized in the text is the need to interface technology and market factors in major decisions related to technology management. First, we will repeatedly note that the goal of technology management is to create value. Second, we will highlight the role played by competitive and customer-related factors in the creation of value through technology management. Third, we will introduce the notion of a technology market matrix as a way of capturing the major factors involved in critical decision making.

THE INFLUENCE OF GLOBALIZATION

A pervasive theme in the book is the globalization of business, in general, and technology, in particular. We will view technology as the leading edge of globalization. This is particularly important to the United States as we enter the twenty-first century: After World War II, during the latter half of the twentieth century, the United States held the dominant role in technology development. In future decades, other nations are likely to challenge U.S. hegemony in specific sectors of technology. Thus, when we discuss technology management, we will point out the influence of globalization.

SIMULTANEITY OF COMPETITION AND COLLABORATION

A fourth theme woven throughout the book is the need to view both competitive and collaborative approaches as potential avenues to value creation. Indeed, we will note that, under appropriate conditions, firms may collaborate with their own competitors. Because the collaborative approach is relatively new to management theory, we will specifically highlight its importance by devoting an entire chapter to it.

SPEED IN PROBLEM SOLVING

Speed has emerged as one of the keys to competitive advantage. Whether it is in new product introductions or responding to customers, what has been termed *fast cycle capability*, or organizational speed, has emerged as a characteristic of successful organizations. Thus, we will note that the problem-solving process in technology management should also be speedy; further, technology managers should emphasize developing a culture of urgency within firms.

MAKE OR BUY

Almost all technology decisions present make-or-buy choices; indeed, it is an avenue to speedy execution. Historically, many U.S. firms developed a culture where in-house development was considered superior and acquiring technology from other firms was not considered a viable alternative. We will argue that the imperative of value creation requires firms to explicitly consider acquisitions as an alternative. In other words, firms have to view themselves not merely as growers of technologies but also as gatherers of technology.

SYSTEMIC VIEW OF MANAGEMENT

As one of the offshoots of the open-systems view of organization, we will argue that technology management requires a systemic view. Two facets of the systemic view will be developed in the book. First, we will view the various activities in technology management—appropriation of technology, deployment in new products and deployment in value chains—as interlinked. Second, we will make technology management an integral element of the activities that create value for a firm.

ROLE OF LEARNING

Fundamental to the management of technology is the process of organizational learning. Learning can come about in several ways: intelligence gathering from outside, imitation of competitors, learning by doing, and problem solving, to name a few. Indeed, we will emphasize that organizational learning is critical for long-run success in the management of technology.

CO-EXISTENCE OF HIGH TECH AND HIGH TOUCH

Finally, we will argue that high technology requires high touch. Learning is a human process; knowledge is a human product. To be effective, high technology requires significant attention to human beings within a corporation. Throughout the book, we will highlight the role played by learning processes in the management of technology. Technology is not a substitute for labor; to be effective, individuals in organizations must perform higher level cognitive functions. This, in turn, requires that the management of technology includes managing the human side of enterprise.

PLAN OF THE BOOK

The text is divided into four major parts: (1) Theoretical Foundations; (2) Technology Strategy; (3) Domains of Technology; and (4) General Management.

In the theoretical foundations, central theoretical ideas are developed; these ideas form the basis for the discussion of the management of technology throughout the book. This part contains five major chapters. In the first of these chapters, the concept of technology environment is developed; the chapter highlights the three major trends—globalization, time compression, and technology integration—that are shaping technology management. In the next two chapters, the processes of technology change—innovation and diffusion—are discussed. The chapter on technology and competition focuses on the impact of technology change on industries and competition. In the next chapter, the impact of technology on value chains and internal organizational characteristics is summarized.

The second part focuses exclusively on the strategic aspects of business. In successive chapters, the text covers the process of gathering technological intelligence and presents an overview of technology strategy and the collaborative arrangements that are currently popular. In addition to the key substantive factors of interest, each chapter deals with approaches to analysis.

In the third part, the focus shifts to the domains of technology management. Thus, successive chapters cover appropriation of technology, deployment of technology in new products, and deployment of technology in value chains.

In the fourth part, we focus on the role of general management. In the chapter on organizing for innovation, we discuss the ways of organizing for technology development and the critical points of managerial intervention. This chapter also covers the role of general manager as an agent of *continual* technological change within his/her organization. In the last two chapters, we deal with intellectual property strategies and the financial aspects of project valuation that concretely link technology management to value creation.

CHAPTER LAYOUT

We begin all chapters with a vignette. In the introductory section, we pose several questions that identify various subtopics and issues that will subsequently be discussed in the book. These questions provide the reader with advanced knowledge of what to expect from the chapter. After reading the chapter, the reader should go back to these questions and try to answer them. This will help the reader to ascertain how much he/she learned from the chapter.

We have used three types of devices to make the reading easy:

1. Figures help summarize the key linkages among the concepts or illustrate a particular point.
2. Tables are summaries of topics presented to help the reader manage the complexity of the topics discussed.
3. We have used three different kinds of boxes. The first one presents examples and illustrations. A second set summarizes research studies. A third set summarizes relatively abstruse technical concepts that are not necessary for the main themes of the book.

Finally, at the end of most chapters, we suggest the major managerial implications; in all the ensuing chapters, we conclude with a summary.

The chapters and the linkages among them are sketched in Figure 1.6.

FIGURE 1.6 PLAN OF THE BOOK

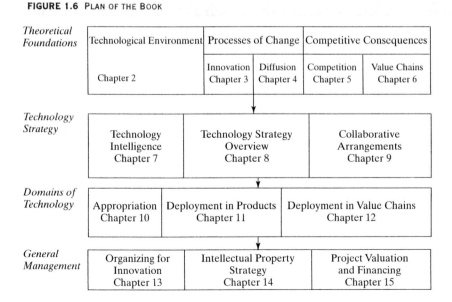

HOW TO READ THE BOOK

So that the reader can master the materials presented, we suggest three guidelines for reading the book:

1. During the first reading, it may be useful to skip all the boxes and complex tables; that is, read only the text portion of each chapter. This should provide the reader with a broad conceptual understanding of the various topics covered in the chapter.
2. The second reading of each chapter should include the complex tables as well as the boxes containing illustrations or examples. During this reading, the reader should reflect upon the example and critically assess how the material in the text sheds light on the example. Where research evidence is presented, the reader should determine the uncertainties yet to be resolved.
3. After the second reading, the reader should return to the introduction and try to answer the questions posed at the beginning of the chapter.

Finally, the summary provided at the end of each chapter should enable the readers to review their learning.

❖ NOTES

1. Reprinted with permission from *America's Network,* Vol. 102, No. 2, January 15, 1998, pp. 30–36. Copyright by Advanstar Communications Inc. Advanstar Communications Inc. retains all rights to this material.
2. Romer, Paul. "The Soft Revolution: Achieving Gold by Managing Intangible," *Journal of Applied Corporate Finance,* Summer 1998, Volume 11 #2, p. 9.
3. Solow, Robert. "Technical Change and the Aggregate Production Function," *A Review of Economics and Statistics,* 1957, Vol. 39, pp. 312–320.
4. See Grant, Robert. *Contemporary Strategy Analysis.* Basil Blackwell, 1991.
5. David Collis and Pankaj Ghemawat. "Industry Analysis: Understanding Industry Structure and Dynamics." In Liam Fahey and Robert M. Randall (eds) *The Portable MBA in Strategy.* John Wiley and Sons, 1994.

THEORETICAL FOUNDATIONS

In this part, we will chart the central theoretical ideas that characterize the practice of management of technology. We will stress three ideas throughout this section:

1. Organizations are open systems; this implies that they are in continual interaction with their environments.
2. Innovation and diffusion are the central activities involved in technology.
3. Finally, the twin processes of innovation and diffusion have competitive consequences for firms: They bring in new products and processes, thereby altering the nature of competition.

In chapter 2, consistent with the theme that organizations are open systems, we will start our discussion of theoretical foundations with a description of technological environment. The technological environment is only one of the environments facing firms, so we will delineate some of the linkages between the technological and other environments facing the organization. We will highlight the key players and issues that pervade the technological environment and some of the major current developments.

In chapters 3 and 4, we describe the two central activities—innovation and diffusion. In both these chapters, we will visualize these activities as being embedded in a technology market matrix, representing the idea that both innovation and diffusion involve changes in technology and in the marketplace.

Finally, in chapters 5 and 6, we will illustrate how innovation and diffusion influence the dynamics of an industry as well as the internal organizational activities of a firm. In chapter 5, we will illustrate the competitive aspects of innovation and diffusion, highlighting the role that technological development plays in the evolution of competitive domains. In chapter 6 we will illustrate how technology influences the configuration of value chains of firms and the internal organization arrangements.

2

TECHNOLOGICAL ENVIRONMENT

In 1980, the race was on between the United States and Japan to develop the "next generation" 64K large-scale integrated (LSI) circuit chip. Past experience certainly favored the United States, because Silicon Valley had produced all prior generations. Yet, by December 1981, the Japanese had introduced the first 64K-memory chip and promptly gained a dominant market position in the industry. It would take U.S. firms another year before they were ready to compete in this market.

The story begins in the 1950s when U.S. manufacturers invented the first transistor. Although transistorized electronics presented enormous possibilities for many new and potentially large markets, U.S. firms instead focused on military applications for these new devices. In essence, U.S. firms chose to ignore any possible consumer applications of transistorized electronics. This left a large technological hole that the Japanese undertook to fill.

During the 1960s, the Japanese pushed numerous applications of the transistor into the consumer marketplace. The result of this move was that by the mid 1970s they had captured most of the consumer electronics market. It was also during the 1960s that U.S. firms developed the integrated circuit. Integrated circuits are computer chips that "integrate" many pairs of transistors on a single semiconductor chip. Though the Japanese had learned to make transistors, they had not yet achieved the technology necessary to produce integrated circuits. Thus, although they dominated the consumer electronics industry, they were forced to import the central component necessary for these products.

Recognizing this market vuinerability, Japanese industry, in partnership with the government, began to learn the technologies necessary to create integrated circuits. Between 1970 and 1975, Japan's Ministry of International Trade and Industry (MITI) provided the equivalent of $10 million in research grants to Japanese electronics firms aimed at developing this national capability. This effort was extremely successful. By the late 1970s, Japanese firms had registered about 1,000 patents associated with this work and developed production capabilities in 16K-chip technology equal to their U.S. rivals. As they had planned, the Japanese had become a serious player in the international semiconductor market.

The result of this series of events was that Japanese industry, facilitated in part by the Japanese government, was able to acquire the technological capabilities necessary to succeed in the development of the next generation of computer chip. This brief history has three important messages for the management of technology:

1. The technological environment can be viewed as a network of organizations consisting of developers and facilitators. In both countries, the developer of integrated circuits was industry. But, in the United States, the military financed the development of applications; in Japan, the facilitator was a government agency concerned with the development of commercial markets. Here we can clearly see the way in which the outcome of technological development may rest on the focus of a facilitator.
2. Technology development occurs in stages. Each stage then provides the basis for development in ensuing stages. In retrospect, it may be easy to determine why an eventual outcome occurred by looking at the stages of development. In "real time," however, it is often difficult to know what the next stage may be.
3. The way in which technology develops is not determined solely by a developer. National, and often international, political considerations will often drive technological development.[1]

As can be seen from the vignette, a number of players are usually involved in the development of a specific technology. Of course, many firms engage in the development of products, processes, and services for commercialization with profit potential in mind. However, events that take place outside the boundaries of a firm often determine the course of development undertaken by the firm: decisions of other developers of technology, policies of governments, or actions of competitors. To manage its technology development effectively, a firm will have to pay attention to developments taking place outside its boundaries. Stated differently, a firm will have to pay attention to its technological environment.

In this chapter, we will focus our attention on technological environment. We will attempt to answer such questions as:

1. What do we mean by environment and technological environment in particular?
2. Who are the main actors in the technological environment?
3. How do changes occur in the technological environment?
4. What are some of the major current developments in the technological environment facing firms?

We have sketched the overview of this chapter in Figure 2.1. As shown in the figure, we will first define technological environment, introducing it as a segment of the macroenvironment surrounding a firm. Second, we will discuss the key actors in this environment and the interrelationships among them. Third, we will summarize the autonomous and in-

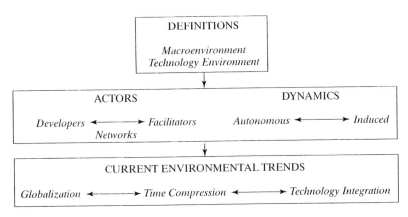

FIGURE 2.1 CHAPTER OVERVIEW

duced evolution of the technological environment, highlighting the role played by political and economic factors. Fourth, we will describe the three major trends—globalization, time compression, and technology integration—currently shaping the technological environment. We will point out key managerial implications and conclude with a summary.

ENVIRONMENT AND TECHNOLOGICAL ENVIRONMENT

As we noted in chapter 1, from an open-systems perspective on analyzing organizations, the performance of an organization is intricately linked with the environments in which it operates. Thus, in all open-systems theories of organizations, the environments of organizations constitute a basis on which internal management actions are designed. The central problem of management is viewed as orchestrating organizational activities to meet the challenges of the environment. These theoretical notions extend to the management of technology. Thus, understanding technological environment is critical to the successful management of technology.

Although the focus of this chapter is on technological environment, we will start our discussion with a description of the various environments facing a firm. We do this because technological environment not only shapes, but also is shaped by, other environments confronting an organization.

LEVELS OF ENVIRONMENT

In theory, almost everything outside the boundaries of a firm constitutes its environment; however, such a description is not useful for understanding the critical environmental influences on organizational functioning. To provide some clarity to understanding the key environmental influences, it is helpful to visualize a firm as being enclosed within three layers or levels of environment: (1) task environment, (2) industry/competitive environment, and (3) general or macroenvironment. These levels of environment are shown in Figure 2.2.

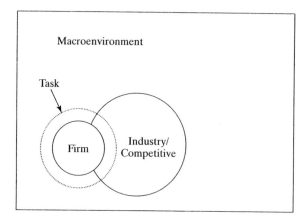

FIGURE 2.2 LEVELS OF
ENVIRONMENT

Task environment refers to the set of customers, suppliers, competitors, and other environmental agencies (such as trade associations) directly related to the firm. Much of the day-to-day operation of a firm involves activities dealing with its task environment: A firm may negotiate a new source of capital with potential investors, enter into a component co-development agreement with its supplier, or attend to upgrading its service to a particular group of customers. The task environment is more or less specific to a firm and is not necessarily shared by its competitors: Customers are often loyal to specific brands, and suppliers may have granted preferred-customer status to the firm.

Beyond the task environment lies the competitive or industrial environment that is comprised of a firm and its competitors functioning in the same industry. At this level, environmental factors directly affect all competitors in the same industry. New entrants, substitute products, suppliers of raw materials or components, customers, and rivalry among competitors influence what happens in an industry.[2] Although factors in the competitive environment directly affect most competitors, they may do so differently. For example, when a new firm is entering an industry, it may significantly affect some competitors in the industry but may have little impact on others.

At the broadest level lies the general or macroenvironment. Macroenvironment affects almost all industries. There are four major segments in the macroenvironment: social, economic, political, and technological. In Figure 2.3, we have sketched the major segments of macroenvironment.

The social environment consists of demographics, lifestyles, and social values. Demographics refer to such items as the population size, age structure or geographic distribution of population, ethnic mix, and/or income levels. Lifestyles represent such elements as household formation, patterns of work, education, consumption, and leisure. Social values include such ideas as the preferences of people for political parties, attitudes toward social habits such as smoking, acceptance of new technologies such as "green technologies," or economic values as reflected in pursuit of economic growth or trade-offs between economic progress and its social costs.

The economic environment consists of the general set of economic conditions facing all industries. It includes the stock, or physical, natural resources and the aggregation of all markets where goods and services are exchanged

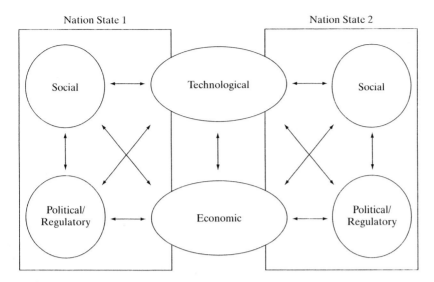

FIGURE 2.3 MACROENVIRONMENT

for payment. The economic activity is reflected in levels and patterns of industrial output, consumption, income, savings, investment, and productivity.

The political environment incorporates all electoral processes that are administrative or regulatory and the judicial institutions that make a society's laws, regulations, and rules. This is perhaps a very turbulent segment of the environment.

The technological environment is concerned with the level and direction of all technological progress or advancements taking place in society, including new products, processes, or materials and the general level of scientific activity and advances in fundamental science (for example in physics).

A simple way to remember the four segments is by the acronym SEPT (social, economic, political, and technological).

Figure 2.3 also underscores two important features of the macroenvironment:

1. The various macroenvironmental segments are interlinked. Thus, for example, the political sector may influence technological and economic environments, whereas the technological environment may influence the lifestyles (by rendering some new products available to consumers) as well as the economic sector of the environment. Thus, when we talk about the technological environment, it is important to appreciate that some of the developments that take place in the technological environment are influenced by the developments that are currently taking place or that have already developed in other segments of the macroenvironment. Put another way, the technological environment is related to other sectors of the macroenvironment.

2. The various segments of the macroenvironment may differ from one nation to another. For example, on the North American continent and especially in the United States, the demographic characteristics are quite different from

the demographic characteristics in the Asian countries: The population growth in many developing nations far outstrips population growth in the United States. In a similar sense, the political and regulatory structures that exist in the various nation states are often very different. The economic and technological environment, however, cuts across nation states. Thus, there is increasingly greater economic interdependence among nations, which causes the economic sector of the macroenvironment to be increasingly global. In a similar sense, although the level of technological development of nation states may often be different, the technological environment pervades all nation states. To cite one example, fax machines are available all over the world; this has made it easier for individuals in various nations to communicate with one another.

TECHNOLOGICAL ENVIRONMENT

Technological environment is thus a major segment of the macroenvironment. This segment is interlinked with the other macroenvironmental segments; nevertheless, it constitutes the primary environmental segment influencing the management of technology.

Technological environment is the most visible and pervasive macroenvironmental segment in a society for three reasons:

1. It brings new products, processes, and materials.
2. It directly impacts every aspect of the society around us—for example, transportation modes, energy, communications, entertainment, health care, food, agriculture, and industry.
3. It alters the rules of global trade and competition.

What makes up the technological environment? It is composed of institutions that participate in the creation of new knowledge (what is often referred to as "science") and the application of that knowledge to develop new products, processes, and materials (what is often referred to as "technology"). Technology development (or development of new products, processes, or materials) consists of two sets of activities: creation of new knowledge and application of that knowledge.

CREATION OF NEW KNOWLEDGE

The knowledge base of technology usually derives from basic research, defined as original investigations of advancement of scientific knowledge that do not have specific objectives or bind this knowledge to practical problems. Basic research focuses on generating scientific knowledge and deals with fundamental questions of science. Scientific research is often cumulative: Research questions begin in some current state of scientific knowledge; these questions stimulate research projects from which scientific results are published in scientific literature. Discoveries in science provide opportunities for technological invention. Thus, most technological innovations can be traced to scientific research activities, although they often result from interplay of scientific method and practical operations.

APPLICATION OF KNOWLEDGE

This consists of investigations that are intended to solve practical problems. Modern inventors must be versed in the latest scientific knowledge and techniques. For this reason, many corporate laboratories are staffed with scientists as well as with engineers.

Scientific knowledge is put into practice in order to design an innovation that will solve a perceived need or problem. Researchers involved in application are the main consumers of basic research. The end result of their efforts is often a product prototype that may have commercial potential.

Application of knowledge itself consists of several activities: applied research development, engineering, and commercialization.

> Applied research usually consists of scientific investigations of known phenomena that do not typically advance scientific knowledge. For example, an oil company may investigate the strength of pollutants of a new type of gasoline.
>
> Development reduces the knowledge to practice in workable prototype form.
>
> Engineering defines the knowledge for commercial exploitation or other practical end users.
>
> Commercialization includes activities such as manufacturing that finally put the technology to use till it becomes adopted and used by others.[3]

During technology development, these activities often overlap; thus, the demarcation line between these activities is often hazy. Nevertheless, a different level of technological skill and business orientation is needed for each. For example, applied research requires expertise in conducting scientific experiments; development needs design skills; engineering requires expertise in process development; and commercialization requires business skills. Hence, these levels are normally performed by different groups of individuals in a society.

The preceding discussion of technological environment does not focus on specific technologies but rather on the organizations and activities involved in the development of new technologies. We have not focused on specific technologies because they are numerous, and the characteristics of each technology are, to a large extent, so unique as to preclude any general description of their characteristics. For example, it is futile to compare genetic engineering with laser technology because they are quite distinct technologies.

ACTORS IN THE TECHNOLOGICAL ENVIRONMENT

TYPES OF ACTORS

Innumerable organizations in the technological environment are directly engaged in developing technology; they are involved in the various activities of creation and application of knowledge. The technological environment also consists of organizations not directly involved in such activities. Indeed, in the introductory vignette, we focused on the role of MITI in stimulating research on microcomputer chips. MITI was not directly involved in creation, but acted as a facilitator. Indeed, throughout this book, the reader will come across the names of many different types of organizations indirectly involved with technology development.

For the purpose of discussion, we distinguish between four types of organizations in the technological environment. These four types of organizations are displayed in

Figure 2.4. As shown in the figure, we distinguish between organizations along two major dimensions: (1) private versus public; and (2) developers versus facilitators.

Private versus public. Technology development is not confined to profit-making enterprises. In addition to large industrial firms, governmental agencies, universities, and many nonprofit organizations carry on the task of technology development. We distinguish between public and private to highlight the differences in the degree of transparency of technology development among organizations. Thus, there is greater transparency and accessibility of technologies developed in public agencies relative to private enterprises.

Developers versus facilitators. The technological environment consists not merely of organizations actually engaged in the task of developing technologies, but also of organizations that facilitate technology development. The facilitators provide information, access, and resources, or sometimes they constrain technology development through sanctions and legal and/or regulatory restrictions.

Figure 2.4 also provides examples of the various types of organizations. Public organizations engaged in technology development include universities and federal research labs. General Electric or former Bell Laboratories are examples of private technology developers. Agencies such as the former Office of Technology Assessment, incubators, or agencies such as Kansas Technology Enterprise Corporation (KTEC) are public agencies created to facilitate technology development. In a similar way, private entities composed of venture capitalists or technology assessment consultants often act as facilitators of technology development.

The different activities involved in technology development—the creation of new knowledge and application of knowledge—are usually performed by different organizations. Public technology developers such as government institutions, independent research agencies (e.g., Batelle Institute), or universities engage in the type of work that we call "basic research." Independent entrepreneurs, business firms, and some governmental agencies play a leading role in applied research as well as development, engineering, and commercialization.

FIGURE 2.4 TYPES OF INSTITUTIONS IN THE TECHNOLOGICAL ENVIRONMENT

	Developers	*Facilitators*
Public	Federal Laboratories University Laboratories	Office of Technology Assessment (OTA)[1] Incubators State Agencies
	National Science Foundation	
Private	Firm R&D Labs R&D Consortia Technological Alliances Partnerships	Venture Capitalists Technology Evaluators

[1]OTA was spun away from the federal government during the 1990s.

As actors in the technology environment, corporations play several roles that lie at the core of management of technology:

1. As technology developers, they are drivers of change in the technology environment. By creating new products, processes, and materials, they alter the rules of competition, transform industries, and create new industries.
2. They are the beneficiaries of technology change initiated by others. By adopting more efficient technologies into their products and processes, corporations can improve their performance and thus create value.
3. They may facilitate technology development by others external to the firm through investments in their research projects.
4. Corporations may also be the victims of technology change created by others. Thus, when a competitor introduces a new product or when new technology transforms industries, corporations may face the threat of obsolescence.

Corporations both shape and are shaped by the changes in the technology environment. At the heart of technology management lie the technology choices made by corporations in their efforts to shape the technological environment, on the one hand, and to adapt to changes in the environment, on the other. Figure 2.5 displays some examples of the organizations arrayed according to the stage of technology development undertaken by them.

INNOVATION NETWORKS

In the technological environment, interlinkages develop between numerous organizations. Thus, organizations with widely differing missions, such as universities, private firms, or government agencies (e.g., NASA)—all part of the technological environment—become connected through networks that facilitate the flow of information, resources,

FIGURE 2.5 TECHNOLOGY DEVELOPMENT: ACTIVITIES AND INSTITUTIONS

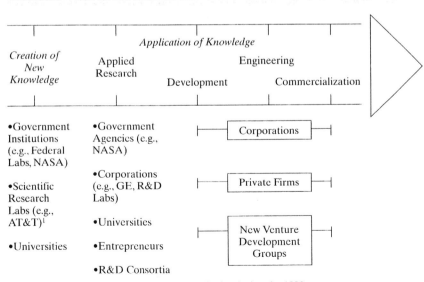

[1]AT&T spun off Bell Labs as Lucent Technologies during the 1990s.

personnel, and other inputs necessary for technology development and diffusion. In addition to the organizations themselves, it is equally important to understand the interconnections that develop among the various organizations to grasp the dynamics of the technological environment. These linkages provide important clues as to the direction and speed with which technologies will be developed by certain groups of organizations. As we saw in the chapter vignette, in the United States, the strong ties between the electronics industry and the military led to the development of technology that is oriented more towards military hardware, whereas in Japan, MITI's role as a facilitator led to the Japanese focus on consumer markets.

Various linkages may arise among developers as well as between developers and facilitators.

INTERCONNECTIONS AMONG TECHNOLOGY DEVELOPERS

Increasingly, linkages are forming among the technology developers, both among private organizations and between private and public organizations. For example, many pharmaceutical firms rely on universities for conducting some basic research necessary for producing commercially viable drugs or therapeutic techniques. In Box 2.1, we have summarized the deepening industry/university relationships for technology development stimulated by the National Science Foundation. Similarly, R&D consortia often form among private firms to pursue a technology development project that cannot be performed solely by the skills or resources available to a single firm.

BOX 2.1

INDUSTRY/UNIVERSITY RESEARCH RELATIONSHIPS

Cooperative research agreements between U.S. industry and universities have existed since Thomas Edison's time. In the 1980s, however, the number of agreements and dollars associated with these agreements began to increase at a rapid rate. Why might this be so? Researchers in this area have suggested that several factors may be responsible for this growth.

Federal funding of university facilities during the 1950s and 1960s built a large capacity for scientific research. As this funding was scaled back in the 1970s, much of the capacity was idle and thus available for alternative uses. Thus, universities began to explore alternative avenues for their outputs.

From the perspective of industry, major advances in such fields as microelectronics,

computer science, and biotechnology during the 1970s, along with expanded globalization of competition, increased the competitive importance of technology, and thus the need for advanced R&D facilities and personnel. Consequently, firms began to search for alternative sources that could rapidly provide a base of necessary but divergent knowledge.

These environmental conditions combine to produce a fertile ground for cooperative agreements between universities and industry. There are clear advantages to such relationships. Industries and universities may approach the same types of problems from differing perspectives. By combining these perspectives, much new knowledge and understanding may be obtainable. Universities may become more

---

Source: From Block, E. and Kruytbosch, C. E. "The NSF role in fostering university-industry research relationships," *IEEE Transactions on Education,* E-29(2): 51–57. © 1986 IEEE. Reprinted by permission.

receptive to the needs of industry to develop commercial applications; industry may begin to recognize the importance of looking beyond these current commercial applications.

Understanding these advantages, the National Science Foundation began a series of programs in the 1970s designed to promote and foster these relationships. Three programs representative of this initiative are summarized.

1. Industry-University Cooperative Research Centers. Under this program, the NSF provides "seed" money to establish university research programs that are consistent with both university research objectives and industry needs. As these centers grow, support for their operations is increasingly provided by their industrial participants, and eventually no funds come from the NSF. By 1984, 20 such centers had been established with research programs focusing on such technologies as polymers, robotics, ceramics, communication and signal processes, and ultraclean manufacturing environments.

2. Small Business Innovation Research (SBIR) Program. This program was established as a result of a directive to the NSF by the U.S. Congress in 1977 to provide research funding to small business firms. Its purpose was to allow small firms to undertake longer term, higher risk research agendas that they could otherwise not pursue without outside funding. Funding is provided in phases, beginning with research on scientific and engineering problems of interest to the NSF and continuing for those projects which appear promising. In the final product development and commercialization phase, funding is provided entirely by private capital, either in the form of venture capital or an investment by a large industrial company.

3. NSF-Industry Cooperation in Materials Research. Materials research, or the understanding of the properties of materials, is a multidisciplinary endeavor. Research scientists and engineers with many varied backgrounds are necessary. Thus, this is an ideal place to foster industry/university cooperative research agreements. The NSF facilitates these agreements by funding multidisciplinary university centers that include university researchers and visiting scientists and engineers from industry.

INTERCONNECTIONS AMONG TECHNOLOGY DEVELOPERS AND FACILITATORS

Technology facilitators such as MITI stimulate technological development by other organizations, creating interorganizational linkages between technology developers and facilitators. The facilitating organizations, be they private or public, function in three major capacities:

Resource providers, who provide resources to developers of technology in order to stimulate technological development in certain directions, as in the example of MITI.

Policy analysts, who may channel the direction of technology development through persuasive argumentation or state direction, as in the case of the Office of Technology Assessment and the National Science Foundation.

Linking organizations, who often link technology developers, resource providers, and entrepreneurs, as in the case of new business incubators.

In Box 2.2, we have summarized the operation of new business incubators, one type of facilitator that stimulates economic development by linking developers and resource providers.

BOX 2.2

NEW BUSINESS INCUBATORS

The new business incubator is a recent addition to the list of technological facilitators. Surfacing in the mid 1970s, incubators provide a sheltered and supportive environment for start-up and emerging businesses. In their basic form, incubators provide development and administrative support for new enterprises. Interested entrepreneurs develop a business petition for membership in the incubator. If the entrepreneur is accepted, the incubator typically provides space, administrative support, and management consulting to the member firm. In exchange, incubator founders and supporters will generally receive an ownership position in the newly formed company.

Incubators have been created through the actions of a number of different sponsors, each with different goals in mind. The four most common sponsors of incubators are universities, communities, corporations, and private investor groups. Examples of each kind are instructive in understanding both the goals of an incubator as well as the way they are organized.

1. Rensselaer Polytechnic Institute. Rensselaer Polytechnic Institute is a private New York state university that has long had a national reputation for excellence in engineering. Prompted by the desire to improve a declining local industrial base, as well as the need to attract top quality faculty and graduate students, the school began exploring ways in which high-technology firms could be developed in, or lured to, the area. In 1980, this evaluation process led to the opening of one of the first incubators in the United States, a place where technically oriented entrepreneurs could be supported and guided by the resources of a technical university.

   In its initial form, the incubator provided inexpensive leased space and tech-

nical support to the start-up company. In turn, these firms were expected, whenever possible, to use university faculty and graduate students as consultants. As the incubator evolved over the next five years, more formal procedures were instituted. Firms wishing to join the incubator were subjected to an evaluation process that included an appraisal of their business plans as well as an assessment of the fit between the proposed technology to be developed and the research being undertaken by the university. Those firms selected to join the incubator are then required to give 2 percent of their equity to the incubator. Rents are assessed on a floating basis, with higher amounts charged to longer term residents (most leave within twelve to eighteen months); support services are charged on an "as used" basis. By 1985, the incubator had sucessfully "graduated" 21 companies, with most remaining in the local area.

2. The Fulton-Carroll Center for Industry. Opened in 1980, the Fulton-Carroll Center for Industry (FCC) was part of a larger urban revitalization project in a slum area of northwest Chicago. The overall purpose of the revitalization project, undertaken by a nonprofit organization known as the Industrial Council of Northwest Chicago (ICNC), was to stem the loss of the inner-city industrial base by retaining existing businesses and attracting new ones. One element of the project was the demolition of dilapidated vacant buildings and the renovation of other facilities. Using a $1.7 million grant from the federal government, the ICNC was able to purchase and renovate one city block of buildings

Source: Adapted from Smilor, R. W. and Gill, M. D. *The New Business Incubator.* Lexington, MA: Lexington Books 1986.

now known as the Fulton-Carroll Center to house a business incubator.

The FCC incubator is primarily composed of light manufacturing firms and provides its tenants with such services as telephone answering, secretarial support, security, and computer services. In turn, tenant firms pay monthly rents at rates substantially lower than those for comparable space. These rental rates increase each year the firm occupies its space.

The project appears to have been a success. The center has been running at almost 100-percent occupancy since it was opened in 1980. During its first five years of operations, property values in the area have risen fivefold. Finally, the majority of firms that have left the incubator have taken space in the same city area. Thus, the goal of urban revitalization through retention and attraction of businesses appears to have been met.

3. Control Data Corporation Business and Technology Centers. The Control Data Corporation Business and Technology Centers (BTCs) were begun by Control Data Corporation (CDC), a *Fortune 500* company, as part of their corporate policy to participate in small business growth. BTC opened its first incubator in St. Paul, Minnesota, in 1979 after purchasing and renovating a building in a deteriorating warehouse district of that city. The initial focus of the incubator was on high-technology start-up businesses, and thus the facility included a clean room, electronics laboratory, technical library, and computer services. The incubator had trouble, however, in attracting high-technology firms, and thus much of the technological support services were eventually removed. BTC officials attribute this situation, in part, to the highly specific research needs of high-technology start-ups.

By 1985, BTC was operating 22 incubators across the nation, generally under franchise agreements with local community governments and economic development agencies. The incubators had more than 700 companies as tenants, occupying over 2 million square feet of operating space. These centers provide not only the typical administrative support services, but also training and consulting on business-related matters. Each center has a support staff, including a manager and a business analyst, as well as an advisory board composed of local businesspeople such as accountants, lawyers, and bankers.

4. The Rubicon Group. Founded in 1983, Rubicon Group, Inc., is a high-technology incubator funded through a private investment pool and operated as a for-profit corporation. Start-up businesses that enter the incubator are funded through a partnership agreement with incubator investors. In exchange for this funding, and the use of incubator resources, the investment partners retain a majority equity share in the new company. By 1986, four of the five start-up companies in the incubator had achieved sales in excess of $500,000.

The relationships among technology developers and between technology developers and facilitators often culminate in the formation of innovation networks, or clusters of organizations that share interpersonal and organizational ties with one another. Silicon Valley in California, Route 128 in Massachusetts, and North Carolina Research Triangle are the most famous innovation networks in the United States. Innovation networks are not confined to high-technology industries but exist in traditional industries also: in furniture (Grand Rapids, Michigan), in carpet (Dalton, Georgia), and in weaving (Northern Italy). Indeed, innovation networks are a major feature of all developed economies.

Networks form when the benefits of proximity to competitors outweigh the costs. New technology that improves the productivity of the industry as a whole gets diffused more easily. As a result, it is easier to determine trends in what buyers want; the arrival of component and services suppliers makes it easier to improve the value chain; and the effects of competing for employees are balanced because qualified people from all over the world gravitate to the cluster.[4]

Networks speed technology development for several reasons:

1. Networks assist in the diffusion of technology.
2. They create a critical mass of skills that speed knowledge development.
3. They provide a social safety net for individuals. Because technology development is risky, victims of innovation failure often can seek employment in an existing labor market that is not controlled by one or two firms.

The networks are valuable sources of technical and market information. The personal linkages that underpin these networks enable speedy sharing of information among organizations that are part of the network. When technological change is rapid, relevant information may be confined to the individuals in the network. Thus, information about choices of competitors, flow of funds into new technology thrusts, or availability of technical expertise is available only through the personal linkages in the networks. These kinds of information are critical in understanding technological environment, making technology-related decisions, and managing their implementation.

Technological development takes place among different organizations that specialize in different stages or levels of technology development. Further, networks develop among these organizations for pursuing specific technology development thrusts. These networks are, to a large extent, formed through temporary arrangements and evolve over time.

CROSS-NATIONAL DIFFERENCES AMONG NETWORKS

As technological developments accelerate, some nations have begun to recognize that national competitiveness requires establishing a national innovation system that speeds the transfer of basic research results to applications, i.e., creation of marketable products and processes. Formalized networks that aid and direct the transfer of technology from the laboratory to industry have therefore begun to take on national significance. At the same time, there is recognition that small and medium-sized industrial firms may represent an important component of a national economy. Yet, these same firms do not have the internal resources necessary to fund any appreciable research and development projects. Thus, some nations have initiated networks that both facilitate the transfer of technology and ensure that this technology is made available to all industrial segments of the economy, especially the small and medium-sized enterprises.

Although the United States has pursued several programs to facilitate technology transfer, they are not formalized to the degree to which some other nations have formalized their national networks. In Japan, we illustrated the role played by MITI. In addition, in Europe, many countries have established nationwide systems designed to promote and facilitate the development and commercialization of new technologies. In Box 2.3, we have summarized the national innovation systems that have been developed over the years in Germany and in the United Kingdom. Although these systems

BOX 2.3

CROSS-NATIONAL DIFFERENCES IN NETWORKS

As technologies change at an ever-increasing rate, nations have begun to recognize that remaining competitive in this environment means establishing systems that allow basic research to be translated into marketable products and processes. Formalized networks that aid and direct the transfer of technology from the laboratory to industry have therefore begun to take on competitive significance. At the same time, there is a recognition that small and medium-sized industrial firms may represent a significant portion of a national economy. Yet, these same firms do not have the internal resources necessary to fund any appreciable research and development projects. Thus, from a national policy standpoint, the concern must be to establish networks that both facilitate the transfer of technology and ensure that this technology is made available to all industrial segments of the economy.

On the national level, the players in the development and commercialization of technology include federal research facilities, universities, state and local governmental units, and industry itself. As we discussed in Box 2.1, the United States has pursued several programs to address the need of technology transfer. Other nations, however, have much more formalized networks to achieve this goal. In particular, Germany and the United Kingdom have established nationwide systems designed to promote and facilitate the development and commercialization of new technologies. A brief overview of these two systems is now provided.

GERMANY

The German system includes the establishment of formal programs at all governmental and geographical levels. These programs result from broad national initiatives and may involve public funds to establish research infrastructure and industry funds to provide for ongoing projects. They may be in the form of direct assistance to university laboratories, or joint research arrangements between industry and universities where matching public funds are made available. In some instances, the government may subsidize company R&D personnel at research institutes or provide financial support for technology-based start-up companies. Inherent in the system is the recognition that some institutions are better equipped than others at certain phases of the process. Thus, universities are assigned basic research agendas; applied research is carried out by research institutes established by the government for that purpose. Finally, this national network specifically includes local and regional governmental entities such as chambers of commerce to ensure that the network is accessible throughout the nation.

What is important to note about this system is that the formalized programs represent a cooperative network across many institutions and geographic locations that can be accessed by all participants in the research, development, and commercialization process. It is a comprehensive system that crosses all institutional and geographical locations in the nation. Industrial firms, including small and medium-sized businesses, do not have to establish their own networks in order to participate in technology development. They need only take advantage of networks that are already in existence. Further, the focus on regional economic development allows technology to spread throughout the economy. Finally, effort is undertaken in those institutions most likely to succeed at a given task.

Source: From Redwood, A. L. 1991. "Innovation and competitiveness through technology transfer and university-industry liaison in Europe." Institute for Public Policy and Business Research, The University of Kansas, Report #184. Reprinted by permission.

Box 2.3 (*continued*)

UNITED KINGDOM

A major focus of the U.K. science and technology policy is on the linkage between university-based and research and industry-based commercialization. To foster these linkages, the government has established several formal mechanisms. These include the establishment of an Industrial Liaison Office at all British universities as well as promoting science/research parks at these universities. They also include the development of a national database of academic research expertise and the formation of the British Technology Group (BTG) to patent and license university research results. Finally, the policies promote the estab-

lishment of university companies to market university research capabilities and commercialize research results.

Again, we note that government policy in the United Kingdom plays a significant role in establishing a national network for research, development, and commercialization. However, the U.K. policies are much more limiting than those in Germany. In the United Kingdom, the focus is exclusively on the flow of research results from the university to industry; critical linkages such as regional economic development and the transfer of technology to small and medium-sized firms is ignored.

are significantly different, both are premised on the idea that government-sponsored organizations can help stimulate technological development among private organizations.

CHANGES IN THE TECHNOLOGICAL ENVIRONMENT

The technological environment is dynamic and evolves over time. Thus, organizations in the technological environment and the linkages among them change. New technologies grow out of the activities of creation and application of knowledge; they enhance human capabilities. Indeed, our interest in the technological environment is due to the dynamic nature of this environment.

Changes in the technological environment often come about in two interrelated ways: (1) induced changes and (2) autonomous changes.

INDUCED CHANGES

Forces in macroenvironmental segments, other than the technological, trigger changes in the technological environment. Induced changes represent the technological consequences created by social, political, or economic forces. For example, demographics and lifestyles, especially through their impact on the political and economic arenas, often influence the nature and direction of technology development. The current interest in women's health issues is a direct result of the demographic changes leading more women into the workforce. Similarly, the aging of the population has caused an upsurge in attention to the problems of the elderly. In turn, one manifestation of these concerns has been the commitment of large amounts of public and private scientific research studying the health issues peculiar to women and the aged. In a similar way, social values directly or indirectly influence technological developments. Changing values, such as concern for the environment, get institutionalized in government policies and structures (e.g., the National Environmental Protection Act).

Although various macroenvironmental segments influence the technological environment, of particular importance is the role played by the political/regulatory and economic environments. Hence, we discuss the influence of these two environmental segments in greater detail.

LINKAGE BETWEEN TECHNOLOGICAL AND THE POLITICAL/ REGULATORY ENVIRONMENTS

Within any nation state, the political/regulatory environment shapes the scope and direction of basic research and the thrust of more applied technological developments. During the first half of the twentieth century, technological development in the United States was, in part, the result of changes that occurred in the competitive and legal environments prevailing in the country:

> First, industrialization of U.S. industry created a need for large firms to perform materials analysis and to establish quality control laboratories. As these production-oriented functions grew in size and frequency, they provided the seed from which corporate laboratories devoted to long-term research would evolve.
>
> Second, U.S. antitrust policy in the late 19th century was focused on preventing inter-firm collusion to control prices and output. This government policy was in part responsible for the merger wave that occurred in U.S. industry during 1895 to 1904. The large firms that resulted from these mergers had a need to develop organizational structures that could coordinate the activities of their many parts. One such activity that required central coordination was the R&D function, and thus industrial research became institutionalized into the corporate structure. In the early 20th century, U.S. antitrust policy was again to play a role as a driver of industrial research. Justice department prosecution for restraint of trade resulting from the acquisition of competitors began to force firms to look for other ways of securing a dominant market position. Industrial research was a way in which firms could achieve growth through innovative developments in their primary industries, as well as diversify into related businesses without undertaking acquisitions.
>
> Third, the strengthening of laws regarding intellectual property rights in the late 19th century increased the competitive importance of internally developed patents. The courts began to uphold the validity of patent protection for goods that were not in production. Thus, the establishment of a broad patent portfolio by a firm provided a strong competitive advantage in protecting market position.[5]

In the last two decades in the United States, there has been ongoing debate about the appropriate role of the federal government in technology development. On the one hand, some have argued that governments should keep their hands off any technology policy and let free markets drive the direction of technology development. On the other hand, some others argue explicitly for a technology policy to bolster national competitiveness. Indeed, President Clinton explicitly argued for such a policy as part of his 1992 election campaign. In Box 2.4, we have summarized the Clinton/Gore technology policy.

BOX 2.4

THE CLINTON/GORE TECHNOLOGY POLICY
FOR AMERICA

In September 1992, presidential candidate Bill Clinton introduced his proposed technology policy for America and declared that U.S. technological leadership would be a national priority of his administration. This policy consisted of six broad initiatives designed to "restore" America's technological leadership by helping Americans "develop and quickly utilize new technologies." The following represents a summary of these broad initiatives.

1. The creation of a twenty-first century technology infrastructure. A twenty-first century infrastructure must encompass the communications, transportation, and environmental needs of the nation in addition to the traditional infrastructures of highways, bridges, and harbors. By directing efforts toward the creation of this infrastructure, the infrastructure itself can act as a *technological driver* for the nation and thus stimulate R&D efforts, private sector investments, and job creation.

2. Establishing education and training programs for a high-skill workforce. Throughout the industrial world, the workplace has become, and will continue to become, more high-skill intensive. For America to remain competitive in this environment, the training of its workforce must keep pace with the technological changes occurring. To do so, both government and the private sector must establish education and training programs centered on meeting the needs that new technologies create.

3. Investing in technology programs that empower America's small businesses. America's small and medium-sized businesses account for a significant portion of GNP, employment, and job creation. Their size, however, may limit their access to technological developments that are needed to remain competitive. This initiative proposes a significant extension to state and local government efforts by establishing a *national technology extension program* designed to provide these businesses with necessary technological knowledge. It would also require that federal agencies set aside a portion of their R&D budgets for small businesses and provide for government investment in private-sector consortia.

4. Increasing the percentage of federal R&D for critical technologies. This initiative proposes a shift in federal R&D dollars currently devoted to defense programs to nondefense programs and refocusing those dollars on *critical technologies* such as advanced materials, information technologies, and new manufacturing processes.

5. Leveraging existing federal investment in technology to maximize its contribution to industrial performance. America's federal laboratories represent a potentially significant resource in the arena of global competition. Yet, their existing Cold War mandate directs approximately one-half of their $23 billion annual budgets toward military applications. This initiative calls for a change in that mandate to include cooperation with industry and universities on technological development for commercial usage.

6. Creating a world-class business environment for private sector investment and innovation. The achievement of technological leadership requires the availability of capital resources for investment. To promote that investment, this initiative proposes tax incentives on plant, equipment, and R&D investments; trade policies that ensure competitive access to foreign markets; and antitrust reform to enable U.S. firms to pool resources and share risks.

Source: The Clinton/Gore position paper on a national technology policy, September 1992.

The influence of political environment is felt not merely through government technology policy. In the United States, because the federal government acts both as developer and facilitator through its various agencies, the influence of the political/regulatory environment is felt in at least three ways:

1. It influences the thrust of major basic research. For example, prior to the discovery of the transistor in 1948, European firms were the equal of U.S. firms in advanced-component technology. In the early fifties, the military services became convinced of the strategic importance of transistors and semiconductor devices. As a result, the Department of Defense financed semiconductor R&D on a large scale. Between 1955 and 1961, direct government funding for semiconductor R&D and production refinement totaled $66 million. Beginning with the transistor, almost all the important inventions and innovations in component technology until the mid-1970s have been made in the United States—most of them consequences of direct and indirect government support.[6] More recently, with the build down of the defense budget, there are pressures on federal laboratories to engage in applied research and away from basic research.

2. Through regulations it can facilitate or impede every phase of technology development. Regulations sometimes impact what research can be worked on, what organizations can work on it, the acquisition and use of patents, and even the diffusion of research outputs and technological changes. Regulatory agencies such as the Federal Drug Administration and the Department of Commerce's Bureau of Standards must give their approval before many of the outputs of technological change can be commercialized.

3. It can act as a facilitator of private sector technology development. Through its authorization of funds and its oversight role of governmental departments and agencies, Congress provides direct and indirect supports and incentives for all phases of technological change. These supports and incentives (e.g., direct funding of R&D, tax policies, technology transfer programs, patent laws) have contributed significantly to the development and diffusion of many technologies.

State and local governments also act as facilitators of technological development. In the 1980s, such an endeavor occurred with the development of North Carolina's renowned Research Triangle Park. This park was a state project designed to foster economic development by establishing an attractive atmosphere for high-technology companies. By building the park and making available the research conducted at Duke University and the University of North Carolina, the state was able to attract such high-technology firms as Northern Telecom, IBM, and Burroughs Wellcome. The area now contains one of the nation's highest concentrations of Ph.Ds.[7] In short, during various time periods, the political environment influences the evolution of technological environment.

LINKAGE BETWEEN TECHNOLOGICAL AND ECONOMIC ENVIRONMENTS

Economic conditions exert a primary causal influence on the level and pace of technological change. Corporations often turn to technology to address the challenges created by economic pressures: They adopt more efficient technology to contain costs or broaden the market presence. Thus, the automobile industry introduced fuel-efficient cars to attract consumers who had become conscious of fuel prices. More recently, Intel's introduction of the Celeron processor in response to the emerging competition from Asia was an acknowledgement of the need for less expensive processors to broaden the consumer market for personal computers. Indeed, it is often suggested that basic and applied research are driven more by the prevailing market or economic conditions than by the availability of scientific and technological knowledge.[8]

AUTONOMOUS CHANGES

In addition to the changes caused by the various macroenvironmental segments, technological environment may also change due to the independent actions of technology developers in their quest for competitive advantage. We term this form of technological change "autonomous"; that is, these changes are initiated by technology developers but are largely independent of the forces in other macroenvironmental segments. In the case of autonomous changes, technological developments feed upon themselves, as if they have a life of their own. These changes are less predictable than induced changes but they can be tracked on an ongoing basis through personal sources of information.

Many examples of technological changes leading to further technological developments could be cited. Advances in semiconductor and microprocessor technology have led to technological developments affecting a wide variety of products, such as computers, electronic equipment, automobiles, refrigerators, and energy control systems. Advances in space-related technology frequently find their way into technological improvements in industrial, commercial, and consumer products. This list goes on.

Whereas other macroenvironmental segments cause induced changes, autonomous changes in technology are drivers of fundamental social and economic change.

SOCIAL CHANGE

Indeed, one group of theorists has traced the development of society along stages, each stage corresponding to a specific technology of production:

1. The first stage corresponds to agriculture.
2. The second stage corresponds to machine production.
3. The third stage refers to the information revolution triggered by advances in computer technology.

These theorists' ideas are summarized in Box 2.5. One of the characteristics of the stages is that as we move from the earlier stages (the first and second stages) to the later stage (the third), the technological environment is increasingly turbulent. First, technology development activities lead to rapidly increasing growth in our stock of knowledge and technology; second, there is greater interconnection among the institutions involved in technology development.

LONG-WAVE THEORY OF ECONOMIC CHANGE

A reciprocal linkage exists between technological and economic segments of the macroenvironment. Indeed, one group of economists has proposed a "long-wave theory" of economic development, arguing that technological innovation lies at the heart of major periods of economic expansion. In its simplified version, the process works as follows:

First, discoveries in science trigger technological innovation, leading to new products and markets.

BOX 2.5

STAGES OF TECHNOLOGICAL CHANGE

The technological environment can be thought of as a subset of the system of social philosophies, norms, dogmas, and ideologies that we group under the broader heading of civilization. Each phase of civilization is grounded in its own system, and these systems change slowly over long periods of time. As new ways of thinking and acting grow in acceptance, they become powerful "waves of change" that first overlap, and then inevitably conflict, with the old system. In a broad sense, technology can be seen as both following and driving these conflicts.

In 1980, Alvin Toffler summarized three "waves of change," and the monumental impact that these waves had on civilization, in a book entitled *The Third Wave*. In essense, Toffler was dividing the history of civilization into three distinct periods of time that he called *waves*. Each of these waves has its own distinct "techno-sphere," or its energy, production, and distribution systems. This techno-sphere in turn drove, or was driven by, the development of a complementary "socio-sphere," or social system of family, workplace, and educational institutions. Thus, broad technological changes can be thought of as being tied directly to broad changes in the social development of society. In Toffler's view, the first three waves are as follows:

The First Wave. The first wave of change occurred in connection with the agricultural revolution, a period in civilization's history from about 8000 B.C. to about A.D. 1700. Prior to the agricultural revolution, humans lived in small, often migratory, groups feeding themselves by hunting, fishing, and foraging. With the agricultural revolution came the technologies that allowed people to "take root" in one place, assured of a reasonably constant food supply, and thus to create what we term a civilization. Technologies that emerged during this wave included levers and hoists, winches and wedges—simple machines designed to amplify the renewable energy sources of human and animal muscle power, wind, sun, and water.

The Second Wave. The second wave of change is often referred to as the *industrial revolution* and occupied a period of time in human development from the 1700s into recent times. In the United States, this wave "crested" in the mid-1950s, but in many parts of the world it is still continuing. This period ended the dominance of agricultural civilization and witnessed the industrialization of society. The technologies introduced with this wave, generally based upon electromechanical machines powered by nonrenewable fossil fuels, produced widespread changes in the makeup of society. Examples of these technologies include the steam engine, the automobile, and electricity. Families became smaller, work shifted from the field to the factory, and education of the young shifted from the home to organized classrooms.

The Third Wave. This wave of change coincides with the postindustrial era, a period beginning in the mid-to-late 1950s and now being experienced by most high-technology nations such as the United States, the countries of Western Europe, and Japan. This era is grounded in electronic systems that foster rapid communication, computation, and dissemination of information. The wide availability of technologies such as computers, telecommunications, robotics, and bioengineering has also begun to leave its mark on the social characteristics of society. Fundamental changes in social behavior can now be seen in such areas as the organization of the workforce, the education of the young, and the diversity in family form.

We summarize the major components of these three waves in Table 2.4.1.

Is there a "Fourth Wave?" Many believe so, but opinions differ regarding the nature of the fourth wave. At least two different types have been proposed: (1) Green Wave and (2) Biological Wave.

Following on Toffler's lead, Herman Maynard and Susan Mehrtens envisioned a

---

Source: Adapted from Toffler, A. *The Third Wave.* William Morrow & Co.: New York, 1980, and Maynard, H. B. and Mehrtens, S. E. *The Fourth Wave: Business in the 21st Century.* Berett-Koehler Publishers: San Francisco, CA, 1993.

Box 2.5 (*continued*)

TABLE 2.4.1   A Comparison of Toffler's Three Waves

	1st Wave	*2nd Wave*	*3rd Wave*
Major Technologies	Levers and hoists, winches and wedges, machines designed to amplify the renewable energy sources of human and muscle power, wind, sun, and water.	Electromechanical machines composed of pulleys, belts, bearings, and bolts powered by nonrenewable, fossil fuels.	Electronic devices that foster rapid communications and computations. Technologies designed to harness renewable energy sources. Biotechnologies focused on improving life.
Technological Development	Providing for the needs of the immediate family and community.	Centralizing technology for mass production and distribution of goods. Work shifted from the field to the factory.	Electronically driven clusters of technology using minimum amounts of energy. The emergence of ecological and humanist concerns. Automation of thought.
Institutions and Networks of Organizations Involved in Technological Development	Small communities and individual craftsmen. The large, "extended" family rooted in one place. Multigenerational households that functioned as an economic production unit. Business undertaken in the form of sole proprietorships and partnerships. Education in the home. Person-to-person communication.	The small, mobile "nuclear" family. Mass education of the young. Long-distance communication. Large factories, mills, foundries, and mines. The large corporation as the unit of business funded by external investors.	Increasing interdependence of organizations. Development of strategic alliances and "virtual" organizations. International mobility of workforces and capital. Increasing collaboration between private and public corporations. The acceptance of the "electronic cottage" as an alternative workplace.

yet-to-be-achieved fourth wave for the future. In their 1993 book *The Fourth Wave,* these authors present a view of the corporation as the steward of global concerns. These organizations will appear more as communities than as business entities, with decisions made in a consensual manner based upon the needs of all people and the environment. Technologies pursued will be "appropriate" to the needs of a world community and in consort with the needs of the planet. Quality of life and alignment with the natural order will be the primary measures of corporate wealth. Ownership will be communal and economic and social justice will be major concerns. In sum, the corporation will view itself holistically as an important guardian of society.

Alternately, some believe that beyond the information revolution or Toffler's third wave lies the biological revolution. At the core of this revolution or fourth wave lie scientific advances in our understanding of human genetic code. Human genome projects and other efforts at mapping the genetic code are expected not only to bring about medical advances, but also to fundamentally change the way we go about living our daily lives. Already this potential has created ethical dilemmas, especially pertaining to cloning. As we deal with scientific developments and solve social and human dilemmas, many believe that we will have arrived at the fourth wave.

Second, new industries are formed around these markets, and continued innovations in these newly formed industries expand the markets.

Third, as technology matures, many competitors enter internationally, eventually creating excess capacity that in turn decreases profitability.

Finally, business failures, unemployment, and attendant economic turmoil in financial markets may lead to depressions.[9]

Both types of change in the technological environment—induced and autonomous—create opportunities and threats for firms operating in various industries. However, they have different implications for the management of technology. Induced changes can be predicted; indeed, firms often construct scenarios of technology futures to develop their technology strategy. Autonomous changes are difficult to forecast because they are the result of the actions taken by technology developers in specific technologies. Firms interested in specific technologies will have to track these changes on an ongoing basis. As we discussed earlier, in the technological environment, information about specific technologies lies with individuals in various organizations—developers and facilitators.

In summary, technological environment is a very dynamic segment of the macroenvironment. Basic and applied research often create technologies with the force of inevitability; however, the direction, thrust, and level of technology development are influenced by a host of factors, especially the political and economic conditions prevailing in a country. We will now sketch some of the key changes currently taking place in the technological environment.

MAJOR CURRENT DEVELOPMENTS IN THE TECHNOLOGICAL ENVIRONMENT

As we enter the threshold of the twenty-first century, technological change is accelerating and becoming increasingly pervasive. The pervasiveness of change makes technological environment very uncertain for the firms that are competing in various industries. Although a large number of specific developments are taking place in different technological sectors and industries, three general trends deserve special mention: (1) globalization, (2) time compression, and (3) technology integration. Figure 2.6 provides an overview of these trends.

GLOBALIZATION

Globalization refers to the process by which the various nations in the world are increasingly being interconnected politically and economically through international trade. Trade relationships have always existed between the United States, Canada, and Europe. Further, since World War II, international trade relations have existed between the North American continent and the Pacific. In recent years, however, interdependence among nations has been growing at a faster rate, especially after the fall of the Iron Curtain and the dissolution of the former Soviet Union.

Four aspects of globalization have significant consequences for the technological environment: (1) the resources allocated to technology development; (2) the location of manufacturing facilities; (3) the role of multinational corporations; and (4) the differing comparative advantage of nations in technology development.

- *Globalization*
  Resource allocated to technology development
  Changing location of manufacturing facilities
  Rise of multinationals
  Comparative advantage of nations
- *Time Compression*
  Shortened product life cycles
  Shortened development times
  Decreasing payback periods
- *Technology Integration*
  Combining technologies to develop new products
  Combining technologies to commercialize products

FIGURE 2.6 OVERVIEW OF TRENDS IN TECHNOLOGY ENVIRONMENT

RESOURCES ALLOCATED TO TECHNOLOGY DEVELOPMENT

The proportion of resources spent on technology development—R&D expenditures—across various countries has been changing in recent years. In Table 2.1, we have sketched the R&D expenditures of selected countries over the past decade. In the United States, just as in Europe, the total R&D expenditures cover both the funds deployed for defense purposes and the funds for research undertaken in industrial corporations. As shown in the table, the amount of resources allocated by the United States for R&D expenditures has plateaued in the last few years; other countries collectively have had large increases in the amount of resources allocated to R&D. Thus, where the United States spent 2.2 percent of the dollars for R&D in 1975 and 2.7 percent in 1989, Japan has increased its share of R&D expenditures from 2.0 to 3.0 percent over the same period.

Because R&D expenditures represent inputs to technology development, we should expect the outputs of technology development efforts to correspond to the trends in R&D expenditures. In Table 2.2, we have sketched the patents—often considered to

TABLE 2.1 National R&D Expenditures (Constant 1989 U.S. Dollars, in billions)

	1975	*1980*	*1985*	*1987*	*1988*	*1989*
United States	$74.9	$92.6	$128.0	$136.1	$137.0	$140.4
France	$12.1	$14.2	$ 19.4	$ 20.7	$ 21.2	$ 21.9
West Germany	$18.6	$24.2	$ 30.0	$ 32.4	$ 33.6	$ 35.0
Japan	$30.5	$43.0	$ 66.6	$ 71.3	$ 78.1	$ 84.6
United Kingdom	$12.7	NA	$ 16.6	$ 18.1	$ 17.9	$ 16.7

National R&D as a Percentage of GNP (Constant 1989 U.S. Dollars)

	1975	*1980*	*1985*	*1987*	*1988*	*1989*
United States	2.2	2.3	2.8	2.8	2.7	2.7
France	1.8	1.8	2.3	2.3	2.3	2.3
West Germany	2.2	2.4	2.8	2.9	2.9	2.9
Japan	2.0	2.2	2.8	2.8	2.9	3.0
United Kingdom	2.1	NA	2.3	2.3	2.2	2.0

Source: The Statistical Abstract of the United States. United States Census Bureau, 1978 through 1992.

TABLE 2.2 Total U.S. Patents Issued Annually to Selected Countries

	1975	*1980*	*1985*	*1987*	*1988*	*1989*
United States		40,800	43,300	47,700	44,600	54,600
France	2,400	2,000	2,400	2,900	2,800	3,300
West Germany	5,800	5,400	6,600	8,000	7,500	8,600
Japan	5,900	6,600	12,800	17,100	17,000	21,100
United Kingdom	3,100	2,300	2,500	3,000	2,800	3,300

Source: The Statistical Abstract of the United States. United States Census Bureau, 1978 through 1992.

be one output of the technology development activity—that were filed in the United States by five select countries. The increasing patent activity of the United States and other countries is evident. Also note that, as was the case with R&D expenditures, Japan has been increasing the outputs of technology development activity.

These shifting trends have two major implications for developments taking place in the technological environment. First, with the greater participation of countries that have hitherto been less active in technological development, the rate of change in the technological environment can be expected to increase. Thus, we should expect the emergence of technologies at a faster rate in the coming years. This is simply a reflection of the increasing amount of dollars—on a global basis—being devoted to technology development. Second, the scope of the technological environment has broadened beyond the borders of the United States and Europe—the traditional strongholds of science and technology for the last two centuries. Technology development is now being conducted all over the world; increasingly, we should expect these developments to emanate from the Pacific region, including such countries as Korea and China. Thus, the scope of the technological environment is now fully global.

LOCATION OF MANUFACTURING FACILITIES

During the last two decades, many firms have shifted their manufacturing capacity from advanced industrialized countries to relatively underdeveloped economies of the world. For example, during the 1960s, U.S. firms in the consumer electronics industry located most of their manufacturing capacity in the United States itself. During the 1970s however, we saw the shift of these manufacturing facilities to the Pacific Rim countries, such as Taiwan. By 1980, roughly all of the manufacturing capacity in consumer electronics was located outside the borders of the United States.

The shift of manufacturing capacity from the advanced to the underdeveloped economies is not confined to U.S. firms but is true of firms from other countries, as well. Japanese firms—to cite a specific case—also exhibit similar patterns. Japanese firms in the automobile industry had initially located their manufacturing capacity almost wholly in Japan. In recent times, the Japanese have begun to locate their automobile manufacturing capacity all over the world.[10]

Although locating manufacturing facilities all over the world heightens global interdependence, it also suggests that some of the improvements in manufacturing will occur in places other than the United States or other advanced industrialized countries. Such improvements may manifest themselves in the techniques to improve productivity, such as quality circles. They might also appear in other areas as improved plant layout, worker skills, or methods of production.

RISE OF MULTINATIONALS

A third factor that is characteristic of globalization is the rise of multinational corporations. By "multinational corporation," we mean those firms that have operations—manufacturing, marketing, and/or R&D—in a number of countries. During the 1960s major multinationals were located in the United States and Europe. However, as we enter the twenty-first century, multinational corporations from other countries are also becoming significant players in international trade. As shown in Table 2.3, in 1970, 57 percent of the *Fortune* list of the 500 largest multinationals were located in the United States; however, this percentage had declined to 33 percent by 1990. An increasing number of multinationals—those belonging to the largest 500 corporations in the world—are located in Japan, Europe, and even the newly industrialized countries.

One of the most significant recent developments in the operations of the multinational firms is the growing research and development activity they conduct outside their host country. According to the data from the National Science Foundation, total R&D expenditures of U.S. firms in foreign countries increased from 2.2 billion dollars in 1978 to more than 6 billion dollars in 1988. On an annual basis, this growth reflects an average increase of 12 percent, compared to an average annual increase in inflation during the same period of about 6.3 percent. By 1988, some industry groups were allocating a larger percentage of their R&D budgets to foreign-based R&D. For example, industrial chemical companies devoted 21 percent of their R&D budgets to international R&D whereas the figures for pharmaceutical and machinery companies were 16 percent and 11 percent, respectively. The increased activity in multinational R&D is not limited to just U.S. firms. The number of Swedish firms performing R&D at foreign locations has increased considerably since the late 1970s. Additionally, multinational R&D is more common for European firms than for U.S. firms. Although Japanese multinationals have traditionally avoided overseas R&D activities due to their emphasis on centralized control, there is some evidence indicating that their approach may be changing, as well.[11]

TABLE 2.3   The Changing Face of the Global *Fortune 500*

Each year *Fortune* publishes listings of the largest industrial firms in the United States and internationally. In the table, we present the number of firms in each of five countries that have been in the list of largest 500 firms as published by *Fortune* three times. *Fortune* uses sales, in U.S. dollars, to rank these 500 firms. Nowhere is the trend towards increasing globalization of industrial enterprise more evident than in the numbers that these lists display.

	1970	*1980*	*1990*
United States	286	219	167
Japan	47	71	111
Great Britain	48	53	43
Germany	27	37	32
France	21	27	29
All Other Foreign Firms	71	93	118

Source: Compiled from *Fortune* magazine's yearly listing of largest industrial firms in the United States and outside the United States, 1970, 1980, and 1990.

The rise of multinationals, and their allocation of R&D expenditures to foreign-based R&D, further heightens the trend toward globalization of the technological environment. Just as we stated earlier, R&D development could no longer be tracked on a local basis; technological development should be tracked on a global basis.

COMPARATIVE ADVANTAGE OF NATIONS

Economists have long recognized that different countries have different comparative strengths. As early as the nineteenth century, David Ricardo advanced the hypothesis of comparative advantage of nations. He argued that, in the bilateral trade between two countries, the relative advantage of one nation over the other should determine the development of specific industries. As globalization has proceeded, both multinational firms and firms following global strategies have begun to take account of the comparative advantage of various countries.

Comparative advantages may accrue from differences in factor costs, such as cost of labor or raw materials. Increasingly, however, comparative advantages also accrue from the ability of nations to create specialized technology-based assets. For example, comparative advantage can result from the presence of world-class institutions that create specific technologies and then continually work to update them. Denmark hospitals that focus on studying and treating diabetes have world-leading export positions in insulin. Similarly, Holland has a premier research institution in the cultivation, packaging, and shipping of flowers: Holland is the world's export leader.[12] Differences in factor costs among countries and the existence of specialized assets in different countries represent two factors that are encouraging firms to locate their technology and product development functions around the globe. For example, Texas Instruments located its software development in low-wage countries to take advantage of the low labor costs among computer scientists.

In summary, globalization has a number of implications for the technological environment. First, the institutions in the technological environment—developers as well as facilitators—have to be tracked on a global basis; they span the entire globe. The increasing trend toward globalization suggests that significant institutions are likely to reside outside the boundaries of any specific country. Second, the interconnections among the organizations in the technological environment are likely to cross the borders of many countries. Increasing globalization is leading to a greater degree of interconnectedness among these institutions. Thus, technology developers in one country (for example, U.S. universities or firms) are likely to consider facilitators (e.g., venture capitalists) from other countries (such as Japan or Europe) to help with financial or knowledge resources in their development efforts.

TIME COMPRESSION

A second major development in the technological environment is time compression, which refers to the rapid decrease in time between critical events in technology development and commercialization. Time compression is reflected in the newly emerging source of competitive advantage of firms—speed; that is, the ability to learn, adapt, and innovate at increasingly faster rates. According to IBM's former chief scientist, Japan's greatest technological strength relative to the United States is the speed with which developments are translated into improved products and processes.[13] Indeed, the outcome of the intense rivalry that currently exists between Japan and the United States in many high-technology industries like computers, electronics, and biotechnology will be determined in part by how quickly each nation's firms can develop and commercialize new products and processes that are central to success in these industries.

We will discuss three facets of time compression: (1) shortened product life cycles, (2) shortened development times; and (3) increased pressure exerted by decreasing payback periods.

SHORTENED PRODUCT LIFE CYCLES

Product life cycle refers to the evolution of sales of a product over time, from its introduction to the time when its market reaches maturity. As early as 1967, Alvin Toffler, a futurist and journalist, popularized the idea that product life cycle is becoming shorter over time. For example, the average time to reach the maximum sales for three groups of household appliances was, respectively, 34 years (those introduced before 1920); 22 years during the period 1920 to 1939; and 8 years (1939 to 1959). Recent studies have provided evidence that the trend toward shorter product life cycles has continued beyond the 1960s. Thus, in 1980, when a group of researchers reviewed the introduction and growth stages for 37 household appliances based upon units shipped during three distinct time periods (1922 to 1942, 1945 to 1964, and 1965 to 1979), they reported a significant decrease in both stages of the product's life cycle. The mean time in years for the introduction stage went from 12.5 to 7.0 to 2.0 years; the mean time in years for the growth stage went from 33.8 to 19.5 to 6.8 years.[14]

SHORTENED DEVELOPMENT TIMES

Whereas product life cycle referred to the speed with which a product penetrates the market, the development time refers to the time taken to develop a specific technology into a marketable product. Just as in the case of product life cycle, the development times of major innovations have been declining. In Table 2.4, we present the development times for certain major innovations marketed in the twentieth century. As can be seen, the development times of major innovations have steadily declined.

In addition, large U.S. firms have been paying attention to the reduction of development times in their organizations. Table 2.5 presents the changes in development times for a select set of U.S. corporations. Such firms as Du Pont and Corning Glass have been able to reduce development costs substantially as a result of shorter development times. Indeed, they are becoming not merely fast but also more efficient in development.

Development times, on the whole, vary across industries as well as countries. Indeed, it is now widely believed that Japanese firms tend to develop and commercialize new products and processes more quickly than their U.S. counterparts. Averaged over

TABLE 2.4   Decreasing Times from Invention to Production

	Technology	Time Lag
1852	Fluorescent	82 years
1887	Radar	46 years
1891	Zipper	34 years
1907	Television	29 years
1940	Transistor	10 years

Source: From *Technotrends* by Daniel Burrus with Roger Gittines. Copyright © 1993 by Daniel Burrus. Reprinted by permission of HarperCollins Publishers, Inc.

TABLE 2.5   Decreasing Development Times

Firm	Product	From	To	Savings
ALCOA	*Can*	6 mos	*2 days*	$98,000
AT&T	*New Phones*	2 yrs	*1 yr*	Unknown
Corning Glass	*New glass*	20 yrs	*3 mos*	$15 Mil
Du Pont	*New material*	5 yrs	*2 wks*	$5 Mil
GE	*Circuits*	3 wks	*3 days*	Unknown
Motorola	*Pager*	3 wks	*2 hrs*	Unknown

Source: From *Technotrends* by Daniel Burrus with Roger Gittines. Copyright © 1993 by Daniel Burrus. Reprinted by permission of HarperCollins Publishers, Inc.

all industries, these time differences may vary between 6 to 18 percent.[15] However, the picture changes from industry to industry. In some industries like machinery, substantial differences exist between Japanese and U.S. firms. In other industries like instruments, no substantial differences appear to exist. In a similar way, Japanese firms also developed and commercialized new products and processes more cheaply than did American firms. This cost differential could range from 10 to 23 percent, according to one estimate. Here also, the situation varies from industry to industry. For example, in machinery and instruments, the cost differential seems substantial, whereas in chemicals there was no substantial differential between the two countries.[16]

DECREASING PAYBACK PERIOD

A third factor that is driving time compression is the pressure exerted by capital markets to yield reasonably quick returns on investments in technology development. In the United States, institutional investors such as pension funds, mutual funds, or other money managers increasingly own the shares of publicly traded companies. In 1950, institutional owners accounted for 8 percent of total equity holdings in the United States; by 1990, the figure had reached 60 percent. The portfolios of these institutional agents are highly diversified in hundreds of different companies. Further, institutional investors tend to base their investment choices on limited information that is oriented toward predicting stock price movements. The system drives them to focus on easily measurable company attributes, such as current earnings or patent approvals. These factors serve as proxies of a company's value on which market timing choices are based. These measures encourage firms to undertake forms of investment for which returns are most readily available.[17]

Although the Japanese and European systems are somewhat different, there is some evidence that the national systems are converging, partly as a result of the general trend toward increasing globalization. A consequence of the reduced payback periods demanded by the external corporate markets is to speed the time compression both in product life cycles as well as in the development times.

Taken together, the shortened product life cycles, development times, and increasingly shorter payback periods demanded by capital markets—in short, time compression—have major implications for the technological environment. When confronted by the need to speed development times, firms have discovered that they cannot engage in technology development by themselves. Instead, they need to collaborate with others, or they need to imitate or borrow technologies from other firms. This, in turn, results in a heightening of the interconnections among the various organizations involved in technology development, both technology developers and facilitators.

TECHNOLOGY INTEGRATION

Every product that appears on the market is composed of a number of distinct and iden
tifiable technologies. For example, at one level of detail, a computer is composed of a
least three technologies: the video display; data processing, memory, and storage; and
the keyboard. In addition, software is needed to run the computer, and several periph
eral products such as printers or scanners are needed to make the computer usable to
the consumer. Of course, each of these items can be further desegregated into specifi
technologies. To produce all these parts, to assemble them into a personal computer, and
market that personal computer requires a number of related technologies in manufac
turing, marketing, sales, and procurement. Although innovation can take place throug
development of very specific technologies, technology integration refers to the idea o
technology development through the combination or reconfiguration of existing tech
nologies. Stated differently, along with the potential for development for specific tech
nologies, there exists a great potential to combine existing technologies into newer and
newer configurations.

In recent years, there has been growing awareness of the potential inherent in tech
nology integration. For example, Daniel Burrus, a futurist and technology forecaster
has suggested that the next decade will witness increasing numbers of applications de
veloped from several core technologies, ranging from engineering to advanced satel
lites. These applications, of course, could vary, and some applications cannot be foresee
even today. The point to remember here is that, by combining core technologies, a larg
number of applications—those that are useful to a group of customers—can emerge
We have showcased Burrus' work in Box 2.6. This box lists 20 core technologies; severa
of their applications hold the potential to transform society in the near future.

Technology integration can take place in two ways: (1) combining technologies t
develop new products; and (2) combining technologies to commercialize a product. W
will discuss each in turn.

BOX 2.6

CORE TECHNOLOGIES THAT WILL SHAPE
THE FUTURE

New products, processes, and services can no longer be seen as being composed of single technologies. Instead, they are packages of multiple technologies working together in a synchronous fashion. One source of competitive advantage may then be the ability to combine various technologies in a workable architecture that is seen as unique or innovative in the marketplace.

Author Daniel Burrus, in his book *Technotrends,* has suggested that there are 20 core technologies that are now poised to profoundly affect the competitive environment in the coming decade. From these core technologies will emerge future competitive products and services. As you review these technologies, note the way in which they tend to integrate several single technologies into unique systems and processes. Note also that practical and significant applications do not yet exist for many of these core technologies. It will be up to future innovators to find these applications and mold them into competitive products and services.

Source: Burrus, D. *Technotrends.* New York: HarperBusiness, 1993.

1. Genetic Engineering: The process of defining and changing specific gene traits. Two current applications are recombinant DNA, the mapping, restructuring, and remodeling of gene codes, and antisense compounds that have the power to block the expression of specific genes.

2. Advanced Biochemistry: The use of advance biological techniques. Although significant commercial applications do not yet exist, we can expect such things as new disease diagnostic systems and highly effective "superdrugs" to evolve from these techniques.

3. Digital Electronics: Digital devices translate signals into a form understandable by computers. In digital form, information of all types such as data, text, sound, and images can be moved from one device to another. Significant commercial applications that are currently emerging include digital imaging, interactive television, cellular telephones, and personal communication networks.

4. Optical Data Storage: Using lasers to read information stored in digital form. Current commercial applications include advanced compact disks that contain large amounts of information.

5. Advanced Video Displays: Current commercial applications include advanced flat-panel displays as used in most laptop computers. High-definition television (HDTV), when commercialized, will also be a product emerging from this core technology.

6. Advanced Computers: Current examples emerging in the marketplace include electronic notepads, multimedia computers, parallel processing computers, and multisensory robotics.

7. Distributed Computing: These devices permit the sharing of information across many individuals. Current examples include desktop videoconferencing and computer-integrated manufacturing.

8. Artificial Intelligence: This core technology represents computers that are able to learn, adapt, recognize, classify, reason, and correct. Commercial applications that have recently emerged include advanced expert systems, advanced simulations, object-oriented programming, and neural networks.

9. Lasers: These devices use highly coherent, high-intensity light. The most significant current commercial application is in advanced compact disks. We might also expect to see commercial applications of holographs in the near future.

10. Fiber Optics: This core technology uses light to transmit digital information. Though fiber-optic telecommunications systems are currently used to transmit telephone data, in the future these systems can also be expected to carry television, radio, and computer data.

11. Microwaves: Significant current applications include transmitting wireless digital information and heating objects. Future applications could include microwave clothes dryers and microwave scalpels to heat inoperable cancerous tumors to temperatures that would destroy the tumor but leave the surrounding tissue unaffected.

12. Advanced Satellites: Satellites can be expected to play a continuing role in communications and in mapping and surveying the earth. Some expected future uses include low earth orbit satellites that would allow worldwide communication between digital cellular telephones and direct broadcast satellites designed to carry strong signals of higher frequency that will be needed for super-VHS-quality pictures and HDTV signals.

13. Photovoltaic Cells: These devices convert sunlight to electricity. Current commercial applications include pocket calculators, refrigerators, and portable communication devices. As technological advances make these cells more efficient, many future uses can be anticipated.

14. Micromechanics: This core technology involves designing and building tiny

Box 2.6 (*continued*)

mechanisms such as valves, sensors, and surgical tools. In the future, these devices may be etched on silicon wafers and used for such applications as giving robots a sense of touch.

15. New Polymers: Polymers are complex chemical structures that can be adapted to many uses. Chemists have currently produced over 60,000 different polymers that can do such things as conduct electricity, dissolve in sunlight, carry light waves, and function as moving parts in automobiles. As this core technology advances, many new commercial applications should emerge.

16. High-Tech Ceramics: Ceramics are hard, chemically inert substances that resist corrosion, wear, and high temperatures. Current commercial uses of this technology include engine components, ball bearings, heat shields, and artificial bone implants. Again, future technological advances hold the potential to span many new commercial applications.

17. Fiber-Reinforced Composites: Composites are materials that have been reinforced with synthetic fibers. These materials are lightweight and often stronger than steel. Current commercial applications include automobile and airplane parts.

18. Superconductors: These are materials that carry electricity without any loss of energy. Currently, these materials must be operated at well below room temperature; the technological push is to create superconducting materials that can operate at higher temperatures. As this technology advances, it will have a great impact on all electrical devices.

19. Thin-Film Deposition: This core technology allows specific materials as thin as one atom to be deposited on almost any surface. One commercial application that is currently emerging is diamond thin-film coating, a process that deposits a diamond film only several molecules thick on surfaces such as razor blades and knives.

20. Molecular Designing: This core technology represents the process of designing new materials at the molecular level. Using lasers, atoms and molecules can be laid down in a precise manner on surfaces to create the desired material's property.

These technologies alone and in combination with one another may generate many new commercially viable technologies in the future.

COMBINING TECHNOLOGIES TO DEVELOP NEW PRODUCTS

Technology development often requires the ability to develop or access different technologies and synthesize them into a product. The technological trends highlighted in Box 2.7 focus exclusively on technology integration at the product level. During technology development, firms occasionally specialize either in a single core technology or in technology integration. For example, many of the small firms in the Silicon Valley are well positioned to develop products in very specific technologies but are not well positioned to combine several technologies into innovations or to generate products from a variety of technologies. On the other hand, many of the Japanese firms such as Sony, Matsushita, Toshiba, and Hitachi have been able to consolidate their lead in television and video electronics by focusing more on technology integration in relationship to their U.S. counterparts. This example is elaborated in Box 2.7. Of course, there are a few firms like IBM or Hewlett-Packard that develop technology along both these lines.

BOX 2.7

TECHNOLOGY INTEGRATION:
U.S. VERSUS JAPANESE FIRMS

Successful new products and process may no longer be based upon single technologies. Instead, they require the integration of various technologies into working systems. The growth of fields such as "mechatronics," the combination of mechanical and computer technologies, and "optoelectronics," combining computer and video technologies, are excellent examples of this trend toward technological integration. When we consider such consumer products as cameras, household appliances, and consumer electronics, along with such industrial products as manufacturing robots and automatic machine tools, this trend towards integration becomes evident.

Recent reports have indicated that Japanese firms are much more adept at these so-called hybrid fields than are their American counterparts. American high-technology firms have tended to focus on specialization in a few distinct technologies. The thrust of technological innovation in these firms has been toward gaining a depth of knowledge in a given technology. As a result, they have also focused on vertical integration strategies that provide control over the resources associated with that specific technology. Japanese firms, on the other hand, are seen as applying a much broader focus to technological innovation. Their strategic orientation appears to be one of adapting technologies to a broad range of applications. In turn, they have focused much more on horizon-

tal integration to bring multiple applications under their control. Two researchers, Richard Florida and Martin Kenney, have suggested that the difficulty that American high-technology firms have in generating systems technologies may be the result of two industry related factors.

First, most firms in the microelectronics field are small and entrepreneurial in nature. American centers of high-technology innovation, such as Silicon Valley and Route 128 outside of Boston, are composed of small firms that lack the scale, resources, and long-term outlook necessary to develop these technologically integrated products. Although this industry characteristic may be important in developing specific technological breakthroughs, it does not facilitate the growth of firms that can then use these breakthroughs in broad applications to commercial products.

Second, the development of America's microelectronics industry was premised upon the notion of specialization. Depth of knowledge in specific technologies was a central concern, so firms relied upon other firms for products and processes outside of their specialized niches. This resulted in the formation of an industry where technological integration could only be accomplished through the collaborative efforts of numerous firms. Thus, the technological knowledge necessary to produce broadly integrated products and processes was spread across numerous, often competing, organizations. The final result is an industry that is fragmented both horizontally and vertically.

Source: Florida, R. and Kenney, M. "Silicon Valley and Route 128 won't save us," *California Management Review* (Fall 1990): 68–88.

INTEGRATION OF TECHNOLOGIES
FOR COMMERCIALIZING PRODUCTS

In order to successfully commercialize a product, a firm has to utilize its product know-how along with such process technologies as manufacturing, marketing, and after-sales support. Technology integration is almost a prerequisite for commercialization. Many small firms that introduce innovative products often do not succeed, primarily because they fail to build or access complementary technologies such as manufacturing.[18] Dean

Schroeder illustrated the role played by complementary process technologies in the case of Automatic Flaskless Matchplate Molding (AFMM); his work is summarized in Box 2.8. As shown in the case, several complementary technologies are needed to successfully commercialize a particular technology.

BOX 2.8

HISTORY AND DEVELOPMENT
OF AUTOMATIC FLASKLESS
MATCHPLATE MOLDING

Automatic Flaskless Matchplate Molding (AFMM)'s development involved two firms: Beardsley and Piper (B&P), a division of Pettibone Corp., and Hunter Automated Equipment Company. The two shared nearly all the market for horizontally parted AFMM machines.

B&P engineers generated the principal concepts of AFMM in the late 1950s and early 1960s. Competing approaches were followed. The first mechanically reproduced the physical actions of molders; the second applied core-blowing technology using compressed air to move and pack molding sand. In 1960, after several learning experiments, the first successful production experiment of the blowing concept was conducted in an Illinois foundry by using two modified core-blowing machines. After this experiment, the task of developing the B&P AFMM machine, trade named "Match-Blowmatic" was assigned to Al Hunter, the chief engineer. Shortly thereafter Hunter, who was the principal champion of the mechanical concept, left B&P and formed Hunter Automated Equipment Company. This stalled B&P's AFMM project until Hunter introduced its competing AFMM unit. B&P responded by rushing the final development of the Match-Blowmatic and introducing it onto the market in 1964 prior to the usual complement of field tests. Early machines, consequently, had various operating problems. The initial difficulties were resolved and important modifications made as operating experience was gained.

Significant developments. Although some minor physical changes were required to improve the innovation's function, the most significant early changes were in the development of operating and maintenance procedures necessary to deal with problems encountered in the field. The new technology proved more sensitive to the harsh production environment than the manufacturer's test environment. Damp, dirty foundry conditions led to revisions in the prescribed cleaning, maintenance, and operating procedures. In the late 1960s, the articulating arm used to move patterns in and out of the machine was replaced by a shuttle framework that resolved persistent alignment and adjustment problems by providing a simple, rigid, and positive pattern movement. The new design also reduced set-up time between jobs.

In 1972, AFMM's operating theory was reconceptualized. Rather than relying on the blowing action to pack the mold firmly (as originally conceived from the core-blower concept), the blow action was used only to fill the mold cavity, and the hydraulic squeeze (originally only for extra packing) was used to supply the compaction force. Although this change only required some adjustments in the control settings, it represented a major shift in thinking that greatly enhanced performance. A consistently higher-quality mold was achieved at lower operating costs. Less compressed air was consumed and there was less pattern wear because the sand was blown at lower pressures. This development also enabled the production of more complex work.

The conceptual change led to a total redesign of the sand blow magazine in 1978. Two aerators were substituted for a mechanical os-cillator intended to keep molding sand from packing in the magazine. The aerators fluidized the sand to flow like water as it was blown into the molding chamber. The aerators lowered maintenance and cleaning requirements, making the unit easier to operate. The fluidized sand further improved mold quality, lowered costs, and allowed for the production of increasingly complex molds.

Machine users and field service engineers initiated a number of improvements in operating techniques and plumbing configurations during the two years following the aerator development. These improvements resulted in more uniform air flows, which further improved AFMM's overall flexibility, reliability, ease of operation, and cost-efficiency while eliminating several expensive valves.

In the early 1980s, advanced electronic programmers and switches replaced electro-mechanical controls in a series of minor refinements. These controls operate more reliably and precisely in the harsh foundry environment, reducing maintenance and further simplifying machine operation. The net consequences of AFMM's continuing development over two decades are (1) increased machine reliability; (2) reduced maintenance; (3) uniformly higher quality molds; (4) increased machine flexibility (through production of more complex casting shapes and rapid job changes); (5) reduced operating costs; and (6) simplification of the required operating and maintenance knowledge. Significantly, one development often led to the next, each building upon the advantages and improvements of its predecessors.

Complementary technologies. A number of complementary technologies and innovations played roles in increasing the viability and performance of AFMM. Three of the most important of these were automated sand mulling, automatic mold handling, and electric furnace melting. All three were needed to achieve AFMM's highest productivity.

- Early bottlenecks limited AFMM's potential. The machine not only needed large quantities of consistent quality molding sand but, unlike the predecessor technology, the operator could not adjust for vari-ation in sand quality. Traditional manually operated sand mulling systems had difficulty providing enough consistent-quality sand. By the late 1960s and early 1970s, innovations in automatic sand quality controls and automated mulling technology emerged and, like AFMM itself, continued to develop and improve. This technology helped overcome upstream bottlenecks and improve mold quality.

- Downstream bottlenecks developed because the innovation produced molds faster than they could be removed and transported to the pouring floor. Consequently, development work began immediately on automatic mold handling systems. The earliest of these were introduced shortly after AFMM itself, with the first really viable systems appearing in the late 1960s and early 1970s. These systems were integrated with the AFMM system to automatically move molds to metal pouring.

- However, one of the limitations of automatic mold handling systems was that they could only hold a limited number of molds. To be efficient, molds had to be moved from the molding machine to the pouring floor, where they were filled with molten metal, allowed to cool, and then discharged into the shakeout machine at a constant and synchronized rate. Little slack is available to hold molds in queue. Thus, having molten metal available at a steady rate throughout the day to match molding and mold handling is critical. Unfortunately, traditional operating practice is to place molds on the pouring floor throughout the day, "pour them off" at the end of the day, and allow them to cool overnight. Essentially, the entire day's production represents one batch. This process matches cupola melting technology, which is a relatively rapid and inexpensive method of melting iron, but has the drawback of spewing a cloud of ash, sulfur dioxide, and smoke into the environment. The solution to the problem of regulating the metal flow throughout

Box 2.8 (*continued*)

the day is electric melting. Although electric furnaces do not melt iron as fast as a cupola, they melt all day long. Unfortunately, electric furnaces are more expensive to buy and operate. The creation of the Environmental Protection Agency (EPA) and passing of the Clean Air Act, both in 1970, altered these economics. New environmental regulations required foundries to retrofit cupolas with expensive pollution control equipment that increased their operating costs. This made purchasing an electric furnace a more viable alternative. The increased demand encouraged electric furnace manufacturers to invest in research on electronic circuitry to develop furnaces with improved performance and lower costs.

The three complementary technologies in sand preparation, mold handling, and metal melting contributed greatly to the success and viability of AFMM. As a package, the four innovations completely altered basic foundry operations, changing them from a batch process to a continuous-flow process.

The economic potential inherent in technology integration has two major implications for ongoing organizations:

1. Historically, organizations have focused on technology development through their in-house research and development activity. To fully realize the potential of technology integration, the firms can no longer take R&D as the sole source of technologies. Instead, they must be able to access technologies from other organizations in a timely manner. Stated differently, organizations should not only farm technologies, but also gather technologies from outside.

2. The potential for technology integration suggests that the main actors in the technological environment—both developers and facilitators—will be increasingly interconnected. Such interconnections will help the transfer of technology from one organization to another, such that the full potential of technology integration can be realized.

In summary, globalization, time compression, and technology integration are creating turbulent technological environment for many organizations. The preceding discussion is summarized in Figure 2.7: how the three major trends are creating greater interdependence among the institutions in the technological environment.

MANAGERIAL IMPLICATIONS

Three significant managerial implications flow from our discussion of the technological environment:

1. Technological environment is dynamic and needs to be tracked on an ongoing basis. From an open-systems perspective, management of organizations, including technology, should be predicated on the environment facing organizations.

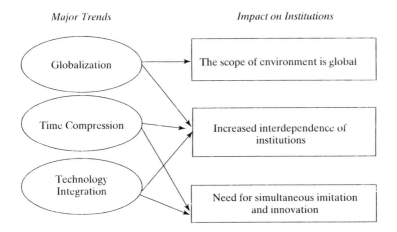

FIGURE 2.7 THE IMPACT OF TRENDS ON INSTITUTIONS

2. Tracking technological changes in the environment requires managers to penetrate the organizations and networks that conduct and facilitate technology development.

3. The three trends—globalization, time compression, and technology integration—require managers to adopt a global perspective, enhance organizational speed of response, and work with other organizations to adapt to technological changes as well as to fully exploit the potential of new technology.

❖ CHAPTER SUMMARY

In this chapter, we identified three levels of environment: task, industry/competitive, and macroenvironment. Macroenvironment consists of four major segments: social, economic, political/regulatory, and technological. Technological environment is defined as institutions linked to technology development activities.

The institutions involved in the technological environment can be classified along two dimensions: public versus private and developers versus facilitators. Technology development in public organizations is, in general, more transparent than in private organizations. Technology developers may be engaged in one or more stages of technology development from basic research to development, engineering, and operations. Facilitators may be resource providers, policy analysts, or linking organizations. Different nations have different interconnections among various organizations in the technological environment.

Changes in the technological environment may come about autonomously, or they may be induced by changes in other segments of the macroenvironment. Especially important is the influence of political/regulatory and economic environments. The political/regulatory environment may influence the thrust of major basic research; it may also facilitate or impede every phase of technology development. In addition, it acts as a facilitator of private sector technological development. There is a reciprocal linkage between economic and technological environments. Thus, major technological innovations stimulate economic development; economic conditions, however, exert a major influence on the pace and level of technological change.

The three major trends in the technological environment are globalization, time compression, and technology integration. As a result of globalization, technological developments occur all over the globe: Thus, the scope of the technological environment is now truly global. Time compression is manifest in shortened product life cycles, development times, and payback periods. The potential inherent in technology integration for new products as well as commercialization is increasingly apparent.

For organizations and managers working for them, the three trends have major implications. First, understanding technological environment requires a global perspective. Second, heightening time compression necessitates faster organizational learning. Third, for the potential of technology integration to be realized, managers need to not only nurture innovation in their organizations, but they must learn to import technology from other organizations, as well.

❖ NOTES

1. Adapted from Betz, F. *Managing Technology: Competing through New Ventures, Innovation, and Corporate Research.* Upper Saddle River, NJ: Prentice Hall, 1987.
2. For a detailed discussion of these forces, see Porter, M. *Competitive Strategy.* New York: The Free Press, 1980.
3. See Quinn, J. B., and Mueller, J. A. "Transferring Research Results to Operations," *Harvard Business Review,* January-February 1963, pp. 49–69.
4. Surowiecki, James. "The Return of Michael Porter," *Fortune* (February 1, 1999): 135–138.
5. From Mowery, D.C. 1990. "The development of industrial research in U.S. manufacturing". *AEA Papers and Proceedings,* 80(2): 345–349. Reprinted by permission.
6. Schnee, Jerome. Government Programs and the Growth of HighTechnology. *Research Policy,* January 1978.
7. See Foust, D. and Mallory, M. "The Boom Belt," *Business Week* (Sept. 27, 1993): 98–104.
8. See for example, Kelly, P., and M. Kranzberg. *Technological Innovation: A Critical Review of Current Knowledge.* National Science Foundation, February 1975.
9. See for example, Mensch, Gerhard, *Stalemate in Technology,* Ballinger, 1979.
10. Indeed there were even predictions that the strengthening of the yen in the early 1990s will accelerate this trend.
11. See for example, National Science Foundation. Research and Development in an Industry, 1990, NSF 90–319, Washington, DC; (2) Cheng, Joseph L. Fee, and Bolon, Douglas S. "The Management of Multinational R&D, A Neglected Topic in International Business Research," *Journal of International Business Studies* (First quarter 1993): 1–18; (3) Behrman, Jack N. and William A. Fischer. 1980. Overseas R&D Activities of Transnational Companies. Cambridge, MA: Oelgeschlager, Gunn and Hain; (4) De Meyer, Arnoud and Atsuo, Mizushima. "Global R&D Management," *R&D Management* (1989): 19:135–46; and (5) Hakanson, Lars and Udo Zander. "International Management of R&D: The Swedish Experience," *R&D Management* (1988): 18:217–26.
12. Michael Porter. "The Competitive Advantage of Nations," *Harvard Business Review,* March-April 1990, 73–93.
13. This quote is taken from Mansfield, Edwin. "The Speed and Cost of Industrial Innovation in Japan and the United States: External versus Internal Technology," *Management Science,* October 1988, Vol. 34, No. 10, pp. 1157–1168.
14. Qualls, W., Olshavsky, R. W., and Michaels, R. E. "Shortening of the PLC—An Empirical Test," *Journal of Marketing,* 45(Fall 1981): 76–80.
15. Ibid.
16. Edwin Mansfield. "The Speed and Cost of Industrial Innovation in Japan and the United States: External Versus Internal Technology," *Management Science,* October 1988, Vol. 34, No. 10, pp. 1157–1168.
17. Porter, Michael. "Capital Disadvantage: America's Failing Capital Investment System," *Harvard Business Review,* September-October 1992, pp. 65–82.
18. David J. Teece. "Capturing Value from Technological Innovation: Integration, Strategic Partnering, and Licensing Decisions," *Interfaces,* 1988, Vol. 18, pp. 46–61.

3

PROCESS OF TECHNOLOGY CHANGE: INNOVATION

An elbow-to-elbow crowd swarmed into the Bell Labs auditorium on the western border of Greenwich Village on June 30, 1948. Onstage before the guests and reporters stood bow-tied research director Ralph Bown—the small sign at his feet telling the story in a nutshell: "The Transistor." The Bell Labs folks would soon launch into full-scale demonstrations of the revolutionary device, invented the previous December. Bown, however, spoke first about how AT&T had engineered its achievement.

"What we have to show you today represents a fine example of teamwork, of brilliant individual contributions, and of the value of basic research in an industrial framework," Bown proclaimed.

It should have been a great moment for Bell Labs. After all, technology revolutions don't happen every day. But from a bottom-line point of view, AT&T's transistor breakthrough was less than transformative. That's because when all was said and done, it's doubtful Ma Bell netted a dime from its invention. Instead, the real winners were the specialized firms with better business plans and focus names like Texas Instruments and Fairchild Semiconductor who won the race to ready the transistor for mass production and distribution.

Granted, the transistor might seem to be a special case, because as part of an antitrust consent decree, AT&T was forced to sell rights to the invention for a modest fee. But to students of the role of science in industrial research, the outcome is all too typical. In fact, for reasons that include corporations' inabilities to embrace radical change and a lack of commercial applications, a number of other profound discoveries have failed to produce big returns on investments. The list includes semiconductor lasers (GE and IBM), cosmic background radiation (Bell Labs), the scanning tunneling microscope (IBM), and even semiconductor and superconductor tunneling phenomena (Sony and GE); the last three won Nobel Prizes.

From the perspective of corporations that sponsor the research, the lesson is clear: Breakthroughs are hard to come by, and the financial payoffs have a troubling tendency to go to someone other than the originator.

This provides some food for thought about today's fervent race to push computing beyond silicon. The field is already littered with failures—think gallium arsenide and optical computers—and current contenders include blue-sky propositions ranging from biological systems to quantum computing. This sort of research fits well in an academic environment, where making money is secondary to the advancement of scientific knowledge (at least in theory), yet much of it takes place in industrial labs. So, because history tells us that the chance of a big payday is remote, why do these companies bother?

The answer is that there are many "hidden" benefits to engaging in basic science, from creating a climate of discovery to staying in touch with the cutting edge. Indeed, the extras are so compelling that the firms bankrolling these studies often don't expect their researchers to produce much of direct market value. "Why is any curiosity-driven research supported in industrial labs?" former IBM vice president for science and technology John A. Armstrong once asked. "There are several reasons, but they do not include the expectation that out of the company's own 'scientific left field,' so to speak, will come new insights or inventions that will radically alter the nature of the company's businesses."

If Armstrong's statement appears to run counter to the popular notion that farsighted corporations invest in basic science to plant the seeds of future growth, it shouldn't. The two views actually complement each other. For one thing, betting on basic research does sometimes pay off financially: DuPont's fundamental polymer studies led to the invention of nylon, and Irving Langmuir's Nobel Prize-winning surface chemistry investigations enabled GE to build a revolutionary lightbulb.

Yet by its very nature, most exploratory work fails. What's more, scientific leadership has never been a prerequisite of marketplace triumphs. Witness Japan's dominance in steel, autos, consumer electronics, and semiconductor memories—or the rise of Dell, Compaq, and Gateway in personal computers.

These truths have led many, Intel cofounder Gordon Moore among them, to conclude that wide-ranging basic research simply isn't worth it. Moore, formulator of the "law" that has long governed semiconductor manufacturing, points to IBM's Nobel Prize-winning invention of the scanning tunneling microscope (STM)—which does not fit into any of the company's business lines—as a case in point. The STM "is really a great tool," he says, "but IBM is not going to get anything out of it." Moore stresses that society benefits tremendously from basic research and that Uncle Sam should support it vigorously. However, don't expect Intel to dive into the realm of biological processing or quantum computing anytime soon.

Still, not every company shares Intel's philosophy. IBM, Hewlett-Packard (HP), AT&T, Lucent-Bell Labs, NEC, and Hitachi are among those supporting world-class investigations into quantum systems, carbon nanotubes, biological processing, molecular computing, or other alternative means of data crunching.

This work is so important to IBM that it went gangbusters to nab quantum hotshot Isaac Chuang 2 years ago, beating out a pack of university and corporate rivals with the lure of a generous salary and state-of-the-art equipment.

Similarly, when HP decided to spin off its measurement and equipment business (now Agilent Technologies), management originally leaned toward placing chemist R. Stanley Williams with the new company. But Williams, whose recent advances in molecular computing received international attention, apparently proved such a hot commodity that he was kept in the HP fold.

All of which underscores the fact that there is more to corporate science than just science. The more subtle payoffs include:

- Covering the corporate backside.
- Building ties to university science.
- Creating a "culture of research.
- Getting a fundamental perspective on commercial problems.
- Public relations.

Beyond all these factors is one critical point: Although places like Bell Labs, IBM, and GE became famous for their basic research, *science alone did not make them great.* Instead, it was their ability to bring together a wealth of talents and viewpoints—scientists with engineers, chemists with mathematicians, deep thinkers with the practical-minded. From that volatile combination—rather than from basic research itself—leaps the spark of discovery.

It often makes perfect sense for a firm to participate in far-out ventures like quantum or molecular computing that may never provide their own revenue streams. Not only does it provide a lot of buzz, the work helps attract good people and researchers probably learn some math, chemistry, or atomic physics that could be applied to more practical problems. Top companies know this and often insist on the full package in research including some blue-sky studies. These efforts never represent a very large fraction of the company's overall R&D budget and they may never yield a Nobel Prize. However even without a scientific breakthrough, the payoffs can be incalculable.[1]

Innovation is one of the engines of economic progress, and we will sketch some broad principles about innovation in this chapter.

In chapter 1, we introduced the theme that the management of technology focuses upon creating competitive advantage for firms by finding effective means to fulfill the wants and needs of customers in the marketplace. Although this involves creating or acquiring technical capabilities, competitive advantages accrue to a firm only when the capabilities are deployed in new products or processes. Thus, we will focus primarily on application of knowledge as the central technological change activity. Successful technological change can take place in different ways: first, when old solutions are applied to new problems; second, when new solutions are found to existing problems; and/or third, a combination of both. Technical breakthroughs sometimes present a firm with opportunities to produce a new product that fulfills an untapped customer want or to produce a product that is superior to the one currently being used by customers. Alternately, technological changes may allow a firm to redesign its processes to be more efficient or more responsive to its customers. Similarly, untapped customer needs often become the basis for directing technological change efforts—both product and process—in an organization.

Technical change consists of two closely linked processes: innovation and diffusion. Although they are tightly linked, for the purposes of discussion, we will deal with them in separate chapters. In this chapter, we will focus on the process of innovation. Specifically, we will address such questions as:

1. What are the different types of innovation?
2. What are the dynamics of technology evolution?
3. What are the characteristics of innovative firms?

The overview of the chapter is presented in Figure 3.1. As shown in the figure, we will portray technological change as emanating from the twin processes of innovation and diffusion. At the firm level, both innovation and diffusion can be described as different ways of technical problem solving. At the industry level, technology evolves as a result of the actions of numerous participants. Although any one firm may successfully innovate at times, some firms register sustained success more than others. The innovative firms generally share a set of organizational characteristics that are shaped by internal management practices.

The scheme of the chapter is as follows. First, we will present an overview of the dynamics of technological change, which consist of the twin processes of innovation and diffusion. Second, we will define innovation, the focus of this chapter; we will also introduce the key components of innovation that we will use throughout the remaining chapters. Third, we will focus on the innovation dynamics at the firm level. Fourth, we will identify the general patterns of technology evolution. Fifth, we will identify the characteristics of innovative firms. We will conclude by pointing out the key managerial implications and including a chapter summary.

FIGURE 3.1 CHAPTER OVERVIEW

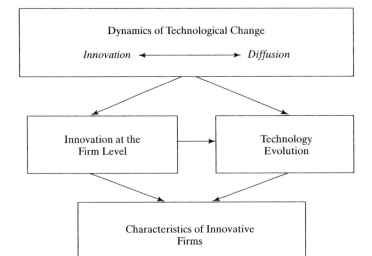

OVERVIEW OF THE DYNAMICS OF TECHNOLOGICAL CHANGE

In our discussion of technological environment, we underscored the fact that numerous organizations participate in the creation and application of new knowledge. Technological change can thus be described at two levels: at the level of the individual firm or at the level of the technology.

FIRM LEVEL

At the level of an individual firm, technological change may be described as a process of problem solving. At a broad level, we can identify four stages in the process of problem solving:[2]

1. **Problem recognition.** Successful technological change begins when a firm recognizes the potential of a technology for new products or process, or when it recognizes a market need that needs to be fulfilled. Where technical feasibility dominates design, we call the process "technology push"; when market demand drives the process, we call it "market pull." Alternately, problem recognition may be triggered by changes mandated by external agencies such as regulatory bodies. The stage is complete when a firm decides that it is in its economic interest to solve the problem.
2. **Technology selection.** During this stage, the firm formulates several design concepts that will serve the market needs. The design concepts are often based on different technologies. The formulation of design concepts tends to be a creative act that also includes a strong judgmental input so that the firm can decide to commit resources to the next stage. Technology choice culminates in the selection of a particular design concept for development.
3. **Solution development.** This stage in problem solving consists of actually fleshing out the chosen design concept. In the case of products, this may involve the development of a prototype. In the case of process innovation, this may involve finalizing a general approach or a blueprint for organizational change. Problem solving may proceed in one of the two ways: (1) A new solution is formulated within the innovating firm; or (2) A ready-made solution is adopted by the firm from outside.
4. **Commercialization/implementation.** The economic benefits of an innovation are never fully realized until an item is actually introduced into the market or cost reductions from the process change are achieved. During this stage, a firm fleshes out the operations and marketing strategy in the case of products, or implements the process change within the organization.

The four stages are presented schematically in Figure 3.2. As shown in the figure, the solution to a problem can be developed in two ways: either by real innovation within

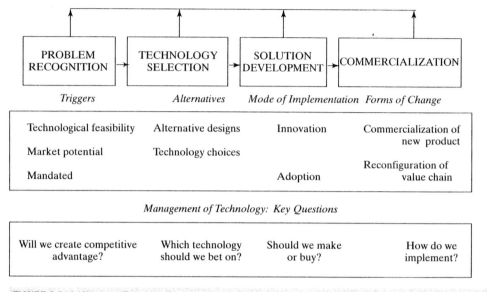

FIGURE 3.2 A MODEL OF PROBLEM SOLVING

a firm or by the adoption of an existing innovation from outside. We will consider adoption of innovation from outside as part of the diffusion process, a second dynamic of technological change.

The four-stage problem-solving model serves three purposes:

1. It provides a unifying framework within which we will be discussing the twin processes of innovation and diffusion;
2. It provides a normative framework for key management of technology decisions, such as new product introduction or value chain configuration; and
3. It helps us to focus on the key questions that need to be answered during management of technology.

In Figure 3.2, we have also summarized the key questions that need to be addressed during decision making in technology management.

TECHNOLOGY LEVEL

Although each firm is trying to seek competitive advantage through its own problem-solving efforts, in most cases technological change is driven by numerous firms and organizations involved in technology development. As a result, at the level of a specific technology (product or process), technology change displays evolutionary dynamics that are not controlled by a single firm. Although breakthroughs are difficult to forecast, once a technology has emerged, the evolutionary dynamics display predictable patterns that enable us to discern the direction of technological change.

Just what drives these changes? We can identify five sets of actors that participate in the evolutionary dynamics:

1. Technology developers, which typically are firms involved in innovation in their pursuit of competitive advantage;
2. Technology facilitators, who may provide the resources for financing and executing the innovation efforts;
3. Customers who are interested in the fruits of technology development and who will shape the direction of development;
4. Regulatory agents, the governmental bodies and others who shape the form of products and processes by establishing standards or specifications; and
5. Other stakeholders, who may be the beneficiaries (e.g., suppliers to the innovating firms) or victims of the technology change (e.g., industries likely rendered obsolete by the technological change).

The dynamics of technological change are complex. We will describe the role of customers in our discussion of diffusion and the role of regulatory agents and other stakeholders in our discussion of competition. In this chapter, we will highlight the role of technology developers.

IMPLICATIONS FOR THE MANAGEMENT OF TECHNOLOGY

The overview of the dynamics of technological change has three major implications for the management of technology: (1) innovation, imitation, and adoption; (2) the role of technology and market factors; and (3) the centrality of learning.

INNOVATION, IMITATION, AND ADOPTION[3]

The two levels of process—firm level and technology level—create opportunities for firms to imitate or adopt innovations from outside. When a firm innovates (e.g., develops a new product), two different groups of players respond to the innovation. One group, the *customers* (either individuals or other firms), makes decisions to adopt or not to adopt the innovation. A second group of players, *competitors,* may decide to copy the innovation and make their own (new) products to compete with the innovating firm. We will refer to this as *imitation*. As illustrated in Figure 3.3, innovation and imitation are supply-side concepts: They refer to firms that *sell* products or services. Viewed within the problem-solving process we described earlier, by imitating, a firm tries to solve a problem without investing heavily of its own resources. Unlike imitation, diffusion is a demand-side concept: It refers to consumers who *buy* products and services. *Diffusion* refers to the technology-level dynamics arising from the adoption decisions that are part of the problem solving; we will discuss this in the next chapter.

THE ROLE OF TECHNOLOGY AND MARKET FACTORS

Successful technological change involves not merely discovering new solutions or adopting seemingly effective innovations but also finding a home for the discovered solution in the marketplace. Stated differently, to be successful, a firm has to manage two related processes: (1) finding effective solutions to a problem and (2) gaining acceptance of the solution in the marketplace. Sometimes, innovations that are considered to be technically superior to existing products and solutions often fail in the market because the consumers do not accept them. The key to effective management of

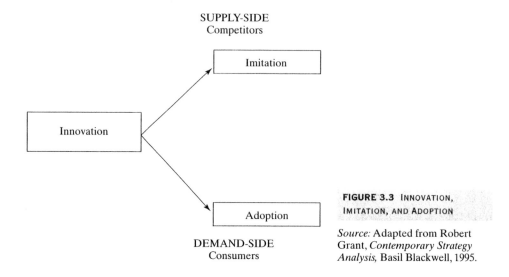

FIGURE 3.3 INNOVATION, IMITATION, AND ADOPTION

Source: Adapted from Robert Grant, *Contemporary Strategy Analysis,* Basil Blackwell, 1995.

technology lies in linking technological solutions to market realities. This is schematically portrayed in Figure 3.4, which displays what we will call in this book, the *Technology-Market (T-M) Matrix.* We will continually refer to this matrix to emphasize the theme that effective management of technology requires simultaneous attention to matters of technology and market.

As shown in the figure, technological change involves two related processes: one along the technical dimension and the second along the market dimension. We will call the processes by which firms arrive at feasible solutions to technical opportunities or customer wants *innovation;* we will call the processes by which the market accepts the solutions *diffusion.* Consistent with our theme, we will describe innovation and diffusion as intertwined, i.e., the two processes mutually influence each other. We will capture this idea by the expression *co-evolution of technology and market;* this simply means that changes in technology and evolution of markets are highly interrelated, each driving the other.

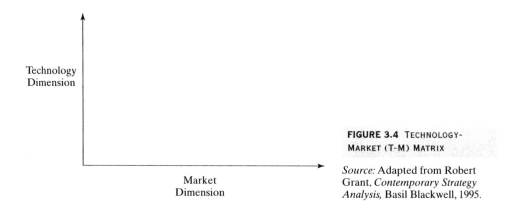

FIGURE 3.4 TECHNOLOGY-MARKET (T-M) MATRIX

Source: Adapted from Robert Grant, *Contemporary Strategy Analysis,* Basil Blackwell, 1995.

We will emphasize that the T-M matrix is a framework for making technology management decisions: All such decisions require weighing both technology- and market-related factors. The specific set of factors may include risk, return, or newness. Indeed, in various chapters we will focus on different sets of factors relevant for the decisions being discussed. Thus, just like the problem-solving model, the T-M matrix is another integrating device that we will employ in our discussion of the management of technology.

THE CENTRALITY OF LEARNING

At the heart of technological change—innovation, imitation, and adoption—lies significant learning by firms, both individually and collectively. Of the many ways to learn, we identify three major mechanisms of learning:

1. Environmental surveillance through technical and market intelligence. Technical intelligence creates awareness within a firm about the availability of scientific and technical knowledge; this alerts the firm to technological feasibility or adoption potential. Market intelligence creates awareness of customer needs and market potential.[4]
2. Experimentation[5] within firms whereby firms can learn problem solving by simulation and by trial and error. Both failures and successes during innovation provide rich avenues of learning about what works and what does not.
3. Imitation[6] through competitive intelligence. Learning from competitors about successful and unsuccessful attempts may enable a firm to learn without the investment required for learning through experimentation.

Multifaceted learning lies at the core of technological change. A central task of management of technology is, thus, to foster an organizational ethic of learning. We will, therefore, describe different types of learning during innovation and diffusion. We will now discuss the first major process of technological change: innovation.

WHAT IS INNOVATION?

DEFINITION

The word *innovation* appears to have its origins in the Latin *innovare,* meaning "to renew, to make new, or to alter." Writings on innovation date as far back as the Roman Empire. Discussion of innovation can also be found in the writings of the early French, the old English, and the colonial United States. Indeed, President George Washington counseled Americans on "preserving a spirit of innovativeness." Although innovation is thus a very common word, it has been used widely in various writings. Definitions differ in two major ways. The first difference relates to what constitutes an innovation; the second relates to the focus of the definition.

Just when can we say a firm has innovated? Some have viewed it as being synonymous with invention; that is, it refers to a creative process whereby two or more existing entities or ideas are combined in some novel manner to produce a configuration not previously known by the firm or person involved. The economist Joseph Schumpeter was the first to draw the distinction between "invention" and "innovation."[7] According to this distinction, invention is a new combination of preexisting knowledge, whereas innovation is a more subtle concept. If an enterprise produces a good or service or uses a system or procedure that is new to it, it makes an innovation. In this view, invention—if present—is part of the process of innovation. Viewed this way, an innovation includes both:

- A technological change new to both enterprise and the economy (e.g., the production of the personal computer by Apple); and
- A change that has diffused into the economy and is adopted by the firm (e.g., the adoption of computers by printing firms for typesetting services or by textile firms for controlling the production of synthetic fibers).

As we have discussed in the previous section, both are ways by which firms solve problems.

Just what is the focus of the term *innovation?* Does it refer to a process, or does it refer to an artifact? One set of definitions treats innovation as a process, that is, as a special case of organizational change, the difference being only in the novelty of the outcome. Others refer to innovation as an idea, practice, or material artifact that is novel—independent of its adoption or nonadoption.[8]

We will employ the term *innovation* to address our preoccupation in the management of technology: effective technological change that involves both the processes of arriving at a solution to a problem and gaining its acceptance among some consumers in the market. Thus, we are interested in both the process and the output of the process. To keep matters clear, we will use the following definition:

> Innovation refers both to the *output* and the *process* of arriving at a technologically feasible solution to a problem triggered by a technological opportunity or customer need.

We will use the term *innovation* in two ways: (1) process and (2) output.

PROCESS
In this meaning of the term, innovation refers to the process by which individuals or organizations arrive at a technical solution. Indeed, the problem-solving model we presented in our overview of the dynamics of technological change is a framework to describe different processes of innovation.

OUTPUT
We will also use the term *innovation* to refer to a product or service, i.e., the output of the process of innovation. According to this use, the personal computer, when it first appeared, was an innovation. In the next chapter, where we discuss diffusion, the term *innovation* is mostly used to refer to an output.

COMPONENTS OF INNOVATION

As *outputs,* all technological innovations have three components:[9]

- A *hardware* component, consisting of the material or physical aspects of the innovation;
- A *software* component, consisting of the information base that is needed to use the innovation; and

- An *evaluation information* component, consisting of the information that is useful for decisions related to the adoption of the innovation.

Four important points need to be remembered about the components of an innovation:

1. The components form a system. In the case of any innovation, if any component of a specific innovation is changed, other components will need to be changed also so as to render the innovation user friendly.
2. The hardware and software components are intrinsic to the technological innovation. For example, we speak of computer "hardware," consisting of semiconductors, transistors, electrical connections, and a metal frame to protect these connections, and computer "software," the coded commands, instructions, and other information aspects that provide instructions to the hardware.
3. Although almost all innovations contain hardware and software components, they may differ in terms of which component is dominant. Indeed, some innovations such as jet engines are hardware dominant. Other innovations such as TQM or process re-engineering, however, are software dominant.
4. The third component—the evaluation information component—is not intrinsic to technology and refers to the information accompanying an innovation that enables firms or individuals to evaluate its usefulness.

Usually, the evaluation information component is a major facet of the marketing strategy of a firm. This component is particularly important during diffusion; hence, we will elaborate on this component in the next chapter.

INNOVATION DYNAMICS AT THE FIRM LEVEL

We will portray the innovation dynamics at the firm level in terms of the drivers, process, and outputs as outlined in Figure 3.5.

DRIVERS OF INNOVATION

Firms innovate in response to environmental demands or opportunistically to shape the environment. We have already noted that innovation can be thought of as a way of problem solving, triggered by a technical possibility or a market need. Recognition of a problem or a need for which a solution is required may be engendered by many

FIGURE 3.5 A FRAMEWORK DESCRIBING FIRM-LEVEL INNOVATION

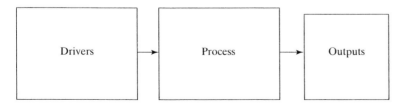

macroenvironmental trends including economic, social, political, and regulatory trends. For example, Ralph Nader's 1965 book *Unsafe at Any Speed*[10] called national attention to the high rate of traffic fatalities occurring in certain automobiles. This, in turn, led to federal laws that required automakers to design safer cars and pushed the highway construction industry to build safer roads. Changes such as these occur but are not commonplace.

On the other hand, two environmental factors very frequently stimulate innovation: (1) market factors and (2) input factors.[11]

1. Market factors appear to have a primary influence on innovation. From 60 to 80 percent of important innovations in a large number of fields have been in response to market demands or needs. This has been true not only in the United States but in other countries as well.
2. Input factors, especially rising costs of inputs, trigger innovations aimed at reducing the use of the expensive inputs. There are two main ways in which this has occurred. First, when labor becomes expensive, firms typically tend to invest in process technology to replace the costly labor. Second, when the raw materials or parts of a product become more expensive, firms search for alternative inputs and work to develop less expensive materials.

In both of the preceding cases, a firm's efforts to innovate were triggered by environmental forces. In addition, a firm may also engage in *autonomous innovation* when it tries to shape the environment to its desired direction. Thus, a firm may recognize a technological possibility, although the market need may not be immediately apparent. Many breakthroughs often do not have any immediate customer demand. For example, when computers were developed, many did not foresee a market for them. Yet, over time, initial beliefs about the innovation proved wrong, and a strong market developed for computers, first in business firms and later among consumers.

PROCESS OF INNOVATION

We may distinguish between two different types of innovation process: (1) market-pull and (2) technology-push.

> *Market-pull* is the advancement of technology oriented primarily toward a specific market need, and only secondarily toward increased technical performance.
> *Technology-push* is the advancement of technology oriented primarily toward increased technical performance, and only secondarily toward specific market needs.

An innovation that is commercially successful often requires making improvements in technical performance while simultaneously fulfilling a market need.

MARKET-PULL INNOVATIONS

In the case of market-pull innovations,[12] the idea for the innovation originates with communication about a customer need, followed by a search for technical solutions to meet that need. Typically, in many organizations, communication about a need quite often seems to be initiated by someone other than the person who generates the idea for an innovation. Such communication may come from users, outside consultants hired by a firm, or individuals who serve in consulting roles and have wide diversity in work assignments. Alternatively, these ideas could emerge from the frequent interaction between users and innovating firms. These sources of ideas have been observed in the case of both product technologies (e.g., gas chromatography, electron microscopy) as well as in process innovations (in the petroleum industry, the chemical industry, and the pultrusion industry). Eric von Hippel pioneered the study of market-pull innovations; his work is summarized in Box 3.1.

TECHNOLOGY-PUSH INNOVATIONS

In the case of technology-push innovations, the opportunity presented by a new technological advance stimulates a firm's search for an application. These innovations, therefore, tend to be driven by manufacturers. For example, during the period from 1944 to 1962, manufacturers dominated innovation in computers. Similar occurrences have also been observed in plastics, scientific instruments, and in chemical processes for producing synthetic fibers.

Indeed, both users and manufacturers can be sources of ideas for innovation. Thus, both market-pull and technology-push innovations can be commercially successful. We can, however, make three broad generalizations about technology-push and market-pull innovation:

1. Market-pull innovations tend to occur when the customers are technologically sophisticated and are, hence, excellent sources of ideas for innovation. Thus, in the case of the scientific instrumentation industry, where market pull was observed, the scientists knew the uses to which new instruments

---

BOX 3.1

MARKET-PULL SOURCES OF INNOVATION

Innovation may come from a number of different sources, some of which may seem unlikely at first glance. One important source of innovation for the firm is its customers. Several studies done by Eric von Hippel in the 1970s highlighted this phenomenon.

In a 1976 study of the scientific instrument industry, von Hippel determined that the source of roughly 80 percent of product innovations in that industry was the customer. These customers invented the innovation, prototyped it, and then field-tested it. Only then did the instrument manufacturer begin production of the innovation. Similarly, a 1977 study of the semiconductor and electronic subassembly industries by this researcher showed that 67 percent of the novel process innovations introduced in these industries were developed in a like fashion by the equipment users. These results suggest that market pull should be viewed as a significant source of innovation.

Ford Motor Company in its development of the highly acclaimed and widely successful Taurus line provides a more recent example of such an approach. From the inception of this product line, the company involved consumers, as well as suppliers, in every phase of its development.

Source: Adapted from von Hippel, Eric. 1977. "The dominant role of the user in semiconductor and electronic subassembly process innovation," *IEEE Transactions on Engineering Management* (1977): 24(2): 60–71.

could be put. On the other hand, technology-push innovations require that the firm's scientists, engineers, and inventors have direct experience with users in order to have the functional focus to create successful applications of new technology.

2. Market-pull innovations tend to occur more frequently in the case of older technologies, whereas technology-push innovations tend to occur in new and emerging technologies. In the case of the latter, technical information resides among the innovators, and the users are likely to be technically unsophisticated. For example, in the case of the computer industry during the period from 1944 to 1960, the users were relatively unsophisticated and, hence, mostly innovators themselves generated the ideas about the innovations.

3. Market-pull innovations most often are incremental innovations because an established market that informs the need bases its perceptions of opportunity on known technologies. Conversely, technology push is often the major source of breakthrough innovations.

TYPES OF INNOVATION OUTPUTS

Innovations differ in terms of the degree to which they introduce practices that depart in a significant way from past practices. Some innovations introduce relatively marginal changes to an existing product or process, whereas others are based on different scientific and engineering principles and thus open up new markets and applications.

However, as we have seen in the last chapter, we are witnessing two different ways in which technology is currently developing. One way is to develop newer principles or specific technologies that replace older ones; the other way is through technology integration, i.e., through configuring existing technologies in different ways. Each of these approaches to innovation may result in new products and/or processes that differ from existing products and processes. Hence, in order to classify an innovation we employ two dimensions:[13]

1. The degree to which specific technologies in an innovation depart from earlier ones, or what we will call *component knowledge;* and
2. The degree to which configurations among technologies in an innovation depart from earlier ones, or what we will call *component configuration.*

The two dimensions of innovation may be arrayed as in Figure 3.6. This classification leads to four major types of innovation: (1) incremental, (2) modular, (3) architectural, and (4) radical.

> *Incremental innovations.* These innovations represent minor improvements or changes to the elements of an existing product or organizational technologies and practices. Their initiation and implementation require little new organizational knowledge, because they are aligned with existing organizational skills and capabilities.

> *Modular innovations.* These innovations refer to significant changes in elements of products, organizational practices, and technologies without significant changes to the existing configuration of the elements. The initiation and implementation of these innovations would thus require an organizational understanding of the new components of the system. No significant new

organizational knowledge concerning the configuration of these components would be required. For example, to the degree that one can simply replace an analog dialing device with a digital one, it can be considered a modular innovation.

Architectural innovations. These innovations use existing organizational practices and technologies but reconfigure them in new or different ways. Thus, their initiation or implementation requires an organizational knowledge of how existing components are to be configured into a new system. No significant new knowledge is required concerning the components themselves. For the maker of large ceiling-mounted room fans, the introduction of a portable fan would be an architectural innovation. Although the primary components would be largely the same (e.g., blade, motor, control system), the architecture of the product would be quite different.

Radical innovations. These innovations represent revolutionary changes that require clear departures from existing organizational practices and technologies. They are typically not aligned with the organization's skills and capabilities and thus require significant new organizational knowledge concerning both the components of a system and the configuration of the system.

In chapter 1, we noted that firms compete by deploying new technologies in products or by reconfiguring their value chains with the help of new process technologies. Both process and product technologies can be classified into the four types of innovation enumerated in Figure 3.6. Figure 3.7 illustrates some examples of both types of innovations. Thus, building a factory run completely by robotics represents a radical process innovation. Further, when quality circles were introduced in the automobile industry in the United States during the early 1980s, they represented a modular innovation. On the other hand, the continuous improvement processes emphasized by total

FIGURE 3.6 CLASSIFICATION OF INNOVATIONS

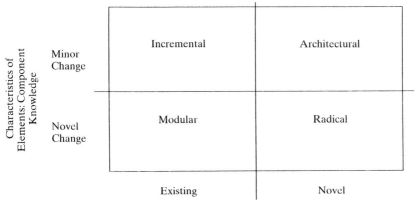

Characteristics of Linkage
Among Elements: Component
Configuration

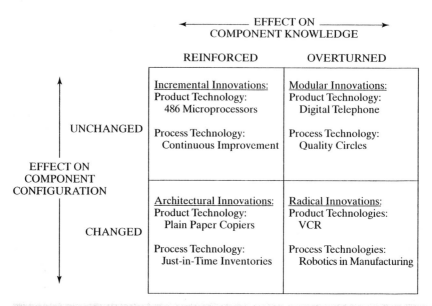

FIGURE 3.7 CLASSIFICATIONS OF INNOVATIONS FOR PRODUCTS, PROCESSES, AND SERVICES

Source: From R. M. and Clark, K. B. 1990. Architectural innovation: The reconfiguration of existing product technologies and the failure of established firms. *Administrative Science Quarterly,* 35: 9–30.

quality management harness the potential for productivity gains through incremental improvements in process technology; so did new automobile factories that employed electronic monitoring of quality.

There are three major reasons to distinguish among innovations as we have done in Figure 3.6. The four types of innovation differ in terms of (1) the process of innovation; (2) the economic impact of an innovation; and (3) the role of a manager in the innovation process.

THE PROCESS OF INNOVATION

The processes by which innovations emerge are somewhat different among the various types of innovations. For example, long-range planning, which assures that requisite technologies will be available and that they will all fit together when the final development stage is reached, is necessary for radical innovations. Success tends to turn on the skills of managers to sort out good approaches from bad ones on a very large scale. Radical innovation is not a common type of innovation in most industrial firms. However, many governmental agencies such as the defense department, NASA, and others are involved in such long-range planning efforts. In relatively mature industries, breakthrough innovations typically come from outside the industry simply because technical people within these industries are apt to be preoccupied with short-term concerns. Their focus will more likely be on product improvement, cross checking, or quality control, all of which fall within their own technical competence. The introduction of radical innovations in mature industries is unpredictable and is predominately the product of the activity of independent inventors or research by firms outside the industry.

Modular innovations may come from inside or outside an industry, but existing firms within an industry can adopt them without too much disruption. Architectural innovations often come from upstart new entrants in an industry seeking a market niche. These involve reconfiguring the existing technologies. Finally, incremental innovations can to a large extent be planned and managed by a firm, because they require only incremental advances to an already existing technology or system.

THE ECONOMIC IMPACT OF AN INNOVATION

Radical innovation and modular innovations extend our technological capabilities and, in general, contribute to the wealth of the society. However, the economic benefits from technology flow not merely from radical and modular innovations but also from the incremental nuts-and-bolts improvements that take place over the course of development of an innovation. Indeed, one estimate suggests that incremental innovations contribute nearly four-fifths of the improvements in productivity in our economy.[14] Similarly, it is expected that great economic potential will be inherent in architectural innovations that require technology integration, a point that was discussed in the last chapter.

THE ROLE OF A MANAGER IN THE INNOVATION PROCESS

The manager's role will change depending on the type of innovation being considered. Many industrial firms encourage incremental innovations that yield immediate market share or productivity gains. These innovations can be planned and managed; indeed, their effective management is crucial to the economic success of a firm. Modular innovations come from central research laboratories in universities, government agencies, or large firms. On the other hand, the radical innovations or architectural innovations often necessitate a much more detailed scanning and understanding of the technology environment in order to gather relevant technologies or, in the case of some select technologies, to grow them internally. Thus, the technological vision of management must be broader and longer term for radical innovations.

TECHNOLOGY EVOLUTION

Technological change has often been characterized in two extreme ways. One view holds that technological change is the result of inspiration or the genius of an individual inventor. A second way of characterizing technological change is to view it as an orderly and planned process.

There is an element of truth in both of these descriptions but technological change is a far more complex phenomenon than is captured in these simple caricatures. To highlight its complexity, in this section we describe six major characteristics or dynamics of technological change: (1) *S*-curve of technology evolution; (2) technology progression; (3) levels of technology development; (4) technology change agents; (5) evolutionary characteristics of technological change; and (6) uncertainty and technological insularity.

S-CURVE OF TECHNOLOGY EVOLUTION

Although the initial development of a new technology often appears to be a random process, once a new technology comes into existence, its evolution over time displays a reasonably stable pattern. These stable patterns may be described in terms of evolution of performance characteristic. *Performance characteristic* refers to a characteristic of interest to the designer of a product or the user of a specific technology. For example, optic fibers have been considered to deliver better quality voice messages relative to the cables that had traditionally been used by telephone companies; in this case, voice clarity is the performance characteristic of interest. In a similar fashion, the speed of computing is typically of interest to the designers of computers. Thus, some computers have lower speeds relative to others, and here computation speed becomes the performance characteristic of interest. What is important is that each technology has a number of performance characteristics associated with it. At any point in time, a product designer or user will be interested in a select few of these characteristics.

Technology evolution refers to the changes in the performance characteristics of a specific technology over time. Figure 3.8 displays the evolution of a typical performance characteristic. Once a new technology has come into existence, the performance characteristics of interest show very little improvement in the early stages of the technology. This initial stage is followed by a second phase of very rapid improvement in the performance characteristic. During the third stage, the performance characteristic continues to improve, but the rate of improvement begins to decline. In the final stage, very little improvement is visible in the performance characteristic. The graph that charts the progress in the performance characteristic of a technology over time resembles an *S* shape; hence, it is called the *S*-curve of evolution.

The *S*-curve of technological evolution summarizes four major stages in the evolution of a performance characteristic:

1. Emergence, when the technology has come into existence but shows little improvement in its performance characteristic;
2. Rapid improvement, when the performance characteristic improves at an accelerating pace;

FIGURE 3.8 S-CURVE: A GENERAL FORM

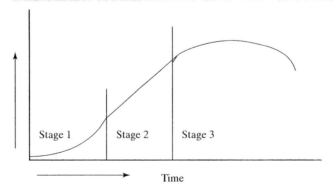

3. Declining improvement, when the pace of improvement declines; and

4. Maturity, when further improvements become very difficult to achieve.

In Box 3.2, we have illustrated the evolution of computing speed of successive genera-tions of computer chips.

Although technologies differ in terms of the time interval between successive stages, virtually all technological developments display the relatively stable pattern cap-tured by this S-curve.[15] In the early stages of development, a technology operates far below its potential, with little improvement in key performance characteristics taking place. During these stages, neither the characteristics of the technology nor its applica-bility to market needs may be well understood. Often, there is a long gestation period before attempts are made to produce a technology, once it has been discovered or in-vented. For example, Charles Babbage invented an analytical computing engine in 1833, but real progress in the development of computing devices became possible only in re-cent decades. A patented design for the modern turbojet had been advanced by 1921,[16] yet the first turbojet-powered flight was possible only in 1939, after nearly two decades of further experimental work. Similarly, the design for radar was conceived many years before a workable model was placed in service.

The outcome of an initial concept of a new product or process is often left un-developed for want of relevant design and production know-how. For example, the biggest obstacle to the development of a satisfactory solar panel was the difficulty in scal-ing up production beyond silicon pellets. The development of the new microcomputer circuit, the 64-K random-access memory chip, has been retarded for want of a reliable and efficient process for its production. During the 1970s, there was great uncertainty in the clarity of optic fibers, partly because the process of manufacturing both the optic fiber and its key components had not been shown to be reliable.

Even the most carefully conceived blueprints seldom prove to be practicable at on-set. Designs must be tried out several times and adjustments and corrections made be-fore designs can be made operational. Many new designs tend to be unreliable, inefficient, and cumbersome. Moreover, their execution into new products generally re-quires special tools, processes, and fixtures. The installation of these new devices is sel-dom possible without giving rise to unanticipated bottlenecks in the production process. As experience is gained, however, it becomes possible to identify and extirpate the bugs. Organizations learn to harmonize production and reduce bottlenecks in operations. The workforce becomes better acquainted with the task at hand, and management finds new ways to improve plant layout and the scheduling of materials, labor, and equipment. All these factors contribute to a stage where firms can pursue successful improvement in performance characteristics.

Once a feasible design and a manufacturing process are established, performance characteristics tend to show steep improvement. As organizations engage in produc-tion, experience accumulates over time. This experience accelerates the improvement in performance characteristics. Often called *learning curve* or *experience curve* effect, this kind of improvement is observed in many industries. Such experience, however, is not limited to production know-how; it may embrace many activities, including design or prototyping. For example, many design practices typically take the form of *rules of thumb,* which are outcomes of a learning process. As new experience is acquired, old rules of thumb give way to new ones. Consider the railroad industry: Until 1930, it was

BOX 3.2

PERSONAL COMPUTER
MICROPROCESSOR SPEED

The "brains," or central processing unit (CPU), of a personal computer is the microprocessor chip. Because essentially all functions performed by the personal computer system are dependent upon the functioning of the microprocessor chip, the speed of this "technology" is an important consideration in the overall performance of the computer.

The most typical measure of computer processing speed is MIPS, or millions of instructions per second. An instruction is one line of software code or the amount the processor can handle at one time. When Intel Corporation introduced the "8086" microprocessor in 1981, its speed was rated at 0.3 MIPS. Since that time, successive "generations" of chips have considerably increased that speed such that the newest generation, known as the Intel Pentium Processor, runs at approximately 100 MIPS, the typical speed of a mainframe computer.

The diagram depicts microprocessor speed (the performance characteristic) across successive generations of chips (8086 or PC, XT, 286, 386, etc.). Note that each generational change results in a significant increase in speed. Further note that between generational changes there are small improvements in the performance characteristic that result from improvements in complementary technologies (hardware and software) and production or process technologies (production techniques and materials used).

If we next overlay the S-curve framework presented in Figure 3.8 on this diagram, it is clear that the microprocessor chip technology is in Stage 2, or the rapid improvement stage. When will this technology reach Stage 3 and begin to show declining increases in performance? At what MIPS will we say that the technology has reached its finite potential?

FIGURE 3.2.1 EVOLUTION OF PERSONAL COMPUTER MICROPROCESSOR SPEED

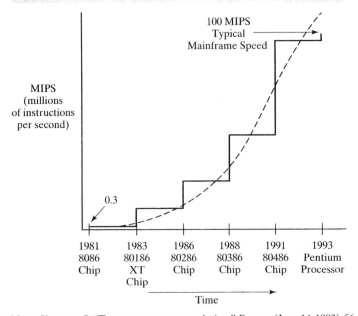

Source: Adapted from Sherman, S. "The new computer revolution," *Fortune* (June 14, 1993): 56–80.

believed that the maximum safe speed in miles per hour of the steam locomotive engine was approximately the same as the number of inches in the diameter of its driving wheels. With experience, this estimate was revised upward by a factor of 25 percent. Typically, learning plays a more important role in improvements in the performance characteristics of so-called science-oriented, high-technology items than it does in the case of traditional techniques.

Every technology is associated with a finite potential of improvement in its performance characteristics. Rapid improvement in performance characteristics first slows and then plateaus when the inherent limits of technology are approached. During this stage of evolution, even if significant efforts are made to improve the performance characteristic, the rate of progress declines. Further improvements will generally not appear until the emergence of a brand new technology.

Why does the performance characteristic exhibit an *S*-shaped curve of evolution? We can attribute the *S*-shaped evolution of performance curve to two effects: (1) learning processes and (2) technology limits.

LEARNING PROCESSES

The slow development in the first stage and the rapid improvement that takes place in the second stage of technology evolution can best be explained by *learning processes*. In the first stage, the learning generates a more or less reliable design and production process. In the second stage, learning curve effects produce rapid improvement in the performance characteristics.

TECHNOLOGY LIMITS

Once a technology has reached its full potential, rapid improvements in performance characteristics will have to wait until a radical breakthrough in technology occurs. During the later stages of evolution, *technology limits* come into play, and improvements in performance characteristics become increasingly harder to come by. The closer to the full potential of the technology, the less rapid the developments that can be achieved.

FIGURE 3.9 TECHNOLOGY PROGRESSION

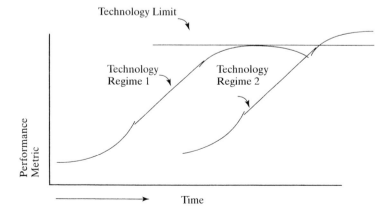

TECHNOLOGY PROGRESSION

Technology progression describes the process by which new technologies emerge to make existing technologies obsolete. Whereas technology evolution describes the incremental improvements in *existing* technologies, technology progression refers to radical breakthroughs that produce *new* technologies. Technology progression may be described using a series of *S*-curves. Figure 3.9 represents technology progression, plotting the evolution of performance characteristics over time. As shown in the figure, the performance characteristics improve along an *S*-curve for each technology. When a radical breakthrough occurs, drastic improvements in performance characteristics are made possible, and the new technology makes the old obsolete. In some cases, drastic improvements in the new technology are needed before it can make an existing technology obsolete; in other cases, a breakthrough technology may, from the very beginning, make an existing technology obsolete.

What do we know about technological progression? First, radical breakthroughs generally appear to be a matter of chance. The primary reason for this is that determinants of new technologies generally tend to be numerous and extremely varied. There are a great many different sources of technical discoveries in any given area. Although some technological discoveries are the result of systematic R&D efforts, others originate during the conduct of day-to-day production and marketing activities. The origin of technological discovery lies, therefore, in complex interactions among a multitude of factors.

Second, technological progression is also the result of an accumulation of relevant know-how or learning. Technological change or breakthroughs occurring without a history of unsuccessful efforts is rare. Lessons learned from mistakes committed in the past constitute an important factor in the process of successful breakthroughs. For example, Fulton's success in building a steamship was preceded by no fewer than 34 distinct attempts that resulted in failure. Similarly, as many as 62 aircraft designs conceived during the period 1927 to 1960 were never used commercially. However, many technological failures are valuable in other respects, because they generate experience on which future developments can be based. Thus, a failure in technological innovation does not constitute failure in the learning sense. Instead, past failures accumulate into valuable lessons for future innovations.

Taken together, technology evolution and technology progression represent two faces of technological innovation. Technology evolution represents the incremental evolution of technology over time; technology progression represents the radical breakthroughs that significantly replace current technologies or make them obsolete. Both occur as a result of organizational and individual learning processes.

LEVELS OF TECHNOLOGY DEVELOPMENT

As we have seen in our discussion of technological environment, the dynamics of technological change are further complicated by the fact that development activities take place at many levels: basic research and applied research, which may occur in areas such as development, engineering, and operations. As we discussed earlier, a different level of technical skill and business orientation is needed for each. Hence, these levels are normally performed by different groups of individuals within a society and also within a firm.

A number of studies have investigated the movement of a technology as it moves from basic research to commercialization. A summary of these studies is presented in Box 3.3. These studies generally reach three major conclusions:

1. Research, especially basic research, is often conducted without a practical application or a problem at hand. Thus, the innovation process does not always begin with a perceived problem or need.
2. A lengthy period often occurs between an invention in basic research and its application in the form of innovation. It seems that basic research results have to "age" before they can be packaged into a useful innovation.
3. Major technological advances (i.e., radical innovations in such fields as military weapons, medicine, or agriculture) require not just one innovation but a cluster of innovations, often as many as a dozen.

As we noted during our discussion of technology progression, radical innovations often *appear* as a matter of chance. This is partly because these innovations often require integrating developments from a number of levels. The synthesis resulting from the integration of developments then gives the appearance of a radical breakthrough. Studies of technological development attest to this fact: A major technological innovation often has to wait until other innovations have taken place in a number of unrelated fields.

TECHNOLOGY CHANGE AGENTS

The agents or creators of technological change are almost innumerable and vary significantly across the levels of technological change. Government institutions such as NASA—or independent research entities such as the Batelle Research Institute, Bell Laboratories, universities, and some large corporations—engage in much of the work dubbed "scientific discovery" or "basic research." Independent entrepreneurs, business firms, and some governmental agencies play leading roles in applied research and commercialization.

EVOLUTIONARY CHARACTERISTICS OF TECHNOLOGICAL CHANGE

Both the coexistence of different types of innovations—incremental, modular, architectural, and radical—and the simultaneous development of innovations at multiple levels by numerous change agents bestow evolutionary characteristics on technological development. Thus, technological developments can be broken down into a series of small steps. In the case of technological change, the distinction between various types of innovation (incremental, modular, architectural, and radical) depends on the location of the observer. As we noted earlier, innovations within an established industry are often limited to incremental improvements of products and processes, and these improvements are the result of accumulation of experience in working with a particular technology. Radical change, on the other hand, is often introduced from outside the established industry. From the perspective of these latter entities—those who are involved in technology development—the so-called radical changes will be seen as an accumulation of incremental innovations. Each of the incremental steps is a creative act and depends on active experimentation, learning, and availability of local information of a specific nature. The accumulation or synthesis of these facts is often not visible to outsiders. This

BOX 3.3

RESEARCH STUDIES

Beginning in the late 1960s, a number of studies have been done on the technology development continuum. These studies have retrospectively traced innovations over time, attempting to reconstruct the series of main events and decisions associated with the innovation-development process. These studies are often referred to as the "tracer studies" (several of the studies were titled TRACES, for Technology in Retrospect and Critical Events in Science).

The first study, appropriately called Project Hindsight, was done for the Department of Defense and focused on the research and development activities associated with 20 major weapons systems, including the Polaris and Minuteman missiles and the C-141 transport plane. Each major system was first broken down into its subsystems and components by a team of experts. From there, the teams identified contributions made by recent science and technology to each of these subsystems and components. In other words, the teams were concerned with identifying scientific and technological events that were necessary to further the overall weapons system development. Thus, the system could be traced back to a series of scientific and technological events, as well as to the individuals associated with those events.

The major findings of the Project Hindsight study, though not particularly surprising, should be noted. First, the development of these sophisticated systems depends on numerous scientific and technological events. Second, these events begin to accumulate as long as 20 years before the actual engineering phase is undertaken. Third, it is the focus of the weapons system project, the applied research, that contributes most to its ultimate development.

Perhaps the most significant result of Project Hindsight is that it spawned numerous other studies of the innovation-development process. Several of these, called TRACES I, TRACES II, and TRACES III, along with a study in England called Project Sappho, improved on the methodologies used in Project Hindsight and extended the domains of the studies of past military weapons systems to include such areas as biomedical, consumer, and agricultural innovations. Consistent with the original study, these extensions showed that major technological advances were dependent upon numerous underlying innovations and that lengthy periods were often necessary between basic research breakthroughs and their technological application.

One final study is worthy of note. In 1977, Julius Comroe published the results of his study tracing the innovation-development process associated with the ten most important technologies in cardiopulmonary medicine that had occurred over the past 30 years. Using what the author called, tongue-in-cheek, a retrospectroscope, the author began with over 4,000 scientific articles and eventually decreased this number to 529 key articles. An article was considered key if it was an important contribution to the scientific and technological process that eventually led to one of the ten important technologies under investigation. Of these 529 articles, 217 or 41 percent, "reported work that, at the time it was done, had no relation whatever to the disease that it later helped to prevent, diagnose, treat, or alleviate." Thus, the innovation-development process does not necessarily need to begin with the identification of a problem.

Source: Adapted from Rodgers, E. M. *Diffusion of Innovations.* 3d ed. New York: The Free Press, 1983; Comroe, J. H. *Retrospectroscope: Insights into Medical Discovery.* Menlo Park, CA: Von Gehr Press, 1977; Isenson, R. S. "Project Hindsight: an empirical study of the sources of ideas utilized in operational weapon systems." *Factors in the Transfer of Technology.* Gruber, W. H. and Marquis, D. G. (Eds). Cambridge: M.I.T. Press, 1969, 155–176.

invisibility often bestows a radical quality on the technological change when it is ultimately presented to outsiders.

UNCERTAINTY AND TECHNOLOGICAL INSULARITY

The evolutionary character of technological change suggests that the individuals and firms that are engaged in solving technical problems face a great degree of uncertainty. They cope with this uncertainty by engaging in a process of learning: gathering information from the technological environment, experimentation, and imitation. The system of information exchange created by firms and individuals while developing technologies is thus a crucial factor affecting innovation. Individuals working on innovation tasks must devote much effort to obtaining and using information concerning

- The performance of innovation they are seeking to create or adopt;
- Materials and components they are fabricating into the innovation;
- Competitors' innovations, the nature of existing patents, and government policies affecting their proposed innovation; and
- The problems faced by consumers in the market and how the proposed innovation might help solve certain of these perceived problems.

In other words, the innovation process is most of all driven by the exchange of technical, market, and other environmental information in the face of a high degree of uncertainty.

The search for or dissemination of technical information embedded in an innovation is governed by the principle of *technological insularity*. This principle suggests that a characteristic feature of technical know-how is that it is not easily transmitted. Thus, the know-how acquired in the development of one innovation may not be fully transferable to the development of another innovation. Pure scientific knowledge, the output of basic research, is equally available to all the actors in the technological environment, although this availability may be spread out over time. However, technical know-how, the output of applied and developmental research, is largely product and process specific and so is highly localized.

There are several reasons why the transfer of technical information may not occur with ease:

1. As we noted earlier, the performance characteristic associated with a specific technology evolves along an *S*-shaped curve, mainly because the accumulated experience of individuals involved in the innovation represents a process of learning by doing. Thus, firsthand knowledge of the innovation is crucial to the evolution of its performance characteristic. This firsthand knowledge is not easily transferred across individuals and firms.
2. Technical and scientific information in the very early stages of research cannot be accessed inexpensively. So, to some extent, the search costs involved reduce the ease of transfer of technical know-how across individuals, firms, and countries.
3. Technical know-how is not often easily accepted by individuals not involved in its production. Such know-how often requires abandoning old concepts or concepts that have not been proven useful. People not engaged in innovation often resist abandoning their cherished ideas.

Thus, the principle of technological insularity arises due to three reasons: The difficulty of transferring first-hand knowledge; the search costs involved in accessing technical information; and the difficulty involved in unlearning or abandoning old concepts.

Technological insularity leads to two characteristics of technological change: (1) spatial clustering and (2) temporal clustering. *Spatial clustering* refers to the occurrence of innovations in clusters around certain regions of a country. An example of this is the case of the U.S. semiconductor industry, which during the 1980s was highly concentrated in the Silicon Valley of northern California (a 10- by 30-mile area between San Francisco and San Jose). All but three of the approximately 75 American semiconductor firms were then located in the Silicon Valley. The semiconductor business—a high-technology industry—has been characterized by continuous innovation, as a larger and larger number of computer functions are put on a tiny silicon chip. In order to compete in this industry, electronics engineers must exchange information with other R&D workers, often in competing firms. Thus, Silicon Valley became an information system for the exchange of technical knowledge. Naturally, a semiconductor industry company wishes to prevent its technological secrets from spreading to its competitors by means of patents, security against industrial espionage, and by other means. But among Silicon Valley R&D workers there was 30 percent job mobility; this shows that one means of obtaining another firm's technical secrets is to hire away its engineers. Thus, the exchange of personnel is facilitated by locating in similar locations, leading to spatial clustering of innovations. The case of spatial clustering in Silicon Valley is further elaborated in Box 3.4.

BOX 3.4

SPATIAL CLUSTERING
AND SILICON VALLEY

An interesting phenomenon that appears in the study of innovation is that innovations often "cluster" in geographic areas. This spatial clustering is quite evident in the case of an area in northern California known as Silicon Valley. This ten-by-thirty-mile area between San Francisco and San Jose is home to all but three of the approximately 75 American semiconductor firms. Further, most of these firms are spin-offs from Fairchild Semiconductor, one of the first firms in the industry.

Several popular theories have been advanced in recent years to explain the success of areas such as Silicon Valley and Route 128 outside of Boston. One of the most popular of these, called the *flexible specialization theory,* suggests

that networks or communities of small firms are a more effective form of economic and technological organization than large integrated firms. In turn, close relationships, shared trust, and intense cooperation generally characterize the networks between firms. Thus, this theory suggests one motivation behind the formation of such areas as Silicon Valley and Route 128.

A second theory, similar in some respects to the one previously noted, has been proposed by economist George Gilder and is called the *law of microcosm.* In this "law," Gilder suggests that small firms are much better suited to new high-technology fields than are the large industrials. This is because the industrials are versed in the production of large things on a large scale, but the

Source: Adapted from Florida, R. and Kenney, M. "Silicon Valley and Route 128 won't save us," *California Management Review* (1990): 33(1): 68–88.

nature of high technology is more focused on miniaturization and specialization. Thus, the small organization has an "economy of microscale." Further, small firms are generally more entrepreneurial in disposition, and this organizational attitude is more suited to the innovative and rapidly changing nature of high technology. In summation then, Gilder suggests that the small, entrepreneurial firm will drive high technology.

Both of these theories help in our understanding of how regional high-technology clusters of firms may come into being. They do little, however, to explain the fierce competition we now witness in the semiconductor industry and see played out in Silicon Valley. Such competition has resulted in high failure rates among firms, constant changes in suppliers and personnel, and price wars throughout the industry. It is difficult to conceive of such an environment as a close network of cooperating organizations. As several authors have recently suggested, "[W]hile this model gives rise to new, highly innovative companies at breakneck speed, it also generates a high degree of internal competition and a serious problem of industrial fragmentation. It can catalyze the world's most advanced breakthrough innovations, but it is unable to generate the small product, process, hybrid, and systems innovations that are needed to follow through on such innovations and turn them into a wide variety of commercial products."

Temporal clustering refers to the occurrence of innovations in clusters around particular points in time. There are two ways in which this takes place:

> First, a major innovation occasionally acts as inducement for a series of minor innovations. For example, developments in semiconductor technology have led to developments in computers, electronics, and military hardware.
> A second way in which temporal clustering takes place is when major innovations themselves come about in clusters.

Temporal clustering also occurs because of technology insularity. Because reaching each small milestone in an innovation is through a random process, we would expect that innovations would eventually be spread in uniform fashion across time, *if* there were no barriers to the diffusion and intermingling of know-how acquired from the development of different techniques. However, as we have seen, there are barriers to exchange of technical information. Just as in the case of spatial clustering, this leads also to clustering of major innovations over time.

CHARACTERISTICS OF INNOVATIVE FIRMS

What makes a firm innovative? In other words, why are certain firms repeatedly successful in innovation? The question has been of interest to scholars and firms over the last century.

As early as 1939, Joseph Schumpeter proposed that innovative success might be related to the *size* of a firm. He outlined two types of innovation from a microeconomic perspective—entrepreneurial innovation and managed innovation:

> Entrepreneurial innovation. *Entrepreneurial innovation* occurs when new technologies and scientific development yield economic opportunities for

proactive entrepreneurs. Small, dynamic, fast-growing firms emerge and become the primary engine of innovation and often generate modular and architectural innovations.

Managed innovation. As the markets mature, the firms that survive tend to become larger, and competition shifts to price. This leads to an era of *managed innovation,* when firms attune their research and development efforts—innovation—to market forces; several incremental innovations result from R&D activity, mainly of large firms. During this era, innovation efforts also become directed away from products and towards cost-reducing process technologies.

Scholars attempting to verify Schumpeter's intuition have tried to assess the relationship between size and innovativeness; this search has had mixed results. Indeed, they have discovered that both small and large firms can be innovative, although the factors that drive small and large firms toward innovation are not always the same. In Box 3.5, we have summarized the research evidence on the relationship between size and innovation.

BOX 3.5

LARGE FIRMS VERSUS SMALL FIRMS

A continuing debate that exists in both the management and economics literature is centered on the question *Are large firms or small firms more innovative?* Economist Joseph Schumpeter spawned much of this debate in the early 1960s when he theorized that large firms would be more innovative than small firms. He argued that there were five primary reasons for this phenomenon:

1. Large firms are likely to have more sustained R&D programs, and this should create more innovations;

2. Economies of scale in large R&D programs should make these programs more efficient and thus result in greater levels of innovations;

3. Larger programs mean that researchers have more colleagues to interact with, and this interaction should result in more innovations;

4. The market power of large firms increases their ability to exploit innovative ideas; and

5. Large firms have the resources to assume greater levels of risk than do small firms.

While these arguments appear sound, the results of empirical studies across large and small organizations have been inconsistent in their findings. Thus, it may not be possible to provide a definitive answer to the large-vs-small question. It may be possible, however, to define the characteristics of large and small firms that may act as drivers of innovation. This approach has been the focus of several recent research efforts.

In a study of small firms (fewer than 500 employees) published in 1989, Khan and Manopichetwattana drew several conclusions concerning the characteristics of these organizations. These researchers found that the in-

Source: Adapted from Hitt, M. A., Hoskisson, R. E., and Ireland, R. D. "Mergers and acquisitions and managerial commitment to innovation in M-form firms," *Strategic Management Journal* (1990): 11: 29–47; Capon, N., Farley, J. U., Lehmann, D. R., and Hulbert, J. M. "Profiles of product innovators among large U.S. manufacturers," *Management Science* (1992): 38(2): 157–169; Khan, A. M. and Manopichetwattana, V. "Innovative and noninnovative small firms: types and characteristics," *Management Science* (1989): 35(5): 597–606.

novative firms in this study generally fell into two distinct groups. The characteristics of the first group, which the authors called the "Young Turks," included being young and proactive, having a strong research orientation, accepting risk taking, and maintaining a focus on product differentiation. The second group of innovators, called "Blue Chips," was characterized by a strong focus on management techniques such as environmental scanning and the integration of decision-making controls and analysis procedures. These firms also had relatively new management teams of very high quality in terms of education, training, and experience. For both types of firms, environmental characteristics seemed to play a role in determining innovative activity. In contrast, non-innovative firms exhibited poor controls, planning, analysis, and integration of strategy. Many tended to ignore their environments entirely, despite the fact that here, too, environmental characteristics appeared to play an important role in determining innovative activity. Management teams in these firms had been with the organizations for longer periods of time. Finally, many of these organizations seemed to survive on past product and market successes. Thus, these researchers point to specific characteristics that may be considered facilitators of innovation in the small firm.

In 1992, researchers Capon, Farley, Lehmann, and Hulbert published their study of innovative activity in a sample of *Fortune 500* firms. For these large firms, this research indicated that environmental, strategic, and organizational characteristics all had a significant bearing on innovative activity. In the environmental context, operating in growing markets and markets in which the firm had dominance appear as facilitators of innovative activity. Strategies focused on heavy investment in product (rather than process) R&D also appeared as a strong facilitator. Finally, organizational structures designed to encourage entrepreneurship and informal organizational atmospheres open to new ideas also appeared as prime facilitators of innovative activity. In contrast, low innovative firms tended to focus on process innovations and pursue strategies associated with existing products in mature markets. Some of the low innovative firms also attempted to substitute acquisitions and contributions to research consortia for innovative undertakings in-house.

Schumpeter suggested that innovation can be of two kinds: (1) managed, or resulting from being in tune with market forces and (2) entrepreneurial, or the type of innovation associated with high risk. Thus, as research continues to show, there may be no definitive answer to the question of which type of firms are more innovative.

Firms, however, do not control size in the short term and, therefore, it is more fruitful to understand how other more managerially controlled internal characteristics of the firm are related to innovation. We can identify four major classes of internal organizational characteristics: (1) organization structure, (2) resources, (3) openness to external information, and (4) informal internal communications.[17]

ORGANIZATION STRUCTURE

The two organization structure variables that have been found to stifle innovation are formalization and centralization.

Formalization refers to the degree of relevant rules, written documentation, and operating procedures within an organization. It represents the degree of bureaucracy that exists in an organization.

Centralization, on the other hand, refers to the locus of decision making. The more centralized an organization is, the more likely it is that decisions are made at the top levels of the organization.

It is often argued that lower formalization and higher decentralization grant lower level individuals greater participation in decision making and thereby a proprietary interest in its outcome. This also facilitates flow of information and free exchange of ideas, which in turn encourage learning and innovation.

RESOURCES

The extent of resources that a firm devotes to innovation is also a determinant of its innovativeness. Resources include financial resources and technical resources. Financial resources take the form of research and development expenditures; technical resources refer to the number of individuals who work on research and development or, in general, the task of innovation within an organization.

OPENNESS TO EXTERNAL INFORMATION

This refers to the patterns of information exchange a firm establishes with its environments, including customers as well as the technical experts outside the firm. Organizational learning is a major factor in successful innovation and, as we discussed earlier, information exchange is a key to facilitating organizational learning. Thus, the higher the level of communication with customers and outside technical experts, the higher the probability of innovation.

INFORMAL COMMUNICATION

In addition to organization structure—the degree of formalization and centralization—the nature of informal communication that exists within an organization also influences innovation. More open climates tend to allow free exchange of ideas within an organization, and thus help the process of innovation. In contrast, closed informal organizations with fewer social ties among members tend to stifle innovation.

Taken together, both environmental and organizational factors influence the process of innovation in an organization. Figure 3.10 summarizes these factors. In Box 3.6, we have illustrated these ideas with the stories of three organizations. As can be seen from these stories, not all factors need to be present for an organization to be successful in innovation.

FIGURE 3.10 FACTORS INFLUENCING THE PROCESS OF INNOVATION IN ORGANIZATIONS

BOX 3.6

TECHNOGENESIS: STORY OF THREE FIRMS

In this and the previous chapter we have been discussing many of the contextual issues, both internal and external, that may facilitate innovation in the organization. The sum of these contextual factors is often referred to as the *technogenesis* in which the firm operates, and its importance can be seen in recent research.

In 1992, several European researchers published the results of a pilot study on the company life histories of three publicly held firms in the Netherlands: Nedap, Van Besouw, and ACF. These researchers used annual reports and in-depth interviews to reconstruct the history of these organizations over a 35-year period. The emphasis of this study was on when, how, and why these firms engaged in innovative activities or strategies within the context of firm-level and environmental-level factors. A brief history of each of these companies is instructive in understanding the outcomes of this study.

NEDAP

Nedap, a manufacturer of electrical equipment and components, was established in 1929, and its life history reflects a company that actively responds to technological change. The company displays a consistent pattern of introducing new products and significant product improvements based upon many new technologies. It successfully made a stepwise transition from mechanical and electromechanical products toward electronic technologies as these technologies were evolving. The company made investments in new products while old products were still profitable, often introducing new products before markets had been fully identified. The company also actively searched for new markets that could be entered with established products. Of the three firms studied, Nedap experienced the highest level of commercial success.

VAN BESOUW

Van Besouw is a carpet and textile manufacturer established in 1836. Its life history shows a firm best characterized as a passive responder to competitive and market pressures. In the 1960s, the company made a small commitment to new synthetic technologies but continued to maintain a primary focus on carpeting and traditional textile materials. In the 1970s, the company was able to introduce a new, high-fashion carpet that resulted in several years of commercial success. However, because the focus of company management was on current operations, they were not alert to competitive pressures such as imitation or the technological opportunities presented by synthetics. As a result, the company entered a period of sustained losses that eventually led to a shift in focus from traditional textiles to synthetics. This shift eventually resulted in a return to commercial success in the mid-1980s.

ACF

ACF was established in 1881 as a manufacturer of chemical products for the pharmaceutical and health care industries. The company's life history shows an organization that was highly innovative in the 1950s and 1960s—over 30 patents were granted to the company during this time. In the 1970s, however, revenues from licenses and profits from existing products began to decrease. In response to this condition, management made two major decisions. First, the company's R&D budget was cut substantially because of the perceived high cost and high risk in a company of ACF's size. Second, management adopted a policy of acquiring access to new technologies through acquisitions in unrelated areas. This second decision eventually led to a widely diversified company in which the original core business held only minor importance. ACF's final acquisition was in the consumer electronics industry in the late 1980s. This acquisition resulted in significant declines in company profits and eventually led to a program to divest unrelated businesses and technologies, including consumer electronics. The company is currently in a restructuring phase, again focused on its core business.

Source: Adapted from Geenhuizen, M. V., Nukamp, P. and Townroe, P. "Company life history analysis and technogenesis," *Technological Forecasting and Social Change* (1992): 41: 13–28.

Box 3.6 (*continued*)

Whereas the small sample size of three companies precludes any definitive conclusions, the results are suggestive of factors that need be considered in building an innovative organization. We briefly list these factors and then summarize them in Figure 3.9.1.

FIRM-LEVEL FACTORS

R&D commitment and intensity. Actively participating in research and development efforts in a steady fashion over the 35-year period seems to have facilitated innovations. Firms that *react* to current market conditions by significantly increasing or decreasing their R&D budgets seem less likely to be innovative in the long run.

Products as a synthesis of many new technologies. Firms that use many new technologies in their products may tend to be more innovative than those that focus on only a few technologies. The use of many technologies may provide the firm with more opportunities to be innovative.

Forward-looking management. In general, a firm's management can either focus on the future and attempt to position the firm for that competitive future, or it can focus on its current commercial success. Those firms that tend to have a forward-looking approach may tend to be more innovative in the long run.

Focused-product/market strategy. Firms that pursue a focused-product/market strategy may be able to build strong technological competencies that would not be available as a result of a broad diversification strategy. Thus, a focused-product/market strategy may be a facilitator of innovation.

Internal development of new technologies. Technologies become available to firms either through internal development or external acquisition. Firms that gain new technologies through internal development may tend to be more innovative in the long run.

ENVIRONMENT-LEVEL FACTORS

Industry technological opportunity. Each industry has its own characteristic set of technologies, and the opportunity to innovate is often driven by these characteristics. Industries that can be characterized by mature technologies and declining demand afford less opportunity to innovate than do new and growing industries. Thus, firms that are able to position themselves in these new and growing industries may tend to be more innovative in the long run.

Spatial and socioeconomic networks. Industries may also be characterized by the types of organizations in the industry, as well as the networks that tie those organizations together. These characteristics may in turn act as facilitators of the innovative process.

FIGURE 3.9.1 SUMMARY OF FACTORS STIMULATING INNOVATION

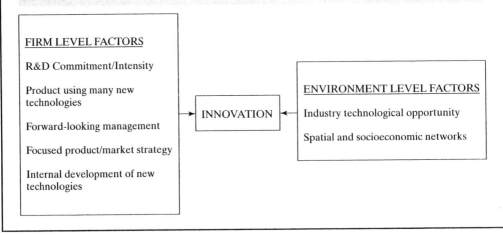

INFLUENCE OF ENVIRONMENTAL TRENDS ON INNOVATION

The three environmental trends—globalization, time compression, and technology integration—are rapidly changing the demand for and occurrence of innovation behavior of firms all over the world.

GLOBALIZATION

We already discussed how innovation in a specific technology might occur in any part of the world; however, different nations tend to develop specialized technology-based assets. One of the significant differences to emerge in recent years is in the relative investments in process versus product innovation. Over the last few years, U.S. firms have under-invested in process technology and over-invested in product innovation relative to their Japanese counterparts. The relevant research is summarized in Box 3.7. As a result, in many, especially mature industries, Japanese firms hold a slight cost advantage relative to their U.S. counterparts.

BOX 3.7

PRODUCT VERSUS PROCESS R&D IN JAPAN AND THE UNITED STATES

The emphasis on product or process R&D may differ substantially across national borders. A recent study of 1,119 large U.S. manufacturing firms indicated that a significant portion of their R&D dollars, approximately 81 percent, was directed at new product development; only 19 percent of total R&D dollars was focused on process innovations. Thus, this study suggests that U.S. firms have a strong preference for product innovations.

In contrast, a similar study of Japanese firms found that 26 percent of the firms focused R&D dollars on manufacturing process innovations, and only 17 percent engaged in new product development (the majority of the firms in this study were focused on incorporating technologies *developed by others*). Clearly, these firms have a much different focus than their U.S. counterparts.

Recent studies have also shown that a dollar spent on R&D in Japan is at least three times more effective in developing international trade than a dollar spent in the United States. One possible explanation for this finding is the noted difference in R&D focus.

Source: Adapted from Caravatti, M. *"Trade and Technology: Strategic R&D Theories and Estimation of the Differential Impacts of Product and Process Innovation on the Bilateral US-Japan Trade Balance,"* UMI Dissertation Service: Ann Arbor, MI, 1992.

TIME COMPRESSION

The pressures of time compression are driving firms to shorten their problem-solving time and, in turn, forcing them to learn smarter and faster. The recent interest in knowledge management and organizational learning is partly a reflection of this necessity. As we have emphasized, organizational learning is central to the successful management of technology.

TECHNOLOGY INTEGRATION

Firms increasingly understand two major implications of technology integration for innovation. First, competitive advantage may be effectively sought by deploying architectural innovations that incorporate known technologies in novel ways. Second, during product and process innovations, alliances with other firms or adoption from external sources is sometimes more economically prudent and faster than in-house development.

MANAGERIAL IMPLICATIONS

Although we have already discussed several managerial implications of the dynamics of technological change, we will reiterate three key themes for emphasis:

1. Successful management of technology requires that the problem solving within the firm should take into account both technical and market considerations. Thus, both technology-push and market-pull innovations can succeed if they are augmented respectively by market and technical considerations.
2. Learning through environmental intelligence, innovation, and imitation are central to effective problem solving. Globalization, time compression, and technology integration are heightening the need for faster and more effective problem solving than in the past.
3. Development of problem solutions can be accomplished either in-house, in collaboration with others, or simply by adopting innovations from outside. The mode of development should be a deliberate managerial choice.

❖ CHAPTER SUMMARY

The dynamics of technological change at the firm level can be described within a four-stage model of problem solving. The first step involves recognition of a problem triggered by market need, technological opportunity, or a change mandated by regulatory bodies or external agents. In the second stage, the firm formulates an idea to solve the problem. The third stage involves bringing the idea into fruition in the form of a prototype or blueprint. The final stage involves commercialization of products or implementation of value chain reconfiguration.

Successful management of technology involves both finding innovative solutions to problems and opportunities and gaining acceptance for them in the marketplace. We capture this idea by the term *co-evolution of market and technology* and represent it on a technology-market matrix.

Innovation is both a process and an output of a firm's attempt to find a solution to customers' needs or a technical opportunity. An innovation has three major components: hardware elements, software elements, and evaluation information components.

At the firm level, we can identify different drivers, processes, and outputs of innovation. The drivers of innovation are usually environmental conditions or autonomous, value-seeking behavior of firms. The major environmental factors are market demand and costs of inputs. The process of innovation may be classified as market pull or technology push.

When the process is initiated by market needs, we call them market pull. Alternately, when a technological opportunity triggers innovation, we have technology-push innovations.

There are two dimensions along which we can classify an innovation output: the degree of novelty in component knowledge and the degree of novelty in the configuration of components. Based on these dimensions, we can identify four types of innovation: incremental, modular, architectural, and radical. These types differ in terms of the process of innovation, their economic impact, and the role of the manager in the innovation process.

Technology evolution can be represented by performance characteristics. The performance characteristics follow an S-curve of evolution with four major stages: emergence, rapid improvement, declining improvement, and maturity. This evolutionary pattern is the result of two major factors: learning processes and technology limits. Learning is inherent in development as are improvements in technology. Every technology has some inherent limits beyond which a specific technology cannot improve. Technology progression describes the process by which new technologies replace older ones. Technology development takes place at many levels. Basic research and applied research, development, and operations are often carried out by different organizations.

Uncertainty is inherent in technology change. Technological insularity refers to the difficulty in transmission of technical know-how from the point of its origin. Costs of information search, knowledge emerging from doing, as well as the difficulty individuals have in abandoning old concepts create technological insularity. Technological insularity generates spatial and temporal clustering. Spatial clustering refers to the occurrence of innovations in clusters around certain regions; temporal clustering refers to clustering of innovation around certain periods in time.

Organization structure (formalization and centralization), resources, openness to external information, and the structure of informal communication within the firm influence the innovativeness of a firm.

❖ NOTES

1. From Robert Buderi, "The Corporate Logic" *Technology Review*, Vol. 103, No. 3, May-June 2000, pp. 88–90.
2. A simplified version of the model developed by Marquis, Donald G. "The Anatomy of Successful Innovations," *Innovation*, November 1969.
3. Adapted from Grant, Robert. *Contemporary Strategy Analysis.* Cambridge, MA: Basil-Blackwell, 1995.
4. This idea will be developed in chapter 7 and is drawn from Fahey, L. and V. K. Narayanan. *Macroenvironmental Analysis for Strategic Management.* St. Paul, MN: West Publishing, 1986.
5. Marquis, D. ibid.
6. This is the basis of institutional theory. See Narayanan and Nath. *Organization Theory: A Strategic Approach.* Homestead, IL: Irwin, 1993.
7. Schumpeter, Joseph A. *Capitalism, Socialism and Democracy.* New York: Harper & Row, 1950.
8. A thorough discussion of the various definitions is found in Zaltman, Gerald, Robert Duncan and Jonny Holbek. *Innovations and Organizations.* New York: John Wiley & Sons, 1973.
9. The description of the components of innovation is drawn from Rogers, Everett. *Diffusion of Innovations.* New York, The Free Press, 1982.
10. Nader, Ralph. *Unsafe at Any Speed.* New York: Grossman, 1965.
11. Marquis. *Ibid.* See also, Myers, S. and D.G. Marquis. *Successful Industrial Innovations.* National Science Foundation (1969): NSF 69-17.

12. von Hipple, E. "The Dominant Role of the User in Semiconductor and Electronic Sub-Assembly Process Innovation," *IEEE Transactions on Engineering Management* (1977): 24(2): 60–71. See also his *Sources of Innovation.*

13. Henderson, R. M. and Clark, K. B. "Architectural Innovation: The Reconfiguration of Existing Product Technologies and Failure of Established Firms," *Administrative Science Quarterly* (1990): 35: 9–30.

14. Marquis. ibid.

15. Perhaps the best empirically and logically developed arguments about the learning process, spatial, and temporal clustering can be found in Sahal, Devendra. *Patterns of Technological Innovation.* Reading, MA: Addison Wesley, 1981.

16. Gohlke. "Thermal-Air Jet Propulsion," *Aircraft Engineering,* 1942, Vol. 14, pp. 32–39.

17. The influence of organizational characteristics has had a long intellectual history starting with Tom Burns and G. M. Stalker. *The Management of Innovation.* London: Tavistock Publications, 1961. For recent works see, Dewar, R. D. and Dutton, J. E. "The Adoption of Radical and Incremental Innovations: and Empirical Analysis," *Management Science,* Vol. 32: 1422–1433; and Damanpour, F. "Organizational Innovation: A Meta-Analysis of Effects and Moderators," *Academy of Management Journal,* Vol. 34, pp. 555–590.

4

PROCESS OF TECHNOLOGY CHANGE: DIFFUSION

In 1965, Dr. Richard Carlson analyzed the spread of modern math among school administrators in Pennsylvania and West Virginia. He studied the opinion leadership patterns related to modern math among school superintendents, characteristics of the innovation, and its rate of adoption.

Carlson's study produced impressive insights about the diffusion networks through which modern math spread from school to school in Allegheny County, Pennsylvania (this county is the metropolitan area for Pittsburgh). Carlson conducted personal interviews with each of the 38 superintendents who headed these school systems, asking each (1) in what year they had adopted modern math, (2) which other superintendents were their best friends, and (3) for certain other data.

Modern math entered the local educational scene of Allegheny County by means of one school superintendent, who adopted in 1958. This innovator traveled widely outside the Pittsburgh area, but he was an isolate in the local network; none of the 37 other school administrators talked to him. The *S*-shaped diffusion curve did not take off until 1959—after a clique of six superintendents adopted; these six included three main opinion leaders in the system. The rate of adoption then began to climb rapidly. There was only one adopter in 1958 (the innovator), five by the end of 1959, 15 by 1960, 27 by 1961, 35 by 1962, and all 38 superintendents had adopted by the end of 1963. Thus, modern math spread to 100-percent adoption in about five years.

The cosmopolite innovator was too innovative to serve as an appropriate role model for the other superintendents. They waited to adopt until the opinion leaders in the six-member clique favored the innovation.[1]

As illustrated in the opening vignette, an innovation or a new idea when it first appears is not accepted immediately by consumers or potential users. Indeed, many innovations fail because they do not get adopted altogether. When successful, an innovation gets adopted over a period of time: Different types of users adopt the innovation at different times. The late adopters sometimes look to the earlier ones for information when trying to decide whether the innovation will be useful to them.

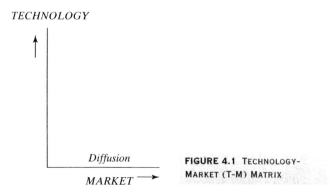

FIGURE 4.1 TECHNOLOGY-MARKET (T-M) MATRIX

In the previous chapter, we noted that a key task in management of technology is to link technological solutions to the needs of the marketplace. We captured this notion by means of the Technology-Market (T-M) matrix, a two-dimensional figure where one dimension represents movement along a specified technical dimension and the other represents movement along a market dimension. This is reproduced in Figure 4.1. We termed the movement along the technical dimension, or the process of finding a technological solution to a problem, *innovation*. From a market perspective, an innovation is the output of that process. The market dimension focuses on the manner in which a firm or an individual customer accepts a technical solution. In this chapter, we will discuss the movement of an innovation along the market dimension; we will term this process *diffusion*.

Taken together, the twin processes of innovation and diffusion capture the dynamics of technological change. Like innovation, diffusion dynamics gets played at two levels. At one level, firms or consumers make decisions about adopting an innovation. This could be a deliberate step in the problem-solving process within firms or it could be individual consumers buying a product or a service. These decisions aggregate to certain predictable patterns of market evolution.

From a managerial perspective, the success of an innovation does not depend only on the technical excellence of a solution but the degree of acceptance in the marketplace. The marketplace is a battleground among firms that compete for the hearts and minds of consumers; consumers may value other factors over technical excellence in their adoption decision. Thus Sony, an otherwise excellent company, engineered a technically superior product, Betamax, only to discover that VCRs were preferred by consumers. In management of technology, we will emphasize the role that market factors play in the success of technology decisions. Learning about markets, customers, and competitors is thus a critical activity in effective technology management. This is in contrast to an engineering perspective, where the technical excellence of a solution is emphasized to the exclusion of market factors.

WHAT IS DIFFUSION?

The original word *diffusion* can be traced to Latin "diffundere," which meant "to put out." In ordinary English language, to diffuse means to spread in all directions. In our discussion of management of technology, we will use diffusion in a more restricted but precise sense:

> Diffusion is the process by which an innovation is propagated through certain channels over time among the units of a system.

There are four major elements in the preceding definition: (1) innovation, (2) propagation through certain channels, (3) time, and (4) units of a social system.

1. *Innovation.* From the point of view of a customer, a technical solution is considered to be an innovation when it is new or perceived as new by the individual or the unit of adoption. It really matters little, so far as human behavior is concerned, whether or not an idea is "objectively new as measured by the lapse of time since its use or discovery."
2. *Propagation.* Propagation refers to the spread of an innovation beyond its inventor. Propagation is the result of a decision to adopt an innovation by an individual or a firm. An innovation presents an uncertain situation to an adopter, and hence the decision to adopt is to some extent influenced by the communication process between the adopter and the individual who has innovated.
3. *Time.* The time dimension is involved in diffusion, because it takes time for individuals or firms to decide to adopt an innovation. Not all adopters adopt an innovation at the same time.
4. *System.* A system is a set of interlinked units that participate in the diffusion process. The members of units of a system may be individuals, informal groups, or organizations.

The term *diffusion* is used restrictively in this definition; it refers only to adoption but not to imitation. We recall your attention to the distinction between diffusion and imitation that was drawn in the previous chapter. We reproduce the schematic representation in Figure 4.2. Thus, when a firm innovates (e.g., develops a new product), two

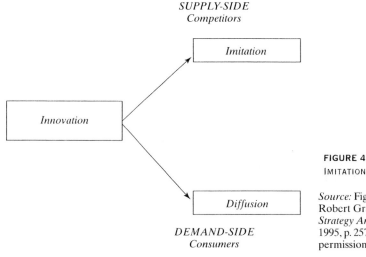

SUPPLY-SIDE
Competitors

Imitation

Innovation

Diffusion

DEMAND-SIDE
Consumers

FIGURE 4.2 DIFFUSION VERSUS IMITATION

Source: Figure adapted from Robert Grant, *Contemporary Strategy Analysis,* Basil Blackwell, 1995, p. 257. Reprinted by permission.

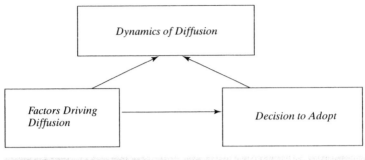

FIGURE 4.3 CHAPTER OVERVIEW

different groups of players respond to the innovation. One group, the customers, makes decisions to adopt or not to adopt the innovation. Diffusion refers to adoption decisions of this kind. A second group of players, competitors, may decide to copy the innovation and make their own (new) products to compete with the innovating firm. We will refer to this as *imitation*. As illustrated in Figure 4.2, thus, imitation is a supply-side concept: It refers to firms that sell products or services. Unlike imitation, diffusion is a demand-side concept: It refers to consumers who buy products and services.

In this section, we will focus on the process of diffusion and describe the ways by which innovations are accepted by the consumers in the marketplace. We will try to answer such questions as:

1. What are the dynamics of diffusion?
2. What attributes of an innovation facilitate or hinder diffusion?
3. What factors drive the processes of diffusion?

The overview of the chapter is presented schematically in Figure 4.3. As shown in the figure, we will first describe the dynamics of diffusion of an innovation through a population of adopters or consumers. Diffusion dynamics arise from a series of individual decisions to adopt. We will summarize this process of (adoption) decision making, anchoring it in the problem-solving model we introduced in the previous chapter. We will then discuss the factors that drive the adoption decision. Next, we will point out the key managerial implications. We will conclude with a chapter summary.

DYNAMICS OF DIFFUSION

Innovations propagate through a population of consumers in the market over time. Not all individuals or firms comprising the market adopt an innovation at the same time; rather, they adopt sequentially over time. This is what we mean by the dynamics of diffusion. Although each innovation diffuses in somewhat unique fashion, there are some general characteristics of the dynamics of diffusion.

We summarize three major characteristics of the dynamics of diffusion: (1) the *S*-curve of diffusion, (2) reinvention during diffusion, and (3) mechanisms of diffusion.

S-CURVE OF DIFFUSION

One facet of the dynamics of diffusion is the manner in which the total number of adopters of an innovation, individuals or firms, changes over time. As shown in Figure 4.4, a plot of the cumulative number of adopters over time displays an *S*-shaped curve. Figure 4.4 also plots the frequency of adoption of an innovation over time. This plot follows a normal bell-shaped curve. Whereas the *S*-shaped curve shows the number of individuals adopting an innovation on a cumulative basis, the bell-shaped curve shows the same data in terms of the number of individuals each year. An *S*-shaped diffusion curve is characteristic of almost all innovations, just as an *S*-shaped curve of improvement is observed in the performance characteristic of innovations over time.

Thus, there are four major eras in the diffusion history of an innovation:

1. Emergence characterized by a slow advance in the beginning, suggesting that adoption proceeds slowly at first when there are few adopters.
2. A rapid growth phase, when adoption rate accelerates until half of the individuals in the system have adopted.
3. A slow growth phase, where the rate of growth declines, but adoption continues.
4. Maturity, the final stage, where the diffusion almost comes to a halt, either as a result of market saturation or the introduction of a new product, process, or service into the market that replaces the existing innovation.

The *S*-curve charts the diffusion of an innovation over time once a few individuals or firms have adopted it. We should remember, however, that there are significant delays between the appearance of an innovation and its first adoption by individuals or firms. As illustrated in our opening vignette, the new math did not diffuse in the school system very easily, even after its adoption by one superintendent. The delays differ from innovation to innovation and are the result of many complex sets of factors.

Although the *S*-curve characterizes the general form of diffusion history for most innovations, the curve also enables us to distinguish between innovations along two factors: (1) the rate of diffusion and (2) the potential set of adopters. The rate of diffusion refers to the speed with which an innovation propagates through a population of individuals or firms. As shown in Figure 4.5, different innovations diffuse through a population at

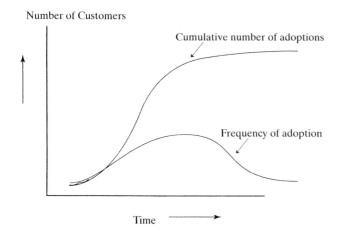

FIGURE 4.4 *S*-CURVE OF DIFFUSION

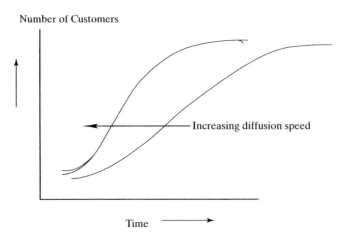

Number of Customers

Time

FIGURE 4.5 DIFFERENCES IN DIFFUSION SPEED

different rates. As an innovation diffuses faster through a population, the *S*-curve shifts toward the left; when the innovation diffuses more slowly through the population, it shifts toward the right. For example, during the 1950s, several manufacturers introduced a washer/dryer for clothes as well as dishwashers for use in the kitchen. Although both of these consumer durable items were based on a similar technological base, the washer/ dryers diffused through consumers much faster than dishwashers did. Consumers were skeptical of the dishwasher's functionality to a much greater extent than that of washer/dryers. As a result, dishwashers diffused much more slowly.

The potential set of adopters refers to the total number of individuals or firms who are likely to adopt an innovation. In a sense, this represents the market potential for an innovation. Some innovations have large market potential; others have low market potential. The height of the diffusion curve is plotted in actual numbers and represents the market potential of an innovation. Taken together, the rate of adoption and the magnitude of potential adopters have been used to describe the *S*-curve mathematically. In Box 4.1, we have summarized the major mathematical formulations of the *S*-curve of diffusion.

During the course of an innovation's diffusion history, an innovation undergoes several changes; further, the forces shaping adoption also change over time. We now turn to these two diffusion-related dynamics.

REINVENTION

Many innovations change over the course of their diffusion history. Reinvention refers to the dynamic by which an innovation is changed or modified by the users as they adopt and use it. There are four ways in which reinvention occurs during diffusion:

   1. The increasing use of an innovation often hinges upon improvement in its functional aspects, an idea that we elaborated in the previous chapter. In many instances, changes in the design and performance characteristics of an innovation are a prerequisite for its further adoption beyond those who

BOX 4.1

MATHEMATICAL FORMULATION OF
S-CURVE OF DIFFUSION: THE BASS MODEL

The diffusion effect or interpersonal inter-action (or the word-of-mouth effect) sug-gested by Rogers has served as the underlying behavioral thesis for building mathematical formulations of innovation diffusion. The *diffusion effect* has been defined as the cumula-tively increasing degree of influence on an individual to adopt or reject an innovation. In fact, Rogers' use of the normal distribution in developing adopter categories is based on the diffusion effect. Articulating the justification for normal adopter distribution, he writes (1983, p. 244):

> ...we expect normal adopter distributions because of the diffusion effect, defined as the cu-mulatively increasing degree of influence upon an individual to adopt or reject an innovation, resulting from the activation of peer networks about the innovation in the social system. This influence results from the increasing rate of knowledge and adoption or rejection of the in-novation in the system. Adoption of a new idea is the result of human interaction through inter-personal networks. If the first adopter of the in-novation discusses it with two other members of a social system, and each of these two adopters passes the new idea along to two peers, the re-sulting distribution follows a binomial expan-sion, a mathematical function that follows a normal shape when plotted over a series of suc-cessive generations. The process is similar to that of an unchecked infectious epidemic.

The key mathematical model that has provided the main impetus for examining the growth of a new product in marketing is the diffusion model proposed by Bass (1969). The Bass model describes the diffusion process by the following differential equation ($p, q \geq 0$):

$$(1) \quad f(t) = \frac{dF(t)}{dt} = [p + q\,F(t)][1 - F(t)]$$

where $F(t)$ is the cumulative fraction of adopters at time t, and $f(t) = dF(t)/dt$ is the rate of diffusion at time t. Bass (1969, p. 217) has referred to p as the coefficient of innovation and q as the coefficient of imitation. If m is the total population of potential adopters, the cumulative num-ber of adopters at time t is $mF(t)$. Inte-gration of equation 1 yields the S-shaped cumulative adopter distribution, $F(t)$, captured by the Bass model. Further dif-ferentiation of $F(t)$ gives the noncumu-lative adopter distribution representing the specified diffusion process. As de-rived by Bass (1969), these distributions are given by:

$$(2) \quad F(t) = \frac{1 - e^{-(p+q)t}}{1 + (q/p)e^{-(p+q)t}}$$

and

$$(3) \quad f(t) = \frac{p(p + q)^2 e^{-(p+q)t}}{(p + qe^{-(p+q)t})^2}$$

The Bass model has been used exten-sively in marketing to estimate the sales of new products. It has also been used to catego-rize different kinds of adopters.

Source: Mahajan, Vijay, Eitan Muller and Rajendra K. Srivastava. "Determination of Adopter Categories by Using Innovation Diffusion Models," *Journal of Marketing Research* (February 1990): Vol. XXVII, 37–50.

have already adopted. These changes require a more detailed specification of the user's requirements; some of the requirements will be known only during its initial use by the potential adopters. For example, although the Remington typewriter was patented in the nineteenth century, it was not until the introduction of QWERTY key configuration that the device began its rapid diffusion through the economy.

2. As an innovation diffuses through a consumer population, a standard model of innovation may emerge and speed the adoption process. This is particularly true in the case of process innovations as they diffuse through a population of firms. For example, as total quality approach to management of organizations diffused through U.S. firms, it became standardized.[2]

3. The widespread diffusion of innovations often requires development of complementary products. Although HDTV has been with us for some time, its diffusion will be rapid as broadcasts suited for the better quality HDTV get developed.

4. In other instances, changes in an innovation make possible new applications, thereby facilitating its adoption beyond the originally conceived scope of its application. An example of this type of reinvention is Velcro, a material originally designed for NASA's space suits and adopted by the commercial textile industry.

There are several reasons why reinvention tends to take place during the diffusion of an innovation. First, as we have discussed in the previous chapter, the principle of technological insularity suggests that it is difficult for knowledge to transfer from the innovator to the adopter of an innovation. Reinvention can occur because adopters typically do not possess detailed knowledge about the innovation; often there is relatively little direct contact between the adopter and/or previous adopters. This learning through reinvention is one of the mechanisms by which the performance characteristic assumes an S-shaped curve during technology evolution. Second, a systemic innovation that has the potential for evolution in multiple directions is more likely to be reinvented during diffusion. When the elements comprising a systemic innovation are loosely bundled (i.e., when the innovation consists of elements that are not tightly interrelated), the innovation can be flexibly suited by adopters to their conditions. Third, reinvention can occur when an adopter uses the innovation to solve a problem for which it was not initially intended. Finally, local pride of ownership in an innovation may also be a cause for reinvention. Here the innovation is modified in certain minor ways so that it appears to be a local product.

An illustration of the local pride of ownership is provided by the diffusion of computers to local governments in the United States. During the 1970s, there was a tremendous expansion in the use of computers for data processing by city and county governments. These organizations soon were spending more than $1 billion per year for computer equipment and computer software programs to perform such data-handling tasks as accounting, payroll, and record keeping. An investigation of how 12 cities and counties adopted the innovation of computer data processing found a surprisingly high rate of reinvention. One of the reasons for such reinvention was that computer programmers working in a local government viewed modifications to innovations as a challenging and creative task. It was more interesting and fun to reinvent a computer program than simply to transfer it from another local government or to purchase it from a commercial supplier, which was viewed as boring and filled with drudgery. Further, local government officials emphasized the degree of reinvention that they had performed, with each of them stressing the uniqueness of their adoption. The relatively petty bells and whistles that they had reinvented appeared to them to be major improvements.[3]

The concept of reinvention suggests that the adopters of an innovation play an active role during the diffusion process. The adopters do not use the innovation passively; they contribute to the development of an innovation or its performance characteristics over time by an active process of modifying and changing the innovation. Recall our discussion of market-pull innovation in chapter 3 (see Box 3.1, featuring von Hippel's work). Thus, the improvement in performance characteristics occurring during the course of technology evolution is partly the result of adopters modifying characteristics during usage.

MECHANISMS OF DIFFUSION

Why do we observe an *S*-shaped curve of diffusion of innovation? The answer to this question lies in two mechanisms by which an innovation propagates through an adopter population: (1) technology substitution and (2) bandwagon effect.

TECHNOLOGY SUBSTITUTION

The mechanism or the key that unlocks the doors of an adopter population for the propagation of an innovation is technology substitution. Technology substitution refers to the actual substitution of a new technique for the old. Many times, a new technology or an innovation displaces an already existing technique or technology during the process of being adopted. As detailed in our discussion of innovation (see chapter 3), an innovation in its early stages suffers from unreliability. Recall also our earlier discussion that an established technology improves radically when confronted with the prospect of being supplanted by a new technology. Thus, the diffusion of an innovation is a process of co-evolution of old and new technologies, involving numerous changes in their performance characteristics. An innovation needs, therefore, to win the hearts and minds of potential adopters against competition from the entrenched older technology. Hence, the rate of adoption of an innovation on an industry-wide basis is likely to be slow at first. Subsequently, as the new technology outpaces the old technology in terms of its performance characteristics, the diffusion of an innovation is expected to take place at a rapid rate. The use of this technology may eventually reach a saturation point as opportunities for its application are exhausted.

BANDWAGON EFFECT

Whereas technology substitution tries to explain why an innovation is adopted in the first place, bandwagon effect is useful for explaining the speed of diffusion. Bandwagon effect focuses on the dynamic by which later adopters, in their decision to adopt an innovation, imitate the behavior of earlier adopters. The experience with the use of an innovation increases as each successive member in the potential adopter population adopts it. As the adopters communicate with each other, either through word-of-mouth communication or through observation of behavior (i.e., they form a network), the networking facilitates the transmission of this knowledge about an innovation in a particular adopter population. Thus, the adoption of an innovation beyond the early stage of diffusion is the result of human interaction through interpersonal or interorganizational networks. The *S*-shaped curve of diffusion "takes off" once interpersonal or organizational networks become activated in spreading knowledge and evaluations about an innovation from one adopter to another in a population. The mathematical models of the *S*-curve featured in Box 4.1 are anchored in the idea that adoption becomes faster as knowledge about the innovation increases and spreads through networks.

The twin mechanisms, technology substitution and bandwagon effect, underscore the roles of (1) uncertainty and information and (2) knowledge and learning in the diffusion process. We observed that during the process of innovation, uncertainty reduction in the early stages or the emergence of an innovation and learning by producers of an innovation leads to improvement in the performance characteristics. Similarly, during diffusion, the accumulated learning that takes place during the course of usage of an innovation by adopters and the amount of information that gets transmitted through the population create the specific pattern of diffusion of an innovation.

Uncertainty-reducing knowledge and learning, therefore, are critical to both the processes of technological change—innovation and diffusion. An innovation presents a novel situation to an adopter, who is faced with uncertainty regarding the performance or usability of the innovation. Technology substitution and bandwagon effect refer to the different facets of learning involved in the decision-making process that leads to adoption:

> The technology substitution refers to the judgment of an adopter or a population of adopters regarding the superiority of an innovation over an existing technology or technique currently in use. For an individual or a firm to adopt an innovation, the adopter has to be convinced that the innovation is superior to something that is already being used by it. Technology substitution focuses on the process of judgment based on the information generated by a unit of adoption. As clear, unambiguous information regarding an innovation's superiority emerges, the adoption decision becomes easier.

> The bandwagon effect refers to the strategy of information collection employed by adopters. Some adopters, especially during the early stages of diffusion history, will have to experiment with an innovation to develop information regarding its superiority. Later adopters may rely on the information generated by earlier adopters to base their judgments about the innovation. Bandwagon effect is the strategy employed by later adopters and focuses on the reliance by adopters on interpersonal and interorganizational networks for information transfer and uncertainty reduction during the adoption decision.

In summary, the two mechanisms, technology substitution and bandwagon effect, underpin the diffusion of an innovation. Both highlight the role of learning and information. Just as learning plays a role in the improvement of performance characteristics of an innovation, uncertainty reduction unlocks the door to propagation of an innovation through an adopter population.

As implied in the preceding discussion, diffusion proceeds as individuals decide to adopt an innovation. Just how does an individual or firm decide whether to adopt an innovation? We will review this topic next.

A MODEL OF INNOVATION ADOPTION

Unlike innovation, diffusion involves two different groups of players: (1) firms that may be employing adoption as a way of problem solving and (2) consumers who may simply be buying a product or service. The decision process that leads either an individual or a firm to adopt an innovation involves five steps: (1) awareness, (2) attitude formation, (3) decision, (4) implementation, and (5) confirmation.

Awareness. In this stage, an individual or firm is exposed to an innovation's existence and gains some understanding of how it functions.

Attitude formation. At this stage, an individual or firm forms a favorable or an unfavorable attitude toward innovation.

Decision. This stage consists of the activities of an individual or firm that lead to the choice of adopting or rejecting the innovation.

Implementation. This occurs when an individual or firm puts an innovation into use.

Confirmation. This occurs when an individual or firm seeks the reinforcement of an innovation decision that has already been made, but the unit may reverse the decision if exposed to conflicting messages about the innovation.[4]

In the case of a firm adopting an innovation, these five steps may be cast within the problem-solving model discussed in the previous chapter. Thus, awareness may trigger problem recognition by alerting the firm to a technical possibility. During attitude formation, the firm may make judgments regarding the appropriateness of the innovation for the problem at hand. If in-house development is judged to be less attractive than the innovation, the firm may move on to the adoption decision phase, followed by implementation and confirmation. This model of the innovation adoption process is schematically presented in Figure 4.6.

We have noted that the key to unlocking adoption of an innovation is the reduction in uncertainty experienced by the unit of adoption. Hence, the information that flows to a potential adopter is a key element characterizing these stages. Table 4.1 summarizes the differences in the characteristics of information sought by the adopters of innovation across the various stages of adoption. For example, in the knowledge stage, the

FIGURE 4.6 STAGES IN DECISION TO ADOPT

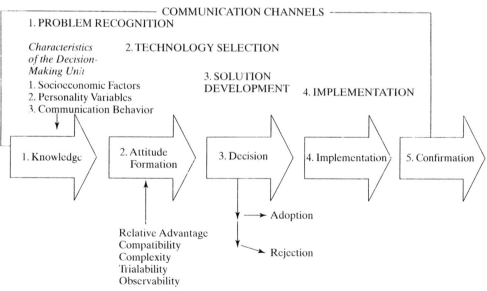

Source: Adapted with the permission of The Free Press, a Division of Simon & Schuster, Inc., from *Diffusion of Innovations, 4th Edition* by Everett M. Rogers. Copyright © 1995 by Everett M. Rogers. Copyright © 1962, 1971, 1983 by The Free Press.

TABLE 4.1   Requisite Information over the Stages of Adoption Decision

Information Characteristic	Awareness	Attitude Formation	Decision	Implementation	Confirmation
1. Level of Knowledge	Ignorance; Existence of New Idea	Positive/ Negative Attitude	Trade-Off	Usability	Lingering Uncertainty
2. Relevant Information Content	Software Elements	Evaluative Information	Cost-Benefit Analysis	Technical Assistance	Disconfirm Better Idea Regulation
3. Sources of Information	Chance	Interpersonal Networks; Peers	Trial Trial by Others	Experience Reinvention	Experience Chance External

adopters particularly look for software information usually conveyed by mass media channels. During the attitude formation stage, they look for evaluation information usually transmitted to them through their interpersonal networks. During implementation the information generated by trying out the innovation becomes key to continued use of the innovation. It has also been observed that, even after an idea has been adopted the adopters sometimes look for information to confirm the value of their decision.

Individual adopters of an innovation differ on (1) the characteristics of the decision making process and (2) the relative importance they attach to each stage of decision making. We will discuss each in turn.

SHIFTING CHARACTERISTICS OF ADOPTERS OVER TIME

As the *S*-curve of diffusion unfolds, different types of individuals adopt an innovation Underlying the *S*-curve is the assumption that the frequency distribution of adopters over time closely approaches a bell-shaped frequency distribution (recall Figure 4.4 Based on this distribution, adopters are typically divided into five adopter categories depending on their speed of adoption: (1) innovators, (2) early adopters, (3) early majority, (4) late majority, and (5) laggards. Actually, there are no pronounced breaks between each of the five categories. The categories represent ideal types—conceptualizations based on observations of reality—that make comparisons possible.

Innovators. Innovators tend to be very eager to try new ideas. They have a wide circle of peer networks. They also have control of substantial financial resources to absolve the possible loss owing to unprofitable innovation. The innovator plays an important role in the diffusion process: They launch the new idea into the system by importing the innovation from outside the system. Thus, the innovator plays a gate-keeping role in the flow of new ideas into a system. The first superintendent to experiment with new math in the opening vignette is an example of an innovator.

Early adopters. Early adopters tend to fall into the category of respectable citizens in the system. This set of adopters has the greatest degree of opinion leadership; others look to early adopters for advice and information about the innovation. This group particularly tends to reduce increased uncertainty about a new idea by adopting it and then conveying an evaluation on the innovation to others through interpersonal networks. The set of six superintendents that followed the innovating superintendent in the opening vignette illustrates this category.

Early majority. The early majority is deliberate in its decision to adopt new ideas. They interact frequently with their peers but seldom hold leadership positions.

Late majority. The late majority adopts new ideas just after the average member of a system. Adoption may be triggered by an economic need or as an answer to increasing network pressures. The late majority approaches innovations with skepticism and caution, and they do not adopt until most others in the system have done so. They have relatively scarce resources; this means that almost all uncertainty about an innovation has to be removed before they feel safe enough to adopt. They primarily rely on bandwagon effect to reduce uncertainty about the innovation.

Laggards. Laggards are the last among a population to adopt an innovation. When laggards finally adopt an innovation, it may already have been superceded by another more recent idea that is already being used by the innovators. The laggards' precarious economic position forces these individuals or firms to be extremely cautious in adopting innovations.

Table 4.2 summarizes the major differences among these adopter categories. Box 4.2 displays the attributes of these adopter categories in the case of consumer durable goods.

RELATIVE IMPORTANCE OF DECISION STAGE

Although each stage of decision making is to some extent visible in every case of adoption, problems of implementation are likely to be more serious when the adopter is an organization rather than an individual. There are two major reasons for this:

1. In an organization, a number of individuals are usually involved in the innovation-decision process, and the implementers are often a different set of people from the decision makers.
2. The organization structure that gives stability and continuity to an organization often resists the implementation of an innovation.[5]

TABLE 4.2   Selected Differences Among Adopter Categories

Factor	*Innovator*	*Early Adopter*	*Early Majority*	*Late Majority*	*Laggards*
1. Socioeconomic Status	High ————————————————————————→				Low
2. Personality Variables	High on • Empathy • Rationality • Abstraction ————————————————→				Low on • Empathy • Rationality • Abstraction
3. Communication Behavior	High on Communication Behavior ————————————————→	High on Opinion Leadership			Low on Communication Behavior

BOX 4.2

ILLUSTRATION OF THE DIFFERENCES
AMONG ADOPTER CATEGORIES

Mahajan, Muller, and Srivastava studied adopters of 11 consumer durable goods ranging from black-and-white TVs, home freezers, steam irons, water softeners, automatic coffee makers, clothes dryers, record players, power lawnmowers, room air conditioners, and electric bed coverings, to electric refrigerators. Based on their analysis, they developed differences among different adopter categories, as follows:

Selected Differences Among Adopters of Consumer Durable Products

Factor	Early Adopter	Early Majority	Late Majority	Laggards
1. *Socioeconomic Status*				
• Age	3.09	2.97	2.90	3.06
• Education	4.12	4.06	3.96	3.78
• Income	4.97	4.73	4.42	4.19
• Occupation	0.60	0.58	0.48	0.44
2. *Reading Habits*				
Number of				
• Computer Magazines	4.32	3.72	3.31	2.79
• Business Magazines	2.99	2.88	2.52	2.11

Averages are reported using the following coding scheme:
Age: $1 = <25$; $2 = 25–34$; $3 = 35–44$; $4 = 45–54$; $5 = >55$
Education: $1 <$ high school; $2 =$ high school; $3 =$ some college; $4 =$ college graduate; $5 =$ master's; $6 =$ Ph.D.
Income in $1,000: $1 < 15$; $2 = 15–24$; $3 = 25–34$; $4 = 35–49$; $5 = 50–74$; $6 = 75–89$; $7 = 100–149$; $8 = 150+$
Occupation as percentage of professionals: $1 =$ professional; $0 =$ nonprofessional
Number of magazines in the last six months

As seen from the table, these researchers were able to track socioeconomic and communication factors enumerated in Table 4.1. Their data generally support that the categorization presented in our discussion was true in the case of these products.

Source: From "Determination of Adopter Categories by Using Innovation Diffusion Models" by Mahajan, Muller and Srivastava, *Journal of Marketing Research* (February 1990): Vol. XXVII, pp. 37–50. Reprinted by permission of American Marketing Association.

This has a major implication for the management of technology. In contrast to product innovation (recall our discussion of the difference between product and process innovation in chapter 3), process innovations are likely to be more challenging to implement, because they will require major internal organizational changes. Several factors influence the decision-making process of adopters at each stage of the model, a topic to which we now turn.

FACTORS THAT DRIVE THE PROCESS OF DIFFUSION

In addition to the characteristics of individual adopters, three sets of factors influence the decisions of adopters over the diffusion history of an innovation: (1) attributes of an innovation, (2) community effects and network externalities, and (3) characteristics of the population through which diffusion occurs. We will discuss each of these in turn.

ATTRIBUTES OF AN INNOVATION

Five attributes of an innovation influence the process of diffusion:

1. Relative advantage is the degree to which an innovation is perceived as being better than the idea it supercedes.
2. Compatibility is the degree to which an innovation is perceived as being consistent with existing values or past experiences and needs of potential adopters.
3. Complexity is the degree to which an innovation is perceived as being difficult to understand and use.
4. Trialability is the degree to which an innovation may be experimented with on a limited basis.
5. Observability is the degree to which the results of an innovation are available to others.

An innovation's performance characteristics, such as technical features or price, may determine the preceding five attributes; however, ultimately, it is the perceived aspect of the innovation that matters. In the case of certain innovations such as new clothing fashions, the social prestige that the innovation conveys to its wearer is almost the sole benefit that an adopter perceives. Indeed, when many other members of a population have also adopted the same fashion, that innovation may lose much of its social value to its adopters. In general, as adopters perceive an innovation to be higher on relative advantage, compatibility, trialability, and observability and lesser in complexity, they will more rapidly adopt the innovation than any other innovations.

As we have noted earlier, an innovation creates uncertainties for a potential adopter: An individual or a firm is likely to be unclear about the potential benefits that are likely to accrue from the adoption of an innovation. An innovation that yields clear advantages but has limited perceived risk is likely to be adopted quickly. The five attributes address the issue of cost benefit and risk:

- The attributes of relative advantage, compatibility, and complexity address the costs and benefits of an innovation. Individuals or firms are more likely to adopt innovations that (1) offer clear advantage, (2) do not drastically interfere with existing lifestyle or organizational patterns, and (3) are easier to comprehend.

- Trialability and observability are both related to risk. Adopters look unfavorably on innovations that are difficult to put through a trial period or whose benefits are difficult to observe. These characteristics increase uncertainty about the innovation's value and thus raise the risk of a decision to adopt.

COMPONENTS OF AN INNOVATION

The hardware (or the material or physical objects that comprise the innovation), the software (which consists of the information base for the use of the innovation), and the evaluation information (which provides the information that is useful for the decision to adopt) components of an innovation may all contribute differentially to the generic attributes of innovation. Figure 4.7 lists some examples of how the three components of innovation can influence the generic attributes of innovations. From the point of view of an innovating firm trying to market its innovation, these generic attributes provide clues to the design and delivery of the product or processes. For example, many software developers jointly develop the products with a select set of customers. This enables them to influence the attributes of the software product and enhance its potential for adoption. It also provides software developers with results of adoption that they can provide later adopters, in an attempt to influence the adopters' perceived observability of the innovation.

COMMUNITY EFFECTS AND NETWORK EXTERNALITIES

Community adoption levels may affect the inherent value and risks of adoption of any class of innovations. Many innovations are associated with increasing returns to adoption or positive network externalities. This means that the benefits of adopting an innovation largely depend on the community of other adopters. This is true for telephones, fax machines, and even Microsoft's operating system. Increasing returns to adoption may ensue from learning by using, positive externalities, and technological interrelatedness.

- Learning by using means that a technology's performance ratio improves rapidly as a community of adopters (vendors and users) accumulates experience in developing and applying the technology. As we described in the previous chapter, market feedback about usability of an innovation leads to improvement in its performance characteristics.

FIGURE 4.7 COMPONENTS OF AN INNOVATION MAPPED TO ATTRIBUTES

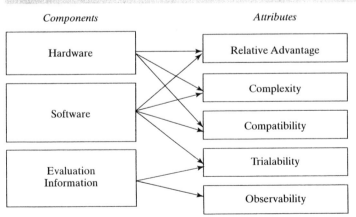

- Positive externalities (sometimes referred to as *network benefits*) means that the immediate benefits of use are a direct function of the number of current adopters. The use of telephone or fax enjoys positive externalities.
- Technological interrelatedness refers to a large base of compatible products needed to make the technology worthwhile as a whole. In the case of Microsoft's operating system, independent software vendors are likely to create applications when they see that sufficient number of users of MS-DOS will buy them. In turn, the users of MS-DOS benefit from the applications.

Four major factors drive community effects:

1. *Prior technology drag.* When a prior technology exists that has already developed a mature adoption network, the disparity in short-term benefits between the old and new technologies is likely to be large, even though the new technology may hold more promise in the long term.
2. *Irreversibility of investments.* When adoption of an innovation requires irreversible investments in areas such as product training and accumulative project experience, it enhances the risk of adoption.
3. *Sponsorship.* This refers to the existence of a single entity (person, organization, consortium) to define the technology, set standards, subsidize early adopters, and otherwise promote adoption of the new technology.
4. *Expectations.* If enough firms hold positive expectations about a technology's chances for dominance, then the technology is likely to enjoy a long honeymoon period, and the adoption is facilitated.[6]

Whereas technology drag and irreversible investments favor existing technologies, sponsorship and positive expectations can overcome these forces. Strong sponsors such as a government agency can tip the cost-benefit equation in favor of the new technology. Similarly, positive expectations can be generated by endorsements of a community and, conversely, reduced by publicizing adoption horror stories. In Box 4.3, we have illustrated how both the attributes of innovation and community effects influence the diffusion of innovations.

BOX 4.3

EXAMPLES OF SOFTWARE
ENGINEERING INNOVATIONS

In this study, the researchers examined three recent candidates competing for dominance in the realm of software engineering: Structured analysis and design methodologies (hereafter "structured methodologies"); production fourth-generation languages (4GLs), and relational database management systems (RDBs).

Each of these innovations was intended to revolutionize a different segment of the software engineering discipline—analysis and design, coding and testing, and data management, respectively. And, like object orientation, each was preceded by tremendous publicity.

Box 4.3 (*continued*)

Structured Methodologies. In the mid-1970s, structured methodologies (such as DeMarco structured analysis and Yourdon/Constantine structure design) emerged to replace the informal analysis and design practices of the day with an engineering style dedicated to rigorous procedures, formal diagrams, and measures of design quality. These methodologies went beyond the mere adoption of a systems development life cycle and prescribed very specific schedules of tasks and activities.

Production 4GLs. Although a wide variety of special-purpose 4GLs had previously existed, it was not until the early 1980s that a new breed of production 4GLs became commercially available. Production 4GLs, unlike end-user query-oriented 4GLs like FOCUS and RAMIS II, are those languages such as Natural, ADS/Online, and IDEAL that were designed to support the development of large-scale business systems, a domain that was then dominated by COBOL.

RDBs. Commercial RDBs emerged in the early 1980s as an alternative to the hierarchical and network model databases such as IMS and IDMS. Although RDBs and production 4GLs emerged concurrently, and some vendors bundled the two technologies together, most vendors took a mix-and-match approach wherein a production 4GL could be used with nonrelational databases, and a relational database could be accessed via 3GLs, especially COBOL.

For structured methodologies, the early adoption window occurred in the mid-1970s, when they were proposed as a replacement for informal (or no) processes. For production 4GLs and RDBs, this window was the early 1980s, when they were slated to replace 3GLs and earlier database models, respectively.

Of the three technologies, only RDBs have proven to be *dominant* in the sense that they replaced the prior technology for new development activities. It is unlikely that an organization would routinely proceed with developing a new application using an older generation (nonrelational) database model, whereas organizations continually choose the older, third-generation languages for new development. Similarly, structured methodologies have not reached the stage of widespread routine use. Many organizations still cling to

ad hoc methods within the life-cycle approach or have abandoned the life cycle altogether for prototyping approaches that make no use of structured methods. The lack of adoption of structured methods has even been cited as a major barrier to the adoption of integrated CASE tools.

The three technologies under discussion are all subject to increasing returns to adoption; they become much more valuable to individual adopters to the extent that others adopt. Widespread adoption leads to faster maturation (learning by using), wider availability of qualified personnel (positive network externalities), and a larger array of complementary products and services (technological interrelatedness). Four factors largely determine whether a technology will achieve critical mass and become a dominant technology: prior technology drag, irreversibility of investments, sponsorship, and expectations.

Production 4GLs stand out among the three technologies as having faced especially severe obstacles from the economics of technology standards view. Production 4GLs faced extensive prior technology drag, required large irreversible investments, were poorly sponsored, and had diminished expectations (due to publicity surrounding adoption fiascoes and the lack of a strong scientific base). When introduced in the early 1980s, production 4GLs were a textbook case of an innovation facing a monolithic installed base, namely, the COBOL programming language. Forgoing the COBOL standard meant missing out on a large network of experienced personnel and compatible tools (e.g., database systems). Hence, prior technology drag was especially high.

Adoption of production 4GLs required largely irreversible investments in staff training and software—specialized assets that lose most or all of their value should the investment project be abandoned later. Naturally, organizations are reluctant to incur the risk associated with such investments, especially when the investment pertains to the technologies that, like most software engineering innovations, require a critical mass of other adopters to achieve full benefits over the long term.

Lack of sponsorship also created a hurdle for 4GLs. A dominant sponsor can advance the adoption of a technology by promoting a unified standard, by subsidizing early adopters, or by making a credible commitment to develop the technology even in the face of expected delays in widespread adoption. In the case of production 4GLs, many languages emerged—none supported by a dominant sponsor. Production 4GLs even lacked a single authority figure to define exactly what capabilities a production 4GL should provide.

Finally, expectations worked against community adoption. Production 4GLs were developed primarily by innovators in the commercial sector and suffered from a lack of scientific support or more objective boosterism from the academic community. Perhaps more damaging, 4GLs experienced some widely publicized adoption fiascoes, such as the infamous New Jersey Department of Motor Vehicles case.

In summary, the failure of 4GLs to achieve critical mass was because of high prior technology drag, large irreversible investments, relatively poor sponsorship, and rapidly diminished expectations.

Structured methodologies and RDBs, on the other hand, would have rated much more favorably. On the first and most important dimension—prior technology drag—structured methodologies were an attempt to impose order on chaos and thus faced essentially no installed base. RDBs faced an installed based of first-generation database systems, although not one so mature and ubiquitous as COBOL. In addition, the first-generation database market was fragmented, meaning that the benefits associated with joining the network of any given database product (e.g., IMS or IDMS) were correspondingly reduced.

As with production 4GLs, RDBs and structured methodologies required largely irreversible investments in staff training. Additionally, adoption of RDBs required the purchase of expensive software. This suggests that the irreversible investments dimension was not a significant discriminator among any of the three

technologies. On the sponsorship dimension, RDBs had a founding father in E. F. Codd, who clearly established the criteria for database management systems (DBMS) to qualify as fully relational. Structured methodologies also had easily identifiable founding fathers (e.g., Ed Yourdon and Tom DeMarco, among others). Although none of the three technologies was strongly sponsored in the traditional sense of a single organization encouraging adoption, RDBs and structured methodologies had widely recognized leaders defining the technology and proselytizing for widespread adoption and therefore rank relatively higher than production 4 on this dimension.

With an unassailable scientific base and near universal support in the academic community, RDBs benefited from high expectations. In addition, the strengths of RDBs—data independence and greatly simplified information retrieval—complemented industry trends toward more data-intensive applications. Structured methodologies were certainly in line with the trend in the 1970s toward large-scale development projects, and they also escaped widely publicized disasters. Therefore, production 4GLs rated the poorest on this dimension.

To summarize, compared with production 4GLs, RDBs faced a much less well-established installed base and had the advantage of positive expectations and a strong sponsor to push forward a cohesive definition of the technology. Structured methodologies had effectively no installed base to overcome, required less in the way of irreversible investments, and were somewhat better sponsored. Hence, other things being equal, we could have predicted a relatively easy community adoption of structured methodologies and RDBs.

Again, however, only RDBs have actually become dominant. Although accurately reflecting the fate of production 4GLs, these factors alone do not effectively discriminate between structured methodologies and RDBs and therefore would have been an inadequate single explanation of the ultimate dispositions of these technologies.

CHARACTERISTICS OF THE POPULATION

Because an innovation permeates a system, the structure of the system accepts an influence on the diffusion process. Of particular importance are three facets of the system: (1) communications, (2) opinion leaders, and (3) cultural norms.

COMMUNICATIONS

Diffusion rates appear to depend on formal and informal communication: Information reduces uncertainty for the adopter. For example, early awareness of an innovation appears to depend on external sources such as advertising and vendors. Adoption of an innovation by an organization, however, seems to also depend to a great extent on the communication networks among technical personnel inside the adopting firm. The communication networks can either facilitate or impede the diffusion of an innovation in the system. In a recent study, researchers found that the firms that refused to adopt innovations from outside tend to have a relatively lower number of information channels with the outside world. This study is featured in Box 4.4. Indeed, in the United States,

---

BOX 4.4

"NOT INVENTED HERE" SYNDROME

Engineers have long recognized the problems facing a technical group should its membership remain constant too long. General folklore among R&D professionals holds that a group of engineers whose membership has been relatively stable for several years may begin to believe that it possesses a monopoly on knowledge in its area of specialization. Such a group, therefore, does not consider very seriously the possibility that outsiders might produce important new ideas or information relevant to the group. This has come to be known in the R&D community as the "Not Invented Here" or "NIH" syndrome.

According to the NIH syndrome, stable project teams become increasingly cohesive over time and begin to separate themselves from external sources of technical information and influence by communicating less frequently with professional colleagues outside their teams. Rather than striving to enlarge the scope of their information-processing activities,

long-tenured groups become increasingly complacent about outside events and new technological developments. The extent to which they may be willing or even feel they need to expose themselves to new or alternative ideas, suggestions, and solutions lessens with time.

In spite of this belief, the fact remains that groups, including those of long-standing membership, must still collect and process information from outside sources in order to keep current technically. Project members rarely have all the required knowledge and expertise to complete their tasks successfully; information and assistance must be drawn from many sources outside the project. Moreover, research findings have consistently shown that personal contacts rather than written technical reports or publications are the primary means by which engineering professionals acquire important technical ideas and information from outside sources. Thus, project groups whose members have been working together

Source: From "Investigating the Not Invented Here (NIH) Syndrome: A Look at the Performance, Tenure, and Communication Patterns of 50 R&D Project Groups," by Ralf Katz and Thomas J. Allen, from *R&D Management,* 12,1, 1982, pp. 7–19. Copyright by Basil-Blackwell Ltd.

over a long period of time (i.e., project teams whose members are averaging high levels of group or project tenure) will have significantly less communication with other professionals both within and outside the organization.

If project communication with internal and external colleagues diminishes significantly as mean group tenure increases, and if such communications are essential to technical performance, then one should also expect a strong inverse relationship between group tenure and project performance. Several studies, in fact, have presented evidence to support such association:

- Shepard was the first to relate performance to mean group tenure as measured by averaging the lengths of time individual members had been working within the group. He found that performance increased up to about 16 months average tenure, but that performance gradually decayed with increasingly higher levels of group stability.

- Pelz and Andrews uncovered a similar curvilinear connection between mean tenure and performance. In their study, however, the "optimum group tenure" seemed to fall at about the four year mark.

- Smith also showed R&D group performance peaking at a mean tenure of about three or four years.

In a general sense, we need to uncover the kinds of managerial pressures, policies, and practices that can be used to keep a project effective and high performing under such tendencies. In addition to such managerial interventions, it would be even more important to determine if and how a project group can keep itself highly energized and innovative. The challenge to industry in general, and to organizations in particular, is to learn to effectively organize and manage projects in a world characterized by a more rapidly changing and complex technology coupled with a more maturing and stable population.

many firms which have an in-house R&D laboratory have been reluctant to adopt innovations from outside: This is often termed the "not invented here" (NIH) syndrome.

OPINION LEADERS

In the communication process within a system, opinion leaders play central roles. Opinion leaders are individuals who influence others' opinions about innovations. Most ideas enter and diffuse through a population because of its opinion leaders. This idea has come to be known as the *two-step flow of communication* in diffusion: The first step in the process is the innovation's being adopted by opinion leaders who, in the second step, transmit it to others in the system. Indeed, opinion leaders are usually among the first ones to adopt a new idea. They have great exposure to mass media; they read widely and watch television; and they are easily accessible to other members of a population of potential adopters.

CULTURAL NORMS

Norms are established behavior patterns among individuals of a population. They define a range of tolerable behavior, serve as a guide for the individuals, and are typified by opinion leaders. Norms may impede or speed the diffusion of innovations. Although boiling water is an important health practice for urban poor, it failed when first introduced as a public program in Peru: Most people associated heat with illness.[7]

Taken together, the attributes of innovation, community adoption, and network externalities and the characteristics of the population drive the speed and pattern of diffusion.

INFLUENCE OF ENVIRONMENTAL TRENDS ON DIFFUSION

Throughout our discussion of the technological environment, we have illustrated how globalization, time compression, and technology integration are key environmental trends influencing the management of technology. These three trends inevitably are reflected in the patterns of diffusion:

1. As a result of globalization, the potential adopters during the diffusion of any innovation are located all over the world. Indeed, diffusion can no longer be conceptualized as movement of innovation from the United States to other advanced economies and to developing countries. Sometimes, and increasingly, adoption of innovation begins outside the United States, and then diffusion spreads back to the United States. For example, Intel was forced to introduce Celeron, a complementary line to Pentium, mostly because of the threat of spread of the lower priced processor from Asia.

2. We have already discussed how time compression has caused the shortening of product life cycles or, in other words, swifter patterns of diffusion. In turn, this is requiring firms to learn about the market evolution faster than before and to develop the capacity for rapid responses. Time compression in diffusion requires rapid responses by firms in three areas: (1) redesign of the evaluation information component of the innovation; (2) adjustment of their marketing strategies; and (3) adoption of relevant innovations faster than their competitors.

3. The potential for technology integration in both process and product arenas is inducing firms to look outside their own organization for appropriate innovations as complements to their in-house development activity. This has intensified the pressure on organizations to institute organizational mechanisms to circumvent the NIH syndrome. As captured in the problem-solving model, "make-or-buy" has become an important choice point in the problem-solving process.

MANAGERIAL IMPLICATIONS

Because the value of technology is ultimately determined in the market, anyone involved in management of technology should have a thorough grasp of the diffusion process. Four major practical implications flow from the discussion of diffusion:

1. Significant attention should be devoted to obtaining market feedback over the course of diffusion in the case of new product or process introductions. The characteristics of the adopters change over time; they reinvent the adoption; and their attitudes toward the innovation are likely to be differ-

ent. Even after a new product is introduced, firms may have to fine-tune the design and delivery of the product over the various stages of diffusion.

2. In the case of firms adopting an innovation, implementation is a challenging task and should be managed carefully. This process is likely to be incremental, and in many cases organizations should be allowed to reinvent the innovation to suit local needs. In addition, because users of innovation are likely to be different from decision makers, sufficient training and incentives should be provided to smooth out the disruptions of adoption.

3. Product design and marketing strategy should reinforce each other as a firm rolls out a new product or process. Both the new product and market strategy should be guided by similar understanding of the five attributes of the innovation that will drive diffusion. For this to happen, coordination mechanisms should be created to foster dialogue between product designers and marketing strategists.

4. When feasible, managers should line up sponsors and create expectations of a technology success to take advantage of community effects in diffusion. They should expect resistance from entrenched players that may retard the diffusion of new technologies. In order to overcome this resistance, managers should recruit the support of powerful sponsors.

❖ CHAPTER SUMMARY

When a new product, process, or idea first appears, different consumers adopt it at different time periods. The process is captured by the S-curve of diffusion very much like the case of innovation, with four major eras: emergence, rapid growth, slow growth, and maturity. During diffusion, its users modify a technology. This reinvention could be due to the difficulty of information transfer to users, flexibility of use of complex technologies, discovery during use of applications not initially intended, and local pride of ownership. Both technology substitution and bandwagon effects are key to unlocking the diffusion potential of an innovation.

The decision-making process that individuals or firms go though during adoption of an innovation may be described as a five-step process: awareness, attitude formation, decision, implementation, and confirmation. The characteristics of adopters shift over the S-curve because of differences in the decision-making process. Five groups of adopters may be identified: innovators, who try out new ideas; early adopters, who are typically opinion leaders; early majority, who are deliberate in their decisions; late majority, who follow the bandwagon effect; and laggards, who are the last of the population to adopt an innovation. The implementation stage is critical in organizations due to resistance from the current organization.

Three major factors determine the speed of diffusion: attributes of innovation, community effects, and characteristics of the population. Five attributes of innovation influence the process of adoption: relative advantage, compatibility, complexity, trialability, and observability. Community effects may arise from prior technology drag, irreversible investments, sponsorship, or expectations. Finally, the communication patterns within the population and opinion leadership may also influence the speed of diffusion.

From a practical point of view, managers of technology involved in new product or process introductions should create market feedback mechanisms for product design and marketing strategy formulation. During the adoption of an innovation, they shoul also be careful about implementation. Finally, managers should recruit sponsors an opinion leaders to overcome resistance from entrenched players in the market.

❖ NOTES

1. Adapted with the permission of The Free Press, a Division of Simon & Schuster, Inc., from *Diffusion of Innovations, 4th Edition* by Everett M. Rogers. Copyright © 1995 by Everett M. Rogers. Copyright © 1962, 1971, 1983 by The Free Press.

2. Westphal, J. D., Gulati, R., and Shortell, S. M. "Customization or conformity? An institutional and network perspective on the content and consequences of TQM adoption," *Administrative Science Quarterly* (1997): 42: 366–394.

3. Danziger, James N. "Computers, Local Governments and the Litany to EDP," *Pub-lic Administration Review* (1997): Vol. 37, pp. 28–37.

4. Adapted from Rogers, Everett. *Diffusion o Innovations.* 3d edition. New York: The Fre Press, 1983, pp. 163–190.

5. Rogers, ibid., p. 174.

6. Fishman, R. G., and Kemar, C. F. "Adoption of Software Engineering Process Innovations: A Case of Object Orientation," *Sloan Management Review,* Winter 1993, pp. 7–22.

7. Illustration from Wellin (1955) referenced in Rogers. *Diffusion of Innovations,* New York: The Free Press, 1983.

TECHNOLOGY AND COMPETITION

Technology can often be a critically important element in the competitive battles between firms. Consider, for example, the case of Xerox and the development of smaller-sized copiers.

Xerox had been the leader in copier technology since it first introduced the model 914 in 1959 and had pioneered the development of the plain-paper copier in the late 1960s. In the mid-1970s, however, competitors began introducing smaller, more reliable copiers to compete with the traditional products of Xerox. The first of these, the Savin 750 built by the Japanese manufacturer Ricoh, was introduced in 1975 and used liquid toner technology that made the machines less expensive to build and more reliable to operate. Several imitations of this product also appeared on the market, including the machines produced by Canon. Xerox considered these machines to be the "low end of the market" and continued to concentrate on the development of their medium- and large-sized copiers. A market for these smaller machines did, however, exist, and in 1976 more than 100,000 Japanese copiers were purchased worldwide. As this market grew year after year, Xerox eventually came to recognize its potential significance in the company's competitive arena.

The Xerox answer to the flood of low-cost Japanese copiers appearing in the marketplace was the 3300 model, introduced in 1979. However, in order to meet the low-end selling price, the machine had been designed with the most inexpensive parts available. As a result, it was extremely unreliable, and in 1980 the company was forced to suspend production and recall close to 4,000 units. The 3300 was subsequently re-engineered and reintroduced in 1982, but the public perception of reliability problems associated with the original unit could not be overcome. The 3300 never became the successful product that had been planned. Further, between 1976 and 1982 the company's share of American copier installations dropped from an estimated 80 percent to 13 percent.

During the 1980s under the direction of new CEO David Kearns, Xerox reinvented itself. By the late 1980s, Xerox had slashed its manufacturing costs by nearly 50 percent, doubled its production, and cut the product development cycle by a full year. By 1990, Xerox was again the producer of the highest quality office products in the world and had gained back the market share from the Japanese.

What is important in this story is the way in which technology plays a significant role in the competitive rivalry that evolves among firms. Through an architectural innovation, Ricoh, then an unknown firm, became a significant force in the copier market. Despite the fact that Xerox was a leader in the core technologies that made up the new smaller copiers, it took the company 8 years to bring a competitive product to the marketplace. And in that period, Xerox lost half of its worldwide market share and experienced severe financial problems. The speed of conduct of business had by then increased; the markets required faster responsiveness by firms. Of course, Xerox's rebound was a function of their embedding new processes and redesigning their value chain in addition to strengthening the new product development efforts.[1]

As described in the opening vignette, the copier industry has witnessed periods of competitive upheavals, characterized by significant technological change. A great deal of uncertainty is associated with technological change: Market positions of firms shift drastically; new firms may enter the market; and even some large firms face the threat of extinction. Technology plays an important role in competition.

In this chapter, we will describe the influence of technology on competition. Specifically, in this chapter we explore such questions as:

1. What are the consequences of technological change?
2. How do industries differ in terms of technological characteristics?
3. What are the systematic patterns of industry dynamics triggered by technological change?

The chapter overview is sketched in Figure 5.1.

In Figure 5.2, we have reproduced the theoretical framework to discuss the role of technology in competitive dynamics. As shown in the figure, we describe how the twin processes of technological change—innovation and diffusion—create opportunities and threats, i.e., competitive consequences for firms in the marketplace.

FIGURE 5.1 CHAPTER OVERVIEW

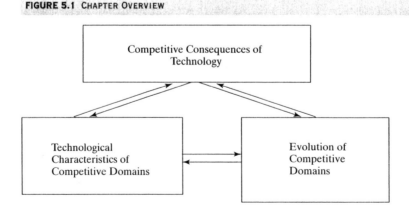

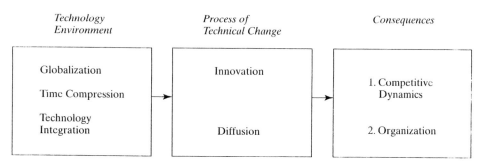

Technology Environment	Process of Technical Change	Consequences
Globalization

Time Compression

Technology Integration | Innovation

Diffusion | 1. Competitive Dynamics

2. Organization |

FIGURE 5.2 THEORETICAL LINKAGES

COMPETITIVE DOMAINS

Throughout this chapter, we will use the term *competitive domains*[2] to refer to arenas where multiple firms compete for the hearts and minds of customers. In many instances, industries constitute the primary competitive domains of technology. However, the term *competitive domain* is more relevant than *industry* for our focus in this chapter for two reasons:

1. Technological change often spawns new industries; leads to industry convergence, whereby several previously unrelated industries merge into one under the influence of technological change; and sometimes destroys industries. A focus on industry obscures the dynamics that lead to the formation, convergence, and obsolescence of industries.
2. Many competitive battles in technology are fought in institutional arenas that are not usually captured in the descriptions of industry. We need a conception of competition broader than the one captured in the term *industry* to describe the competitive dynamics triggered by technology.

Within the analysis framework for management of technology, why should we concern ourselves with the dynamics of competition? We have emphasized that the primary objective of technology management should be the creation of value for a firm. Value creation is, however, tied to the competitive advantages that a firm can create in the marketplace or, more precisely, in the firm's competitive domains. Customers judge a firm's offerings in relation to those of its competitors; therefore, a firm has to win the hearts and minds of its customers in competition with other firms. As we saw in the introductory vignette, technology creates and destroys competitive advantage. It is important to understand the mechanisms by which technology influences the competitive dynamics. This logic that we introduced in chapter 1 is reproduced in Figure 5.3.

The visible battlegrounds in competitive domains are product markets, where firms fight to get their product designs accepted as the standard, attempt to overcome switching costs and win customers, and gain market share and brand loyalty. Technological and organizational capabilities are a prerequisite to the successful deployment of technology in products. Thus, a more subtle and less transparent battleground in the competitive domains is the acquisition of technological and organizational capabilities.

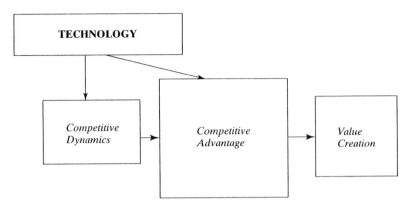

FIGURE 5.3 TECHNOLOGY AND COMPETITIVE ADVANTAGE

We may array acquisition and deployment of technology in the Technology-Market Matrix, as illustrated in Figure 5.4. Acquisition of capabilities, technological and organizational, can be portrayed along the technology dimension and deployment, which is dictated by the market realities, along the market dimension. Recall the story of Microsoft and its acquisition of the technological capability for WebTV from Perlman that we summarized in our introductory vignette to chapter 3. We will deal with the strategic considerations involved in the acquisition of technological capabilities, be it from outside or through in-house development, in chapter 10. In chapter 6, we will summarize a framework for analyzing the organizational capabilities ushered in by technological advances.

In our discussion of innovation and diffusion, we underscored the central importance of learning for successful management of technology. Thus, we illustrated different kinds of learning that need to be nurtured during the evolution of technology and market. Learning is central to the creation of value in competitive domains—learning about competitors, relevant external stakeholders, and the central institutional players that influence the course of competitive domains.[3]

The scheme of the chapter is as follows. First, we will sketch the consequences of technological change—how technological change spawns new industries and affects

FIGURE 5.4 TECHNOLOGY-MARKET MATRIX

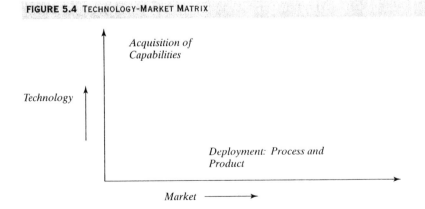

competition within industries. Second, we will summarize the key technological properties of industries. Third, we will discuss the industry dynamics triggered by technological changes. Finally, we will point out the major implications of technological change for competition among firms.

COMPETITIVE CONSEQUENCES OF TECHNOLOGICAL CHANGE

Technological change ushers in new products and processes, simultaneously destroying the existing order, or the status quo. Joseph Schumpeter was the first to recognize this dual tendency of technological change when he described technological change as "creative destruction." Technological change includes both innovation and diffusion. Innovation brings in its wake new ideas in the form of products and processes that invariably replace existing products and processes. In a similar way, whenever a firm adopts new ideas from others—when diffusion takes place—it abandons the existing way of doing things in favor of the idea, the practices, or the tools that it has borrowed from its environment.

Four clusters of consequences evolve from technological change: (1) creation of new products, (2) changes in the value chain, (3) changes in value constellation, and (4) competitive rivalry.

CREATION OF NEW PRODUCTS

New products represent arguably the most visible battleground in the marketplace. Product improvements through incremental and modular innovations, architectural innovations that open up new market segments, the introduction of radically new products that render existing products obsolete, and technology convergence are the manifest ways that product competition evolves.

1. Product improvements have helped firms extend the market reach of their products. Industries in the mature stage can often be rejuvenated by an infusion of newer technologies into their products. For example, during the last 3 decades, the watch industry has been dramatically rejuvenated by the evolution of technologies from mechanical through electronic, quartz, and digital technologies. Similarly, in videotape recorders, firms have prolonged the product life cycle through the introduction of technology-based features.
2. Architectural innovations provide opportunities to serve previously untapped market segments and enable firms to change their competitive positions. Recall the story of Ricoh and their battle with Xerox that we summarized in our opening vignette.
3. Technological innovation sometimes spawns totally new products. By opening up possibilities hitherto unavailable, these new products enable human beings to extend their mastery over their environment. For example, advances in computing are increasingly making it possible for human beings to focus on nonroutine tasks, releasing them from (automated) routine analysis tasks.

4. Technology integration or the opportunity to develop new products and processes by synthesizing a set of existing technologies often leads to convergence. For example, convergence is now taking place in the computer, telecommunications, and entertainment businesses: It is expected that over the next 3 to 5 years, technological developments will lead computers, telecommunications, and entertainment to converge to form an "information industry." Similar convergence is also taking place in biotechnology industries; genetics, agriculture, and pharmaceuticals are beginning to converge to form a biotechnology industry.

Technological change can, however, also make existing products obsolete. Technological progression—a mechanism of the process of innovation—inevitably destroys inferior technologies and ushers in superior technologies. Similarly, during technology substitution (one of the mechanisms of diffusion), firms adopt a newer technology in favor of a technology that is currently being employed in the firm. Thus, both technological progression and technology substitution result in the displacement of existing technologies by newer or superior ones. In turn, this renders existing products obsolete. For example, with the advent of personal computers, personal calculators have become almost obsolete.

CHANGES IN VALUE CHAIN

Technological changes enable firms to reconfigure their value chains, thus influencing the cost and speed of doing business. For example, continuous improvement practices—often the cornerstone of total quality management (TQM)—enable a firm to incrementally capture the productivity that is embedded in its existing value chain. Alternatively, a firm may substitute a newer technology for an existing one to enhance its speed of operations. For example, optical scanners used in retail outlets enabled faster and more accurate recording of transactions than manually operated checkout counters.

We may identify two ways in which value chains are transformed: (1) automation and (2) reconfiguration of processes.

AUTOMATION

Automation refers to the replacement of labor with less expensive capital-intensive technologies. Automation has been an ongoing phenomenon in developed countries during the twentieth century, with capital-intensive equipment and machinery replacing blue-collar jobs. Indeed, in the technology-induced wave theories of society, automation has been featured as the driving force behind society's movement from the First Wave—the agricultural era—to the Second Wave—the industrial era (see Box 2.5). In the United States, automation was a primary reason for the declining blue-collar workforce: With the increasing adoption of automated factories and the use of robotics, the need for a blue-collar workforce has declined.

In recent years, however, as a result of developments in information technology (IT), automation has been extended to white-collar jobs. With the advent of distributed computing and faster processing of information, organizations have been able to replace whole layers of management with information technology. As illustrated in Box 5.1, office automation has begun to yield productivity gains in the last 5 to 6 years.

BOX 5.1

THE PRODUCTIVITY ENHANCEMENT
FROM OFFICE AUTOMATION

Productivity enhancement is a key element in developing sustainable competitive advantage. One clear way in which technology has made, and will continue to make, major impacts on productivity is in the area of office automation. Consider how the following technological developments in computers have changed the way office work is performed:

First, graphical user interfaces such as icons allow all workers, regardless of technical literacy, access to the system. Next, computer networking has increased the speed and flexibility of communicating data and correspondence throughout the organization. Similarly, imaging software that converts documents to electronic images also facilitates the rapid movement of information. Finally, flexible databases expedite the storage and retrieval of vast amounts of information, making it instantly available to all who need it.

Despite the obvious ties between office automation and productivity, it is important to understand that implementing automation does not in itself result in simultaneous productivity enhancement. Like any new process adoption, the productivity enhancement that results from information technologies can come only after an organization has learned and adapted a system to fit its own unique operational needs. We can see the way in which this learning phenomenon has played out on a national level in recent times. During the 1980s, U.S. businesses spent more than $1 trillion on information technology. Yet, productivity remained stagnant and in fact declined during the final years of that decade. It was not until 1992 that serious increases in productivity could be seen. Although there may be numerous reasons for national productivity improvement, many business experts suggest that recent increases may largely be attributed to the automation investments made in the previous decade.

SUPERIOR PROCESSES

Firms also reconfigure their value chains by introducing superior processes into their operations. Superior processes may evolve from technology progression or technology evolution.

A radically different process could replace an existing process. For example, when airline industry deregulation took place, many of the large airlines altered the nature of their flight schedules to what became known as the "hub-and-spoke" system. This allowed the airlines to move a large number of passengers with fewer flights. Box 5.2 illustrates the shift to the hub-and-spoke system in the airline business. As was expected, when the flights were arranged according to the hub-and-spoke system, significant productivity gain was possible.

Alternatively, an existing process may be made efficient through the naturally occurring learning that results from its continued utilization. Thus, TQM methods help to incrementally harness the productivity gains inherent in existing processes.

CHANGES IN VALUE CONSTELLATION

The value constellations of firms are often upset by technological developments in three ways: (1) shifting balance of power, (2) potential for outsourcing, and (3) different ways of managing value constellations.

BOX 5.2

COMPETITION IN SERVICE INDUSTRIES—
THE CASE OF THE U.S. AIRLINE INDUSTRY

When the U.S. airline industry was deregulated in 1978, experts expected that, along with lower airfares, there might also be a reduction of flights to smaller communities. This latter expectation proved wrong because of the unexpected emergence of an innovative service form—the "hub-and-spoke" system of route networks. Under this routing system, a large number of cities (the "spokes") are connected by one-stop service through a centrally located airport (the "hub"). This allowed the airlines to greatly increase the number of flights between *pairs* of cities: Instead of offering limited point-to-point service, fliers from a variety of origination points could be aggregated at the central hub and then flown to a common destination. Thus, this represented a more efficient routing approach, because it permitted an airline to link pairs of cities that would otherwise have been uneconomical to service.

Before deregulation, only the smaller, regional carriers utilized a hub-and-spoke system. The major airlines focused primarily on offering point-to-point nonstop service between major cities and emphasizing their connecting flights. In contrast, the smaller volumes handled by the regional carriers necessitated an efficient approach to routing. Because the hub-and-spoke system reduced the number of aircraft needed while increasing the number of passengers on those aircraft, and because it centralized maintenance and other service functions, it was clearly the more economical approach. During the recession in the early 1980s, this became evident when the majority of large carriers experienced losses; the regional carriers that were profitable flew hub-and-spoke routes. By 1986, the hub-and-spoke system had become the dominant route design in the airline industry.

Source: Adapted from Allred, C. M. "The U.S. Airline Industry in 1987: Seven Years after Deregulation," 1986.

---

1. Technological developments shift the balance of power between firms and their suppliers and distributors. For example, consumer goods firms such as Procter and Gamble have discovered that, with the advent of optical scanners, their distribution outlets have better consumer information and thus greater clout. Previously, the distribution channels had been the recipients and beneficiaries of the knowledge created in the corporate market research departments of the consumer goods firms; however, with the advent of optical scanners, the distribution channels can now easily capture knowledge about consumers. This has also resulted in a concentration of the distribution outlets; firms like Wal-Mart have been able to reap the benefits of economies of scale inherent in the deployment of scanners and related information technologies.

2. As a result of the market forces and the standardization of production processes, firms are discovering opportunities to outsource many activities that had hitherto been conducted in-house. For example, by outsourcing component manufacturing, automobile firms such as General Motors are breaking up their integrated manufacturing operations.

3. The widespread adoption of IT is enabling firms to better plan and manage their supplier and distributor relationships. The just-in-time processes are

enabled by computer-based systems that cut across organizational boundaries to include the various players in the value constellation.

COMPETITIVE RIVALRY

Product and process innovations are two means by which the competitive game is
played and won. These innovations enable firms (1) to erect entry barriers to competitors; (2) to bring about product and process substitution; and (3) to redefine the rules
of competition.

1. *Barriers to entry.* The patents resulting from technological development and
    the economies of scale present in the research and development (R&D) ac-
    tivity are sometimes significant barriers to entry into an industry. In the
    pharmaceutical industry, for example, many large firms are dependent on
    patents for a significant percentage of their cash flows. If the patents are not
    renewed as they expire, small generic drug manufacturers enter, thereby de-
    creasing the profitability of the drug. In many competitive domains, where
    firms compete on the basis of know-how generated from their research and
    development activity, new entrants also will have to compete with high
    R&D dollars; this poses a significant barrier to entry for them.

2. *Product and process substitution.* Technological change is often one of the
    most important factors giving rise to product substitution and product dif-
    ferentiation. For example, plastics have replaced many uses of steel; word
    processors have replaced typewriters; and microwave ovens are now fre-
    quently substituted for conventional ovens. In the videotape recorder
    market, firms have sought to differentiate their products through the intro-
    duction of technology-based features: longer recording time, longer ad-
    vanced time-setting, sharper picture production, clearer sound, and so on.
    Similarly, process innovations and innovations in raw materials may enable
    a firm to enhance its competitive position—sometimes by improving qual-
    ity, sometimes by reducing its cost structure. For example, automation, ro-
    botics, and CAD/CAM have bestowed cost and quality advantages on many
    firms. Japanese automobile manufacturers have gained a significant com-
    petitive edge over their U.S. counterparts through the adroit use of this
    form of technological change.

3. *Redefine the rules of competition.* Firms may find themselves in a different
    business due to technological changes that they or others have initiated. As
    we saw in the introductory vignette, many U.S. firms were forced to redefine
    their business following the success of Japanese firms in miniaturizing prod-
    ucts, in part through technological advances. Thus, because some Japanese
    firms introduced smaller copiers, Xerox found itself selling to different cus-
    tomers with different needs through different distribution channels and
    competing on a different basis. In the steel industry, the availability of a dif-
    ferent process technology—mini-mills—made possible the emergence of
    new competitors in the United States.

Box 5.3 presents the story of a mini-mill in the United States. As described in the box,
mini-mills redefined the rules of competition in the United States.

BOX 5.3

PROCESS INNOVATIONS AND CHANGES
IN COMPETITION—THE CASE OF MINI-MILLS

Process innovations can significantly alter the nature of competition in an industry. One often-cited example of this phenomenon is the introduction of "mini-mills" into the U.S. steel industry.

Until the 1970s, steel had generally been manufactured in very large "integrated" mills by using iron ore processed in blast furnaces. However, the competitive pressures at that time made this industry ripe for a change. Market shares of U.S. firms continued to erode to international competition despite attempts by these firms to encourage import quotas. Demand had fallen to levels well below industry capacity as labor and material costs continued to rise. In turn, little profit or capital was available to modernize existing plants.

It was into this environment that the first "mini-mills" were introduced in the 1970s. These facilities were much smaller than the traditional integrated mills and relied on electric arc furnaces to process scrap steel. They thus took advantage of the wide availability of electricity, the power source, and scrap steel, the raw material needed to feed the process. Further, these plants were able to incorporate newer production technologies and thus were designed to be more highly automated than the older, integrated facilities against which they competed. As a result of these process innovations, the average cost per ton of steel produced by a mini-mill was approximately one half the cost of a ton produced by an integrated facility. Some companies, such as Nuclear Corporation of America (NUCOR), were able to achieve additional reductions in cost through further re-engineering efforts. By the end of the decade, mini-mills had captured a 17 percent share of domestic steel shipments, and this percentage was expected to rise in the 1980s.

Mini-mills were not, however, immune from competitive forces. During the 1980s, international competitors continued to put downward pressures on prices. The large integrated mills, recognizing their threatened positions, began large-scale plant modernization projects and worked toward renegotiating labor contracts. Many of the mini-mills could not remain competitive and were forced to close. Further, the technology employed in mini-mill production limited the types of steel products that could be produced (primarily bar steel). Flat-rolled steel, the thin sheet steel used in such products as automobile bodies and refrigerators, represented the largest U.S. market for steel products at approximately 50 percent. Mini-mill technology did not permit the production of this type of product, and thus this market appeared to remain a safe haven for the large, integrated mills. But this also was to change.

NUCOR, the company considered to be the leader in mini-mill technology, set out to attack this market. Using high-tech German casting equipment and sophisticated computer control technology, the company opened the first mini-mill for manufacturing flat-rolled steel in 1989. This mill produced a 2″-thick ribbon of steel, which required much less processing to achieve the $\frac{1}{10}$″ sheets sold to customers than the conventional 10″-thick slabs produced in integrated mills. As a result, mini-mill production costs for flat-rolled steel were approximately 25 percent less than steel produced in integrated mills. Again, we see the innovative use of technology threatening the competitive position of existing firms in an industry. Further, by some estimates NUCOR, which did not open its first steel mill until 1968, will become the 4th largest steel producer in the United States by 1997.

Source: Adapted from Barnes, Frank C. "Nucor in 1991," In Hill, C. W. and Jones, G. R., *Strategic Management: An Integrated Approach.* Boston, MA: Houghton Mifflin Company, 1992; Magnet, M. "Meet the New Revolutionaries," *Fortune,* February 24, 1992, p. 94.

Thus, technological change shapes the evolution of competitive domains. It brings about product substitution and differentiation, changes the price and quality relationships among products, reconfigures value chains and constellations through process innovations, and enables firms to redefine the rules of competition.

TECHNOLOGICAL CHARACTERISTICS OF COMPETITIVE DOMAINS

Different competitive domains require firms to employ different modes of competition to gain competitive advantage. Further, competitive rivalry is dynamic; effective modes of competition will change as the domains evolve over time. Six characteristics of competitive domains influence the rivalry: (1) technological opportunity, (2) appropriability, (3) resource requirements, (4) collateral assets, (5) institutional milieu, and (6) speed.

TECHNOLOGICAL OPPORTUNITY

Technological opportunity refers to the degree to which innovation potential exists in an industry. Thus, innovation may be possible in the form of new products, new services, or new processes; but, the opportunity for developing competitive advantage will differ from one competitive domain to another.

- Significant competitive advantages for a pharmaceutical company may derive from breakthrough drugs that require significant outlays of R&D expenses.
- Process innovations leading to cost reductions may lie at the heart of successful competition in the case of many commodity chemicals.
- In many low-tech settings, real estate, faxes, cellular phones, voice mail, and the like become competitive tools, because they enable firms to be responsive to their customers.

Thus, competitive domains differ in terms of the windows of opportunity provided by technology. We will emphasize that these windows of opportunity should be judged attractive not merely by the technical and scientific feasibility of an innovation, but by the extent to which they can serve marketplace needs. Successful competition depends on a thorough grasp of these windows of opportunity. However, technological opportunity is not a guarantor of competitive advantage; hence, we look to a second characteristic—appropriability.

APPROPRIABILITY

Appropriability refers to the degree to which the potential economic benefits from an innovation can be appropriated by the firms engaged in technology development. Where appropriability is high, firms can reap the benefits of their innovation; in low appropriability environments, the profit potential of innovation is dissipated through imitation by other firms or ceded to suppliers, distribution channels, or customers. When patents are obtained in the pharmaceutical industry, the developing firms reap the benefits of innovation. Even in high-technology sectors, technological appropriability is often vastly different for various competitive domains. To illustrate this point, in Box 5.4

BOX 5.4

THE APPROPRIABILITY OF TECHNOLOGY: BIOTECHNOLOGY VERSUS SOFTWARE INDUSTRY

In the text, we have discussed the notion of appropriability of the benefits of technology and noted the importance of this concept in obtaining competitive advantage. With increased levels of competition, and swifter changes in technological frontiers, the ability of firms to appropriate long-term benefits from innovation has been eroded.

Thus, many of the economic benefits associated with innovation are the result of proprietary intellectual property. The more proprietary the innovation, the greater will be the competitive advantage provided to the firm. The ability of a firm to protect these intellectual property rights is then key to its ability to appropriate long-term benefits from the technology. In some industries, such as biotechnology, patent protection may exist for these intellectual property rights. However, if other firms are able to "engineer around" these patents, the patent provides little long-term assurance of appropriability. Further, in industries such as software and information technologies, the underlying innovation may be easily duplicated. In these cases, patents or copyrights may provide no protection at all.

Source: Rosenbloom, Richard. "The Future of Industrial Research." Talk given at the University of Kansas Center for Management of Technology Workshop Series, January, 1994.

---

we contrast biotechnology and information technology sectors, both deemed to be high technology domains, highlighting the different appropriability regimes that currently exist in these industries.

RESOURCE REQUIREMENTS

Competitive domains differ in the magnitude of resource commitments required to bring about an innovation. In those domains where fundamental research is required the resource commitments are relatively higher; where product development is the key focus, resource commitments may not be as large. For example, in the pharmaceutical industry, where considerable basic research is needed before drugs can be produced, significant resource commitments are needed for innovation. One estimate puts the average cost of development of a new drug at $300 million.[4] On the other hand, in the software industry, much lower resource commitments are enough for innovation. Broadly, the more the requirements for basic research, the more resource commitment are required to produce an innovation.

Competitive domains differ in terms of the resources flowing into technology development. Table 5.1 presents the research and development (R&D) expenditures in different industries for the year 1990. As shown in the table, there are significant differences among industries in terms of their R&D expenditures—expressed in absolute terms or as a percentage of sales. For example, chemical and allied products, machinery and electrical equipment, and professional and scientific instruments incurred significant research and development expenditures. On the other hand, firms in industries such as food and allied products, textile mills, or primary metals spent relatively little on

TABLE 5.1   R&D Expenditures by Manufacturing Industries

Industry	Total R&D Funds as a Percent of Net Sales		
	1970	*1980*	*1990*
Stone, clay, and glass products	1.8	1.4	(D)
Primary metals	0.8	0.7	(D)
Fabricated metal products	1.2	1.4	1.2
Machinery, except electrical	4.0	5.0	8.9
Electronic and other electric equipment (Electric equipment)	7.3	6.6	7.3
Transportation equipment (missiles) [added 2 together]	18.7	18.6	14.3 + (D)
Instruments and related products (Professional and scientific instruments)	5.7	7.5	7.7
Food and kindred products	0.5	0.4	(D)
Textile mill products	0.9	1.0	0.8
Chemicals and allied products	3.9	3.6	5.7
Oil and gas extraction, petroleum products (Petroleum refining and extraction)	1.0	0.6	0.9
Rubber and miscellaneous plastics products	2.3	2.2	(D)

Source: The Statistical Abstract of the United States, 1992, U.S. Department of Commerce.

R&D. R&D expenditures represent only the in-house development activities; they do not reflect the investments in technology purchased from outside via acquisitions or mergers or through investments in information technology or new capital equipment. Nonetheless, Table 5.1 reflects our major point: The competitive domains differ vastly in terms of their resource requirements and commitments.

In Table 5.2, we have presented the patent statistics that firms in various industries have filed during the year 1990. Whereas R&D expenditures represent the inputs to

TABLE 5.2   Patents by Selected Industries

Industry	*1970*	*1980*	*1990*
Stone, clay, and glass products	1,227	1,281	1,738
Primary metals	639	674	895
Fabricated metal products	5,142	5,201	7,038
Machinery, except electrical	15,758	14,337	18,796
Electronic and other electric equipment	13,038	10,687	19,179
Transportation equipment	3,053	2,913	4,400
Instruments and related products	7,293	7,395	12,289
Food and kindred products	488	482	726
Textile mill products	480	420	501
Chemicals and allied products	8,806	9,828	12,417
Oil and gas extraction, petroleum products	829	729	831
Rubber and miscellaneous plastics products	2,478	2,592	3,834

Source: U.S. Patent and Trade Office, *Patenting Trends in the United States, State Country Report,* 1963–1990.

technology development activity, patent statistics typically reflect the outputs of the technological activity of firms. As shown in the table, there are also significant differences among industries in terms of the patents they have filed. Industries that spend a higher percentage of sales on R&D expenditures typically also tend to have a larger number of patents.

COLLATERAL ASSETS

Another characteristic of competitive domains is the need and availability of collateral assets for an innovation to yield a firm competitive advantage. Collateral assets may be complementary products or complementary value constellations. Consider the case of high-definition television (HDTV). Arguably, some television manufacturers have been well positioned to introduce HDTV for over a decade. Yet, without supportive television broadcasts, the superior television is useless to consumers.

INSTITUTIONAL MILIEU

In many competitive domains, technology-based rivalry gets enacted not merely in the marketplace but in the institutions that are linked to the technology, as well. Three sets of institutional players are important:

1. Market participants, such as suppliers and distributors;
2. Nonmarket institutions, such as standard-setting organizations and governmental agencies; and
3. Enabling institutions, such as industry and trade associations, scientific and technical associations, and data sources, such as influential trade journals.

The relevance of various institutional players for competitive action changes with the evolution of the technology, but the actions in the institutional arena are significant enablers of the pursuit of competitive advantage. Conversely, many corporations have found themselves ultimately outmaneuvered in the marketplace by the adept actions of their rivals in the institutional milieu.[5]

SPEED

Competitive domains also differ in terms of the speed of execution they demand of competing firms. Speed, or "clockspeed," refers to the velocity of change in a competitive domain that sets the pace of the internal operations of the competing firms.[6] In recent years, time compression has forced many firms to improve their speed of execution of new product development activity, value chain activities, and technical support operations. We will elaborate on the capabilities that enable a firm to enhance its speed of execution in the next chapter.

The three industry types identified in chapter 1—capacity intensive, customer intensive, and knowledge intensive—differ in several technological characteristics of the competitive domains. Consider two illustrations:

In knowledge-intensive industries, resource commitments required for successful competition are significantly higher than in capacity- and customer-driven industries (see Table 5.1). Thus, in the pharmaceutical industry, each new drug requires an R&D investment of $300 million. On the other hand,

TABLE 5.3   Industry Types and Characteristics of Competitive Domains

Characteristic	Capacity Driven	Customer Driven	Knowledge Driven
1. *Opportunity*	Process	Process Product improvements	New products
2. *Appropriability*	Variable	Variable	Short run
3. *Resource requirements* *for technology*	Low	Moderate	High
4. *Institutional milieu*	Markets	Markets	Markets and technological communities
5. *Clockspeed*	Low	Moderate	High

innovations in the low-technology sector, such as junk bonds in the financial services sector, require relatively limited developmental expenditures.

The windows of opportunity for infusing technology are different across industry types. Knowledge-intensive industries require firms to devote significant attention to the innovative activity: both basic and applied research. For example, in electrical equipment manufacturing, significant applied research is needed before product development can take place. In contrast, many low-technology industries focus on adopting innovations that are created elsewhere. Thus, firms in the oil extraction industry typically adopt new machinery that is developed in the mechanical instruments industry.

We have summarized the major differences among the three types of industries in Table 5.3.

The technological characteristics of competitive domains are important in forging a technology strategy; however, these characteristics change as technology evolves over time. What are the mechanisms of technological change that transform these characteristics? In chapters 3 and 4, we discussed the twin dynamics of technical change—innovation and diffusion. Although innovation and diffusion are the central mechanisms of technical change, the dynamics of change of competitive domains is far more complex: In addition to innovation and diffusion, these dynamics include actions of competing firms and those of numerous other actors. We now turn to the dynamics of technology-induced change in competitive domains.

DYNAMICS OF CHANGE
IN COMPETITIVE DOMAINS

Technology change can create turbulence as well as predictable incremental change in competitive domains. During certain periods, radical innovations create upheavals within an industry, and the patterns of technology change drive the evolution of competitive domains. During other periods, we witness predictable evolution of technology, when existing characteristics of industries exert a major influence on technology development. These two periods correspond respectively to the two types of innovation identified by Joseph Schumpeter: entrepreneurial innovation and managerial innovation. Thus, the relationship between technology and industry is not a straightforward one; each influences the other during different periods of time.

It is useful to think about technology-induced changes in competitive domains as evolving over two major phases. During the first phase, when a radical innovation appears, high levels of turbulence characterize the competitive domains; during this period, the "concept of industry" has probably not emerged with clarity.[7] During the second phase, when the characteristics of the competitive domains have stabilized, a conception of industry would have developed around the innovation. During this phase, the industry characteristics exert influence on the technology development. We call these two phases the technology emergence phase and the incremental change phase.

> The technology emergence phase[8] begins with the appearance of a radical innovation, spans the period of upheaval and turbulence, and ends when the competitive domain has stabilized. During this phase, the competitive domains undergo significant change but do not exert a profound influence on the evolution of the technology. Technology evolves autonomously, i.e., due to the actions of the individuals and firms developing the technology and more or less uninfluenced by market forces. There is significant ambiguity in what constitutes an industry. We call it the technology emergence phase because various technology developers shape the evolution of technology and competitive domains.

> The incremental change phase refers to a period when technology evolution is relatively predictable. By now, the various players have converged on a relatively clear definition of the industry. The relatively stable characteristics of the industry influence the developments of technology within it; that is, technology evolution is now induced.

We will discuss each of these two phases in turn. The two phases are pictorially represented in Figure 5.5.

THE TECHNOLOGY EMERGENCE PHASE

One of the consequences of technological change is that a radical innovation often gives rise to the emergence of an entirely new competitive domain. Sometimes, the emergence of the new domain results in new rules of competition in established industries; at other times, it creates totally new industries. The beginning of a new competitive domain is characterized by a high degree of uncertainty. This uncertainty is felt at two levels:

1. Technical uncertainty. Technical uncertainty pertains to the performance of an innovation; during the early stages, the functionality of a radical innovation is unreliable and undeveloped.
2. Market uncertainty. Also during this stage, there will be fewer buyers for the innovation because the diffusion process has not actually begun; market uncertainty pertains to the competitive avenues to be pursued by firms interested in commercializing the innovation.

Thus, the appearance of a radical innovation corresponds to the early part of the S-curve of innovation and diffusion, as we discussed in chapters 3 and 4. Recall the advent of

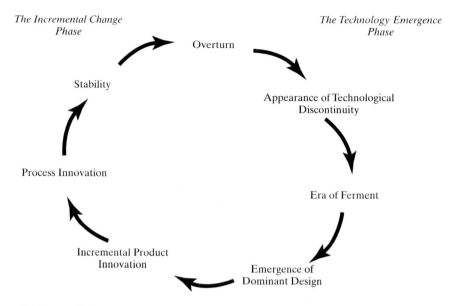

*The Incremental Change
Phase*

*The Technology Emergence
Phase*

Overturn

Stability

Appearance of Technological
Discontinuity

Process Innovation

Era of Ferment

Incremental Product
Innovation

Emergence of
Dominant Design

FIGURE 5.5 EVOLUTION OF COMPETITIVE DOMAINS

Source: Anderson, P. and M. Tushman, "Technological Discontinuities and Dominant Designs: A Cyclical
Model of Organizational Change," *Administrative Science Quarterly* 35 (1990), pp. 604–33.

microchips. This led to a competitive scramble among several firms in both fronts: (1) the
designs of personal computers and (2) different ways of configuring the value chains
to deliver the product to the consumers. During the technology emergence phase,
firms in the industry deal with both technical and market uncertainties triggered by an
innovation.

We will discuss four major topics to describe the technology emergence phase:
(1) the key time periods in this phase; (2) a framework for understanding industrial
emergence; (3) the role of technological communities; and (4) the response of threatened industries.

KEY TIME PERIODS

The technology emergence phase begins when a radical innovation first appears and
ends when the market has converged on a standard product design. We may identify
three time periods during this phase: the appearance of technological discontinuity, the
era of ferment, and the emergence of dominant design.

The Appearance of Technological Discontinuity   With the appearance of radical innovation, a few new firms have been founded, and the technology race begins. This is a
period of very high technical uncertainty, when solutions to product problems are arrived at through trial and error. The period culminates in significant learning about design and production.

The radical innovations could be either competence enhancing or competence destroying.[9] Thus, a competence-destroying innovation renders obsolete the skills required to master the technology that it replaces. For example, the skills of mechanical
watch manufacturers or vacuum tube producers were rendered obsolete by quartz

watches and integrated circuits, respectively. A competence-enhancing discontinuity builds on the know-how that is embodied in the technology it replaces. For example, the turbofan advance in jet engines built on prior jet competence. Similarly, the series of breakthrough advancements in mechanical watch escapements built on prior mechanical competence.

Era of Ferment   Each radical innovation inaugurates a technological cycle, which begins with an era of ferment following the introduction of a radical innovation. At the time it is introduced, a radical innovation is likely to be crude and experimental, but it ushers in an era of experimentation, and less radical, follow-on innovations are introduced.[10] Many new firms enter the technology race and develop their own variants of the basic innovation, which is gradually improved through R&D and by closer attention to marketing. The new firms are often spin-offs from existing companies. For example, most of the Silicon Valley semiconductor firms, when founded, were spin-offs from Fairchild Semiconductor, one of the first firms in the industry.[11]

Two distinct competitive processes characterize this era: competition between technologies and competition within the radical innovation.

1. *Competition between technologies.* When a radical technology is a substitute for an existing technology, there ensues fierce competition between the old and new technologies. New technologies are disparaged when they are introduced because they frequently do not work well and are based on unproven assumptions. Also, they require competence that is different from the one associated with existing technologies. The response of firms competing with older technology is often to increase the innovativeness and efficiency of the existing technologies. For example, mechanical typewriters, piston jets, telegraphy, gas lighting, mechanical watches, and sailing ships all experienced sharp performance advances in response to product substitution threat.[12]

2. *Competition within the radical innovation.* Concurrent with competition between the old and new technologies is the process of competition that ensues among differing designs within the new innovation. Several versions of the radical innovation appear both because the technology is not well understood and because each firm has an incentive to differentiate its variant from its rivals'. For example, once the first personal computer appeared in the mid-1970s, it was followed by a host of different models with different microprocessors, disk formats, and operating systems.[13]

During this stage, there is substantial variation among the product designs, and the technical uncertainty is quite high. Thus, during this stage in a technology's evolution, both producers and customers are experimenting. As new companies enter with uniquely designed products, established firms perfect their original designs and continue to introduce new models. Indeed, fierce struggle ensues as each firm tries to get market acceptance for its own version of the product. Customers, on the other hand, are not yet so wedded to any particular design or company that they will not experiment with something new. Industry standards at this stage are usually rudimentary, if they exist at all.

The Emergence of Dominant Design   As different firms try to capture the hearts and minds of the customers with different product variants, and as customers experiment with the products marketed by different firms, the competitive domain begins to converge on a dominant product design.

A dominant design is defined as the product design that wins the allegiance of the marketplace, the one that competitors and innovators must adhere to if they hope to command a significant market following.

The dominant design usually takes the form of a new product or a set of features synthesized from individual technological innovations introduced independently in prior product variants. For example, in the history of the typewriter industry, Underwood Model 5 emerged as the dominant design: It was enormously well received by the marketplace, and the subsequent introduction of copycat models by its major rivals, both of which trailed Underwood sales by a wide margin, only confirmed its dominance. In a similar way, the IBM PC format quickly became the dominant design in its market. The PC, like the Model 5, offered the market little in the way of breakthrough technology, but it brought together familiar elements that had proven their value to users: a TV monitor, standard disk drive, QWERTY keyboard, the Intel 88 chip, open architecture, and MS DOS operating systems. Taken together, these elements came to define the idea of the personal computer for at least 80 percent of the market.

How does a dominant design occur? When we introduced the Technology-Market Matrix, we underscored the point that success in technology management arises not merely from the technological characteristics of an innovation, but often from events and actions in the marketplace. This is true in the case of dominant design as well: A dominant design occurs not merely because of the technical excellence of a firm or superior product features, but also due to the influence of market forces. Thus, the idea of a dominant design is conceptually broader than technical competition and progress, as captured by the S-curves described in chapter 3.

Four factors other than technology influence which product design emerges to be dominant: (1) collateral assets, (2) regulation and government intervention, (3) strategic maneuvering by individual firms, and (4) communication between producers and users.

Collateral assets. When a firm possesses collateral assets such as market channels, brand image, and customer-switching costs, it will have some advantage over its competitors in enforcing its product as the dominant design. One of the reasons the IBM PC emerged as the dominant design, when it first appeared on the market, was because of the collateral assets that IBM possessed. To the buying public, the name IBM had tremendous brand value. As a huge firm, its entry meant that replacement parts and service would be available and that application software would begin to appear, encouraged by industry standards that will conform to IBM's machine.[14] The dominant design model is better suited to mass markets, where consumer tastes are relatively homogeneous.

Regulation and government intervention. Regulation has the power to enforce a standard and to define a dominant design. For example, during the early 1950s when the FCC approved the RCA television broadcast standard, it worked to the advantage of RCA by establishing its design as the standard for the emerging television industry. Today, efforts by governments around the world to define standards for HDTV will certainly heavily influence the dominant design that emerges.

Strategic maneuvering at the firm level. Sometimes, a firm that pursues a particular product strategy relative to its competitors may succeed in establishing its design as the dominant one. For example, in one analysis of the videocassette recorder industry, the researchers found that Sony's betamax lost to the VHF system backed by JVC. JVC's strategy of establishing alliances first in Japan, then in Europe, and then in the United States succeeded, whereas Sony's attempt to go it alone, trusting its reputation and avoiding alliances or contracts, failed in the marketplace.

Communication between producers and users. As we discussed in chapters 3 and 4, one of the characteristics of innovation is the evaluation information associated with it, that is, the information that is provided by producers to their customers to influence the latter's purchase behavior. Although the evaluation information is not intrinsic to the product but is dependent on the actions of the firm, it sometimes exerts an influence in the emergence of a dominant design. Thus, the way a firm manages its communication with its customers may have a significant effect on its ability to impose a dominant design. Similarly, staying close to customers makes it possible for producing firms to observe how their evolving products are actually being used, how they are succeeding or failing to satisfy customer requirements, and how design changes might close the gap between product capability and user requirements.

A dominant design emerges due to a host of factors: the technical merits of an innovation, market forces, the role played by the government, the strategies of firms in affected industries and chance factors. Box 5.5 discusses three alternative perspectives on the factors determining the emergence of a dominant design.

Given the magnitude of the technical and market uncertainty surrounding the emergence of a dominant design, it is unlikely that a manager will be able to forecast or predict its emergence with any degree of confidence. One thing however is clear: Firms tracking the emergence of a dominant design need to focus their attention on factors over and beyond the technical features of innovation. Because information sources have not stabilized, and unknown upstart firms sometimes enter the competitive fray during the technology emergence phase, intelligence gathering—market and technical—is a challenging task. Error in terms of detection of the dominant designs by firms is a common occurrence.

What does the dominant design do? It serves four major functions:

1. Dominant designs provide for the standardization of a product, reducing variation in products and, thus, uncertainty in the product class.
2. They permit firms to design standardized and changeable parts to optimize organization designs for volume and efficiency.
3. They permit more stable and reliable relationships with suppliers, vendors, and customers.
4. From the customers' perspective, dominant designs reduce confusion among products and promise decreases in product cost.

Once a dominant design emerges in an industry, it is difficult to dislodge it. Firms that are well positioned to take advantage of the dominant design continue to improve the innovation through the production process changes; other firms, including some of the smaller ones, find it difficult to enter the industry. Finally, because dominant design dispels confusion among customers regarding the product features, the process of innovation diffusion

BOX 5.5

THREE PERSPECTIVES ON THE FACTORS DETERMINING THE DOMINANT DESIGN

For managers, of course, the important question is whether a dominant design can be seen for what it is when it first appears or is discernible only in retrospect. If the emergence of a dominant design is a signal that an important shift is about to take place with respect to the pace of innovation and the number of competing firms, the ability of managers and industry watchers to receive that signal—or even better, to predict the emergence of a dominant design—should be important with respect to their product designs, R&D, and process development. There are three schools of thought on this question.

1. Some believe that dominant designs are the result of chance events. In this sense, their appearance cannot be predicted (though they may be recognized). This school would say that the QWERTY keyboard would be a curiosity piece today had August Dvorak and his ideas for keyboard design been on the scene earlier, during the period of experimentation with the first typewriters. Steel-bodied automobiles, the norm since Dodge's all-steel innovation of the 1920s, may have been dictated by the high cost of aluminum relative to steel at that time. Certainly aluminum, then as now, had tremendous performance advantages over heavier steel. Today, when the cost difference is not as great, the tradition of steel auto bodies is difficult to change.

2. The second school of thought has a deterministic viewpoint—i.e., something inherent in the technology determines the outcome with respect to the dominant design. The laws of nature, for example, fairly dictate that only a few

synthetic materials (nylon, rayon, and polyester) have chemical structures that support the spinning of long-fibered material. Thus, the technological trajectory accommodates only a few possible candidates for the dominant design.

3. Others suggest that social and organizational factors work together to determine dominant design. Here, again, come into play arguments, such as the early success of the QWERTY keyboard having created an investment in particular typing skills and barriers to other designs. The same may apply to the IBM PC; IBM's stature can be said to have led to an industry standard around which small competitors and software writers naturally gravitated.

None of these three schools of thought is entirely right or entirely wrong. Each, in fact, contributes to our understanding of the facts. But no matter how a dominant design is determined, it is doubtful that it can be recognized except in retrospect. Attempting to define or anticipate the appearance of a dominant design simply by mapping features and functions of the product alone is doomed to frustration. However, design simplicity and so-called technological elegance are clearly characteristics of many dominant designs, the DC-3 aircraft being a notable example.

Our inability to immediately perceive a dominant design for what it is in no way diminishes its impact on the evolution of innovation and competition in an industry. For assembled products, as later chapters will show clearly, the appearance of a dominant design ushers in a period in which the rate of product innovation slows and the rate of process innovation increases.

Source: Utterback, James. *Mastering the Dynamics of the Innovation.* Boston, MA: Harvard Business School Press, 1994. Adapted with permission.

speeds up, and the rapid growth phase of the industry begins. Finally, the emergence of a dominant design assures an era of incremental innovation within the industry.

Table 5.4 summarizes our discussion of the stages involved in technology emergence phase and lists representative industries in each stage.

We have already mentioned that two levels of competition break out during the technology emergence phase: (1) among the variants of the radical innovation and (2) between the new and old technologies. The competition gets played out in several arenas, and once threatened, the firms that employ older technologies enter the competitive fray. We now discuss each one of these topics.

TECHNOLOGICAL COMMUNITIES

During the technology emergence phase of an industry, technological competition for the hearts and minds of the customers is fought and won in arenas often far removed from the R&D labs of firms or the marketplace itself. These arenas include:

1. Regulatory bodies, where battles for standards are often waged;
2. Trade associations, where industry players coalesce to promote their product designs; and
3. Scientific advisory boards, which provide valuable sources of information as well as legitimacy to emergent developments in technology.

Taken together, these arenas—public regulatory agencies, industry associations, and scientific groups—are called technological communities.

Technological communities serve several functions:

1. They serve as important mechanisms of information transfer, enabling firms that are included in those communities to obtain up-to-date information about technology or industry.
2. They serve as forums for testing ideas, especially in the early stages of technology emergence.
3. They play a significant role in legitimating technology and product specifications. Thus, the stamp of approval from a scientific advisory body for a

TABLE 5.4   Examples of Industries in Various Stages of Technological Development

Stages in Technological Development of a New Industry	Representative Industries
1) *Appearance of Technological Discontinuity:* A period of very high uncertainty in which trial-and-error problem solving leads to the innovation.	Multimedia, reflecting the convergence of computers, telecommunications, and entertainment.
2) *Era of Ferment:* When there is decreasing technical uncertainty as many new firms enter the industry and develop their own variants of the basic innovation, which is gradually improved through R&D and by closer attention to marketing.	Bioengineering industry, in which the basic invention of recombinant DNA is applied.
3) *Emergence of Dominant Design:* Dominant design emerges, which standardizes the product features.	Windows operating environment for microcomputers.

particular class of product designs is often a powerful tool a firm can employ to promote its preferred product designs.

4. They serve as arenas for standard setting, where rules and regulations are made.

Thus, participation in technological communities often enables firms to skew the emerging competitive domains in their favor and away from their competitors. Indeed, gaining access to and participating in technological communities is an important managerial activity for firms involved in industry emergence.

We have noted that, during the technology emergence phase, competition ensues not merely among variants of a radical innovation but also between the innovation and the old technology that it seeks to replace. Technological substitution often involves retaliation by the entrenched firms that employ older technologies. The response of threatened firms is another important dynamic characteristic of the technology emergence phase of an industry.

RESPONSE OF THREATENED INDUSTRIES

As we have seen, a radical innovation, having been pioneered by a new firm, often originates outside an existing industry. Although initially unreliable, crude, and expensive, the new technology expands through successive markets. When incumbent firms recognize the threat of technological substitution by a new technology, this recognition stimulates further development of the old technology. Indeed, the old technology typically continues to be improved and reaches its highest stage of development in terms of its performance characteristics after the new technology is introduced. For example, the smallest and most reliable vacuum tubes ever produced were developed after the introduction of the transistor.

Once the threat is recognized, a traditional firm can go one of two routes. Either it decides not to participate in the development of the new technology, or it may choose to participate in the new technology in some fashion.

If a firm chooses not to participate in the new technology, its management might elect one or a combination of the following specific actions:

1. Do nothing;
2. Monitor new developments in the competing technology through vigorous environmental scanning and forecasting activity;
3. Seek to hold back the new threat by fighting it through public relations and legal action;
4. Increase flexibility in order to be able to respond to subsequent developments in the new technology;
5. Avoid the threat through decreasing dependence on the most threatened submarkets;
6. Expand work on improvement of existing technology; or
7. Attempt to maintain sales through actions not related to technology, such as promotion or price-cutting.[15]

Alternatively, a threatened firm may decide to participate in the development of the new technology. This participation is clearly fraught with challenges and pitfalls. Broadly, the participation requires three sets of decisions:

1. *Time of entry.* The firm can enter early in the development of the technology or much later, after the technological uncertainties are worked out in the industry.

2. *Magnitude of commitment.* The firm must determine the amount of resources to commit to developing the new technology.
3. *Degree of organizational separation.* The firm must decide the degree to which the strategies pursued should be coupled to those of its existing lines of business.

The threatened firms often commit three types of errors while making these decisions. First, when firms enter early, they usually underestimate the resources and skills required for overcoming the initial technical obstacles; as a result, they often become disenchanted when the market does not develop quickly. Second, when firms make limited early commitments but then mount a more vigorous effort as the industry develops, they allow new competitors to establish formidable technical leads; it then becomes much more difficult for firms to establish a viable long-term competitive position. Third, close linkages between new and traditional activities appear to be fairly common among these firms. There are often synergies to be gained from utilizing an existing organization for the new product; hence, managers have an incentive to fit the new technology within the existing organization. However, tight linkages lead to a problematic situation: When firms develop a strategy for competing in the new field, they use the same basic approaches that were successful in established industry, i.e., they fold the new product into the traditional strategy. In Box 5.6, we have showcased the Purdue study of firms' responses to technological threats, documenting these pitfalls.

In summary, in this era of technology emergence, when a new technology first appears, intense competition ensues among start-up firms, culminating in a dominant design. This competition takes place not only along the technical features of the technology or factors in the marketplace but also in other arenas, such as technological communities. In addition to the competition between variants within the new technology, the firms that are threatened by the new technology begin to improve the performance characteristics of the old technology that the new one seeks to replace. Alternatively, some of the older firms might themselves decide to develop the new technology.

INCREMENTAL CHANGE PHASE

Once a dominant design has emerged in an industry, further technological progress is driven by numerous incremental innovations. These improvements elaborate the dominant design and do not challenge the industry standard with new rival architectures. The focus of competition shifts from higher performance to lower cost and to differentiation via minor design variations and strategic positioning tactics. This incremental change phase corresponds to Schumpeter's managed innovation, and it persists until it is ended by the advent of another major innovation.

With emergence of dominant design, the performance criteria that serve as a primary basis for competition become well articulated. The market has formed its expectation of the product in terms of features, form, and capabilities. By now, a definition of the industry has emerged that is clear to the participants and other players in the marketplace. The avenues for product innovation become much fewer than during technology emergence, and the focus of R&D narrows to incremental improvement of existing features. Smaller firms find it difficult to enter the industry, and competition eliminates continuing firms that cannot succeed in making important incremental

BOX 5.6

RESPONDING TO TECHNOLOGICAL CHANGE

Significant technological change within an industry presents a serious threat to the competitive position of established firms in that industry. In the text, we have discussed the ways in which a threatened firm might respond to these technological changes. Recent research on this subject provides interesting insights into the way this process might develop.

Professors Arnold Cooper and Clayton Smith have recently investigated the ways in which established firms have responded to technological changes in eight industries. The industries and technological changes investigated were diverse and ranged from the impact of ballpoint pens on the fountain pen industry to the impact of transistors on receiving tubes. The researchers focused on 27 firms that were established players in these 8 industries (e.g., Eversharp and Parker Pen in the fountain pen industry; G.E., R.C.A., and Ratheon in the receiving tube industry) at the time of the major technological change. Four attributes of the decision to participate by each of these established firms was explored: (1) timing of entry in the new field; (2) the magnitude of commitment to the new technology; (3) the degree of organizational separation between new and traditional product activities; and (4) the competitive strategy for the new business. Several of the findings of this research have important implications for the management of technology.

1. The timing of entry and the commitment level of the 27 firms studied varied widely. However, it was evident that few of the established firms were able to display the vision and know-how necessary to produce commercially viable products from the new technologies. Early product versions produced by incumbent firms were poorly designed and did not meet customer needs. The established firms appeared to regard the new technologies as only ancillary add-ons to their traditional product lines and did not see them as threatening to their established businesses. As a result, the first commercially viable products using the new technologies often came from firms outside the established industry. For example, Papermate, a firm not involved in the fountain pen industry, was the first to produce an acceptable ballpoint pen. Similarly, mechanical typewriter companies such as Remmington and Royal could achieve only poorly designed versions of the electric typewriter. The first commercially successful electric typewriter came instead from IBM, a firm that had never produced a mechanical version.

2. Most of these firms attempted to capitalize on existing organizational and management structures in order to develop, produce, and distribute products using the new technologies. Thus, RCA placed transistor activities within its established vacuum tube division; Smith-Corona handled production, sales, and distribution of its electric typewriter through its mechanical typewriter departments. However, in cases where the new technology was fundamentally different from the traditional technology, this tie to existing organizational structures was often counterproductive. Existing administrative systems and cultures tended to make decisions regarding the new products in the same fashion as was appropriate for existing lines, often with disastrous results.

3. Established firms often found themselves bound by their existing approaches to competitive strategy. They seemed unable to fundamentally rethink their businesses based upon the new technologies. For example, the first

Source: Cooper, A. C. and Smith, C. G. "How established firms respond to threatening technologies." *Academy of Management Executive* (1992): Vol. 6: 55–70.

Box 5.6 (*continued*)

microwave ovens produced by Tappan and General Electric were styled as "built-ins" to conventional ovens. Thus, customers would be required to replace their entire cooking unit. It was not until Raytheon/Amana entered the market with a countertop design—an approach that supplemented rather than replaced existing appliances—that wide market acceptance occurred. Similarly, Friden, a manufacturer of mechanical calculators, emphasized their repair staff in marketing the newer electronic calculators. However, the use of electronic compo-

nents made the new calculators much more reliable than their mechanical counterparts, and thus there was little need for service.

These research findings seem to suggest that established firms have significant problems in responding to technological threats in their industries. Indeed, of the 27 firms investigated, only 7 were able to successfully make the transition to producers of products using the new technologies. The importance of technological change to competitive positioning in an industry should never be underrated.

improvements on the basic innovation. Thus, the industry tends increasingly to be composed of a fewer number of players than during the technology emergence phase.

During the incremental innovation phase, however, innovations are far from over; indeed, important changes continue to take place in the industry. We will discuss these innovations along three lines: (1) product versus process innovation; (2) the role of architectural innovation; and (3) sustained innovation. Whereas the product-process linkages are observed in most industries, sustained innovation and architectural innovations are special cases, confined to a limited number of industries.

PRODUCT VERSUS PROCESS INNOVATION

After the emergence of a dominant design, once the energies that characterize the period of great product innovation begin to fade, process innovations begin to assume greater importance. The shift from product to process innovation is schematically presented in Figure 5.6. As shown in the figure, during the technology emergence phase, the rate of product change is expected to be rapid; however, process innovation generally takes a backseat to product innovation. For instance, major changes in product design and specifications are a hindrance to standardizing the production process.

Once a dominant design has emerged, however, product and process innovation start to become more salient. Materials become more specialized; expensive specialized

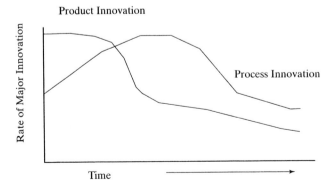

FIGURE 5.6 THE DYNAMICS OF INNOVATION IN INCREMENTAL ERA

Source: Reprinted by permission of Harvard Business School Press. From *Mastering the Dynamics of Innovation; How Companies Seize Opportunities in the Face of Technological Change* by James M. Utterback. Boston, MA 1994, p. xvii. Copyright © 1994 by the President and Fellows of Harvard College; all rights reserved.

equipment is brought into the manufacturing plant; islands of automation begin to appear; and managerial action is suddenly seen as important. During the incremental innovation phase, as the rate of product innovation decreases, there is a corresponding
increase in the rate of process innovation. For example, in the case of incandescent lighting, once a dominant design emerged, several processes appeared: specialized glass-
blowing equipment, high-capacity vacuum pumps, and manufacturing improvements.
The number of steps in the manufacturing process dropped from 200 to 30 between 1880
and 1920. Specialized equipment replaced common tools, and workers became less
skilled. Lamp production moved from custom production to batch and later to semi-
continuous production.[16] In Box 5.7, we illustrate the evolution of product and process
technology in the automobile industry.

During the incremental innovation phase, product innovations are relatively infrequent; a small number of firms begin to dominate the industry; and competitive shifts
within the industry are not likely. However, during this phase, two types of product innovations may upset the competitive equilibrium within industries: (1) architectural innovation and (2) sustained innovation. Each of these may occur in some industries. We
will briefly discuss each one of these, in turn.

BOX 5.7

AN ILLUSTRATION OF THE EVOLUTION
OF PRODUCT AND PROCESS INNOVATION—
THE AUTOMOBILE INDUSTRY

In the text, we have described the evolutionary nature of product and process innovations in an industry. Studies of such diverse
industries as processed foods, semiconductors, electric light bulbs, and commercial air-
liners all reflect patterns of development
similar to this evolutionary model. Consider
the following short example from the research of Professors William Abernathy and
James Utterback on the early development of
internal combustion engines for the automotive industry:

Product and process evolved in a similar
fashion in the automobile industry. During a
4-year period before Henry Ford produced the
renowned Model T, his company developed,
produced, and sold five different engines, ranging from two to six cylinders. These were made
in a factory that was flexibly organized much as
a job shop, relying on trade craftsmen working

with general-purpose machine tools not nearly
so advanced as the best then available. Each engine tested a new concept. Out of this experience
came a dominant design—the Model T; and
within 15 years, 2 million engines of this single
basic design were being produced each year
(about 15 million all told) in a facility then recognized as the most efficient and highly integrated in the world. During the 15-year period,
there were incremental—but no fundamental—
innovations in the Ford product.

These researchers go on to note that with
the emergence of a dominant design, and the
focus on process efficiencies that then followed, the Model T experienced price reductions from $3,000 to less than $1,000 (in 1958
dollars). So, in the automobile industry, as well
as in many others, we can see the life cycle of
products and processes following a rather predictable path.

Source: Abernathy, W. J. and Utterback, J. M. "Patterns of Industrial Innovation," in Tushman, M. L. and
Moore, W. L. (eds). *Readings in the Management of Innovation.* 2d ed., New York: Harper, 1988.

COMPETITIVE DYNAMICS OF ARCHITECTURAL INNOVATION

Once a dominant design has emerged in a competitive domain, the hardware and software elements of the innovation do not change drastically. Over time, these elements and the linkages between the two are taken for granted and may even become the tacit knowledge shared by competitors and customers. Henceforth, the firms are likely to engage in incremental innovation, neither of which upsets the taken-for-granted linkages.

Architectural innovations, on the other hand, invoke different linkages among the components of an innovation. New entrants—like Ricoh—typically introduce architectural innovations to an industry. The incumbent firms within an industry often have trouble spotting architectural innovations and adapting to them for several reasons:

1. The introduction of new linkages is quite hard to spot. Because the logic of the prevailing dominant design remains untouched, the firm may mistakenly believe that it understands the new technology. The development of the jet aircraft industry illustrates the impact of unexpected architectural innovation. The jet engine initially appeared to have important but straightforward implications for airframe technology. Established firms in the industry understood that they would need to develop jet engine expertise; however, they did not comprehend how its introduction would change the linkages between the engine and the rest of the airplane in complex and subtle ways.[17] Indeed, Boeing's rise to leadership in the aircraft industry is often attributed to the failure of incumbent firms to grasp the potential of the jet engine.
2. Even if an organization recognizes the nature of an architectural innovation, it is hard to build and apply new architectural knowledge effectively. A new learning cycle has to begin, and this is made very difficult by two factors: First, an organization must switch from one mode of learning to another; second, it must build the new architectural knowledge in a context in which some of its old architectural knowledge may still be relevant.
3. The building of a new architectural innovation takes time and resources. Although new entrants into industry must also build the architectural knowledge, they have no existing assets and, hence, they can optimize their organization to exploit the potential of a new design.

Thus, architectural innovations may upset the competitive equilibrium within an industry by favoring the emergence of new firms over existing ones. The established firms may interpret the innovation as an incremental extension of the existing technology or underestimate its impact on their embedded architectural knowledge. Thus, new entrants to the industry may be well positioned to exploit its potential much more effectively, because they are not handicapped by a legacy of partially irrelevant architectural knowledge. Indeed, in the story of the competition between the Japanese and Xerox described in the opening vignette, the architectural nature of innovation inherent in small copiers played a significant role in allowing the Japanese entrants to gain a foothold in the U.S. market. This is summarized in Box 5.8.

THE COMPETITIVE DYNAMICS OF SUSTAINED INNOVATION

In competitive domains characterized by sustained innovation, windows of opportunity for drastic, sequentially ordered improvements in product persist for a prolonged period of time. This results in new generations of the product that have significantly enhanced performance over previous generations of the product. The movement from one product gen-

ARCHITECTURAL INNOVATIONS
AND COMPETITION

In chapter 3, we introduced the notion of architectural innovations and defined them as a reconfiguration of existing organizational technologies. Because the primary components remain the same, no significant new knowledge is needed concerning these components: The components are just put together in a different fashion. From this definition, it would seem that architectural innovations would have little impact on the nature of competition in an industry. This is not, however, the case.

Consider again the story that was presented in the opening vignette to this chapter. Xerox was confronted with competitors offering copiers that were smaller and more reliable. These copiers were based upon the same core technologies that Xerox had pioneered and, thus, required little new scientific or engineering knowledge on the part of the company. Yet, as we discussed, Xerox seemed unable to reconfigure these technologies into a viable product until well after the competition had gained a significant lead. Thus, in the case of small copiers, the emergence of an architectural innovation changed the face of industry competition in two ways:

1. It allowed new entrants with no previous position in the industry to gain solid market holds in a short period of time.

2. It provided the conditions that forced the undisputed industry leader, Xerox, to fall to a position best described as that of a "slow follower."

The point to remember is that any innovation, occurring in or outside of an industry, whether incremental, modular, architectural, or radical, can dramatically change the nature of competition in an industry.

Source: Adapted from Henderson, R. M. and Clark, K. B. "Architectural innovation: the reconfiguration of existing product technologies and the failure of established firms," *Administrative Science Quarterly* (1990): 35: 9–30.

eration to another is responsible for changes in the characteristics of competitive domains. For example, the very first dynamic random access memory (DRAM) was introduced in the early 1970s. From 1934 to 1988, we have seen sustained innovation as DRAM devices improved from 4K to 4Mb, as product generations moved from large scale integrated (LSI) to very large scale integrated (VLSI) through ultra large scale integrated (ULSI).

Sustained innovation provides opportunities for firms to shift their competitive position within an industry. This could occur in two ways:

1. In the presence of sustained innovation, an innovative firm grows at the expense of non-innovative firms. Thus, these growing firms will be able to acquire resources necessary to continue innovation and, as a result, should emerge as winners.

2. Each new innovation provides a window of opportunity for a firm lagging in the current product generation to attempt to gain on the leading firm and overtake it with an innovation of the next product generation.

In Box 5.9, we have described the evolution of the DRAM industry, illustrating how large firms continue to be innovative and how the competitive positions of firms shifted over successive product generations.[18]

BOX 5.9

SUSTAINED INNOVATION AND THE DRAM MARKET

In chapter 3, we discussed the nature of innovation and noted that very few innovations can be considered "radical." Instead, most innovations are "incremental" and represent improvements to the performance characteristics of products and processes. We often refer to these improved versions as "new generations," and the sequential process through which these new generations emerge may be referred to as "sustained innovation." One prominent example of sustained innovation is the evolution of the market for dynamic random access memory (DRAM) integrated circuits (ICs).

As shown in the table, the DRAM IC has developed in a sequential fashion from the introduction of the 4K large scale integration (LSI) circuit in 1974 through the introduction of three versions of the very large scale integration (VLSI) circuit in 1978, 1980, and 1985. The DRAM is currently at the 4Mb ultra large scale integration (ULSI) stage of its evolution. This process of sustained innovation has created many new applications for this technology. This sequential, evolutionary pattern of innovation provides a useful example to investigate the ways in which sustained innovation might impact upon the competitive arena of the IC industry. Professor Methé of the University of Michigan recently undertook such an investigation. Several important findings of this study are noted.

1. As the technology moves from one generation to another, the financial resources necessary to compete in the technology increase dramatically. For ex-

ample, the estimated cost of establishing a state-of-the-art fabrication facility in 1977 was $10 million; by 1989, this figure had reached $250 million.

2. Relatively small firms, as measured by market share, dominated the early LSI era. It was not until later innovations that large firms began to dominate this market. Further, those firms that were "prime movers" in one generation were not, in general, also prime movers in successive generations. Thus, first to market in one innovation does not necessarily guarantee the same status in later generations.

3. Despite the increased costs of entry and the growing dominance of large firms, as each IC generation evolved, more firms were entering the marketplace. This was the result of rapidly increasing demand as the number of applications of the technology increased.

4. Throughout this innovation life cycle, firms have both entered and exited the market. This suggests that entry and exit barriers are not yet high enough to preclude movement of firms into and out of the industry. It also reflects an important issue in understanding the linkage between technology and competitive strategy: As each successive generation has evolved, existing firms are faced with a new set of competitors. Thus, sustained innovation results in a competitive arena that changes and evolves over time.

Year	DRAM Device	Technology	Applications
1974	4K	LSI	Mainframe, Minicomputer
1976	16K	LSI	Mainframe, Minicomputer, Graphics
1978	64K	VLSI	Mainframe, Minicomputer, Personal Computer, Graphics
1980	256K	VLSI	Mainframe, Minicomputer, Personal Computer, Portable Computer, CAD/CAM, Robotics, Graphics
1985	1Mb	VLSI	Mainframe, Minicomputer, Personal Computer, Portable Computer, CAD/CAM, Robotics, Graphics
1988	4Mb	ULSI	Mainframe, Minicomputer, Personal Computer, Portable Computer, CAD/CAM, Robotics, Graphics, Laptop Computer, HDTV

Source: Adapted from Methé, D. T. "The influence of technology and demand factors on firm size and industrial structure in the DRAM market—1973–1988," Research Policy (1992): 21: 13–25.

TABLE 5.5   Evolving Characteristics of Competitive Domains

Characteristic	Technology Emergence	Incremental Innovation
1. Opportunity	Product designs Technology push	Product improvement Process improvement Market pull

2. Appropriability	Limited by:
	    Size of the market
	    Retaliation of older firms
		Contingent on the nature
		    of the industry

3. Resource requirements	1. Technical talent 2. Financing 3. Suppliers	Same as before

4. Institutional milieu	Arenas for major
	    competitive battles
		Markets are the primary
		    battlegrounds

5. Clockspeed	High	Variable

In summary, once a radical innovation has appeared, the characteristics of the competitive domains evolve over the two major phases: technology emergence and incremental innovation. In Table 5.5, we have summarized the preceding discussion: how technology emergence and incremental innovation phases differ along the characteristics of the competitive domains enumerated earlier. These characteristics have significant implications for competitive strategy during different phases. During the technology emergence phase, technology-push strategies dominate; during the incremental innovation phase, market-pull strategies become increasingly necessary.

A FRAMEWORK FOR THE ANALYSIS OF TECHNOLOGY EMERGENCE

We have seen that during the technology emergence phase it is difficult to predict the emergence of a dominant design, because it is dependent on factors other than the technical features of the innovation. Although chance plays an important role in technology emergence, salient characteristics of the environment in which the firms are embedded also play a role in the evolving dynamics of the competitive domains. Structural analysis of industries (see chapter 1 for a summary) is not adequate to handle the significant technical and market uncertainties during the era of emergence; it is, however, useful for competitive analysis during the incremental innovation phase.

To capture technology emergence, an alternate framework has been proposed by Van de Ven, which is presented in Figure 5.7. It offers a tool for managers to track and analyze technology emergence.

As shown in the figure, Van de Ven's framework focuses on three major components of the environment: (1) institutional arrangements, (2) public resource endowments, and (3) technical economic activities.

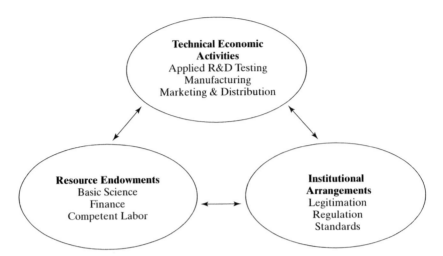

FIGURE 5.7 A FRAMEWORK FOR UNDERSTANDING INDUSTRY EMERGENCE

Source: Adapted from Van de Ven, A. H. and Garud, R. "Innovation and industry development: The Case of Cochlear Implants," in Burgehman, R. and Rosenbloom, R. (eds.) Research on *Technological Innovation, Management and Policy,* Vol. 5, Greenwich, CT: JAI Press, 1993.

INSTITUTIONAL ARRANGEMENTS

These arrangements serve to regiment, regulate, and standardize a new technology. The ultimate authorities that serve these functions are governmental organizations, professional trade associations, and scientific communities that society recognizes as its delegated agencies. Firms may either adapt to the requirements imposed by these institutional authorities or attempt to build their goals and procedures directly as rules and institutional arrangements. Thus, firms compete not only in the marketplace, but also in technological communities. Rival firms often cooperate by collectively manipulating their institutional environment to gain access to resources necessary for their collective survival and to legitimize their innovation.

RESOURCE ENDOWMENTS

Three kinds of resources are critical to the development of almost every technological innovation:

1. Advancements in basic scientific or technical knowledge;
2. Financing and an insurance mechanism; and
3. A pool of competent human resources.

Although private entrepreneurs engage in the development of these resources, public organizations—usually external to the competitive domain—play a major role in creating and providing these public resources. In our terms, resource endowments are built up by technology facilitators (chapter 2) in the technological environment.

TECHNICAL ECONOMIC ACTIVITIES

The commercial component of the framework focuses on the traditional definition of an industry that consists of the set of firms developing product innovations that are related to or are substitutes for each other. If they persist in developing technology, they subsequently develop a line of products and gain access to the complementary assets of functions (manufacturing, marketing, distribution, etc.) necessary to establish an economically viable business.

The three elements—institutional arrangements, resource endowments, and technical economic activities undertaken by the firms within a competitive domain—continue to evolve and influence each other during the course of a technology's emergence. Numerous events need to take place to develop institutional arrangements, resource endowments, and economic activities, particularly because they require the involvement of many actors from public and private organizations over an extended period of time. Individual events are often not widely known, and various insights pertaining to technical, resource, and institutional capabilities are often required to overcome bottlenecks.

These processes could begin with the intentions and inventive ideas of entrepreneurs, who undertake a stream of activities to gain the resources, competencies, and endorsements necessary to develop an economically viable enterprise. However, the process can begin any number of ways and vary by the technology being developed. In Box 5.10, we have employed the framework to describe the emergence of the cochlear implant industry.

BOX 5.10

THE EMERGENCE OF THE COCHLEAR IMPLANT INDUSTRIAL SECTOR

As we have discussed, major technological changes evolve through two broad phases: (1) a technology emergence phase, during which necessary complementary technologies and infrastructures are created and the market reaches consensus on dominant design; followed by (2) a period of incremental technological change. Although technological changes occurring during the second phase are usually evident in the changing products in the marketplace, those occurring in the first phase are more likely to be subtle changes taking place in diverse locations over long periods of time. Recent research on the development of the cochlear implant industrial sector will help in understanding the importance of this social construction phase.

Cochlear implants are a biomedical innovation used to provide hearing to many profoundly deaf people. The underlying premise of the innovation is that electrical stimulation can be used to simulate normal hearing. The device consists of a small microphone, sound processor, and transmitter that acts like a miniature radio transmitter. A miniature receiving antenna and related circuitry are implanted in the user's head adjacent to the ear canal. An electrode then passes electrical impulses from the receiver, through the ear canal, and into the cochlea in the inner ear.

Professors Andrew Van de Ven and Raghu Garud have recently concluded a historical investigation of the way in which this innovation was developed and eventually came to market. Events surrounding this innovation, and occurring from 1955 until the present, were studied in detail. In this research, Van de Ven and Garud described a period called "Creation of Resource Endowments" that preceded commercial activity involving the private sector.

The period, Creation of Resource Endowments, lasted from 1955 to 1976. The primary participants during this period were universities and basic research institutes that focused on advancing the scientific knowledge

---

Source: From Van de Ven, A. H. and Garud, R. 1993. "Innovation and industry development: The case of Cochlear implants." in Burgelman, R. and Rosenbloom, R. *Research on Technological Innovation, Management, and Policy.* Volume 5, Greenwich, CT: JAI Press.

Box 5.10 (*continued*)

associated with cochlear implants. Research was occurring in multiple locations (e.g., the United States, Australia, and Austria), with researchers using different assumptions and pursuing fundamentally different technological designs. For example, an early disagreement between researchers centered on the type of device, single or multiple-channel, that was most appropriate.

At the same time, there were some minor financing activities, primarily in the form of research contracts and grants from public research foundations, and legitimation activities, such as journal papers and presentations at professional association meetings. Thus, we see a period of development during which the public sector focuses on scientific knowledge and disseminates that knowledge through institutional mechanisms. In turn, this dissemination then contributes to building the other resource endowments, financing and human competence, which further fuels other basic research.

By the late 1970s, seven leading research units—worldwide—had developed prototype devices for human implantation. However, human implantation required regulatory approval (e.g., the FDA) to move forward to an incremental improvement era. By the mid-1980s, the FDA had approved two devices for large-scale commercial sales (both a single- and double-channel design). However, despite marketing projections, these products were not widely accepted by the deaf population. At the same time, the institutional arrangements that had made the development of this innovation possible now came to constrain further new design efforts. It appears as if a "technological path" had become locked-in.

The importance of this historical illustration is that all sectors of the social system continually interact as the development of an innovation goes forward.

The framework identifies three major managerial challenges to be addressed by firms involved in the development of a radical innovation:

1. It points to a set of forces that the firms need to track in order to be successful in an emerging industry, especially during the era of technology emergence.
2. It points to the difficulties in navigating this era or highlights strategic uncertainties faced by a firm. The information necessary to make decisions is going to be limited, because many actors involved in the process of industry emergence are likely to be unrelated to each other or, in some cases, unknown to each other.
3. It highlights the importance of the role played by technological communities. The framework suggests that firms need to compete in this arena to gain endorsements and legitimacy for their products and sometimes obtain scarce labor talent and venture capital funds.

INFLUENCE OF ENVIRONMENTAL TRENDS ON COMPETITION

How are the major trends in the technological environment shaping the competitive domains? All three trends—globalization, time compression, and technology integration—are redefining the competitive landscape.

GLOBALIZATION

The scope of competition is increasingly global—a fact that has profound implications for the battles being waged in many competitive domains. Consider just three major implications:

1. Competitors from all over the world can potentially compete on many technological battlegrounds. They bring different assumptions and styles of competing, increasing the diversity among competitors.
2. Technological competition is not confined to markets but extends to the institutional milieu; institutions in different parts of the world follow different practices, regulations, and approaches. Knowing each one of them is a formidable task.
3. On the positive side, globalization has provided opportunities for rapidly acquiring collateral assets, because the number of possible alliances has increased considerably.

Globalization has introduced significant complexity and, in its wake, uncertainty and turbulence to the competitive domains.

TIME COMPRESSION

Time compression is creating the need for speed in competitive responses among firms; thus, the technology emergence phase is rapid. Just as we witnessed in the case of product life cycle, the industries, once formed, mature faster. Problem solving, learning, and competitive responses by firms are therefore forced to be more rapid than was the case earlier.

TECHNOLOGY INTEGRATION

Different phases in technology evolution open up possibilities for technology integration, both process and product. During the phase of technology emergence, smaller firms such as Artemis can join with Microsoft to complete their value chains. Conversely, large firms may find smaller ones useful to complete their technology portfolios. Technology integration potential at the product level continues well after the formation of an industry; this may enable firms to enhance product features and create differentiation.

MANAGERIAL IMPLICATIONS

Implications for four key managerial actions—competitive strategy, investment in innovation, learning, and internal operations—flow from the preceding discussion.

1. *Competitive strategy.* As the characteristics of competitive domains shift over time, firms will have to alter the course of their competitive thrusts. For example, during technology emergence, competition gets played out in product designs and in arenas such as technological communities. However, during the incremental innovation era, the focus shifts to the marketplace and

increasingly to process innovation. Firms that are insensitive to these shifts may discover that their competitive positions are eroded by rivals' actions.

2. *Investment in innovation.* In our discussion of technical change as problem solving, we noted how the problem recognition phase involves decision making to proceed with technology choice and solution development. The decisions require careful weighing of the potential for the value creation.

   The characteristics of competitive domains provide a set of five questions to help make the decision: (1) Where is the technological opportunity? (2) Once developed, will we be able to appropriate value from the innovation and, if so, how? (3) Can we access collateral assets needed to extract value from our technical change efforts? (4) How and in which institutional milieu—technological communities—should we compete in addition to the marketplace? (5) How fast should we execute?

3. *Learning.* As described in Van de Ven's framework, firms will have to orchestrate rapid learning about technological communities, resource endowments, and competitors during the technology emergence phase.

4. *Internal operations.* A key implication is that competitive domains demand certain speed of execution; managers will have to build the requisite organizational capabilities for rapid response in many competitive domains. We will, of course, discuss this issue extensively in the next chapter.

❖ CHAPTER SUMMARY

Technological change plays an important part in competitive dynamics. The change has several consequences. First, it brings in new products and processes. Second, it alters the value chains and value constellations of firms. It also alters the nature of the rivalry among firms.

Five technology-related characteristics are important for the analysis of competitive domains. First, technological opportunity refers to the potential for innovation along the value chain of firms within an industry. Second, competitive domains differ in terms of the degree of appropriability of the benefits accruing from the innovative activity. Third, resource commitment required for success varies over competitive domains. Science-based industries that demand basic research may require greater resource commitment than technology-based industries involving applied research and development. Fourth, significant rivalry is often played out in institutional settings far removed from the marketplace. Finally, different competitive domains demand different speeds of execution.

We can identify two broad technology change regimes: the technology emergence phase, followed by a phase of incremental change. The technology emergence phase begins with the appearance of a major radical innovation, when a few firms have pioneered a new product or process. This is followed by a stage of tremendous ferment within the industry, when a large number of firms enter into the market with somewhat different product designs. Competition among these product designs comes to an end when a dominant design has emerged in an industry. The factors that drive emergence of a dominant design are not exclusively the technical characteristics of the innovation but market-related factors, strategic moves of firms, the role played by the political institutions, and chance factors. Industry emergence due to a radical innovation should be conceptualized within a framework comprised of three major components: institutional arrangements, technical economic activity, and resource endowments.

During the technology emergence phase, competition among technologies takes place simultaneously at two levels. The first level of competition takes place among the variants of the product designs embodying the radical innovation. This competition is not merely at the level of product features but also is played out in technological communities. A second level of competition takes place between the radical innovation and the industries threatened by it. The threatened industries often improve the performance characteristics of the older technologies they employ. Broadly, they have two responses available to them: First, not to commit resources to the new innovation and, second, to participate in the development of the new industry. Participation in new industry requires decisions related to timing of entry, intensity of commitment, and the degree of separation between organization for the new technology and the one for the existing technology.

Following the technology emergence phase of an industry, there ensues a period of incremental innovation. During this stage, the rate of product innovation declines but is accompanied by a corresponding increase in process innovation. The focus of competition shifts from product features to pricing and cost decision of firms within the industry. This phase of incremental change continues until another radical innovation appears and upsets the competitive equilibrium within an industry.

During the incremental innovation phase, the industry reduces to a few firms, and the competitive position of firms will remain stable for long periods of time. However, in industries characterized by sustained innovation—where successive product generations make previous generations obsolete—windows of opportunity exist for firms to shift their competitive position within the industry. In a similar way, the ability to introduce an architectural innovation into a mature industry often yields new entrants advantages over existing firms, thus upsetting the competitive equilibrium within the industry.

❖ NOTES

1. Adapted from Kearns, David and Nadler, David. *Prophets in the Dark*. Harper Business, NY: 1993, pp. 89–91, 108–109, 134–135. And Henderson, R. M. and Clark, K. B. "Architectural innovation: the reconfiguration of existing product technologies and the failure of established firms," *Administrative Science Quarterly* (1990): 35: 9–30.

2. Fahey, Liam. Competitors, New York: John Wiley & Sons, 1999.

3. Fahey, L. ibid., see chapter 2.

4. Narayanan, V. K., John Charnes, George Pinches, and Susan Mercer. *A Retrospective Analysis of Fast Cycle Teams*. Institute of Public Policy and Business Research. KS. September, 1998.

5. Winning in the institutional arena is increasingly addressed in the rubric of political strategy. See John Mahon, Barbara Bigelow, and Liam Fahey. "Political Strategy: Managing the Social and Political Environment,"

The Portable MBA in Strategy. Liam Fahey and Robert Randall (eds.) New York: John Wiley & Sons, 1994.

6. See for example Mendelson, Haim and Ravindran R. Pillai. "Industry Clockspeed: Measurement and Operational Implications," *Manufacturing & Service Operations Management*, Vol. 1, No. 1, 1999, pp. 1–20.

7. Hence our preference for using the more embracive term, *competitive domains.*

8. This phase has been named the *social construction phase* in academic writings. I have used a simpler term that is more easily understood by the readers.

9. Anderson, Phillip and Tushman, Michael L. "Technological Discontinuities and Dominant Designs: A Cyclical Model of Technological Change," *Administrative Science Quarterly* (1990): Vol. 35, pp. 604–633.

10. Mueller and Tilton. "Research and Development Costs as a Barrier to Entry,"

Canadian Journal of Economics (1969): Vol. 2, pp. 517–579.

11. Everett, M. Rogers, et al. *Modeling Technological Innovation in Private Firms: The Solar and Microprocessor Industries in Northern California.* Stanford, California, Stanford University, Institute for Communication Research, Report, 1980b.

12. Bright, James. *The Electric Lamp Industry.* New York: MacMillan, 1949; Hughes, Thomas P. *Networks of Power.* Baltimore: Johns Hopkins University Press, 1983; Landes, David. *Revolution in Time.* Cambridge, MA: Harvard University Press, 1983.

13. Freiberger, Paul and Swaine, Michael. *Fire in the Valley: The Making of the Personal Computer.* Berkeley, CA: Osborne/McGraw-Hill, 1984.

14. The term *collateral assets* was used by James Utterback and borrowed from the term *co-specialized assets* coined by David Teece in his paper, "Profiting from technological innovation," *Research Policy,* 1986, Vol. 15, No. 6.

15. Cooper, Arnold C. and Schendel, Dan. "Strategic Responses to Technological Threats," *Business Horizons,* 1976, pp. 61–69

16. Utterback, James M. *Mastering the Dynamics of Innovation.* Cambridge, MA: Harvard Business School Press, 1994.

17. See for example, Ronald Miller and David Sawyers. *The Technical Development of Modern Aviation.* New York: Praeger, 1968; Gardiner, J. P. "Behind Victories and Airplanes and Automobiles during the Past Fifty Years," *Design, Innovation and Long Cycles in Economic Development.* Christopher (ed.), London: Francis Pinter, 1986.

18. Henderson, Rebecca M. and Clark, Kim B. "Architectural Innovation: The Reconfiguration of Existing Product Technologies and the Failure of Established Firms," *Administrative Science Quarterly* (1990): Vol. 35, pp. 9–30.

6

PROCESS INNOVATION, VALUE CHAINS, AND ORGANIZATION

Technology has always had a significant role in shaping work, organizations, and management practices. The shift from the First Wave to the Second Wave, characterized by the automation of labor, led to the creation of routine tasks, emergence of the blue-collar workforce, and the modern factory as the major organizational form. In the Third Wave, the information technologies are shaping work and organizations.

The impact of technology on organizations during the Third Wave can be illustrated by the manner in which computers have begun to reshape the nature of work. Consider the following three examples:

> American Airlines, which reshaped the travel industry in the 1960s by introducing a computerized reservation system, is making big strides in the use of information technology to train employees. A recent course on security procedures for gate agents on international flights, for instance, included sessions with interactive CD-ROMs. Computer-aided instruction, as it is called, increased the retention rate for agents and shortened training time.

> Cigna, the giant property and casualty insurer, is transforming its procedure for developing group policies for corporate customers with the help of artificial intelligence. The old method, still standard practice for most insurers, had been to send each proposal through ten or more departments, sequentially—sales, underwriting, policy service, claims, and so on. Each department would revise the proposal in light of its own responsibility, information, nomenclature, and schedules. The inevitable result: confusion and delay. Now, teams made up of a representative from each department assemble new policies with the help of a system programmed with insurance knowledge. At once highly flexible and quietly disciplined, the system can call up, correlate, and display descriptions of all existing insurance coverage and options. The team constructs the policy from alternatives the system suggests; the system then distributes the proposal electronically throughout the

corporation for the necessary approvals. Proposals are finished faster and conform better to customers' needs, yet cost less because they reuse work that has already been done.

By linking its computers with those of major retail chains, a top consumer products company manages its inventory from the moment goods are produced until the consumer takes them through the checkout line. The system helps cut costs every step of the way: It enables the factory to produce just what the market needs, saving on inventory and warehouse space; it computes optimal truck loads and delivery schedules; it allows the retailer to tie up less shelf space by guaranteeing that the stock will be constantly replenished. As a result, the "replenishment cycle"—the period between the moment when a consumer takes a product off the shelf and the time a replacement arrives—has shrunk from 12 days to five. Everybody wins. Manufacturer and retailer share the cost savings, and the consumer enjoys lower prices.

There are several important issues to note from these examples and to consider as you read this chapter. First, technologies cross all areas of the organization, and, thus, all areas of work may be enhanced by their use. Second, computer networks allow for interorganizational information flows. They thus allow the "value chains" of various organizations to be connected and managed simultaneously. Finally, technologies in general—and more specifically, computers—allow the intellectual activity of work to be disconnected from its physical location. As we will see, technology has profoundly changed the nature of work and the workplace, and this is the subject we will explore in this chapter.[1]

As can be seen from the vignette, technological changes are transforming the value chain configurations of firms. In turn, these transformations of value chain configurations are altering the nature of jobs, the way work is performed, the design of organizations, and the processes by which decisions are made by top-level managers. In this chapter, we will discuss the influence of technology and technological changes on the internal organization of a firm.

In the previous chapter (chapter 5), we discussed the role played by technology in the dynamics of competition that unfolds in an industry. Thus, the management of technology is crucial to a firm's competitive success within its industry. This success, however is derived not merely from new products, but also from a firm's (internal) processes, organization, and management of its operations. Because the changes in internal operations of a firm are often not immediately visible to competitors, the benefits of internal changes are less quickly dissipated by imitation. Thus, firms need to exploit the opportunities opened up by technological change to improve their internal organization.

In this chapter, we will try to answer questions such as:

1. What are the drivers of technological change in processes and organizations?
2. What are the major shifts in value chains configurations that we have witnessed as a result of technological advances?
3. How do technological changes influence the internal functioning of an organization—nature of work, organizational structures, and decision processes?

An overview of the chapter is presented in Figure 6.1.

Changes in an organization ensue from several sources, some strategic and others technological:

- During the last 2 decades, many diversified corporations have been organized into business units for sharper market focus. This change is not necessarily triggered by technology.
- Other firms have restructured to take advantage of innovations in process technology. For example, through re-engineering, firms try to reap the benefits of information technologies.

In our discussion, we will focus primarily on changes triggered by facilitating process technologies.

As illustrated in Figure 6.2, technology enables a firm to introduce change in its value chain, and just as in the case of product introductions, such changes provide a firm with windows of opportunity to create competitive advantage. Process technology innovations that reconfigure value chains and value constellations lie at the heart of many fundamental organizational changes.

Intra-organizational learning is central to the creation of competitive advantage through value chain reconfigurations and organizational rearrangements. This learning falls into two types: first order and second order.

1. First-order learning focuses on learning by doing and incremental innovations within the existing value chain configuration.
2. Second-order learning focuses on the fundamental reconfiguration of value chains and value constellations.[2]

Both types of learning confer productivity benefits to firms, facilitating their pursuit of competitive advantage. In our discussion of the S-curve of innovation, we pointed out that significant shifts in performance of technologies come about in two ways: the appearance of breakthrough technologies and incremental improvement in those technologies.

FIGURE 6.1 OVERVIEW OF THE CHAPTER

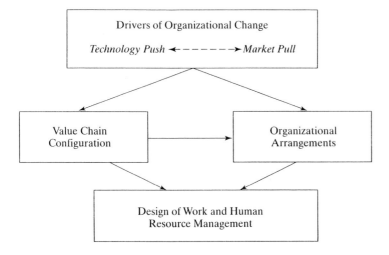

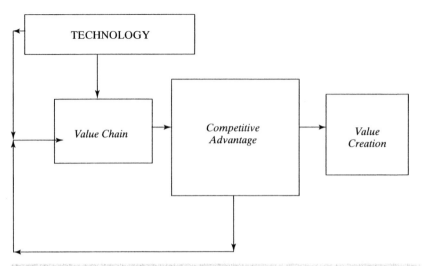

FIGURE 6.2 TECHNOLOGY, VALUE CHAIN, AND COMPETITIVE ADVANTAGE

- First-order learning is analogous to the incremental improvement and, just as in the case of *S*-curve of innovation, contributes to significant productivity gains. The learning may occur in processes of design, manufacturing, or marketing and, in short, the entire value chain of the firm.
- Over the years, process innovations have brought several fundamental shifts in value chain configurations. This has been due to the confluence of several technological breakthroughs, or technology integration. These shifts, once adopted by firms, necessitated fundamental shifts in organizational practices. The shifts, in turn, have resulted in major leaps in productivity.

The scheme of the chapter is as follows. First, we will discuss the major drivers of change in value chains and value constellations. Second, we will describe the four major modes of value chain configuration. Third, we will develop the linkages between value chain configurations and organizational characteristics. Fourth, we will summarize how changes in value chain configurations are transforming the nature of work and careers in organizations. The ensuing sections will respectively deal with the influence of environmental trends on organizations and the key managerial implications flowing from our discussion of the influence of technology on organizations. We will conclude with a summary of the chapter.

DRIVERS OF CHANGE IN VALUE CHAIN

PROCESS INNOVATION AND VALUE CHAIN

At the heart of our discussion of the linkage between technology and organization lie process innovation and adoption. The concepts of value chain and value constellation together provide a convenient way to describe process innovation or diffusion. Thus process innovations enable firms to introduce changes in the value chain that, in turn, affect the design of work, organizational structure, and processes.

Process innovations may be either hardware dominant or software dominant. Recall that hardware-dominant process innovations infuse a higher level of technology in terms of equipment or other physical characteristics, sometimes replacing labor, as in the case of automation. Software-dominant process innovations, on the other hand, may require a firm to create not only new skills but also new attitudes and mindsets among its employees. Figure 6.3 shows examples of different types of hardware- and software-dominant process innovations (using the classification scheme for innovations we developed in chapter 3). Indeed, many firms adopt both hardware- and software-dominant process innovations to enhance their competitiveness in an industry.

Process innovations help firms accomplish the reconfiguration of value chains in three major ways:

1. New technologies change the way in which firms actualize the primary value chain activities. Thus, process innovations can be employed to restructure major functions such as manufacturing, marketing, or R&D. Consider the following examples:

   • Advances in electronic technology are drastically reshaping the way stocks are traded in the United States and around the world. Computerization has radically changed the speed of stock trading and allowed colossal sums of capital to flow daily through the markets. Technology is now one of the most important determinants of how the next stage of the market evolution will be managed.[3]

   • Justice Records recently signed a deal with CompuServe, Inc., the vast computer network owned by H & R Block. It gives CompuServe customers access to an electronic record store—where they can browse through a catalogue, read biographies of the featured acts, and check out the album's finer notes. Compact disks ordered by modem come by mail within two weeks.[4]

FIGURE 6.3 TYPES OF PROCESS INNOVATION

		Technology Elements	
		Existing	New

Linkage among Elements	Existing	Hardware Dominant
		    Upgrading of Equipment
		
		Software Dominant
		    Training Programs
			Hardware Dominant
			    Voice Transmission
			
			Software Dominant
			    Quality Circles
			    Job Design

	New	Hardware Dominant
		    Evolution of Information Architecture
		
		Software Dominant
		    1. Socio-Technical Systems
		    2. TQM
			Hardware Dominant
			    AI
			    Robotics
			
			Software Dominant
			    Re-engineering

2. Process innovations, especially in information technologies, can be used to change the conduct of secondary value chain activities. Consider:

   • Total quality management (TQM) has been successfully applied in several finance departments. Both (a) major public firms, such as AT&T, Campbell's Soup Co., Federal Express Corp., IBM Corp., Motorola, Inc., Procter & Gamble Co., Westinghouse Electric Corp., and Xerox Corp. and (b) small enterprises such as Baldridge, Globe Metrological Inc., Harley-Davidson, Inc., and Analog Devices, Inc., had all reaped substantial benefits from TQM application.[5]

   • User-friendly software and huge databases allow just about anyone to access information directly. Advances in this technology have generated do-it-yourself marketing research that threatens the jobs of researchers. Eventually, the user-friendly systems will be augmented by an expert system full of artificial intelligence to answer many of the same questions that a product manager used to ask a marketing consultant.[6]

   In recent years, IT-augmented process innovations have been at the center of the re-engineering activities in corporations that have led to delayering and downsizing.

3. Finally, process innovations also enable firms to redefine their scope, i.e., reconfigure the value constellation, by outsourcing or in-sourcing of value chain activities.

   • As technologies have matured, automobile firms have discovered that outsourcing component manufacture is more cost-effective than manufacturing the components in-house.

What drives firms to adopt these changes? We summarize the reasons for the changes next

DRIVERS OF CHANGE

As in the case of products, both technology-push and market-pull sources of process innovation may alter the value chains and value constellations of firms. See Figure 6.4 Process innovations, both technology push and market pull, can result in one or more desired consequences:

   • Enhance the speed of operations and customer responsiveness;
   • Reduce the cost position of firms relative to competitors;
   • Incorporate product features; and
   • Increase the flexibility of the workplace.

As also shown in the figure, technology-push innovations involve investment in newer organizational capabilities made possible by technological advances. These organizational capabilities and the ensuing value chain changes enable firms to alter the rules of competition in the marketplace. For example, the electric process in global steelmaking enabled Japanese firms to alter the rules of the game in their favor in the steel industry

   Product-market and strategic considerations dictate market-pull innovations Broadly, we can identify four major considerations:

1. *Phases of technology evolution.* The nature of process innovation changes over the development of an industry. During the technology emergence phase, process innovations are tightly coupled to design and engineering

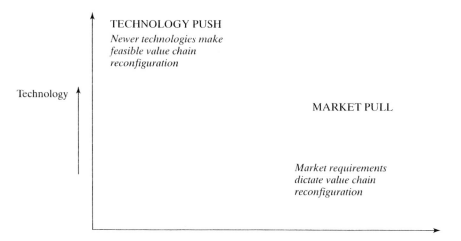

FIGURE 6.4 TECHNOLOGY-MARKET MATRIX

during product development and marketing and distribution during commercialization. Indeed, during this phase, firms experiment with different value chain configurations to commercialize the new and often radical product innovations. During the incremental innovation phase, as industry matures, the focus of process innovation shifts to cost control to compete successfully in the market.

2. *Characteristics of competitive domains.* The characteristics of competitive domains may propel firms to undertake process innovations and value chain reconfigurations. Technological opportunity may rest in possible cost reductions across the value chain or the need to add product features. Institutional milieu may force firms to adopt innovations, as in the case of ISO 9000 certification. Finally, industry clockspeed may require that firms revamp their value chains by adopting process innovations that enhance the speed of their own operations.

3. *Changes in products.* The most obvious change in value chains is derived from the changes in firms' product portfolio: extensions, deletions, and modification through redesign, or addition of features.

4. *Other strategic reasons.* Other reasons, especially human resource considerations, may prompt a firm to adopt process innovations and value chain changes. In response to the changing labor markets, firms have employed process innovations to enhance the flexibility of the workplace. Practices such as telecommuting, flextime, and job sharing have been adopted to attract and retain scarce human talent.

In spite of the potential benefits, firms are often reluctant to introduce process innovations. Two major factors impede the adoption of the innovations:

1. Process innovations and value chain reconfigurations typically require investment of financial and human resources, and the benefits of the investment are sometimes far in the future. This fact slows the adoption of technology-push innovations.

2. The implementation stage of process innovations requires careful managerial attention (see the discussion in chapter 4 on diffusion), because
   it involves realigning the workforce and organizational structure and
   process—tasks that often meet with organizational resistance.

Many incremental process innovations may affect only some parts of the value chain
and do not require organizational overhaul. Sometimes, these incremental innovations
accumulate over time to create an entirely new mode of configuring value chains. At
other times, a breakthrough process innovation alters the relationship between product
and processes and may require a fundamental shift in the mode of value chain configuration: The extent of change may be so broad as to embrace the entire value chain and
value constellation. Indeed, four distinct modes of value chain configuration have
emerged over the years, a topic to which we now turn.

MODES OF VALUE CHAIN CONFIGURATION

Broadly, there are four distinct modes of configuring value chains and value constellations: (1) craft production, (2) mass production, (3) lean production, and (4) mass
customization.

CRAFT PRODUCTION

For centuries, value chain configuration was based on the notion of craft. Everything
was crafted by the hands of someone who had the requisite materials, tools, and most
importantly, skills. Craftsmen, who were also called *artisans,* used their skill or know-
how to turn raw materials into finished goods; their craft was both an art and a source
of pride. For example, before the advent of the sewing machine, dresses or suits were
tailored according to the craft production model. Here, a customer picked a type of material (texture, color, etc.) and then negotiated with the tailor about the design of the
suit or dress—as well as the price. The tailor made the dress or suit in conformity to the
specifications of the customer; the article of clothing was tested on the customer himself
(or herself). This model of value chain configuration resulted in a large variety in the design of a suit or dress. However, because craftsmen did most of the tailoring manually,
the process itself was slow—the production of clothing took as long as a month or two.

Craft production was the predominant mode of configuring value chains during the
First Wave (recall our discussion of waves of change in chapter 2). Thus, craft production utilized human sources of energy and the skills, knowledge, and attitudes of the
craftsman rather than utilizing a physically embodied technology. In other words, the
level of technology associated with craft production was relatively low. As a result, craft
production allowed only small batches to be produced at a time; products could not be
turned out in large volumes. Craft production also required that the suppliers of goods
and services interface with the customers quite frequently. It produced a large variety
of goods and services, because each product was customized to the specific needs of
the customer. These two factors related to the product—small batch and high variety—
meant that the value chain operation was relatively slow.

In the history of economic affairs, craft production is probably the oldest and perhaps the most pervasive form of organization. However, during the Second Wave, the
industrial revolution made possible the replacement of human sources of energy by mechanical sources; for example, hand tools were increasingly replaced by machinery. This
led to a revolution in the mode of configuring value chains. This revolution followed two
distinct paths.

1. The first was a continuation of the basic idea of craft production. It was
   founded on the idea that machines and processes could augment the craftsmen's skill by allowing the worker to embody his source of knowledge in
   more varied products. Thus, the more flexible the machine, and the more
   widely applicable the process, the more it expanded the craftsman's capacity
   for productive expression.[7]
2. The second path took the form of mass production. Its guiding principle was
   that the cost of making any particular good could be dramatically reduced if
   only machinery could be substituted for the human skills needed to produce
   it. In economic terms, technology enabled the scale of production operation
   to be higher, or the development of what we call economies of scale.

The differences between these two paths are still visible, for example, in the different
management systems that produced a Rolls Royce and a Chevrolet; a Paris designer
original and an off-the-rack dress from T. J. Max; and a five-course meal at a 5-star
restaurant and a cheeseburger and fries at McDonalds.[8]

In the early days of the industrial revolution, the two paths were less distinct,
blurred by the simultaneous use of high-skilled workers and mechanization. However,
as the United States began to grow into economic prominence, mass production became
the pervasive mode of configuring value chains. Craft production has continued in specific instances: architecture, urban development, and value-added services, for example.

MASS PRODUCTION

As the United States moved into the twentieth century, craft production processes became unable to support the growth of large industrial enterprises as they sought to meet
the demands of a growing and geographically dispersed population. Mass production
practices arose partly in response to the demand for producing goods on a larger scale
and volume. Although mass production can be traced back to the beginnings of the late
1800s, it reached its full development during the 1910s and 1920s under the leadership
of Henry Ford. Ford and his cadre of production engineers, notably Charlie Sorenson,
put mass production to full use in the Model-T assembly line. This rearranged the organization of their factory into a moving line where each worker assembled a piece of
the car; the car then moved to the next worker for the next assembly part, and so on.
This innovation became synonymous with mass production.

When Ford's engineers introduced the assembly line to Model-T production, the
amount of labor time spent making a single car dropped from 12 hours and 8 minutes
to 2 hours and 35 minutes. Six months later, Model Ts could roll off the assembly line at
the rate of 1,000 a day, with the average labor time dropping to just over 1½ hours.[9]

Mass production relied on several principles relating to the configuration of value
chains and the system of management.

THE VALUE CHAIN CONFIGURATION

Mass production was based on five major principles of value chain configuration:

1. **Interchangeable parts.** Each product part needed to join to other parts without hand fitting. Thus, parts of a product had to be produced to tight tolerances. This requirement led to the principle of interchangeable parts.
2. **Specialized machines.** Specialized machines were necessary in order to produce parts to the tight tolerances required to eliminate hand fitting.
3. **Focus on the process of production.** Rather than simply providing isolated craftsmen with all the materials they needed to manufacture a product one at a time, a firm should focus on the entire value chain and how full value chain operations can be managed to greater efficiency.
4. **Division of labor.** As the processes related to primary value chain operations became standardized, workers were required to focus on only a piece of the product. In turn, this quite naturally brought about greater efficiency.
5. **Flow.** The product should move automatically and systematically from worker to worker.

Along with this mode of configuring the value chain, a system of management and several principles to manage the operations were also developed.

THE SYSTEM OF MANAGEMENT

Mass production involved seven major principles of management:

1. **Focus on low cost and low prices.** Mass production focused on reducing the cost of a product and passing the benefits to the customers in the form of low prices.
2. **Economies of scale.** The larger the enterprise, and the greater its output, the lower its cost should be.
3. **Product standardization.** An enduring principle of mass production is producing standardized products for homogenous markets; standardized products reduced the complexities associated with custom work and helped in lowering costs.
4. **Degree of specialization.** To reduce costs, the workers should be specialized so that, under the close direction of the supervisor, they should perform the smallest of functions over and over.
5. **Focus on operational efficiency.** The value chain operation should be controlled so that a factory can be maintained at near capacity.
6. **Hierarchical organization with professional managers.** An administrative structure of professional managers arranged along a single hierarchy needs to be developed to control increasingly complex value chain operations.
7. **Vertical integration.** To ensure an adequate supply of raw materials and components, as well as a stable marketplace in which to sell finished products, mass producers became mass suppliers and distributors, as well. This grew out of the need to control production and is influenced by the rise of large hierarchical organizations.

During the 1920s and 1930s, as well as during the years after World War II, mass production diffused throughout the American economic system. It also became the dominant management philosophy. In Box 6.1, we have sketched the underlying logic of the system of mass production.

THE UNDERLYING LOGIC
OF MASS PRODUCTION

The process of mass production that fueled the growth of industrial nations for so many years is based upon an underlying logic, or thought process, of what makes a business successful. This logic is sequential and reinforcing in the sense that it results in products that, over time, come closer and closer to achieving the ultimate goals of mass production: higher volumes, more efficient manufacturing processes, lower costs, and larger stable markets. We present this sequential thought process here. As you work through this logic, you may wish to consider the environmental and technological changes that have tended to make many of the assumptions that underlie this model obsolete.

1. A company must make profits to stay in business; the more profits, the more successful is the enterprise. Profits come from selling the most number of products, which are produced at the lowest cost.

2. The product can be sold in large, homogeneous markets.

3. High product volumes result in reduced manufacturing costs through economies of scale.

4. Demand is elastic; lower prices will bring higher volume that, in turn, results in higher profit. Lower prices

FIGURE 6.1.1 THE UNDERLYING LOGIC OF MASS PRODUCTION

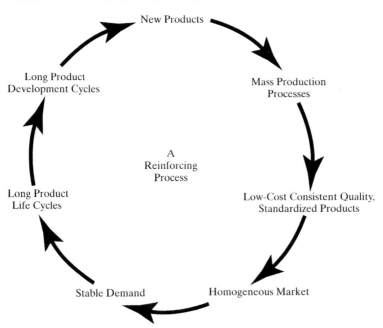

Box 6.1 (*continued*)

also result in a broadening of the market, and thus the market becomes more homogeneous.

5. Niche markets represent relatively low volume and thus should be ignored.

6. The lowest possible costs can be achieved through automation. This results in high fixed costs but low unit costs, which, in turn, reinforces the need for high volume.

7. Efficiency of the production process is of major importance. The process must run smoothly with no delays, interruptions, or surprises. So,
    a. Inputs must be stabilized; supplier and wage prices must be controlled.
    b. The process itself must be stabilized through product standardization and worker and machinery specialization.
    c. Output must be stabilized through control of demand and inventory level.

8. Product life cycles should be lengthened in order to reduce per unit development

costs and investments in product and process technologies. The experience curve must be allowed to operate at its fullest. R&D should be focused on new product breakthroughs that can be mass produced; minor changes and improvements just add cost and, thus, should be avoided.

9. The profits produced from this sequence of events allow for long product development times. Thus, a steady stream of new product developments can be readied for the marketplace. This will then provide the stability necessary for long-run profitability.

The figure presents this underlying logic in graphic form. New products manufactured using mass production processes result in the lowest cost, highest quality, standardized products targeted for a homogeneous market. This results in stable demand, which in turn allows long product life and development cycles. From this process, new products emerge that continue along the same path, thus reinforcing the logic.

As shown in the box, the underlying management philosophy can be summed up with the phrase "efficiency through stability and control": The efficiency of the value chain operation must be maintained through stability in, and control of, the firm's inputs, process, technologies, and outputs. If this is achieved, profits will naturally follow. And, indeed, for mass producers throughout most of the twentieth century, profits have followed. Those organizations that adopted it first and managed it best became the giants of industry, the *Fortune 500* companies. Among their members were Ford, General Motors, U.S. Steel, Standard Oil, IBM, AT&T, Texas Instruments, Du Pont, Xerox, Eastman Kodak, Procter & Gamble, Goodyear, and General Electric.

Relative to craft production, mass production had four distinct features:

1. The level of physically embodied technology involved in mass production was considerably higher than in the case of craft production. The beginning of specialization of men and machinery clearly differentiated mass production from its predecessor. Although interchangeable parts greatly simplified the production process and significantly reduced the amount of labor, it required specialized machines to produce the parts to the tight tolerances required to eliminate hand fitting. In the case of craft production, the machines that were used were general-purpose machines that could be adapted to all sorts of specialized functions throughout the production process.

2. Mass production led from artisans responsible for producing an entire product by their own means, and at their own pace, to groups of craftsmen interdependently working together on a defined product or at least a significant component of one. This also led to workers becoming so specialized that, under the close supervision and direction of a supervisor, they performed the smallest of functions.

3. The volumes involved in mass production produced a corresponding need to inventory products to prevent disruptions of supply in the market. Thus, the interaction between customers and suppliers became much less frequent than it had been in the case of craft production. Indeed, mass production enabled the suppliers of goods and services to control the marketplace by developing a homogenized product that the customers had to buy. Thus, product design became a specialized function within the organization; it was at this point in time that the desires of the customers were incorporated into the product.

4. Finally, wherever mass production was adopted, the cycle time for producing a product declined considerably; so also did the costs associated with the product.

The first challenge to mass production arose with the Japanese system of lean production, which was specifically created to compete with U.S. mass producers by achieving lower costs at smaller volumes with higher quality.

LEAN PRODUCTION

Toyota is often credited with pioneering the key elements of the lean production model. Toyota Production System evolved the key principles of mass production, adapting them to the Japanese context. Toyota adapted the large-scale, highly efficient, constant flow production philosophy of the Ford Rouge complex to its small-scale facilities in an interesting way. Unable to achieve either a high level of vertical integration or large volumes, Toyota built up a local network of adaptable suppliers and integrated them with assembly plants. Building on the benefits of standardization and assembly line—essential elements in mass production—Toyota, in addition, engaged the minds of the workers characteristic of the days of craft production. There were four major ideas in lean production:

1. *Team organization.* Workers were organized into teams that were largely autonomous. Teams were composed of four or five workers under a team leader. Teams took on responsibilities not normally the province of line workers in U.S. auto plants, in particular for quality assurance, preventive maintenance, and internal job rotation schedules. If a worker was absent without notice, the team would fill in; repair areas were minimal because it was believed that quality should be achieved within a process, not within a rectification area.

2. *Training.* Unlike thinking of workers as cogs in a machine as in the mass production era, management trained each worker for a variety of jobs and skills—not just for production tasks but maintenance, record keeping, quality control, and more.

3. *Continuous improvement.* Rather than delegating the task of productivity improvements to industrial engineers, management gave the workers the responsibility for continuous improvement through such mechanisms as quality control, suggestion boxes, etc.

4. *Just-in-time manufacturing system (JIT).* Working with a network of adaptable suppliers, inventory levels were kept at an absolute minimum so that costs could be shaved and quality problems detected and solved. Assembly lines, with little inventory, were thus bufferless, yet ensured continuous flow.[10]

In the United States, the best-documented lean production manufacturing plant is New United Motor Manufacturing, Inc., (NUMMI) in California, a joint venture between Toyota and General Motors (GM). After the start of pilot production in 1984, NUMM has recorded lower employee hours per vehicle (20.8 hours in NUMMI versus 43.1 at the old GM–Fremont plant), lower inventory levels, and fewer defects. Also, absenteeism rates have been low, and the employee surveys showed improvements in morale.[11]

Although lean production tried to harness the human potential within an organization, as well as the potential inherent in some of the emerging information technologies, it is being replaced by mass customization, a fourth stage in the evolution of production organizations.

MASS CUSTOMIZATION

The fourth stage, mass customization, can be seen as a synthesis of two long-competing systems of management that we have previously discussed: craft production and mass production. Specifically, mass customization involves the value chain operations in individually customized goods and services on a mass scale. It has come to represent the mode of value chain configuration of the Third Wave. In this mode, information and other technologies enable firms to customize goods and services to meet consumer demand, often at prices at or below those of mass producers.

As we move from mass production to mass customization, all aspects of the value chain—from inbound logistics to outbound logistics—may be affected as shown in Figure 6.5.

In mass production, low costs are achieved primarily through economies of scale in contrast, economies of scope drive the low costs in mass customization. Economies of scope are said to exist when a single process can be employed to produce a greater variety of products or services more cheaply and more quickly. Often, companies can achieve economies of both scale and scope. Whereas economies of scale can be realized in the mass production of standardized parts, these parts may, in turn, be combined in a myriad of ways in order to achieve economies of scale.

Just as in the case of mass production, mass customization relies on several principles related to the system of value chain configuration and the system of management

THE VALUE CHAIN CONFIGURATION
The production system involves five major principles:

1. *Flexible manufacturing systems.* In manufacturing industries, computer numerical control, direct numerical control, and industrial robots greatly increase manufacturing flexibility by controlling parts manufacture through software programming. Flexible manufacturing systems extend this flexi-

Impact of Mass Production

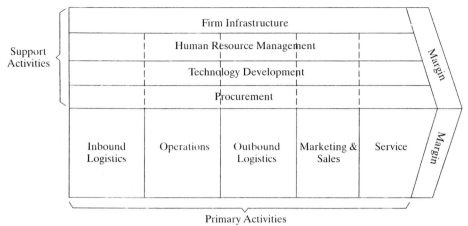

Impact of Mass Customization

FIGURE 6.5 IMPACT (SHADED) OF MASS PRODUCTION AND MASS CUSTOMIZATION ON THE VALUE CHAIN

bility by allowing all members of a family of parts to be manufactured at will and at random.

2. *Computer-aided design/computer-aided manufacturing (CAD/CAM).* Design modifications and even new designs can be completely developed by the computer; the manufacturing requirements can be automatically generated from the design specifications.

3. *Computer-integrated manufacturing.* Computer-integrated manufacturing links all the disparate computer controls needed for automation into a single integrated system that is fast, responsive, flexible, and very low cost at high volumes.

4. *Use of information and telecommunication technologies.* The instant application of information technologies allows the production process to

respond quickly to changes in demand and design. Thus, its use can constantly lower the cost of increasing differentiation in service as well as manufacturing industries.

5. *Use of computerized databases.* Computerized databases enable firms to respond instantly to individual requests for information.

In Box 6.2, we have illustrated how mass customization has been put into operation in one firm. As shown in this box, the firm combines a number of technologies to allow a product to be produced to individual customer specifications.

BOX 6.2

MASS CUSTOMIZATION AT NATIONAL PANASONIC BICYCLE

In the 1980s, National Panasonic Bicycle (NPB), a wholly owned subsidiary of the giant Matsushita Electronics Industries, found itself in a mature market characterized by sluggish demand and falling prices. New market segments such as sports cycles (for example, mountain bikes) were beginning to emerge and cause fragmentation in customer demands. As with many markets, customers had come to expect a wide variety of choice, low cost, and high quality, as well as fast delivery times. Faced with these market conditions, NPB recognized that it could no longer remain competitive using typical mass and lean production techniques. Instead, it would have to find ways of delivering customized products at reasonable cost in a timely manner.

FIGURE 6.2.1

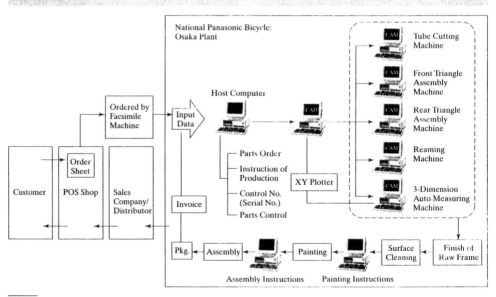

Source: Reprinted from *European Management Journal*, Vol 11 No 1, Roy Westbrook and Peter Williamson, "Mass Customization: Japan's new frontier," pp. 38–45, Copyright 1993, with permission from Elsevier Science.

To accomplish this task, NPB established a pilot plant within their Osaka factory. The backbone of this plant was the Panasonic Order System, or POS. Under this system, a customer could walk into any bicycle shop displaying the POS sign in Japan and the United States and get measured on a special frame for a bicycle that would fit the individual proportions of the customer. Note that the entire frame is sized to fit the customer, a concept far advanced from that of mass production, which allowed differences only in frame height. Beyond the sizing of the frame, the customer also selects from 18 different base models, several different handlebar and handle stem configurations, 199 different color patterns, various pedal and tire types, and even the type of calligraphy and placement of the manufacturer's logo. In total, more than 11 million different combinations of system components are available to create a customized bicycle.

The customer's information is faxed to the Osaka factory on the same day that the order is placed at the bicycle shop. At the factory, the customer's specifications are entered into a central computer, which assigns an order number and produces a listing of required parts and instructions for production. All information is captured in bar-code format so that, as the unit moves from station to station, detailed instructions for the next step can be scanned into the computer controlling that station. No prefabricated frames exist when the order arrives; each frame is individually cut from 20-foot lengths of metal tube as determined by a computer-assisted design program based upon the customer's proportions. Each of the following steps in the manufacturing process is then controlled by computer-assisted manufacturing programs based upon customer specifications. This process is summarized in the figure.

The result of this order and manufacturing process is that the customer receives a truly customized product within 2 weeks in Japan and 3 weeks in the United States. Although the cost of the end product is somewhat higher than its mass-produced counterpart (average cost is approximately 15 percent above the best mass-produced cycle), the extra value added by customizing the product to fit the buyer's size and taste appears to outweigh this difference. In 1991, NPB sold approximately 15,000 of these customized units. Mass customization also changes the nature of competition in an industry; retailers can now emphasize a differentiated product to their customers and not rely strictly on cost as a way of competing. Finally, these customized products have raised the image of NPB in the eyes of consumers, resulting in a spill-over effect of increased sales in their off-the-shelf line of bicycles. In 1991, sales of these units posted a strong increase to approximately 723,000 bicycles.

THE SYSTEM OF MANAGEMENT

In addition to value chain configuration, mass customization also relies on several principles of management:

1. *Just-in-time delivery.* This processing of materials and components eliminates process flaws and reduces inventory-carrying costs.
2. *Reducing set-up and changeover times.* These reductions directly lower run size and cost of variety.
3. *Compressing cycle times.* This eliminates waste and increases flexibility and responsiveness while simultaneously decreasing costs throughout all processes along the value chain.
4. *Production to order.* Production is based upon receipt of an order instead of forecasts. This lowers inventory costs, eliminates fire sales and write-offs, and provides the information necessary for individual customization.[12]

Mass customization as the primary mode of value chain configuration is being adopted in many industries. Consider the following examples:

- In the automobile industry, Toyota is reportedly offering customers 5-day delivery. This cycle time is from the time the customer personally designs his/her own customized car (from modular options) on a CAD system (in a dealer showroom or in the customer's own home by a traveling salesman) through order processing, scheduling, manufacture, testing, and delivery.[13]
- In another industry, telecommunications, the number of innovations is increasing dramatically, and availability of options and opportunities for customization are skyrocketing.
- In home telephone service, customizing options include call waiting, call forwarding, caller identification, caller ID blocking, multiple phone lines (different rings), and voice mailboxes.

Mass customization is also visible in consumer markets:

- In the beverage industry, Pepsi and Coca-Cola used to be the leaders in the soft drink market, with an assorted number of off-brand colas and an allotment of other flavors comprising the rest of the market. Today, the basic cola segment has fragmented into diet and non-diet, caffeinated and decaffeinated, with and without fruit juice, and so on.
- Similarly, in 1980, only 88 brands of breakfast cereals were available in the United States; by 1990, 205 brands were being sold.
- Finally, attempts at customization are also seen in such consumer products as toothbrushes. Until the late 1970s, only two major innovations, nylon bristles in 1938 and electrical toothbrushes in 1961, marked the toothbrush industry. With the advent of bristle design as a differentiating factor when Johnson & Johnson brought out its Reach brand in 1977, even the toothbrush industry has been characterized by continuous incremental innovations.

Thus, mass customization has brought about a different mode of value chain configuration. Through the application of technology and new management methods, mass customization relies on creating variety and customization through flexibility and quick responsiveness. The practitioners of mass production share the common goal of developing, producing, marketing, and delivering goods and services at prices low enough that almost everyone can afford them. On the other hand, mass customization focuses on developing, producing, marketing, and delivering affordable goods and services with enough variety and customization that almost everyone finds exactly what they want. We have summarized the differences between mass customization and mass production in Table 6.1.

When we discussed craft production, we cited the example of tailoring a suit or dress. In Figure 6.6, we have charted the evolution of the apparel industry in the United States from the eighteenth century on. As can be seen from the chart, prior to the eighteenth century, craft production was the dominant mode of production in the apparel business in the United States. Starting around 1890, mass production began to dominate; this resulted in the declining unit cost of apparel as well as a decline in the variety of clothes produced. However, post-1990, we begin to witness not only a further reduc

TABLE 6.1 Comparing Mass Production and Mass Customization

	Mass Production	*Mass Customization*
Focus	Efficiency through stability and control	Variety and customization through flexibility and quick responsiveness
Goal	Developing, producing, marketing, and delivering goods and services at prices low enough that nearly everyone can afford them	Delivering, producing, marketing, and delivering affordable goods and services with enough variety and customization that nearly everyone finds exactly what they want
Key Features	Stable demand	Fragmented demand
	Large, homogeneous markets	Heterogeneous niches
	Low-cost consistent quality, standardized goods and services	Low-cost, high-quality, customized goods and services
	Long product development cycles	Short product development cycles
	Long product life cycles	Short product life cycles

Source: Reprinted by permission of Harvard Business School Press. From *Mass Customization, The New Frontier in Business Competition* by B. Joseph Pine II. Boston, MA 1992, p. 47. Copyright © 1992 by the President and Fellows of Harvard College; all rights reserved.

tion in cost, but also an increase in the variety of apparel produced. It is expected that the post-1990 era will be dominated by mass customization as the dominant form of production. Thus, the apparel industry in the United States has come a long way from the days of craft customization; the industry went through an era of mass production and is currently at the doorstep of mass customization. Lean production methods have not been pervasive in this industry in the United States.

FIGURE 6.6 PRODUCTION TECHNIQUES AND PRODUCT VARIETY IN THE U.S. APPAREL INDUSTRY

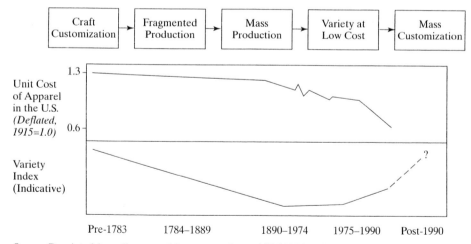

Source: Reprinted from *European Management Journal,* Vol 11 No 1, Roy Westbrook and Peter Williamson, "Mass Customization: Japan's New Frontier," pp. 38–45, Copyright 1993, with permission from Elsevier Science.

DIFFERENCES AMONG THE FOUR MODES OF VALUE CHAIN CONFIGURATION

Craft production, mass production, lean production, and mass customization represent four fundamentally different approaches to the value chain configuration. The four modes incorporate specific new technology, but the configuration of these technologies is associated with a particular philosophy of management needed to operate the respective organizations. We can identify five major dimensions of difference that separate the four modes of value chain configurations: (1) the linkage between a firm and its market; (2) product-process linkage; (3) the relative mix of labor and capital content in the production process; (4) the mix of software and hardware elements of new technology; and (5) the nature of the social system in the workplace.

THE LINKAGE BETWEEN A FIRM AND ITS MARKET

In different modes of value chain configuration, a firm develops different relationships with its customers. In craft production, where products are produced according to the needs of the individual consumer, there is frequent interaction between the supplier of goods and services and the customer during the production process—from initiation of the order to the delivery of the order. In mass production, where customers are provided a more or less homogenized product, the interaction between the firm and its customer is confined primarily to the design activity and then secondarily during the after-sale service activity. As a result, the linkage between the supplier of goods and services and its customers is lower than during craft production; interactions are buffered by means of inventory. Lean production enables greater variety to be built into products and services, so that they are more responsive to customers' needs. And mass customization, which is built around the idea that customers will almost always get the kind of product that they want, further tightens the linkage between the firm and the customer.

PRODUCT-PROCESS LINKAGE

In general, certain product strategies employed by a firm may necessitate a corresponding process technology. However, as the level of technological sophistication increases, these relationships are altered. Thus, the technological sophistication increases over the four modes of value chain configuration—craft, mass, lean production, and mass customization. With this increase, different linkages between products and processes have emerged. These linkages may be described with the help of a product-process matrix, as shown in Figure 6.7. In this matrix, one axis refers to the nature of the products (ranging from one of a kind, to higher volume, and finally to standardized commodity); the other axis refers to processes (job shop to batch processing, to assembly line, and finally to continuous flow).

Historically, stages one and two corresponded to craft production, whereas stages three and four were associated with mass production technology. The competitively viable decisions were generally regarded to be on the diagonal, with other positions typically considered to be inefficient mismatches of product and process: One-of-a-kind products, for example, should optimally be produced in job shops, not on assembly lines. Within this perspective, as the product strategies moved from stage one through stage four, the value chain activities were typically more automated, especially in design and manufacturing. These historical linkages are severed under mass customization. As shown by the arrow, mass customization makes it economically possible to consider the commercialization of less standardized products in a quasi-continuous process.[14]

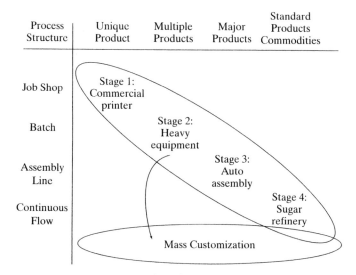

Process Structure	Unique Product	Multiple Products	Major Products	Standard Products Commodities
Job Shop				
Batch				
Assembly Line				
Continuous Flow				

Stage 1: Commercial printer

Stage 2: Heavy equipment

Stage 3: Auto assembly

Stage 4: Sugar refinery

Mass Customization

FIGURE 6.7 THE EVOLVING PRODUCT-PROCESS MATRIX

Source: From Adler, P. A. 1988. "Managing Flexible Automation." Copyright © 1988, by The Regents of the University of California. Reprinted from the *California Management Review,* Vol. 30, No. 3. By permission of The Regents.

THE RELATIVE MIX OF LABOR AND CAPITAL

The nature of the workforce required for running the various forms of organization also varied. In craft production, skilled artisans using general-purpose machines are required. During mass production, the labor content declines, and capital content increases; skilled workers doing repetitive jobs using specialized machines are required. In the case of lean production, although more labor content or capital content is introduced, enhanced social skills of the workers (communication, teamwork, etc.) are mobilized to advance the cause of effectiveness and responsiveness to the customers. Finally, with the coming tide of mass customization, an additional influx of technology will still further replace skilled labor.

SOFTWARE AND HARDWARE ELEMENTS

The replacement of labor is made possible by increasing levels of sophistication of process technology. Combinations of both hardware-dominant and software-dominant technologies make possible the shift from one mode of value chain configuration to another. Thus, the shift from custom production to mass production is accomplished by a heavy dose of hardware-dominant technologies in the production process. These technologies come in the form of specialized machines and assembly lines, which control the flow of production between workers. Much documentation exists as to the effect of this shift in technology: Mass production brought in its wake higher levels of absenteeism, lower levels of job satisfaction, and what sociologists call "anomie," or meaninglessness. Software-dominant technologies enable the shift to lean production. Employees are required to learn the skills necessary for communication, teamwork, and so forth. Finally, mass customization is accomplished not merely by adopting software-dominant technologies but by a further influx of hardware-dominant technologies, such as information technologies (e.g., manufacturing systems, computer-integrated manufacturing, electronic databases, and telecommunications).

THE NATURE OF THE SOCIAL SYSTEM IN THE WORKPLACE

The nature of the relationships among employees shifts over the four modes of value chain configuration. Mass production heightens the interdependence among individuals involved in the manufacturing process, although the system itself does not encourage social relationships in the workplace. Work is defined in terms of the repetitive jobs to be performed by an individual. Lean production tries to marshal the potential for productivity inherent in the social system—the relationships that exist among the workers. It also allows individuals greater control of work and pushes supervision of testing, quality control, and productivity enhancement methods down to the lowest possible level. The full implications of mass customization are yet to be known; however, it is expected that the widespread adoption of mass customization will lead to a further release of individuals from repetitive and routine tasks.

In summary, we have witnessed four distinct modes of value chain configuration made possible by advances in process technology. These differences are summarized in Table 6.2. These changes also bring about attendant changes in organizations. We will focus on the major characteristics of these changes and then discuss their implications for organizations.

VALUE CHAIN CONFIGURATION
AND ORGANIZATIONAL CHARACTERISTICS

Technology affects almost all facets of an organization and, thus, technological changes bring about changes in many internal characteristics of the organization. When organizational changes are triggered by technology, value chain configuration determines the organizational structure and functioning. We will summarize the influence of value chain configurations on (1) organizational structures, (2) organizational processes, and (3) the role of the manager.

ORGANIZATIONAL STRUCTURE

As technology enables changes in value chain configurations, it also brings about changes in organizational structure. Organizational structure is usually reflected in an organizational chart, which is a visible representation of underlying value chain activities and processes in the organization. Organizational structure typically consists of three components:

1. Basis of subunit formation, or the grouping of individuals into departments and the grouping of departments into the broader organization;
2. Degree of centralization, which refers to the locus of decision making—the more decentralized the organization, the more decision-making authority is transferred to lower levels of the organization and vice versa; and
3. Degree of hierarchy, which refers to formal relationships, including the number of levels in the hierarchy and the span of control of managers in the organization.

Joan Woodward, an industrial sociologist from England, conducted the first major study of the influence of technology on organizational structure. In her 1950s study, Woodward classified technology into three groups: small-batch and unit production; large-batch and mass production; and continuous process production. This classification closely corresponds to the distinction between craft production and mass production that we discussed earlier.

TABLE 6.2 Summary of Differences in Production System Dimensions

Production Systems

Dimensions of Production	Craft Production	Mass Production	Lean Production	Mass Customization
Linkage Between Organization and Market	Frequent interaction; close relationships	A buffered relationship; customers may be involved in design, but little involvement thereafter	Increased focus on customer needs	The organization tightly attuned to the marketplace
Linkage Between Products and Processes	Each product unique and produced one at a time	Standardized products produced by standardized processes	Focus on the more efficient production of standardized products	Production processes are flexible and change rapidly to accommodate customized products
Mix of Labor and Capital	Labor intensive	Capital intensive; in many cases, capital replaced labor; specialized machines and labor come into existence	Increased labor and capital; social skills of workers become important	Technology replacing specialized labor
Mix of Hardware and Software Elements of Technology	Primarily software intensive; technology imbedded in the craftsman	Hardware intensive; production processes built into equipment	New technologies are software dominant	New technologies include both hardware and software elements
The Nature of the Social System in the Workplace	Close interaction among craftsmen	Workers become interdependent but socially separated	Social systems seen as key to productivity	Further reliance on the potential benefits inherent in the social system

in this chapter. Woodward argued that technical complexity increases as we move from small-batch and unit production to continuous process production.

Woodward's work showed that production technology has a systematic relationship with organizational structure and management characteristics. For example, the number of management levels and the manager-to-total personnel ratio shows definite increases as technical complexity increases from unit production to continuous process. This indicates that greater management intensity is needed to manage complex technology. Further, direct-to-indirect-labor ratio decreases with technical complexity, because more indirect workers are required to support and maintain complex machinery. Other characteristics such as span of control, formalized procedures, and centralization are high for mass production technology but low for craft and continuous process technologies. Unit production and continuous process technologies require highly skilled workers to run the machines. Also in these technologies, level of communication will have to be higher to adapt to changing conditions. In contrast, in mass production technology, tasks are standardized and organized, so few exceptions occur, little level of communication is needed, and employees are less skilled.[15] In Box 6.3, we have summarized Woodward's findings, along with those of a following study by the Aston Group.

In the years since Woodward's research, new developments have occurred in modes of value chain configuration. As we saw in the rise of mass customization, computer integrated manufacturing (CIM), CAD/CAM techniques have now become prevalent. Thus, raw materials, machines, product design, and engineering analysis are all coordinated by a single computer in computer-integrated manufacturing. Although research into the relationship between technologies anchored in mass customization and organizational structure has not been as systematic as Woodward's research, some patterns are beginning to emerge. These patterns suggest that mass customization is associated with an emphasis on teamwork, decentralized decision making, and highly skilled workers. We may discuss these implications along the three dimensions enumerated earlier—basis of subunit formation, degree of decentralization, and degree of hierarchy.

BASIS OF SUBUNIT FORMATION

Two major innovations have transformed the basis of subunit formation in lean production and mass customization:

1. Team-based structures. In the last decade, changes in process technology have facilitated the increasing adoption of team-based structures within an organization. Unlike mass production where specialists work in their own functional areas, there is a shift in modern process technologies toward specialists from different disciplines working together within a team. For example, at one Westinghouse plant, 65 percent of the 830 employees are involved in a system of task forces that handle daily problems and promote product innovation.
2. Information technologies. The coordination among teams or within the organization is further facilitated by the adoption of information technologies.

The work-team approach is used in many large organizations, such as Procter & Gamble, Cummings Engine, Xerox, Polaroid, and Ford. Information technologies are now so prevalent that almost all organizations use some form of it all of the time.

DEGREE OF DECENTRALIZATION

The hardware- and software-dominant process technologies that have been sweeping the workplace during the last decade have resulted in pushing decision making down the

BOX 6.3

STUDIES ON THE IMPACT OF TECHNOLOGY
ON ORGANIZATIONAL STRUCTURE

Joan Woodward was a British industrial sociologist and one of the first researchers to tie organizational structure to technology. Along with her research team, she began studies in 1953 in South Essex, England, to understand the administrative practices of local firms. The prevailing wisdom at the time was contained in universal principles of management propagated by the classical theorists. Woodward wanted to gain firsthand experience of the management practices of firms.

The research team studied over 100 firms, which constituted 91 percent of all firms in that area of England with at least 100 employees. Data was obtained through interviews, observation, and analysis of company records. The researchers then attempted to group the firms based upon classical management principles, such as number of management levels, span of control, and the ratio of direct to indirect labor. However, no distinct groupings emerged: The 100 firms studied differed widely along all the dimensions suggested in classical management theory. Nor did the data correlate with either firm size or nature of the industry. Thus, the researchers were left with no explanation of why firms might structure their organizations in the ways that they were observed.

Eventually, the researchers thought of attempting to classify the firms based upon the technologies that they employed. Specifically, they classified the firms into three categories based upon the complexity of technology:

Unit and small-batch production, which consisted of job shop operations that manufacture and assemble small orders to meet the specific demands of customers. Products were custom-made and thus could not be inventoried in any appreciable amounts. This form of production constituted the lowest level of technology.

Large-batch and mass production, which were characterized by long production runs of standardized parts. Because the products are standard and production runs are long, the output is typically inventoried. Examples of firms studied using this production technique included automobiles and cotton mills.

Continuous production, which represented mechanization and standardization beyond that of mass production. This was the highest level of technology observed by the researchers. Examples included chemical plants and oil refining.

When firms were grouped according to the production technologies employed, certain systematic regularities in management practices began to emerge. For example, the continuous production firms had the highest number of levels and, from the CEO's point of view, the widest span of control. At lower levels of the organization, the span of control varied in a curvilinear fashion, with job shops and continuous production technologies having the lowest span and mass production having the highest span of control. We summarize several of the findings of the Woodward studies in the table.

What is important to note from the work of these researchers is that technology may play a large role in the way an organization is structured and managed. In other words, management structure may be contingent upon technology rather than any universal theories of management.

In the 1960s, a research team from the University of Aston in Birmingham, England, extended the work of Woodward. Called the Aston Group, these researchers noted that the Woodward studies did not include service firms, and thus they set out to gather data about technology and structure in both service and manufacturing firms.

Service firms are characterized by simultaneous production and consumption, and thus the product or service cannot be inventoried.

Source: From Narayanan, V. K. and Raghu Nath, *Organization Theory: A Strategic Approach.* Chicago, IL: Irwin, 1993. pp. 114–117.

Box 6.3 (*continued*)

TABLE 6.6.1   Woodward's Findings

Structural Characteristics	Unit Production	Mass Production	Continuous Process
Number of Management Levels	3	4	6
Supervisor Span of Control	23	48	15
Direct/Indirect	9:1	4:1	1:1
Labor Ratio: Manager/Total Personnel	Low	Medium	High
Workers' Skill Level	High	Low	High
Formalized Procedures	Low	High	Low
Centralization	Low	High	Low
Amount of Verbal Communication	High	Low	High
Amount of Written Communication	Low	High	Low
Overall Structure	Organic	Mechanistic	Organic

This form of business is quite different from the batch and continuous production technologies found in the Woodward studies. Thus, these researchers had to measure technology in a different fashion. Specifically, the Aston Group noted three characteristics of technology that are pertinent to both service and manufacturing firms:

Automation of equipment, which represents the amount of activity performed by machines relative to that performed by human beings.

Work-flow rigidity, which represents the degree to which the sequence of operations is tightly interconnected and unalterable.

Specificity of evaluation, which refers to the extent that work-flow activity can be evaluated using precise, quantifiable measurements as opposed to subjective evaluations by managers.

The Aston Group discovered that these three characteristics are closely related; hence, they created a single technology variable, which they called *work-flow integration*. Scores on this single variable were closely related to Woodward's scheme in classifying the complexity of technology: As the sophistication of technology increased, so did work-flow integration. Thus, unit and small-batch production technologies had low work-flow integration scores, and continuous production technologies had high scores.

In general, the firms studied by the Aston Group showed that service firms used lower levels of technology than did manufacturing firms. Service firms were characterized by less automation, less work-flow rigidity, and less precise measurements than were their manufacturing counterparts. Further, like Woodward's studies, the Aston study showed a similar correspondence between technology and management structures: As work-flow integration increased, so did bureaucratic characteristics.

One major difference in findings between Woodward and the Aston Group did emerge. The Aston findings suggest that technology is only one factor influencing management structure. In fact, it may be less important than other variables, such as firm size. The Aston Group noted that technology affects those aspects of management structure that are close to the work flow. Because the firms in the sample employed by Woodward were primarily small, it is likely that the overall management structure would be more greatly affected by technology. Thus, the size of the organization may be a more critical factor in determining management structure than is technology. However, technology still is an important factor to be considered.

lower levels in the organization. Thus, we have witnessed increasing levels of decentralization. For example, in organizations that have adopted the new factory technologies (flexible manufacturing systems, CAD/CAM, or CIM) decisions tend to get made at lower levels. The responsibility for operations is increasingly being delegated to autonomous units.

1. In socio-technical systems or in team-based structures, the work teams need authority to make decisions, and most managers use participatory management techniques that involve workers.
2. As a consequence of re-engineering, corporations have further pushed the levels of decision making to those in the organization closest to the customers.

The higher levels of decentralization enable organizations to be more responsive to the needs of the customer and to meet the demands of the competitive markets.

DEGREE OF HIERARCHY

As the bases of subunits and the levels of decentralization have shifted, they have in turn influenced the number of levels and supervisory spans of control within an organization. As firms adopted lean production over mass production, the team concept was used to derive the benefits of incremental innovation to enhance productivity. During mass customization, two different trends have appeared:

1. The re-engineering movement has made it possible to delayer a corporation— to remove an entire hierarchical level within a corporation.
2. Flexible manufacturing systems usually require shorter spans of control than in mass production—usually 15 or fewer subordinates report to a supervisor. This span of control in the manufacturing activity allows for a quicker response time from managers when serious problems erupt.

The adoption of information technologies and team concepts and the decentralization of decision making across the entire value chain have led to lower levels of hierarchy in the firm. This is associated with fundamental changes in organizational processes.

ORGANIZATIONAL PROCESS

Processes such as decision making, communication, and conversion of inputs into outputs are influenced by technological changes. As we have seen earlier, when design changes are frequently needed, mass customization works much faster than mass production to deliver the requisite products to the customers, once orders have been initiated. The shift to mass customization, increasing adoption of information technologies, and software-dominant technologies (such as re-engineering) have led to shorter development cycles, faster communications, and faster decision making. Consider the following examples:

- Adoption of satellite technology and the peripherals required to run a satellite have enabled Wal-Mart to inform its retail store managers all over the country about such decisions as prices, products, delivery, and marketing tactics. As a consequence, it can initiate changes in all its U.S. stores in a relatively short time—20 minutes, for example.

- Similarly, utilization of software-dominant technologies, such as groupware for interfunctional work teams, has speeded the development time for products in organizations.

In short, higher levels of customer responsiveness and speed of internal operations are associated with the shift to mass customization.

THE ROLE OF THE MANAGER

Recent trends indicate that process technology changes necessitate a more highly skilled workforce and different forms of managerial practices. Organizational structures have responded to those changes by taking advantage of increased worker skill to enhance the productivity of the organization as a whole. A by-product of the change in organizational structure and process is that the role of the manager has begun to change. Further, the managerial styles have shifted from one of command and control during mass production to a more participative style in team-based structures common in lean production. Managers tend to be less involved in running and controlling day to-day operations and instead act as facilitators, insuring that the teams have necessary resources.[16] Additionally, in mass customization, the role includes a conceptual dimension, both interfacing with external entities in the value constellation on a frequent basis and anticipating resource requirements and importing newer technologies for speed and customer responsiveness. The differences in organizational characteristics over the four value chain configurations are summarized in Table 6.3.

TABLE 6.3   Value Chain Configurations and Organizational Characteristics

Characteristics	Craft Production	Mass Production	Lean Production	Mass Customization
Organizational Structure:				
1. Subunits	Small, few subunits	Based on similar activities	Overlay of teams on existing groups	Team structure
2. Locus of Decision		Centralized	Increasingly decentralized	Highly decentralized
3. Degree of Hierarchy	Low	High	Moderate	Low
Organizational Process				
1. Speed	Low	Low	Low to moderate	High
2. Customer Responsive-ness	High	Low	Moderate	High
Management Role	Participative Supervisory	Directive	Facilitative Participative	Conceptual Facilitative Participative

DESIGN OF WORK AND CAREERS

The most visible influence that technology has on an organization is in terms of how it affects the design of work and careers within that organization. As we have seen in the various modes of value chain configurations, during craft production, many of the tasks were performed by human beings. During mass customization, most of the routine tasks were absorbed by technology. In addition to the nature of tasks, the value chain configurations have influenced the careers of individuals in firms, with attendant consequences for human resource management practices. We will deal with these topics in turn.

DESIGN OF WORK

Broadly, the influence of technology on the design of work can be observed along three dimensions: (1) task characteristics, (2) interdependence among tasks, and (3) requisite skill levels.

TASK CHARACTERISTICS

We will discuss technology's influence on task characteristics by using the framework developed by Charles Perrow—a framework that has had the greatest impact on our understanding of the task characteristics. The framework is displayed in Figure 6.8. Perrow specified two dimensions of tasks that were relevant to organizational structure and process: variety and analyzability.

FIGURE 6.8 MATRIX OF TASK CHARACTERISTICS

	Low ← Task Analyzability → High	

High
 	
Task Variety
 	
Low
	Nonroutine
	  Frequent face-to-face
	    meetings; group
	    meetings
	  Unscheduled meetings
	  MIS, DIS support
		Engineering
		  Large computer bases
		  Written and technical
		    materials
		  Frequent statistical
		    reports
		  MIS support

	Craft
	  Personal observation
	  Occasional face-to-face;
	    group meetings
	  Telephone
		Routine
		  Written reports
		  Rules and procedures
		  Some statistical data
		  MIS support

Source: From Richard L. Daft and Norman B. MacIntosh, "New Approach to the Design and Use of Management Information." Copyright © 1978, by The Regents of the University of California. Reprinted from the *California Management Review,* Vol. 21, No. 1. By permission of The Regents. All rights reserved.

1. Variety refers to the number of exceptions in the task, or the frequency of unexpected and novel events that occur during the normal course of doing the task. When an individual encounters a large number of unexpected situations with frequent problems, variety is considered to be high. When there are few problems and when the day-to-day activities are repetitious, tasks contain little variety.

2. The second dimension of the task concerns analyzability of the work activities. When the production process is analyzable, the work can be reduced to mechanical steps, and participants can follow an objective computational procedure to solve the problems. Problem solution may involve the use of standard procedures, such as instructions and manuals or technical knowledge such that in a textbook or handbook. On the other hand, some work is not analyzable. When problems arise, it is difficult to identify the correct solution. There is no store of techniques or procedures to tell a person exactly what to do. The cause or solution to a problem is not clear, so employees rely on their accumulated experience, intuition, and judgment.[17]

Based on these dimensions, four types of major tasks can be identified: routine, craft engineering, and nonroutine.

Routine tasks are characterized by little task variety and use of objective computational procedures. The tasks are formalized and standardized. Examples include automobile assembly lines and the bank teller department.

Craft tasks are characterized by a fairly stable stream of activities, but the task is not analyzable or well understood. Tasks require extensive training and experience, because employees respond to intangible factors on the basis of judgment and experience. For example, steel furnace engineers continue to mix steel based on judgment and experience; pattern makers for apparel firms still can work rough designer sketches into saleable garments.

Engineering tasks tend to be complex, but there is substantial variety in the task performance. However, the various activities are usually handled on the basis of established formulas, procedures, and technical experience. Engineering design and accounting tasks usually fall in this category.

Nonroutine tasks have high task variety, and the tasks themselves are not analyzable or very well understood. Basic research, strategic planning, and other work that involves new projects are examples of nonroutine tasks.

Perrow's framework can be used to highlight how changes in process technology impact the nature of the tasks within organizations. As a result of the change from craft production to mass production techniques, there was an increase in routine tasks. With the arrival of information technology and its applications in the form of CAD/CAM, many engineering tasks could also be automated. Finally, artificial intelligence techniques currently being developed try to codify the tacit knowledge and experience accumulated by individuals (for example, physicians) so that some of the craft tasks could also be automated. Thus, changes in process technology influence the variety and analyzability of tasks within an organization. Although such changes could, in general, move the tasks from one category to another, during the last few decades the technological developments have increasingly automated more and more jobs that are highly analyzable; currently, they are transforming many of the less analyzable jobs into the analyzable ones.

INTERDEPENDENCE AMONG TASKS

Transformations in value chain configurations alter the interdependence among tasks that exist within an organization. For example, we have seen that, as we moved from craft to mass production, the introduction of the assembly line heightened the inter-dependence among the various tasks performed on the production line. Team-based structures also enhance the interdependence among individuals who work on the same task team. This increase in interdependence heightens the need for communications within an organization. Advances in information technology enhance the organizational capability for communication; for example, voice mail, electronic mail, and personal schedulers enable messages to be inventoried, whereas teleconferencing capability makes possible face-to-face communications across long distances.

REQUISITE SKILL LEVELS

As the characteristics of tasks change due to technological progress, different skill sets are required within an organization. A process of creative destruction is at work here: Some skills become obsolete while additional skills are required for running an organization. For example, as technology automates many of the analyzable jobs, individuals who perform repetitive tasks and even many engineering tasks may no longer be required in an organization. However, this same automation makes it necessary to have in organizations individuals who can work with more sophisticated technologies (for example, computers and robotic machinery). Similarly, adoption of software-dominant technologies such as work teams requires individuals who have requisite interpersonal skills (communication, teamwork, etc.) necessary to operate in this environment. The forces of creative destruction are not only remaking the jobs required in organizations but are also fundamentally altering the career paths available to individuals.

CAREERS IN ORGANIZATIONS

As technological progress influences skill levels required, it alters the career paths in organizations. In Box 6.4, we present Walter Keichel III's summary of how changes in information technology have affected the work and career of managers.

The career paths demand adaptive capabilities but offer work-related flexibility, and they have altered the nature of the economic contract between employees and firms.

ADAPTIVE CAPABILITIES

As process innovations and value chain reconfigurations continually redefine the tasks and the requisite skills keep changing, there is greater emphasis on life-long learning as opposed to training for specific jobs, which was characteristic of firms organized in the mass production mode. Individual learning and organizational learning have become important, and a major component of managerial tasks is to encourage, facilitate, and capture this learning and transform it into competitive advantage for the firm.

FLEXIBILITY

Process technologies have made it possible to enhance workplace flexibility for individuals working in an organization. During mass production, jobs had to be performed at certain locations (e.g., the factory floor) and at certain times (e.g., shift work). Over the years, technology has made it possible to relax the restrictions on both time and location. During the 1970s, the concept of flexible working hours diffused throughout the U.S. economy. This concept was made possible by electronic tracking of work hours

o BOX 6.4

THE CHANGING FACE OF MANAGERIAL CAREERS

In this chapter, we have discussed many of the ways in which changes in technology have impacted the nature of work in organizations. *Fortune* editor Walter Kiechel III recently summarized three major changes that we have seen in the workforce:

- The new economy is increasingly driven by the convergence of telecommunication and computer technology. Thus, the ability to function in any organizational position will depend upon an individual's understanding of how to use these technologies.

- The use of teams of specialists to solve organizational problems is expanding. These teams are specifically configured to solve unique problems and are then disbanded once the problem is solved, with the individuals moving to other teams. So, the ability to function in an environment of constantly changing relationships and responsibilities will be a key factor in an individual's success.

- As the pace of change in organizational missions and structures increases, the likelihood of 30 years of employment with 1 organization decreases. Successful careers will thus be based upon a lifetime of learning and gaining skills as individuals move through a series of positions and organizations.

These broad changes in the nature of employment have significant consequences for the careers of managers in organizations:

- The increased use of information technology spreads information needed for decision making throughout and deeper into the organization. At one time, a manager's prime responsibility was the assimilation of information from divergent sources needed to make informed decisions. Now, the information needed to make informed decisions resides throughout the organization. Thus, the managerial role becomes one of providing resources to those in the best position to make decisions.

- Next, the increased reliance on teams will move the role of the manager away from direction and supervision and more toward one of facilitation. Managers will need to know how these teams of specialists can be formed and facilitated in the most efficient and effective manner.

- Finally, the success of a manager's career will also depend upon the learning and skills that they gain over a variety of positions and organizations. A steady progression up the corporate ladder is likely to involve lateral movements throughout different areas, as well as movement between organizations.

As many organizational scholars have noted, the importance of a job will not be lifetime employment, but instead the acquisition of additional skills and knowledge necessary to be employable in the next position.

Source: Adapted from Kiechel, Walter. "A manager's career in the new economy," *Fortune*, April 4: 68–72.

clocked by an employee. The flexible working hour system relaxed the rigid time re strictions imposed on employees.[18] With the adoption of lean production methods employees could work on different tasks; the flexibility with respect to job selection in creased. With the advent of information technologies, it has now become possible to a ford flexibility to employees with respect to their job location. As illustrated in Box 6.5

BOX 6.5

THE GROWTH OF THE HOME OFFICE

As these examples have illustrated, advancements in technology have allowed the convenience associated with a home office to grow. However, the use of home offices might well be the result of necessity rather than convenience. Consider a recent example:

On January 17, 1994, a major earthquake measuring 6.6 on the Richter scale struck Los Angeles. Although surprisingly few lives were lost in this disaster, large portions of the city's infrastructure were significantly damaged. In particular, a major portion of one of the world's most complicated and sophisticated highway systems was left unusable. As with most large cities, the majority of people who worked in the metropolitan areas lived outside of the city limits. Thus, the commute to work that once took 45 minutes now required up to 6 hours, an amount of time

that was clearly untenable for both employees and employers.

Some companies attempted to cope with this situation by establishing busing and car-pool systems for their employees. However, this approach resulted in only limited reductions in travel time. Others adopted a more technologically oriented approach. Because many employees had microcomputers, modems, and fax machines in their homes, much of their daily work could be done from that location. This removed the lengthy commuting times and also reduced the number of vehicles that traveled on a highway system that was now inadequate to handle the volume of traffic to and from the city. As we have discussed, the notion of telecommuting from home to the workplace has been around for some time. In the case of Los Angeles, a natural disaster made this form of work organization a very viable alternative.

Source: As reported on *All Things Considered.* National Public Radio, January 27, 1994.

---

firms are increasingly making it possible for individuals to stay at home, yet fulfill their workplace obligations. One of the consequences of the technological change has been the rapid rise in home offices.

EMPLOYMENT CONTRACTS

As we noted earlier, technological change creates the need for different types of skills, destroys some types of jobs, and creates other types. In recent years, since technological change has been rapid, the nature of employment contracts between a firm and its employees has undergone a fundamental shift. Instead of offering the security of lifetime employment, many firms are building their human resources practices with the concept of employability as security. Firms such as General Electric used to offer, implicitly or explicitly, the promise of lifetime employment. They are abandoning lifetime employment as part of their employment contracts and, in its place, are offering employees a workplace where they can continue to learn and update their skills. This issue was recently addressed by one of America's most noted and respected CEOs, Jack Welch of General Electric. In his words:

"What we have to do now is educate our people. Companies have to get involved in the school system, with dollars and volunteers. Within GE, we've got to upgrade workers' skills through intense and continuous training. Companies can't promise lifetime employment but, by constant training and education, we may be able to guarantee lifetime employability. We've got to invest totally in our people."[19]

These organizations hold the view that in today's world of rapid technological change, employability is the main source of security for their employees. In recent times, one consequence of this shift in employment contracts has been the creation of a temporary, or contingency, workforce. In Box 6.6, we have summarized the emergence of the contingency workforce due to technological change.

Technological progress and the shifts in value chain configurations have created changes in the very nature of work. These changes have, in turn, resulted in dramatic

---

BOX 6.6

TECHNOLOGY AND THE CONTINGENCY WORKFORCE

Over the past decade, U.S. industry has witnessed a marked increase in the use of temporary personnel, a situation many see as a permanent and significant change in the nature of employment in America. The growth in the so-called contingency workforce—part-timers, freelancers, subcontractors, and independent professionals that provide skills and services on an as needed basis—is evident on many fronts. Consider the following statistics:

- In the past decade, the number of people working for temporary agencies is up 240 percent.

- Temporary or part-time positions accounted for 20 percent of the new jobs created in the past 10 years.

- Manpower, the largest of the U.S. temporary-employment agencies, is now the largest private employer in the nation, with roughly 600,000 people on its payroll.

- Current estimates suggest that contingency employees represent one in four workers, and projections suggest that by the year 2002 this ratio will be one in two.

- The demand for temporary employees is now at every level of the organization, including top management—over the past few years, the number of agencies specializing in professionals and executives has increased threefold.

The growth in the contingency workforce can be seen as one fall-out of the large-scale corporate downsizing that began in the 1980s and continues today (since 1979, the *Fortune 500* industrials have eliminated 4.4 million jobs, roughly 1 in 4 that they once provided). Faced with global competition and rapid technological change, large firms needed to find ways of increasing efficiency. One such way was to reduce fixed labor costs. Because temporary workers often are paid less, and almost always receive no benefits, their use can reduce fixed labor costs and increase organizational flexibility. The result is a growing dependence on this type of workforce in the marketplace.

The continuing movement toward contingency workforces has clear implications for the financial and social security associated with careers and permanent employment. How can contingent employees find this security? Harvard researcher Rosabeth Moss Kanter has suggested that when security cannot come from being employed, it must come from being employable. She believes that the new appropriate career foundation will be based upon employability security—the knowledge that today's work will enhance the person's value in terms of future opportunities. Thus, personal security will come from the accumulation of human capital—the skills and reputation needed for future employment.

Source: From Joan Woodward, *Industrial Organization: Theory and Practice.* London: Oxford University Press, 1965, with permission.

TABLE 6.4   Design of Work under Differing Production Regimes

Dimensions of Work Design	Differing Production Regimes	
	Mass Production	*Mass Customization*
Task Characteristics	Formalized and standardized; low variety and high analyzability	Less routine and specialization; computer automation provides greater analyzability
Requisite Skill Levels	Limited and very specialized	Broadened to encompass many stages of the production process; higher level of technical and personal skills
Task Interdependence	Assembly lines heighten interdependence among tasks	Heightened interdependence, but communication becomes critically important
Flexibility	Very inflexible; locations and times were set	Technology allows flexibility in both time and location
Employment Contracts	Stable ladders of career progression within narrowly defined functions	Skills needed in multiple functions so lateral progression becomes important
Adaptive Capabilities	Little need for adaptive capabilities	Workforce must be highly adaptive

changes in the career paths available to individuals. The notion of a 30-year career with one firm, characterized by steady progression up a functional ladder, is no longer the norm. Instead, lateral movement between functions and organizations designed to enhance an individual's learning and skills will be the order of the day. Thus, individuals build their human capital by gaining knowledge in different functions or, in some cases, different locations of an organization. The design of work and careers under different value chain configurations is summarized in Table 6.4.

INFLUENCE OF ENVIRONMENTAL TRENDS

Implicit in the preceding discussion is the influences of the three trends—globalization, time compression, and technology integration—on value chains and organizations. These influences can be summarized thus:

1. *Globalization.* Globalization has extended the scope of an organization, with two major implications. First, the potential of process innovations is increasingly spread all over the world. Second, the geographic scope of both the value chains and value constellations of firms is now truly global. Both add complexity to organizational characteristics; firms are employing communication technologies (e.g., videoconferencing) to manage the complexity and different competitive tactics, such as global switching, exploit the value potential.

2. *Time compression.* Time compression has resulted in faster industry clock-speeds and, in turn, the need for increasing the speed of internal operations and customer responsiveness in organizations. Mass customization tactics are increasingly employed to accomplish this. Additionally, time compression has resulted in two related requirements: first, the need for faster organizational learning, resulting from faster waves of technological change; second, the need for heightened adaptive capabilities among employees and progressive human resource policies.

3. *Technology integration.* The scope of the value chains is constantly shifting as technological change alters the economics of make-or-buy decision making with respect to value chain activities. This, in turn, is forcing firms to develop different relationships with suppliers and organizational mechanisms to absorb process innovations from outside. Significant organizational learning has become necessary to overcome the NIH syndrome ("Not Invented Here") that we described as a barrier to diffusion in organizations.

MANAGERIAL IMPLICATIONS

Value chain configuration, internal organization, and human resource practices can be transformed by process innovations. These changes enable a firm to add product features, reduce cost, compete on the basis of speed and customer responsiveness, and, in many cases, retain employees with the promise of flexibility and opportunities for learning. Three major managerial implications are worthy of repetition:

1. *Choice of value chain configurations.* Different value chain configurations are appropriate for different competitive domains and strategic purposes. Increasingly, technology-augmented craft production is restricted to value-added services, such as architecture. Mass production continues to be relevant for low-cost production in low price segments of the mass markets and lean production when cost reductions from software-dominant technologies are used as a competitive weapon. Finally, mass customization is required when competition is on the basis of niche markets and low costs. In competitive domains where speed is necessary for survival, managers should be on the lookout for process innovations on a continuous basis.

2. *Change in organizational characteristics.* Changes in value chain configuration necessitate changes in organizational structure and process. For the full value impact of reconfigurations, a total organizational plan must be drawn up and implemented. This may require redesign of structure and process and human resource alignment: the selection of appropriate managers and employees with requisite skills.

3. *Flexible workplace.* The changing demographics and lifestyles of employees are increasingly necessitating flexible work arrangements. Technology can enable the development of these arrangements. Managers must be on the lookout for process innovations to provide a more flexible workplace. This

may be a source of retaining scarce talent in many industries, such as the information sector. In turn, this may lead to competitive advantage for firms.

Implementation of value chain configuration is a challenging task. We will deal with this topic in chapter 12, which focuses on deploying technology in value chains.

❖ CHAPTER SUMMARY

Over the years, we have witnessed four modes of value chain configurations: craft production, mass production, lean production, and mass customization. In craft production, custom products are designed and produced primarily with human energy. During the 1910s, mass production practices began to be adopted, partly in response to the demand for producing goods and services on a large volume. Mass production is based on five principles of value chain configuration: interchangeable parts, specialized machines, focus on the process of production, division of labor, and flow. During the latter half of the twentieth century, mass production began to be modified in favor of the Japanese lean production. Lean production relies on four major ideas: team organization, training, continuous improvement, and just-in-time manufacturing system (JIT). We are currently witnessing the emergence of a fourth mode of value chain configuration: mass customization. Mass customization involves flexible manufacturing systems, computer-aided design and manufacturing, computer-integrated manufacturing systems, use of information technologies, and the use of computerized databases. The system of management provides just-in-time delivery, reduced set-up time and delivery, compressed cycle time, and production to order.

The four stages differ in terms of the linkage between a firm and its market, product-process linkage, the relative mix of labor and capital content in the operations, the mix of software and hardware elements of technology, and the nature of the social system in the workplace. As we move to mass customization, the firm is tightly linked to customers and becomes technologically more intensive (increasingly employing both hardware and software elements), and the system shifts from individual to team organization.

Changes in process technology have altered organizational characteristics and the nature of work and careers in firms. Four major organizational changes have occurred as a result of value chain reconfigurations. First, re-engineering approaches have made it possible to delayer a corporation—to remove an entire hierarchical level within a corporation. Second, in the last decade, changes in value chains have necessitated the increasing adoption of team-based structures within an organization. Third, the hardware- and software-dominant process technologies that have been sweeping the workplace during the last decade have resulted in pushing decision making down to lower levels in the organization. Finally, technological advances have speeded organizational processes such as decision making and communications.

Both the designs of work and careers have changed, as well. First, technological advances have increasingly automated repetitive and engineering tasks and, with the advances in artificial intelligence, have begun to automate tasks that incorporate human judgment. Second, interdependence among tasks has increased as a result of process innovations. Third, tasks require not merely advanced technological know-how but "soft skills" such as teamwork, as well. Fourth, technological advances have infused greater flexibility in time and place for individual employees. Fifth, career progression is increasingly horizontal, with greater skills serving as a benchmark for advancement; thus employabi ity, rather than lifetime employment, is being emphasized in organizations. Altogethe technological advances have stretched the adaptive capabilities of individuals.

❖ NOTES

1. From von Simon, Ernest, "Customers will be the innovators," *Fortune* Magazine, Autumn 1993. Time Inc. Reprinted by permission.
2. See Argyris, Chris and Schön, Don. *Organizational Learning: A Theory of Action Perspective.* Reading, MA: Addison-Wesley, 1978.
3. Wright, David J. "Technology and Performance: The Evolution of Market Mechanisms," *Business Horizons,* Nov/Dec 1989, pp. 65–69.
4. Newcomb, Diedre. "Endangered Species?" *Forbes,* July 20, 1992, pp. 52, 53.
5. Schneider, Alan J. "TQM and Financial Function," *Journal of Business Strategy,* Sept.-Oct. 1992, Vol. 13, No. 5, pp. 21–25.
6. Cebrzynski, Greg. "Expert Systems or Replacements," *Marketing News,* February 27, 1987.
7. Piorie, Michael J. and Sabel, Charles F. *The Second Industrial Divide: Possibilities for Prosperity.* New York: Basic Books, 1984, p. 19.
8. Pine, Joseph B. *Mass Customization: The New Frontier in Business Competition.* Cambridge, MA: Harvard Business School Press, 1993, p. 10.
9. Chandler, Alfred D., Jr. *The Visible Hand: The Managerial Revolution in American Business.* Cambridge, MA: The Belknap Press of Harvard University Press, 1977, p. 280.
10. Krafcik, John F. "Triumph of the Lean Production System," *Sloan Management Review,* Fall 1988, pp. 41–52.
11. Adler, Paul S. and Cole, Robert E. "Designed for Learning: A Tale of Two Auto Plants," *Sloan Management Review,* Spring 1993, pp. 85–94.
12. Pine, B. Joseph. *Mass Customization: The New Frontier in Business Competition.* Cambridge, MA: Harvard Business School Press 1993, pp. 48–50.
13. Goldhar, Joel B. and Schlie, Theodore W. "Computer Technology and International Part II: Managing the Factory of the Future to Achieve Competitive Advantage," *Integrated Manufacturing Systems,* Vol. 2, No. 2, 1991, p. 27.
14. Hayes, R. H. and Wheelwright, S. C. *Restoring Our Competitive Edge.* New York: John Wiley and Sons, Inc., 1984; Ferbowes 2 Technology-Push strategies for manufacturing. *Pijdschrift Voor Economie en Management,* 28 2 (1983).
15. Daft, Richard L. *Organization Theory and Design.* St. Paul, MN: Best Publishing, 1989
16. Hull, Frank M. and Collins, Paul C. "High technology batch production systems: Woodward's missing type," *Academy of Management Journal,* Vol. 30, 1987, pp. 786–97. Also Alphea Jones and Terry Webb. "Introducing Computer Integrated Manufacturing," *Journal of General Management,* Vol. 12, 1987, pp. 60–74.
17. Daft, Richard L. *Organization Theory and Design.* St. Paul, MN: Post Publishing, 1989.
18. Narayanan, V. K. "A Contingency Model of Assessment of Flextime: A Field Experiment." Unpublished Ph.D. Dissertation, Graduate School of Business, University of Pittsburgh, PA, 1979.
19. Adopted from "Jack Welch's lessons for suc cess," *Fortune,* January 25, 1993, pp. 86–93.

TECHNOLOGY STRATEGY: BASICS

In the following three chapters, we will discuss the basic ideas that constitute technology strategy, and the key steps involved in its formulation. We will emphasize three main themes throughout our discussion that are consistent with the open systems perspective developed in theoretical underpinnings.

1. We will emphasize the role of environmental intelligence in the formulation of strategy.
2. We will portray technology strategy as a key driver of competitive advantage, and hence its value creation for many firms.
3. We will highlight the role played by collaborative strategies in the technology arena.

In chapter 7, we will describe the process of environmental-intelligence gathering that should precede strategy formulation. Readers are urged to revisit the chapter on environment (chapter 2), because we build on the ideas developed in that chapter to describe a process of gathering information and analysis. The advent of the Internet has made the task of gathering information both easier and more difficult. It is easier because there is a wealth of information available in electronic form; it is more challenging because personal sources may have to be tapped because almost everyone has access to many of the electronic sources.

Chapter 8 lays out the fundamental concepts of strategy, and the steps involved in formulating it. In addition, it highlights the three domains in which technology strategy is played out: research and development (R&D), new-product development, and value-chain configuration.

Chapter 9 focuses on the collaborative strategies that are increasingly common in the technology arena. We will summarize the various forms of collaboration in all three domains of technology.

TECHNOLOGY INTELLIGENCE

THE DAWN OF KNOWLEDGE NETWORKING

During the 1990s AT&T became interested in the convergence of three technology drivers: personal computing, video, and telecommunications.

MULTIMEDIA EVOLUTION

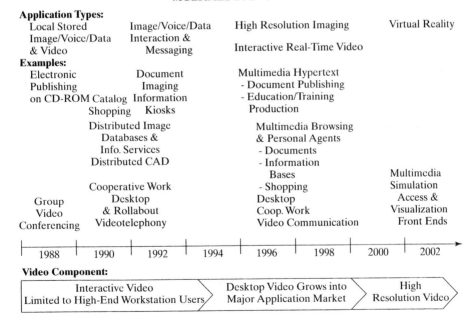

To understand and exploit the convergence, AT&T initiated a project titled "Plan 2000 Customer Research" to give focus to their business development efforts. By 1992, the firm had identified several applications/technology directions:

- Electronic image capture would be exploding and image networking rapidly emerging;
- Visual communications would be ready to emerge;
- Multimedia communications would emerge by mid-decade;
- Multimedia/video information services would be viewed as post-1995 requirements;
- Client-server, distributed database networking would be routine;
- Mobility applications would grow but would be both customer and function-driven; and
- Speech-recognition would be operational.

These trends were anchored in AT&T's forecast of technology. The forecast, titled "Multimedia Evolution," consisted of (1) identifying several application types, (2) the technologies that would need to be developed to produce the applications, and (3) establishing some probable time lines by which the technologies would come to be operational. See the chart below.

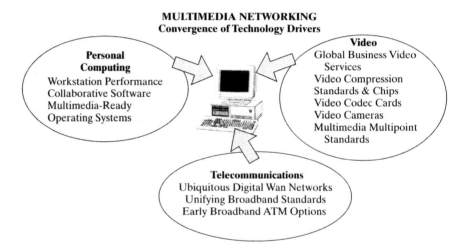

MULTIMEDIA NETWORKING
Convergence of Technology Drivers

Personal Computing
Workstation Performance
Collaborative Software
Multimedia-Ready
Operating Systems

Video
Global Business Video Services
Video Compression Standards & Chips
Video Codec Cards
Video Cameras
Multimedia Multipoint Standards

Telecommunications
Ubiquitous Digital Wan Networks
Unifying Broadband Standards
Early Broadband ATM Options

Based on this predicted convergence of hitherto independent industries, AT&T created a vision of the future, where what they call the "Phone Call of the Future" will involve voice, data, video and images in any combination anywhere, at any time with convenience and economy.[1]

As illustrated by the AT&T case, significant business development efforts require among other things, careful attention to technology forecast. Critical business decisions—business strategy decisions, authorization of a major research program, or decision to launch a new product initiative—need to be anchored in technology intelligence. Technology intelligence may reside inside the firm; but more likely, such information will come from the external technology environment.

Broadly speaking, most strategic decisions require two kinds of external intelligence: technology related and market related. Thus, intelligence needs may also be cap tured within the T-M matrix, as shown in Figure 7.1. However, in this chapter, we will address only the technology dimension, leaving the reader to other sources that deal with market intelligence.

Technical intelligence is a primary input into technology strategy formulation. Those responsible for investing in technologies must understand what others are doing and how it might affect them. For example:

- What new technologies are likely to emerge in the near future that might affect our business?
- What advances are being made in our core technologies? Which of our key technologies are maturing, and what will replace them?
- What capabilities do our competitors have, and how might they use them against us? Are we about to be blind-sided?
- Who is working on technologies that could benefit us, and how might we access them?[2]

The importance of finding accurate and timely answers to these questions is critical: If a firm misses answers to these questions, it may forever miss the opportunity to exploit new technologies or forfeit by default its position in the marketplace. If a firm invests in the wrong technologies, it may never recover its investment. Technology strategy should thus be anchored in technology intelligence. Hence, as shown in Figure 7.2, we have portrayed technology intelligence gathering as the first step in the formulation of technology strategy.

In this chapter, we will discuss the steps involved in gathering technology intelligence for making strategic decisions. We will answer such questions as:

1. What is technology intelligence? What are the different levels of technology intelligence? What functions do they serve?
2. How do we gather and analyze technology intelligence? How do we incorporate the intelligence into decision making?
3. What organizational challenges need to be met for the technology intelligence to meaningful to the decision makers?

Before you read this chapter, it is useful to refer to both chapter 2, "Technology Environment," where we have described some of the general characteristics of the technological environment; and chapter 5, "Technology and Competition," where we have described the influence of technology on industry dynamics.

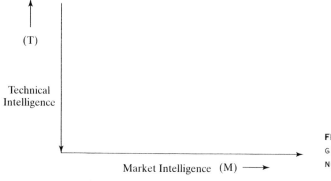

FIGURE 7.1 EXTERNAL INTELLIGENCE ARRAYED ON THE TECHNOLOGY-MARKET MATRIX

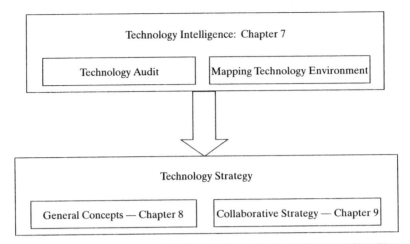

FIGURE 7.2 TECHNOLOGY INTELLIGENCE AND STRATEGY FORMULATION

Figure 7.3 presents the overview of this chapter. As shown in the figure, we first de fine technology intelligence and enumerate the different levels of technology intelli gence. Second, we describe the process of gathering technology intelligence, highlighting the differences between the different levels. Third, we discuss the major mechanisms of data collection. Fourth, we sketch the major forecasting and assessment tools. Fifth, we summarize the key challenges in managing the intelligence gathering activities in orga nizations. We conclude with managerial implications and the chapter summary.

FIGURE 7.3 CHAPTER OVERVIEW

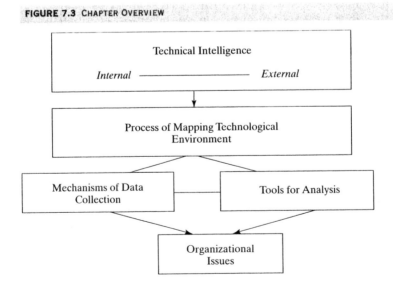

TECHNOLOGY INTELLIGENCE[3]

SIGNALS OF NEW TECHNOLOGY

New technology might require years to develop, so effective technology intelligence frequently focuses on very early indicators of change. However, these early signals of technology change are often very weak and difficult to relate to potential consequences such as product launches, that may occur many years later. The first signs often emerge in scientific and technical discussions, "gray literature," or statements that resources are being directed toward certain areas of science or technology. These signals might be weak; but gathering, assessing, and communicating this information are crucial objectives of technology intelligence programs, especially those that uncover and anticipate precommercial developments. For instance, small business innovation research (SBIR) grants are often awarded to one-or two-person companies with not much more than an idea. Firms can monitor those ideas related to their businesses and join the development as partners when progress occurs.

Later signals include scientific publications, which might appear 1 to 2 years after the research is completed. This delay is rapidly decreasing due to instant electronic communication of technical results; and effective technical intelligence now requires thorough integration with electronic sources of technical information. The Internet is now a key source of new research interests and programs at universities. Firms sometimes visit a foreign university to discuss potential collaborations, armed with the current research interests of professors downloaded from the Web.

Rumors or announcements of R&D alliances, joint ventures, or partnerships often follow valuable scientific reports. Later, patents will begin to be issued; these patents can easily represent work performed 3 to 4 years earlier and are clearly not timely indicators for identifying and addressing technology changes. Next, process development efforts on the new technology might be rumored. Finally, near the end of the development cycle, the strongest signals occur perhaps involving a product announcement, competitive product sales, and loss of business.

As can be seen, there is plentiful data about technology, but obtaining useful information for decision making—technology intelligence—is a significant challenge.

WHAT IS TECHNOLOGY INTELLIGENCE?

By technology intelligence, we refer to technology-related information that is useful and utilized by firms during strategic decision making. As illustrated in the opening vignette, technology intelligence provides

1. Descriptions of technology-related changes currently taking place;
2. Harbingers of potential changes in the future; and
3. Alternative descriptions of future change.

Together, they provide descriptions of alternative futures. Such descriptions provide organizations with lead time to identify, understand, and adapt to technological changes that most often occur externally; to anticipate the consequences of technology trends and to develop well-thought-out plans and policies.

In this and following chapters, we will use the term *intelligence* as opposed to *data* or *information*. We do this because we want to underscore the idea that the information should be useful to strategic decision making. Abundant data is often available from various sources concerning both the technological environment as well as competing firms. Not all the data is useful for making strategic decisions. Sometimes, a firm has to weave through available data; at other times, it will have to search or discover the data that are important for crucial decisions.

Technology intelligence arises from technical data but is imbued with interpretation and judgment by decision makers. The relationship between data, information, and intelligence can be described with the help of Figure 7.4. A large amount of data is usually available about various technologies and technological environment. Consider a biotechnology firm, such as Amgen. A significant amount of data is available about Amgen, including details of patents issued or patent statistics, research and development expenditures, names and quality of the key scientific personnel, scientific papers published by the scientists, and so on. When a firm interprets the data to mean that Amgen has certain key strengths and weaknesses (e.g., in proteins), the data becomes information. Further, when the firm infers that Amgen has a development lead in a particular drug that needs to be counteracted or overcome, the information is transformed into intelligence. Thus, technological intelligence has decision implications.

IMPORTANCE OF TECHNOLOGY INTELLIGENCE

Technology intelligence serves three major functions.

1. The intelligence provides an understanding of current and potential changes taking place in the environment. We have emphasized "current" to highlight that changes taking place currently are an important guide to anticipating the future, and "potential" to underscore the idea that strategic decisions should cover a time frame from short run to long run.

FIGURE 7.4 RELATIONSHIP BETWEEN DATA, INFORMATION, AND INTELLIGENCE

Infer

Intelligence

Interpret

Information

Data

Gather

Intelligence Gathering Activities   *Outputs*

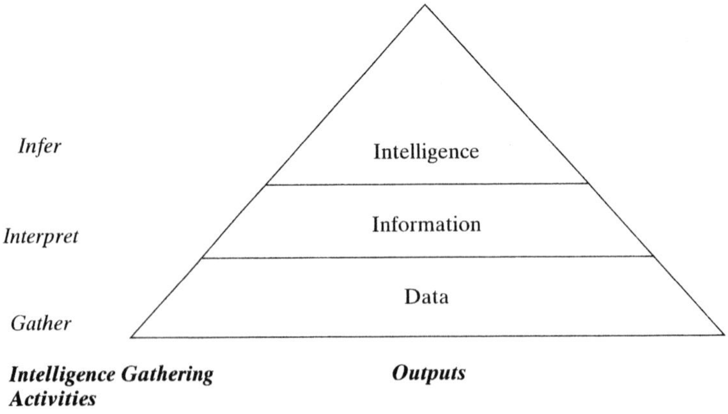

2. Technology intelligence provides important information for strategic decision makers. The technological information is often intrinsically interesting, but the primary goal is the generation of information not for its own sake, but information that is of use in determining and managing a firm's strategies.

3. Finally, the intelligence facilitates and fosters strategic thinking in organizations. The intelligence is typically a rich source of ideas and understanding of the context in which a firm operates. It should also challenge the current technology strategies by bringing fresh points of view into the organization.

The value of technology intelligence lies not merely in the information but in the process of generating it. When conducted properly, the process of generating technological intelligence leads to enhanced capacity and commitment to understanding, anticipating, and responding to external changes on the part of a firm's key strategic managers. Responsiveness is achieved by inducing managers to think beyond their immediate circumstances, often forcing them to change major courses of action. In Box 7.1, we have summarized the story of a firm that changed its course of technology development as a result of a critical piece of technology intelligence. As illustrated by the story, the technological intelligence gathering in the firm started when a piece of data was shared by a potential competitor (the manager of the Far Eastern company). As the

---

BOX 7.1

THE VALUE OF TECHNICAL INTELLIGENCE

A company's vice president for R&D had just given an exciting talk on what the firm believed would be the next major technological breakthrough in its business—one that would establish the company as the industry's technological leader and lay the groundwork for a marketing plan to introduce a new system based on that technology. But during the Question and Answer session, a manager from the Far East commented that his firm had also investigated such an approach and had found that the technology could be produced.

The vice president asked his intelligence director to check that out. The company reviewed the competitive intelligence files and conducted a patent search, but found nothing. However, a scan of foreign language literature—which had to be translated into English—and some intelligence gathering in the Far Eastern firm's home country revealed that the firm had indeed been active in the field for

a number of years. An assessment by the company's intelligence department and the R&D staff concluded that this firm had at least an 18-month jump on it in terms of research and product development.

The company compared the two organizations' current and projected technological positions and concluded that the costs of catching up were prohibitive. It weighed the possible threat posed by the small foreign competitor against the potential risk of another major competitor acquiring the technology. The company decided to acquire the smaller firm.

This allowed the company to reassign the majority of scientists and engineers involved in R&D to other projects. The remaining engineers used the Far Eastern firm's technology to develop the company's own advanced system—and move the introductory date up by at least a year.

Source: Herring, Jan P. "Scientific and Technical Intelligence: The Key to R&D," *Journal of Business Strategy,* May/June 1993. Vol. 14. No. 3, pp. 10–12.

firm gathered requisite data, it better understood the nature of the threat. This, in turn led the firm to acquire the smaller firm, thus cutting down the time to market and potentially thwarting a major competitor from entry through acquisition.

We have seen that, when an industry reaches maturity, the major technological threats are likely to come from outside the industry, but incumbent firms are unlikely to detect these threats. Such blind spots are reduced with appropriate technology intelligence. In short, at the process level, technology intelligence gathering offers one basis for organizational learning.

LEVELS OF TECHNOLOGY INTELLIGENCE

We may identify three broad types of intelligence suitable for different types of strategic decisions: (1) macrolevel, (2) industry or business level, and (3) program or project level.

Macro-level technology intelligence refers to broad technology trends that are developing in an economy, which may influence the functioning of national economies, specific industrial sectors, and specific industries within them.

Industry or business-level intelligence refers to technology trends and factors that affect or are likely to affect specific industries.

Program or project-level intelligence refers to technology-related factors for a specific technology-related program or project.

These three levels of technology intelligence differ in terms of (1) the characteristics of intelligence and (2) the level of applicability.

CHARACTERISTICS OF INTELLIGENCE

The levels of intelligence differ in terms of three characteristics: breadth of technologies, clarity of trends, and the degree of precision of trends.

At the macro level, technology trends are typically likely to be general, imprecise, ambiguous, and often directional. For example, one such trend may be the emerging influence of biotechnology in agricultural industries; this, however, does not specify which technologies are likely to be useful to agriculture, nor does it tell when such technologies will begin to industry in the future. As summarized in the opening vignette, AT&T focused on the convergence of three hitherto unrelated industries—computers, video, and telecommunications; this convergence is an example of a macro-level trend.

Industry or business-level intelligence focuses on specific technologies, although the trends may be quite imprecise. For example, the multimedia evolution portrayed by AT&T involves fairly specific technologies; however, the exact nature of the relationships that are developing between computers and the telecommunications sector is still open and likely to be subjected to the actions taken by the firms within these two industries.

Project or program-related technology information has to be, by its very nature, very specific. For example, if a firm is designing an "environment-friendly" (green) product, very specific technologies need to be tracked, technologies that are useful for developing the product. Further, the intelligence that is needed at this level has to be precise and timely so that immediate action can be taken by a particular firm.

LEVEL OF APPLICABILITY

Macro-level technology environment trends are particularly useful for two types of decisions. First, the regulatory agencies or federal government often track macro-level intelligence to advise on national technology policy decisions. Similarly, firms use macro levels of technology intelligence as inputs to long-term strategy development. For example, a firm that is in agriculture may want to develop a technology strategy to incorporate biotechnology trends within its operations. This is likely to be a long-term strategy, and macro-level intelligence is particularly useful for making such decisions. As seen in the AT&T example, macro-level intelligence is fueling its Year 2000 strategy. The industry or business-level intelligence is probably useful for firms engaged in strategy formulation in specific industries. They are more useful for medium-term decisions. Finally, project-level intelligence is applicable primarily for short-range decisions at the operating level. Such decisions may include specific new products, specific plans, or process changes being contemplated in organizations.

We have discussed the three levels of intelligence to highlight the point that technology intelligence should be useful for the kinds of decisions under consideration in an organization. Table 7.1 summarizes the differences among the three levels of intelligence.

EXTERNAL VERSUS INTERNAL TECHNOLOGY INTELLIGENCE

It is useful to distinguish between external and internal intelligence: External intelligence focuses on developments taking place outside a firm; internal intelligence focuses on projects and technologies within the firm. During technology strategy formulation, both types of technical intelligence—external and internal—are needed. As shown in Figure 7.2, generating external technology intelligence is called "mapping" the technology environment, whereas internal intelligence generation is referred to as "technology audit." Firms may differ in terms of their need for formal processes of gathering external and internal technical intelligence.

- In small firms, where the entrepreneur is chief technologist, she holds in her head the relevant internal technical intelligence. As the focus of small firms tends to be relatively narrow, the entrepreneur may have the requisite external intelligence necessary for making key decisions. This is especially true if she is working on a new technology or a new product using state-of-the-art technology. Usually, elaborate mapping of technology environment or technology audit is not necessary in the case of start-ups or relatively small firms.

TABLE 7.1   Differences Among Levels of Intelligence

Level	Characteristics	Applicability
Macro	General technology trends Directional, imprecise, ambiguous	Long-range focus National and corporate levels
Business	Specific technologies General trends	Medium-range focus Business strategy
Program/Project	Specific technologies Specific trends	Short-range focus Product, process, and materials

- In large firms operating in a single industry, mapping the technology environment may be critical and a formalized activity within the R&D or strategic planning departments. In these firms, the firm's R&D division will have the requisite internal intelligence; therefore, formal technology audits may not be required.
- However, in diversified firms with many divisions, various technologies are often dispersed among divisions, and the key decision makers are several steps removed from the scientists and technologists working at the cutting edge of technology. In these firms, for long-range decisions a technology audit is often necessary in addition to external technology intelligence. For example, when NASA launches a major initiative such as the space station program, it usually starts with a technology audit before significant technology decisions—those that consume billions of dollars—are made.

Because a firm has relatively easier access to internal technology intelligence, in thi chapter we will devote most of our attention to the process of generating external tech nology intelligence.

MAPPING TECHNOLOGY ENVIRONMENT[4]

Mapping technology environment refers to the process of gathering external data an analyzing it to derive intelligence for major strategic decisions. As portrayed in Fig ure 7.5, technology intelligence for major strategic decisions involves both the macro technology environment as well as the industry environment. For ease of exposition, w will first discuss a general model of intelligence gathering and then pinpoint some o the unique challenges involved in mapping the macro- and industry-levels of techno ogy environment.

FIGURE 7.5 MAPPING TECHNOLOGY ENVIRONMENT

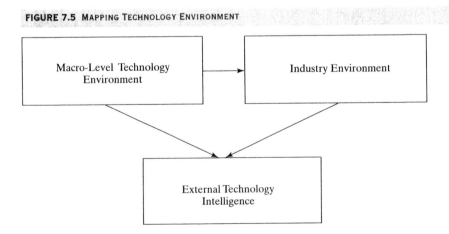

STEPS INVOLVED IN MAPPING THE TECHNOLOGY ENVIRONMENT

Conceptually, the process of mapping the technology environment consists of four interlinked steps:

1. Scanning the environment to detect ongoing and emerging change;
2. Monitoring specific environmental trends and patterns to determine their evolution;
3. Forecasting the future direction of environmental changes; and
4. Assessing the current and future environmental changes for their strategy and organizational implications.

SCANNING

Organizations frequently scan the environment in order to identify indicators or precursors of current and potential change and issues in the technological environment. The intent of scanning is to alert an organization to predictable changes in its environment so that it will have as much lead time as possible to consider alternative courses of action. Indeed, the most successful scanning draws an organization's attention to particular changes and events—both fortuitous and calamitous—well before they reveal themselves in an obvious way to all other organizations.

Ideally, scanning feeds early signals or indicators of potential technology change into monitoring and forecasting. Scanning is especially useful when changes in the technological environment take time to unfold. An organization gains valuable lead time to understand the implications and consider its options for action. Scanning might find signs of technological change, such as an emergence of a new technology (for example, biotechnology). Once an organization has become aware of this potential change, it can begin to monitor its development, project its evolution, and examine its implications.

On the other hand, scanning may unearth discoveries that require immediate action. For example, a scan may detect a new product in the market incorporating newer technologies that may cause the core technologies of the focal firm to become obsolete. Such a change may have evolved to the point where it is actual or imminent, rather than likely, at some unspecified date.

MONITORING

Monitoring involves tracking technology change over time. Specifically, the focus during monitoring is on charting the evolution of trends, such as the development of a specific technology. The trends, events, and activities that the organization tracks may have been identified during scanning; the organization may accidentally become aware of them; or they may be brought to the organization's attention by outsiders.

The intent of monitoring is very different from that of scanning; it is to assemble sufficient data so that a firm can discern whether certain patterns are emerging. It is important to note that these patterns are likely to be a complex of discrete trends. Monitoring ensures that the hunches and intuitive judgments about weak signals observed during scanning are brought to the attention of the organization. These hunches and judgments need to be tracked for confirmation, elaboration, modification, and validation or invalidation.

In monitoring, the data search is more focused and more systematic than in scan
ning. The search is usually guided by prior hunches (seat-of-the-pants hypotheses) gen
erated during scanning or brought to the organization's attention by consultants o
academics. As monitoring continues, trends accumulate into patterns. A picture o
change in progress that may have been hazy and uncertain when first uncovered durin;
scanning could easily become imbued with clarifying details during monitoring.

FORECASTING

Forecasting involves the task of laying out possible evolutionary paths of anticipatec
change in the technology environment. The intent of forecasting is to develop possiblc
projections of the scope, direction, speed, and intensity of technology change:

> Scope refers to the substance of what is being forecast—whether it is a
> narrowly defined trend, such as the *S*-curve evolution of a particular perfor-
> mance characteristic, or a broadly conceived pattern, such as the emergence
> of a major core technology.
> Direction describes the nature of the specific trend and pattern.
> Speed describes how quickly or slowly a trend or pattern is projected.
> Intensity describes the strength of the forces propelling a trend or pattern.

There are two distinct types of forecasting. The first involves projections based o
trends that are relevant and can be expected. For example, once a technology has come
into existence, the performance characteristics associated with it can be predicted to fol
low an *S*-shaped curve. It is often possible to project all such technological trends as the
rates of diffusion of new products or evolution of a performance characteristic.

The second type of forecasting prepares alternative futures. They are based on cur
rent trends and on judgments regarding events that may take place or that may be made
to happen by the firm itself or by other entities such as competitors, customers, suppli
ers, or other environmental actors. Alternative futures are thus brought by the interac
tion of many different institutions in the environment. Alternative futures are obviousl}
more complex and more uncertain than projections. As a consequence, they are consid
erably more difficult to envision and construct. Scenarios serve as the analytical mean:
by which many organizations conceive and elaborate alternative futures. A scenario i:
simply a depiction of how one future might unfold. Many firms routinely develop mul
tiple scenarios that depict possible future shapes of technology.

ASSESSMENT

Assessment involves identifying and evaluating how and why the ongoing and antici
pated changes in the technology environment affect the strategic decisions of the orga
nization at present and in the future. During assessment, the frame of reference move:
from understanding and interpreting the environment—the focus of scanning, moni
toring, and forecasting—to identifying the implications of technology trends for the
firm. In linking technology intelligence and strategic management, the critical question
is "What are likely to be the positive or negative impacts of change in the technology
environment on the organization's current and future strategies?"

To explain the concepts of scanning, monitoring, forecasting, and assessment, we in
troduced them during the preceding discussion as if they were distinct analysis activi
ties. In practice, however, they are inexorably intertwined. This is shown in Figure 7.6
For example, scanning often generates surprises and signals of change that lead firms to

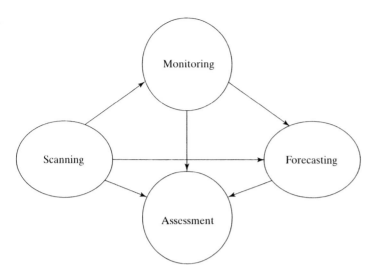

FIGURE 7.6 STEPS IN GATHERING TECHNOLOGY INTELLIGENCE

assess their impact on the industry and the firm's future strategies. Forecasting requires some initial assessment in order to ensure that the organization expends its efforts on the most critical issues.

Having discussed the steps involved in generating external technology intelligence, we will now highlight the unique challenges presented by the macro-level environment and the industry-level environment.

MACRO-LEVEL ENVIRONMENT

We have enumerated several key features of the technological environment in chapter 2, "Technology Environment." These features have four major implications for the tasks of intelligence gathering:

1. The conception of technological environment as a set of interconnected actors—both technology developers and facilitators—suggests that the data sources for intelligence are many and, in some cases, personal rather than impersonal sources.
2. Because technology development takes place over several stages—from basic research to applied research—and because different groups of players get active during different stages of technology development, communication with differing experts is necessary for intelligence gathering. This communication is rendered obscure, especially for basic research: Experts speak a language with jargon and specialized terms that are often obscure to most of the players. Similarly, personal sources of information are usually going to be secretive about many technology developments, because, without patent, many actors try to protect their knowledge advantage.
3. The stages of development further suggest that there is a significant time lag between the appearance of basic research findings and applied applications;

further considerable time elapses between the initiation and applied research project and the appearance of a product innovation in the market.
4. Because technology changes can both be induced and autonomous, only
   some of the technological changes are predictable.

In Table 7.2, we have summarized the linkages between the characteristics of the macro
technological environment and their implications for intelligence gathering.

INDUSTRY-LEVEL ENVIRONMENT

There are two major differences in terms of intelligence gathering at the industry leve
relative to the macro-technological environment:

1. Firms that have operated in their industry for a long period of time will
   have developed sources of information for data gathering. Thus, to some extent the task of developing data sources is much easier at the industry level
   of environment than at the macro-environmental level.
2. Intelligence gathering at the industry level is particularly important to
   medium-term strategy decision making. Industry-level intelligence is much
   less applicable to long-term decision making, unlike the intelligence gathered at the macro-environmental level.

Drawing on our discussion of the impact of technological change on competition (the
readers may want to refer to chapter 5), we highlight the influence of two factors on the
process of technology intelligence gathering: (1) the type of industry and (2) the stage
of industry evolution.

INDUSTRY TYPE

The significance of technology intelligence varies across industry types. We categorized
industries according to three types: capacity-driven, customer-driven, and knowledge
driven industries. Obviously, the role of technological intelligence is far more significan
in knowledge-driven industries relative to customer-driven or capacity-driven indus

TABLE 7.2 Overview of Challenges in Mapping Macro-Level Environment

Characteristics of Macroenvironment	Implications for Intelligence Gathering
1. Developers and Facilitators	Data sources: many; personal and impersonal
2. Stage of Development	Sources are secretive
Basic vs. Applied	Appearance of innovation usually at advanced stages
	Difficulty of communicating with scientists
3. Autonomous vs. Induced Change	Not all changes are predictable
4. Globalization, Time Compression, and Technology Integration	Global search, speedy responsiveness needed
	Process and product reconfiguration likely

tries. This however, does not obviate the necessity for intelligence gathering for all types of industries; however, the nature and frequency of technology intelligence gathering varies across the type of industries.

Capacity-driven industries, where the role of technology in competition is probably the weakest, may rely on infrequent, broad scans of technology environments for strategic decision making. Although these firms may gather intelligence at the industry level, much of this intelligence will focus on the capacity positions of competitors, shifts in industry structure, and competitive moves taking place within the industry.

Customer-driven industries, where the focus of competition is on deriving some temporary advantages, may gather more frequent technology intelligence. Such intelligence will be of a specific nature and be designed to help firms make product-related decisions (for example, new product introductions). Thus, these firms will not only engage in broad but infrequent technological scans at the macro-environmental level, but they will also engage in frequent scanning of specific technologies. Such frequent technology intelligence gathering is oriented toward business decisions designed to capture temporary advantages over competitors.

Knowledge-driven industries will require frequent technology intelligence gathering. Both broad technological trends and specific trends will need to be tracked on an ongoing basis. Because knowledge is the key to competition in these industries, any long-range plan should include broad-based technology trends. Similarly, specific business decisions also will require incorporation of technology trends of a very specific kind.

Table 7.3 summarizes the relative importance of technology in intelligence gathering among the three types of industries.

STAGE OF INDUSTRY EVOLUTION

During initial stages (the social construction phase), a new, perhaps undeveloped, technology has appeared on the horizon. Most of the data pertaining to the technology is fragmented and conflicting. These data reside in technological communities as well as among technology facilitators. This means that, during scanning, the data sources available to attract the specific technology are highly personal, and performance indicators

TABLE 7.3 Industry Types and Intelligence Gathering

Industry Type	*Focus*	*Illustrative Issues*
Capacity Driven	Infrequent, broad	Position of competitors Shifts in industry
Consumer Driven	More frequent, specific	Decision to capture temporary advantages
Knowledge Driven	Frequent, broad, and specific	Decision to incorporate technology trends

have not yet evolved. The monitoring of the technology is rendered difficult by the lack of indicators; this requires that firms pay attention to multiple indicators of performance rather than focus exclusively on one or the other performance characteristic. Forecasting activity is also difficult, because numerous firms experiment with different configurations of design or product specifications. Finally, the systematic assessment based on forecasts is almost impossible during this stage. Further, during this phase the firms need to be able to respond quickly to marketplace needs and, therefore, the scanning–assessment linkage is likely to be very strong.

However, during the incremental change phase, after a dominant design has appeared, industry developments can be tracked on a regular basis: Most of the developments are predictable. During this phase, firms can utilize secondary data sources because most of the industry data will be available from published sources. In a similar sense, with performance characteristics now clearly available, indicators are also available, and monitoring can proceed much more smoothly than during the crucial construction phase. Forecasting is rendered easy because the changes are induced by industry structure; technology does not evolve autonomously within the industry. As a result, the scanning, monitoring, forecasting, and assessment cycle can be performed with ease during the incremental phase.

It is important to remember two factors that are crucial for the success of technology intelligence activities during this phase: (1) process technology changes and (2) industry obsolescence.

> Process technology changes assume greater importance during the mature stages of an industry. Such changes may come not merely from within an industry but also from outside the industry. Because the process changes taking place within an industry are not well publicized, they are often much more difficult to track than product changes; competitors are often not forthcoming with information about process technology developments. These changes do not appear in the form of products in the marketplace; therefore, detecting these changes is much more difficult.
>
> As industry matures, it faces the threat of obsolescence due to the appearance of newer technology, even though such technology in the initial stages is inferior to the existing ones. As noted earlier in chapter 6, disruptive or discontinuous technological changes often have their origins outside of a firm's industry. Hence, during the incremental phase the scope of scanning should be broad in order to include industries far outside a firm's field of operations or base technology. For example, analysis of technological change in the textile industry may require that the chemical, plastics, paper, and equipment industries be included. Analysis of technological change in the electronics industry requires a scan of technological developments related to component, circuit, and software producers. In the electronics industry, changes in the field as far away as biological sciences may have implications.

Table 7.4 summarizes the differences in technology intelligence gathering effort between the two broad stages of industry evolution.

TABLE 7.4   Industry Stages and Intelligence Gathering

Intelligence Gathering Characteristics	*Stage of Technology*		
	Early	*Middle*	*Mature*
Focus	Broad	Monitoring	Problem solving
	Precommercial science	Technologies in development	Products/services
	Potential competitors		
	Opportunity generation	Actual/potential competitors	Actual competitors
Types of Information	Developments/abstracts/ inventions/expertise	Customer/supplier	Costs
		Technology trends	Market/industry trends
	Science trends/ breakthroughs	Competitor technologies	
Benefits	Save time	Avoids surprises	Marketing strategy
	New options	Early trend identification	Early warning of obsolescence

Source: Adapted from Brenner, Merrill S. "Technology Intelligence and Technology Scouting," *Competitive Intelligence Review,* 1996, Vol. 7 (3), pp. 20–27.

MECHANISMS FOR DATA COLLECTION

The value of technology intelligence depends to a great extent on the quality of the data that serve as inputs for interpretation and inference. As we saw in our discussion of the steps involved in mapping the technology environment, gathering data and tracking indicators are the primary activities during scanning and monitoring. In this section, we will discuss (1) the challenges of data collection, (2) the sources of data, (3) the organizational arrangements for gathering data, (4) key principles of data collection, and (5) the role of the technical library.

CHALLENGES OF DATA COLLECTION

The challenges of data collection differ over the stages of development of technology.

EARLY TECHNOLOGIES

The data about specific technologies in their embryonic stages is difficult to obtain because much of the evolution of technological change is not in the public arena. This is especially true for developments in basic research. Thus, the data is confined to specialists, scientists, researchers, consultants, academics, and relevant government personnel. The data pertaining to fundamental research primarily reside in scientific communities, whereas technology specifics reside within many specific application-oriented organizations such as corporations, consulting firms, and some research organizations. Tapping these data sources poses at least four challenges.

1. Effort is required to locate these sources of data.
2. The specialists use much technical jargon, which makes communication difficult; even in the case of technological change in the innovation and diffusion stages, a lot of highly local knowledge may not easily be transmitted, but remain in the minds of the individuals.
3. Many technology experts are not forthcoming with the information, as technological developments are frequently shrouded in secrecy and deemed confidential. This is true even for some government sources, especially when technological developments are tied to issues of national security and defense.
4. Indicators such as performance characteristics are often specific to individual technologies. The relevant indicators may vary over the stages of technology evolution; in the early stages, uniform, complete, credible, and timely data are often absent, and standard formats for data collection do not exist.

The secrecy of technology development in the early stages poses critical challenges for firms interested in scanning the technological environment. Yet, intelligence is so important to many firms that they go to unusual lengths to gather such intelligence. In Box 7.2, we have illustrated these efforts by focusing on the industrial espionage conducted by many firms trying to access technology.

MATURE TECHNOLOGIES

Data pertaining to technologies at advanced stages of development are much more easily available. At the national level, macro-level (nation by nation) data pertaining to R&D expenditures—broken down by industrial sectors—level of scientific development, level of R&D, level of scientific education, and government expenditures for R&D are typically available in advanced economies. Such data provide indicators of technological development and are often useful for identifying patterns of changes in the long run—patterns that are becoming increasingly important as we move toward a more globally interdependent economy.

Extensive data on specific technological developments, especially in advanced stages of development, also exist at the national or federal level. Many federal agencies provide considerable data pertaining to their domains (for example, the Department of Energy, the Environmental Protection Agency, and the National Institutes of Health). Some federal agencies primarily address technology issues (for example, the Office of Technology Assessment). Note also that many nongovernmental institutions play major roles in shaping technology developments. For example, the American Cancer Society plays a key role in cancer research.

In summary, data about embryonic or early stage technologies are more difficult to obtain. Yet, for many firms, such data may be crucial in developing a technology strategy: Technology intelligence regarding early stage technologies provides requisite lead time for taking actions in the marketplace.

There are several sources from which data for technology intelligence can be gathered. These sources may be classified according to two factors: (1) the characteristics of the data—personal versus impersonal, and (2) proximity—directly from a technology developer or indirectly from a technology facilitator. Table 7.5 presents examples of different types of data sources.

Impersonal data sources are probably the most commonly used because the information is relatively easy to collect. With the advent of the Internet, search of impersonal

BOX 7.2

TECHNOLOGY INTELLIGENCE GATHERING— INDUSTRIAL ESPIONAGE IN SILICON VALLEY

FBI agents assert that more than half the nations in the world are running industrial espionage against U.S. firms. They all aim at the technology and trade secrets of high-tech firms. Allies as well as traditional U.S. rivals are trying to steal critical aerospace technologies like radar, navigation, communications encryption, and electronic warfare systems. Consider the following examples:

1. French engineers of a governmental agency tried to pry information on the secret chemical coatings of radar-evading aircraft from several firms, including Dow Corning.

2. After an agreement with Japan limited the technology Japan can access as it develops its own fighter planes, the forbidden technology became a high-priority target for the Chinese, Koreans, Taiwanese, and even the Japanese.

3. According to the FBI, of more than 125 firms owned by citizens of the People's Republic of China, many are set up specifically for the purpose of collecting information on certain technologies. Mainland Chinese students compile lists of Chinese ethnics working at U.S. firms. Some are invited to come to China at no cost. The entire price they have to pay is to meet with colleagues in the areas of nuclear physics or microelectronics in Beijing.

4. The French intelligence agency Direction Generale de la Securite Exterieure (DGSE) has also been involved in industrial espionage incidents with techniques such as offering draft deferments to French graduate students in exchange for stolen information. DGSE has considered it usual business to acquire personal computer technology from French nationals working for IBM in France and to pass it on to IBM's French competitors.

Companies are considered especially vulnerable in foreign operations and joint ventures. U.S. businesses are sometimes required to hire nationals planted by local governments to pass on information. Thanks to the personal computer revolution, information once protected in minimal access mainframe computers is now promiscuously distributed on networks among desktop users. Critical information may sometimes be leaving a corporation on a floppy disk.

Although several spies have been clearly identified, in only a small number of cases is there a clear tie to a foreign government. When allies are involved, the incidents are handed to the State Department for secret diplomatic resolution. Some firms, though allegedly victims of espionage, prefer resisting any comment. They do not want to offend the spies, especially if they are big customers.

Source: Alster, Norm. "The Valley of the Spies," *Forbes,* October 1992.

data sources has become increasingly easy. In Box 7.3, we have listed the addresses of popular Web sites for gathering technical information.

Unfortunately, the information is usually not current and cannot be tailored to the specific decision level. Relatively, direct personal sources are more reliable and timely; however, they can be time-consuming. Personal contacts must be handled carefully to avoid accusations of industrial espionage. For these reasons, professional information consultants are usually commissioned to do the intelligence gathering. Such indirect

TABLE 7.5   Sources of Data

	Proximity	
	Direct	**Indirect**
Personal	Personal networks	Venture capitalists
	Sponsored research	Consultants
	Visits	Suppliers/vendors
	Trade shows	Expert panels
	Universities	Editors
	Entrepreneurial firms	Retired executives
Characteristic		
Impersonal	Patent statistics	Industry surveys
	Literature searches	Trade journals
	Reverse engineering	Government records
	Marketing material	UN reports
	World Wide Web	Newspapers

Source: From Paap, Jay. "Technology Management and Competitive Intelligence: Strategies for a Changing World," 1997. Copyright Jay Paap, Paap Associates, Inc., 351 Waban Avenue, Waban, MA 02468. Reprinted by permission.

sources can also be useful in filtering out extraneous information, although some firm prefer to gather the information themselves to avoid losing details filtered out b experts.[5]

ORGANIZATIONAL ARRANGEMENTS FOR GATHERING DATA

Data gathering usually takes a great deal of effort. According to one estimate, in Mo torola the ratio of data gatherers to managers involved in the analysis is about one t five.[6] As a result, firms use a variety of organizational mechanisms to gather data. Thes mechanisms can be arrayed along two dimensions: (1) the time frame of data collectio and (2) the level of commitment of a firm to the technology of intelligence gathering.

1. Time frame of data collection refers to whether the data about technology is collected exposed (that is, after the technology has appeared) or ex ante, where a firm tries to anticipate the development of a specific technology.
2. Level of commitment refers to the importance that a firm attaches to technology intelligence gathering.

We have provided examples of organizational mechanisms in Figure 7.7. Thus, th mechanisms may vary from reverse engineering, which involves taking apart a con petitor's product to understand the product architecture, to chartering organization locations, whereby an organization sets up a lab to provide a window on technology de velopment. For example, W. R. Grace's laboratory in Japan was partly established t serve as a window on technology development in Japan. Similarly, Rockwell establishe an office of external technology development to ensure a continuing exchange of in formation, in their case, from Europe.[7]

BOX 7.3

POPULAR WEB SITES

CI COMPANIES/ORGANIZATIONS

- CHI Research—CHI's strengths are in Patent Citation analysis. http://www.obiresearch.com/
- CI Source—Provides links to CI articles and resources. http://www.cisource.com
- Dataquest Interactive— http://www.dataquest.com/
- Dialog Corporation— http://www.dialog.com

PATENT INFORMATION

- Derwent Scientific and Patent Information—Comprehensive site with search engine for patents and patent related information. http://www.derwent.com/
- IBM Patent Server Home Page—Fast and free access to patent info—including images—copies by fax or mail at modest cost. http://patent.womplex.ibm.com/
- Intellectual Property Reference Library—Patents, Trademarks, Copyrights and more. http://www.servtech.com/public/mbobb/
- Japanese IP—info on Japanese IP and other Asian IP sites. http://okuyama.com
- MicroPatent—free search and modest cost for download or e-mail of patents, patent applications, and trademarks. http://www.micropat.com/
- Questel-Orbit Patent and Trademark Welcome Page—Links to worldwide patent resources. http://www.questel.orbit.com/
- U.S. Patent Boolean Search Page— http://patents.cnidr.org/access/search-bool.html
- United States Patent and Trademark Office—http://www.uspto.gov/
- Where to find patent information on the Internet—Links to worldwide sites. http://www.epo.co.at/epo/online/index.htm

SEARCH ENGINES AND LIST OF SITES

- ABCs of Search Engines: Search Engine Watch—Search Engine News, Search Engine Tips and more about search engines. http://searchenginewatch.com/
- AltaVista Search: Main Page— http://www.altavista.digital.com/
- AT&T WorldNet(sm) Service Business— http://www.att.net/explore/business
- BizTech Network—extensive links to business and technology sites. http://www.brint.com/
- USLIB-L—Business Librarians' Discussion List—http://www.tile.net/tile/listserv/buslibl.html
- Competitive Intelligence— http://crrm.univ-mrs.fr/vl/tech.html
- Deja News—The Source for Internet Newsgroups!— http://www.dejanews.com/
- Galaxy—broad coverage of business. http://galaxy.einet.net/images/bgalaxy/3dswatch.gif
- HotBot—http://www.hotbot.com/
- Internet Business Research Hot List (Montague Research Institute)— http://www.montague.com/scip/cihot1.html
- TheIreConference—Tips for Searches—How to article on finding info on companies and people. http://www.access.digex.net/~schlein/TheIreConference.html
- kim-spy—Here is the "real" intelligence stuff. http://kimsoft.com/kim-spy.htm
- KnowledgeExpress—Provides searchable link to growing number of companies—large and small—sorted by technology. http://www.knowledgeexpress.com/
- Liszt, the mailing list directory— http://www.liszt.com/

Box 7.3 (*continued*)

- My Virtual Reference Desk—My Search Engines—http://www.refdesk.com/newsrch.html
- Northern Light—Excellent search of web and thousands of journals and business pubs. Free abstracts and inexpensive article copies. http://www.nlsearch.com
- ProFusion—Multiple search engine driver. http://profusion.ittc.ukans.edu
- SCIP Web Journal Home Page—http://www.montague.com/scip/scipweb.html

GOVERNMENT SITES

- FedWorld—collection of government sites including bulletin boards. http://www.fedworld.gov/
- Government Resources on the Web—Worldwide government links. http://www.lib.umich.edu/libhome/Documents.center/govweb.html
- How To Effectively Locate Federal Government Information on the Web—Tutorial on using government Web resources. http://gort.ucsd.edu/pcruse/universe/intro.html
- Library of Congress—http://www.loc.gov/
- Library of Congress Experimental Search System—http://lcweb2.loc.gov/ammem/booksquery.html
- The Great American Web Site—Links to Government—http://www.uncle-sam.com/
- U.S. Census Bureau Home Page—Source of basic demographic data. http://www.census.gov/
- U.S. Federal Government Agencies—http://www.lib.lsu.edu/gov/fedgov.html
- U.S. Securities and Exchange Commission—Contains links to EDGAR search (for online copies of all SEC filed documents), plus one of the best links to other government sites (look under other sites of interest). http://www.sec.gov/
- U.S. Naval Observatory—Check your system clock. http://tycho.usno.navy.mil./Timecheck.html

- USPS ZIP Code Lookup and Address Information—Find zip codes for any address. http://www.usps.gov/ncsc/
- Welcome to the White House—Good links to some major government sites. http://www.whitehouse.gov/

GENERAL COMPANY INFORMATION

- Access Business Online&trade—http://www.clickit.com/touch/home.html
- ABI—SalesLeadsUSA—Search of business basics—profiles available at $3. http://www.salesleadsusa.com/
- Breakthrough!—Newsletter on S&T "breakthroughs." http://www.lucifer.com/~sean/BT/
- British Science—Access to articles, links to sites, and monthly newsletter of British Technology. http://britcount/science
- Business Information sources on the internet—comprehensive links to multiple sources. http://www.dis.strath.ac.uk/business/index.html
- Business Wire—Basic profiles for major corporations; links to corporate web pages; press releases going back several years. http://businesswire.com/
- CompaniesOnline Search—Basic info on firm plus web sites. http://www.companiesonline.com/
- CorpTech Database of 45,000 U.S. Technology Companies. http://www.corptech.com/index.cfm
- Corporate financials online—http://www.cfonews.com/
- Corporate information—Links to profiles available on line from other sites. http://www.corporateinformation.com/
- D&B's Online Access for the BBR $—D&Bs available through credit card. http://www.dbisna.com/dbis/product/secure.htm
- EDGARSCAN—Java and HTML interactive search of EDGAR database. http://bamboo.tc.pw.com/edgarscan.html

- EUROPAGES: The European Business Directory—comprehensive source for European business firms
- Surfy.com—Comprehensive search engine linked to multiple other sources—good first cut. http://surfy.com
- Washington Researcher's Search Engine Reference—http://www.researchers.com/searcheng.html
- Yahoo—still one of the best. http://yahoo.com

TRADE SHOWS

- ASAE on the Net!—http://www.asaenet.org/
- EventSource—Your First Source for Planning Meetings, Trade Shows and Conventions. http://eventsource.com/
- EXPOguide Home Page—http://www.expoguide.com/
- TechCalendar—database of technology events, listing of over 2000 technical events worldwide. http://www.techweb.com/calendar/
- TechExpo—Technical Conference Information Center—http://www.techexpo.com/

- TradeShow Central Home Page—http://www.tscentral.com/
- TSNN—The Trade Show News Network—http://www.tsnn.com/

VENTURE CAPITAL

- San Jose Mercury News: Money Tree/Venture Capital—menu driven summaries of new investments limited to last 4 quarters (edit location line and substitute past year date for older listings). http://www1.sjmercury.com/business/venture/
- Price Waterhouse Venture Capital Survey—http://www.pw.com/vc/
- Venture Capital—links to venture capital sites. http://www.killshot.com/vc.htm
- Venture One—http://www.ventureone.com

This resource list was prepared as a student reference for the two day executive program on "Competitive Technical Intelligence," offered by the Industrial Relations Center at Cal Tech Several times a year. For further information on the course, please contact Delores Lee at Cal Tech (626-395-4043), or Jay Paap directly (617-454-1122).

FIGURE 7.7 ORGANIZATIONAL MECHANISMS

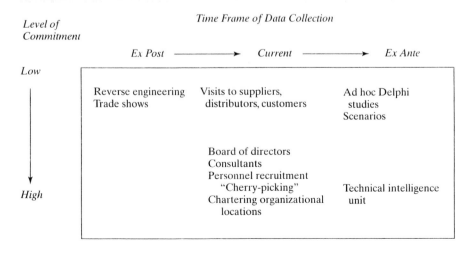

KEY PRINCIPLES FOR DATA COLLECTION

Based on the preceding discussion, we can summarize four major principles to be observed when developing a strategy of data collection.

1. The data collection should be guided by the kind of decision for which technology intelligence is sought. For macro-level decisions, general trends are useful. For industry/business strategy, current and prospective data regarding specific technologies may be needed; for specific projects, unambiguous technical information about specific technologies may be necessary.
2. Scanning in the technological arena should have an investigative element. Data sources must be identified, and primary sources must be consulted. Primary sources are critical, because the appearance of technological developments often takes place at the innovation and diffusion stages, at which time a firm would have lost considerable lead time for strategic action.
3. Because the technology environment consists of both technology developers and facilitators, the analyst should focus not merely on those engaged in technology development, but also on facilitators of technology development. These facilitators, who have access to information regarding technology developments, may often provide critical sources of information that are often kept secret by the technology developers themselves.
4. An array of organizational mechanisms is available for gathering technology-related data. The choice of mechanism will depend on the importance attached to technology intelligence by a specific firm.

These principles are evidenced in the discussion of Air Products and Chemicals, Inc and the signals of new technology and sources of technology intelligence employed to track them. We have showcased the key details in Box 7.4.

THE ROLE OF THE TECHNICAL LIBRARY

The technical library is a gateway to all types of technical information. In tandem with the Internet, the technical library is a key resource in developing technical intelligence. In addition, the library professionals are often essential in identifying the most effective sources of information on technology intelligence. They can organize information and put it in a user-friendly context. Increasingly, they are helping to build the intranet—critical organizational mechanism for developing technical intelligence. In major research institutes such as Battelle, the technical library is staffed with qualified people who understand information technology and resources and who know where to go to get information.[8] In short, the technical library and its staff should be a major source of data and assistance in intelligence gathering activities.

ANALYTIC TOOLS

Two different classes of analytical tools are employed in generating technology intelligence:

BOX 7.4

TECHNOLOGY INTELLIGENCE GATHERING AT AIR PRODUCTS AND CHEMICALS, INC.

Air Products and Chemicals, Inc. proactively searches for new precommercial opportunities, innovations that are perhaps researched and ready for development, product extensions, and technology improvements and peripheral know-how that its researchers and business developers can pursue. It concentrates on unusual sources of information, such as gray literature and human networks.

APTECH, the Air Products Technology ClearingHouse, is a technology search operation currently scouting for more than 10,000 specific interests of 1,300 Air Products people worldwide. It searches for technology using more than 140 regular sources, as many occasional sources, and thousands of network contacts.

This effort has been remarkably successful. More than 500 unique and over 1,000 information items reach *more than* 400 Air Products people each year. The internal customers respond that 75 percent of this information has not been seen elsewhere and that 94 percent of the information *is* valuable. Thirty percent of the responses are "hits": that is, a technology judged by the Air Products recipient to be both "not seen elsewhere" *and* a "good opportunity—will follow up." In other words, more than twice each week, it finds a new technology opportunity important enough for its researchers and developers to spend *their* time pursuing. Many of these hits progress through confidentiality agreements, physical testing, and further development to be integrated into process and product technologies.

Source: Brenner, Merrill S. "Technology Intelligence and Technology Scouting," *Competitive Intelligence Review,* 1996, Vol. 7 (3), pp. 20–27.

1. Tools that assist in developing technology forecasts from the trends identified from the data collected during scanning and monitoring; and
2. Tools that are useful in generating the implications of the forecasts for the firm, or its industry.

TOOLS FOR FORECASTING[9]

The approaches to technological forecasting vary with the stage of technological development and the intent of the forecast.

1. Forecasts of basic research generally fall into the category of informed opinion. This requires a thorough grasp of some science or engineering discipline. These forecasts may take the form of one person's opinion or be Delphic, where the opinions of a number of experts are pooled or averaged. Many business-related technology forecasts (i.e., that focus on applied research) focus on the rate and the direction of diffusion. This makes pragmatic sense: The time period of diffusion is often long, so there is still time to take action. Approaches to forecasting diffusion differ. One approach utilizes historical diffusion curves (S-curves that we discussed in chapter 4, for example). A second approach focuses on diffusion of technology on an industry-by-industry basis.

2. Because technology development is quasi-autonomous, forecasting in the business arena often involves either the delineation of future states of the world or the creation and diffusion of new products, processes, and materials. In the first case, extrapolative tools such as trend extrapolation or scenarios are useful. The creation of these technological changes is not merely the result of natural processes but of creative acts on the part of individuals and organizations. The technological change is very much open to influence by a firm regarding its future evolution. Here, creative methodologies such as morphological analysis are often employed by firms to invent new technologies or products.

In Table 7.6, we have compared several forecasting tools that are used in generating technology intelligence. Of these tools, the most frequently used are the *S*-curve trend extrapolation and the Delphi technique and scenarios; these are employed to forecast not only the technological but the other segments of the macroenvironment, as well. Morphological analysis is uniquely suited for the technological segment and offers great potential in new product/process development. We will sketch these techniques in somewhat greater detail.

THE DELPHI TECHNIQUE

The most common of the qualitative methods, the Delphi technique, was developed by Olaf Helmer, Nicholas Rescher, and others at the RAND Corporation. In this technique, the experts doing the forecasting form a panel and then deal with a specific question, such as when will a new process gain widespread acceptance, or what new developments will take place in a given field of study. Rather than meeting physically to debate the question, however, these experts are kept apart so that their judgments will not be influenced by social pressure or by other aspects of small group behavior. An example of how this approach has been used should demonstrate its procedural characteristics.

Phase 1: The experts on the panel (numbering five) were asked in a letter to name inventions and scientific breakthroughs that they thought were both

TABLE 7.6   Forecasting Tools

	Characteristics		
Tool	**Objective**	**Quantitative**	**Stages of Applicability**
1. Time Series	Objective	Quantitative	Growth/Maturity
2. *S*-curves	Objective	Quantitative	Growth/Maturity
3. Simulation	Objective	Quantitative	Business situation
4. Scenario	Mixed	Quantitative and judgmental	Wide applicability
5. Delphi	Subjective	Qualitative	Early stage technology
6. Morphological analysis	Objective	Quantitative	Developing new products, processes, or materials

urgently needed and could be achieved in the next 50 years. Each expert was asked to send his list back to the coordinator of the panel. From these lists, a general list of 50 items was compiled.

Phase 2: The experts were then sent the list of 50 items and asked to place each of them in one of the 5-year time periods into which the next 50 years had been divided, on the basis of a 50-50 probability that it would take a longer or shorter period of time for the breakthroughs to occur. Again, experts were asked to send their responses to the panel coordinator. (Throughout this procedure, the experts were kept apart and asked not to approach any other members of the panel.)

Phase 3: Letters sent to the experts told them on which items there was a general consensus and asked those who did not agree with the majority to state their reasons. On those items on which there was no general agreement, the experts were also asked to state their reasons for their widely divergent estimates. As a result, several of the experts reevaluated their time estimates, and a narrower range for each breakthrough was determined.

Phase 4: To narrow the range of time estimates still further, the phase 3 procedure was repeated. At the end of this phase, 31 of the original 49 items on the list could be grouped together as breakthroughs for which a relatively narrow time estimate of their occurrence had been obtained. Thus, the government exercise was able to obtain considerable information about the major breakthroughs and, for at least 31 of them, when they were most likely to occur.

The Delphi method, unlike many forecasting methods, does not have to produce a single answer as its output. Instead of reaching a consensus, the Delphi approach can leave a spread of opinions, because there is no particular attempt to get unanimity. The objective is to narrow the quartile range as much as possible without pressuring the respondent. Thus, justified deviant opinion is allowed by this approach.

A variety of situations exist within business or nonprofit institutions in which the Delphi technique can be utilized. In the business setting, this technique is generally used by groups of experts both in and outside the company. An important aspect of such a group is that each expert need not be well qualified in exactly the same area. Rather, each can be qualified in only subparts of the area of concern, with at least one expert in every subpart. In this way, the entire problem area is covered, and information can be processed about several areas of interest. The initial questionnaire distributed to the group of experts might seek to establish the general products or production processes for which there will be future demand. The subsequent phases would then give the panel members feedback on the results of the first phase and would attempt to have the panel reach some consensus on the problem. The final phases might seek to detail some of the specific products and processes on which there was a consensus and attempt to discover the best of the available alternatives and the time at which they could be expected to be ready. An example of the application of the Delphi technique in nonprofit or governmental institutions is the U.S. Air Force's Project Forecast, where opinions were gathered from experts about developments of new physical phenomena, and forecast implications for future systems, such as aircraft, were derived.

Despite its widespread use, the Delphi method has some disadvantages. The general complaints against it have been insufficient reliability, oversensitivity of results to

ambiguity of questions, difficulty in assessing the degree of expertise, and the impossi
bility of taking into account the unexpected. These complaints are only relative, and the
Delphi method should be judged in terms of the available alternative. The same objec
tions apply even more critically to the less systematic methods of forecasting.

THE *S*-CURVE APPROACH

One of the most applicable and frequently used curves by technological forecasters i
the *S*-curve. As we saw in our discussion of innovation (chapter 3, "Process of Technol
ogy Change: Innovation"), *S*-curve implies a slow start, a steep growth, and then a
plateau; this curve shows a characteristic form for many technological development
and for the sales of several products. The use of an *S*-curve in representing growth can
be applied to product sales and technology and pertain even more broadly to a given
parameter; for example, the *S*-curve has been applied to such things as the maximum
speed of transportation. Figure 7.8 shows the time period from trains to nuclear rock
ets. By connecting the tangents of each of the individual growth curves in the figure, an
envelope *S*-curve can be developed. In this particular case, the upper limit of the curv
can be recognized as the absolute or natural limit on transportation speed, such as th
velocity of light or the exhaustion of some fixed resource. In most instances, howeve
predicting the point at which one finds oneself on such an envelope *S*-curve may be ex
tremely difficult. Nonetheless, the insights generated by the approach are usually valu
able for planning technology investment.

SCENARIOS

Scenarios represent hypothetical descriptions of the sequences of future events an
trends, that is, plausible alternative futures. They typically include trends, patterns
events, assumptions pertaining to these, conditions in the current environment, and th
dynamics that lead from the current state of the environment to some future state.

Scenarios serve several purposes:

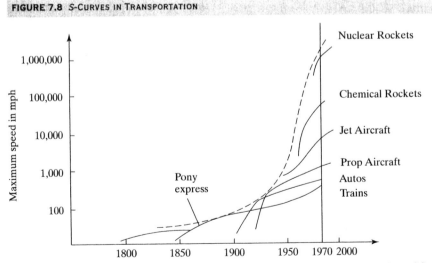

FIGURE 7.8 *S*-Curves in Transportation

Source: From *Forecasting Methods for Management 5th Edition* by Steven Wheelwright and Spyros Makri
dakis, 1989. Reprinted by permission of John Wiley & Sons, Inc.

- They provide an opportunity for a firm to describe or lay out possible blue-prints of the future. In so doing, they allow the firm to examine the future by searching for and postulating linkages among different aspects of the macroenvironment.
- They serve as an explicit context for identifying assumptions, clarifying perceptions about the environment, and assessing risks and implications of environmental change.
- Scenarios provide a context for using other environmental analysis techniques: They serve as a collection of insights for evaluating, adjusting, and making sense out of more formal analytical techniques, such as the Delphi technique.

Developing a scenario is usually done in seven steps:

1. *Identify the strategic decision context.* Scenarios lay out alternative plausible futures that will serve as a context within which strategic decisions facing the organization will be made. The content of scenarios should be guided by the strategic decisions under consideration. For example, if some strategic decisions are strongly impacted by technological change, scenarios may be focused upon likely developments in the technology arena and their impacts on the organization.

2. *Identify key industry, competitive, and organizational forces.* The first step can be further refined when we remember that strategic decisions are impacted by the industry, competitive, and organizational context within which they are made.

3. *Identify key macroenvironmental forces.* In this step, the challenge is to identify the forces in the macroenvironment that will impact the forces in the industry and organizational context.

4. *Analyze key forces.* In this step, the firm develops an understanding of the interrelationships among the macroenvironmental forces identified in the previous step: To what extent are the forces reinforcing, opposing, or disjointed? By identifying forces that tend to reinforce each other or are opposing, the number of scenarios that are created in the next step may be considerably reduced.

5. *Develop scenario logics.* This step is the core of the scenario process. It involves building a scenario around a set of relationships among the macroenvironmental forces noted in the previous step. By the word *logic,* we mean the rationales or glue that holds the story line in the scenario together. The logic provides the explanations for how the elements in the scenario fit together. Creating a small number of logics (i.e., different scenarios) is usually useful. Different logics identify different linkages among the macroenvironmental forces, different assumptions, and possibly different scenario outcomes. These differences help to sharpen the insight into the relationships among the scenario's elements. The most difficult part of selecting scenario logics is to incorporate the dominant environmental forces in consistent ways without creating too many scenarios or different logics. The primary output of this step is skeletal scenarios. This implies relatively simple causal statements that show the logic linking the key environmental forces.

6. *Elaborate the scenarios.* The skeletal scenarios may be elaborated in varying degrees of detail, depending on the knowledge base of the scenarios' users and providers. Scenarios can range from simple descriptions or summaries of the major environmental forces and the logics connecting them to highly complex and detailed analyses of the interactions of the environmental forces and their impact on the decision variables.

7. *Identify implications for strategic decisions.* In this step, the implications of alternate scenarios for the relevant decision context must be clearly identified. Thus, the purpose of this step is to move from the outside-in perspective of the previous four steps to an inside-out perspective: What do the scenarios imply for the decision context of the organization?

Scenarios are used in product planning (Morris 1982) and in creating end-centu[ry] narios (Martin and Mason 1982). In Box 7.5, we have illustrated a recent use of s[cenar]ios in technology planning at Noranda.

Morphological Analysis

The morphological method was developed by the well-known Swiss astro[nomer] Zwicky in his work in the field of jet engines. Morphological research concern[s] with the development of the practical application of basic methods that will allo[w] discover and analyze the structural interrelations among objects, phenomena, an[d con]cepts and to explore the results gained for the construction of a sound world. Suc[h de]finition of the morphological method goes beyond just another forecasting appli[cation] to a systematic approach toward thinking and finding ways to solve problems. The [tech]nique has been applied to industrial situations as well as to a number of purely [theo]retical ones in the area of technological possibilities.

Zwicky distinguishes five essential steps that constitute the morphological m[ethod]

Step 1: The problem must be explicitly formulated and defined.

Step 2: All parameters that may enter into the solution must be identified and characterized.

Step 3: A multidimensional matrix (the morphological box) containing al[l] parameters identified in step 2 must be constructed. This matrix will contain all possible solutions.

Step 4: All solutions of the morphological box should be examined for their feasibility and analyzed and evaluated with respect to the purposes to be achieved.

Step 5: The best solutions identified in step 3 should be analyzed, possibl[y] in an additional morphological study, according to their feasibility and the r[e]sources and means available.

In Box 7.6, we have illustrated how morphological analysis was used to deve[lop a] jet engine.

An attractive characteristic of morphological research is the assessment of th[e like]lihood that a future technology (or a square in the morphological box) will be re[alized]. This is calculated as a function of what Zwicky calls morphological distance. (I[t is the] number of parameters by which the existing technology differs from a speci[fied]

BOX 7.5

SCENARIO FOR PLANNING
NORANDA'S FUTURE

At the beginning of 1996, Noranda Inc. was searching for a new strategy. With revenues of $9.7 billion (Canadian) and operating assets of $14.9 billion, Noranda was a diversified natural resources giant. It ranked 18th in R&D spending in Canada. Business magazine surveys identified Noranda as one of the most respected companies in Canada. Its operating businesses were grouped into mining and metallurgy, forest products, and oil and gas. However, Noranda's rate of return was unsatisfactory: Over the previous decade, its ROE had been only 6 percent.

At the time, Noranda began to consider using scenario planning, although few industrial companies had worked with the discipline.

In February and March 1996, Noranda decided to test the field. Consultations opened with then-chairman David Kerr and heads of Noranda's constituent companies. Although the participants agreed to take tentative moves on scenario planning, most believed at the time that it was to be a leap of faith. At the time of inception, no one within the company had any idea of what the results of the process would be, or even if anything practicable would emerge.

The work began in June 1996. Courtney Pratt served as champion for the process, the key sponsor and coordinator. He assembled 45 people to form a steering committee. The group was composed of senior executives from across the Noranda group, as well as senior executives from the holding company, Noranda Inc. Each business unit nominated a person from among Noranda's best and brightest: 15 managers or senior professionals with keen minds and the ability to think laterally. The amount of work required that they commit 75 percent of their time to scenario planning for 6 months.

The scenario group had 6 months to develop stories about probable futures. Determining the key question to be answered by scenario planning was essential if the entire exercise was to have meaning. The group decided that asking what the world would be like in 10 to 15 years *in ways that are relevant to Noranda* was essential. The scenarios had to have practical value. They had to answer such questions as: Which businesses have the most growth potential; which offer the greatest competitive advantage; which will produce the greatest returns for shareholders?

The range of influences on the questions required a matrix. The most difficult exercise of all was deciding on the *drivers* that would make up the matrix axes. The drafting team identified a broad range of candidates.

They were grouped into the predictable (such as demographics) and unpredictable (such as geopolitical developments). Understanding unpredictable factors is a key to determining influences. Just arriving at this point required 3 to 4 months of extensive research and discussion. Determining the axes was by trial and error. Some choices, although obvious topics of interest to Noranda (such as the environment), didn't work. Rather, they seemed more results than drivers.

Geopolitics emerged as one axis. Geopolitical developments would definitely affect Noranda. Would they experience an expansion in the free flow of goods, capital, ideas, and people around the world? Would they experience coordinated global trade policy? Could there be a possible reversal of such liberal trends?

Technology emerged as the other axis. The degree to which technology would deliver its full potential—whether there would be quantum leaps in technical development;

Source: From "Planning Noranda's Future," by Courtney Pratt, *Research Technology Management,* Jan-Feb 1999. Reprinted by permission.

Box 7.5 (*continued*)

whether it would increase productivity, have a positive result on jobs, the environment and overall quality of life—all made a compelling case for a technology axis. Technology could bring quantum improvements for everyone, it might have only incremental benefits, or it could have deleterious effects in the form of, say, job losses.

Scenario-driver teams grouped issues and outcomes into related clusters to develop the scenario outline, and they developed rich and detailed stories for each scenario. The following summarizes the four scenarios that emerged.

1. Power shift—This scenario essayed a fundamental change in global economics. The first world of the United States, Japan, and Europe would lose dominance to less developed regions. Deregulation and freer trade policies would increase trade and investment. The new economies would apply the best technology in key industries. New markets and open borders would steady economic growth among regions, with the highest rates occurring in developing economies and lower but stable growth among developed ones.

2. Technoglobe—In this scenario, most regions of the world would be connected by a reinforcing cycle of economic growth, freer trade, and political liberalization. Change would be most significant by individual sector. Technology would boost productivity and shake up industries. Despite sector and market volatility, businesses adjust. Freer trade, freer information, political liberalization, and broad distribution of technology would allow for fast adjustments. Employees displaced by technology would find new jobs in emerging sectors. A positive world convergence would be the result.

3. Islands—This scenario suggests that despite the opportunity and promise of technology, and the general global growth it would create, regions of the world would differ greatly in economic prospects, creating distinct islands. Islands of wealth, such as North America, would contrast with islands of poverty in parts of Africa. Regional disparities would be aggravated by small elites within the poor zones enjoying wealth and technology, with large underclasses either displaced by it or unable to find better opportunities. Restricted global trade would erode employment opportunities.

4. Stagnation and fragmentation—The fourth and darkest scenario supposes a world of barricaded economic frontiers with slow and volatile economic growth. The developed world would plod along modestly and erratically. In the face of rising unemployment, the United States and Europe would elect protectionist governments. Other nations would retaliate, crippling international trade and forcing a prolonged recession. Emerging economies would grow slowly and be disrupted by tribal conflicts and wars. International regulators and standard-setters would lose relevance as nations opted for self-interest.

After the four scenarios emerged, Noranda wanted a sense of which seemed most probable. The assessment team created the notion of momentum trajectory: certain forces already at work that would push the world in a particular direction over the medium term (5 to 7 years). Over the short term, it was concluded, the world would move along a trajectory toward *power shift*. Over the longer term, the trajectory arc was judged to move toward *technoglobe*.

MORPHOLOGICAL ANALYSIS AND THE
DESIGN OF THE JET ENGINE

An example of the morphological analysis is the attempt of Zwicky in the late 1930s to identify possible propulsive power plants that could be activated by chemical energy. He distinguishes six parameters that define all possible jet engines that can be activated by chemical energy.

P_1: The medium through which the jet engine moves. Four components relate to the first parameter:

 P_{11}, denoting that the jet engine moves through a vacuum,

 P_{12}, denoting that the jet engine moves in the atmosphere,

 P_{13}, denoting that the jet engine moves in large bodies of water, and

 P_{14}, denoting that the jet engine moves in the solid surface strata of the earth.

P_2: The type of motion of the propellant in relation to the jet engine, with the following four components:

 P_{21}, denoting a propellant at rest,

 P_{22}, denoting a translatory motion,

 P_{23}, denoting an oscillatory motion, and

 P_{24}, denoting a rotary motion.

P_3: The physical state of the propellant, with the following three components:

 P_{31}, denoting a gaseous physical state,

 P_{32}, denoting a liquid physical state, and

 P_{33}, denoting a solid physical state.

P_4: The type of thrust augmentation, with the following three parameters:

 P_{41}, denoting no thrust augmentation,

 P_{42}, denoting no internal thrust augmentation, and

 P_{43}, denoting no external thrust augmentation.

P_5: The type of ignition, with the following two parameters:

P_{51}, denoting a self-igniting engine, and

P_{52}, denoting an external ignited engine.

P_6: The sequence of operations, with the following two parameters:

 P_{61}, continuous operation, and

 P_{61}, intermittent operation.

From this morphological box of six parameters, we can identify 576 combinations of parameters ($4 \times 4 \times 3 \times 3 \times 2 \times 2 = 576$), which might represent different jet engines. Each would have to be studied for its feasibility and analyzed and evaluated with respect to its ability to achieve a specific set of objectives. The large number of alternatives makes impossible the examination of all of them (step 4); therefore, Zwicky had to pick some of them at random and start studying them or discover some principle that would relate a number of possible alternatives so that he could study them as a group. Thus, the aim is to reduce as far as possible the number of alternatives to be evaluated.

Even after that, Zwicky was still faced with a large number of engines that had to be carefully studied to determine their characteristics, desirability, feasibility with existing or developing technologies, costs, and the possibility that a certain combination of factors would have a high chance of combining in the near future. If it is possible to solve the problem related to the huge amount of work required, we can then utilize the morphological method successfully. Zwicky, for example, was able with this analysis to suggest several radical new inventions that were sound, at least conceptually, and many of which were later developed successfully. He also mentions 16 patents that were granted to him as a result of his study of jet engines, and he claims that they were obtained mainly because of the use of the morphological approach.

Source: Wheelwright and Makridakis. *Forecasting Methods for Management.* 3rd ed. 1980.

inside the morphological box.) The greater the distance, the smaller the chance of that technology being realized. In a similar fashion, technological opportunities can be evaluated as a function of the number of combinations existing in the neighborhood of the technology that would depend on it. The greater the number, the higher the chance that the technology will materialize either by accident or because it will be needed before some future developments can occur.

Morphological research can be viewed as a kind of checklist that in a systematic manner enumerates all combinations of technological possibilities. Its major advantage is that it allows the user to identify "hidden," missed, or rare opportunities of technological factors that can be profitably developed. It is from this checklist, or morphological box, that both the search for new technologies and their chances of being materialized are calculated. Even though morphological research is simple in nature, it can be a powerful tool in the search for a clearer picture of the future. It is particularly useful in the search for new products, processes, or materials.

All technology forecasts—both macro-level forecasts as well as development of a specific technology—are fraught with error, because technology development generates consequences not anticipated during the time of the forecast. Given the difficulties in forecasting, scanning and monitoring assume importance. Tracking the technological environment on an ongoing basis is necessary, given the "noise" level in technological forecasts and predictions. Forecasts of the future should be regarded as assumptions rather than definitive postulations of what will transpire.

ASSESSMENT TOOLS

The intent of forecasting the technological environment is to provide inputs into strategic decision making. The technological information is transformed into intelligence when the firm draws implications from the technological forecast or outputs of scanning for business strategy decisions. Because technological developments are increasingly accelerated due to time compression, assessment involves not merely deriving the implications of technological forecasts but also, in many cases, relying on the outputs of scanning to inform strategic decision making. As developments accelerate, the firms will have relatively less time to forecast, but they may require adaptation to the rapid developments taking place in the environment. This is much more so with respect to changes in applications than with respect to basic research.

The technological developments may affect industries in several ways (see also chapter 6, "Technology and Competition"):

1. They can affect whole industries in three ways: They can rejuvenate existing industries, make them obsolete, or bring into being totally new industries.
2. Technological change has implications for industry boundaries.
3. Technological developments have implications for the business definition.
4. Technological developments have implications for product substitution and product differentiation.
5. Technological developments may influence industry structure, strategic groups, and competitive rivalry.

One useful means of integrating the preceding analysis is to develop issue-impact matrices. These matrices detail the effect of each of the major technological trends on in dustry- and firm-level factors. Matrix displays of the type shown in Figure 7.9 enable firms to systematically assess the impacts of technology. These assessments should include not only the general direction of change but its timing and intensity, as well. Such assessments form a critical input for formulating technology and business strategies.

MANAGING ENVIRONMENTAL ANALYSIS IN ORGANIZATIONS

Organizational factors strongly influence how well macroenvironmental analysis is conducted and to what extent it is integrated into strategy analysis. The intelligence gathering and analysis need careful managerial attention. Three key organizational tasks can be highlighted: (1) the design process, (2) the internal management, and (3) managing linkages.

1. *Managing the design process.* It is important to manage the process of setting the overarching premises of technology intelligence gathering. Setting these premises is not an exercise in rational analysis, but it should be viewed as an educational effort: The key individuals who play a role in strategic analysis need to be educated about the role of technology intelligence. Managing the expectations about the role, scope, and nature of technology intelligence is a key to the success of intelligence gathering efforts.
2. *Managing the internal process.* The process of technology intelligence gathering also is an issue that needs managerial attention. Two issues related to technology intelligence activities deserve mention:

   - The individuals responsible for intelligence gathering are expected to exercise judgment, intuition, and sometimes speculation. This necessitates internal operating procedures different from those in many firms. Procedures that emphasize decisiveness, specificity, and consensus are not always functional; in contrast, norms of reflection, ambiguity, and legitimacy of differences need to be nurtured.

FIGURE 7.9 ISSUE-IMPACT MATRIX

	Impacts on				
Issue	*Industry Structure*	*Strategic Groups*	*Success Factors*	*Profitability*	*Opportunity/Threat*
Issue 1					
Issue 2					
Issue 3					
Issue N					

- It is critical to manage the time frame of those engaged in technology intelligence activity. It is always easy to focus on the current environment, because data is plentiful and analysis is relatively straightforward; but as time horizons lengthen, data becomes murky, and interpretations are much more difficult. Where individuals are rewarded on short-term considerations, the focus will be predominately shorter. It is, therefore, necessary to manage the reward systems so those individuals are focused not merely on the short term, but also on the long term.

3. *Managing linkages.* The technology intelligence should be a significant input into strategic decisions. Managing this process of linkage by which technology intelligence is both useful and utilized in strategy analysis requires attention to four key tasks:

- The technology intelligence should have direct utility to strategy problems being confronted by a firm. Thus, the kind of outputs useful for corporate strategy is likely to be different from those of the business unit at functional levels. Loss of linkage results when outputs are mismatched.
- Technology intelligence should be timed to fit into different planning cycles. The short-, medium-, and long-term characterization of environmental issues is useful for different planning horizons.
- The form of technology intelligence should be understandable to those engaged in strategy analysis. Although analysis requires the use of several methodologies and its own jargon, the outputs of these are not necessarily intelligible to those not familiar with them.
- The technology intelligence should be given visibility at all stages of strategy analysis. This is especially true for knowledge-driven industries.

HERRING MODEL

In recent years, the Herring Model, developed by Jan Herring, has been used to organize the technology intelligence process. The Herring Model consists of five steps:

1. *Needs Assessment.* What do the decision makers want to know? What problem do they need to identify? What decisions do they need support for?
2. *Planning.* How are we going to find the answers that will supports these decisions? What sources are we going to use? Who can I talk to? Where do I go to find basic secondary information that will give me leads of additional people to talk to so that I can start my primary data collection activity? How will the data be analyzed? What is the time frame?
3. *Collection.* Getting the information in; database searches, phone interviews, working the network and the Net.
4. *Analysis.* Organizing the data into something that is meaningful and that will support the decision you have been asked to support. Looking at it backward and forward, and creating new insights and conclusions.
5. *Presentation.* Communicating what you have found to the decision maker who is going to use that intelligence to make a decision, providing suggestions for action.

The Herring Model is presented schematically in Figure 7.10.

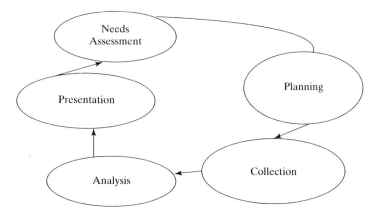

FIGURE 7.10 HERRING MODEL

EVALUATION OF INTELLIGENCE GATHERING ACTIVITIES

It is of particular importance to organizations where technology intelligence gathering activities have been in existence as a formalized process to periodically evaluate their performance. Technology intelligence activity should be audited with a view to assess its contribution to strategy analysis. For example, as the environment changes, previously held definitions of technology environment will have to be discarded. We have seen that in recent years the scope of technology environment has become global, rather than purely domestic, even for U.S. firms. At the organizational level, structures and processes will have to be changed, given the particular set of circumstances facing the organization.[10]

CONTEMPORARY CHALLENGES IN MAPPING THE TECHNOLOGY ENVIRONMENT

Globalization has rendered the mapping of the technology environment more complex and challenging. It is now evident that many advanced economies are participating in technology development. More importantly, firms in these economies are also undertaking significant technology intelligence activities.

- Japan. The development of science and technology intelligence in Japan began in the late 1950s, when the government recognized that its industries needed advanced Western technology to modernize. In 1957, the Japanese government established the Scientific Information Center (SIC). Initially, much of the foreign S&T information was gathered by the government. The Center provided the means for disseminating information throughout various Japanese industries. Today, all Japanese companies involved in international business and trade have their own intelligence units. Typically, they are located in the companies' planning departments. Both trading firms and manufacturing companies use some form of foreign-based intelligence collection. Trading companies have dozens of offices abroad and hundreds of people devoted to this task. Manufacturing companies often use a "listening post"—an office located in their competitors' local regions—to gather both business and technical intelligence, which is then used to improve product and performance. More recently, Japanese firms have established overseas R&D centers, where local researchers are assigned to develop both new and older technologies—often based on what they had created for previous employers. This is transferred back to Japan to be studied and incorporated into products and processes.

- Germany. According to a 1991 study of the technology intelligence activities of German companies conducted by Klaus Brockhoff of the University of Kiel, these programs appear to be isolated from government activities. Over half the companies surveyed have formalized their S&T intelligence programs. About one-third centralized the activities in specific departments. In one fairly advanced program, a German chemical company computerized its early-warning system and prepared a number of countermeasures and actions to be taken.[11]

The technology intelligence activity is thus truly global.

The three environmental trends—globalization, time compression, and technolog integration—have clear implications for the intelligence gathering activity:

1. The scope of gathering intelligence should mirror the globalization of technology development.
2. Given time compression, intelligence gathering efforts should be frequent to spot fast developments and rapid changes taking place in the technological environment.
3. Finally, because technological changes are not always predictable, scanning is perhaps the key to understanding the technological environment. Surprises unearthed during scanning may require immediate action by the firms, skipping the stages of monitoring and technology forecasting.

MANAGERIAL IMPLICATIONS

Although this chapter has been about the steps involved in gathering technology intelligence, and thus primarily pragmatic and managerial in orientation, we will reiterat three key managerial implications:

1. Technology intelligence should constitute a critical input into all major strategic decisions. Thus, managers involved in such decisions should insist that they have the very best technology intelligence in their technology choices that underpin major decisions.
2. Technology intelligence will require tapping a mix of secondary and primary data sources. Thus, maintaining access to secondary data sources and having a network of personal contacts outside the firm are critical to the flow of timely technology information to the firm.

3. Managers should employ systematic approaches to incorporating technology-related information into action alternatives. The systematic approaches should enable them to assess the consequences of technological trends, as well as the consequences of their technology choices.

❖ CHAPTER SUMMARY

Technology intelligence is a critical input into strategic decisions. The technology-related data is interpreted to yield information and intelligence results from inferences of implications from the information. Technology intelligence falls into three levels: macro, industry, and program/project-related. Technology audit refers to the process of gathering intelligence internal to a firm, whereas mapping refers to gathering intelligence about the external environment.

Four steps are involved in gathering intelligence: scanning, monitoring, forecasting, and assessment. Scanning and monitoring focus on data gathering. In technology-related matters, data need to be collected from both personal and secondary sources. The sources may be developers or facilitators, either private or public (see chapter 2, "Technology Environment"). Secondary sources are made easier with the advent of the Internet. The most useful forecasting techniques are the Delphi technique, scenarios, *S*-curves, and morphological analysis. Issue-impact matrices facilitate systematic analysis of the implications of technology forecasts.

The process of technology intelligence generation should be carefully managed. The Herring Model's five steps—needs assessment, planning, collection, analysis, and presentation—provide a useful way of organizing the activity. In today's environment, intelligence gathering should be global and frequent; also, firms have to act quickly on the information thus obtained.

❖ NOTES

1. Mortenson. Robert F. "The Dawn of Knowledge Networking," Session W-39-A, September 30, 1993.
2. Paap, Jay E. "Technology Management and Competitive Intelligence: Strategies for a Changing World," 1997.
3. This section is adapted from a much more extensive discussion of macroenvironmental analysis in Fahey, L. and V. K. Narayanan. *Macroenvironmental Analysis for Strategic Management*. St. Paul, MN: West Publishing Co., 1986.
4. Ibid.
5. Paap, Jay. ibid.
6. Bryant, Patrick J., John Chu, Jan Herring, and Jay Young. "Starting a Competitive Technical Intelligence Function: A Roundtable Discussion," *Competitive Intelligence Review* (1998), Vol. 9(2), pp. 26–33.
7. Contractor, Farok J. and V. K. Narayanan, "Technology Development in the Multinational Firm: A Framework for Planning and Strategy," *R&D Management*, Fall 1991.
8. Bryant, et al. ibid.
9. This section is drawn from Wheelwright and Makridakis. *Forecasting Methods for Management*. 3rd ed., New York: John Wiley & Sons, 1980.
10. V. K. Narayanan. "Managing Environmental Analysis: Organizational Prerequisites," in Liam Fahey (ed.) *The Strategic Planning Management Reader*. Upper Saddle River, NJ: Prentice Hall, 1989, pp. 124–128.
11. Herring, Jan P. "Scientific and Technical Intelligence: The Key to R&D," *Journal of Business Strategy* 11. (May/June 1993), Vol. 14 (3), pp. 10–12.

TECHNOLOGY STRATEGY: OVERVIEW

Motorola, Inc., has been one of the very successful businesses in the United States. The company's evolution and the changing nature of its products reflect the impact of the electronics industry on many aspects of life in the twentieth century.

Motorola began in 1928, when Paul V. Galvin and his brother Joseph E. Galvin purchased the battery eliminator business from the bankrupt Stewart Storage Battery Company in Chicago. The brothers incorporated it as Galvin Manufacturing Corporation on September 25, 1928. It had five employees, assets worth $565 in cash, $750 in tools, and a design for the company's first product, a battery eliminator. The product enabled battery-operated home radios to operate on an ordinary household current. As the battery-powered radios became obsolete, so did the battery eliminator.

During the 1930s, Galvin Manufacturing Corporation produced the first practical and affordable auto radio. Because auto radios were not available from automobile manufacturers, the Galvin auto radio was sold and installed as an accessory by independent auto distributors and dealers. By 1936, Motorola had entered the new field of radio communications with the announcement of *Police Cruiser,* an AM auto radio that was preset to a single frequency to receive police broadcasts. Over the years, Motorola introduced several firsts—new features such as push-button tuning, vibrator power supply, fine-tuning, and tone controls—in the auto radio market.

During the 1940s, Motorola established a research function and hired Daniel E. Noble, a pioneer in FM communications, as its director. The company continued its product development with the introduction of the first handheld two-way radio for the U.S. Army Signal Corps and the first portable FM two-way radio. The company made its first public offering, and the company name was changed to Motorola, Inc. The decade also witnessed the firm's entry into the television business and a product flop—an automatic push-button gasoline car heater. By 1949, Noble had built a research facility in Phoenix, Arizona.

In the 1950s, the company continued its product development efforts with a mixed record. Some of its products, a 3-amp power transmitter, transistorized auto radio, and a pager, met with success. However, its entry into color television was lackluster. At the end of the decade, the company began to face competition from overseas manufacturers.

The 1960s witnessed several strategic moves by Motorola, Inc. First, it continued its process development efforts. It was the first manufacturer to introduce the epitaxial method to mass-produce semiconductors; it also pioneered several other low-cost production methods. Several new products were also introduced—a Motorola transponder for Mariner II on its flight to Venus, a fully transistorized portable two-way radio, the *Pageboy* radio pager, and the first all-transistor color television sets. Second, it entered into several strategic alliances. Its joint venture with National Video developed the first rectangular picture tube for color television, which quickly became an industry standard. In a joint program with Ford and RCA, Motorola designed the first 8-track tape players for the automotive markets. Third, it began globalizing its operations. During the years from 1967 to 1978, Motorola set up plants in Australia, England, Germany, Israel, Malaysia, Mexico, and Puerto Rico.

During the 1970s, Motorola continued its evolution. It moved into related areas of operations, such as the manufacture of components for battery-powered watches. Between 1971 and 1979, the company gained critical experience in producing and supplying integrated circuits, quartz crystals, and miniature motors to manufacturers such as Timex, Benrus, and Bulova. It continued its product development efforts—the 68000 microprocessor; a high-capacity radiotelephone system, computer-controlled radio systems, and products that use the trunking method. In 1974, Motorola exited the television business, selling off Quasar to Matsushita. In 1977, it acquired the Codex Corporation and, in 1978, Universal Data Systems. In 1979, Motorola initiated the quality initiative—the company-wide quality program.

In the 1980s, Motorola rolled out several new products—electronic engine controls for the automotive market, the *Dyna-TAC* cellular system, 32-bit microprocessors, low-cost secure telephone terminals, and RISC microprocessors. Motorola exited from the auto radio business and divested itself of its display systems business, as well as its automotive alternator and electromechanical meter product lines. In 1986, Motorola launched a major employee reeducation program. Its quality initiative was recognized in 1988, when Motorola won the first Malcolm Baldridge National Quality Award. It undertook several reorganizations, as well.

During the 1990s, the company continued the reorganization efforts it started earlier. It also launched new products—wristwatch pagers, third generation 32-bit microprocessors, and *Iridium,* a cellular communication system. In 1991, Motorola opened the Motorola Museum of Electronics.[1]

As can be seen from the vignette, firms continually make decisions involving technology; these decisions often lie at the heart of the firm's competitive advantage and, in turn, the value created by the business. Thus, Motorola's success depended critically on its technology-related decisions, such as the choice of appropriate technologies, as well as the divestiture of technologies whose time had run out. These decisions involve investing in programs to develop technologies for commercial applications, the kind of technologies that are embodied in the products marketed by the firm, as well as the choice of technologies to deploy in its value chain. The decisions may also in clude the appropriate mode of implementation—whether a firm decides to implemen the decision by itself, in conjunction with others through strategic alliances, or throug outright acquisition. In short, technology is the cornerstone of many strategic decision made by a firm.

We will use the term *technology strategy* to describe the strategically importan technology choices made by a firm. Thus, Motorola's success highlights the fact that a firm's technology choices have significant competitive implications. In many competi tive domains, the outcomes of rivalry are determined by technology choices—the suc cess of products and processes that leads firms to secure competitive advantage in thei respective competitive domains. Thus, a firm's choice of technologies influences its cur rent and future competitive position within an industry. In short, the technology strat egy of a firm is a fundamental driver of its profitability.

As shown in Figure 8.1, the technology intelligence gathering activities describe in the previous chapter precede the development of technology strategy. In this chap ter, therefore, we will assume that the requisite technology intelligence for strategy for mulation is available to the firm.

In general, firms execute various pieces of their technology strategy-—R&D, nev product development, or value chain configurations—in two modes. In one mode, a firn implements its strategy all by itself, relying on its own internal value chain and organi zation. As illustrated in the opening vignette, Motorola developed a number of tech nologies in-house and successfully deployed them in products and processes. A secon mode is collaborative: A firm executes its strategy with the help of others. Motorola als had a number of strategic alliances for developing technology. In this mode, the deci sions made by a firm yield benefits both to itself and to its strategic partners. In recen years, the collaborative mode has become widespread partly due to the pressures c time compression and the potential inherent in technology integration. Given its in creasing prominence, we will deal extensively with this mode of implementation in th next chapter.

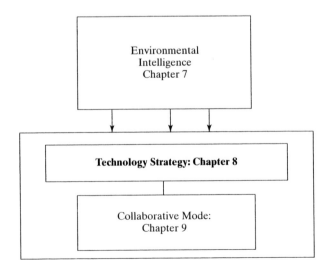

FIGURE 8.1 LINKAGE TO ENVI-RONMENTAL INTELLIGENCE

In this chapter, we will discuss the central ideas behind the concept of technology strategy. We will try to answer such questions as:

1. What is technology strategy?
2. What are the principles underlying the formulation of technology strategy?
3. What are the steps involved in formulating a technology strategy?

Figure 8.2 provides an overview of the chapter. The scheme of the chapter is as follows. First, we will summarize the primary connections between technology and the business strategy of a firm and articulate the reasons for the concept of strategy. Second, we will define the concept of technology strategy and explain its significance. Third, we will describe the major principles that should guide technology choices. Fourth, we will enumerate the primary technology strategy types and their appropriateness for different strategic contexts. Fifth, we will outline a process of arriving at a technology strategy for firms. We will conclude with a summary.

TECHNOLOGY-BUSINESS CONNECTION

THE DOMAINS OF TECHNOLOGY CHOICES

Firms make myriad technology choices as they compete in the marketplace. Broadly, such choices are made in three domains:

1. Technology appropriation, or commitments to build technological capabilities;
2. Deployment in products, or commitments to exploit technological capabilities through new product development; and

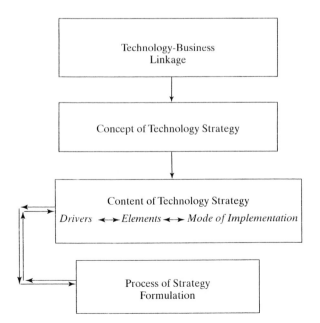

FIGURE 8.2 OVERVIEW OF THE CHAPTER

3. Deployment in value chains, or commitments to exploit technological capa-
    bilities in operations.

TECHNOLOGY APPROPRIATION

A firm's technology appropriation decisions often lie at the core of its future successes.
These decisions influence the ability to create new businesses, to pioneer new markets,
and to discern new strategic directions. Historically, firms aspiring to develop strong
technological capabilities have relied on strong in-house research and development
functions; increasingly, they are also relying on collaborative arrangements to accomplish the same objectives.

Technology appropriation choices embrace both software- and hardware-dominant
technologies. For example, during the 1970s Boeing's aerospace division invested significantly to develop program management capabilities. Similarly, Koch Industries is
committed to developing market-based management, a software-dominant managerial
technology. In contrast, Kodak's definition of leadership in the imaging industry is driven more by investments in hardware-dominant technologies. Box 8.1 presents an example of the set of technology appropriation decisions that led to the phenomenal
success of NEC, a major Japanese firm.

Even when technological capability is not viewed as a source of future competitive
advantage, firms may need to appropriate technological capabilities for several reasons:

1. In some industries, the acquisition of certain capabilities is necessary for
    survival. For example, in the airline industry, computer reservation systems
    have become an integral part of the value chain constellations. It is difficult
    to operate in the industry without acquiring the capability to handle infor-
    mation systems. Similarly, JIT (just-in-time) inventory is now considered a
    prerequisite to be a tier-one supplier to the auto industry. It is the price one
    has to pay to stay in the game.
2. Second, acquisition of capabilities often enables a firm to manage its value
    chain more efficiently and effectively. Indeed, the speed with which Wal-
    Mart can make rapid changes on the shop floor is to some extent attribut-
    able to its capability at telecommunications and its satellite communication
    capability.
3. Finally, acquisition of capabilities sometimes enables firms to redesign exist-
    ing products or to develop new products so that they can differentiate them-
    selves in the marketplace.

Appropriation of technology capabilities is not confined to high-tech technology industries. Even in low-technology industries, certain firms may choose to develop technological capabilities for deployment in their own businesses or for development of
newer businesses. For example, in a capacity-driven industry like agriculture, some firms
are beginning to acquire biotechnology capabilities in order to transform the agricultural sector.

DEPLOYMENT IN VALUE CHAIN

Every activity in the value chain of a firm uses some technology to combine raw materials or components and human resources to produce some output. This technology may
be a simple set of procedures for hiring or may involve complex technologies like logistics, which combines such disciplines as industrial engineering, electronics, and ma-

NEC: STRATEGIC TECHNOLOGY APPROPRIATION TO CREATE CORE COMPETENCY

A core competency requires the management of complex, iterative processes; the bundling of technologies; and the integration of learning in different areas of an organization. A core competency results only when a firm learns to harmonize multiple technologies. It intends to synergistically manage these technologies in conjunction with customer knowledge and marketing intuition. When developed, it provides specific differential advantages over other competitors in the industry and is difficult to imitate.

A strategic architecture allows firms to identify which core competencies they have and the ones they need to develop. The key characteristics of core competencies can be revealed to determine whether the competence is a significant source of competitive differentiation and whether it generates distinct value and benefits for customers. The firm should also try to discover whether the competency provides access to a variety of product marketplaces and whether it is difficult for others to imitate.

An example of strategic architecture is NEC's concept of computing and communications, C&C. NEC believes that the evolution of computing is being driven by two market driven forces: the need for decentralized processing and the rapid changes in communication and component technologies. NEC asks three preliminary questions to define the basic stepping-stones in the evolution of an industry or in the evolution of a series of technologies:

1. What are the new technological possibilities?

2. How might these technologies or different combinations of them change the interface with customers?

3. How are our current and future competitors positioning themselves to approach this industry?

To graphically represent the NEC concept of C&C, the evolution of the computer and communications industry is displayed around a joining path of common discoveries. The stepping-stones in each industry are shown along time axes to find the natural main events to follow. These events converge along the common discoveries. Around the joining path of the tube, the transistor appears. IC, LSI, and VLSI occur. The computer industry develops from the electronic computer through single-function, multifunction, centralized processing, and distributed processing to the recent advances in intelligent processing. The progress of the communication industry, starting with the telephone, is displayed in three different paths:

- Data communication, facsimile, and image communications.

- Crossbar switching, space division electronic switching, and time division electronic switching.

- Analog transmission, digital transmission, and digital transmission network. These three paths converge to the current integrated communication network.

The discoveries in the common path and in the communications and computer paths signal the evolution of both industries. The framework of C&C has been used in NEC as a central organizing idea behind the firm's strategy, providing consistency and direction to complex decision making involving individual markets, customers, and technologies across multiple business units.

Source: The material is drawn from Prahaled, C. K. "A Strategy for Growth: The Role of Core Competencies in the Corporation," in Fahey, L., and Randall, R. M. (Eds.) *Portable MBA in Strategy,* New York: John Wiley & Sons, 1994, pp. 249–269.

terial technology. Figure 8.3 illustrates the range of technologies typically represented in a firm's value chain.

A firm's value chain, as currently configured, represents innumerable technology choices made over a period of time. For example, the value chain configuration in Figure 8.3 suggests multiple opportunities to render each one of the activities faster, more efficient, and more effective. The substitution of fax machines for mail delivery has speeded the handling of documents and information. Computer-aided design, which came into pervasive use in product development efforts, replaced traditional ways of developing new products, and made the design function faster, more effective, and more efficient.

As we have seen in Chapter 6, reconfiguring a firm's activity value chain may occur along two dimensions:

1. Whether specific activities are modified, either on an incremental or on a radical basis;
2. Whether the linkages among the activities themselves are modified, either on an incremental or radical basis.

Technology deployment at the value chain level includes not only specific technologies embedded in the activities but also potential for improvement by judicious combination of existing activities. Thus, a movement from mass production to mass customization represents a radical overhaul of a firm's value chain and requires the firm to make significant investments in technology. On the other hand, TQM focuses on reaping the benefits of continuous improvement within the existing value chain of a firm. In general, technology selection decisions in this domain focus not merely on the choice of specific technology but on the potential for significant technology integration, as well. In Box 8.2, we have illustrated the changes in value chain by deploying newer technologies.

Indeed, for many smaller players in an industry, the decision to deploy technology in the value chain may be a lasting source of competitive advantage. Consider the story of Crown Cork and Seal (CC&S), a firm operating in the metal container business. The firm lacked in-house research and development capabilities; however, CC&S focused instead on building a highly competent technical sales force and an applications oriented engineering group and then forged strong links between the two groups. As a result, CC&S could provide complete technical solutions for its customer's filling needs. Further, Crown Cork and Seal decided to stick to its traditional strengths in the value chain; its competitors directed their attention to diversification and gradually lost interest in the metal can industry. As a result, CC&S is now the only remaining metal can company of the four original major players.

DEPLOYMENT IN PRODUCTS

Deployments of technology in products or new product introductions are a firm's technology choices that are most visible in the marketplace. Technology deployment could focus on:

1. Incremental innovation, or the introduction of new products either through addition or enhancements of existing features. Because every product is composed of a number of different technologies, each product offers a number of avenues for enhancement of its features. For example, intelligent terminals consist of at least five identifiable technologies: storage,

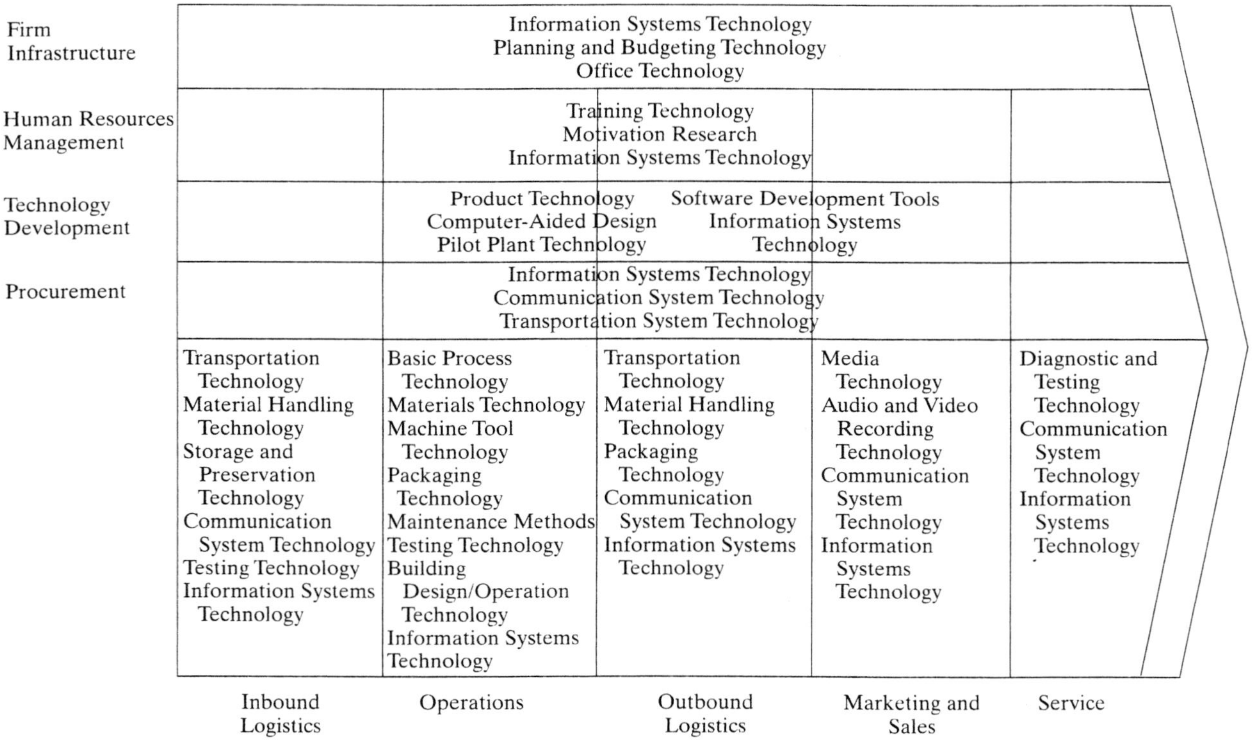

FIGURE 8.3: TECHNOLOGIES IN A VALUE CHAIN

Firm Infrastructure	Information Systems Technology / Planning and Budgeting Technology / Office Technology				
Human Resources Management	Training Technology / Motivation Research / Information Systems Technology				
Technology Development	Product Technology / Computer-Aided Design / Pilot Plant Technology	Software Development Tools / Information Systems Technology			
Procurement	Information Systems Technology / Communication System Technology / Transportation System Technology				
	Transportation Technology / Material Handling Technology / Storage and Preservation Technology / Communication System Technology / Testing Technology / Information Systems Technology	Basic Process Technology / Materials Technology / Machine Tool Technology / Packaging Technology / Maintenance Methods / Testing Technology / Building Design/Operation Technology / Information Systems Technology	Transportation Technology / Material Handling Technology / Packaging Technology / Communication System Technology / Information Systems Technology	Media Technology / Audio and Video Recording Technology / Communication System Technology / Information Systems Technology	Diagnostic and Testing Technology / Communication System Technology / Information Systems Technology
	Inbound Logistics	Operations	Outbound Logistics	Marketing and Sales	Service

Source: Porter, Michael. *Competitive Advantage.* New York: The Free Press, 1986.

243

BOX 8.2

DEPLOYMENT OF TECHNOLOGY IN THE VALUE CHAIN

In 1985, when the former material manager for Computer Systems Manufacturing became head of Distributed System Manufacturing (DSM), he was charged with doubling the return on assets and achieving a 10 point annual improvement in margins over 5 years, while keeping head count untouched. DSM, a producer of network products within the System Manufacturing Group of Digital Equipment Corporation (DEC), had a constantly increasing demand, annual growth rates of 40 percent to 60 percent, and $1.5 billion expected revenue for 1990.

The new management prepared a 5-year strategic plan to make dramatic changes in three key processes: managing supply and demand, manufacturing, and new product development. The plan, based on a vision of a virtually integrated enterprise termed *End Point Model,* was set to reduce manufacturing cycle time and time to market by 50 percent and to triple new product introductions. A systems and information management tools component required the implementation of computer-aided design, computer-integrated manufacturing, artificial intelligence, group technologies, and other advanced manufacturing systems.

In 1988, DSM had achieved the following results:

	Process
Cycle Time	−52%
Time to Market	−30%
Quality	+95 to 99%
Delivery	+85 to 95%
Product Intros	2.5X
Financial	
Inventory	−60%
Revenue	+2X
ROA	+25 points
Margin	+25 points
Head-count	Flat

Success criteria within DSM were redefined from:

Old	New
Supply/Demand	Demand/Supply
Number of suppliers	Number of alliances
Partial Orders	Complete Orders
Delivery to Commit	Delivery to Request
Cost	Margin
Quality at Dock	Quality at Customer
Percent Build-to-stock	Percent Build-to-order

Concurrent engineering and design for manufacturability are widely advocated means for reducing cycle time, using as primary enablers computer-aided design and engineering tools and cross-functional teams. Consider the following examples:

- Nissan, considered a leader in the use of computers to integrate the design process, claims to have reduced design cycle time by 40 percent.

- To facilitate the new product development process, Xerox has created a prototype expert system to facilitate design for manufacturability that will help engineers evaluate alternative designs by using internal Xerox information about existing or easily sourced components.

- Rank Xerox, after finding that its order to delivery cycle took as much as 40 days, introduced process innovations that have reduced it to 4 days for many products. When Xerox redesigned its order management process, it created a list of specific "empowerments" for frontline personnel, allowing broad price flexibility.

- IBM is one of the firms that have decided to outsource outbound logistics, engaging Federal Express to manage and deliver spare parts for computers. To redesign the order management process to be fully executed by one individual or team, the role of the "case manager" has been created. Though IBM Credit Corporation has used this concept successfully, the company believes that it must move generation out to the field sales force.

- Digital Equipment Corporation has used the expert systems technology throughout the order management process, as in the case of the XCON configuration, which saved Digital millions of dollars and many expensive configuration mistakes.

In all of the preceding examples, deployment of technology in the value chain enabled a firm to support its existing business by providing efficiencies or building competitive advantage.

microprocessor, integrated circuits, CRT displays, and keyboards. Each of these technologies may offer differing potential for improvement.

2. Radical or architectural innovations, or the introduction of drastically new products. Firms may pursue entirely new product designs either through architectural innovations by combining existing technologies or through technology substitutions, which render some of the existing products obsolete.

In Box 8.3, we have summarized how Sun Microsystems and Digital Equipment Corporation embedded Reduced Instruction Set (RISC) architecture in workstations, their major product line. The domains in which technology strategy gets enacted also determine whether a firm is technology push or market pull. In a relative sense, technology-push companies tend to pay greater attention to appropriation of technology, whereas market-pull companies are likely to be driven by deployment of capabilities in products and processes. Table 8.1 illustrates the patterns of relationships that are likely to be exhibited by two different technology strategies.

In summary, firms enact technology choices in a number of domains. We may broadly group the various domains into two categories: appropriation of technological capabilities and deployment in value chain and products. These technology choices may be arrayed on the Technology-Market Matrix, as shown in Figure 8.4.

These technology choices lie at the heart of competitive advantage for many firms in their competitive domains, a topic to which we now turn.

LINKAGE BETWEEN TECHNOLOGY CHOICES AND COMPETITIVE ADVANTAGE

As shown in Figure 8.5, broadly, the technology choices in various domains allow a firm to secure competitive advantage in three ways: (1) by creating fundamentally new businesses and competitive domains; (2) by altering the rules of rivalry in the existing competitive domains; and (3) by supporting existing businesses.

1. *Creating fundamentally new businesses.* Firms often pursue basic and applied research, which enables them to discover opportunities for totally new businesses. As described in our discussion of the impact of technology on

---

BOX 8.3

TECHNOLOGY DEPLOYMENT IN PRODUCTS

Sun Microsystems and Digital Equipment Corporation (DEC) product family strategies provide an example of two leading firms in the same industry that were confronted with a technological discontinuity.

- Sun continued extension of its Complex Instruction Set (CISC)-based products effectively up to the point where Reduced Instruction Set (RISC) technology created a discontinuity. Sun developed a new family of workstations with the RISC architecture, based on a microprocessor of its own design: the Sparc chip. In two years, Sun was able to make a clean break with its older-generation workstations, dedicating all of its energies to the family of products that emerged from the new architecture.

- DEC, having a wide range of minicomputers and workstations, had a long-standing strategy of supporting compatibility among its own products and those of major competitors. Its large established base of customers and installed equipment presented an obstacle to the transition to the new RISC architecture, threatening continuity and compatibility. DEC maintained its commitment to its existing family of VAX-station products, slowly entering the RISC technology and planning for the future a new generation of workstation based on a proprietary Alpha chip. DEC had built its empire on the VAX architecture and was not able to find a painless transition for the company and for its customers. It played a dual strategy of sustaining both the new and the retiring product at a time of radical change. It almost lost the company for waiting too long to make the necessary transition.

TABLE 8.1   Technology Push vs. Market Pull

Elements	Technology Push	Market Pull
Scope	Broad and Focused Defined by firm's technology needs	Focused Defined by project level needs
Leadership	1. Seeks leadership in a set of technologies 2. Routinely seeks leadership in product deployment	1. Does not usually seek leadership 2. May often seek leadership in product deployment
Mode of Implementation	In-house R&D and strategic alliances	In-house R&D less important

competition, many new businesses have emerged from technological capabilities that were embodied as products and brought to the market by pioneering firms.

2. *Altering the rules of rivalry in existing competitive domains.* Firms also use technology to alter the rules of rivalry in the existing competitive domains. In these cases, the underlying customer functionality is not new to the marketplace, but through the deployment of technological capabilities in prod-

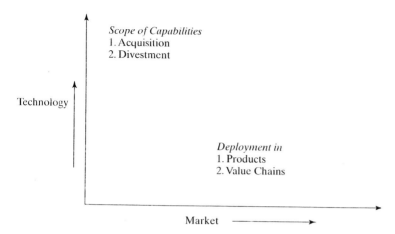

FIGURE 8.4 TECHNOLOGY-MARKET MATRIX

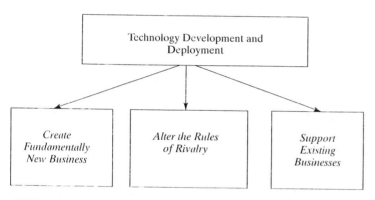

FIGURE 8.5 TECHNOLOGY-BUSINESS LINKAGES

ucts or in value chain configurations, firms may acquire market position to the detriment of their competitors.

3. *Supporting existing businesses.* This option includes both product and process innovations. Product innovation may focus on enhancing product features or improving customer acceptance. Process innovations may focus on improvements in manufacturing processes or on using different or new raw materials. Both are oriented toward improving a firm's competitive position within the existing competitive domains.

Thus, there is a reciprocal relationship between technology choices and corporate strategy. As shown in Figure 8.6, the relationships can be summarized in terms of the three technology-related pathways to competitive advantage.

1. Technology choices, especially in the form of radical innovations from basic research, typically drive business/corporate strategy when fundamentally new businesses are created. Thus, during the emergence of new

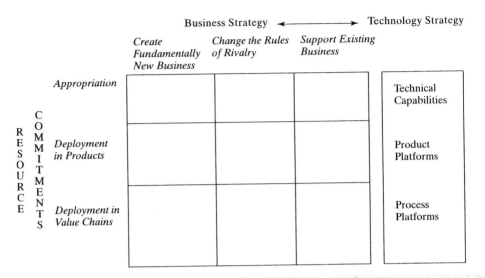

FIGURE 8.6 TECHNOLOGY-BUSINESS LINKAGES

competitive domains or when a firm's primary mode of strategy formulation is technology push, technology choices are the primary determinant of competitive advantage.

2. Technology choices in the form of both process and product innovations also influence business strategies when a firm decides to change the rules of rivalry. However, unlike that of fundamentally new businesses, some features of the strategy game are already formed in the case of existing businesses. Therefore, in this case, business fundamentals assume greater significance in the strategic choices of firms.

3. In their support of business strategy, technology choices are driven by the demands of business/corporate strategy. In this case, decisions related to which technologies to acquire, which ones to upgrade or downgrade, and which ones to divest are determined by business strategy considerations.

The connections between technology choices and competitive advantage are dynamic, i.e., they undergo significant change over time. This dynamism is fueled by the changes in competitive domains and the evolution of firms:

1. As we saw in our discussion of the influence of technology on competition, many competitive domains emerge when technologies create fundamentally new businesses, but over time, as the era of incremental change sets in, business considerations tend to drive technological developments.

2. The connections also undergo change during the evolution of a firm. Recall the history of Motorola that we summarized in the opening vignette. Through its research function, Motorola created several fundamentally new businesses, including most recently Iridium. During the 1970s, Motorola narrowed its technological capabilities by exiting from the television business. Technological capabilities were deployed in products and processes to alter the rules of rivalry in several businesses, and of course, Motorola

wielded technology as a competitive weapon in several existing businesses. Technology appropriation, abandonment, and deployment in products and processes were the primary drivers of Motorola's success.

Thus, there is a reciprocal relationship between the technology choices and business/corporate strategies of firms. When the relationship is fully exploited, as in the case of Motorola, technology is a significant source of the competitive advantage for firms. To exploit the full potential of technology choices, however, there should be close linkage between technology and business strategy decisions. Specifically, we can put forth four reasons for closer connections:

1. Technology directly affects the competitive position of firms. As seen in the preceding discussion, technology lies at the core of a firm's success in its competitive domains. Defining the firm's technology as it affects the ability to maintain competitive advantage is therefore central to market success.
2. Technology competes for resources within a firm. Each firm must decide how to deploy its resources in light of the available opportunities. Selection of one investment area normally precludes an investment in another. Thus, technological opportunities must be judged in relation to other opportunities within the firm.
3. Structure, processes, and information systems for managing technology are costly. The administrative costs of organizational structures and processes and the information requirements for reducing technological uncertainty are quite high.
4. Technology decisions are strategic in nature. These decisions span long time frames, deploy significant resources, and are often irreversible, i.e., difficult to change once commitments are made.[2]

Yet, in many firms there is a fundamental lack of integration between technology and strategy: Indeed, strategists and technologists exist as two separate communities. Ideally, the two groups should maintain close communication on matters of strategy formulation; in practice, however, the two groups are not often well integrated.[3] The concept of technology strategy arose from the need for building closer connections between technology choices and strategy formulation.

TECHNOLOGY STRATEGY: DEFINITION

Technology strategy is a relatively recent concept. After World War II, firms such as Westinghouse and General Electric pursued paths of diversification through internal research and development (R&D) efforts. Although the concept of technology strategy was not prevalent at that time, the roots of the concept can be traced to the R&D practice and the writings about the strategies used to manage research and development in large diversified firms. Later, arising from recognition that technology is an important determinant of the competitive rivalry in high-technology industries, scholars and practitioners began to focus on business strategies, which incorporate the technology dimension. These writings focused on technological innovation and attempted to classify firms according to their innovativeness.[4] The focus of innovation in these writings was the development of new products and processes for competing within technology-based businesses. The idea that technology strategies can exist in industries other than high-technology businesses was not recognized in these writings. It was during the 1980 that the concept of technology strategy came to be advocated and developed.[5]

> *Technology strategy* is the revealed pattern in the technology choices of firms. The choices involve the commitment of resources for the appropriation, maintenance, deployment, and abandonment of technological capabilities. These technology choices determine the character and extent of the firms' principal technical capabilities and the set of available product and process platforms.

Four important points are captured in this definition:

1. Technology strategy focuses on the kinds of technologies that a firm selects for acquisition, development, deployment, or divestment. For example, R&D strategies, which involve investments in the further development of selected technologies, are embraced by this definition. Also, the technologies that are embedded in products, as well as those that constitute the value chain of a firm, reflect the firm's technology strategy.
2. Commitments surrounding technology selection define technology strategies. We used the term *revealed pattern,* i.e., patterns that are not merely intended but accomplished. Execution implies commitment of resources; by commitments, we refer to the decisions to invest or not invest. For example, firms may choose to invest in technologies to be first in the market with a product, or they may decide to adopt a "me-too" strategy. Alternately, they may invest in a major test facility or a flexible factory.
3. Technology strategies are not confined to high-technology industries. Even a capacity-driven industry or a customer-driven industry requires a technology strategy. Such strategies may be implicit and may not reflect the conscious decisions by executives, but nonetheless they determine the choice of technical capabilities and available product and process platforms of the firms. For example, in a service industry like banking, a firm may decide to invest in information technology or adopt ATMs as a way of interfacing with the customers. Similarly, they may also invest in developing the technological capabilities for financial management (for example, neural networks or quantitative analysis groups). Although they are often not conceived as technology strategies by the firms themselves, according to our definition they reflect a firm's technology strategy.[6]
4. Finally, technology strategies embrace both the hardware and software elements of a technology. Although the term *technology* is often associated with hardware elements, the preceding definition of technology strategy includes both software and hardware elements.

TECHNOLOGY STRATEGY AND THE DOMAINS OF TECHNOLOGY CHOICES

As discussed earlier, a firm makes technology choices in each of the appropriation and deployment domains; together, this array of choices is linked to the three fundamental business objectives of the firm. Technology strategy is revealed in the pattern of these choices and reflects the technical capabilities and the available process and product platforms. It could be a driver of business decisions and be driven by it.

THE ROLE OF THE CHIEF TECHNOLOGY OFFICER

In many firms, technology strategy is decided at the top levels of an organization, and chief technology officers serve as the champions of technology strategy. Indeed, technology strategy constitutes the primary task of the chief technology officers. In different firms, different individuals perform the role of the chief technology officer. Titles such as "chief information officer" or CIO (in charge of the information systems design and architecture), "chief technology officer" or CTO (in charge of the R&D function of an organization or the operating characteristics of an organization) or "R&D manager" are now common. Technology strategy encapsulates the important functions performed by these individuals. They provide top management with requisite intelligence and sponsor specific technology selection decisions within an organization.

We will first articulate the key principles that should guide the technology selection decisions and then describe the process of technology strategy formulation.

THE KEY PRINCIPLES UNDERLYING TECHNOLOGY STRATEGY

We have schematically presented the flow of discussion of the central principles that underlie technology choices in Figure 8.7. As shown in the figure, we will respectively summarize the objectives, drivers, decision criteria, and the choice outcomes.

OBJECTIVES

The fundamental objective of any firm is the creation of value for its customers and its investors. This objective is the cornerstone of the contemporary approaches to management of technology. Thus, technology appropriation and deployment, the central activities in management of technology, are to be judged effective to the extent they serve as the instrument for value creation.

The link between management of technology and value creation in many instances is not direct. For example, investment in developing technologies creates the possibility of new competitive capabilities, but they are not real until the firm actually deploys them in the marketplace. Marketplace strategy is driven by the search for competitive advantage, which is the prime driver of value creation. Technology choices are one instrument available to a firm in its pursuit of competitive advantage. In other words, *a*

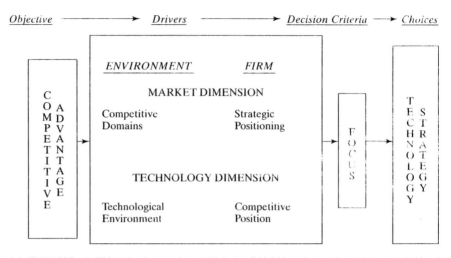

FIGURE 8.7 A SCHEME FOR ARRAYING THE PRINCIPLES

firm should commit resources to technology appropriation and deployment only if th
commitments are judged to result in significant competitive advantage in the marketplace

DRIVERS

Because competitive advantage is the primary objective in technology management
both technology and strategic considerations should be weighed in the process of ar
riving at the technology choices. The process should focus on two major questions:

1. Does the environment offer sites for value creation? If such profitable sites
   don't currently exist, can they be created?
2. Is the firm well positioned to exploit the sites?

ENVIRONMENT

Technological opportunity and appropriability, two characteristics of competitive do
mains that determine the availability of sites where value can be created, are driven b
both the technology and market conditions.

Technological opportunity.   Every product is made up of numerous technologies; nu
merous technologies are embedded in the value chain that delivers the product/servic
to the customers. Potentially, each of the technologies may provide opportunities fo
substitution by superior technologies or improvements in performance and architec
ture, although this may depend on the stage of evolution of the competitive domain. W
have seen that during the era of technology emergence, product architecture and valu
chain configurations offer the targets of opportunity, whereas during the era of incre
mental change, product improvements and process changes become necessary.

However, technological opportunity also depends on the availability of technolc
gies for displacing some or all of the product/processes in the competitive domain. Cer
tainly, the technological environment generates the possibilities for improvements i
product/processes, or alterations in the rules of competition. Because most technologie
evolve along an *S*-curve, the potential benefits of innovation are unevenly distribute

over the life of the technology. *Thus, technological opportunity lies at the juncture of technical feasibility and the requirements of the marketplace.*

Appropriability. The appropriability of the competitive domain will also depend on the market and technological factors. Both factors may enable a firm to appropriate value from its development efforts and prevent the value from being dissipated by imitation. For example, the availability of patents, regulatory entry barriers, lead time in technology development, resource requirements in development, or scarce collateral assets may enhance the appropriability of the competitive domain. Conversely, when barriers to imitation do not exist or cannot be erected, profitable sites do not exist, even when there are opportunities for innovation. For example, in the lobster industry, where there are hardly any barriers to entry or potential to insulate product innovations from competitive imitation, Prelude, which invested heavily in research and development, was unable to appropriate the value from its investment in R&D.

For committing resources to a technology path, it is necessary, but not sufficient, for a profitable site to exist. The firm under consideration must be appropriately positioned to exploit the technology to its advantage.

FIRM

Just as in the case of environment, both technological and strategic factors determine whether a firm is appropriately positioned to exploit the profitable sites. Because technology choices focus on development and deployment, we will deal with each of them.

Technology Development. Different firms are differentially positioned to exploit profit sites through the development of a specific technology. The principle of comparative advantage would suggest that the relative technology capabilities of firms should drive their technology development choices. That is, a firm should have a dominant technological strength relative to its competitors in a technology in order for it to commit resources for the development of that specific technology. Otherwise, the firm should let the competitors do the development.

As we have noted, when successful, technology development leads to three outcomes: creation of new competitive domains, alterations in the patterns of rivalry in the existing competitive domains, and support for firms' strategies. Small firms are unlikely to have the resources to invest in technology development to create fundamentally new competitive domains. In addition to the relative resource positions, technology development for operating in current competitive domains should be guided by characteristics of the marketplace.

Technology Deployment. Technology development creates the possibilities for new competitive capabilities, but they are not real until the firms deploy them in products or value chain configurations. The deployment also requires a firm to commit resources so that the technological opportunity is exploited. The deployment leads to competitive advantage only if it is supported by a firm's strategic positioning within its competitive domain. For example,

1. The firms should have the relevant collateral assets needed to exploit the deployment. During the emergence of the personal computer business, Apple's operating system was technically superior to Microsoft's, but the network of software programmers that supported Microsoft gave it a distinct strategic advantage over Apple.

2. The resource requirements for technology development must be consistent with resources available to the firm.

3. The deployment should deliver value to the customers that can be appropriated by the firm. In other words, the firm's strategic positioning should be such that the value created by the deployment is neither negotiated away by the customers due to their bargaining position nor imitated away by the competitors.

In other words, the firm should be appropriately positioned strategically and technologically to exploit the profit site.

Taken together, our discussion of the drivers highlights the principle that technology choices should interface with business/corporate strategy formulation.

DECISION CRITERIA

Technology choices imply commitment of limited resources. Firms channel their resources to those alternatives that promise the most effective route to competitive advantage. Technology choices compete with other alternatives for resources, on the one hand, and among themselves, on the other. The underlying logic of technology strategy is one of focus: The resources of a firm should be focused on a limited number of choices where the firm can expect to gain significant competitive advantage based on the availability of profit sites and the firm's strategic position.

TECHNOLOGY STRATEGY TYPES

The specific technology choices made by a firm may be deliberate or emergent: In some cases, considerable thought is given to the analysis of alternatives to guide choices; in others, actions are taken, and firms later discover that they had been following a particular strategy. Either way, specific technology choices exhibit a pattern over time. Broadly, these patterns may be classified along two dimensions: scope and leadership.

Scope. Although there may be a number of technological sites available for commercial exploitation, a firm will have to focus on a limited number in its pursuit of competitive advantage. Scope decisions refer to the answer firms develop to the question: What technologies should we be in?[8] Some firms, such as Hewlett-Packard in the electronics industry or Merck in the pharmaceutical industry, have pursued technology strategy of broad scope.

Leadership. Technology leadership refers to a firm's commitment to a pioneering goal in the development or exploitation of a technology as opposed to a more reactive goal. Specific corporate examples are NEC's goal of leadership in computers and communication and Kodak's intent to remain a world leader in imaging. Increasingly, leadership is defined in global terms: The firms chose to be technology leaders globally, by which they mean that they will acquire or develop technologies ahead of their competitors all over the world. However, firms may deliberately choose followership as the critical element of their technology strategy: They avoid the costs of pioneering, but instead focus on exploiting the technologies available from external sources.

Based on the two dimensions, four broad types of technology strategies are available to a firm:

1. Technology leadership strategy consists of establishing and maintaining through both technology development and deployment a preeminent position in the competitive domain in all the technologies for a dominant market position. Technology is the primary instrument for creating and maintaining competitive advantage for these firms.
2. Niche strategy consists of focusing on a limited number of critical technologies to seek leadership. Technology development is selective, and deployment is oriented toward exploiting the technological strength of the firm in selected technologies to create competitive advantage.
3. Follower strategy consists of maintaining technological adequacy in a broad set of technologies. This strategy is focused on deployment, avoiding the risks of basic research. For these firms, technology is not their primary instrument for seeking competitive advantage.
4. Technology rationalization involves maintaining adequacy only in a select set of technologies. For these firms, their technology deficit should be compensated by other competitive strengths in order for them to survive in many competitive domains.

We have sketched the four types in Figure 8.8.

Thus, technology leaders view technology appropriation as a source of future competitive advantage in the markets in which they choose to operate. Technology followers, on the other hand, typically view acquisition of capabilities as subordinate to their business- or corporate-level strategies. Further, niche developers and technology leaders differ fundamentally in their deployment of products and processes:

FIGURE 8.8 TECHNOLOGY STRATEGY TYPES

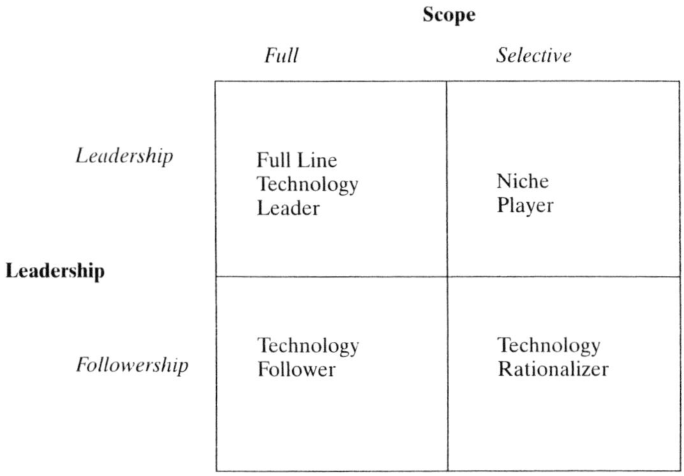

	Scope	
	Full	*Selective*
Leadership	Full Line Technology Leader	Niche Player
Followership	Technology Follower	Technology Rationalizer

Leadership (vertical axis label)

Source: From A. D. Little, "The Strategic Management of Technology," material originally presented at the 1981 European Management Forum in Davos. Reprinted by permission.

- Firms following niche strategy typically adopt the innovative first-to-market strategy. The route through which they can win market share from market leaders is often to be the first in a competitive domain with an innovation and to build a reputation as an innovative producer. In our discussion of architectural innovations, we highlighted the fact that new entrants employ such innovations to gain a foothold in the market.
- Technological leaders can often adopt a second-to-market approach for several reasons. First, they know that the market will be waiting for their entry. Second, they can avoid the risks associated with rushing an innovation to the market. Third, they can leapfrog and come up with a superior product that will render the first innovation obsolete. Finally, by not rushing to the market, they can focus on compatibility, costs, and standardization and thus create superior value.

APPROPRIATENESS OF TECHNOLOGY STRATEGY TYPES

The various strategy types are appropriate for different strategic contexts, characterized by the stages in technological evolution of competitive domains and the strategic positions of firms.

1. In the era of incremental innovation, technology leadership strategy is appropriate for firms that have strong technological and market positions. Niche strategy is recommended for technologically strong but competitively moderate positions. Technology followership requires a strong competitive position in the markets, although the firm may lack technological superiority. If the firm is competitively weak, then it may be forced to adopt a technology rationalization strategy.
2. In the era of technology emergence, the leader strategy is much more broadly applicable, because the technologies and markets tend to be highly fluid. Thus, there are more opportunities to gain competitive advantage.

These prescriptions are summarized in Figure 8.9.

DIVERSIFIED FIRMS

The preceding discussion of technology strategy types primarily focused on single industry businesses. In diversified firms, i.e., firms that operate simultaneously in several industries or competitive domains, technology strategy is obviously more complex than in single industry businesses. Each of the businesses in a diversified firm may pursue its own technology strategy depending on its competitive domain and strategic position within it. In addition, diversified firms may try to exploit the potential synergies among the technologies of various businesses. The connections among the technology strategies of businesses depend on the type of diversification pursued by the firm:

- In technology-related diversifiers, there are significant synergies among the technology strategies of various businesses. These firms typically have core technological competencies; as a result, each business benefits from the technology development and deployment of other businesses. Businesses built around large complex systems such as aircraft, automobiles, or telecommunications switches must be able to apply and integrate distinct

ERA OF TECHNOLOGY EMERGENCE

COMPETITIVE POSITION

TECHNOLOGY POSITION	STRONG	MEDIUM	WEAK
STRONG	LEADER	LEADER	FOLLOWER
MEDIUM	LEADER / FOLLOWER	NICHE	ACQUISITION
WEAK	NICHE	JPOINT VENTURE	RATIONALIZATION

LATE STAGES OF INCREMENTAL CHANGE

COMPETITIVE POSITION

TECHNOLOGY POSITION	STRONG	MEDIUM	WEAK
STRONG	LEADER	FOLLOWER	ACQUISITION
MEDIUM	NICHE	FOLLOWER / RATIONALIZATION	RATIONALIZATION
WEAK	JPOINT VENTURE	RATIONALIZATION	DIVESTMENT

FIGURE 8.9 APPROPRIATENESS OF TECHNOLOGY STRATEGY

Source: Adapted from A. D. Little, "The Strategic Management of Technology," material originally presented at the 1981 European Management Forum in Davos. Reprinted by permission.

types of expertise. Thus, General Electric was able to bring high-powered mathematical analysis from its military research to bear on the development of computerized products in its medical equipment division.[9]

- In market-related or conglomerate diversifiers, the technology strategies of various businesses tend to be unrelated. Even when there are potential synergies among various businesses, conglomerates leave the businesses to run by themselves, deliberately refusing to explore the synergies, if any. This choice is, of course, dictated by the corporate strategy of the firms.

A carefully orchestrated technology strategy that exploits the synergies among businesses can bring about a significant transformation of companies. In Box 8.4, we have showcased the story of Perkin-Elmer which, over a 20-year period, orchestrated such major transformation. As illustrated in the box, technology strategy was the centerpiece of this transformation.

A FRAMEWORK FOR FORMULATING TECHNOLOGY STRATEGY

Technology strategy is usually formulated over four stages: (1) strategic diagnosis, (2) formulation of technology strategy, (3) crafting an implementation approach, and (4) execution. Figure 8.10 sketches the four stages involved in formulation.

STRATEGIC DIAGNOSIS

During the first stage of formulation of technology strategy, a firm focuses on addressing the technological and the business context of the firm. This involves two major activities:

1. Environmental assessment, both technological and competitive, and
2. The competitive position of the firm in both the technologies and markets.

ENVIRONMENTAL ASSESSMENT
Operationally, this means identifying actual and potential technologies inside and outside the firm, assessing the applications that might emerge from them, and determining the impact of these applications on current and future competitive domains. This stage consists of three steps:

1. Technology intelligence. This is the process of identifying technologies and their potential impact on the current and future competitive domains. This process was described in detail in the last chapter.
2. Profiling competitive domains. This step involves the requisite intelligence to interface technology intelligence with the opportunities and threats faced in a commercial context.
3. Identifying profit sites. In this step, technology intelligence and competitive intelligence are interfaced to generate potential profit sites where technology choices are necessary. Choices may lead to ideas for fundamentally new businesses; ways to alter the rivalry in current competitive domains; and

PERKIN-ELMER'S STRATEGIC EVOLUTION (1962–1980)

Over a period of 2 decades (1960–1982), Perkin-Elmer (PE) accomplished a major transformation from a $100 million to a billion-dollar corporation. This was the result of a carefully planned strategy of internal product development and well-calculated acquisitions. The company strategy focused first on strengthening its baseline operations in optical devices and avionics and then expanded into new fields, ranging from analytical instrumentation and small computers to flame sprays.

Consider PE's acquisition history during the period:

1960–1965	1966–1970	1971–1975	1976–1980
Automium	Boller Chivens	Metco	Wangco
Solid State Materials	Ultex	Nester & Faust	Physical Electronic
Penn Optical	Aerospace Division	Randex	Etec
ERS&Gray		Photometrics	
Coleman		Interdata	

These acquisitions take on a pattern when organized by business segment.

1. Penn Optical, Boller Chivens, Aerospace Division, Randex, and Etec belonged to the Optical Systems and Precision Optics Division;

2. Ultex and some other parts of the Aerospace Division fell to the Avionics Division;

3. Coleman Instruments, Photometrics and Physical Electronic were organized into Analytical Instruments;

4. Interdata and Wangco became part of the minicomputers and peripheral division; and

5. Metco became part of Flame Spray Equipment and Materials.

Specific technology and market linkages characterize the company's seemingly diverse technology forays during this time period. Consider two examples:

- The technology linkage between optics and analytical instruments provided access to markets for a yet third technology-dependent product: minicomputers.

- The optics and aerospace defense businesses provided the technology base and market experience for a venture into low-light systems for the military.

Taken as a group, PE's acquisitions demonstrated a close fit on two fronts: They were well aligned with the company's long-term strategy, and they complemented the baseline operations in terms of technological and market linkages. As a result, the company that resulted from the repositioning process was not only greatly expanded but also far better positioned—both strategically and technologically. This is a reflection of the underlying strategic intent. A CEO's active participation in directing technology and market investments is vital in a repositioning program. Thus, PE's repositioning could not have succeeded without top management's involvement.

Source: Adapted from William P. Sommers, Joseph Nemec Jr., and John M. Harris. "Repositioning with Technology: Making it Work," *Journal of Business Strategy*, pp. 16–27.

• Technology Intelligence
• Profiling Competitive Domains
• Identifying Profit Sites

ENVIRONMENTAL ASSESSMENT

• Technology Inventory   • Appropriation of Technology   • Mode of Implementation
• Firms' Competitive Positions   • Deployment in Products   • Organizational Strategy
• Technology Requirements   • Deployment in Value Chains   • Intellectual Property Strategy

COMPETITIVE POSITION OF
FIRM

FIGURE 8.10 FORMULATION OF TECHNOLOGY STRATEGY

methods to improve the competitive position of firms in their current competitive domains.

THE COMPETITIVE POSITION OF THE FIRM

During this stage, a firm assesses its technological strengths relative to its competitor and the technological requirements of its strategic position in the market. This, in turn involves three steps:

1. **Technology inventory.** Technology inventory refers to the process of identifying all technologies throughout the firm. It may appear surprising, but many companies do not know what is in their technology portfolio. For instance, Martin Marietta's portfolio of businesses includes aerospace as well as construction aggregates obtained from quarrying operations. In defense-related applications, the aerospace division had developed ultra high-speed imaging techniques to track missiles and projectiles. By defining the technology rather than the business as a unit of analysis, the company spotted the capability of this new technique for the construction aggregate division. Consequently, quarrying efficiency was improved by 15 to 30 percent.[10]
2. **Profiling a firm's competitive position in current and future technologies.** What are the relative technological strengths of a firm in each of the technologies? This requires comparing the firm's technological strengths against its competitors.
3. **Charting the technological requirements of strategic positioning.** What technological requirements are imposed by the firm's strategy in its current competitive domains? During this stage, significant input from the business strategy function is needed, so that information about industry context, and firm resources and capabilities, is brought to bear on the answers to these questions.

The assessment of the competitive position enables a firm to discover (1) the profit sites that it is well positioned to exploit and (2) the enormity of the task should the firm want to venture into areas where it is not currently strong. Both environmental assessment and firm's position are the primary inputs into the formulation of technology strategy.

FORMULATION OF TECHNOLOGY STRATEGY

During this stage, a firm decides to commit resources to a select set of technology choices—the set of technologies to be appropriated, deployed in products and value chains, marketed, or simply abandoned. They become the basis on which to mount R&D programs, new product development efforts, value chain changes, and licensing of technology. Three major areas of decisions are involved:

1. Appropriation of technology. Technologies to be acquired and those technologies that need further development are translated into specific R&D programs or acquisitions strategies of firms. Resources are negotiated between this activity and the remaining operations of the firm. A firm may also decide to exploit current technologies through mechanisms such as licensing or divesting specific technological capabilities.
2. Deployment in products. Technologies to be embedded in products either through product enhancement or new product development efforts are identified and, along with industry and competitor analyses, are used to develop a product development program.
3. Deployment in the value chain. Opportunities for enhancing competitive advantage through process innovation—either through radical innovation or through improvements in specific value chain activities—are identified, and programs are developed for implementing them.

These choices that determine the scope and leadership dimensions of a firm's technology strategy are influenced by the availability of financial resources: In general, the broader the scope and the greater a firm's commitment to leadership position, the greater the resources it will have to commit. In addition to financial resources, existing organizational resources also influence the technology strategies of firms. Thus, a firm's capabilities may be rooted in science (for example, pharmaceutical firms), engineering (for example, semiconductor firms), manufacturing (for example, Japanese firms), or marketing (for example, the cosmetic industry). Indeed, resources and capabilities interact: Technology strategies that require capabilities far outside a firm's traditional capabilities need an enormous commitment of resources.

Although industry and technological context, and resources and capabilities, need to be taken into account in the formulation of technological strategy, firms have a fair amount of discretion in their technology choices. The exercise of this discretion reflects the ambitions and objectives of the key decision-makers in an organization. In the case of Crown Cork and Seal, a firm we discussed earlier, the architect of technology strategy was its chief executive officer, John Connelly, who took over the company in 1957. He chose to build on Crown's existing skills in metal formation and specialized "hard to hold" applications for tin cans. He discontinued Crown's R&D efforts and instead developed strong links between the technical sales force and the engineering group so that it could provide technical solutions for customers. As aluminum companies introduced a 2-piece can, an external innovation, Crown mobilized its own capabilities as well as those of its steel suppliers to adapt the innovation for use with steel. Indeed, pur suit of technological leadership or followership is motivated not merely by industry or technology-related factors but also by the values and objectives of top decision maker.

CRAFTING AN IMPLEMENTATION APPROACH

The technology choices once formulated reflect the *intended* technology strategy of the firm. They need to be implemented in order to contribute to the competitive advantage of firms. During implementation, a firm has to address three major questions pertain ing to the mode of implementation, ways to protect the value from technology choices and the organization for implementation:

1. Should we go it alone or should we collaborate with other firms in order to execute the decision?
2. How should we protect the investments in technology choices from being dissipated through various means?
3. How should we organize internally for implementation?

MODE OF IMPLEMENTATION

Firms may choose to implement their technology strategy either by going it alone or collaborating with other firms. A firm can implement its technology strategy by collab orating with other firms potentially in almost all domains of technology strategy. Dur ing the last decade, collaborative strategies have been increasingly prevalent due t globalization, time compression, and potential for technology integration. However technology leadership position may necessitate that a firm pursue an in-house strateg in at least some selected set of technologies.

INTELLECTUAL PROPERTY STRATEGY

Intellectual property protection refers to the actions that a firm takes to prevent th value derived from its technology choices from being dissipated by the forces of imita tion or holdup. In many industries such as computers, semiconductors, pharmaceutical or chemicals, intellectual property protection has become an important component of the technology strategy implementation. As the number of technologically proficien firms has increased globally, as competitors are better able to assimilate and reproduc technology, the importance of intellectual property rights and protection is keenly fel For example, patents are used to stake out a market, to negotiate licensing arrang ments, and for technology and territorial swaps rather than for cash value.

ORGANIZATION FOR IMPLEMENTATION

Technology choices to be implemented require proper planning and organization. Be in-house research and development, product development, or value chain reconfigura tion, the organization required for execution is usually different from the operating o ganization. This is further complicated by the fact that the three domains of technolog choices are themselves interrelated. Thus, technology development needs to interfac with deployment in products and processes; product development almost always re quires value chain changes; and the value chain reconfiguration inevitably affects proc uct launches.

EXECUTION

During execution, a firm develops detailed operational plans and human resource deployments necessary for the execution of the technology choices. During this stage, significant interaction needs to take place between implementers of technology strategy and those performing key business functions: marketing, manufacturing, finance, and strategy. Success and effectiveness of technology strategy require regular monitoring, careful assessment, and evaluation of the various technology programs developed in stage two.[11]

One final point: As we have noted, the environmental context and the connections between technology and business strategies of a firm evolve over time. A major implication of this observation is that the technology strategy formulation, just like business strategy formulation, should be an ongoing activity within a firm. In Box 8.5, we have showcased how Lucent Technologies continued to evolve its technology strategy in the wake of deregulation of the telecommunications industry. This deliberate evolution was a major factor in its successes.

❖ CHAPTER SUMMARY

A firm makes technology choices in three major domains: appropriation that determines its technological capabilities, deployment in products that determines its product platforms, and deployment in value chains that determines its process platforms. These decisions may create fundamentally new businesses, alter the rules of rivalry in their competitive domains, or support the current business strategies. The connections between technology and business change with time as competitive domains evolve and firms change their business strategies.

Technology strategy is the revealed pattern in the technology choices of firms. The choices involve the commitment of resources for the appropriation, maintenance, deployment, and abandonment of technological capabilities. These technology choices determine the character and extent of the firms' principal technical capabilities and the set of available product and process platforms. Technology strategy is the primary responsibility of the chief technology officer.

Several major principles should guide the formulation of technology strategy. First, the quest for competitive advantage should be the primary objective of technology strategy. Second, both technological and market environments at the firm and industry levels should guide the formulation of strategy. Third, profitable sites for technology strategy should exhibit not merely opportunity but appropriability by the firms, as well. Fourth, firms should be competitively positioned both technologically and strategically to exploit the technology choice. Finally, because technology choices involve commitment of financial resources, the firms should focus their resources on a select set of choices to get the maximum benefit from technology development and deployment.

There are four major types of technology strategies: technology leadership, niche, technology follower, and technology rationalizer. During the era of technology emergence, there are numerous opportunities for technology leadership; however, during the era of incremental change, technological leadership requires dominance in both technology and markets. Niche is preferred when the firm is competitively positioned, but not dominant. When the technological positions are weak, the firms may be forced to adopt followership or rationalization.

BOX 8.5

TECHNOLOGY STRATEGY—
LUCENT TECHNOLOGIES

The future of AT&T Bell Laboratories, the precursor to Lucent Technologies, was uncertain in January 1984, when AT&T was broken up. Having produced the transistor, the laser, the solar cell, and the first communication satellite, as well as sound motion pictures, the science of radio astronomy, and crucial evidence for the theory that a Big Bang created the universe, some believed that, without the revenue base provided by the parent company, Bell Lab's immense production might begin to fade. The result has been that AT&T's support did not waver. Basic research came through the breakup largely unscathed, but Bell Labs began branching into new commercial areas and looking into licensing for companies as far afield from telecommunications as airlines and shipping firms.

Historically, engineers at Bell Labs had always worked on applications. But, basic research has always been an attention-getter because of its unmatched results and epochal discoveries: Several Bell Lab scientists have won Nobel Prizes. Bell Labs had been strong in the transfer of research results into products and considered research not a luxury but a strategic necessity. With a long-term view, Bell Labs executives tailored basic research more closely to company needs. They scrutinized research activities for their contribution to the parent company's business, which was defined as management and movement of information.

The scope of research remained wider than at most other industries and even some universities. Bell Labs' method had always been to assemble many specialists who interact closely. The most basic work has a way of merging into development, though that is not evident from the activities of some of the basic scientists. One area of study could be, as once reported, the activities of ants in the jun-

gles of Brazil; another could be observing faint galaxies at the edge of the universe from observatories in Chile and Hawaii. Bell Labs considers it part of its business strategy to have a few scientists do work that connects Bell Labs to universities and the rest of the scientific community.

A 1956 consent decree that AT&T signed with the Department of Justice banned AT&T and Bell Labs from operating in any field outside telecommunications and obligated Bell Labs to share any discoveries it made with the world at large. After the breakup, Bell Labs no longer had to give away its discoveries, as it famously did with the transistor. (Sony secured the rights in the 1950s with a $25,000 down payment on royalties and thereby ignited the consumer electronics revolution with transistor radios.) The breakup opened different windows into the marketplace; competing globally has taught Bell Labs' product developers to couple R&D even more closely to manufacturing and market needs. In the past, technology drove Bell Lab's development: Now, the customer does. Bell Labs does not allow too long for a product to pay for itself. Just as it opened the world of microelectronics by inventing the transistor, Bell Labs is now far along in harnessing the electron's ephemeral cousin, the photon, for the task of information movement and management. Bell Labs has brought impressive products, such as a gigantic computerized system, the 5 ESS, that allows customers to transmit both voice and data directly in digital form; and the integrated services digital network (ISDN), designed to connect 7,500 McDonald's hamburger outlets with the company administrative offices. Bell Labs has worked for years on an optical computer that, using laser beams instead of electrical connections, would work 1,000 times faster than the electronic variety.

There are four steps in formulating a technology strategy. The first consists of diagnosis, understanding the environmental context and the firm's strategic position. The second step involves the commitment of resources to certain technology choices. Third, the mode of implementation, intellectual property protection plans, and organization for execution of the technology choices are determined. The final step involves the execution of the choices.

❖ NOTES

1. "A Time Line of Motorola History," Motorola Museum of Electronics, IL.

2. See Goodman, R. and M. W. Lawless. *Technology and Strategy: Conceptual Models and Diagnostics.* New York: Oxford University Press, 1994.

3. Weil, E. and R. Cangemi. "Linking Long Range Research to Corporate Planning," *Research Management,* 1983, Vol. 26, pp. 32–39. See also Goodman and Lawless, ibid., p. 35.

4. Ansoff, I. and J. Stewart. "Strategies for a Technology Based Business," *Harvard Business Review,* Vol. 45, No. 6, Nov-Dec 1967.

5. Rosenbloom, Richard S. "Rethinking Technology Strategy." Paper presented at the Academy of Management, Technology and Management Division, distinguished speaker session, Atlanta, Georgia, August 9, 1993.

6. Rosenbloom, Richard S. "Rethinking the Technology Strategy," ibid.

7. Little, A. D. "The Strategic Management of Technology." Material originally presented at the 1981 European Management Forum in Davos.

8. Rosenbloom, R. S., and Cusumano, M. S. "Technological Pioneering: The Birth of the VCR Industry," *California Management Review,* December 1987, Vol. 24, No. 4, pp. 51–76.

9. Rutenberg, D. "Umbrella Pricing." Working paper, Queens University, 1986.

10. Westwood, A. "R&D in a Multi-industry Corporation," *Research Technology Management,* May–June, 1984, pp. 23–26.

11. Contractor, F. J. and Narayanan, V. K. "Technology Development in the Multinational Firm: A Framework for Planning and Strategy," *R&D Management* (1990): 2. Ford, E. "Develop Your Technology Strategy," *Long Range Planning* (1988): Vol. 21, No. 5, pp. 85–95.

CHAPTER 9

TECHNOLOGY STRATEGY: COLLABORATIVE MODE

Faced with pressure on all fronts to do more with less, a growing number of today's business schools are pooling their resources with other institutions as part of "learning alliances."

The trend presents a powerful paradox—success achieved through cooperation among business schools—even between institutions that are simultaneously engaged in stiff competition for top students. Counterintuitive as it may seem, many experts predict that this describes the future of management education.

This definition of learning alliance varies, but it generally describes a collaboration between two or more business schools to jointly offer educational programs, whether they be regional executive education programs or ambitious international linkages with schools in Asia, Europe, South America, or elsewhere in the world.

Although joint programs are not new, learning alliances are different—characterized by institutions truly integrating their intellectual, financial, and physical resources on every level of the joint venture—from establishing research agendas to marketing plans.

The goal is to make better, more efficient use of shrinking resources and to create high-quality educational programs that are greater than the sum of their parts, rather than continue the linear transfer of students, faculty, or other resources between institutions that has defined most partnerships in the past.

In the past, when business schools cooperated in any manner, it most likely was with foreign partners—for the sake of "internationalizing" their programs. Seldom did domestic schools link their programs with other American schools, either to expand their international relationships or create new educational programs targeted exclusively toward domestic students. But the learning alliance approach now is increasingly evidenced in a variety of domestic linkages, as well.

For example, the University of Michigan business school is the lead institution in a new consortium that includes business schools at New York University, the University of California at Berkeley, and eight European universities.

The consortium's objective is to establish an MBA/EMS (Certificate in European Management Studies). The certificate program will provide an opportunity to those MBA students who wish to extend their normal 2-year MBA program by spending several semesters of study at two European Community schools of management.

The recently established International Campus Consortium (ICC) created by the American Graduate School of International Management (Thunderbird) is another example. It will include a group of U.S. business schools linked in a partnership to assist in the development of international programs at their schools.

The Ohio School of International Business, a new project funded by the Ohio state legislature, brings together business faculty from Kent State University, the University of Akron, Cleveland State University, and Youngstown State University in an effort to provide international business education and executive education to the growing number of Ohio companies involved in exporting. The presidents of the four collaborating universities serve as the board of trustees of the new consortium.

Although the four schools actively compete for students, a sense for the greater need to use scarce resources to address a critical need for more focused "real world" international management education outweighed competitive concerns when this program was established, according to Frank E. Vaughn, interim dean of the new school.

"We were driven by the understanding that it doesn't make sense for every institution to develop a specialty—particularly in the international arena—on its own," said Vaughn. "There is a critical need for a resource to train students to work in the international environment and to help companies better prepare to compete globally. It just makes more sense to cooperate under one center, with intellectual resources coming from each university."

There are other alliances formed exclusively to present programs targeted toward the domestic market. In Oklahoma, for example, the business schools at the two state universities recently held, for the sixth year, their joint Management Development Program, which features business faculty from both the University of Oklahoma and Oklahoma State University coming together to present an extensive development program to a large group of the state's senior executives.

Yet another example is a consortium of business schools at Oregon's three largest public universities, in which they jointly offer the Oregon Executive Education MBA. Students earn an MBA degree from the University of Oregon but receive their education via courses taught by faculty from all three schools at a nonuniversity executive education center located in Portland.

What ultimately will determine the success or failure of the learning alliance concept in the United States is the ability to accept cooperation as a new component of competition—both internationally and within the domestic market, according to Michael A. Goldberg, dean of the Faculty of Commerce and Business Administration at the University of British Columbia. Goldberg also is chairman of the Canadian Federation of Deans of Management and Administrative Studies (AACSB's counterpart in Canada).

"What it is going to take to foster a greater state of cooperation among U.S. schools is individual deans who have confidence in their skills and who have some scar tissue from trying to establish linkages in the past," said John C.

Ivancevich, dean of the College of Business Administration at the University of Houston. "They realize that today's schools simply can't support a large volume of joint programs, and that true alliances must be formed in order for everyone to compete successfully in the future."[1]

As illustrated in the vignette, universities in the United States that in the past have competed among themselves are learning the advantages of collaboration from the experience of business firms. Indeed, in the arena of technology, firms not only compete among themselves, but they also find avenues to cooperate. Globalization, time compression, and potential for technology integration are driving firms to find collaborative approaches for the appropriation of technology and their deployment in new product and value chains. During the 1980s, the trend toward collaborative relationships among firms, some of them competitors, accelerated.

In this chapter, we will focus on the collaborative mode by which technology strategy is implemented. We will answer such questions as:

1. What is a collaborative arrangement?
2. Why do firms collaborate?
3. What are the different types of collaborative arrangements?
4. What are the risks of collaboration?

The chapter overview is presented in Figure 9.1. First, we will define collaborative arrangements and highlight the key trends in collaborative arrangements among firms in the United States. Second, we will present the reasons for the collaborative mode of implementation of technology strategy. Third, we will enumerate the major types of collaborative arrangements. Fourth, we will enumerate the major types of risk associated with collaborative activity. Fifth, we will summarize the impact of globalization on

FIGURE 9.1 CHAPTER OVERVIEW

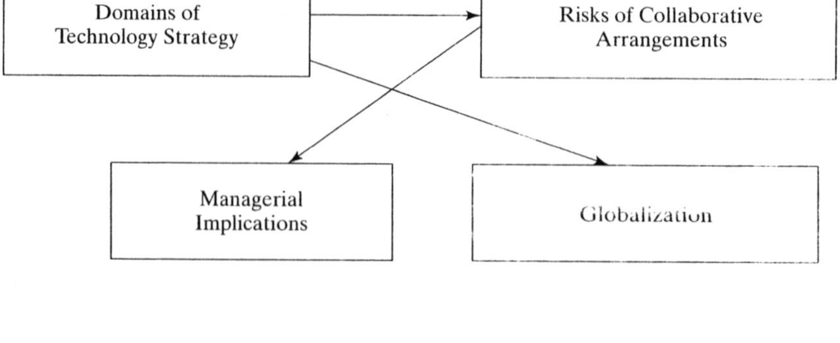

collaborative arrangements. Finally, we will pinpoint the key managerial implications and conclude with a chapter summary.

COLLABORATIVE ARRANGEMENTS: DEFINITION AND TRENDS

Collaborative arrangements involve two or more firms in which the partners hope to learn and acquire from each other the technologies, products, skills, and knowledge that are not otherwise available. The partners may range from suppliers and customers to competitors, unrelated firms, or organizations in the public sector. Although such arrangements are pervasive in the day-to-day operations of a firm, in matters related to technology two special characteristics can be observed:

1. One of the major functions performed by collaborative arrangements is the transfer of knowledge from one organization to the other. Unlike a supplier-customer relationship, the transfer of knowledge requires that the individual firms understand the operations of their partners much more intensely than in the case of the supplier-customer relationship.
2. The choice of the partners is determined greatly by strategic reasons. Thus, whereas firms may avoid competitors in their day-to-day operations, many technology-related collaborative arrangements are between competitors.

In the United States, domestic firms are increasingly collaborating, not only among themselves but also with foreign partners for technology appropriation and deployment. Recent years have witnessed four distinctly *new* trends in collaborative arrangements: (1) R&D alliances, (2) marketing alliances, (3) outsourcing arrangements, and (4) collaboration between small and large firms.

R&D ALLIANCES

R&D alliances represent the formation of collaborative arrangements between two or more firms to conduct research and development. Previously, in the United States R&D collaboration between competitors had been restricted by antitrust regulations; but, antitrust provisions were relaxed as a result of the National Cooperative Research Act of 1984 (NCRA), allowing competitors greater freedom to collaborate on R&D ventures. In Box 9.1, we have summarized the provisions of NCRA. As a result of the act, the number of R&D strategic alliances (RDSA) in the United States has been increasing over the past decade. In Figure 9.2, we have displayed the formation of R&D strategic alliances; as shown in the figure, R&D strategic alliances have been on the rise.

MARKETING ALLIANCES

Firms are also increasingly employing marketing alliances to exploit the outcome of research and development through marketing channels. These alliances could take the form of licensing or teaming up with firms that have marketing expertise. For example, a lot of drug developers are teaming up with domestic firms with mass distribution expertise.

BOX 9.1

THE NATURE OF THE NATIONAL COOPERATIVE RESEARCH ACT OF 1984

The NCRA of 1984 was an effort to change the public perception that the United States antitrust laws deter competitive joint research and development activities. To correct the perception problem, the law explicitly states that "a joint research and development venture shall not be deemed illegal per se; such conduct shall be judged on the basis of its reasonableness, taking into account all relevant factors affecting competition . . . ."[a] The law, however, limits its benefits only to "joint R&D programs," a specially designed term to include those collaborative innovative efforts that U.S. firms undertake to compete globally and exclude others that may have potential anticompetitive concern.

Specifically, Congress sought to address three major issues through the 1984 Act. First, it is intended to provide valuable direction on the application of the rule of reason standard to R&D joint ventures. Section 2 states that no joint R&D venture shall be condemned as illegal per se, but shall be judged based on its reasonableness. The Act thus codifies the rule of reason as the substantive standard that would encourage joint ventures.

The second major issue is the exemption from treble damages. Section 3 of the NCRA states that a plaintiff can only recover actual damages and attorney's fees (plus interest on actual damages in order to provide a more fully compensatory remedy) if he can prove he has been injured. Section 5 of the NCRA awards costs, including a reasonable attorney's fee, to a prevailing defendant if the claimant's conduct during the litigation was frivolous, unreasonable, without sound foundations, or in bad faith. Any award to a prevailing plaintiff may be discounted in favor of any other party if a plaintiff is found to be frivolous, unreasonable, without sound basis or in bad faith. Section 5 applies to all joint research and development ventures.[b]

The third issue is the requirement for filing a written notification of any R&D joint ventures with the Department of Justice and Federal Trade Commission, to be published in the Federal Register. Such a disclosure will assure the firm of its exemption of trebling of damages and attorney's fees.

---

[a]S. Rep. No. 427, 98th Cong., 2d Sess. 4, reprinted in 1984 U.S. Code Cong. & AD. News 3105, 3108.
[b]NCRA, Pub. L. No. 98–462, § 4(d), 98 Stat. 1815, 1817.
Source: Stoltenberg, C. D., and Yang, X. "A Multidisciplinary Approach Toward Understanding R&D Strategic Alliances: Experience From Changes In American Antitrust Laws." Paper presented at the Information and Technology Management Group (Track ITM-11) at the 1994 Association of Management Meeting in Dallas, Texas.

OUTSOURCING ARRANGEMENTS

U.S. firms are sourcing particular components and production processes from other firms, including foreign partners. In consumer electronics alone, no U.S. manufacturer currently produces its own color television sets, VCRs, stereo equipment, or compact disc players. All electronic products sold under the Eastman Kodak, General Electric, Zenith, or Westinghouse brands are made by their foreign alliance partners and imported into the United States. Similar trends are being repeated in the electrical power generation and distribution industry and in factory automation.

Year	Number	Percent
1985	49	15.6
1986	15	4.8
1987	24	7.7
1988	32	10.2
1989	33	10.5
1990	43	13.8
1991	56	17.8
1992	61	19.5
Total	313	39.9

Source: From Stoltenberg, C. D., and Yang, X. "A Multidisciplinary Approach Toward Understanding R&D Strategic Alliances Experience from Changes in American Antitrust Laws" Paper presented at the Information and Technology Management Group (Track ITM-11) at the 1994 Association of Management Meeting in Dallas, Texas. Reprinted by permission.

FIGURE 9.2 GROWTH OF RDSA BY YEAR (1985–1992)

COLLABORATION BETWEEN SMALL AND LARGE FIRMS

Small firms have been growing in importance as leaders in technology development. However, because the ability of small firms to compete in the global markets is constrained by conditions both internal and external to the firm, inter-firm collaboration for innovation has become a major vehicle by which small firms overcome some of these barriers. Collaboration between large and small firms is becoming a very significant force in many industries today.[2] In Box 9.2, we have showcased the advantages of inter-firm collaboration by size and industry.

REASONS FOR COLLABORATIVE ARRANGEMENTS

In principle, there are three major reasons why firms seek collaborative relationships with other partners, including competitors:

1. The resources required for a particular venture are so high that no single firm can do it alone. For example, many competitors join together to bid for contracts with major federal agencies such as the Department of Defense or NASA.
2. The risks associated with a venture may be so high that firms may want to incur only a portion of the total risk of the venture. For example, in the case of oil drilling, a number of firms typically join together because the probability of striking oil is often very low.
3. Different firms have different capabilities, and some ventures may require pooling the capabilities of different firms for successful implementation.

Taken together, pooling of resources, sharing of risk, and leveraging the individual firm's capabilities are the primary reasons that firms undertake collaborative strategies.

BOX 9.2

ADVANTAGES OF INTER-FIRM
COLLABORATION BY SIZE AND SECTOR

SMALL FIRMS

Small-Large Firm Collaboration: Electronics

To exploit new technology

Build company resources

Access to expert user

Open new markets

Product development

Potential sales to partner

Access to EC funding

Management strategy, company evolving from followers to leaders in technology

Approached by larger company to develop prototype after DTI recommendation

Solve partner's technical problems through joint development and acquire new product as a result

Extend client base

Gain major overseas principal

Extend range of company and increase distribution network

Gain better access to partner's technical needs

Develop new products with user and sell to partner

Approached by major company to develop product jointly

Small-Large Firm Collaboration: Biotechnology

Objective of becoming major pharmaceutical company

Collaboration finances company development and provides access to partner's resources, e.g., as clinical trials, marketing

LARGE FIRMS

Large-Small Firm Collaboration: Electronics

Access to people with right combinations of skills to develop new products

Increase company range, provide customers with better service

Strategic decision to invest in a key technology. Exploitation needed specialized resources of smaller company

Gains early look at technology and equipment

Access to smaller firm's expertise for product development

Provided solution to technical problem

Better service for customers—hence an improved competitive position

Entry to U.K. market

Access to expertise at precompetitive research stage

New products

Access to technology which would facilitate in-house project development

Large-Small Firm Collaboration: Biotechnology

Develop major new product range

Access to expertise to develop products jointly in order to maintain market share

---

Source: Reprinted from *Research Policy,* Vol. 20, Smith, Helen L., Dickson, K. and Smith, Stephen L., "There are two sides to every story: Innovation and collaboration within networks of large and small firms," pp. 457–468, copyright 1991, with permission of Elsevier Science.

In several arenas of technology management, sharing of resources, pooling of risks, and leveraging each other's capabilities prompt firms to undertake collaborative arrangements. We may classify these arrangements into two broad categories: (1) strategic and (2) operational.

STRATEGIC

Collaborative arrangements are particularly useful for firms to accomplish three strategic long-term objectives: (1) controlling the evolution of competitive domains, (2) acquiring knowledge, and (3) developing institutional links with other institutions.

CONTROLLING THE EVOLUTION OF COMPETITIVE DOMAINS

Collaborative arrangements often emerge when a group of firms ally to compete with another group in an attempt to influence environmental agents for favorable treatment. Four major arenas of collaboration have been common: (1) dominant design, (2) establishment of standards, (3) cooperative research to compete with other firms in technology development, and (4) obtain favorable treatment from the government.

1. **Dominant design.** Although competition among groups of firms may break out during various periods of industry emergence, industry growth, and transition, the competition for the attention of key environmental agents is intense during the early stages of what we have characterized as the era of technology emergence. As we have seen in chapter 5, during this era different product designs compete for dominance until a dominant design emerges. During this era, therefore, firms find it useful to collaborate with certain other firms for gaining acceptance of their designs as the industry standard. For example, in the early stages of the personal computer industry, even after Apple's successful introduction of its Mac, IBM PC became the de facto standard. A major anchor of IBM's strategy to win the race for dominant design was the set of collaborative relationships that it established with other firms, including Microsoft. Although these relationships themselves may not be enduring for long periods of time, they skew the characteristics of a competitive domain to be, over the long run, more favorable to one group of firms than others.
2. **Establishment of standards.** Because standards reduce the uncertainty not merely for the customers but for the supplier firms, as well, firms collaborate to establish standards. For example, automobile firms often collaborate to get environmental emission standards established (in their favor) by the government.
3. **Technology development.** During various points in the evolution of an industry, firms may band together to gain favorable treatment from other environmental agents. For example, the formation of SEMATECH was based on the premise that to compete with global competitors, the U.S. government and U.S. firms could collaborate for technology development. In doing so, the group of companies that formed SEMATECH also gained access to federal funds to support their own research.
4. **Favorable treatment from the government.** In 1995, the Clinton administration's threat to impose sanctions on Japanese imports was partly stimulated

by the collective lobbying efforts of U.S. auto manufacturers, who stood to gain from the imposition of sanctions. Similarly, firms in the tobacco industry persistently lobby Congress to alleviate regulations that might adversely affect the market of cigarettes.

KNOWLEDGE ACQUISITION AND TRANSFER

A second strategic objective that motivates a firm to pursue collaborative arrangemen is the acquisition or transfer of knowledge needed to operate in an industry or a pa ticular value chain activity. Thus, a firm may attempt diversification into another indu try, away from its base of operations, by collaborating with other firms either throug joint ventures, equity investments, or acquisitions. Consider the following:

- When United Telecom (UTI) entered into a joint venture with GTE— what is now known as Sprint—it was with the specific purpose of obtaining the size required to operate in the emerging long-distance telecommunications market.
- Procter & Gamble's diversification into the biotechnology industry was implemented through a series of acquisitions that enabled the firm to understand the dynamics of the biotechnology industry.
- Finally, 3M routinely invests in small firms to gain technology in the form of products and processes.

Some collaborative arrangements result in technology transfer to developing nations

- India's truck and auto industry has been booming over the last decade with the help of Indo-Japanese joint ventures, which extend to some of the supplier firms. Such alliances helped the industry make about 30 years of technological progress within about 10 years.[3]

LINKS TO ENVIRONMENT

Firms have always understood that collaborative ventures are one mechanism by whic they can maintain links to people and information. Thus, large firms encourage their sc entists or senior science personnel to become active in advisory committees in unive sities or government agencies. This kind of participation enables the firms to gain acce to information that otherwise would not have been easily available. Furthermore, suc participation also allows the firms to gain access to personnel whose expertise can k tapped as and when the firms need it.

- For example, in the pharmaceutical industry, membership on the advisory committee in a university enables a senior scientist to have close interaction with university professors, thereby enabling them to cherry-pick the students from that particular university.

In Box 9.3, we have sketched the evolving relationships between IBM and U.S. unive sities. As can be seen from the box, during the 1980s IBM strongly believed that cc laborative research was an especially promising area that could bring industries ar technical applications strength into academia, and the creativity of that environme into the industry.

BOX 9.3

IBM AND U.S. UNIVERSITIES

IBM has supported higher education for many years and in many forms. But in recent years, as they have recognized new academic exposures and dependencies, IBM has stepped up its support and attempted to be more innovative in encouraging the development of education and research in some much-needed areas.

Increasingly, IBM's university programs focus on working with the faculty and students of the universities, as well as responding to proposals from presidents and deans.

Probably the most important feature of IBM's activities is their "grass roots" character. Under general company policies intended to ensure that both the university's and IBM's needs and objectives are protected, local IBM laboratories are encouraged to identify opportunities for cooperative activities and work out suitable arrangements. Even the program of corporate contributions to educational institutions has its origins primarily in suggestions from IBM operating units, as well as from the universities themselves.

The totality of IBM's contributions and cooperative research is, then, the aggregation of a set of activities initiated in a "bottom-up" environment. Both IBM and the research-intensive universities are highly complex, decentralized organizations. This situation can lead to creativity, but it makes coordination of many different projects difficult for all concerned. This difficulty is, however, an acceptable price to pay for the level of originality and creativity reflected in such a highly diverse set of relationships.

IBM develops these relationships through the Research Division, technology development laboratories, Academic Information Systems business unit, and through branch office organizations. IBM administers corporate policy and programs and monitors university interactions from the corporate level through various groups: University Relations, Personnel and Technical Personnel Development staffs, and an executive Education Relations Board.

Under the Technical Interchange Program, for example, each of IBM's development labs has established close technical ties between the company and one or more major research universities. For each school, a scientist or engineer is assigned to monitor and encourage the IBM technical community's interactions with that university. Forty-three research universities are covered, in all. In addition, many senior IBM executives maintain personal contact with the academic administration and monitor IBM relationships in major universities.

Overall, IBM is attempting to manage relationships with universities to address some very real IBM needs that are mirrored in the economy as a whole. IBM makes no apology for the fact that these programs not only respond to the schools' needs but are very much in IBM's own self-interest. Indeed, most universities prefer that self-interest be manifest, because that provides the strongest basis for lasting relationships.

During 1985 (see the table), IBM contributed a total of $71 million in cash, equipment, and salaries of IBM-loaned experts to educational institutions and organizations in the United States to help support fellowships and organizations, faculty and curriculum development, and advanced instructional programs and research. Of that amount, more than $45 million was earmarked for science and technology, and the largest donations generally fall in this area.

Listed separately in the table is cooperative research with universities, which has grown very rapidly in recent years. Since 1980, more than 1,100 projects, representing a total commitment of over $130 million, have been initiated with over 200 U.S. institutions.

Source: From Branscomb, Lewis M. "IBN and US Universities—An Evolving Partnership," *IEEE Transactions on Education,* Vol. E-29, No. 2. © 1986 IEEE. Reprinted by permission.

Box 9.3 (*continued*)

Major IBM Support to U.S. Education in 1985
Contributions

Support to leading universities for graduate fellowships, faculty and curriculum development, and research programs, particularly in high-technology areas important to the nation's future, such as computer-aided design and manufacturing, manufacturing systems engineering, magnetic recording technology, management of information systems, advanced education projects, etc.	$ 40,400,000
Support for 2-year college curricula in computer-aided design and drafting.	$ 800,000
National Achievement Scholarships, salaries of loaned IBM employees, and other support for education of minorities, women, and handicapped students in technical and business fields.	$ 7,400,000
IBM Departmental Grants and IBM Faculty Development Awards.	$ 3,600,000
IBM two-for-one Matching Grants to Education.	$ 9,700,000
Other (National Merit Scholarships, support for independent College Funds of America, leading liberal arts colleges, schools, etc.)	$ 9,100,000
Total	$ 71,000,000
Cooperative Research Contracts	
624 active projects with 158 universities (cost shown is IBM multiyear commitment)	$107,000,000

OPERATIONAL

Operational or short-term objectives focus the accomplishment of specific milestone or objectives in a firm's implementation of technology strategy through collabora tive arrangements with other firms. We can identify four major operational objective that may prompt a firm to undertake collaborative arrangements with other firm: (1) competitive benchmarking, (2) time to market, (3) extract operating efficiencies, an (4) capture value from existing technology.

COMPETITIVE BENCHMARKING
In an effort to improve their current operations, firms are increasingly adopting th benchmarking of other firms' activities. Benchmarking practices involve a firm's im porting the "best in the world" practices in a specific value chain activity and institu tionalizing these practices in the normal operating procedures.

- For example, when General Electric wanted to benchmark its distribution system, it studied Wal-Mart and L. L. Bean. Presumably, such relationships enabled General Electric to benchmark its operation against world-class op erators and thus begin a process of continuous improvement.

OPERATING EFFICIENCIES
Because comparative advantage of firms is shifting due to the rapid changes in the mai ketplace, firms often find it useful to outsource some of the activities in the value chai that they had previously performed in-house.

- For example, banks are finding it economical to outsource many of the ac tivities involved in the management of information systems.

- During its much-celebrated turnaround, Laura Ashley outsourced its logistics function to Federal Express. Federal Express was considered to be a world-class performer (and, thus, much better than Laura Ashley) in the logistics function.

These new outsourcing relationships require the partners to understand each other's operations in greater depth than in a typical customer-vendor relationship. For example, outsourcing information technology requires that the vendor understand the operations of the banks. Similarly, Federal Express had to be intensely aware of the particular market characteristics of Laura Ashley for it to be useful to Laura Ashley in its logistics function.

TIME TO MARKET

Firms are also using collaborative mode to cut the time to market. Reduction in time to market is accomplished by using a variety of mechanisms ranging from outsourcing to joint development to equity purchase.

- For example, major pharmaceutical firms have begun to outsource some of the routine operations involved in drug development (e.g., clinical trials for animal testing).
- In joint development efforts, firms bring in both suppliers and customers to develop a product, so that during scale-up and manufacturing, the time for communicating the firm's requirements to the outside entities is made much easier and, therefore, much faster.
- 3M takes equity position in several small entrepreneurial ventures with the intention of acquiring them should the products turn out to be a success. In short, time compression has been a major driving force in the increasing frequency with which firms participate in collaborative arrangements.

CAPTURING VALUE FROM TECHNOLOGY DEVELOPMENT

Collaborative arrangements also provide firms one avenue by which the benefits of in-house technology development can be realized.

- Spin-offs represent a mechanism whereby a firm can reap the value of technology developed in-house that does not fit with the corporate or business strategy of the firm. In this case, the firm might take a key position in a new firm created by the people who were involved in the development of the technology.
- Transfer of technology through projects such as turnkey projects or construction of manufacturing facilities is another way by which firms have reaped the benefits of technology developed in-house.
- During the 1950s, RCA successfully licensed the black and white television vacuum tube to Japanese and U.S. manufacturers to stimulate TV sales.
- Finally, some firms may sell consulting services based on the know-how developed in-house.

As in the case of outsourcing, these relationships are much more intense than the customer-supplier relationship; they require a greater degree of understanding and collaboration between the firms involved.

Indeed, firms employ a multiple set of collaborative arrangements to enhance both the strategic and operational objectives. In the next section, we summarize the diverse set of arrangements that are typically employed in managing technology.

COLLABORATIVE ARRANGEMENTS IN DOMAINS OF TECHNOLOGY STRATEGY

Collaborative arrangements may be employed in any one of the four domains of tech nology strategy: appropriation of technological capability, deployment in new products deployment in the value chain, and marketing of technology.

APPROPRIATION OF TECHNOLOGY

In the United States, the appropriation of technology has historically been accomplishe through in-house research and development; most of the joint R&D, when it occurred consisted of contractual joint development of a new applied technology by two compa nies at different stages in the value chain of the industry. Thus, if the manufacturer of photolithography tool made by contractual agreement worked jointly with a semicon ductor device manufacturer, and the larger firm was then purchased from the forme photolithography tools would embody the jointly developed technology. Collaboratio among competitors in competitive arenas has been relatively rare except in oil explo ration and defense-related industries. Historically, fears of antitrust legislation and stron; managerial resistance to collaborative ventures have severely limited joint R&D activity

However, recently, joint R&D involving collaboration among three or more firm including competitors, has emerged in a variety of industrial sectors.[4] Starting in 1984 the National Collaborative Research Act (NCRA) was passed to clarify the legal statu of joint R&D and encourage its use where appropriate. As we saw earlier (Figure 9.2) the relaxation of antitrust provisions has led to the increasing adoption of joint R&I ventures in the United States. By and large, the microelectronics industry leads all othe industrial sectors in the number of collaborative organizations.[5] As noted earlier, severa factors have stimulated collaborative R&D: the desire to pool scarce resources, sprea risks, reduce duplication of effort, establish technical standards, and lessen developmen time for new generations of products and processes.

Broadly, in their efforts to appropriate technology, firms may participate in tw forms of collaborative endeavors: collective research and strategic alliances.

COLLECTIVE RESEARCH

In response to intense global competition, many companies are establishing cooperativ research and development organizations whose objective is to enhance the competi tiveness of the industries in which they operate. All collective research organization want to strengthen the technical infrastructure of their respective industries. In realit however, collective research organizations have focused primarily on (1) precompet tive research or (2) noncompetitive research:

1. Traditional research organizations have centered their activities on the non-competitive technical phase of an industry: basic research, education, health, safety, and dissemination of technical information. For example, Portland Cement Association conducts noncompetitive technical activities, albeit with a modest budget. These organizations have recently joined forces in toxicology and in meeting federal regulations for environmental quality.

2. More recently established research organizations emphasize the development of a strong technical base to improve productivity and enhance international competitiveness. An example is the Semiconductor Research Corporation. These organizations strengthen members' competitiveness by conducting R&D and by permitting each member to concentrate its resources on those areas crucial to its competitive position.

Collective research organizations share four major features:

1. These organizations pursue activities that range from fundamental research to testing and measuring, with many associations engaging in more than one activity.
2. Collective associations use a variety of facilities for their technical programs: the organizations' own in-house sites, member firms' facilities, universities, independent nonprofit institutes, commercial laboratories, and government installations.
3. A strong relationship exists between collective research organizations and universities.
4. Finally, these organizations also have strong relationships with government facilities. Federal laboratories hold two attractions for research groups: availability of unique or very expensive research facilities and leverage of related government-conducted federal programs.

Collective research organizations fall into five major categories.

1. Trade associations and research divisions or foundations. These groups pursue both technical and nontechnical activities. The American Iron and Steel Institute is an example.
2. Industry associations. These are established to fund and/or conduct research programs. The program itself may take place at a university facility, as in the case of the Semiconductor Research Corporation, or be owned by a university facility, as is the case of Electric Power Research Institutes.
3. University-based centers. These may be either mission-oriented centers established with National Science Foundation seed money and phased in by industry or institutions established with a large portion of funds from interested companies. The University of Rhode Island Center for Robotics is an example of the first kind of facility, and the Stanford University Center Integrated Systems is an example of the second.
4. Company-funded research institutes. These organizations pursue technical advances and applications or research related to the public welfare and, hence, are nonproprietary programs. The Sulfur Institute and the Chemical Industry Institute of Toxicology are examples.
5. Research corporations. These groups are funded by a group of companies to perform both proprietary and nonproprietary research that contributes to members' technical competitiveness. Examples in this category are Micro Electrics and Computer Technology Corporation, Eugenics, and American Welding Applications Center.[6]

Research corporations are a new phenomenon in the United States. In Box 9.4, we have featured MCC, a for-profit research corporation in Austin, Texas, with its own facilities

---

BOX 9.4

MICROELECTRONICS AND COMPUTER TECHNOLOGY (MCC)

MCC is the first major for-profit research consortium in the United States established to enhance the competitiveness of U.S. high-tech firms. It consists of 100 member companies (22 shareholders, 48 associates, 18 small business associates, and 12 universities). The success of Japan's VLSI project was a prime impetus to the formation of MCC. Benefits of MCC include shared costs and risks, exploration of new ideas, pooling of scarce talent, shared research or manufacturing facilities, research synergy, and diversification of technology portfolio.

The initial goal of MCC was to ensure that only participating companies benefited from MCC's research efforts. This challenge was sometimes difficult to meet. Additionally, it was difficult to structure MCC so that the member companies shared research without abandoning competition in the marketplace.

Since its founding in 1983, MCC has had three leaders: Admiral Inman (1983–1986);

Grant Dove (1987–1990); and Craig Fields (1990–present). As of late 1993, MCC had about 35 separate research projects grouped under the High Value Electronics (HVE) Division and the Information Systems Division. MCC's technical expertise and testing facilities were being hired out in a bid to speed up the process of technology transfer. MCC holds all intellectual property rights to technology developed at the consortium. The technology could be licensed to a third party.

MCC was created as an experiment in collaboration on R&D projects focusing on *precompetitive* research in areas judged to be critically important by its shareholder companies. MCC's greatest impact has been through the transfer and application of technologies. MCC has had the greatest impact on its member companies through learning about the process of collaborating on the technologies that have the potential to increase U.S. industrial competitiveness.

Source: Gibson, David V. and Everett M. Rogers. *R&D Collaboration on Trial.* Boston, MA: Harvard Business School Press, 1994.

---

and technical research teams. In Table 9.1, we have provided a comparative analysis of the various cooperative research organizations. As shown in the table, some organizations like trade associations or industry associations are ideally suited for influencing the regulatory or other environmental entities in terms of standard setting and industrial policy decision making. On the other hand, some of the other research organizations are focused more on competitive research and are therefore more suited for long-term objectives such as knowledge acquisition or building the competitive infrastructure of industries.

STRATEGIC ALLIANCES

As part of their technology strategies, firms often undertake joint endeavors with other firms for appropriation, deployment, and marketing of technologies. These we term *strategic alliances.* Unlike cooperative ventures, where a number of firms join together to further their technical capabilities, both noncompetitive and competitive, strategic alliances are forged specifically to further the competitive objectives of the participating firms. The benefits of strategic alliances are strictly proprietary and mostly confined to the alliance partners.

TABLE 9.1 Comparative Analysis of Cooperative Research Organizations

	Trade Associations/ Foundations	Industry Associations	University-Based Centers	Company-Funded Research Institutes	Research Corporations
1. Objectives	Noncompetitive research	Competitive research	Competitive research	Noncompetitive research	Competitive research
2. Focus of Activity	Technical and non-technical activity	Research programs	Mission-based	Technical advance, research related to public welfare	Technical
3. Facilities	Mostly owned	University-based or owned	University-based	Owned	Owned
4. Funding by	Member companies	Member companies	Seed money from NSF; phased-in industry support	Member companies	Group of companies
5. Proprietary	Mostly nonproprietary	Mostly nonproprietary	Mostly nonproprietary	Nonproprietary	Proprietary and nonproprietary

Source: Fusfeld, H. I. and Haklisch, Carmela S. "Cooperative R&D for Competitors," Harvard Business Review, November-December 1985, pp. 60–75.

There are three major types of strategic alliances: (1) corporate venturing, (2) join technology development, and (3) outsourcing.

1. *Corporate venturing.* Corporate venturing involves relationships between a large company and a small company. The large company either founds the smaller company through spin-offs or provides capital and sometimes marketing capabilities to a small company that brings out innovative products. For the large firm, this provides the mechanism for flow of technology from external sources; for the small firm, the arrangement presents much-needed capital and marketing expertise. Capital and corporate venturing may assume the form of financial participation by large firms, merger, or acquisition. For a large company like 3M, corporate venturing provides a window on the real world of technology development, as well as a plug for product/technology gaps in its portfolio.

   Box 9.5 lists some of the overseas corporate venturing activities undertaken by 3M Company.

2. *Joint technology development.* In this form of strategic alliance, two or three firms come together for a limited period of time to conduct research projects whose benefits flow back to the partners themselves. The alliances could vary from joint R&D projects, teaming agreements, and technology exchange contracts, to joint ventures. In the case of joint ventures, two or three firms float a separate firm (joint venture), and all partners hold shares in the newly created venture. Partners may, however, differ in terms of the kind of competence they bring to the venture: Some may bring technology expertise; others may bring marketing expertise; and still others may bring management and operating expertise.

3. *Outsourcing.* Outsourcing involves one firm contracting out some activity in technology appropriation, deployment, or marketing. Outsourcing in the

---

BOX 9.5

3M OVERSEAS INVESTMENTS

France	Paribas
	Patricof
	Soginnove
Germany	Technoventures
Italy	Finprogetti
Japan	Paribas
The Netherlands	Euroventures
Spain	Advent
Switzerland	Genevest
United Kingdom	Cygnus
	Phildrew

Source: From Hegg, G. L., "A Corporate View of Venture Capital," The Conference Board and Industrial Research Institute, New York City, March 20, 1989.

case of appropriation or deployment of technology usually takes place on a case-by-case basis. For example, pharmaceutical companies sometimes outsource clinical trials involved in the drug development.

Table 9.2 summarizes the differences between the various forms of strategic alliances.

DEPLOYMENT OF TECHNOLOGY IN NEW PRODUCTS

Speeding the time to market and creating potential for new products through technology integration are also propelling firms to undertake joint activities with other firms in the domain of technology deployment in product markets. Some firms in the United States have always practiced acquisition of new products through equity participation or mergers. Increasingly, however, firms are also engaging in inward technology licensing and joint development of products.

Inward technology licensing (ITL). This refers to a contractual arrangement whereby one firm (licensee) obtains the rights to use technology (in the form of patents, trademarks, manufacturing, marketing, and technical expertise) from another firm, organization, or individual (the licensor). ITL has several advantages, as well as disadvantages, over internal product development:

1. The capital investment in the case of ITL is generally believed to be less than in the case of new product development. One estimate puts the costs of acquiring a new product through ITL at 2 to 10 percent of the internal development cost.[7]
2. Unlike internal new product development, ITL is a faster method of acquiring and upgrading internal capabilities, entering new markets, and filling product gaps.
3. A firm that uses ITL has a relatively lower degree of control over the technology than in-house new product development. Thus, when a firm licenses in a new product technology, the licensor may impose restrictions on its use in such areas as export, purchase of raw materials, grant-back provisions, pricing, quality control, and production limits.
4. ITL may also involve transaction costs such as costly and lengthy negotiations, overseas travel, and the risk of the licensor licensing out the same product to a competitor.
5. Finally, ITL has not allowed the licensee to gain substantial expertise in the area.

The technology that is inherent in ITL agreements usually is in the mature stages and, therefore, does not offer a major technological lead for the licensee over its competitors.

Joint technology development. When firms want to have a technological lead over their competitors in new product development efforts, they usually undertake joint development efforts or in-house development as alternatives. Joint development efforts are very common in fast-changing industrial sectors: electronics, computers, telecommunications, and biotechnology. Joint development efforts may take place between firms pursuing complementary products, as in the case of the joint venture efforts between IBM and Microsoft in the early 1980s, or among competitors, as in the case of IBM and Apple in recent years.

TABLE 9.2 Comparative Analysis of Types of Strategic Alliances

	Corporate Venturing	Technology Appropriation	Outsourcing	Marketing of Technology
1. Objectives	Enabler of technology strategy	Joint development of products, processes	Building relationships to perform key activities	Appropriating value from technology developed in-house
2. Typical Arrangements	Financial participation, equity purchase, acquisition	Joint venture, joint R&D, teaming agreements	Manufacturing capacity utilization	Licensing consulting services
3. Type of Arrangement	Long-term exclusive			Case-by-case nonexclusive

In Table 9.3, we have summarized the key differences between inhouse product development, inward technology licensing and joint technology development.

DEPLOYMENT OF TECHNOLOGY IN THE VALUE CHAIN

As firms are faced with changes in technology that render traditional technologies and competencies obsolete, they are undertaking joint efforts with other firms to carry out many of the activities in the value chain. Advances in information technology and the rise of global competitors have been the primary drivers of this trend. Three major forms of alliances have appeared in recent years: (1) logistic alliances, (2) information partners, and (3) outsourcing.

LOGISTIC ALLIANCES

Many manufacturers and vendors are employing logistics alliances as a way to lower distribution and storage operating costs and to improve the quality of customer service. The principals in a typical agreement are a provider of customized logistic services and a producer of goods that jointly engineer and launch a system to speed goods to customers. In logistic alliances, the service provider usually assumes a certain amount of risk through an agreement calling for a penalty, such as an automatic reduction in revenues, if performance is worse than specified. On the other hand, the agreements often include rewards for superior performance, such as a greater than expected percentage of on-time delivery. Of course, the risks may also include a capital investment on the provider's part. Consider the following example:

- In early 1990, American President Companies started a double-stack container rail service from Woodhaven, Michigan, to Ford Motor Company's auto assembly plant in Hermosillo, Mexico. APC coordinates all the information, transportation, and inventory handling necessary to pick up parts and components from vendors and sequence-load them into containers for delivery on a just-in-time basis to Hermosillo. The movement includes coordination over four railroads and with Mexican customs officials for delay-free clearance. At the plant, Ford has built a state-of-the-art stack train terminal to smooth the flow of sequence parts into assembly operations. APC provides cranes and management to break down containers. The partners collaborate to return containers to the United States carrying components produced in the Maquiladora region.

TABLE 9.3   Differences Between Inward Technology Licensing, Joint Development, and In-House New Product Development

	In-House New Product Development	Joint Development	Inward Technology Licensing
Control	High	Medium	Low
Resource Commitment	High	Medium	Low
Strategic Flexibility	Low	Medium	High
Risk Exposure	Low	Medium	Low

Several forces have created a favorable environment for logistics alliances:

1. The legal and political environment of the 1980s stimulated the development of integrated-service practices. Thus, deregulation of transportation and communications, coupled with relaxed antitrust enforcement, generated an atmosphere conducive to innovation.
2. The explosion in information technology has made computerization cheap, and computers hold logistic alliances together.
3. Today's emphasis on low-cost operation has sensitized managers to turn to the opportunities inherent in using external specialists to solve problems outside the organization's sphere of expertise.
4. Competitive forces are causing firms to do all they can to become low-cost competitors, including efficient logistics operations.[8]

INFORMATION PARTNERS

Information technology developments have created a new form of joint efforts: the information partnership, facilitated by the sharing of customer data. Consider the following example:

- In a partnership between American Airlines and Citibank, air mileage credit in the airline's frequent flyer program is awarded to credit card users: 1 mile for every dollar spent on the card. American has thus increased the loyalty of its customers, and the credit card company has gained access to a new and highly creditworthy customer phase for cost marketing. This partnership has been expanded to include MCI, a major long-distance phone company, which offers multiairline frequent flyer miles for each dollar of long-distance billing. Recently, Citibank, the largest issuer of VISA and Master Card, initiated a partnership to steer its 14.6 million VISA holders to MCI, a response to AT&T's entry into credit cards.

Four different kinds of information partnerships have emerged: (1) joint marketing partnerships, (2) inter-industry partnerships, (3) customer-supplier partnerships, and (4) IT vendor-driven partnerships.[9]

1. *Joint marketing partnerships.* In marketing partnerships, the partnering firms gain access to new customers and territories and to economies of scale through cost sharing. For the provider of the data channel, sharing offers an opportunity to sell excess capacity in the channel, to ensure that the company's image and marketing position are not compromised, and to extend their reach to customers once thought too expensive to reach. The effort by IBM and Sears to make Prodigy is an example of such an effort. At the expense of more than $500 million, these companies assembled a package of over 400 electronic data services to be delivered across a standard telephone network to millions of American homes. Taken individually, this service is used so infrequently that customers would be unlikely to find any of them worthwhile. However, IBM and Sears have perceived that these services have considerable appeal when bundled together.
2. *Inter-industry partnerships.* These partnerships evolve among small or midsized competitors who see an opportunity or a need to pool resources. They, thus, collect the capital and skills required to create a new technology

infrastructure for an entire industry. In one case, 18 mid-sized paper companies jointly developed a global electronic information system to link themselves with hundreds of key customers and international sales offices. Another partnership among competitors is the insurance value added network services (IVANS) linking a roster of insurance companies to hundreds of home offices of thousands of independent agents. In the auto parts industry (MEMA)/transnet—connecting manufacturers and thousands of retailers—resulted from actions by Motor Equipment Manufacturers Association (MEMA).

3. *Customer-supplier partnerships.* These partnerships evolve from data networks set up by suppliers to service customers. For example, Baxter Healthcare, a major medical and health care supplier, is offering its customers office supplies and even medical supplies of a competitor through its direct electronic customer channel. The system has created a platform, a single interface, for buyers to reach their many suppliers; participating supplier organizations now reach new customers at lower costs. For its part, Baxter has developed a new revenue stream, offering a mighty package of vendor services.

4. *IT vendor-driven partnerships.* Sometimes, a technology provider may bring its technology to a new market and provide a platform for uninitiated industry participants to offer novel customer services. For example, ASAB, a large European welding supplies and equipment company, tripled in size as a result of an alliance with a large independent network vendor. It used its ally's information services to facilitate acquiring and rationalizing failing companies all over Europe: closing their plants, moving production of what had been a local plant to a central plant, and providing old customers an on-line ordering service. Sometimes, an information vendor may form a research alliance with a major customer, establishing joint information research projects through beta sites, where a manufacturer tests a new technology with selected clients to debug it or understand more fully how it may be used. Vendors gain valuable insight into the practical field problems associated with their technology, whereas the customer learns about a new technology that may otherwise be beyond its skill and financial resources.

Information partnerships are a phenomenon of the 1990s, created by advances in low-cost information technology triggered by computerization.

OUTSOURCING

Outsourcing involves subcontracting one or several activities in a firm's value chain to other firms. U.S. firms have employed outsourcing as a mechanism in a number of industries, including consumer electronics, heavy machinery, power generation equipment, composite materials, factory equipment, and office equipment. Although outsourcing of production and distribution has had a long history, one of the new functions being outsourced in recent times is information technology.

- Consider the Kodak story: In 1989, Kodak decided to outsource IT. Kodak's chief information officer (CIO), who had been a general manager rather than a computer professional, took an aggressive stance in outsourcing mainframes, telecommunications, and CPS.

- In the last few years, a number of banks have outsourced their information technology operation to firms such as IBM, in the hope that the contracting company can perform the IT function more effectively than the banks themselves.

Unlike a customer-supplier relationship, these outsourcing contracts require the two firms to work together at a more intense level: The contracting supplier has to understand the operations of the banks at a level not necessary in a typical customer-supplier relationship. Two factors have affected the growth of all IT outsourcing—the recognition of the value of strategic alliances and the changes in the technological environment. Thus, firms and managers have come to recognize the value of strategic alliances. Second, the rapid fusion of computers and telecommunications technologies has led many firms in the difficult position of needing to integrate both internal and external computers so that they can effectively function in the global marketplace. This integration is putting extraordinary pressures on firms that are trying to keep the old service running while developing the interconnections and services demanded by the new environment. Thus, outsourcing has become a viable alternative for those firms to gain access to appropriate skills and to speed up the transition reliably and cost-effectively.[10]

MARKETING OF TECHNOLOGY

The marketing of technology represents the opposite side of outsourcing: Firms that have technology capabilities partner with firms that need the requisite technology for mutual benefit. The major mechanisms by which firms market technologies are (1) licensing of technology, (2) provision of consulting services, and (3) sale of technology through divestiture.

There are several reasons why firms may choose to sell technologies:

1. Firms want to appropriate the best value from their technology development efforts, especially those technologies that they know have no immediate relevance to their own lines of business. For example, General Electric developed a microorganism that destroys oil spills by digesting it. However, GE decided to offer the technology for sale because it did not fit the company's major lines of business.
2. Some technologies developed in-house may not pertain to a company's overall strategy because the market for their application may be too small or undesirable. As an instance, GE sold off its mature Fluidics technology because it no longer contributed to the company's major strengths or strategies.
3. A company may not have the complementary assets needed to produce and market a product. Sinclair Radionics, a small British company in the consumer electronics industry, made a breakthrough in the technology of flat-screen color TV. However, Sinclair lacked the resources to market the screen; therefore, it had to seek joint venture arrangements with large multinational electronics companies as a way of combining resources.
4. Antitrust regulations and other regulatory restraints may prevent a firm from exploiting its technology. For example, in some of the Third World countries, licensing is probably the only way by which a firm can offer its products.[11]

Marketing of technology may span the whole spectrum of outright sale, as in the case of General Electric's microorganism, to licensing of technology to partners both domestic and global. Licensing is particularly common in the technology arena. For example, Magnavox widely licensed its video-game patents, reasoning that it could expand the market faster through encouraging competitors to introduce a wide range of products. Similarly, AT&T and IBM may award a license in return for a license of another firm's technology. The pioneers of VHS and beta formats in videocassette recorders licensed them widely to promote standardization, because standardization was so critical to increasing the availability of software.

RISKS OF COLLABORATIVE ACTIVITY

From a strategic viewpoint, collaborative mode is undertaken by firms when the economics of collaborative mode enhance the firm's value more than the alternative mode of a firm undertaking implementation all by itself. Thus, the choice of the mode of implementation resembles many make-or-buy decisions made by firms where a firm chooses between performing an activity or making a component in-house over finding a subcontractor. However, the decision is complicated in the technology arena, because the nature of the interrelationships between collaborating firms is far more intense than in the case of a component or some particular raw material. The joint nature of the activity in the collaborative mode introduces three major risks for the participating firms: (1) intellectual property right risks, (2) competitive risks, and (3) organizational risks.

INTELLECTUAL PROPERTY RIGHT RISK

The knowledge gained through the appropriation, deployment, sale, or marketing of technology is referred to as intellectual property. Intellectual property may be hardware- or software-dominant property:

* A prototype that results from product development efforts is often hardware dominant.
* The information that is obtained from implementing a technology or research and development activities—information about how to implement change or a particular scientific process—often resides in the heads of individuals involved in the process and, hence, will be software dominant.

When a firm undertakes the appropriation or deployment of technology in-house, the rights to the intellectual property, that is, the economic returns accruing from ownership of the intellectual property, rest exclusively with the firm that holds such property rights. However, in the collaborative mode, because a number of firms are jointly engaged in the technology effort, the question of intellectual property rights and their subdivision among the partners is an important problem to be resolved by the collaborating firms.

We can identify three forms of intellectual property: (1) private property, (2) public property, and (3) leaky property:

> *Private property* is any intellectual property that a private party practically or legally appropriates; private property may be transferred to others at the owner's wish.

Public property cannot practically be appropriated by the inventor for even a short period of time. In the United States, the means for producing public property has been to grant public funds to universities and nonprofit research organizations, or to sponsor government-owned laboratories.

Leaky property refers to knowledge that can be appropriated by another through imitation, observation, or by hiring people away. It can effectively be appropriated by a private party, but only for a short period of time. The prospective inventor foresees that the invention will be successful and have substantial value to its users. He also realizes, however, that he may be unable to monopolize the returns sufficiently to justify his investment.[12]

Different forms of intellectual property arise from different institutional arrangements. Figure 9.3 arrays the three classes of property against the appropriate institutional forms: the private firm, joint undertakings, and university or government laboratory. Joint undertakings—technology strategy through collaborative mode—lead to leaky property, which places the partners or the private firms engaged in the collaboration in a weak position to appropriate the benefits of the joint endeavor. In particular, because R&D or technology management has a complex and uncertain set of outcomes, contractual agreements will be difficult to specify and monitor; the partners can behave opportunistically both during, as well as after, the joint effort. Thus, the collaborating firms run the potential risk of erosion of their intellectual rights, due to the sharing of intellectual property rights and the threat of opportunistic behavior by their partners.

COMPETITIVE RISK

In many domains of technology strategy, joint efforts pose an additional risk to the partners: Because collaborative efforts require a deeper interdependence among partners than that existing in the case of typical customer-supplier relationships, each of the partners gets a window to the knowledge base of the other. Such a knowledge base may pertain to products both current and planned, as well as information that is useful in research and deployment of technology. Thus, competitive risk refers to the danger that one of the partners may imitate another's technology and attempt to compete with the firm in which it acquires the relevant know-how.

The competitive risks can be dangerous, particularly for small firms. For example, small companies have lost valuable technical advantage to competitors through intentional and unintentional revelation of commercial secrets.[13] Of course, a common

Type of Property	Organizational Form
Private Property	For-profit corporation
Leaky Property	Collaborative arrangements
Public Property	Government, nonprofit educational institutions

Source: From Ouchi, W. G. and Bolton, M. K. "The Logic of Joint Research and Development." Copyright © 1988, by The Regents of the University of California. Reprinted from the *California Management Review*, Vol. 30, No. 3. By permission of The Regents.

FIGURE 9.3 INTELLECTUAL PROPERTY

problem small companies face is that they lack experience or resources to protect their intellectual property. Failure to protect the rights at the outset has meant that companies have lost out on a share of ownership and have devoted resources to projects only to find themselves in dispute later.

ORGANIZATIONAL RISK

Because joint efforts require coordination between partners who are autonomous entities, the modes of behavior that are required for effective performance on the joint effort are somewhat different from the normal operations of an organization. Organizational risk refers to the problems that appear due to the way in which joint efforts are managed. Broadly, such risks arise from four factors: (1) differing priorities, (2) differing behavior styles, (3) lack of performance of one partner, and (4) relationships among people.

1. *Differing priorities among partners in joint efforts.* In one example, a joint venture between a small and large company, the smaller company was invited to help develop a product, an automatic blocking machine, on the basis of previous interaction. Problems arose when a short-term solution was found that did not involve the full development of the instrument and for which the smaller firm needed the larger company's knowledge of the process involved. Eventually, the product was completed, but the smaller company had lost time in getting the instrument to market.[14]

2. *Differences in behavior style.* Because joint efforts require a greater degree of trust than that in typical customer-supplier relationships, high-handed behavior on the part of one or both partners can be ruinous to the venture. For example, a large European electronics firm had been working on a data station for use in laboratories—a project that needed software inputs too sophisticated for in-house capacity. For 3 years, the company embarked on a joint venture with a firm in the United States; but, the U.S. firm failed to deliver on its promise. It was decided that the firm would approach a British company so that communication and monitoring would be easier. The British firm was chosen by the in-house people because of their technical competence. However, problems arose out of initial advantage the smaller company had seized when a partner heard how desperate the larger firm was for a signed formal agreement. With this knowledge, the smaller firm was able to impose terms on the larger; however, this simply created a lack of trust in the longer term.[15]

3. *Lack of performance.* Because technology ventures are often fraught with uncertainty, lack of performance by one or both firms involved in a joint effort can be a major risk to the development effort. For example, Apple's laser writer is a case in point. Apple persuaded Canon to participate in the development of the laser writer. Canon provided subsystems from its copiers, but only after Apple contracted to pay for a certain number of copiers. In short, Apple actually took a good deal of financial risk in order to induce Canon to assist in the development and introduction of a laser writer. Yet, there are risks for both sides. It is difficult to write, execute, and enforce complex development contracts, particularly when the design of the

new product is still floating, which is often the case, even after commercialization. Apple was exposed to the risk that its co-innovator Canon would fail to deliver, and Canon was exposed to the risk that Apple's design and marketing effort would not succeed.

4. *Relationship among people.* Personal relationships are not only an outcome of collaboration, but also a key element in its success. For example, the director of a research institute had for some time bought equipment from Browns and had been impressed by the quality of their back-up service. He was able to go into a partnership with Browns to develop a novel piece of equipment that had considerable market potential but that needed the technical expertise of both firms. However, the opportunity for Browns came only after larger firms, which had been approached by the director, had rejected the project as having insufficient potential. The smaller company in this case had committed itself to a long-term development project requiring considerable investment of resources.[16]

In Box 9.6, we have summarized how, in recent years, some of the domestic strategic alliances have experienced problems due to organizational issues.

In summary, the collaborative mode of implementation of technology strategy poses three sets of risk for the firms engaged in the collaboration: intellectual property loss, competitive risk, and organizational risk. These returns and risks differ among the

---

BOX 9.6

PROBLEMS IN JOINT VENTURE

Scores of high-tech companies have set up joint ventures and alliances in the past few years, deciding it makes sense to work together on risky projects. But, as narrated in a recent *Wall Street Journal* article, many of the groupings have faltered.

An example is Kaleida, formed in 1991 as part of an alliance between Apple Computer, Inc., and International Business Machines Corp. It was supposed to develop a software language that would allow personal computers, video-game machines, and other devices to play the same multimedia programs, mixing sound, text, and video.

But Kaleida was rocked by management shake-ups and conflicting agendas of its parents:

1. John Sculley, then Apple CEO, announced a product delivery schedule be-

fore Kaleida had hired its first employee. After that, the venture was faulted for running 2 years behind schedule.

2. When the product was ready, IBM and Apple, intent on protecting other parts of their businesses, hindered the creation of programs for Kaleida-equipped devices.

3. Inside Apple, one software group opposed Kaleida because it competed with their own work.

Kaleida is not the only one to fail. Alliances between US West and Time Warner Inc.; Prodigy, the alliance between IBM and Sears; General Magic (backed by AT&T and Sony)—the list could go on. All have met with failures.

Source: Republished with permission of Dow Jones & Company, from Bart Ziegler, "How Do Joint Ventures Go Wrong? Ask Kaleida," *The Wall Street Journal,* 1995, page B1; permission conveyed through Copyright Clearance Center, Inc.

various domains of activity in the technology strategy: appropriation of technology, deployment in new products or value chains, and marketing.

APPROPRIATION OF TECHNOLOGY

Joint R&D efforts between competitors should address the technical goals, intellectual property rights, and the organizational arrangements required to implement the technical goals. In a recent study of joint R&D activity, Ouchi and Bolton discovered that establishment of a delicate balance between competition and team work is a major challenge for participants in joint R&D efforts. They also found each collaboration must locate the domains between research, which is overly basic—and thus of little interest to participants—and that which is overly proprietary.[17] As we had indicated, successful resolution of the dilemmas posed by the three types of risks—intellectual property, competitive, and organizational risks—is a prerequisite to the success of the collaborative effort during appropriation of technology. In Box 9.7, we have showcased the Corporation for Open Systems, a joint R&D effort in the United States, by outlining the technical goals, organizational forms, and intellectual property rights.

JOINT PRODUCT DEVELOPMENT

In addition to the risk posed by a loss of intellectual property and organizational risk, joint development efforts provide firms with a window to their partners, processes, and capabilities, and, therefore, induce greater levels of competitive risk. However, they also give firms the opportunity to produce new products by exploiting complementary strengths and technology integration.

OUTSOURCING

Outsourcing creates direct and indirect windows of opportunity for gaining access to a partner's skills, technologies, competencies, and even strategic direction. Consequently, there are risks involved in outsourcing, especially loss of intellectual property and competitive risks.

First, outsourcing may lead to the loss of intellectual property. The loss of intellectual property can take place in two ways:

1. When firms concentrate their efforts on designing, distributing, and marketing new product ideas, thereby outsourcing the production of these products, the ensuing division of labor results in a steady deterioration of firms' production skills and technologies that are important sources of organizational learning. For example, consumer electronics firms, such as General Electric, Westinghouse, and Zenith, often enter into supply arrangements with Japanese and Korean partners because of their inability to build low-cost high-quality components at home. This form of outsourcing may actually accelerate the "hollowing out" of a domestic industry precisely because foreign partners are able to develop the kinds of human resource skills and technologies needed to enter into an industry on their own.

2. Sometimes the partner is able to learn from a firm that often has seriously undervalued the technology's potential use in other product applications. This was the case with GE's early joint venture with Citizen of Japan. GE believed that tuning fork technology developed for watches had little use elsewhere; Citizen applied the manufacturing skills learned from working with miniaturized tuning forks to other electronic applications.[18]

BOX 9.7

OFFICE SYSTEMS

The Corporation for Open Systems (COS) in Alexandria, Virginia, emerged to accelerate implementation of industry standards that would permit electronic equipment, computers, and telecommunication equipment manufactured by different companies to interconnect and to be interoperable. Members believe that the growth of the "information" industry depends upon development of these standards.

In May 1985, the Computer and Communications Industry Association sponsored the formation of task teams among 17 companies to study the "open systems" concept promulgated by the International Standards Organization and by another international telecommunications standards body, the CCITT. In September, the task teams reported that each company had been individually participating in these standards bodies for 7 years. In that time, only two applications had matured sufficiently; agreement on implementation of standards had led to the actual offering of products incorporating those standards.

Galvanized by this recognition, the group reconvened in October, established long-range goals, and appointed an executive committee. In January 1986, the founding companies hired an external program management firm to provide a rapid start and began an intensive membership drive. By March, COS was formally incorporated, and a president was hired in April. COS's initial annual budget was established at approximately $8 million, provided by 41 members.

Technical Goals. The task teams identified eight critical areas of need, from which specific sets of protocols were selected for development. They agreed to develop the capability to test and certify equipment meeting those standards. Once these goals have been attained, each company may then independently develop its own products, which will be interoperable with the products of other manufacturers.

COS established the following specific technical goals:

- to deliver a file transfer applications package;
- to deliver an electronic mail applications package; and
- to deliver document management, virtual terminal, network management, and directory service applications packages.

Organizational Form. COS is in its infancy, and its ultimate form is yet to be realized. It appears, however, that compared to other collaboratives, its structure and governance mechanisms are somewhat more complex. A board of directors, with one representative from each member company, provides governance. Additionally, an 11-member executive committee elected from the board has been established. The strategy forum, also composed of one representative from each company, meets more frequently and oversees the technical subcommittees.

Most of the technical work of COS occurs within the in-house laboratories of each member company, augmented by support from the testing lab at COS. Companies will develop specific protocols, develop "test beds" on which new products can be demonstrated, and develop testing capabilities. The COS staff and committees oversee these efforts, share information, and communicate with the relevant international standards bodies. COS is neither a directorate like PRADCO nor an operating entity like the VLSI Association or MCC, but combines features of each type. COS elected a hybrid structure because it must serve as an intermediary between the international standards bodies, which set basic standards, and the individual firms, which design and manufacture products that embody those standards. COS included both large and small companies

Source: Ouchi, William G., and Bolton, Michele K. "The Logic of Joint Research and Development," *California Management Review,* Spring 1988, pp. 20–21.

in its membership, thereby increasing the difficulties of reaching agreement. The development of several membership categories permits representation of all who wish to be included. Relatively more influence may be concentrated in the hands of the larger firms, who otherwise might not have joined COS.

Intellectual Property. COS has determined that it will own the intellectual property that it produces and license that property to member companies. Because of its newness,

however, more specific agreements have yet to be consolidated.

COS emerged because the international standards bodies were slow to translate conceptual agreements on standards into specifics. The disparate goals of the many COS member firms, however, require relatively intricate governance mechanisms. The tension between equitable participation by all members and efficient administration poses a significant managerial challenge.

Second, there may be competitive risks. For example, partners in an outsourcing alliance could emerge as competitors in the future. In addition to this obvious risk, outsourcing often limits a firm's future strategic discretion. For example, in the course of the joint venture between Matsushiba and NB Philips in compact disc technology, Philips lost many sources of initiative and now serves as a distributor of Matsushiba across several lines of compact disc products. Matsushiba had a window of opportunity to learn about future Philips developments and strategic direction in related technologies.

Finally, in outsourcing alliances, performance risks are also present. Such performance risks exist in the case of logistics and IT outsourcing alliances. For example, many small banks that have outsourced IT face the risk of changes in software and resulting disruptions when their partners make internal decisions related to the information system that they have to subcontract.

LICENSING OF TECHNOLOGY

Just as in the case of any other domain, marketing of technology, especially through licensing, also has its risks. Perhaps the most significant is the competitive risk. Licensing may unnecessarily create competitors in the process and cause a firm to give away its competitive advantage for a small royalty fee. Licensing often is an easy way of increasing short-term profits, but it can result in long-term erosion in profits and dissipation of a firm's competitive advantage. For example, during the late 1970s, Fiat faced in its Western European car markets fierce competition from its licensees in the Soviet Union and Poland. Similarly, many firms have licensed to firms in other industries only to have the licensees ultimately enter their own industry. Because a licensee can learn everything possible, not only about the license source technology but about its other value activities as well, the licensee can decide to attack the licensor successfully and become a serious competitor. Asian firms that have licensed widely have sometimes used licenses in this way.[19]

INFLUENCE OF ENVIRONMENTAL TRENDS

The three environmental trends—time compression, potential for technology integration, and globalization—are indeed related to the increasing emphasis on the collaborative mode of implementation of technology strategy. As we have seen, knowledge

acquisition and transfer lie at the center of many such arrangements. Similarly, reducing time to market has also driven such arrangements. Because we have discussed the
influence of time compression and technology integration, we will focus in this section
on globalization.

Two major facets of globalization of collaborative activity deserve mention: R&D
collaboration in other parts of the world and global technology alliances.

R&D COLLABORATION IN JAPAN AND EUROPE

Although we have discussed cooperative research organizations developed in the
United States, similar modes of collective research are evident in other countries as well.
For example, in Japan these activities fall roughly into three institutional categories:

1. Government establishments affiliated with the technical ministry;
2. Centers directed by local and regional authorities, and
3. Semipublic centers.

The Japanese system represents a widespread network for collective research in which
government serves as an integrating influence and private sector participation varies.
Collective industrial research in Europe operates primarily on three levels:

1. Traditional collective research associations that perform research for companies in a single industry sector;
2. National programs to coordinate R&D between industry and academic consortia within a single country, and
3. Community-wide programs to promote research consortia that cross national boundaries.

In 1984, the European Community and European private industry launched a new
model for cooperation: the European Strategic Program for R&D in Information Technologies (ESPRIT). It focuses on long-lead-time R&D in basic technologies and on free
competitive technical areas in fields like advanced microelectronics, data and knowledge processing, and office and factory automation. Further, the collaborations among
countries are also growing, a point to which we now turn.

GLOBAL TECHNOLOGY ALLIANCES

In the wake of the pressures created by globalization, strategic alliances among partners domiciled in different countries are becoming increasingly common. We will call
them *global alliances*. Global alliances have sprung up between partners in Western
countries, between firms in Western countries and Asian countries, and between small
and large companies. Consider the following examples:

> Western partners. Through its alliance with France's state-owned FMECMA,
> General Electric produced a low-pollution engine for high-performance air-
> craft. Both sides agreed to share the estimated $800 million development costs,
> an amount neither company was prepared to commit on its own.
>
> Alliances with Japanese. By 1990, Borden, Inc., based in Columbus, Ohio,
> and Meiji Milk products company of Japan were entering the 20th year of a
> major collaborative agreement. Meiji Milk, established in 1917, ranked as the

second largest dairy producer in Japan and handled three products under the Borden brand name—margarine, ice cream, and cheese.

Alliances with Eastern Europe. Although more recent, firms are also developing strategic alliances with partners in Eastern Europe, stimulated by the fall of the Berlin Wall. For example, Denver Moscow Inc. is a Colorado corporation, founded in 1991. A subsidiary, Siberia West Ltd., also a Colorado corporation, is jointly owned with Sibtecom, a private corporation in Krasnoyarsk, Russia. As a result of an unusual opportunity to restore a historic site near Kaluga, Russia, some of the U.S. partners in Denver Moscow have formed a nonprofit company called Pushkin Goncharop Historical Foundation. All three of these firms—Denver Moscow, Siberia West and the Foundation—are located in Colorado.

Alliances between large and small firms. In 1985, Juan Rodriguez started Exabyte, a company that manufacturers high-capacity 8-millimeter computer tape drives that back up and store huge amounts of data, unattended. Unable to strike deals with American companies, Exabyte turned to Japanese firms instead. Sony now provides the 8-millimeter mechanical disk for Exabyte's drives. Kabota manufacturers 60 percent of the product and distributes Exabyte's tape drives in the Far East. Increasingly, many of the small firms, especially in the United States, are turning to global partners for capital and marketing expertise.

Table 9.4 illustrates the many industries with strategic alliances between U.S. firms and foreign partners.[20]

In many ways, global alliances are similar to domestic alliances: They offer sharing of returns for the participating firms and pose similar risks—intellectual property loss, competitive risk, and organization and management risk.[21] However, in one area, global alliances produce an additional level of complexity: Partners from different countries bring different cultural assumptions into an alliance. Such cultural assumptions may focus on management approaches as well as appropriateness of various governance mechanisms.

1. Global partners may bring to the alliance differing solutions for managing complex organizations. For example, firms in the United States have often focused on command and control systems for handling increased information-processing demands necessary for coordination and control. On the other hand, the solutions for managing complex organizations from Japanese firms have often been premised on a trust-based community model of collaborative behavior.[22]
2. Similarly, North Americans have historically harbored the belief that power, not parity, should govern collaborative ventures. In contrast, Europeans and Japanese often consider partners as equals, subscribe to management by consensus, and rely on lengthy discussion to secure stronger commitment to share the enterprises.[23]

For example, in a recent study of the relative importance of 22 joint venture determinants with American and Japanese managers, it was discovered that, whereas honesty, reliability, mutual trust, and confidence were among the determinants paramount in

TABLE 9.4   Areas of Growing U.S. Dependency

Consumer Electronics	**Composite Materials**
GE-Hitachi (TVs)	GE-Asahi Diamond (Industrial Diamonds)
Westinghouse-Toshiba (TVs)	Corning Glass-NGK Insulators (High-Energy Ceramics)
GE-Samsung (Microwave Ovens)	Hercules-Toray (Specialized Chemicals)
GE-Matsushita (Room Air Conditioners)	Armco-Mitsubishi Rayon (Composite Plastics)
RCA-Matsushita (VCRs)	**Factory Equipment**
Kodak-Canon (Photographic Equipment)	GE-Fanuc (Controllers)
Kodak-Matsushita (Camcorders)	GM-Fanuc (Robotics)
Kodak-Philips (Photo-CD Players)	GM-Hitachi (Robotics)
Heavy Machinery	Bendix-Murata (Machine Tools)
Allis Chalmers-Fiat-Hitachi (Construction Equipment)	Cincinnati Milacron (Semiconductors, Automated Equipment)
Ford-Fiat (Farm Equipment)	Kawasaki-Unimation (Robotics)
Caterpillar (Growing Outsourcing)	Fujitsu-McDonnell Douglas (CAD/CAM Systems)
Dresser-Komatsu (Construction Equipment)	IBM-Sankyo Seiki (Robotics)
Deere-Hitachi (Farm Equipment)	Houdaille-Okuma (Machine Tools)
Clark-Samsung (Forklift Trucks)	Allen Bradley-Nippondenso (Programmable Controls)
Power Generation Equipment	Bendix-Yasegawa Tools (Robotics)
Westinghouse-ABB (Heavy Power Equipment)	**Office Equipment**
GE-Toshiba (Nuclear Equipment)	AT&T-Ricoh (Fax Machines)
GE-Hitachi (Nuclear Equipment)	Kodak-Canon (Mid-range Copiers)
GEO-Mitsubishi (Motors)	Fuji-Xerox (Small Copiers)
Westinghouse-Komatsu (Motors, Robotics)	3M-Toshiba (Copiers)
ABB-Combustion Engineering (Power Equipment)	Apple-Toshiba (Printers)
	RCA-Hitachi (PBX Controls)
	Hewlett Packard-Canon (Laser Printers)
	Xerox-Sharp (Low-End Copiers)

Source: From Lei, David and Slocum, John W. Jr. "Global Strategy, Competence Building and Strategic Alliances." Copyright © 1992, by The Regents of the University of California. Reprinted from the *California Management Review,* Vol. 35, No. 1. By permission of The Regents.

importance regardless of national and organizational background, cultural influences were linked to different concepts of teamwork and collaboration.[24] These differences enhance the organizational risk of global technology alliances.

MANAGERIAL IMPLICATIONS

Obviously, firms should explicitly consider the collaborative arrangements as a means to implement their technology strategy. Beyond this, two major managerial implications can be suggested: (1) the choice of the form of arrangement and (2) attention to execution.

THE FORM OF COLLABORATIVE ARRANGEMENT

The appropriateness of the collaborative arrangement for a particular firm may be determined with the help of the Technology-Market (T-M) Matrix. The critical factor is a firm's familiarity with the technology and its markets. When the technology and markets are familiar, a firm may be better off developing or deploying them internally. The less familiar the firm is with technology and markets, the more difficult it is to develop them internally: The firm may be better off cooperating with another firm that has them.

The form of collaborative arrangement may vary from joint ventures, acquisitions, licensing, corporate venturing, and nurturing and educational acquisitions. In Figure 9.4, we have summarized the optimal mechanisms for collaborative arrangements.

1. If the technology and market are familiar, internal development is preferred, because the firm has the capability to execute the technology strategy. If the market is familiar and the technology is new but familiar, acquisition and licensing may be feasible in addition to internal development. Similarly, acquisition (in addition to internal development) is a viable alternative in new but familiar markets where the firm knows the technology.
2. As either the markets or the technologies become less familiar, internal development is less feasible. Here, joint venture becomes an attractive mechanism. Joint ventures are thus formed between partners with complementary capabilities. When a firm is familiar with technology, it seeks a firm with marketing capabilities, and vice versa. When both technology and market are new but familiar, a firm may also use acquisitions or internal ventures. Internal ventures are separate entities set up within a firm to develop a new product, usually employing entrepreneurial individuals in a firm.
3. As both technologies and markets become unfamiliar and new, the firm is moving into radical innovations. Here, venture capital, venture nurturing, and educational acquisitions are the appropriate mechanisms. In venture capital, as in the case of 3M, a larger firm takes a small minority position in a young firm that has the capabilities to exploit the innovation. In venture nurturing, the investing firm also gives managerial assistance, in addition to capital. Educational acquisition is when a firm buys another not to keep it as a subsidiary, but with the sole purpose of learning from it.[25]

Market		Existing	New but Familiar	New and Unfamiliar
New and Unfamiliar	Joint venture	Venture capital Venture nurturing Educational acquisition	Venture capital Venture nurturing Educational acquisition	
New but Familiar	Internal market development Acquisition	Internal venture Acquisition Licensing	Venture capital Venture nurturing Educational acquisition	
Existing	Internal development (or acquisition)	Internal product development Acquisition Licensing	"New style" joint venture	

Technology

FIGURE 9.4 APPROPRIATE FORM OF COLLABORATIVE ARRANGEMENT

Source: Reprinted from "Entering New Businesses: Selecting Strategies for Success," by E. B. Roberts and C. A. Berry, *Sloan Management Review,* 1985, Vol. 26, pp. 3–17 by permission of publisher. Copyright 1985 by Sloan Management Review Association. All rights reserved.

EXECUTION

Success in reducing organizational risk collaborative arrangements results from good management practices that remove organizational and strategic differences as obstacle from collaborating with partners. Four key success factors are necessary for the success of a strategic alliance:

1. From the beginning, both partners need to define clearly the technical objectives of the collaborative arrangement, the scope of the business, and the responsibilities of each side in order to minimize the potential divergence of interests, in the long term.
2. From the start of the collaborative arrangement, top management of both parent companies must commit themselves to the success of the alliance and contribute most of their best managers to staff the new company.
3. Both parents should agree to start small, to treat the collaborative arrangement as truly independent and not to interfere in its day-to-day management.[26]

4. Because the alliance evolves over time, there is need for continuous, open, timely communications among partners.

Although these steps may seem commonplace, differences in the assumptions brought to bear on the alliance by the managers of the different partners necessitate very careful attention to the management of the four activities.

❖ CHAPTER SUMMARY

In this chapter, we have outlined the key ideas behind the collaborative mode of implementation of technology strategy. In recent years in the United States, there has been a growth in R&D partnerships, marketing alliances, outsourcing, and alliances between small and large firms.

There are three overriding reasons for collaborative arrangements: sharing of risks, pooling of resources, and leveraging of individual firms' capabilities. Both strategic and operating objectives propel a firm to undertake collaborative arrangements. Strategic objectives include controlling the competitive domain, knowledge transfer and acquisition, and maintaining institutional links to technology environment. Operational objectives may be competitive benchmarking, capturing operating efficiencies, time to market, and capturing value form technology development.

Collaborative arrangements are visible in the appropriation of technology, deployment of technology in new products and value chains, and marketing of technology. Cooperative research and strategic alliances are the usual forms of arrangements in technology appropriation. Inward technology alliances and joint product development are common in new product development. Outsourcing is increasingly common in value chain activities. Finally, licensing is a major way by which firms extract value from technology developed in-house.

All collaborative arrangements involve three types of risk: loss of intellectual property, competitive risk, and organizational risk. The risks are present in all the domains of collaborative arrangement: appropriation, deployment, and marketing.

Cooperative arrangements in technology development are common in Japan and Europe. In recent years, global technology alliances have also become common. Global alliances have sprung up between partners in Western countries, between firms in Western countries and Asian countries, and between small and large companies.

Managerially, different forms of arrangements are appropriate under different technology and market conditions. When the technology and market are familiar to the firm, internal development is encouraged. When either one is new or unfamiliar, joint venture or acquisition is an alternative. When neither the technology nor the market is familiar to a firm, acquisition, venture capital, or educational acquisitions are needed. The execution of collaborative arrangements requires specification of clear objectives, top management commitment, and clear and open communications.

❖ NOTES

1. From *Newsline,* "Learning Alliances: Cooperation Enters the Business Education Vocabuary," Vol. 24, No. 3, Spring 1994, pp. 1–5. *Newsline* is a publication of AACSB-The International Association of Management Education. Reprinted by permission.

2. Botkin, K. W. and Matthews, J. B. *Winning Combinations.* New York: John Wiley, 1992;

Smith, H. L., Dickson, K., and Smith, S. L. "There Are Two Sides to Every Story: Innovation and Collaboration within Networks of Large and Small Firms," *Research Policy,* 1991, Vol. 20, pp. 457–468.

3. Schroeder, Dean. Personal communication.

4. Peck, M. J. "Joint R&D: The Case of Micro Electronics and Computer Technology Corporation," *Research Policy,* October 1986, Vol. 15, No. 5, pp. 219–231.

5. Hakisch, C. S., Fusfeld, H. I., and Levenson, A. "Trends in Technical Projects by Industry Groupings," NYU Center for Technology Policy, December 1984, pp. 38–41.

6. Fusfeld, H. I. and Haclich, C. S. "Cooperative R&D for Competitors," *Harvard Business Review,* November-December 1985, pp. 60–76.

7. Morehead, John W. "Advantages of new product search," *Les Nouvelles,* June 1984, Vol. 19, pp. 100–102.

8. Bowersox, D. J. "The Strategic Benefits of Logistic Alliances," *Harvard Business Review,* July-August 1990, pp. 36–45.

9. Konsynski, B. R. and McFarlan, F. W. "Information Partnerships—Shared Data, Shared Skill," *Harvard Business Review,* September-October 1990, pp. 114–120.

10. McFarlan, Warren, and Nolan, R. F. "How to Manage an IT Outsourcing Alliance," *Sloan Management Review,* Winter, 1995, pp. 9–23.

11. Ford, D. and Bryant, C. "Taking Technology to Market," *Harvard Business Review,* March-April 1981, Vol. 59, No. 2.

12. Ouchi, W. G. and Bolton, N. K. "The Logic of Joint Research and Development," *California Management Review,* Spring 1988, pp. 9–38.

13. Smith, H. L., Dickson, K. and Smith, S. L. "There are Two-Sides to Every Story: Innovation and Collaboration within Networks of Large and Small Firms," *Research Policy,* 1991, Vol. 20, pp. 457–468.

14. Smith, et al., ibid.

15. Smith, et al., ibid.

16. Smith, et al., ibid.

17. Ouchi and Bolton, op. cit.

18. Magaziner, I. C., and Patinkin, M. "Fast Heat, How Korea Won the Microwave War," *Harvard Business Review,* January-February 1989, Vol. 63, pp. 83–93; Lewis, J. D. *Partnerships for Profit: Structuring and Management Strategic Alliances.* New York NY: The Free Press, 1990.

19. Porter, M. E. *Competitive Advantage.* New York: The Free Press, 1985, p. 193.

20. Lei, D. and Slocum, Jr., J. W. "Global Strategy, Competence Building and Strategic Alliances," *California Management Review,* 1992, pp. 81–95.

21. Perlmutter, H. B., and Heenan, D. A. "Cooperate to Compete in Global Economy," *Harvard Business Review,* March-April 1986, pp. 136–138; Huerman, A. G. "Creating an Effective Interface with Russian Technology." 3rd. Biannual High Technology Management Conference, June 16–18, 1993, University of Colorado at Boulder; Botkin, J. W. and Matthews, J. P. op. cit.

22. Wallace, A. "American and Japanese Perspectives on the Determinants of Successful Joint Ventures." Working Paper Series, International Management Research Institute, International University of Japan. No. 1993-003.

23. Perlmutter, H. W. and Heenan, D. A., op. c

24. Wallace, op. cit.

25. Roberts, E. B. and Berry, C. A. "Entering new businesses: Selecting strategies for success," *Sloan Management Review,* 1985, Vol. 26 (3), pp. 3–17.

26. Turpin, B. "Strategic Alliances with Japanese Firms: Myths and Realities," *Long Range Planning,* 1993, Vol. 26, No. 4, pp. 11–15.

PART III

DOMAINS OF TECHNOLOGY STRATEGY

In this part, we will elaborate on the content and process of strategy formulation in the three domains of technology strategy. It is in these domains that technology strategy is played out in concrete terms. Put another way, whereas our delineation of technology strategy in the previous three chapters was relatively abstract, our discussion of technology-strategy domains will link the abstract ideas to the concrete decisions made in organizations.

Although all three domains of technology strategy have concepts developed in related disciplines (e.g., new-product development in marketing or value chain in operations), we will highlight three themes in discussing these domains.

1. We will illustrate the importance of strategic concepts on managing these three domains in the pursuit of competitive advantage.
2. We will illustrate that although the three domains are treated separately, they are interconnected to varying degrees.
3. We will illustrate the influence of the key environmental trends—globalization, time compression, and technology integration—on each of the three domains.

In chapter 10, we will discuss research and development. The chapter discusses the movement to third-generation R&D, a relatively recent concept in R&D. Third-generation R&D ideas are

closely aligned with the central thrust of this book: Technology strategy's primary focu
is the creation of value through competitive advantage.

In chapter 11, we will focus on new-product development, and illustrate the man
ways technology is infused into new products to create competitive advantage. In chap
ter 12, we will focus on infusing technology in the value chain. In both of these chapter
we will enumerate the ways by which organizations can speed up the execution o
strategies.

10

APPROPRIATION OF TECHNOLOGY

IBM's research, development, and engineering expenses amounted to over $5 billion in 1993, over $4 billion in 1994, and over $6 billion in 1995. These expenditures covered research and development related to basic scientific research and the application of scientific advances to the development of new and improved products and their uses (over $5 billion in 1995, $3 billion in 1994, and over $4 billion in 1993). In addition, expenditures for product-related engineering included in these amounts were over $700 million, $900 million and $1 billion in 1995, 1994, and 1993, respectively. Finally, the R&D expenditures also included over $1 billion charge in process research and development in connection with the acquisition of Lotus in July 1995.

For the past several years, IBM has led in the number of patents awarded by the U.S. Patent Office. Last year in the United States, IBM more than doubled its hiring of people with Ph.D.s in electrical engineering and computer science—and hired a full 10 percent of the total number of these Ph.D.s entering the workforce.

What drives these investments? According to IBM, two intertwined forces are at play in terms of technology: (1) digitization and (2) radical reshaping of networks. Digitization refers to the conversion into bits that gives information a digital passport to travel across global networks—such as the Internet—to digital devices like PCs or TV sets. Similarly, powerful new communications technologies are giving networks the speed they need to handle rich but space-consuming content like movies, MRI scans, or great works of art. And, with the speed to support the interaction, communication and collaboration is possible over the network. Based on this forecast for the future, IBM is committed to creating network-centric computing. Simply stated, the network is the unifying strategy of IBM. It drives investments; it touches virtually every product in their portfolio.

Of course, IBM also recognizes that in a company of its size and breadth, not every project and priority fits neatly under the network-centric computing pattern. Therefore, with vigor and determination, they continue to pursue basic research as well as emerging market and consumer strategies.[1]

As illustrated in the vignette, IBM identified a technology future consisting of digit zation and reshaped networks; based on this forecast, IBM redefined its technolog strategy in three domains: the appropriation of technological capabilities, their deplo ment in new products, and their deployment in the value chain. In this chapter, we w focus on the appropriation of technology. We will deal with the deployment of techno ogy in products and in value chains in the ensuing chapters. As seen in the IBM stor the decisions related to what kinds of technologies to acquire and how to acquire the are increasingly linked to the corporate strategy of a firm.

The appropriation of technology refers to the acquisition of technology by a fir in two ways: (1) from in-house R&D and (2) from external sources by acquisition strategic alliances. Historically, the in-house R&D function has been the prima source of technology for many firms. Increasingly, due to the pressures of time cor pression and the potential for technology integration, firms are augmenting their i house R&D function with external sourcing of technology. Thus, as we saw in t opening vignette, IBM's R&D expenditures in 1995 included both in-house R&D ar $1 billion in purchased R&D. Hence, in our discussion of technology appropriation, v will focus on both the in-house research and development function as well as extern sourcing of technology.

The decision to appropriate different technologies may be driven by technolog push or market-pull considerations. As shown in Figure 10.1, technology push involv appropriating capabilities to push the technology frontier; market pull involves the a quisition of capabilities to meet the needs of deployment in products and/or val chains. There are, of course, trade-offs in appropriation between developing technolog cal capabilities (T axis) and meeting market needs (M axis). These trade-offs reflect th balance that a firm strikes between technology-push or market-pull orientation. F example, in the case of IBM, the debate between technology-push and market-pull a vocates ended when IBM chief executive officer Louis Gerstner resolved the trade-c in the following fashion.

FIGURE 10.1 TECHNOLOGY-MARKET MATRIX

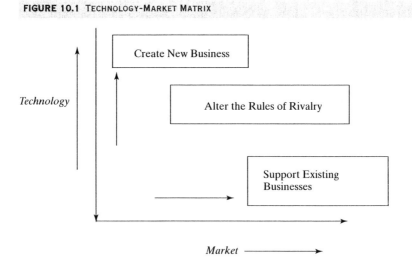

IBM has two fundamental missions:

1. They strive to lead in the creation, development, and manufacture of the industry's most advanced information technologies, including computer systems, software, network systems, storage devices, and microelectronics;
2. They translate these advanced technologies into value for customers through professional solutions' businesses worldwide.[2]

Figure 10.2 reproduces the stages involved in formulating technology strategy. As shown in the figure, the appropriation of technology is one of the key domains in which technology strategy gets enacted. Strategic decisions with respect to the appropriation of technology are broad and directional; these decisions need to be broken down into specific projects and plans for implementation. The projects and plans should, in turn, be consistent with the direction set by the strategic considerations.

Traditionally, the appropriation of technology has been the primary function of research and development (R&D) groups within a corporation. Although some firms such as IBM carried on basic research, most R&D departments focused on applied research, not basic research. Applied research involves embedding the fruits of basic research in new products, which are then commercialized, or new processes, by which the value chain configurations of a firm are transformed. In small and medium-sized firms, the R&D departments focus primarily on product development. In large firms, R&D departments continue to play a significant role in technology appropriation, although other departments or subunits of firms may now share this activity.

During the current decade, two significant shifts have been taking place in the manner in which a firm appropriates technological capabilities:

1. In many organizations, the R&D function is being redefined to incorporate not merely in-house development activity but also external sourcing of technology.
2. Firms are paying increased attention to improving the productivity of the appropriation function: To what extent is the appropriation of capabilities creating value?

In this chapter, we will answer four interrelated questions:

1. How should a firm determine the set of technology appropriation projects that it should invest in?
2. How should it determine the mode of appropriation with respect to each of the specific projects in its desired portfolio?
3. What are firms doing to enhance the productivity of the appropriation function?
4. How have firms responded to the trends of globalization, time compression, and technology integration?

The chapter overview is presented in Figure 10.3. As shown in the figure, we will first review the evolution of technology appropriation principles from their origins in industrial R&D. We will present the third generation principles currently gaining popularity in industry as a managerial approach that is appropriate for technology appropriation. We will detail how the principles underpin two key decisions in appropriation: project portfolio selection and the mode of implementation. Finally, we trace the influence of the environmental trends on technology appropriation.

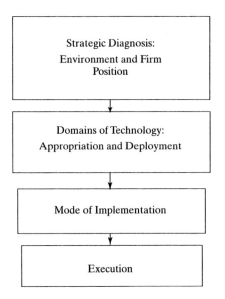

FIGURE 10.2 STAGES OF TECH-NOLOGY STRATEGY FORMULATION

FIGURE 10.3 CHAPTER OVERVIEW

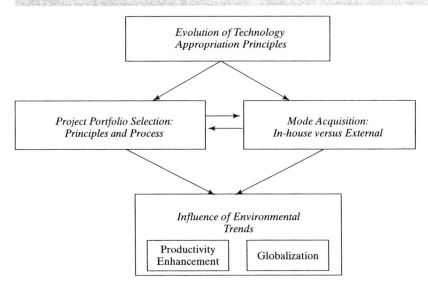

EVOLUTION OF TECHNOLOGY
APPROPRIATION PRINCIPLES

INDUSTRIAL R&D

The appropriation of technology has historically been conceived as being the domain of industrial R&D. In the United States, the beginnings of industrial R&D can be traced to Thomas Edison's Menlo Park laboratory, established in 1876. By 1899, nearly 139 industry-based laboratories were engaged in applied science. However, the era of large laboratories was ushered in only when General Electric (GE) established its research laboratory in 1901. The GE lab grew from 8 to 555 scientists by 1929. During the 1930s, a handful of companies—AT&T, DuPont, Dow Chemical, and GE—carried on research in their central laboratories.

With the onset of World War II, the era of big science was born in the United States. Government defense expenditures and high investments in R&D stimulated the research in aerospace, electronics, and related industries. The age of big science saw the rapid accumulation of knowledge, which continued after World War II. Companies such as Westinghouse, GE, and RCA exploited the fruits of the age of big science by diversifying into technology-related products. Indeed, during most of the 1950s, 1960s, and the 1970s, appropriation of technology was mostly conceived of as in-house R&D.

However, beginning in the 1980s, we began to witness an age of fragmentation in industrial R&D. During this period, there were cutbacks in central laboratories and an increase in contract research among large firms. Additionally, small and medium-sized firms began to capture a greater share of the innovation in the United States. Several potential reasons accounted for the age of fragmentation:

- The capital markets began to exert pressures on the operation of large firms, holding them more accountable for the returns on invested capital. This led to the externalization of R&D, and firms began to outsource R&D activities in areas where they only had a small degree of expertise.
- Many of the R&D laboratories in large firms began to be held accountable for the resources they consumed by their top management, who made sure that a large chunk of the R&D budgets came from the operating divisions.
- Finally, the introduction of internal market concepts, where research contracts to central laboratories were allocated on a competitive basis, also led to the further fragmentation of research and development in the United States.

In Box 10.1, we have showcased the evolution of industrial R&D, with a forecast of the changes for the future.

The historical evolution of the central laboratories and industrial research reflects changes in managerial philosophies that underpin the conduct of technology appropriation.

FROM FIRST TO THIRD GENERATION

As industrial R&D evolved from the benign environment of the 1930s to the stringent environment of the 1980s and 1990s, the managers of technology-driven companies in the United States are having to struggle to get more out of less or the same investment

BOX 10.1

THE TRANSFORMATION
OF INDUSTRIAL RESEARCH

The dominant market positions of corporate research cushioned budgets from the pressures of narrow margins and facilitated the fullest appropriation of profits ensuing from new technologies. As deregulation and the rise of global competition have forced greater corporate attention to the bottom line, discretionary expenditures such as research have come under closer scrutiny. The changes have been most severe among those firms most notable for their prior accomplishments in creating new technologies. For example:

- Overall employment at IBM's research division was cut by nearly 20 percent in 1993. An atmosphere once characterized as "IBM University" vanished. The situation changed by 1999.
- The David Sarnoff Research Center, under RCA ownership a pioneer in electronics technology (inventing liquid crystals, for example), has become a contract research organization dependent on government funds for its long-term research.
- The continuing restructuring of AT&T led to the spin-off of Bell Laboratories into Lucent Technologies.

Of course, there are also countercurrents. Some seasoned companies have continued to support pioneering research; Hewlett-Packard, for example, intensified its research commitment in the 1990s. New actors on the technology frontiers are beginning to play a role. Prominent among them is Microsoft, which recently established a substantial research organization focused on technologies likely to be significant 5 to 10 years in the future. But, many of the new breeds of high-technology firms in electronics and information technologies have eschewed traditional research organizations and chosen other strate-gies. U.S. leaders in the semiconductor industry, including Intel, Motorola, and Texas Instruments, now cooperate to fund research in universities and to develop precompetitive manufacturing technologies.

There are multiple forces at work shaping these changes. The U.S. system of industrial innovation was built on the strong interplay of scientific institutions in industry, universities, and the public sector. But the end of the Cold War is reshaping the allocation of federal resources for science and advanced technology within that system, with undoubted consequences in the laboratories in the private sector. The new competitive environment raises questions about the benefits of investment in research. Firms now compete in the global marketplace with rivals that do no fundamental research but are quick to exploit developments made elsewhere. The success of these free riders deters further investment by traditional pioneers in industrial research.

The character of innovation has also changed, reducing the incentives for investment in climbing up what Ralph Gomory, a former IBM research director, calls the "ladder of science." The nature and scale of investments now required for commercialization of fundamentally new technologies have changed the game. Rarely is a single firm able to dominate; instead, numerous firms with comparable technological capabilities must coordinate their activities and find ways to share the costs and benefits. Consider the recent case of advanced television systems. What started out as a contest among companies to be first with a new system was transformed into a "grand alliance" of firms pooling their capabilities and sharing royalties. Contrast this with the mid-century establishment of current standards, in which the winner, RCA, took all the spoils. What was once a race has become more like a rugby match.

Source: From "The Transformation of Industrial Research" by Richard Rosenbloom and W. J. Spencer, *Issues in Science and Technology,* Volume XII, No. 3, Spring 1996. Reprinted by permission.

in technology appropriation. To describe the evolution, the practice of technology appropriation has recently been classified into three generations: the first, the second, and the third.[3]

First generation. In the first generation, a company's future technology is decided largely by the R&D function alone. General management participates very little in defining programs and projects, and R&D is viewed as a cost center. There is limited evaluation of the contribution of R&D to shareholder value, other than by those involved in R&D. There is little communication from R&D to other parts of the organization. The current year's budget provides the total framework for R&D spending, and the general management stands aside and provides little guidance. Thus, the first generation R&D, which is a holdover from the 1950s, is characterized by the lack of a strategic framework for the management of technology.

Second generation: A transition state between the first and third generations, the second generation approach to technology appropriation is practiced by companies that (1) recognize the interrelationships among various organizational functions and (2) seek to introduce greater order into their management. In this generation, there is a strategic framework for managing technology at the project level, and managers seek to enhance the communications between business and technology management. The long-range plans in these companies recognize projects as distinct and discrete activities. This represents an advance from the first generation, because both business and technology management cooperate in the joint consideration of individual projects—their cost over lifetimes, their impact on the businesses, their uncertainties in management and execution. However, because projects are considered on a project-by-project basis, this generation omits the strategic dimension dealt with in the third generation management: the interrelationship among projects within a business, across businesses, and the corporation as a whole.

Third generation: In this generation, management of the firm seeks to create across the corporation a strategically balanced portfolio of technology appropriation projects, formulated jointly in a spirit of partnership between general managers and technology managers. Both strategic and operational partnerships exist between technology managers and the rest of the organization. Technology managers both challenge and help define the company's real business needs, both today and tomorrow, in addition to helping meet those needs.

The third generation approach, thus, differs significantly from first and second generation approaches in both the managerial philosophy, as well as in how the firms operate. Table 10.1 provides a comparison of the characteristics of the three generations of technology appropriation. As shown in the table, the third generation approach relies on a strategic framework that is built on true partnership between business and technology management; it thus breaks the isolation of the technology appropriation function that has traditionally existed in the first generation management. The project selection and the nature of the funding are based on the degree to which a project meets the business and technological objectives of a firm. Third generation principles are

TABLE 10.1 A Comparison of the Characteristics of the Three Generations of Technology Appropriation

Characteristics	First	Second	Third
A. Management and Strategic Context		**Technology Appropriation Generation**	
Philosophy	• No long-term strategic framework • In-house R&D is an overhead cost • R&D decides future technologies • Business decides current technology objectives	• Transition state • Partial strategic framework • Judge-advocate management/R&D relationship • Customer-supplier business/R&D relationship	• Holistic strategic framework • Partnership
Organization	• Emphasis on cost centers and disciplines • Avoid the matrix	• Centralized and decentralized • Matrix management of products	• Breaks the isolation of technology and R&D
Technology/R&D Strategy	• No explicit link to business strategy • Technology first, business implications later	• Strategic framework by project • No integration business—or corporate-wide	• Technology/R&D and business strategies integrated corporate-wide
B. Operating Principles			
	• Lacking combined business • Fatalistic	• Distinguish between types of R&D • Combined business/R&D insights at project level	• Combined R&D/business insights across the spectrum
Funding	• Line item in annual budget • Fund what you can afford	• Funds based on needs and risk sharing • Different parameters by R&D type	• Varies with technology maturity and competitive impact • Based on balancing of priorities and risk/reward
Resource Allocation	• At the discretion of R&D • No upward visibility	• To fundamental R&D by central R&D management • To other R&D jointly by customers and suppliers	
Targeting	• Is anathema for fundamental and radical R&D • Business and technological objectives sequential	• Consistent business and R&D objectives by project for incremental and radical R&D	• All R&D has defined, consistent business and technological objectives
Priority Setting	• No strategic priorities • Priorities vary with operational circumstances	• For fundamental R&D by central R&D management • For other R&D jointly by customers and suppliers	• According to cost/benefits and contribution to strategic objectives
Measuring Results	• Expected results not defined precisely • Measurements often misleading	• Quantitative for incremental R&D • "Market intelligence gap" for radical R&D	• Against business objectives and technological expectations
Evaluating Progress	• Ritualistic and perfunctory • Periodic	• Formalized peer reviews • Good communications with businesses for incremental and radical R&D projects	• Regularly and when external events and internal developments warrant

Source: Reprinted by permission of Harvard Business School Press. From *Third Generation R&D* by Roussel. P. A., K. N. Saad and T. J. Erickson, Boston. MA 1991. Copy-

312

based on the premise that a close linkage between technology strategy and corporate strategy of a firm leads to the greatest value for the firm.

As a corollary to this premise, loss of linkage is likely to lead to significant value erosion for the company. The value erosion may come from a number of sources:

1. **Drift.** The technology appropriation moves away from business purposes, and the personnel involved in the function conduct research for its own sake without necessarily tying it to the strategic needs of the business.
2. **Inability to market or exploit technological capabilities.** When there is loss of linkage, R&D generates products or processes that a firm does not have the capability to exploit commercially. This leads to significant lost revenues and, in turn, losses in value.
3. **Conflict and communication breakdowns between technology managers and the corporate office.** As the linkage is lost, both technology appropriation or R&D and the corporate office begin to develop stereotypes of the other as being obstructionist, thus leading to significant communication breakdowns. This leads to unnecessary loss of time in negotiations, meetings, and, in general, the inability to incorporate each other's views into the decision-making process.
4. **Strategic failures.** Especially in high-technology organizations, the in-house R&D usually has an important role to play in the business direction. Lack of linkage often leads to strategic failures.

For example, during the 1980s, given the difficulties involved in the Palo Alto operation of Xerox laboratories, Xerox lost significant opportunities to improve their position in the copier, electronics, and computer businesses. Xerox lost several billion dollars as a result of the technology appropriation being carried out in isolation of the general management and strategic concerns of the firm. Box 10.2 summarizes the experience of Xerox.

BOX 10.2

XEROX AND THE PALO ALTO RESEARCH
CENTER DURING THE 1980s

The importance of linking and integrating research and development efforts with the strategies and capabilities of the rest of the organization is clearly illustrated through the experience of Xerox Corporation and its Palo Alto Research Facility, known as PARC. Xerox founded PARC during 1969 in the innovation-rich Silicon Valley, well divorced from their Stamford, Connecticut, corporate headquarters. The corporation wished to be a leader in computerized office systems and charged the new research center with developing the technologies that Xerox would need to achieve this goal. To foster an innovative environment, the elegant three-story facility featured amenities such as rock garden atria and beanbag chair

Source: Uttal, B. "The lab that ran away from Xerox," *Fortune,* September 5, 1983; Markoff, J. "And not a personal computer in sight," *The New York Times,* October 6, 1991.

Box 10.2 (*continued*)

conference rooms, with corporate headquarters promising a "hands-off" policy. In short time, PARC was able to attract some of the nation's leading computer scientists.

The innovative environment and absence of corporate interference allowed the researchers to explore and develop blue-sky concepts for personal computing. Such innovations as word processing software, icon-based programming, large-scale integrated circuits, and graphical computer displays with windows were initially conceptualized and developed at PARC. Indeed, PARC researchers developed the first networked personal computers, known as the ALTO, which was soon in use throughout Xerox. In short, researchers at PARC conceptualized and developed a large proportion of the innovations that have driven the personal computing industry for the last two decades.

Yet, by the mid-1980s, it became clear that Xerox was unable to capitalize on the majority of these innovations. Researchers, frustrated with the company's apparent inability to commercialize their inventions, left to join firms such as Apple, Microsoft, and Digital Equipment Corporation. As a result, many of PARC's innovations were brought to commercial reality by other firms. What follows is a partial list of such innovations:

Technology
Modern chip-making technology
Portable computing
Bit-mapped screen displays
Mouse-and icon-based computing
Ethernet office network
"WYSIWYG" word processing
Postscript printer language

Commercializing Firm
VLSI Technology
Grid Systems
IBM, Apple Computer
Apple
3COM
Microsoft
Adobe Systems

Why was Xerox unable to leverage the wealth of intellectual capital created by PARC into competitive advantage in the marketplace?

- First, Xerox is a large organization, and its sheer size slowed decision-making processes. It was thus unable to react to rapidly changing market conditions.

- Second, the company viewed itself as a risk-averse maker of photocopying equipment. This strategic focus prevented management from grasping the commercial implications of the personal computer, and so many of the related innovations simply languished in the research lab.

- Third, although PARC's isolation from corporate headquarters served to foster a creative environment, it also provided researchers with little strategic focus to guide research efforts. As a result, researchers pursued innovations that were incompatible with the product development and marketing capabilities of the firm, leaving it unable to capitalize on these innovations in the marketplace.

In the case of PARC, the absence of linkage and integration between the lab and the strategies and capabilities of the overall organization resulted in a very expensive strategic failure for Xerox.

In the 1990s, Xerox continued to look to PARC to develop technologies that will guide the next generation of products for the company. However, several corrective actions have been taken to prevent the types of failures that occurred in the past.

- First, product development is no longer isolated from basic research. Marketing personnel have been placed in PARC as a liaison between research and operations.

- Second, many of Xerox's product development operations, such as software development, have now been located adjacent to the PARC facility in an attempt to further integrate the lab with the operations of the company.

There is increasing recognition among technology managers that the third generation principles are the appropriate way to manage the appropriation of technology.
They note that, in the earlier generations of R&D, the absence of linkages between the
appropriation of technology and the corporate strategy often led to problems of communication between technology managers and general management; this resulted in the
inability to appropriate value from the fruits of in-house research and development.

THIRD GENERATION APPROACH
FOR THE APPROPRIATION OF TECHNOLOGY

The third generation approach to the appropriation of technology focuses on linking
the business strategy and the technology appropriation decisions of a firm in a systematic manner to create competitive advantage and, consequently, value for the firm. The
concept of a project portfolio is basic to the third generation approach. We will first articulate this concept, summarize the key principles for portfolio selection, and then describe a generic process for portfolio selection.

THE CONCEPT OF PROJECT PORTFOLIO

During any specific period of time, a firm will be pursuing a number of technology appropriation projects that have different strategic implications and technical characteristics. Classifying the projects into three classes can highlight these differences:

1. **Fundamental.** This type of project involves the creation of new knowledge,
   creation of knowledge new to the company and/or new to the world. Projects of this type enable a firm to create fundamentally new businesses.
2. **Radical.** This type of project involves creation of knowledge new to the
   company and enables the firm to alter the rules of rivalry in its existing competitive domains.
3. **Incremental.** This involves the exploitation of the existing scientific and engineering knowledge in new ways and helps support the firm's existing
   businesses.

Strategically, technology appropriation projects serve one of three major purposes: to
create fundamentally new business; to alter the rules of rivalry; or to support—defend,
maintain, and expand—existing businesses. The three types of technology appropriation projects also differ significantly in terms of their probability of success and the potential risk and rewards. In Table 10.2, we have summarized the major differences
among the three types of projects. As shown in the table, incremental projects provide
modest returns characterized by low risk; the fruits of fundamental projects are highly
uncertain, although the resulting payoff may indeed be quite high.

During any specific time period, a firm may have several potentially attractive technology appropriation projects, some of which are incremental; others, radical; and even
a few fundamental in character. One of the major decisions any firm faces is the selection of the mix of projects for implementation. Because every firm has limited resources
and capabilities, a choice often has to be made from a number of attractive project

TABLE 10.2   Differences in Types of R&D Projects

| | *Type of R&D Projects* | | |
Characteristics	*Incremental*	*Radical*	*Fundamental*
Business Objectives	Support existing businesses	1. Alter the rules of rivalry 2. Create new businesses	Enhance technical capability
Probability of Success	High	Moderate to low	Low
Potential Rewards	Low	Medium to high	High
Risks	Low	Moderate to low	Uncertain

opportunities. This involves some harsh trade-offs among the differing criteria of project attractiveness. The resulting mix of projects that the firm decides to pursue will be referred to as its *project portfolio.*

The concept of the project portfolio is employed in third generation approaches to highlight three key points:

1. The technology appropriation decision should focus on the portfolio, not individual projects alone. The portfolio concept emphasizes both the strategic and technological interrelationships among the projects.
2. The resources available to a firm for pursuing technology appropriation are limited; hence, the projects should be judged relative to other opportunities. In other words, the resources should be focused in the areas where the firms can derive the best value.
3. The firm's project portfolio represents its optimum choice between risk and reward, on the one hand, and stability and growth, on the other. The definition of optimum, of course, varies as widely as the goals, aspirations, competence, mission, and culture of individual firms.

The focus in third generation approaches, therefore, is on the portfolio, not merely on the individual projects.

KEY PRINCIPLES

During our exposition of technology strategy, we articulated several key principles that should guide the formulation of technology strategy. The third generation approach emphasizes these principles in the evaluation of projects and the choice of the project portfolio. As applied to technology appropriation, these principles may be summarized as follows:

1. Market and technological considerations together determine the technological opportunity and appropriability.
2. A firm's technological capability should be factored into the choice of the projects.
3. The choice of project portfolio should be guided by the principle of focusing resources.
4. Both in-house R&D and external sourcing should be viewed as alternative implementation modes for the appropriation of technology.

MARKET AND TECHNOLOGICAL CONSIDERATIONS

We have seen that competitive domains and markets evolve over time, and the patterns of products and process innovation should evolve with the competitive domains in which a firm is operating.

- The role of technology appropriation varies over the evolution of competitive domain: To launch a new business during the era of technology emergence; to grow and improve a firm's competitive position during the growth phase; to sustain or defend a firm's competitive position when the industry arrives at maturity; and finally, to abandon the existing technologies or to find other technologies to renew an aging industry are all roles of technology appropriation.
- During the earlier phases of an industry, product innovations dominate, whereas in the later stages process innovations become more significant for enhancing the competitive position of a firm. Both of these, of course, may be process or product innovations.

In Table 10.3, we have given examples of the differing emphasis on technology appropriation at the different stages of industry development.

Thus, the competitive impact of specific technologies varies over competitive domains. Put another way, different technologies have differing potential to influence the nature and pace of competition. Indeed, in many competitive domains, there is a progression over time from pacing to key to base technologies:

> Pacing technology has the potential to change the entire basis of competition, but it has not yet been embodied in a product or a process.
>
> Key technology is most critical to competitive success, because it offers the opportunity for meaningful product differentiation; this technology yields significant competitive advantage.
>
> Base technology, although necessary and essential to practice, will offer little potential for competitive advantage. This is typically widespread and shared among the various incumbents in the industry.[4]

This march of technology from pacing to key to base can be observed in many, many industries. For example, the 35mm camera of today can be compared to the best of 20 years ago. Similarly, the first mechanical typewriters reflected young and key technologies—the transition of mechanical action of the fingers to printed type; this was vastly superior to the pens they displaced. Over time, these technologies aged and

TABLE 10.3   Appropriation over Stages of Technology

Stages	Type of Projects Needed
1. Technology Emergence	Product Design Process Design for Reliable Manufacturing Technology Integration
2. Incremental Change	
A. Product Improvement Stage	Market-Pull Product Improvement Modular and Architectural Innovation
B. Process Improvement	Cost/Strategy-Driven Process Improvements

became the base technologies, because they were well known and practiced by all com
petitors. In time, the electric typewriter incorporated some new and key technologies t
displace the mechanical systems.

The strategic mission of the technology appropriation function is to exploit the pc
tential for improvement in technology to enhance a firm's competitive position. Thu
key technologies are vitally important, followed by pacing technologies; a firm withou
competence in the base technology is not likely to be a player in the respective industr

Technologically, the concept of the *S*-curve of innovation describes the evolution of
performance characteristic over time, from the embryonic stage through growth and ma
turity, and finally to decay or its supplanting by superior technology. As we have seen, ever
technology can be characterized by a set of performance characteristics, each following i
distinct *S*-curve of evolution. In the real world of technology, the climb toward maturity
a series of steps contributed to by several different researchers working in different firm
Thus, the *S*-curve of innovation represents a set of distinct types of learning by firms.

The potential for further advances in a specific technology is limited by its positio
on the *S*-curve. In Figure 10.4, we have reproduced the *S*-curve to highlight the impl
cations for project selection. As shown in the curve, during the very early stages (for ex
ample, the embryonic stage), the potential for a vast improvement in technology is high
in the later stages (for example, maturity), the advances in technology come about onl
slowly. In other words, when a firm is allocating its limited funds, the returns from in
vestment are likely to be higher in the early stages than in the later stages.

Technological maturity is intrinsic to a technology regardless of the industry in whic
it is applied. The competitive impact of the technology is, however, extrinsic; that is, th
impact is closely dependent on the industry that applies it. The third generation approac
emphasizes the importance of taking into account both factors in the selection of project

FIRM'S TECHNOLOGICAL CAPABILITIES

Competitors often differ in their capabilities in specific technologies that are impo
tant for the business. Relative technological competitive strength is a measure of th
degree to which a firm has mastery in a specific set of technologies relative to its con
petitors. The relative competitive strength of a firm may vary from weak to domina
along a continuum:

FIGURE 10.4 *S*-CURVE AND TECHNOLOGY DEVELOPMENT

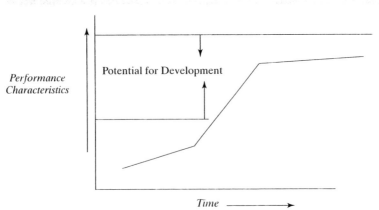

Weak. Here, the firm's line of business is difficult to turn around; its product processes and costs are slipping relative to its competitors; it has adopted a short-term focus; and the technical output relative to competitors is of declining quality.

Tenable. The firm is behaving in a catch-up mode, unable to set independent goals. It may be able to maintain the competitiveness of its business but unable to differentiate it from its competitors.

Favorable. A firm has strengths that can be exploited into technological competitive positions. It may not be a technological leader except in some developing niches, but it is able to sustain its competitiveness in the markets that it serves.

Strong. Here, the firm is able to express independent technical action and set new directions. It has made a significant commitment to technologies, and these commitments enable it to distinguish itself from lesser competitors.

Dominant. Dominant firms are technological leaders in their industry and are characterized by high commitment, large allocation of funds, manpower, and creativity to R&D. They are well recognized in the industry, and they set the pace and directions for technological development. As a result, competitors consistently seek to catch up with the dominant firms.

Technological competitive position thus measures the size and quality of the technical resources that a firm can deploy to achieve business success. A favorable to strong technical competitive position is generally a precondition for the technical success of its projects. Stated differently, a firm is better off by concentrating its resources and focusing them where they can have the most competitive impact. Of course, applying this idea often demands difficult, even painful choices between projects competing for limited resources.

FOCUSING OF RESOURCES

Modern financial theory would argue that the higher the risk associated with a project, the higher the returns that it should deliver. Three broad generalizations regarding risks and rewards can be made for specific technology appropriation projects:

1. Technological uncertainty is high during the early stages of the development of a technology.
2. A firm's technological position is an indicator of its ability to complete a technical project. For example, dominant competitors are well positioned to exploit specific technologies in which they have competence.
3. Technology appropriation projects need to be evaluated not only in terms of their technical uncertainty, but also with respect to the market uncertainty. This will require a thorough analysis of the industry context.

Further, because a firm's financial and human resources are limited, the focal point of deliberation is not merely a specific appropriation project, but the firm's portfolio of projects. To evaluate a project portfolio, a technology appropriation project may be evaluated on its position on a risk-return matrix, such as the one shown in Figure 10.5. As shown in the figure, where returns are high and the risks are low, projects are deemed to be attractive; high risk/low return projects are not deemed worthy of funding by a firm.

In summary, during a specific period of time, a firm will be pursuing a number of technology appropriation projects with differing competitive impacts, risks-returns, trade-offs,

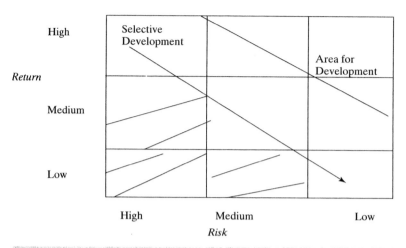

FIGURE 10.5 RISK-RETURN MATRIX

and varying levels of technological maturity. A project portfolio expresses the technolog
appropriation strategy of a firm. It represents the resource commitments that the firm i
willing to make in pursuing various technology development directions. The firm's projec
portfolio represents its optimum choice between risk and reward, on the one hand, an
stability and growth, on the other. The definition of optimum, of course, varies as widel
as the goals, aspirations, competence, mission, and culture of the individual firm. The cor
cept of portfolio further recognizes that the resources available to a firm for pursuing tech
nology appropriation are limited. Thus, a technology portfolio is not an aggregation of a
the in-house R&D projects proposed by various individuals within the firm; it represent
a careful balance of choices made by senior management.

MODE OF IMPLEMENTATION

All of the three functions of technology appropriation—supporting existing busines
starting new business, and enhancing technology capability—can be implemented ei
ther through in-house research and development or acquisition through externa
sources. As we discussed in chapter 9, collaborative approaches are increasingly be
coming part of a firm's technology strategy. Although in external sourcing a firm has t
share the technological capability with its allies, the potential for technology integratio
(ability to use different pieces of technology or know-how to configure new product
and processes) suggests that external sourcing may lead to advantages for the firm i
specific competitive domains.

PROCESS INVOLVED IN ARRIVING AT THE PORTFOLIO OF TECHNOLOGY APPROPRIATION PROJECTS

How should a firm design its portfolio of technology appropriation projects? We ma
identify five major steps involved in portfolio planning. Figure 10.6 outlines the majo
steps involved in the design of a project portfolio.

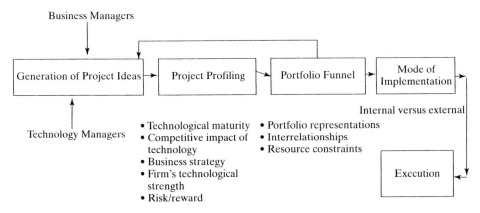

FIGURE 10.6 PROCESS OF DETERMINING A PORTFOLIO

1. *Generation of project ideas.* The technology appropriation projects usually originate from two sets of sources: (1) the technologists and technology managers, who are exposed to the developments in the technological environments and (2) the business managers, who understand the technological and competitive requirements of their businesses. During the idea generation stage, it is important for project ideas to bubble up from both sides so that a firm will have a rich initial set of technology appropriation projects.
2. *Characterization of each project.* Each individual project is characterized in the terms of the portfolio variables that are appropriate for the firm. Factors such as technological competitive strengths of the firm, technological maturity, competitive impact of technology, and risk/reward ratios are established at this stage.
3. *Portfolio funnel.* The total set of R&D projects is subjected to a series of increasingly demanding screens to enhance the probability that the project ideas that emerge from the screening are likely to serve business strategy most effectively. This requires that all the projects be assembled into portfolio representations that answer various strategic and operational questions.
4. *Mode of implementation.* Each project in the portfolio is further scrutinized in order to determine which one is a candidate for external sourcing and which one should be pursued internally.
5. *Execution.* During the execution, appropriation organizational mechanisms are put in place, and the project progress is continuously monitored.

The process is often iterative, and there may be cycling between the steps. For example, if, based on a portfolio funnel, the senior management is not satisfied with the set of projects it is discussing, it may ask for additional projects. In Box 10.3, we have summarized how one company—Westinghouse—determines its technology appropriation portfolio.

BOX 10.3

USING R&D PORTFOLIO EVALUATIONS
AT WESTINGHOUSE

As discussed in the text, the use of formal portfolio analysis advanced in the third generation approach is one management tool available to increase the effectiveness of R&D. By focusing attention on such issues as technological maturity, competitive impact, and estimated return and risk, these analysis techniques represent an important addition to the set of tools currently being employed in linking the efforts of R&D to the business strategies of the organization.

At Westinghouse, corporate R&D must evaluate specific projects proposed by the operating business units (that is, market-pull technologies) and basic technology projects proposed by the lab itself (that is, technology-push projects), deciding which of these represent the best potential use of resources. For both types of projects, the lab uses an adaptation of portfolio analysis in making its determination.

With regard to projects proposed by the business units, unit managers are required to detail their strategic goals, indicating general technology advances they feel are necessary in achieving those goals. Business unit engineers then indicate the specific technology advances and approaches that are needed. The analysis then focuses on the market impact that each project may have. Those projects with high

and medium market impact receive priority over those that are considered lower impact. In this way, corporate-level and business-level resources can be concentrated on projects that are more likely to have strong impact on the future of the business. It also means that business managers must give more thorough consideration to a project before it is proposed to the R&D lab.

R&D project proposals for basic technologies that arise in the lab itself are evaluated in a similar fashion. Again, the focus is on the overall competitive impact that may accrue from the technological advance. In particular, the analysis is concerned with how the company will be positioned with respect to the technology (that is, will it be a leader, a significant player, or merely a follower) and the potential size of the market(s) that can be exploited. Those projects that both position the company as a leader in a technology and are focused on high-potential markets receive greater priority. As potential market size and positioning decrease, avenues other than full development (e.g., alliances or industry exit) are explored. Through this evaluation process, the lab is better able to focus its resources on those technologies that will grow and shape the organization in the future.

Source: From "Making R&D more effective at Westinghouse" by T. M. Foster, *Research Technology Management,* Jan/Feb, 1996. Reprinted by permission.

EXTERNAL SOURCING OF
TECHNOLOGICAL CAPABILITY

External sourcing forms an important mechanism by which a firm appropriates technological capabilities. As we saw in chapter 9, two external sourcing approaches have been common in the domain of technology appropriation: collective research and strategic alliances. Recall that in collective research, firms often ally with rivals in a con-petitive domain to create mostly public property to the common good of the allies. To acquire technological capabilities unique to a firm requires the firms to focus on strategic alliances and other forms of external sourcing. Strategic alliances and collaborative approaches are, thus, often critical to building a firm's technological capabilities, and these external sources are an alternative to in-house R&D. Indeed, most innovations in firms result from borrowing or imitation rather than in-house R&D.[5]

The ability of a firm to recognize the value of new external technology, assimilate it, and apply it to commercial ends is often called *absorptive capacity*.[6] Indeed, absorptive capacity is now recognized to be increasingly important, as globalization of the technology environment continues and the market for technology expands. Successful external sourcing requires a firm to answer three questions:

- How does a firm choose between in-house R&D and external sources for a specific appropriation project?
- What are the external sources of technology?
- How do firms insure effective absorption of technology from external sources?

We will discuss these questions in this section.

CHOICE OF EXTERNAL SOURCING VERSUS IN-HOUSE DEVELOPMENT

External sourcing in conjunction with in-house R&D may be used to extend a firm's technological capability over time. For example, over a period of 2 decades, Corning Glass developed a full capability in clinical and toxicological testing services. This was initiated in the early 1970s with a small investment in MedPath, an emerging leader in nationwide clinical testing of biological specimens such as blood and urine. After observing the company for some time, Corning acquired MedPath. Further, in 1987, Corning acquired Hazelton, a leader in toxicological testing services. Corning thus parlayed its initial experience in laboratory glassware to knowledge about producing analytical instruments; it progressed to clinical and diagnostic instruments and then became an expert in reagents.[7]

To create value for a firm, as in the case of Corning, the choice of external sourcing of technological capabilities must be based on a sound rationale. Clearly, external sourcing should be a speedier or a less costly alternative for the appropriation of the specific technological capability relative to internal R&D without compromising the competitive advantage of the firm. This depends on two sets of factors:

1. What is the firm's competitive position in the specific technology?
2. How important is the technology to the firm?

Competitive position. As we saw in the discussion of R&D project portfolio, a company's competitive position in a technology requires placing its knowledge of the technology under the harsh light of competitive realities. Benchmarking against the best of class in other industries helps managers calibrate a technological capability.

Strategic importance. Equally important is the degree to which the technology is strategically important to a firm. On the one hand, a firm may have enough expertise in one technology, but that technology may not really be important for the strategic direction of the firm. On the other hand, technologies that may really be important for corporate strategy may not be within the existing capabilities of the firm.

The two dimensions of strategic importance and technological competitive position of a firm may be juxtaposed to yield four potential technology-sourcing situations. Figure 10.7 displays these situations. As shown in the figure, technologies may be classified into four groups: (1) candidates for internal R&D, (2) candidates for external acquisition, (3) candidates for disinvestment, and (4) candidates for limited investment.

Internal R&D. Technologies where a firm has a strong competitive position, and which are important to the strategic direction of the firm, represent the firm's core competence. These technologies need to be nourished in-house.

Candidates for external acquisition. As shown in the figure, the greatest need for external acquisition is where there are capability gaps: Strategic importance is high, but the company's internal knowledge is incomplete or out of date.

Candidates for disinvestment: These technologies, in which a firm is both familiar and capable but that are extremely low in strategic importance, may be marketed or licensed to specialist firms.

Limited investment. There is little reason to invest in a technology that is not strategically important and with which the firm has little experience.[8]

Two important observations can be made about the matrix shown in Figure 10.7:

1. When a firm has a dominant position in a specific technology that is also strategically important to it, it should continue to develop its internal capability. This will not only ensure its continued leadership in that technology, but it may also prove to be a lower cost option. For example, technological

FIGURE 10.7 EXTERNAL SOURCING

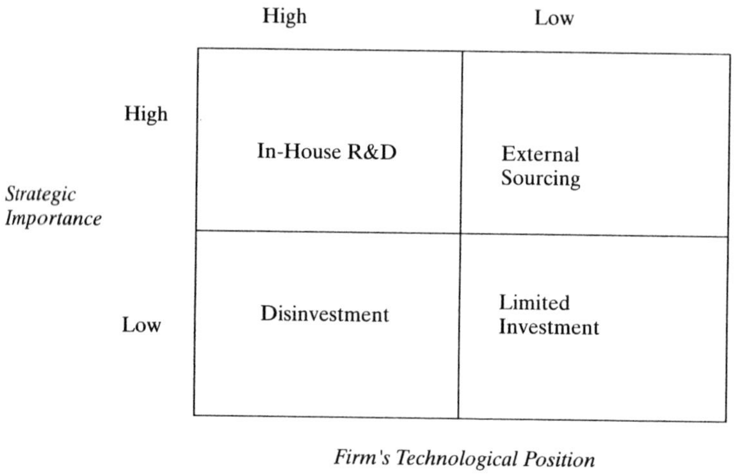

Firm's Technological Position

competitive position may enable a firm to develop its base of knowledge faster and relatively more cheaply than external sources.

2. It is preferable to seek external sources of technology when a firm is not dominant in a particular technology. External sources may be relatively more inexpensive and also a faster way of acquiring that specific know-how.

External sources differ in terms of the potential for erosion of intellectual property and in terms of barriers to the transfer of technological capabilities, a topic to which we now turn.

SOURCES OF EXTERNAL TECHNOLOGY

Broadly, there are three sources of external technology: (1) other companies, including competitors, (2) universities, and (3) government laboratories.

1. *Other companies.* As we saw in chapter 9, inter-company relationships structured as cooperative research or strategic alliances have been on the increase ever since the passage of NCRA in 1984.
2. *Universities.* They are another set of partners, and the depth of this partnership is on the increase. Partnering with universities may assume the form of consulting, licensing, applied research contracts, and use of specialized facilities.
3. *Government laboratories.* They are a relatively new set of partners. Only the government can afford some of the facilities that are vital to industry: high-intensity gray-light sources, enormous banks of high-end computers, and specialized radiation sources, to name just a few.

Three challenges have to be addressed during the appropriation of technology from the external sources of technology: (1) intellectual property, (2) secrecy, and (3) procedural details.

1. *Intellectual property.* Both universities and government laboratories are public institutions and, hence, are devoted to public property. In sourcing technology from these organizations, who owns the intellectual property is a significant source of tension.
2. *Secrecy.* Indeed, there is certainly an inherent conflict between industry's need for secrecy, as it tries to gain competitive advantage, and a university's need to publish. In the case of government laboratories, the right-to-know laws cause the businesspeople to be concerned about the risk of working with the laboratories.
3. *Procedural details.* Other barriers to university partnerships include responsiveness, i.e., the confidence that the time to produce results will be respected; cost, where universities and businesses have differing perspectives on costs; and termination clauses, which spell out clearly the procedures under which an alliance or a contract is terminated. In a similar sense, barriers to alliances with government laboratories include suspicions on the part of government personnel, the sensitivity of government labs to the political climate, and limited access to seed money.[9]

Success like Corning experienced in building its technological capability over time depends on a number of factors, a point to which we now turn.

IMPORTING TECHNOLOGICAL CAPABILITIES FROM EXTERNAL SOURCES

Simply importing technology from external sources does not guarantee the kind of success Corning Glass experienced in its clinical and toxicological testing services. The success depends also on the absorptive capacity of the firm, its ability to absorb a new technological capability. Five managerial behaviors are needed to build a true absorptive capacity:

1. **Scan broadly.** Because technological knowledge comes from innumerable sources, firms need to scan broadly so that they can catch a valuable technology. Indeed, technology scanning is one of the most important activities that a firm needs to undertake before it formulates a strategy.

2. **Provide for continuous interaction.** A characteristic of companies skilled in importing knowledge is that they allow for continuous interaction with outside sources. Studies on information flows in research laboratories demonstrate that such continuous interaction benefits performance.[10]

3. **Nurture technological gatekeepers.** Technological gatekeepers are self-selected individuals who expose themselves to more outside sources than their colleagues. They are also excellent technical performers who keep their colleagues apprised of the latest developments in their respective fields. Nurturing technological gatekeepers is an important managerial activity leading to a firm's absorptive capacity.

4. **Nurture boundary spanners.** Boundary spanners are people who understand the source and the receiver and can translate as well as disseminate knowledge. Multiple boundary spanners are needed to avoid bottlenecks.

5. **Fight Not Invented Here Syndrome.** Many organizations experience resistance from their personnel to the knowledge or technological capability imported from outside. This is often referred to as Not Invented Here (NIH) syndrome. The most successful anecdote to NIH is an organizational culture that embodies a sense of urgency for innovation, encourages interactions with outside sources of knowledge, and helps employees understand that success never comes in isolation.[11]

External sourcing of technological capability is increasingly employed by firms to build up competitive advantage faster, take advantage of the opportunities for technology integration, and as a source of value enhancement for the firms, in general. At the same time, firms are also adopting mechanisms to enhance the productivity of the in-house R&D function.

PRODUCTIVITY OF IN-HOUSE R&D

In recent years, with the shift toward the third generation principles and the pressure of the capital markets, firms have been focused on the productivity of the in-house R&D function. This search for productivity has proceeded in two directions: (1) benchmarking and (2) deployment of quality principles.

BENCHMARKING

In response to the increasing emphasis on productivity of R&D organizations, a number of firms have begun to benchmark their activities within the R&D function against those of their competitors, as well as against those of the best performing firms. One consequence of this has been the development of metrics, or measures, to capture various facets of R&D. Indeed, the Industrial Research Institute's Technology Value Program captures over 50 measures to benchmark a firm's in-house R&D practices. These efforts are in the early stages of development, and firms are exploring various ways to measure R&D productivity.

In Box 10.4, we have illustrated one company's—Westinghouse Corporation's—attempts to measure the productivity of R&D and the learning associated with its experience.

BOX 10.4

WESTINGHOUSE'S APPROACH TO IMPROVED R&D EFFECTIVENESS

We discussed earlier the steps taken by the Westinghouse Science and Technology Center to streamline R&D project selection. In a broad sense, the purpose of corporate R&D is the creation of new business endeavors and/or the establishment of competitive advantage. Unfortunately, these outcomes may take years to accomplish, so determining the effectiveness of R&D in the short term represents a management problem. Further, it is difficult to establish the degree to which R&D efforts are responsible for successful business outcomes.

In an attempt to monitor and improve their own in-house R&D effectiveness, the Westinghouse Science and Technology Center (the company's corporate R&D lab) has developed a series of policies and steps focused on four areas:

1. Suitable measures of performance,
2. Linking outcomes to incentive compensation,
3. Project management training, and
4. The transfer of culture from operating units to the R&D lab.

Each of these policies and steps is designed to bring a business orientation to corporate R&D and to align the activities of the lab with the needs of the operating organization.

To develop effectiveness measures in a more timely manner, lab manager Ted Foster began by recognizing that operating business units are the customers of the lab and, thus, in the best position to provide immediate and concrete measures of R&D effectiveness. Although the number or value of businesses created, the value of business unit sales that result from developed technology, and the number of technologies transferred are more difficult to measure, they are critical elements in establishing the effectiveness of the lab. How did Foster do it?

- First, business units are asked to provide periodic assessment of the lab's performance rated against ambitious quantifiable objectives for these measures.

- Second, business unit managers and technical personnel are asked to complete customer satisfaction surveys, rating the lab on planning and preparation, responsiveness, and technical performance.

- The lab also attempts to get feedback on what business unit presidents say to the

Source: Foster, T. M. "Making R&D more effective at Westinghouse," *Research Technology Management,* January-February 1996, pp. 31–37.

Box 10.4 (*continued*)

CEO regarding their contributions to successful operations. Foster believes that this latter measure may be the best in establishing the lab's effectiveness.

- Some traditional measures of effectiveness—such as outside orders, sales and operating cost variances, patents filed, and papers published—are also considered, but these are considered to be of lesser importance than the business unit assessments.

Having established timely effectiveness measures, the lab next linked these measures to incentive compensation. Lab department managers are, in part, compensated on how business unit assessments of their effectiveness rate against the objectives established for the department. By tying a significant portion of the department manager's compensation to the success of R&D projects, the manager's goals become more aligned with those of the operating business unit.

A further step taken to increase R&D effectiveness concerned project management training. Westinghouse's corporate R&D lab has a large number of both scientists and engineers. As a result, two separate cultures had appeared, one grounded in scientific thinking

and one grounded in engineering approaches. The scientists did not understand the need to manage R&D projects, and the engineers could not understand why the scientists did not take budgets and schedules seriously. To correct this dysfunctional situation, the lab developed a course to teach basic project skills to both groups of individuals; topics included systematic project planning and execution, team building, responding to changes in plans, and keeping the project on target in terms of performance, schedule, and cost. This training has since increased planning and execution effectiveness and developed an understanding of cultures between the two groups.

As discussed in Box 10.3, when R&D labs are divorced from ongoing operations, they often develop cultures that are inconsistent with the needs of the overall organization. These inconsistencies decrease the effectiveness of R&D programs. To avoid this situation, Westinghouse initiated a program whereby representatives of the operating groups were installed in the R&D lab. This process provides a means by which the culture of the lab can be more business-oriented, and the business units feel secure that their interests are being heard. In turn, business unit acceptance of corporate R&D has been dramatically improved.

DEPLOYMENT OF QUALITY PRINCIPLES

During the last decade, the application of quality principles has gained a sudden and significant presence in R&D settings.[12] Although many firms had in the past conceived of the quality in R&D as the effective transfer of R&D results to commercial applications, application of quality principles embraces four dimensions:

1. Strategic decisions, which include choice of appropriate technologies, strategic value of R&D information and applicability, and transferability of R&D results;
2. Administrative and research processes, including definitions of clients' expectations, participation of clients, evaluation of R&D processes and reviews, and information systems and training;
3. Cross-functional integration and project management, including interfunctional integration of R&D with manufacturing, marketing and engineering, reduction in time to delivery, and control of projects; and

4. Participation of scientists in the design and execution of research programs and training of scientists.

Because quality principles have been applied to the R&D setting only recently, the effectiveness of this approach in R&D is yet to be determined. Early indication, however, is that the productivity of R&D has been enhanced in many organizations by the adoption of quality principles.[13]

THE INFLUENCE OF ENVIRONMENTAL TRENDS

The three environmental trends—globalization, time compression, and technology integration—have been influencing the appropriation of technology. As shown in Figure 10.8, both time compression and the potential for technology integration have intensified the search for collaborative arrangements to appropriate technology. Time compression, especially the influence of capital markets, has induced firms to apply quality principles and benchmarking to shorten the development time and enhance the productivity of the in-house R&D function. Because we have discussed these changes in the previous section, we will now focus on the globalization of the in-house R&D.

GLOBALIZATION OF R&D

Consistent with the environmental trends we observed in chapter 2, firms are increasingly globalizing their R&D activities. Foreign R&D potentially combines both improved linkage of technology investment to local market needs, as well as improved leverage from accessing multiregional resources for technology strategy. Both U.S. firms and Japanese firms have been increasing the scope of their R&D operations abroad.

- In 1988, U.S. companies spent 10.5 percent of their R&D budget abroad, up from 7.6 percent in 1985. This pattern continues with R&D expenditures from major U.S. firms rising about 5.7 percent annually from 1990 to 1992 abroad versus 3.5 percent domestically.

FIGURE 10.8 INFLUENCE OF ENVIRONMENTAL TRENDS

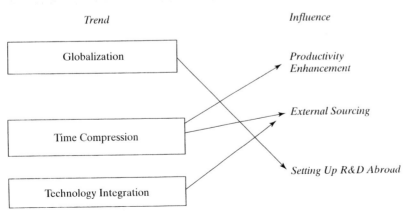

- Japanese firms have increased the rate of establishing U.S. basic research labs in electronics and biotechnology, in addition to increased Japanese-U.S. university research and company alliances. This is paralleled, in part, by the rise of foreign R&D centers in Japan, as reported by its ministry of international trade and industry, especially in the fields of chemicals and pharmaceuticals.[14]

A recent survey suggested that the R&D based in foreign countries is growing, but the percentages for all regions remain considerably smaller than their overall foreign capital investments or, in particular, their foreign revenues. Figure 10.9 sketches the percentage of total R&D based in foreign countries.

Why do companies establish R&D operations in foreign countries? Five different reasons motivate firms to invest in global R&D:

1. To be responsive to national markets;
2. To establish an R&D base in the region. An example is IBM's Yamato laboratory, which conducts supply research for IBM's operations in Japan and other Asian markets;
3. To cooperate with host country laboratories. Several Japanese companies established R&D facilities in the United States for working with other research institutes or institutions like U.S. research universities.
4. To employ host country R&D personnel.[15]
5. To serve as a window on the developments in the respective region.

There are, of course, important differences between Japanese, European, and U.S. approaches to their R&D facilities abroad.

FIGURE 10.9 R&D PATTERNS IN EUROPE, JAPAN, AND NORTH AMERICA

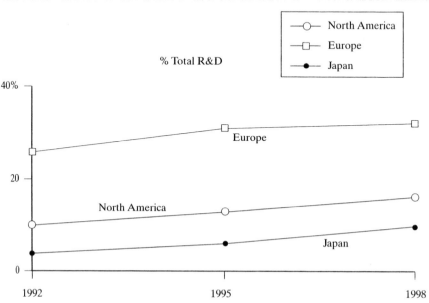

Source: From "Benchmarking the Strategic Management of Technology," by Ed Roberts, *Research Technology Management,* Jan-Feb 1995. Reprinted by permission.

- U.S. R&D facilities in Japan tend to work in fewer areas and on fewer projects. Matsushita has several R&D facilities in the United States working on a number of specialized projects (for example, Burlington, New Jersey, for HDTV; Princeton, New Jersey, for computer software; San Jose, California, for semiconductors and software). Digital Equipment Corporation conducts multiple R&D projects in computer hardware and software (for example, hardware design, large systems integration, software design, and advanced development) in its single facility in Akikawa, Japan.
- Relative to both Europe and the United States, the Japanese tend to engage in more joint R&D cooperative arrangements with other U.S. organizations.

What does the globalization of R&D mean for the technology appropriation function? We may point to three major implications:

1. In light of the growth of the multinational involvement in foreign-based R&D, firms that continue to concentrate their R&D in the home country may well be advised to reexamine their position for lost opportunities.
2. Industrial research executives could benefit from addressing the impact on their business of the growing R&D presence of foreigners in the United States.
3. Finally, U.S. firms may wish to establish R&D facilities in foreign countries so that they can learn from the successes and failures of the U.S. companies abroad, not merely in R&D, but in business as a whole. The potential for enhanced learning as a result of globalization of R&D is quite high.

In Box 10.5, we have sketched how one company—Asea Brown Boveri—manages global R&D. Although ABB's approach does not save cash in the short term, ABB attributes the significant percentage of orders coming in 1994 for its new models of gas turbine to its decision to globalize R&D.

BOX 10.5

THE GLOBALIZATION OF R&D AT ABB

Asea Brown Boveri Ltd. (known as ABB) is a Zurich, Switzerland-based conglomerate with 1,300 companies in 140 countries. The company's primary areas of operations are power plants, power transmission and distribution, industrial and building systems, and transportation. For 1993, revenues totaled $28.3 billion, and the company employed 206,000 individuals in its factories, laboratories, and offices worldwide. At ABB, business-level and corporate-level R&D represent a primary source for the development of its new products.

The operations of ABB are widely diversified, both in terms of product/markets and geographical location. Key to the company's success has been its ability to move to markets quickly with products that are tailored to meet local demand conditions. To accomplish these twin objectives, the company operates as a "multidomestic" organization—that is, they establish complete operating units in each major national market; very little in the way of operations is centralized at corporate headquarters. The company's approach to R&D mirrors that

---

Source: From "Managing 'multidomestic' R&D at ABB," by P. Gwynne, *Research Technology Management*, Jan/Feb 1995 Reprinted by permission.

Box 10.5 (*continued*)

of its operations, with 90 percent of R&D being done at operating units throughout the world. The remaining 10 percent, representing corporate R&D, is accomplished at six laboratories in six different countries.

As expected, the geographical and cultural diversity of the firm's R&D operations could create problems if resources are not consistently focused on activities congruent with its overall strategies. To avoid such problems, ABB has taken several steps to help assure that all labs are following the same basic "playbook."

- First, lab directors often are chosen from the operations side of the business. This helps ensure a business orientation in R&D activities.
- Second, the company pursues an aggressive job rotation program. Scientists are moved from the lab to operating divisions for short periods of time so that they themselves can develop a business orientation. In some instances, bright young scientists are assigned to follow top executives around for 3 months to develop insight into operations.
- Third, individuals from both operating and corporate R&D units participate in

an annual strategic technology planning process. Planners address key technological areas (e.g., combustion, fluid mechanics, and computational dynamics), analyzing the competitive positioning of the company with regard to the state of the art. In this way, attention is focused on the company's current activities, its need to allocate resources to certain areas, and potential products and markets that should be explored.

Although these activities contribute to focusing the overall R&D resources and efforts of the organization, basic cultural differences between personnel in the various labs can also create problems. Recognizing this, the company has undertaken several other activities to help in smoothing over any cultural differences that may appear. Specifically, the company attempts to build trust between labs with a policy stating that information in any lab is available, on a need-to-know basis, to any other of the company's labs. Further, the company periodically organizes team-building exercises, both athletic and cerebral, to foster collegiality among lab personnel.

MANAGERIAL IMPLICATIONS

Although this chapter has mostly discussed managerial choices, we will highlight four major points to be considered in the technology appropriation projects:

1. Technology appropriation projects should be decided only by juxtaposing technological possibilities and business considerations. This implies that technology managers and business managers should be jointly involved in the selection of technology projects.
2. All three purposes of technology appropriation should be explicitly evaluated: creation of fundamentally new business, altering the rules of rivalry, and supporting the existing businesses.
3. Technology appropriation should focus on the portfolio of projects, not merely on each project. This is necessary for focusing of resources to gain the best value for the firm from its appropriation activities.
4. External sourcing should be explicitly considered to build technological capability and to speed execution.

❖ CHAPTER SUMMARY

Appropriation of technological capability serves three basic purposes: to create fundamentally new businesses, to alter the rules of rivalry in existing competitive domains, or to support existing businesses. Over the years, firms have been moving toward the third generation principles that emphasize bringing technology appropriation into close linkage with business strategy formulation. Third generation principles view technology appropriation projects as a portfolio, interrelated among themselves and with business objectives.

Four major principles are involved in the decision to adopt a portfolio of technology appropriation projects. First, the competitive impact of technology and the magnitude of the possible technological advance determine technological opportunity and the appropriability of the value that can be derived from the project. Second, firms should undertake to develop technology only in areas where they have relative competitive strength. Third, the portfolio of projects should be evaluated for the potential risk/reward trade-offs. Finally, the external sourcing should explicitly be evaluated as an alternative mode for implementation.

The process of decision making involves five steps: generating ideas for technology appropriation projects, profiling each project according to its technological and strategic characteristics, determining the portfolio, choosing the mode of implementation, and execution. When a firm has a dominant position in a technology that is also strategically important to it, it should continue to develop its internal capability. It is preferable to seek external sources of technology when a firm is not dominant in a particular technology.

The major external sources of technology are other firms, universities, and the government. Intellectual property, secrecy, and procedural barriers are significant arenas of tension that need to be resolved in external sourcing. To enable a firm to get the most from external sourcing, the firm should scan broadly, provide for continual interaction between technology managers and the environment, nurture gatekeepers and boundary spanners, and fight the NIH syndrome.

Recently, firms have begun to pay close attention to their in-house R&D function. They have continued to benchmark their performance against the best in class as a way of stimulating higher productivity. They have also been employing total quality principles in the operation of R&D function. Increasingly, R&D is becoming globalized, and large firms are conducting their R&D in several locations in the world.

❖ NOTES

1. IBM. Annual Report, 1995.
2. IBM. Annual Report, 1995.
3. Roussel, P. A., K. M. Saad, and T. J. Erickson. *Third Generation R&D*. Cambridge, MA: Harvard Business School Press, 1991.
4. Roussel, P. O., K. M. Saad, and T. J. Erickson. *Third Generation R&D* 1991. Cambridge, MA: Harvard Business School Press, 1991, p. 64.
5. Von Hippel, E. *The Sources of Innovation.* New York: Oxford University, 1988.
6. Cohen, W. M. and B. A. Levinthal. "Absorptive Capacity: A new perspective on learning and innovation," *Administrative Science Quarterly,* Vol. 35, 1990, pp. 128–52.
7. MacAvoy, P. C. "Technology Strategy for a Diversified Corporation." Unpublished papers, Darden Graduate School of Business, University of Virginia 1989.
8. Leònard-Barton, D. *Wellsprings of Knowledge.* Cambridge, MA: Harvard Business School Press, 1995.

9. MacLachlan, A. "Trusting Other Outsiders to Do your Research: Does Industry Learn to do it?" *Research Technology Management,* 1995, Vol. 38, pp. 48–53.

10. Allen, T. *Managing the Flow of Technology: Technology Transfer and the Dissemination of Technological Information within the R&D Organization.* Cambridge, MA: MIT Press, 1977.

11. Leònard-Barton, D. *Wellsprings of Knowledge.* p. 160, op. cit.

12. Davidson, J. M., and Truden, A. L. "Quality Deployment in R&D Organizations," *Re-search Technology Management,* January/February 1996, p. 49.

13. Miller, R. "Applying Quality Practices to R&D," *Research Technology Management,* March/April 1995, pp. 47–50.

14. *Inside R&D,* May 13, 1992, p. 3; *Inside R&D,* April 29, 1992, p. 7; *Science* 258, November 27, 1992, pp. 1428–1433; *R&D Magazine,* May 1992, p. 21.

15. Serapio, M. G., Jr. "Growth of Japan-U.S. Cross Border Investments in the Electroni Industry," *Research Technology Management,* November-December 1995, pp. 42–4

11

DEPLOYMENT IN NEW PRODUCTS

Chrysler's drive back to the top has been a long and winding road. Quality management, new product development, and cross-discipline creativity have turned the company around, and they're speeding down the road to success.

The man who led Chrysler back to the top was Chrysler Corporation President Robert A. Lutz. Child of a Swiss banker and product of the U.S. Marine Corps—where he served as a fighter pilot, many credit his drive and determination for saving the number three U.S. carmaker. Yet in 1991, Lutz almost walked away from Chrysler. Long seen as the heir apparent to Chrysler's legendary chairman Lee Iacocca, Lutz was passed over in favor of an outsider, Robert J. Eaton. Lutz confounded industry skeptics, announcing, "Being a team player, which I am, you don't sulk and quit when someone else is selected captain of the team." Staying on as Chrysler's number two man, Lutz proved that teamwork might be the single best way to compete.

In the early 1980s, Chrysler barely avoided bankruptcy with the help of a billion-dollar federal bailout. But by 1989, the automaker again tottered over the abyss. Chrysler had to survive on its own that time, and it wasn't easy. American consumers had turned their backs on Chrysler's stodgy outdated passenger cars, and with its debt rating in the junk bond cellar, banks were turning down the loans Chrysler needed to develop a new generation of vehicles.

Chrysler managers knew it was time to make the proverbial "sea change," and so they reached out across both the Atlantic and Pacific Oceans. Having years of experience in Europe with companies like BMW and Ford of Europe, Lutz knew that the best automobiles were "products that stand out and are truly focused. They don't try to please everybody by being all things to all people but provide the customer with a very clear-cut choice." Chrysler's long-time Japanese affiliate, Mitsubishi Motor Corporation, provided another role model. Program manager G. Glenn Gardner spent several years as Chrysler's top representative at the Diamond-Star Motors plant, a Chrysler/Mitsubishi joint venture in Bloomington, Illinois. It provided a unique chance to learn the Japanese concepts of lean management and lean production.

A big influence was a 2-year benchmarking study of the Honda Motor Co. "They saw themselves more like Honda," noted auto analyst Maryann Keller of Furman-Selz, Inc., "with a limited product line and about the same size.

Honda doesn't have rich parents to support it like Mitsubishi does. And it doesn't have the keiretsu system." That's a closely linked network of wholly or partially owned suppliers that Japanese automakers like Mitsubishi or Toyota rely on to offset product development costs.

Chrysler began developing its own keiretsu-like network, tapping the brainpower of outside suppliers who provide 70 percent of its components. And, in the process, Chrysler "leaned out" its own operations.

Consider the genesis of the Chrysler New Yorker and LHS and their mid-size siblings, the Chrysler Concorde, Dodge Intrepid, and Eagle Vision. Collectively known as the L/H line, they pioneered a concept called "cab-forward design." The engine and front tires were moved as far forward as possible, translating into a well-appointed, near full-sized cabin on a midsize platform. But the most significant changes weren't visible to consumers.

"They put together a product development system that's really better than anybody else's in this country," proclaimed David Cole, director of the Office for the Study of Automotive Transportation at the University of Michigan. At peak, the L/H program employed just 744 engineers and support staff, but budgeted for 1,500. The difference was in the way the L/H program was structured.

Traditionally, the Big Three carmakers have been organized in a "chimney" structure. There was little communication between, say, someone assigned to design a dashboard and an engineer working on the heating system. So a minor change in an air conditioner duct could delay the dashboard—indeed, the entire program—by 6 months. There was even less contact between marketing and design, design and engineering, and manufacturing, and that meant no sense of ownership, or responsibility, for the way a particular vehicle turned out.

So, Chrysler knocked down the chimneys and tore out the walls, reorganizing the L/H staff into cross-disciplinary teams. Then it empowered those teams to challenge the limits. Take the case of the PRNDL display, the indicator showing the gear the automatic transmission was in. Mechanical readouts were often inaccurate, but electronic displays cost more and "we rejected that because we couldn't afford it," said Interior Engineering Chief Craig Love. Instead of taking no for an answer, "The guys said we made a bad decision and took it upon themselves to find a more cost-effective approach. What they came back with had all the benefits of an electronic indicator but was cheaper than a mechanical one."

Ultimately, this team approach permitted Chrysler to design and engineer the L/H line for just $1.7 billion, barely a third of the cost of past programs. Meanwhile, Chrysler slashed the lead time on the project—the time from concept approval to production—from 5 years to 39 months. In 1993, Chrysler would unveil its first cab-forward subcompact. Total investment for the Neon: $1.3 billion, meaning it could become the first American-made small car to earn a profit in decades.

Lutz warns that it will take more than just a sound business plan to ensure Chrysler's long-term success. It also takes something less tangible. "You can only get there by using your right brain," he suggests, referring to the side of the brain devoted to creativity. "A lot of people think the car business is just technology, an accumulation of assembly plants and money. It's all those things, but it's fundamentally a lot like the movie business. You must have the creativity, people who passionately love automobiles. And I think we have a corner on the market." Chrysler certainly proved that with the Viper. Deftly modeled after the legendary Shelby Cobra, this two-seat roadster made its debut as a concept car at the 1989 Detroit Auto Show, triggering a flood of mail—and checks. "People ask us what made us do the Viper. Nothing! We just thought it up," Lutz recalled. The Viper went into limited production in the fall of 1991. Even at $50,000, it was not likely to make much of a profit, but "that doesn't really matter," laughed Lutz, who personally conducted much of the initial road testing of the model. "You can't measure the impact in terms of the money you've made. If you consider what it's done in terms of image, prestige, and morale, the car is priceless."

In 1993, Chrysler was making money on a long list of other new products. There was reportedly a waiting list for the Jeep Grand Cherokee, which by some estimates earned an average $7,000 profit per vehicle. Chrysler's share of the booming minivan market had steadily grown to more than 50 percent, despite an increasing number of competitors, and the sales of the L/H sedans were so strong that Chrysler would soon add a second assembly plant.

That's not to say all its troubles were over. It wouldn't take the competition long to copy the cab-forward concept, so Chrysler would need to raise billions to maintain an aggressive product development program. But rising health care costs, which in 1992 added more than $700 to the cost of every car it built, stretched its budget. And because of a decade's cutbacks, Chrysler now had nearly two retirees collecting pensions for every active employee, another overwhelming burden.

Yet somehow the company had managed to pull off a profit, even while some of its toughest competitors around the world slipped into the red. It's been 10 years since the industry's doomsayers were readying Chrysler's obituaries. Under the 1991 headline, "Chrysler's Stock Offering Is a Risky Ride for Investors," *The Wall Street Journal* stated that "this Chrysler bet isn't for the fainthearted."

By 1993, everyone was applauding. "I used to be a doubter," said auto analyst Keller. "I'm not anymore."[1]

As described in the vignette, Chrysler's drive back to the top of the automobile industry had been a long and winding road. A significant factor in this transition had been the introduction of new cars into the market, designed with new technology, and managed with cross-disciplinary creativity and quality management. Indeed, by 1993, among the U.S. auto manufacturers, Chrysler had the shortest product development time, along with some of the most profitable car lines.

New products have always been a significant source of sales and profits for companies. Among major firms, the sales attributable to new products in recent years have been around 5 percent. The patterns of new product introductions by U.S. firms are presented in Table 11.1. As shown in the table:

- During the 1980s, the trend had been for firms to introduce on average more products per year.

TABLE 11.1 New Products Introduced Annually

	Year							
	1989		*1988*		*1987*		*Average*	
SBU Type	*All New Products*	*Innovative Products*	*All New Products*	*Innovative Products*	*All New Products*	*Innovative Products*	*All New Products*	*Innovative Products*
Service	5 (3)	1.4 (1.3)	4 (3)	0.8 (1.4)	4 (4)	0.7 (1.2)	4	1.0
Package Goods	12 (24)	2.5 (4.4)	9 (19)	1.5 (2.6)	7 (13)	1.4 (3.5)	9	1.8
Durables	6 (9)	1.4 (1.8)	6 (8)	1.7 (2.0)	4 (4)	0.8 (0.9)	5	1.3
Industrial	13 (54)	2.8 (9.0)	6 (18)	1.2 (2.3)	6 (19)	1.6 (4.2)	8	1.9
Total	10 (35)	2.1 (6.0)	6 (14)	1.3 (2.1)	5 (13)	1.2 (3.0)	7	1.5

Source: Reprinted from *Journal of Product Innovation Management*, Vol. 9, 1992. V. Mahajan and J. Wind, "New Product Models: Practice Short-comings and Improvements," pp. 128–139. Copyright 1992, with permission from Elsevier Science.

- There are differences in the number of new product introductions among industry types. For instance, there were more introductions in packaged goods industries than in many other industries; and service industries showed the smallest number of new product introductions.[2]
- The table also distinguishes innovative products from product refinements; note that truly innovative products comprised only a very small number of new product introductions.

As this discussion suggests, deploying technology in the market through new product introductions is a frequently employed tactic by many firms.

In this chapter, we will focus on the deployment of technology in new products. Specifically, we will try to answer such questions as:

1. What are the different types of new product introductions?
2. What factors should a firm consider in the decision to launch a new product?
3. How can firms reduce product development times?

We will describe new product introductions by using the Technology-Market (T-M) matrix, as shown in Figure 11.1.

- In the case of some products, a firm searches for an appropriate market opportunity to commercialize a technology that it has either developed in-house or acquired from outside. These technology-push products may require the redesign of a firm's value chain for the manufacture and delivery of products.
- On the other hand, market-pull products may require firms to search for appropriate technologies to solve market needs. This approach may also require the redesign of the value chain. Thus, new product introductions often require coordination with both the appropriation of technology as well as the deployment in the value chain.

The chapter overview is presented in Figure 11.2. The scheme of the chapter is as follows. First, we will describe the key concepts and ideas necessary to anchor our discussion of new product development. Second, we will discuss the means of technology infusion into new products. Third, we will summarize the principles and process of new product development. Fourth, we will summarize some major approaches to speeding product development time. Finally, we will outline how large multinational firms are globalizing their new product development activity.

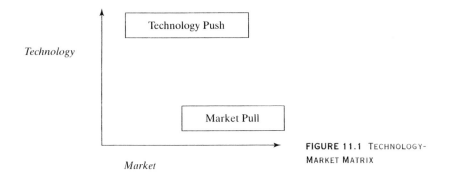

FIGURE 11.1 TECHNOLOGY-MARKET MATRIX

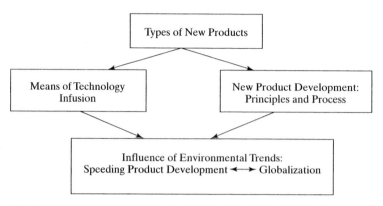

FIGURE 11.2 CHAPTER OVERVIEW

NEW PRODUCTS: DEFINITIONS

TYPES OF NEW PRODUCTS

Unlike Table 11.1, where we distinguished innovative products from other new products, firms often employ a broader set of characteristics to describe new product development activity. Some commonly accepted categories of new products are as follows:

- New-to-world products. Products that are inventions. Examples include the first Polaroid camera, the first car, rayon, the laser printer, and in-line skates.
- New category entries. Products that take a firm into a new market segment. Such products are not new to the world, but, instead, are new to the developing firm. Examples include P&G's entry into the shampoo market, Hallmark's development of gift items, and AT&T's introduction of the universal card.
- Additions to product lines. Products that are line extensions in the firms' current markets. Examples include Tide, liquid detergent; Bud Lite, beer; and Apple's Mac 2SI, computers.
- Product improvements. Current products made better. Virtually every product on the market today has been improved, often many times.
- Repositioning. Products that are retargeted for a new user application. A classic case is Arm & Hammer baking soda, which was repositioned several times as a drain deodorant, refrigerator deodorant, etc.[3]

Three observations may be made with respect to such commonly used categories:

1. In the preceding classification, products are categorized from the developing firms' point of view and not necessarily from the perspective of the market or the customers. For example, the "new category entries" are strictly existing products; they are not likely to be perceived as "new" by the market or the customers.

2. Some new product activity within a firm is focused on imitating its competitors. As we will discuss later in the chapter, smart followership is a profitable strategy, and some recent evidence suggests that, in certain conditions, a firm first to enter into a market does not often do very well.[4]
3. Different categories represent different degrees of difficulty in the product development process. As a general rule, additions to product lines, product improvements, and repositioning are less difficult and less expensive to develop than are new-to-world products or new category entries.

In chapter 3, we identified four different types of innovation: incremental, modular, architectural, and radical. According to this classification, product improvements represent incremental innovations. New category entries and additions to the product line may represent, at best, incremental innovations; repositioning is *not* considered an innovation. Further, when a firm talks about new-to-world products, such products may represent modular, architectural, or radical innovations. All of the three types of new-to-world products, therefore, require some emphasis on technology, either through a specific set of technologies (as in modular or radical innovations) or on technology integration (as in architectural innovation). Further, these three types of innovations have different competitive implications: Radical innovations may open up new industries, whereas architectural innovations and modular innovations may open up new market segments. In spite of differences in products, a firm's product lines are often related; so, it is useful to talk about a product family.

THE CONCEPT OF PRODUCT FAMILY

Firms, especially the large firms, pursue multiple development projects either sequentially or concurrently. Many of these development projects are related, because they rely on a common set of capabilities or technologies. Consider the following:

- Hewlett-Packard built on a foundation of capabilities in scientific instruments to create families of computers and peripherals, as well as to enter into the medical systems business.
- Similarly, Canon built on its copier and facsimile machine platforms to create laser printer and panel businesses.

The term *product platform* is often used to connote this common technological base, which encompasses design and components shared by a set of products. For example, Chrysler's three lines of cars, the Chrysler Concord, Eagle Vision, and Dodge Intrepid, are all based on a common platform that shares the same basic frame, suspension, and drive train.

Products that share a common platform must have specific features and functionality required by different sets of customers; these are called a *product family*. A product family addresses a market segment, and specific products or groups of products within the family target niches within that segment. The commonality of technologies and markets leads to efficiency and effectiveness in value chain activities such as manufacturing, distribution, and service when the firm tailors each general value activity to the needs of specific customer groups.

The concept of product family draws our attention to two different types of learning that take place during a new product development process.

1. The first occurs within an existing family. Here, renewal is achieved by integrating the best components in new structures or proprietary designs to better serve evolving customer needs. Integration improves all products within the family.
2. In addition, a second kind of learning requires development of new product families. Indeed, in terms of creating new businesses, new product families branch from existing ones, expanding on their technical skills, market knowledge, and manufacturing capabilities. This focuses development of new technologies.

In Figure 11.3, we have portrayed the relationship between products to product families and product platforms.

The twin concepts of product families and product platforms are useful for illustrating four major implications:

1. A product platform is a valuable resource that a firm can deploy to compete in the market, especially in the new product development process.
2. Competitors' product families need to be analyzed, because successive generations of products may be introduced more efficiently and effectively as a result of continual improvement of the existing product platforms.
3. Reliance on the existing product platforms for successive generations of products may shorten the product development time.
4. For a firm to maintain technology leadership, it may be important to begin work on the next product platform while completing specific products based on the current platform.

In summary, firms may pursue, concurrently or sequentially, several different types of new product introductions ranging from incremental to modular, architectural, and radical. The products of any single firm are often related to one another through a common platform; the related products constitute a product family.

MEANS OF TECHNOLOGY INFUSION INTO PRODUCTS

How does a firm compete with technologies in new product development activity? Two approaches are becoming increasingly prevalent: (1) bundling and (2) disruptive technologies. Bundling involves some form of technology integration, whereas disruptive technologies focus on modular or radical innovations.

BUNDLING

An increasing number of companies have come to realize the value of combining separate elements of their product lines into bundles. A bundle is a group of products and/or services offered to the market as a package. Bundles display a wide variety of features including items that are not available separately, and are offered at a price that is less than the sum of the prices of the individual items. Creating a bundle is like creating a

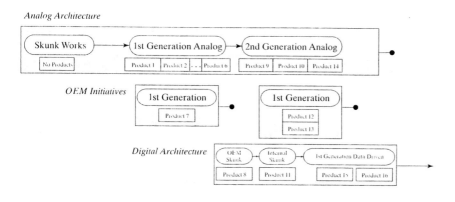

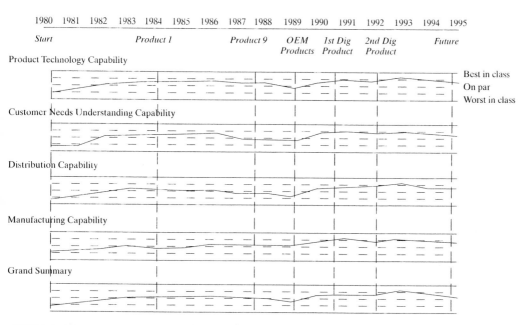

FIGURE 11.3 PRODUCT PLATFORM AND PRODUCT FAMILY

Source: Reprinted from "Product Family and the Dynamics of Core Capability," by Marc H. Meyer and James M. Utterback, *Sloan Management Review,* Spring 1993, p. 32, by permission of publisher. Copyright 1993 by Sloan Management Review Association. All rights reserved.

new product. However, although a new bundle acts like a new product in the marketplace, from the point of view of the developing firm, bundles are typically much less expensive and risky to create.

Box 11.1 narrates the story of how Chrysler turned around its nonprofitable Dodge Omni and Plymouth Horizon product lines by using the tactic of cost reduction bundling.

Bundling offers three opportunities for a firm in its product development activities: (1) cost reduction, (2) market expansion, and (3) product enhancement.

BOX 11.1

CREATING NEW PRODUCTS
WITH BUNDLING

In 1983, the Dodge Omni and Plymouth Horizon were endangered products. With the base car priced at $7,000 and all options separately priced (i.e., itemized pricing, where the price of a bundle is the sum of the individual component prices), Chrysler could not compete effectively with less expensive imports.

At this time, these cars were available with a wide variety of individual options; indeed, more than 8,000,000 varieties of individual cars were possible. To become competitive, Chrysler switched to bundling and offered only 42 varieties. The results were rather remarkable. Chrysler was able to reduce the price of the car, including a typical package of options, by more than $1,000. New market segments were attracted to the product, and the profitable product life was extended by several years.

The price reductions were made possible by reduced manufacturing costs. The primary sources of savings were from reduced set-up costs because of longer production runs; better quality based on the reduction in interactions; and a $2,000,000 per year savings from reduced carrying and shipping costs.

Note that Chrysler presented the consumer a new menu of choices at new prices, i.e., they introduced new products.

Dramatic turnaround for the Dodge Omni and Plymouth Horizon was possible when bundling was implemented. By aggressively trimming its product line of the separate components and presenting the consumer with fewer choices, Chrysler staved off product extinction and extended the profitable life of the car dramatically.

Source: Hanson, Ward A., Eppen, G. D., and Martin, R. K. "Mining Your Product Line: Creating New Products with Bundling," Paper No. 972, Institute for Research in the Behavioral, Economic and Management Sciences, West Lafayette: Purdue University, April 1990.

COST REDUCTION BUNDLING

As shown in the Chrysler story in Box 11.1, a firm may reap the benefits of enhanced profitability through aggressively pruning its product line of separate components. As a consequence, the consumer is presented with fewer choices. Often, the cost savings from bundling are so substantial that items can, in a sense, be given away to the consumers.

MARKET EXPANSION BUNDLING

A firm may also reap the benefit of expanding its market when consumers value bundles more than individual items (mass market bundles). Restaurants have successfully used mass market bundling by offering items separately or by bundling them together. Recently, automobile companies have been employing a similar approach in terms of the features they allow in a car. Bundling may also enhance sales by reducing customer switching to competitors' products. Building manufacturer loyalty, or encouraging switching only among a single manufacturer's offerings, is an objective for many consumer package group firms.

PRODUCT ENHANCEMENT BUNDLING

It is often possible for firms to use performance enhancement bundling as a market entry strategy. Personal computer companies have repeatedly been successful in using this strategy. In 1981, Osborne Computer came on the scene, rapidly growing enough to set landmarks for sales for a start-up company. Much of its success was credited to a unique bundling of adequate hardware and leading software. In 1987, the Next Computer Company achieved recognition for its bundling of advanced drive technology and unique software programs with its computer system. In 1990, Headstart Computer Systems introduced CD-ROM technology to the mass market together with its basic computer system, bundling extensive software databases such as an encyclopedia, writers' reference tools, business databases, and entertainment packages.[5]

A fundamentally different technology offers firms the opportunity to introduce technology through modular and radical innovations.

DISRUPTIVE TECHNOLOGIES

Radical innovations typically, and sometimes modular or architectural innovations, find their way into the market through the deployment of disruptive technologies in new products. Different technologies influence product performance in different ways.

- On the one hand, *sustaining* technologies tend to maintain a rate of improvement, thereby giving customers something more or better in the attributes they already value.
- On the other hand, *disruptive* technologies introduce a package of attributes very different from what the mainstream customer historically values, often being inferior along one or two performance dimensions that are particularly important to the customers. This, of course, is another way of paraphrasing our discussion of the innovation process: A technology, in its infancy, is likely to be inferior to an existing one that it eventually displaces.

Typically, mainstream customers are unwilling to use a disruptive product in applications they know and understand. This means that disruptive technologies will tend, at first, to be used and valued only in new markets or new applications. In fact, they generally make possible the emergence of new markets. At the same time, once these technologies become established, they make it possible for the developing firms to invade their competitors' markets and often to dethrone longtime market leaders.

How could disruptive technologies threaten market leaders?

First, once a disruptive technology gains acceptance in a new market, its performance enhancements begin. Often, the *S*-curve of performance characteristic improvement is so steep that the disruptive technology soon outperforms the existing technology. It can thus satisfy the needs of customers in established markets.

Second, market leaders' revenue and cost structures have been built around the existing technology. These revenue and cost structures, thus, play a critical role in the market leader's discounting of disruptive technologies. That is, disruptive technologies look financially unattractive to established companies. For example, as illustrated earlier in Box 8.3, DEC found it difficult to transition to RISC architecture in its workstations. However, to managers of the new entrants, the world looks quite different. Without the high-cost structures of their established counterparts, these companies find the emerging markets appealing. In Box 11.2, we have illustrated the story of Seagate Technology and the impact of disruptive technologies on its performance.[6]

BOX 11.2

SEAGATE TECHNOLOGY
AND THE HARD-DISK MARKET

To illustrate the disruptive effects a change in the core architecture of a technology can have on the new product development process, consider the case of disk drive developer Seagate Technology. The California-based company, started in 1980, pioneered the development of the 5.25-inch hard disk drives that had been the standard for personal computer manufacturers. By the mid-1980s, Seagate was the leading manufacturer of these drives, with sales in excess of $700 million. By all accounts, its future looked bright.

A brief history of the hard-disk drive industry is helpful in understanding events at Seagate in the late 1980s. The architecture of the hard-disk drive had gone through a number of changes since the mid-1970s. The original drives were 14 inches and designed to service the needs of mainframe computer manufacturers. The late 1970s saw the architectural change to an 8-inch drive, which was smaller and required less power to operate. However, the storage capability of the new drive was substantially less than that of the older architecture and thus not of interest to the customers of the 14-inch drive manufacturers. Further production of the new drives required substantial changes in existing manufacturing systems. These conditions led manufacturers of 14-inch drives to ignore this architectural change in technology. As 8-inch drives were further developed, their capacity was increased, and they became the standard for the next generation computer, known as the "mini." In this new market, original manufacturers of 14-inch drives were no longer key players. Instead, new firms that focused their efforts on the new architecture were to lead the way.

This scenario was played out again with the next architectural change—from 8-inch drives to 5.25-inch drives during the early 1980s. As the performance characteristics of these new drives were enhanced, they became a key component in the new personal computer. As noted earlier, Seagate had focused its attention and resources on this architecture, becoming the pioneer and leading producer in the market. In the mid-1980s, another new architecture began to appear—the 3.5-inch drive. Seagate was second in the industry in developing a working prototype of the drive, and by 1985 they had developed more than 80 models using the new architecture. However, as with its predecessors, early versions lacked the storage capacity that Seagate's customers were demanding. Further, large-scale production of these units would require a retooling in the production process. The expected low sales volume and high unit cost of the 3.5-inch drive led management to shelf further development of the unit. Instead, they focused their development efforts on further increasing the performance characteristics of the 5.25-inch drives.

By 1987, the storage capacity of 3.5-inch drives had increased sufficiently to compete in the mainstream personal computer market. The small size of the new units also made them ideal for the next generation of computer—the portable or laptop computer. It was only then that Seagate took its 3.5-inch technology off the shelf for further development. However, by that time Conner Peripherals and Quantum Corporation had already established market leadership by focusing their development efforts on the new architecture. As a result, Seagate had become a second-tier supplier in the new portable computer market.

Source: Adapted from Bower, J. L. and Christensen, C. M. "Disruptive technologies: Catching the Wave," *Harvard Business Review,* January-February 1995, pp. 45–49.

Two further points can be made about the infusion of technology into new products.

1. Bundling and use of disruptive technologies are not mutually exclusive tactics. In many new products, firms successfully bundle known technologies while simultaneously introducing disruptive technologies to create new product features.
2. Indeed, as we have seen, disruptive technologies often render an existing platform obsolete. Hence, firms need not only exploit their existing product platforms but must continually replenish them by adding newer capabilities.[7]

PRODUCT DEVELOPMENT: PRINCIPLES AND PROCESS

The choice of products to launch into the marketplace is determined not merely by the technical characteristics of the product but also by a set of strategic factors that will help ensure its market success. In the previous section, we have underscored the many ways in which technology can be embedded in a product. Thus, technology intelligence is critical input into the decision to develop a new product.

Similarly, attention to strategic factors is equally important, because new product launch is an inherently risky process. Three interrelated sets of strategic factors need to be considered in the decision to develop a new product: (1) strategic context, (2) technology leadership, and (3) timing of product launch.

STRATEGIC CONTEXT

What is the business rationale for launching new products? Recall the theme that we have emphasized throughout the text: The test of technology management is the degree to which it enables value creation. This is true in the case of new product introductions, as well. Whether a new product creates value depends at least on three factors: business strategy, risk-return trade-off, and resources.

BUSINESS STRATEGY

Except in the case of radically new products—that lead to the creation of new industries—new product introductions reflect the business strategy that a firm is currently pursuing. As shown in Figure 11.4, business strategies may be classified into four types based on two dimensions:

1. Scope (broad versus narrow), and
2. Focus (cost versus differentiation)

Although new product development may take place in any of the four strategic types, the thrust of new product development will differ across the four strategic types. For example,

> Cost leadership. This strategy necessitates that product development efforts be oriented toward cost reduction by lowering material content, facilitating manufacturing ease, or simplifying logistical requirements.

Focus

	Cost	Differentiation
Broad	Cost Leadership	Differentiation
Narrow	Cost Focus	Differentiation Focus

Scope (label on left axis)

FIGURE 11.4 BUSINESS STRATEGY AND PRODUCT DEVELOPMENT

Differentiation. Differentiation requires that product development enhance product quality, features, or availability.

Cost focus. Here, the product development may focus only on designing enough performance for the target segment's needs.

Differentiation focus. Rather than broadly targeting customers, the firm may focus its product design to meet the needs of a particular segment.

Unlike new product introductions in established industries, radically new products frequently open new industries. Although a firm's extant value chain may influence its strategy for the new product, it is difficult to predict the evolution of a new industry in its embryonic stages. Hence, introducing firms may have to reformulate their business strategies as industry evolution proceeds.

RESOURCES

A decision to proceed with new product development implies commitment of resources, both financial and human. Resource commitment varies from industry to industry and across new product types. A new drug in the pharmaceutical industry may require commitment of over $200 million on average, whereas a line extension of the same drug will cost much less. When a firm is pursuing a number of projects—a portfolio of new product development projects—it is often necessary to prioritize the projects and to allocate the resources according to the prioritization scheme.

RISK-RETURN TRADE-OFF

New product introductions are risky; many of them, indeed, fail. At the same time, as we have noted, their development involves commitment of resources that, in many cases, could be substantial. Therefore, a decision to proceed with new product development should be anchored in an assessment of expected returns against the planned commitment of resources and the riskiness of the project.

The three factors enumerated previously should be considered during the decision to launch any new product. They can be summarized as three questions to be answered during the decision to initiate new product development:

1. How does the new product development fit with our business strategy?
2. How many resources will need to be committed to the development project?
3. What is the expected risk-return trade-off in the project?

There is emerging evidence that financial markets reward firms that utilize their resources to bring out innovative new products into the market with both higher returns and lower risks. In Box 11.3, we have summarized a recent study that explores the response of the capital markets to new products.

TECHNOLOGY LEADERSHIP VERSUS FOLLOWERSHIP

A second factor that must be considered in a firm's decision to launch new products concerns its technology objectives: its decision to position itself as a leader or follower. If a firm seeks to be the first to introduce new products, then it is pursuing a strategy of product leadership. Here, the strategic choice is between pioneering an innovation or waiting for others to be the pioneer.

The choice of whether to be a leader or a follower should be based on three factors: (1) sustainability of the technological lead, (2) first mover advantages, and (3) first mover disadvantages. Because of the importance of these considerations, we will discuss each in some detail.

SUSTAINABILITY OF THE TECHNOLOGICAL LEAD

For a firm to justify pursuing product leadership, the technological lead must be sustainable. That is, either competitors cannot easily duplicate the technology or, if they can, the firm can innovate faster than competitors in successive generations. Sustainability of a technological lead is a function of four factors:

1. *The source of technological change.* A firm will find it relatively easier to sustain its technological lead if its technology is developed in-house. When important sources of technology are external to an industry (or a firm), sustaining a lead is generally more difficult.
2. *The presence or absence of a cost differentiation advantage in technology development activity.* When product development costs are high, a firm with a large share of new product development activity in the industry has proportionally lower R&D costs than a smaller share firm. It may thus be able to spend more money on R&D in order to maintain its technological lead without a cost penalty. For example, Honda has reinforced its competitive advantage in motorcycles through a continual stream of new models.
3. *Relative technological position.* Firms that pursue and nurture their technological dominance are more likely to sustain their technological lead. Such firms do not cut back R&D in industry downturns and maintain relationships with leading scientific centers in appropriate fields. NEC, for example, is the company most highly ranked by engineering graduates in Japan. This contributes to its ability to attract the best graduates, reinforcing its strong R&D capability.
4. *Rate of technology diffusion.* The diffusion of technology may undermine a technology leader's efforts to sustain its technological advantage. Diffusion can occur when it is easy for competitors to observe the leader's product and methods of operating; when technology transfer can take place through equipment suppliers or other venders; through industry observers, such as

BOX 11.3

INVESTIGATING NEW PRODUCT STRATEGIES OF LARGE MANUFACTURING FIRMS

At the individual project level, the outcomes of new product development efforts within any given firm are likely to differ. That is, any one new product development may bear little resemblance to other products developed during the same period of time. However, at the firm level, there is likely to be some overall focus or direction that drives the development of new products in the firm. This overall orientation and direction can be conceptualized as a firm's new product strategy[a] and should become apparent by looking at the aggregate pattern of product introductions that emerge from the organization over time. Further, it is also likely that relationships exist between the new product strategy a firm is pursuing, and the shareholder value it is able to create.

To investigate the new product strategies of large manufacturing firms, as well as explore the connection between strategy and capital market outcome, researchers at the University of Kansas analyzed 459 new products introduced over a 5-year period by 18 *Fortune 500* firms. The researchers characterized each product along three scales: how new the technology embodied in the product was to the developing firm; how new the intended market was to the developing firm; and how innovative the product was in the overall marketplace. These characteristics were then aggregated for each firm to produce a profile of its new product strategy. The 18 firms were then grouped or "clustered" based upon similarities in their new product strategies.

The results of these procedures identified four different types of strategies being pursued by the 18 firms. These strategies included "Innovators," those firms producing products considered highly innovative in the marketplace using their existing technologies; "In-vestors in Technology," those firms that acquired or developed technologies new to them in order to introduce moderately innovative products; and "Business as Usual" firms that used their existing technologies to develop lines of products that displayed little innovation in the marketplace. Another group of firms, which did not display any strong characteristic or focus in their development efforts, was also identified in the sample. The researchers titled this group of firms "middle-of-the-road." So, these results support the notion that, at the firm level, identified patterns of new product developments can be identified. That is, different firms pursue different new product strategies.

The research next attempted to link these new product strategies to capital market outcomes, measured as both shareholder value creation and perceived riskiness of the strategy. The findings illuminate the relationships between strategies and outcomes. Specifically, firms that introduced new products that were highly innovative in the marketplace tended to display higher levels of shareholder value creation. Capital markets did not tend to reward those firms that acquired or developed technologies new to them if the products resulting from that technology were not also innovative in the marketplace. Further, firms that lacked a strategic focus (i.e., middle-of-the-road firms) were considered more risky by the capital market; firms that used their existing technologies to develop highly innovative products were among the least risky. In short, using a firm's existing resources to produce products that are innovative in the marketplace may be an important consideration in securing higher returns with lower risk.

Source: Adapted from Firth, R. W. and Narayanan, V. K. "New product strategies of large, dominant product manufacturing firms: An exploratory analysis," *Journal of Product Innovation Management* (July 1996): 13(4): 334–347.

[a]Cooper, R. G. "New product strategies: What distinguishes the top performers?" *Journal of Product Innovation Management* (September 1984): 1(3): 151–164.

consultants; or through buyers who desire another qualified source. Faster diffusion may also result from spin-off firms or public statements and papers delivered by a leader's scientific personnel. On the other hand, patents, in-house development of prototypes and production equipment, vertical integration in key parts that embody or give clues to the technology, and personnel policies that retain employees may retard such diffusion of technologies.[8]

FIRST MOVER ADVANTAGES

Competitive advantages that result from being a technological leader are commonly referred to as *first mover advantages*. These advantages allow a leader to translate technology gaps into other competitive advantages that persist even after the technology gap closes. In general, a first mover gets the opportunity to define the competitive rules in a variety of areas. There are several important sources of first mover advantages.

1. *Reputation.* First movers may establish a reputation as the pioneer or leader. Leadership places a firm in a position of being the first to serve buyers and, thus, establish relationships that may build loyalty.
2. *Preemptive positioning.* First movers may preempt attractive market positions, forcing competitors to adopt less desirable ones. They are also positioned to be the first to increase capacity, preempting competitors from expanding profitably.
3. *Switching costs.* A first mover can lock in later sales if switching costs are present, that is, when a customer finds it unattractive, or increased costs in moving, switching from one competitor to another.
4. *Channel selection.* A first mover may be able to choose the best brokers, distributors, or retailers; followers must either accept second best or persuade the channels to shift or divide their loyalties.
5. *Proprietary learning curve.* When there are experienced curve effects in value activities, the first mover starts the learning curves first in the affected activities and will gain a cost or differentiation advantage.
6. *Favorable access to facilities inputs or other industry resources.* First movers often enjoy cost advantages due to favorable access to facilities and inputs. The firm may get its pick of sites for facilities, for example, or favorable deals with raw material suppliers eager for new business. In the airline industry, the early no-frills carriers required cheap surplus aircraft and low-cost terminal space, and hired out-of-work pilots.
7. *Definition of standards.* The ability to define standards may make a firm's position more sustainable. For example, RCA defined the standards in color TV, which meant the competitors had to go down the learning curve far behind RCA rather than create a new one.
8. *Institutional barriers.* First movers may secure patents or, being first into the country, may receive special status from the government. Such factors may also facilitate the first mover's ability to define standards, as well.
9. *Early profits.* In some industries, the first mover may be in a position to enjoy temporarily high profits from its position. It may be able to contract with buyers at high prices because the new item is relatively scarce or sell to buyers who value the new technology very highly.[9]

First mover advantages need to be weighed against the potential disadvantages that ar associated with being a pioneer.

FIRST MOVER DISADVANTAGES

First movers often face disadvantages as well as advantages. These disadvantages com from three sources: (1) the cost of pioneering, (2) the risks ensuing from uncertain con ditions, and (3) low-cost imitation.

1. *The costs of pioneering.* A first mover often bears substantial pioneering costs. The pioneering costs are often engendered by the need to gain regula-tory approval, educate buyers, develop infrastructure in such areas as ser-vice facilities and training, develop inputs such as raw material sources and machinery, and the higher cost of early inputs because of the scarcity of sup-ply or small scale of needs.

2. *Risks.* The first mover often faces three different types of risk created by un-certain conditions. First, the first movers bear the risk of uncertainty over future demand, especially because buyer needs may change. Second, the first movers may be at a disadvantage if early investments are specific to the current technology and cannot be easily modified for later generations. Fi-nally, technological discontinuities work against the first mover by making obsolete its investments in the established technology.

3. *Low-cost imitation.* The first movers expose themselves to followers who may be able to imitate the innovation at lower costs than the cost of innovating.[10]

All three factors—sustainability of technological need, first mover advantages, and firs mover disadvantages—combine to determine the best choice for a particular firm Hence, all three need to be analyzed concurrently in order to decide whether the firr should pursue a leader versus a follower strategy in its new product launches. Decision may vary from industry to industry as well as from product launch to product launch.[11]

Impressive evidence exists concerning the impact of pioneering on new product per formance. In one study of 40 industrial product entries, pioneering entrants generally main tained their market share advantage. Similarly, in another study of 174 industrial product pioneering was discovered to be one of the major determinants of long-term success of new product. In the case of consumer products, it was discovered that second entrants ob tained, on average, only about three-quarters of the market share of the pioneer, and late entrants were able to capture progressively smaller shares. However, there are also studie that uncover significant first mover disadvantages. For example, in the study of the ciga rette market, it was found that later entries in rapidly growing markets or entries that wer significantly differentiated from existing products could gain substantial shares; this re moved the first entrant from its dominant position. These studies generally show that th decision to be a pioneer or a follower is a complex one and should not be taken lightly.[12]

TIMING OF NEW PRODUCT LAUNCH

Whether a firm chooses to be a pioneer or a follower, it still has to determine the spe cific timing of its product launch: When should a new product enter the market? A po tential leader must determine its entry time so as to balance the opportunities o benefits of an innovation with the risks and costs associated with product developmen and marketing. A potential follower must consider not only the marketing activities o the early entrant and the evolution of the industry, but also the competition of other potential entrants.

The timing of new product introduction is a balancing act, and a firm has to weigh the risk of premature entry against the problems of missed opportunity.[13] The risks are determined by several factors, including R&D capabilities, demand potential, market evolution, and marketing rivalry. These factors have different implications for pioneers, early followers, and late followers:

> *Pioneers.* The potential pioneer in an industry should spend time and money to build expertise in R&D, engineering, production, and marketing before entering the market. The decision to pioneer a new product in the market is justified only if the expected return from the firm's investment in various activity is high enough to offset the risk of being preempted by a competitor.

> *Early followers.* An early follower who intends to enter the market in the introduction or growth stage of the product life cycle should hasten its new product entry unless its expertise in R&D, engineering, and production can be significantly enhanced by a short delay in entry time. In many situations, the benefits from market development by the pioneer can be easily and quickly capitalized, whereas additional return from further R&D and marketing effort is not very high.

> *Late followers.* A late follower that imitates early entrants during the late growth or the maturity stage of the product's life cycle should also enter the market as early as possible. The benefit from further market development becomes marginal, and the penalty for late entry increases rapidly.

In Box 11.4, we have showcased a study that examines the market entry–performance relationship in a systematic manner. The study generally confirms the need to balance the costs and risks of pioneering for leaders, early followers, and late followers.

PRODUCT DEVELOPMENT PROCESS

The product development process is a sequence of steps or activities that a firm employs to conceive, design, and commercialize a product. Broadly, we may group the activities into a two-step model of the development process. As illustrated in Figure 11.5, the process of product development consists of two major phases: the strategic phase and the operational phase.

STRATEGIC PHASE

During the strategic phase, the critical objectives of new product development in the firm are determined. During this phase, top management establishes focus and critical guidelines that drive the product development process in the operational phase. Five major questions are debated and settled in this phase:

- Where does new product development fit with the corporate and business strategy of the firm?
- What are our expectations regarding risk and return?
- How does a firm's decision to be a technology leader or follower shape the development process?
- How much resource is a firm willing to devote to the process?
- When should we time the introduction of the product in the market?

BOX 11.4

STUDYING THE TIMING OF COMPETITIVE MARKET ENTRY

The timing of market entry is a critical element in the eventual success or failure of a new product. To determine what factors might be important in establishing the "right" time of entry, researchers at Pennsylvania State University and the University of Lowell recently studied the timing and relative success of 112 new industrial products introduced by 52 French firms. The firms were selected from diverse industrial sectors including electronics, chemicals, construction, transportation, and agricultural. The data was collected through personal interviews with members of the participating firms.

The results of this study suggest several interesting implications for alternative entry strategies (i.e., pioneers, fast followers, and slow followers):

- First, the timing of entry must balance the risks of being premature to the market against the costs of missing the opportunity to be the market leader. A pioneer's success is more likely when it has solid expertise in R&D, engineering, production, and marketing. Because of the importance of these activities, entry should be delayed until the necessary expertise is developed. The high returns

that result from sound expertise offset the risk of being overtaken by potential competitors.

- Second, the earlier the entry of a follower, the more likely the success of the product. Thus, the strategy of being a "fast" follower is an important one. This is particularly true in markets that are in their introduction and growth stages; fast followers will have less market impact during the mature and declining stages of the life cycle. However, if by delaying entry the follower can make significant improvements to the project, entry should be delayed.

- Finally, with respect to late followers, success becomes less likely as the market moves through its life cycle. Entering as early as possible is critical to the success of the product. Further, delaying entry in order to make improvements to the product does not appear to be a successful strategy in the latter stages of the product life cycle.

Thus, in general, this research suggests that sooner, rather than later, is important to a follower's success.

Source: Adapted from Lilien, G. L. and Yoon, E. "The timing of competitive market entry: An exploratory study of new industrial products," *Management Science* (1990): 36(5): pp. 568–585.

This phase is critical for two major reasons:

1. It determines the profit potential of the new product and, thus, its success.
2. This phase offers top management greater leverage (than the operational phase) in influencing the success of new product development by defining the guidelines under which the development process will proceed.

OPERATIONAL PHASE

This phase assumes that corporate or business strategies have already been formulated–thus, the focus, goals, and broad guidelines for the product development process have already been established. The operational phase can be broken down into five major step

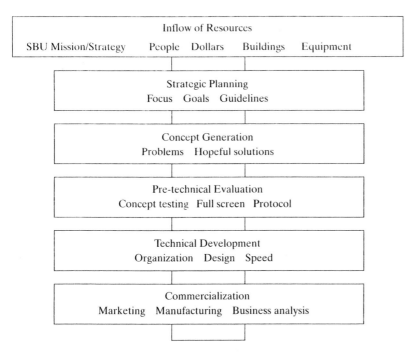

FIGURE 11.5 STAGES OF NEW PRODUCT DEVELOPMENT

Source: From Crawford, Merle C. *New Product Management,* Chicago, IL: Irwin, 1997, p. 43. Reprinted by permission of The McGraw-Hill Companies.

1. *Concept development.* "Product concept" is a description of the form, function, and features of the product. During concept development, the needs of the target market are identified, alternative product concepts are generated and evaluated, and a single concept is selected for further development. The technology infusion into new product takes place at this step.

2. *System-level design.* This step consists of the definition of the product architecture and the division of the product into components and subsystems. The final assembly scheme for the production system is also usually defined during this step.

3. *Detail design.* During this step, the materials and tolerances of all the unique parts of the product are completely specified, and all the standard parts purchased from the suppliers are identified. A process plan is established, and tooling is designed for each part to be fabricated within the production system.

4. *Testing and refinement.* Testing and refinement involve the construction and evaluation of multiple preproduction versions of the product. Early prototypes of the product are usually built with production parts, i.e., parts with the same properties as those intended for the production version of the product. We may distinguish between two types of prototypes. Alpha prototypes are tested to determine whether or not the product will work as

designed. Later, beta prototypes are usually built with parts supplied by the intended production processes but may not be assembled using the intended final assembly process. Customers in their own use environment often test beta prototypes.

5. Production ramp-up. In this step, the product is made using the intended production system. The purpose of the ramp-up is to train the workforce and to work out any remaining problems in the production process. The transition from production ramp-up to ongoing production is usually gradual and continuous. At some point in this transition, the product is launched and becomes available for widespread distribution.[14]

The generic development process closely resembles the one used in a market-pull situation, where a firm begins with a market opportunity and then seeks out the technologies required to satisfy the market need. However, the development process may vary from firm to firm and, indeed, from project to project. In general, we can identify three variants of this process: (1) technology-push products, (2) platform products, and (3) customized products.

1. Technology-push products. Here, a firm begins with a new proprietary technology and looks for an appropriate market in which to apply this technology. The technology-push process begins with an additional phase to match a given technology with a market opportunity.
2. Platform products. A platform product is built around a preexisting product platform. In one sense, platform products are very similar to technology-push products: A product development team begins with the assumption that the product concept will embody a particular technology.
3. Customized products. Customized products are slight variations of standard configurations and are typically developed in response to a specific order by a customer. When a customer requests a new product, a firm executes a structured design and development process to create the product to meet the customer's needs.

Table 11.2 provides a summary of the variants of the generic development process.[15]

APPROACHES TO SPEEDING PRODUCT DEVELOPMENT

Increasingly, firms are trying to improve the product development process. By improvement we refer to both the speed of introduction of products (or reducing the product development time) and the commercial success of the new product launches. These efforts are triggered by three major factors.

1. The outcome of the intense rivalry in high-technology industries like computers, electronics, and biotechnology is determined in part by how quickly and economically firms can develop and commercially introduce new products and processes that are central to success in these industries.

TABLE 11.2 Summary of Variants of Generic Development Process

	Generic (Market Pull)	Technology Push	Platform Products	Customization
Description	The firm begins with a market opportunity, then finds an appropriate technology to meet customer needs.	The firm begins with a new technology, then finds an appropriate market.	The firm assumes that the new product will be built around the same technological subsystem as an existing product.	New products are slight variations of existing configurations.
Distinctions with Respect to Generic Processes		Additional initial activity of matching technology and market. Concept development assumes a given technology.	Concept development assumes a technology platform.	Similarity of projects allows for a highly structured development process.
Examples	Sporting goods, furniture, tools	Gore-Tex rainwear, Tyvek envelopes	Consumer electronics, computers, printers	Switches, motors, batteries, containers

Source: From Ulrich. Karl T. and Eppinger, Steven D. *Product Design and Development.* New York: McGraw-Hill, 1995, p. 20. Copyright © 1995 by McGraw-Hill, Inc. Reprinted by permission of the McGraw-Hill Companies.

2. The potential for improvement in the commercial success of new products is quite high; on average, the success rate of new product introductions in the United States has often been estimated to be less than 12 percent.
3. It is believed that different nations have differential advantages in product development, with Japanese firms' greatest technological strength often attributed to the speed with which developments are translated into improved products and processes.[16]

Indeed, in one carefully documented study, Japanese firms were found to have introduced new products and processes more cheaply than American firms; averaged over all industries, the resource cost differential was 23 percent. The situation, however, varied from industry to industry; for example, in machinery and instruments the cost differential seems substantial, whereas in chemicals there were no indications of any substantial differentials. This study is profiled in Box 11.5.

The increasing importance of product development in many industries has prompted firms to adopt new approaches to the product development process during the operational phase. These approaches have pursued one or more of the following objectives: speeding the process of development from concept development to production ramp-up; reducing the development and commercialization cost; and reducing the risk of new product failure. Broadly, these approaches may be classified according to two dimensions.

1. Technology versus organization. Is the focus on technology or on organizational mechanism?
2. Internal versus external. Does it invoke collaborative approaches?

Figure 11.6 identifies examples of approaches according to the preceding classification. We will discuss the major approaches in some detail.

INTERNAL ORGANIZATIONAL MECHANISMS

Internal organizational mechanisms for organizing the new product development process vary from the redesign of the process, partially as in concurrent engineering, or wholly as in quality function deployment (QFD), to building interfaces and linkages among various functions within the organization, as in early manufacturing involvement (EMI) or manufacturable design.

CONCURRENT ENGINEERING

As we discussed in Figure 11.5, the operational phase consists of several steps starting from concept development through system-level design, detail design, and testing and refinement, and culminating in production ramp-up. In the traditional product development process in the United States, these steps were viewed as sequential, with various functions from design to manufacturing being involved in different steps in the process. For example, the design is thrown back and forth between design and manufacturing. The result of such a process has often been extended design lead times, high reject rates, extensive paperwork, high warranty costs, and antagonism between design and manufacturing.[17] One mechanism to avoid these pitfalls, often used in U.S. organizations, is concurrent engineering. In concurrent engineering, concept and process design stages are allowed to overlap, thus making the steps in the operational phase parallel instead

BOX 11.5

STUDYING THE TIME AND COST
OF INNOVATION IN U.S. AND JAPANESE FIRMS

Japanese firms develop and commercialize new products and processes more quickly and more cheaply than do their American counterparts. To understand what factors might be responsible for differences in time and cost in product development, Professor Edwin Mansfield of the University of Pennsylvania randomly surveyed 60 firms—30 from the United States and 30 from Japan. Data was gathered regarding the time and costs associated with the development and commercialization of product innovations, as well as the source of the technology upon which the product was based (i.e., whether the technology was internally developed or externally acquired). The technology was considered externally acquired if only a minor portion underlying the innovation was developed within the innovating firm. When a major portion of the new technology underlying the innovation was developed by the innovating firm, the technology was considered internally developed.

By classifying the underlying technology as either internally developed or externally acquired, the study was able to shed light on the differences observed in the time and cost of innovation between U.S. and Japanese firms. For internally developed technologies, the time and cost of innovation did not differ significantly across the two nationalities. However, with regard to products based upon externally acquired technology, Japanese firms required significantly less in the way of time and money to bring an innovation to market. Although the time and cost of innovation between internal and external technology differed little for U.S. firms, in Japan product innovations based upon external technology required about 25 percent less time and 50 percent less money than did those based upon internally developed technology. In essence, Japanese firms have been more efficient in employing external technology in product innovation than their American rivals. Thus, one important factor in understanding the differences in time and money is the source of the technology on which the innovation is based.

This research also investigated whether time and cost differences occurred in the development stage of product innovation (i.e., from the start of R&D to the development of a product) or in the commercialization stage (i.e., from product development to commercial introduction). For both Japanese and American firms, the development stage takes longer and requires more money when the product innovation is based upon an internally developed technology. However, a Japanese firm is able to commercialize a product innovation in about 10 percent less time using more than 50 percent less money if the innovation is based on an externally acquired technology. In contrast, American firms require about as much money and more time to commercialize a product innovation if it is based on an externally acquired technology. That is, although Japanese firms find it easier to commercialize a product innovation based on externally acquired technology, American firms tend to find it more difficult to do so. It is in the commercialization of product innovations based upon externally acquired technology that Japanese firms have gained a time and cost advantage over their U.S. counterparts. It appears that U.S. firms tend to invest more heavily in marketing start-up costs than do the Japanese.

To summarize, Japanese firms develop and commercialize product innovations more rapidly using fewer dollars than American firms. However, the time and cost advantage appears to be limited to product innovations based upon externally acquired technology; for internally developed technology, little difference is found between the two nations. Finally, the Japanese advantage observed in using externally acquired technology seems to occur during the commercialization stage rather than the development stage of product innovation.

Soure: Adapted from Mansfield, E. "The speed and cost of industrial innovation in Japan and the United States: External vs. internal technology," *Management Science* (1998): 34 (10): 1157–1168.

In-House	Off-the-Shelf Technology Utilizing Technologies	QFD/Concurrent Engineering EMI/Design for Manufacturing Cross-Functional Teams
Collaborative	Inward Technology Licensing	Joint Development with a. Customers b. Suppliers

FIGURE 11.6 SPEEDING TIME TO MARKET

of sequential. Usually, this is done by cross-functional teams with manufacturing engineering being represented in the product design team. It is expected that the use of cross-functional teams with representation from manufacturing engineering will lead to three benefits:

1. Manufacturing can inform design about its manufacturing capabilities so that design can take these capabilities into account during the design.
2. Manufacturing can also suggest ways to design the product for ease of manufacturability.
3. Manufacturing can learn enough about the product to design the manufacturing process while the product is being developed.[18]

Although some of these benefits may accrue from better inter-functional communication, the emphasis on overlapping phases and cross-functional teams has given concurrent engineering a distinct popularity among firms. Indeed, concurrent engineering teams now allow their major vendors on the teams. Even in the aerospace industry, where firms tend to be conservative for fear of not living up to government regulations, the practice is catching on. For example, Boeing invited BP Chemical's Advanced Material Division to solve some of the problems on components of 747 and 777 aircraft. BP is reported to have suggested that Boeing qualify one new adhesive and apply another in a wholly new area.[19]

QUALITY FUNCTION DEPLOYMENT (QFD)

QFD is a formal management process currently being implemented in many U.S. companies to improve product development. Mitsubishi's Kobe Shipyards are credited with developing QFD in 1972. Over the years, several firms have adopted QFD: Toyota, in 1978; Fuji-Xerox, in 1983; and Ford, in 1983. Since 1983, major U.S. firms including

Cummins Engines, Digital Equipment Corporation, General Motors, Hewlett-Packard, Proctor & Gamble, and Polaroid have adopted QFD.[20]

QFD employs four ideas to reduce development time and enhance the success rate of new product launches:

1. QFD tries to capture and convert the voice of the customer into the product and process requirements throughout the development process.
2. It employs fully empowered cross-functional teams to move product development activities from a sequential to a parallel mode.
3. It provides a coherent process to encourage integration across individual functional aspects of new product development (e.g., marketing research and engineering design).
4. It emphasizes the need to anchor development activities on systematically collected and ordered data.

Thus, QFD allows development teams to bring together and manage all elements needed to define, design, and deliver products that will meet or exceed customer needs.

A unique feature of QFD is the visual data presentation format that both engineers and marketing personnel find easy to use. QFD invokes the House of Quality, which consists of four houses, as shown in Figure 11.7.

FIGURE 11.7 QUALITY FUNCTION DEPLOYMENT

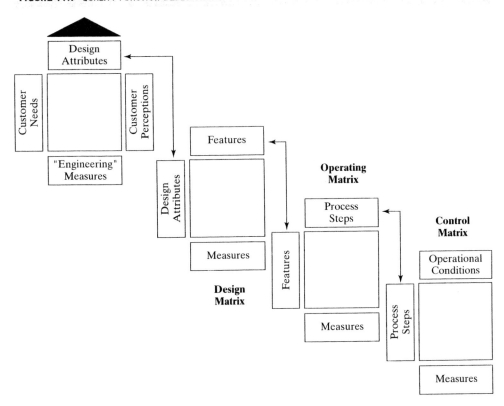

1. The First House of QFD links customer needs to design attributes. Design attributes are the engineering measures of product performance.
2. The Second House of QFD links these design attributes to actions the firm can take.
3. The Third House of QFD links actions to implementation decisions, such as manufacturing process operations.
4. The Fourth House of QFD links the implementation (manufacturing process operations) to production planning.

The cross functionally developed matrix nature of QFD is expected to lead to several specific process-related benefits.

- First, the matrices bring together all the data required to generate good product definition, design, and production and delivery decisions in a highly visual and compact form. Assumptions behind each decision are linked to expressed customer wants and needs.
- Second, the linkage charts quickly highlight any areas where the development team needs to acquire additional information to bolster the validity of the decision-making process.
- Third, the matrices store the plan so that none of the details are lost over time.
- Finally, the charts quickly communicate the plan and its assumptions to management, new team members, and those responsible for implementing the results later in the development process.

In Box 11.6, we have illustrated how Puritan-Bennett used the house of quality. In general, QFD has led to impressive results: A recent study of 35 projects that employed QFD in U. S. firms demonstrated shorter development time and measurable impacts on product development performance.[21]

Both QFD and concurrent engineering aim to speed the new product development process, as well as improve its success. Other approaches to organizing new product development emphasize inter-departmental and inter-organizational cooperation.

INTRA-ORGANIZATIONAL COORDINATION MECHANISMS

Four methods of intra-organizational coordination have been identified and implemented to improve the success of new product development programs: (1) R&D marketing interface, (2) early manufacturing involvement, (3) manufacturable design, and (4) culture based on shared commitment.

R&D marketing interface. R&D/marketing integration refers to the extent to which marketing and R&D share information, as well as how closely R&D and marketing work together on specific new product development tasks. Approaches to building integration may include give-and-take interactions between the departments through job rotation, early joint involvement in new product development, and high levels of conflict resolutions between the two departments.[22]

Early manufacturing involvement (EMI). Another approach by which product development times are cut and manufacturing costs are reduced is to have the manufacturing personnel be involved in the product development

BOX 11.6

USING THE "HOUSE OF QUALITY" AT PURITAN-BENNETT

The method of organizing the new product development process known as QFD is dependent upon four interrelated and integrated "houses." The first of these houses is the "House of Quality," and its purpose is to link the voice of the customer to design attributes that need to be met by engineering. Attention is thus first focused on identifying, structuring (i.e., categorizing), and prioritizing customer needs. When customer needs have been established, the design attributes of the product necessary to meet those needs are then defined. This box showcases how one firm used the house of quality to accomplish a necessary redesign on a primary product.

In 1990, faced with aggressive competition, medical equipment manufacturer Puritan-Bennett (PB) used the house of quality to redesign one of its products. The company manufactured several models of spirometers (devices to measure the volume capacity of the lungs), each priced at about $4,500. The primary market for these devices was made up of hospitals and physicians that specialized in respiratory illnesses; the cost and size of the units made them unappealing to a growing market of general practitioners that needed to use the devices only occasionally. Unable to tap the general practitioner market, PB saw its market share slip from 15 percent in 1988 to 7 percent in 1990. Further, in 1990 a competitor introduced a new model that would sell for under $2,000, a price PB could never meet with its current spirometer designs. Management realized that an entirely new design approach was needed if the company wished to remain competitive.

PB began the house of quality process by establishing a cross-functional product development team. Team members were appointed from marketing, customer service, sales, engineering, R&D, manufacturing, and management. The use of team members from throughout the organization fostered full communications so that the needs of the customer could effectively be matched with the final design of the new unit. To bring the "voice of the customer" into the design process, the team used focus groups and telephone interviews to detail a list of customer needs. A total of 26 needs were identified through this process. These needs were then categorized and prioritized to establish a vision of the new product as perceived by the customer.

With customer needs now detailed, the team turned to identifying design attributes (i.e., generic descriptions of the new product) that would fulfill these needs. The team identified 56 engineering design attributes in this fashion. The next step in the house of quality was to develop a product definition matrix that listed customer needs on the vertical axis and design attributes on the horizontal. Where a need intersected an attribute that could fulfill it on the matrix, weighting was scored based upon how well the attribute fulfilled the need. This product definition matrix, also known as the body of the house of quality, now provided a visual depiction of the design attributes that were most important, somewhat important, and of only marginal utility in meeting the needs of the customer, as well as how important each of those needs was. It thus served as a roadmap for the design process that followed, focusing attention on meeting the needs of the customer.

Using the house of quality, PB was able to develop, in record time, a unique design for a new spirometer. Its innovative modular design created instant interest in the industry when it was first introduced. The new design also meant that the base unit could be sold for less than $1,600, substantially underpricing PB's competition in the general practitioner market. When the unit received final FDA approval in late 1991, sales orders rapidly exceeded the company's manufacturing capacity, and market share began to rise. In this case, using the house of quality resulted in a rapid positive economic outcome for the developing firm.

Source: Adapted from Hauser, J. R. "How Puritan-Bennett Used the House of Quality," *Sloan Management Review*, Spring 1993, pp. 61–70.

process right from the concept formulation stage. This is often referred to as early manufacturing involvement. In most product development approaches, the manufacturing personnel in the product development team may have limited roles to play; however, as the product concept is defined and as it moves into the design stage, they become active, not only influencing the design but linking the manufacturing requirements of the product to their respective manufacturing departments, as well.

Design for manufacturing. Because manufacturing cost is a key determinant of success of the product, economically successful design is about assuring high product quality while minimizing manufacturing costs. Design for manufacturing (DFM) is a methodology for achieving this goal. DFM utilizes information of several types including (1) sketches, drawings, product specifications and design alternatives; (2) a detailed understanding of production and assembly processes; and (3) estimates of manufacturing costs, product volumes, and ramp-up timing. DFM efforts commonly draw expertise from manufacturing engineers, cost accountants, and production personnel in addition to product designers. Many companies use structured team-based workshops to facilitate the integration and sharing of views required for DFM.

Shared commitment. Building a culture of collaboration and commitment to long-range success of the firm reduces problems of interorganizational cooperation. In successful Japanese companies, for example, inter-functional cooperation is based on a shared commitment and is reinforced through participative decision making, job rotation, and the use of joint reward systems. This is a long-term strategy as opposed to the project-specific approaches outlined in concurrent engineering or QFD.

In summary, internal organizational mechanisms focus on enhancing the speed and success rate of new product launches by developing organizational arrangements that induce parallel phasing of steps in the operational phase; improving communication among functional departments; and, in general, enabling decision making to be more objective and data-based.

EXTERNAL ORGANIZATIONAL MECHANISMS

External organizational mechanisms emphasize the inclusion and integration of agents outside the firm, such as suppliers or customers, in the process of new product development. This is expected to enhance the success of the new product as well as to reduce the development time. Two specific external agents are often included: customers and suppliers.

CUSTOMERS

Involving customers in the innovation process or the product development process can perhaps be the easiest way of increasing quality, decreasing cost, and speeding the product development time. As a result, market-driven managers are bringing customers into their new product development processes earlier and providing them greater opportunities for contributing, not only to new product ideas, but also to the development process used in the company. This involvement, however, may vary from situation to situation. In Figure 11.8, we have illustrated five different situations: (1) user-driven enhancement, (2) developer-driven development, (3) user-context development, (4) new application, and (5) technology/marketing coevolution.

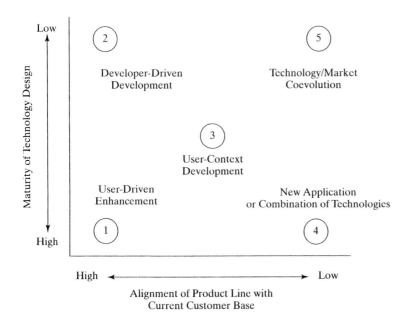

FIGURE 11.8 NEW PRODUCT DEVELOPMENT PROCESSES ON TECHNOLOGY-MARKET MATRIX

Source: From Dorothy Leonard-Burton. *Wellsprings of Knowledge,* 1995, Boston, MA: Harvard Business School Press, p. 184.

User-driven enhancement. When explicit customer demands drive improvements in current products, developers establish user needs in reactive mode: Competition defines the performance characteristics on which the development team attempts to achieve parity, if not superiority.

Developer-driven development. When the technology is relatively young, users often lack the ability to translate their needs into a request for a specific solution. Here, the developers may proactively decide to delight their customers with leaps in performance that no competitors have attempted, and no users have directly requested.

User-context development. User needs may exist for years before a technological solution is presented, as in the case of Post-it notes.

New application. Here, developers take an application of a technology that is mature and well understood in one domain and apply it to an entirely different one—for a totally new set of users.

Technology/market coevolution. At times, technologists run far ahead of consumers by developing an application for which they initially target the wrong market. These technology-push inventions present several new products for which there was initially no user demand, but that many people now concede to be revolutionary such as xerography.

In Figure 11.8, we have also illustrated appropriate methods by which we can incorporate information about customers in each one of these situations into the new product development process. These methods can be classified in three ways: (1) inquiry, (2) empathic design, and (3) market creation.[23]

Inquiry. When the current customer set is targeted for an extension of a well-established product line, inquiry methods are appropriate; this is the major province of traditional market research tools. Three major types of tools are usually employed. First, customers can refer to a known product, surveys, focus groups, and mall studies (whereby new products or prototypes are taken to a shopping mall for testing and soliciting shoppers' reactions) when appropriate. Second, in fast moving high-technology industries where new models may differ quite radically from the old, lead users usually face needs in the marketplace, but they face them months or years before the bulk of the marketplace encounters them; they are also well positioned to benefit significantly by obtaining a solution to those needs. Third, some techniques are designed to probe users' desires less directly and thereby uncover latent and less readily articulated needs.

Empathic design. Empathic design is the creation of product or service concepts based on a deep understanding of unarticulated user needs. Because empathic design is based on observed customer behavior, it arises from the interaction of developers, on the one hand, and users, on the other. For example, in Hewlett-Packard, several new product ideas originated with the engineers who wanted such equipment for themselves. Another way is to partner with existing customers. For example, Alza Corporation is noted for its partnerships with specific customers to design customized delivery systems for a particular drug.

Market creation. When the technologies and customers are new, inquiry and emphatic design are impossible. Therefore, customer information needs to be sought through extrapolating from today to imaginable possible futures or else seeking information through trial, error, and success. Firms are using several approaches. First, by extrapolation of societal, technological, and political trends, product developers attempt to foresee what users in a current market will need in the future. Second, formal scenario construction techniques are often used; the intent of such scenarios is less to predict the future state than to stimulate consideration of nonobvious futures. Finally, for short lead time items that can be quickly manufactured, marketers and developers engage in experimentation, that is, they test a fully functioning product in the real marketplace.

All of the preceding methods provide ways by which firms collaborate with customers to develop new products. In Box 11.7, we have outlined one approach by which customers are induced to collaborate developing products—technical market research.

SUPPLIERS

Bringing suppliers into the product development process offers several advantages.

- First, suppliers can provide access to a wealth of in-depth technical knowledge.
- Second, inclusion of suppliers may reduce replication of suppliers' expertise in the buyers' development organization.
- Third, it may enhance the speed of introduction of new products.
- Finally, the new product development cost may be lower.

BOX 11.7

THE TECHNICAL MARKET RESEARCH
PROCESS AND "ANTENNA SHOPS"

Technical market research (TMR) is yet another process that attempts to bring the customer into the new product development process. As with other techniques discussed in this chapter, the process begins with the appointment of a cross-functional product development team. Next, the team attempts to determine customer wants and needs as a basis for the initial product concept. However, TMR goes beyond QFD in this area by seeking to develop an understanding of the customers' latent expectations—that is, what the customer may want from the product in the future. In this way, product development efforts can focus on technologies that need to be developed to meet customer needs in the next generation of products.

A unique aspect of TMR is its use of so-called "antenna shops." Once the initial product concept has been developed through extensive consumer input, a 3-dimensional computer graphic model of the product is constructed. Consumers are then brought into a marketplace R&D laboratory, or antenna shop, where they interact with the product in a "virtual" computer environment. Using computer-aided design and engineering (CAD/CAE) software, the computer makes changes in the design based upon customer input. The changed product is immediately displayed as a 3-dimensional graphic, and its new performance characteristics are calculated. The customer continues to interact with the computerized model until they achieve a design which best fits their perceived needs. A competitor's product may also be displayed so that designers can better understand how consumers interact with those products. While the customer is interacting with the on-screen model, the computer is also recording all actions and preferences in a marketing database. This database can then be used to better refine the designer's understanding of the needs and wants of the customer. In essence, the antenna shop combines design, engineering, and marketing software that is run by the potential consumer. Although other new product development processes use extensive customer input only in the conceptualization stage, TMR makes extensive use of customer input in the design stage, as well.

The concept of an antenna shop was originally developed by innovative Japanese firms and is beginning to gain credence as an important new product development tool. Mazda Motor Corporation has formed a new company called M2 Incorporated that will run a design center based upon the antenna shop concept. The center will use extensive consumer input to design products well aligned with the potential customer's image and identity. Several other Japanese firms have established antenna shops in California to design consumer electronic products. Preschool toy manufacturer Little Tikes provides employees with free daycare for their children and uses the daycare center as a form of antenna shop to test new product concepts, prototypes, and design improvements. Designers and engineers monitor how the children interact with the toys and talk to them about their "toy experience." Finally, Rubbermaid is considering the use of factory outlet stores as a form of antenna shop. The company's newer merchandise (including prototypes) would be featured, and customers would be invited to be involved in surveys and focus groups to help guide the R&D efforts of the company.

Source: Adapted from Lauglaug, A. S. "Technical market research—get customers to collaborate in developing products," *Long Range Planning* (1993): 26(2): pp. 78–82.

Today, several labels are being used to refer to the involvement of suppliers in produc development. *Black box sourcing* refers to the practice of treating a precise part or as sembly as a black box, i.e., the supplier is provided with functional and interface re quirements of assembly and is expected to design the rest. Black box sourcing has three distinct characteristics:

1. Early involvement of suppliers in the new product development process,
2. Clear communication of the customer's design-related requirements, and
3. Extensive design-related responsibility taken on by the suppliers.

As is obvious, the customer relies on the supplier to produce a high-quality design, test the design, and build the prototype, all within the time frame that is stipulated well in advance Black box sourcing requires organizations to develop a complex interface with each of its suppliers. The reason for the complex interface is that the process is rife with commercial and technical risks. Technically, managers are forced to coordinate decisions and informa tion flows when many outside organizations have a hand in the process. Commercially, there is the problem each organization has in protecting its business and commercial interests.[24]

INTERNAL TECHNOLOGY APPROACHES

These approaches focus on harnessing the potential of technology available in-house to speed the new product development process. In the case of specific projects, firms have used three approaches to speed the new product development process: (1) use of off-the-shelf technology, (2) technology tools to speed the process, and (3) product mapping

OFF-THE-SHELF TECHNOLOGY

Earlier, we discussed the two means by which technology permeates new products: bundling and disruptive technologies. Bundling, or the use of technologies currently de ployed in other products or existing product platforms, reduces both technology devel opment time and the technical risks during product development.

In addition, in the case of firms with strong in-house technology development capabil ities, technology that has hitherto not been exploited may be available, partly because the firm was unsure of its potential applications. In some cases, these off-the-shelf technologies may be employed in new products to better the competition, at the same time cutting down the product development time involved in creating new technology from the start.

USE OF TECHNOLOGY TOOLS

Multimillion dollar investments and CAD/CAM/CAE (computer-aided design, computer-aided manufacturing, computer-aided engineering) have helped manufacturers improve productivity in the new product development process. Indeed, some have claimed that con current engineering, coupled with advances in CAE/CAD/CAM, presents the single great est opportunity for manufacturers to improve the new product development process.[25]

In addition to such product-specific approaches to incorporating technology, some firms also adopt longer term strategies for enhancing the organizational capability for speeding the product development process. One such approach is product mapping.

PRODUCT MAPPING

Product mapping assumes that planned renewal of product platforms, combined with sustained development of core abilities, allows a firm defense against technological sur prise and obsolescence. Thus, a disciplined approach to developing and extending prod uct families presents a basis for achieving rapid development times.

Product mapping is often used to plan next product family platforms. The family is represented in four hierarchical levels: (1) the product family itself, (2) platforms with the family, (3) product extensions, and (4) specific products. Product family maps convey a sense of continuity, or lack thereof, in product development. This provides a way for management to intervene in the product platform development, to either continue the level of development or to bring new thought processes into new product development. Box 11.8 describes the evolution of a product family in one company.

EXTERNAL TECHNOLOGY

Although suppliers and, in some cases, customers serve as sources of technology-related ideas (as we saw in the section on external organizational mechanism), firms may also acquire technology from outside through collaborative arrangements such as inward technology licensing or acquisitions. We have detailed many of these collaborative approaches in chapter 8. Unlike supplier or customer arrangements, these approaches rely on contractual agreement and therefore do not require heavy commitment of management time for monitoring the performance. Indeed, there is some evidence to suggest that when the appropriate technology is outside their corporate abilities, firms are better-off relying on external acquisitions or licensing to acquire the technology during their new product development efforts.

In summary, several approaches are being used in organizations to improve the new product success rate as well as speed the development process. Indeed, two further points can be made with respect to the array of techniques available:

First, many firms use them in combination. Thus, it is believed that concurrent engineering—an internal organizational mechanism—coupled with advances in CAE/CAD/CAM tools present the single greatest opportunity for manufacturers to come along in decades.[26]

Second, different combinations may be appropriate for different product development projects within the same corporation. Figure 11.6 provides a simple way of classifying the array of techniques for consideration during the design of the new product development process.

BOX 11.8

MAPPING PRODUCT FAMILIES
AND PLATFORMS

New product developments represent the tangible embodiment of a firm's technological resources and capabilities. They do not, however, arise in isolation. Instead, most new product developments belong to a family of products and are based upon a product platform in that family. Product families are groups of products directed at a particular market segment or customer group; a product platform is a particular architecture (i.e., shared designs and components) from which individual products are developed. For example, the Sony Walkman represents a product family for that company targeted at the

Box 11.8 (*continued*)

portable tape cassette market segment. The product design is based upon a product platform that was enhanced with four major technical innovations from 1980 to 1990. These platforms provided the core architecture for the development of more than 160 variations of the product during that period of time. To understand how a particular firm's resources and capabilities have changed through the sequential launch of products within a product family, and to shed light on what resources and capabilities might require further development, it is often helpful to chronologically "map" the family and its platforms. The figure below presents a mapping of one product family for a firm that develops and manufactures

electronic imaging equipment. Professors Meyer and Utterback at M.I.T. developed this mapping as part of a research project on the evolution of product families and platforms.

For this product family, four product platforms were developed or acquired.

• The first platform, based on an analog architecture, was begun in 1980, when the concept and initial development were undertaken in a skunk works. This work led to the first generation platform in late 1993, from which six new product developments emerged.

• In 1984, management recognized that a digital (rather than an analog) architec-

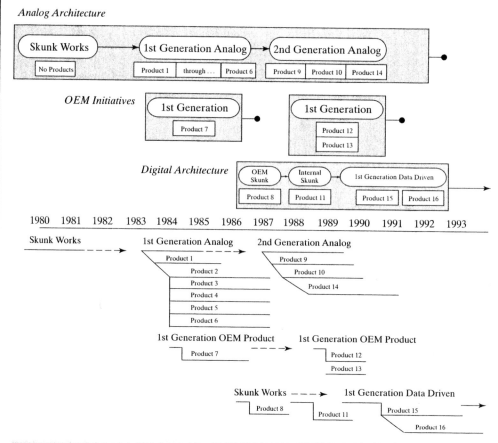

FIGURE 11.8A PRODUCT FAMILY AND PLATFORMS

Source: Meyer & Utterback, *Sloan Management Review*, 1993, p. 35.

ture was more likely to meet the needs of future users. However, the company's concentration on developing its analog architecture precluded an in-house development of digital products in the short term. So, the company acquired a platform based on an early digital version of the architecture from an outside vendor. Using this platform, the company developed "Product 7." Between 1986 and 1988, the company pursued research efforts on its own digital platform, from which products 8 and 11 were developed. Concurrently, the company pursued a platform extension of its analog architecture, with

products 9, 10, and 14 flowing from this technology.

- Between 1989 and 1990 the company acquired a second digital platform from an outside vendor that resulted in products 12 and 13. Further, the first generation of their in-house digital platform was completed, and products 15 and 16 were generated.

- Finally, the company abandoned its analog architecture in 1993.

Though the figure visually displays the firm's continuity in its product development efforts for one product family, it also shows how certain resources and capabilities were developed at the same time.

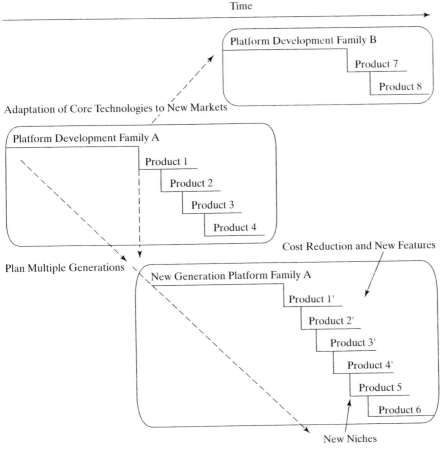

FIGURE 11.8B THE PRODUCT FAMILY

Source: Meyer & Utterback, *Sloan Management Review,* 1993, p. 32.

INFLUENCE OF ENVIRONMENTAL TRENDS

Time compression has forced organizations to adopt methods to accelerate the product development process, whereas the potential for technology integration has led to external collaborative arrangements with other firms and the infusion of technology through bundling and use of disruptive technologies. In a similar way, globalization is altering the product development approaches of many firms.

GLOBALIZATION OF NEW PRODUCT DEVELOPMENT

The globalization of new product development activity is most visible in the case of large multinational corporations with operations spread throughout the world. This globalization of new product development has assumed two forms: (1) integrated product development and (2) global focusing.

INTEGRATED PRODUCT DEVELOPMENT

Firms are adopting globally integrated new product development activity to benefit from the economies of scale involved in the development process. They particularly employ cross-functional teams, with membership from the various sites across the world in which they are operating. Such teams are typically called global product development teams. Unlike the case of local product development—where product development is confined to one or two sites—global product development teams enable faster wrap-up on a global basis by drawing up manufacturing and commercial plans from all the sites during the product development process itself. In addition to the speed of wrap-up, global standardization in components and assembly lead to reduction in cost of the new product development activity. For example, firms in the pharmaceutical industry employ global product teams to speed the worldwide submission of new drug application. Although there are differences in submission requirements among countries, there is also enough commonality in science among the regions to allow the company to take advantage of global product development teams to launch the product faster.

Currently, product development teams are the most common means by which firms globalize their product development activity. However, during the last decade, firms have employed another mechanism to globalize product development activity: global switching.

GLOBAL SWITCHING

Increasingly, large multinationals have the ability to switch R&D/sales sequencing across national boundaries. Thus, R&D may be undertaken in one country; initial production may scale up in another; full production and related component production may occur in still other countries; and the first market launch will be held in a completely different country. Despite difficulties in coordination and integration of the functional phases, switching provides considerable economic benefits for corporations: They are able to exploit the different technical manufacturing and marketing skills of the various sites and ease the problems of international compatibility. Consider the experience of Glaxo:

- Global switching was reportedly employed by Glaxo Wellcome as it developed the antiasthma drug, salmeterol. The product involved R&D at a Glaxo site in the United Kingdom, followed by extensive clinical trial studies at sites across the world. The scale-up of production for active ingredients of the drug was transferred to Montrose in Scotland, which then moved into full-scale primary production. Another production site in Singapore was also expected to help, and both the Montrose and Singapore factories were expected to supply production and packaging operators in France and in the United Kingdom.

In the United States, Hewlett-Packard and Texas Instruments have also been reported to employ the tactic of global switching in new product development.[27]

❖ CHAPTER SUMMARY

New products have always been a significant source of sales and profits for companies. Firms usually classify products into five types: new-to-world products, new category entries, additions to product lines, product improvements, and repositioning. Product improvements represent incremental innovations. New category entries and additions to the product line may represent, at best, incremental innovations; repositioning is *not* considered an innovation. New-to-world products may represent modular, architectural, or radical innovations. Firms, especially the large firms, pursue multiple development projects either sequentially or concurrently. The term *product platform* is often used to connote the common technological base that encompasses design and components shared by a set of products.

Technology is infused into new products in two ways: bundling and the use of disruptive technologies. Bundling involves some form of technology integration, whereas disruptive technologies focus on modular or radical innovations. Bundling offers three opportunities for a firm in its product development activities: (1) cost reduction, (2) market expansion, and (3) product enhancement.

Three interrelated sets of strategic factors need to be considered in the decision to develop a new product: (1) strategic context, (2) technology leadership, and (3) timing of product launch. Whether a new product creates value depends at least on three factors: business strategy, risk-return trade-off, and resources. The choice of whether to be a leader or a follower should be based on three factors: sustainability of the technological lead, first mover advantages, and first mover disadvantages. A potential leader must determine its entry time so as to balance the opportunities and benefits of an innovation with the risks and costs associated with product development and marketing. A potential follower must consider not only the marketing activities of the early entrant and the evolution of the industry, but also the competition of other potential entrants.

The process of product development consists of two major phases: the strategic phase and the operational phase. During the strategic phase, top management establishes focus and the critical guidelines that drive the product development process in the operational phase. The operational phase can be broken down into five major steps: concept development, system-level design, detail design, testing and refinement, and production ramp-up.

The increasing importance of product development in many industries has prompted firms to adopt new approaches to the product development process during the operational phase. Four different types of approaches are increasingly common. Internal organizational mechanisms include concurrent engineering, quality function deployment (QFD), and building interfaces and linkages among various functions within the organization, as in early manufacturing involvement (EMI) or manufacturable design. External organiza tional mechanisms emphasize the inclusion and integration of agents outside the firm, suc as suppliers or customers, in the process of new product development. Internal technolog approaches include use of off-the-shelf technology and technology tools to speed th process and product mapping. Firms may acquire technology from outside through co laborative arrangements such as inward technology licensing or acquisitions.

Globalization is altering the product development approaches of many firm Multinational firms have globalized new product development in two ways: (1) inte grated product development and (2) global focusing.

❖ Notes

1. "The Driving Force Behind Chrysler's Turnaround," in *Hemisphere,* June 1993, by Paul A. Eisenstein, publisher of TheCar Connection.com. Reprint by permission.
2. Mahajan, V. and Wind, J. "New Product Models: Practice, Shortcomings and Desired Improvements," *Journal of Product Innovation Management,* 1992, Vol. 9, pp. 128–139.
3. Crawford, C. M. *New Products Management.* Chicago, IL: Irwin, 1997, p. 9.
4. Golder, P. N. and G. J. Tellis. "Pioneer Advantage: Marketing Logic or Marketing Legend?" *Journal of Marketing Research,* May 1993, pp. 158–70.
5. Hanson, W. A., G. D. Eppen, and R. K. Martin. "Mining Your Product Line: Creating New Products with Bundling." Paper No. 972, Institute for Research in the Behavioral Economic and Management Sciences, Krannert Graduate School of Management, April 1990.
6. Bower, J. L., and C. M. Christensen. "Disruptive Technologies: Catching the Wave," *Harvard Business Review,* January-February 1995, pp. 43–53.
7. Meyer, M. H. and Utterback, J. M. "The Product Family and the Dynamics of Core Capability," *Sloan Management Review,* Spring 1993, pp. 29–47.
8. Michael Porter. *Competitive Advantage.* New York: The Free Press, 1995.
9. Ibid.
10. Ibid.
11. Porter, M. E. *Competitive Advantage.* New York: The Free Press, 1985.
12. See 1) Biggadike, E. R. *Corporate Diversification: Entry Strategy and Performance,* Cambridge, MA: Harvard University Press,

1976; 2) Dillon, W. R., Calantone, R., and Worthing, P. "The New Product Problem: An Approach for Investigating Product Failures," *Management Science,* Vol. 25 (December 1979), pp. 1184–1196; 3) Urban, Glen L., Carter, T., and Gaskin, S. "Market Share Rewards to Pioneering Brands: An Empirical Analysis and Strategic Implications," *Management Science,* Vol. 32 (June 1986), pp. 645–659; 4) Whitten, I. T. *Brand Performance in the Cigarette Industry and the Advantage to Early Entry,* 1913–1974, Federal Trade Commission, Bureau of Economics, June 1979. For a recent summary, see Kevin, Roger A., Varadarajan, P. R., and Peterson, R. A. "First-Mover Advantage: A Synthesis, Conceptual Framework, and Research Propositions," *Journal of Marketing,* Vol. 56 (October 1992), pp. 33–52.
13. Lillien, G. A. and Yoon, E., "The Timing of Competitive Market Entry: An Exploratory Study of New Industrial Products," *Management Science,* May 1990, Volume 36, pp. 568–585.
14. Ulrich, K. T. and S. D. Eppinger. *Product Design and Development.* New York: McGraw-Hill, Inc., 1995, pp. 16–18.
15. Ulrich, K. T. and S. D. Eppinger. *Product Design and Development.* op cit.
16. Clark, K., R. Hayes, and C. Lorenz. (eds.) *The Uneasy Alliance.* Boston: Harvard Business School, 1985, p. 139.
17. Liker, Jeffrey K. and Mitchell Fleischer. "Organizational Context Barriers to DFM," in Gerald I. Susman (ed.) *Integrating Design and Manufacturing for Competitive Advantage.* New York: Oxford University Press, 1992, pp. 228–264.

18. Susman, Gerald I. and James W. Dean, Jr. "Development of a Model for Predicting Design for Manufacturability Effectiveness," in Gerald I. Susman (ed.) *Integrating Design and Manufacturing for Competitive Advantage.* New York: Oxford University Press, 1992, pp. 207–227.

19. "Concurrent engineering brings new faces to aerospace development teams," *Machine Design,* March 7, 1994, p. 156.

20. Griffin, A. "Evaluating QFD's Use in U.S. Firms as a Process for Developing Products," *Journal of Product Innovation Management,* 1992, Vol. 19, pp. 171–187.

21. Griffin, A. ibid.

22. Song, X. M. and M. E. Parry. "How the Japanese Manage the R&D Marketing Interface," *Research Technology Management,* 1993, Vol. 36, pp. 32–39.

23. Leonard-Barton, D. *Wellsprings of Knowledge.* op. cit.

24. Liker, J. K., Kamath, R. R., Wasti, F. N. and Nagamachi, M. "Suppliers Involvement in Product Development: Are there still large U.S.–Japan differences?" *Best Paper Proceedings,* Academy of Management, Annual Meeting, Dallas, 1994.

25. Fischer, R. A. "Can Technology Improve Product Development?" *Machine Design,* May 1993, p. 202.

26. ibid.

27. Howells, Jeremy and Michelle Wood. *The Globalization of Production and Technology.* New York: Belhaven Press, 1993, pp. 146–149.

12

DEPLOYMENT OF TECHNOLOGY IN THE VALUE CHAIN

In 1993, Property and Casualty (P&C) was in dire straits. From 1989 to 1993, the 8,000-person business unit had lost $1 billion. *Standard and Poor* had downgraded P&C from A to BBB+. High prices had left the division with a business that no one else in the industry wanted. Numerous changes had drained the organization's critical underwriting skills and capabilities. Though the organization suffered from redundancies at the home office, it faced highly downsized and stretched field staff. All these factors contributed to the organization's inability to react to market changes.

A new division president along with two direct reports was hired from a competing insurance company in the winter of 1993. Within 2 months, the senior management team announced a new vision and business strategy. The vision was to become a top-quartile performer in all businesses P&C participated in, and the unit would transform from a generalist to a specialist organization (i.e., P&C would target certain market segments). The new strategy called for fundamental conversion in products, customers, mindset, processes, behaviors, and technology.

The first step in implementation was to reorganize the division into three separate profit centers in order to more easily gauge performance and analyze trends in the business. Field operations were also restructured to transform relationships with producers (i.e., distributors) and customers.

The second step was to use re-engineering to actuate the structural changes.

The new specialist strategy would require P&C employees to do their jobs in a new way. The division president Gerry Isom summarized the challenge: "How do we get an underwriting assistant in Harrisburg to think and act like a specialist?" The challenge was particularly difficult because the business unit was paralyzed by the fear of what might happen. Over the previous 5 years, employees had been told again and again that "the building's burning down"—but having seen so many fire-fighting efforts fail, they were going to take their time accepting, and attempting, any new fix.

The re-engineering project was initiated in October 1993. The division president referred to the effort as "transformation." He elaborated,

From the start we knew the change effort at P&C, the Operational Alignment Review (OAR), would be like few others. The traditional goal of re-engineering has been to increase an organization's efficiency, either by reducing costs, improving cycle times, enhancing quality, or upgrading service levels. But P&C needed to improve its overall financial picture . . . to create structures for growth and revitalization and to position us for a healthy future.

Tom Valerio, the Head of Transformation, designed a two-phased approach for OAR that would strive for both restructuring and revitalization, over time. Phase I, a 10-week effort that began in October 1993, focused on analysis and design. Phase II, implementation, began in January 1994.

Phase I. A broad range of analytical techniques, at multiple levels, was used in Phase I. Over a 7-week period, 30 different diagnostics were carried out. Among them were 1½ to 2-hour confidential interviews with 113 CIGNA employees, 343 organizational effectiveness surveys, 4 full-day customer workshops (two with producers and two with policyholders), over 40 key producer phone interviews, and so on. Nineteen different processes were also mapped on brown paper to understand their broken parts.

A "brown paper" fair was conducted in December. Over 450 feet of brown paper showed the explicit details of how, for better and for worse, P&C actually worked; 626 employees registered for the fair; and about 200 additional employees attended but did not register because the registration lines were long. The employees posted from 800 to 1,000 Post-it notes to brown papers commenting on the current processes.

All P&C employees also received a monthly newsletter on the project. Employees, anonymously or unanimously, were encouraged to send e-mail or faxes and/or to call the project office. Answers to the most commonly asked questions were circulated organization-wide. Over all, employees were told early and repeatedly that the project was expected to result in a downsized and streamlined home office and that nearly everyone in the division would have to learn new skills.

Because the effort was division-wide, the implementation would have to occur in slices to be manageable. The end-to-end process analysis of Phase I helped to identify the most broken business. This business, or the slice, would be the initial focus of implementation. The slice cut horizontally across functions but focused on one profit center of the business. That slice represented 3,000 employees, or 25 percent of the P&C premiums. Because each of the P&C profit centers shared the same high-level processes, the lessons from fixing the slice would be used to create a template that, with slight modifications, could be applied to the remaining slices of the business.

Phase II. The implementation was structured as six projects, or streams. A dedicated implementation team was assigned to each stream. Three of the streams were division-wide initiatives (leadership and governance; support function alignment; and information systems) and three were more specific (producer management, claims, and underwriting). The P&C vision of top-quartile performer was translated into a set of quantifiable measures that were cascaded throughout the organization. The measures were, in turn, linked to performance models, which were associated with drivers and levers. This top-down view helped to ensure that, rather than optimizing any particular area or function, the OAR effort would optimize the end-to-end value chain.

Over 20 "best" performers from business and systems worked full-time on six implementation teams. Additional employees participated part-time. Each team was aided by outside consultants and had two sponsors who reported directly to the division president and were expected to be in daily contact with their teams. All the sponsors as a group reviewed the project weekly.

Because of the short implementation time frames, the IS personnel on each implementation team had to be proactive in identifying the technology support requirements and launching appropriate development efforts. The IS members met weekly to exchange information to ensure integration and minimize redundancy across teams. The teams were also holding special 2-day work sessions to identify the information support requirements for new processes. It was decided that although the new systems were being developed to deliver the information, the organization would use existing things, like telephone, faxes, and e-mail, to get the information to the people who needed it.

A separate team was formed to revisit the divisional IS strategy. Another systems team was developing a methodology to evaluate the business value of applications currently under development. The goal of the methodology was to prioritize the projects and make sure that resources were allocated to applications with the highest business value. Re-engineering also presented a large added responsibility to the P&C division information system officer. She devoted 30 percent of her time to the re-engineering effort.

Much attention was devoted to creating a new culture that promoted learning and innovation. Learning and training programs were instituted to strengthen the weakened underwriting skills. Best practices were documented and diffused throughout the division. A new information culture promoted sharing of information across the groups.

In April 1994, the division president summarized the progress made:

> We sense that things are moving as they should, and on schedule, and that resistance is being replaced by cautious receptivity. The project will be successful when everyone in the P&C organization understands our strategy, where they fit, and how they contribute. In the rapidly changing world, success will only be sustained if the transformational thought process becomes a basic work style.

Stewart, the chief financial officer, made the following prediction:

> The project will be a success because the management demands that it work. Sponsorship is real; management won't quit until the changes have happened. Field involvement has built ownership from both the top and the bottom.

The implementation plan for P&C's transformation project called for changes in 12 to 24 months. The fast pace of the project was attributed to management's willingness to address staffing issues early. The division president noted: "Management has to address the staffing issue right in the beginning. Otherwise, your hands are tied. I changed four out of the eight senior executives to ensure a unified front."[1]

During the 1990s, many firms have employed re-engineering to restructure their operations and to enhance productivity. As illustrated in the vignette, the re-engineering process harnesses the potential of information technology (IT) for redesigning work activities and simplifying procedures in order to enhance operating efficiency. Re-engineering, however, is only one means by which technology is deployed in a firm's value chain.

In this chapter, we discuss how technology is deployed in the value chain activities of a firm. In Figure 12.1, we reproduce the domains of technology to remind the reader that the deployment of technology in value chains is one of the key domains in which technology strategy is enacted. Consistent with our discussion of technology strategy, we will highlight three themes in our discussion of the technology deployment in value chains:

1. Decisions about the kinds of technology to be deployed in value chains are constrained by the broader technological and business strategy of firms;
2. Value chain activities may be performed either in-house or in collaboration with other firms; and
3. There are interrelationships among the decisions in the three domains of technology strategy: deployment in the value chain, appropriation, and deployment in new products.

FIGURE 12.1 DOMAINS OF TECHNOLOGY

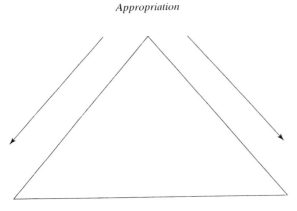

Appropriation

Deployment in Products ⟶ *Deployment in Value Chains*

Choices of the technology to be deployed in a firm's value chain may correspond either to the technology [T axis] or to the market [M axis] dimensions of the T-M matrix. Just as in the case of product development, market considerations and business strategies of a firm dictate many of the value chain decisions. For example, market responsiveness may require that a firm restructure its activities. A differentiation strategy may necessitate customization of a firm's products. What is often not fully appreciated is the fact that technology deployment in the value chain may also enhance the capability of a firm, as well. As we noted in our discussion of the S-curve of innovation, significant advances in performance characteristics of a technology are made possible through incremental advances (when the technology reaches its growth stage). Continuous improvement processes introduced by a firm in its value chain activities capture the potential for incremental advances that are inherent in any technology. Thus, technology decisions with respect to the value chain may be guided by the twin objectives of enhancing responsiveness and building firm capabilities to be deployed later in the market.

Value chain reconfiguration requires changing the usual ways of doing business within a firm. This upsets the status quo and often invites organizational resistance. These resistances need to be anticipated and, when they occur, dealt with in order for the full exploitation of the deployment of new technologies. Thus, more so than in any other domain of technology strategy, execution is central to the success of value chain deployment.

In this chapter, we try to answer three questions:

1. What factors determine the choice of technologies to be deployed in the value chain?
2. What are the different classes of technologies firms thus deploy?
3. How does a firm manage the process of implementation of these choices?

Three observations are in order with respect to the discussion of technology choices in this chapter. First, the focus of the chapter is on value chain, not just operations. The reader may want to refer to the discussion of the value chain in chapters 5 and 6. Second, we will focus both on the activities performed within a firm and the activities that the firm undertakes jointly with other firms in order to meet its business objectives. Third, we confine our discussion to technology choices and their implementation and do not focus on the ongoing management of value chain activities. As illustrated in the vignette, our focus in this section will be on the decision to re-engineer and the means by which the decision is implemented. However, once re-engineering has been accomplished, the focus shifts to managing the reconfigured value chain; we will not focus on these management activities in this chapter.

The chapter overview is presented in Figure 12.2. The scheme of the chapter is as follows. First, we will enumerate the major factors that drive the choice of technologies to be deployed in the value chain. Second, we will present a framework for organizing the various technology alternatives confronting a firm. Third, we will highlight the key issues that a firm has to address during the implementation of technology choices. Finally, we will trace the influence of globalization on a firm's value chain.

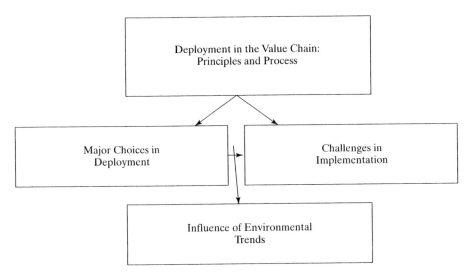

FIGURE 12.2 CHAPTER OVERVIEW

PRINCIPLES OF TECHNOLOGY DEPLOYMENT IN THE VALUE CHAIN

The choice of which technologies to deploy in the value chain is guided by environmental and firm-related factors, both market and technology related. Broadly, these factors can be captured by the answers to the following four questions:

1. Where in the value chain are the opportunities for deployment of technology?
2. Which technologies are available?
3. What are the reasons for deploying technology?
4. Do we have adequate resources to do so?

Figure 12.3 reproduces these questions; we will now discuss each of the related factors.

ENVIRONMENTAL CONTEXT

The industry and technology factors in Figure 12.3 constitute the environmental context in which technologies to be deployed in the value chain are chosen. These factors are not necessarily coupled: Technology environment may evolve independently of the industry, and vice versa. Thus, technology intelligence—outputs of the analysis of technology environment—and the analysis of competitive domains should inform these decisions. In short, as shown in Figure 12.4, the decisions involve interfacing technology and market intelligence.

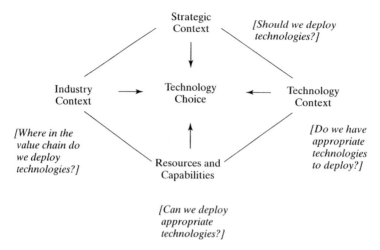

FIGURE 12.3 Drivers of Technology Strategy in the Value Chain

TECHNOLOGY CONTEXT

The technology context determines the availability of the technologies that are appro priate for a firm to deploy in its value chain. These may be technologies that are avail able in-house or technologies that can be acquired from outside. For example, we have seen that there are four ways of configuring value chains: craft, mass production, lean production, or mass customization. The movement of a firm from craft to mass produc tion mode requires significant investment in assembly line techniques; lean production requires introduction of software technologies; and mass customization is based on the introduction of flexible operations and information technologies. As shown in Table 12.1, the product-market scope of a competitive domain may determine the adoption of any one of the configurations:

1. Craft model is appropriate in the case of high value-added single-unit cus- tom products;
2. Mass production works best in high-volume homogeneous markets in the low-price segments;
3. Lean production is needed when the simultaneous demands of low price and high quality in homogeneous markets require firms to control costs through incremental innovation;

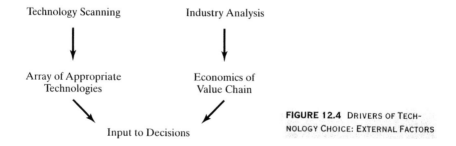

FIGURE 12.4 Drivers of Tech- nology Choice: External Factors

TABLE 12.1   Product-Market Scope and Value Chain Configurations

Dimension	*Value Chain Configuration*			
	Craft Production	*Mass Production*	*Lean Production*	*Mass Customization*
Market	Niche	Mass	Mass	Niche
Market Segments	Single unit	Homogeneous	Homogeneous	Many
Customization Required	High	Low	Low	High
Value Added Due to Customization	High	Relatively low	Relatively low	Moderate
Quality Emphasis	High	Low	Moderate	High
Cost Emphasis	Low	High	High	High
Technology Emphasis	Moderate	High	High	High

4. Mass customization is needed in domains with high clockspeed and markets that require persistent customization, but have ceilings on the price that will be borne by the customers.

COMPETITIVE DOMAINS

On the other hand, the characteristics of competitive domains determine where in the value chain the firm should deploy its technologies so as to support its corporate strategy. They dictate the deployment of specific technologies and offer opportunities for changing the nature of rivalry.

- We have seen that base technologies are needed in order for firms to be in the competitive game in specific domains. Increasingly, in the national trucking sector, large customers such as Wal-Mart are requiring tracking capabilities by its trucking firms. This means that computer-based tracking systems are a base technology: You need to have it to be in the game, although this does not ensure that a firm will be successful.

As shown in Table 12.2, the emphasis on different activities in the value chain shifts over the evolution of competitive domains. Thus, during the era of technology emergence, design and process engineering are critical challenges. As the era of incremental change sets in, product features first—and later, streamlining the value chain activities—gain importance for the competitive advantage of firms.

Competitive domains may also provide opportunities to firms for the deployment of technologies in value chains to gain competitive advantage. For example, in industries where there are significant learning curve effects, it pays to invest in significant process innovation to capture those learning curve effects; this is central to the success of firms whose strategy is one of being a low-cost producer. In the electronics business, Texas Instruments pursues a strategy of low-cost producer by successfully reaping the learning curve effects in markets where the product life cycles have historically been short.

FIRM-RELATED FACTORS

A firm's strategic context and its resources and capabilities represent the managerial dimension in the technology deployment in the value chain. These factors are interrelated:

TABLE 12.2 Value Chain Focus and Evolution of Competitive Domains

Eras of Evolution	Research and Development	Value Chain Activity		
		Manufacturing	Marketing	Service
Technology Emergence	Product Design Institutional Milieu	Process Engineering Scale-up of Manufacturing	Establishing Market Channels Market Feedback for Design and Service	Limited
Incremental Change	Product Improvement Process Innovation	Learning Curve Capacity Buildup Cost Reduction	Aggressive Growth Branding Efficient Marketing	Service Setup

On the one hand, the strategies a firm pursues are dependent on its resources and capabilities; on the other hand, the strategies it pursues may, in turn, enable it to build its resources and capabilities. This two-way interrelationship is portrayed in the T-M matrix shown in Figure 12.5. Thus, technology choices in the value chain may reflect both attempts to build resources and capabilities (or movement along the T axis) and deployment of existing value chain elements to further business strategies (or movement along the M axis).

In addition, firms need to emphasize four unique principles in their deployment of technologies in value chains:

1. The thrust of technology deployment should be based on a firm's business strategy;
2. During the implementation of business strategy, broad objectives need to be broken down into very specific, clearly articulated objectives;
3. Technology deployment in the value chain requires inter-functional integration.
4. Finally, new product introductions require changes in the value chain configuration as the new product moves from the design to the commercialization phase.

BUSINESS STRATEGY

The business strategy—low cost versus differentiation—pursued by a firm has an important influence on the scope and timing of technologies to be deployed in the value chain. In Table 12.3, we have illustrated how the business strategy of the firm influences the choice of value chain elements, as well as the decisions related to technology leadership.

In recent years, *competitive benchmarking* has become increasingly common as a tool by which companies try to achieve their value chain objectives. Competitive benchmarking involves analyzing the performance and practices of the best-in-class companies. Their performance becomes a benchmark to which a firm can compare its own performance, and their practices are used to improve the focal firm's own practices.

FIGURE 12.5 T-M MATRIX: DEPLOYMENT OF TECHNOLOGY IN VALUE CHAINS

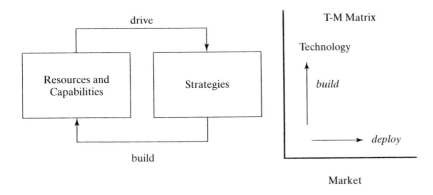

TABLE 12.3   Strategic Context and Technology Choices

	Scope	
Strategic Focus	*Broad*	*Narrow*
Low Cost	Broad Deployment	Niche/Focus Selective Deployment
Differentiation	Broad Deployment	Niche/Focus Selective Deployment

The choice of the specific best-in-class firm may depend on the firm's own competitive position:

1. When a firm has a technology leadership in some of its value chain activities, the competitive benchmarks are likely to come from outside the industry. For example, Xerox compared its warehousing and materials handling activities with those of L.L. Bean and its building practices with those of Federal Express. Similarly, Texas Instruments targeted Eli Lilly, a drug manufacturer, as a benchmarking partner for analyzing receiving transactions on the loading dock. Henry Ford studied Sears Roebuck's mail order plant in detail before adapting it to the automobile industry.

2. On the other hand, when a firm is pursuing a technology followership, it is more likely to emulate the best in class within its own industry.

SPECIFIC OBJECTIVES

To be implementable, the objective behind technology deployment in the value chain needs to be operationalized in concrete and specific terms. Broadly speaking, one can identify four specific objectives that can lead to a low cost or differentiation strategy. Figure 12.6 sketches the specific objectives. As shown in the figure, low cost or differentiation can be achieved through superior efficiency, superior quality, superior customer responsiveness, or superior innovation.[2] Superior efficiency enables a company to lower its costs; superior quality lets it both charge a higher price and lower its costs; superior customer responsiveness allows it to charge a higher price; and superior innovation can lead to higher prices or lower unit costs.

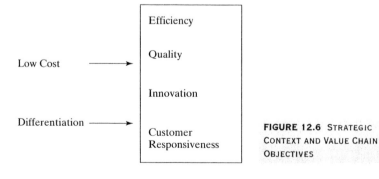

FIGURE 12.6 STRATEGIC CONTEXT AND VALUE CHAIN OBJECTIVES

INTER-FUNCTIONAL INTEGRATION

The specific goals—efficiency, quality, innovation, and customer responsiveness—require technology strategies that embrace several distinct value chain activities. In other words, these goals need to be regarded as cross-functional goals that cut across different value activities within the company and require substantial cross-functional integration. Indeed, in Table 12.4, we have illustrated how various specific goals of technology choice may impact different value chain elements within the firm.

PRODUCT-VALUE CHAIN LINKAGE

Indeed, the characteristics of competitive domains and the kind of products that a firm produces have a major influence on the kind of technologies that get embedded in the value chain. One of the developments in the last decade has been the increasing automation of activities that have usually been considered to be separate activities: new product development or product design. There are significant differences between knowledge-intensive and capacity-intensive industries in terms of the technologies that are being adopted in the value chain of firms. For example, knowledge-intensive industries are critically dependent on the use of information technologies, unlike the capital-intensive technologies employed in the latter. Thus, the complexity of the value chain is, to some extent, determined by the nature of the products and the type of industry in which a firm operates.

DECISION CRITERIA

Four major criteria should drive the decision to deploy a specific technology in the value chain activities of a firm:

1. To what extent does it accomplish the objectives? How do the various technologies perform in terms of the specific objectives: efficiency, quality, customer responsiveness, or innovativeness? In some cases, staying competitive in the industry requires a firm to adopt specific technologies. To gain competitive advantage through low cost or differentiation, a firm will have to reconfigure value chains through technology deployment.

2. To what extent do we have the resources to deploy the technology? Both hardware- and software-dominant technologies require resources for deployment. Hardware-dominant technologies require a significant investment in equipment or, in general, physically embodied technologies; software-dominant technologies require a significant investment in time for such things as training or organizational transformation.

3. Cost-benefit analysis: Do the benefits outweigh the costs? Can we appropriate enough benefits from the deployment to offset the costs?

4. Can we implement the deployment fast enough to accomplish the objectives? Because the value chain reconfiguration involves organizational changes, resistance from within a firm is common. The decision to implement should weigh the ability of the firm to overcome the resistance in a timely manner so that the benefits of deployment can be realized.

TABLE 12.4 Specific Goals and Value Chain Deployment

Specific Goal	Value Chain Activity			
	Procurement	Research and Development	Manufacturing	Marketing
Superior Efficiency	JIT	Design for manufacture Process innovation	Pursue experience curve Flexible manufacturing	Delete marginal accounts
Quality	Rationalize suppliers Help implement TQM	Design for manufacture	Trace defects to source Install TQM	Customer feedback on quality
Innovation	Supplier co-development	New product development	Process innovations	Customer feedback on product ideas
Customer Responsiveness	Install MIS with JIT	Customer co-development	Mass customization with FMS	Voice of the customer

Source: Adapted from Hill, C. W. L. and G. R. Jones. *Strategic Management.* Boston, MA: Houghton Mifflin Company, 1995, pp. 130–165.

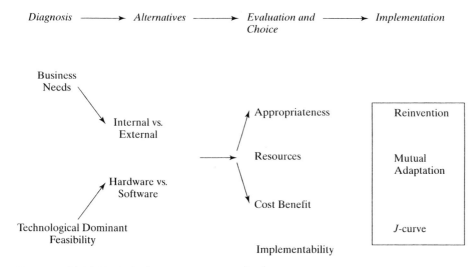

FIGURE 12.7 DEPLOYING TECHNOLOGY IN VALUE CHAINS: DECISION-MAKING PROCESS

PROCESS

We can summarize the sequence of steps in the decision process to deploy technologies in value chains of firms as shown in Figure 12.7. The decision involves four steps:

1. *Diagnosis.* This consists of assessing the environmental and firm contexts to identify the opportunities for technology deployment and establishing the objectives of the value chain reconfiguration. Both technological and market considerations are to be factored in the assessment of opportunity and value appropriability of the specific technology deployment. Firms' strategic positioning enters into the objectives of deployment.
2. *Alternatives.* The specific technological approaches to be considered are profiled. Four broad sets of alternatives (to be described in the ensuing section) are candidates for deployment.
3. *Evaluation and choice.* Each alternative is subjected to the four decision criteria: appropriateness in the light of objectives; availability of resources; cost-benefit analysis; and implementability.
4. *Implementation.* Because the technology deployment in the value chain involves changes in organizational structures and routines, implementation of the change is critical to the success of the deployment.

A FRAMEWORK FOR TECHNOLOGY ALTERNATIVES IN THE VALUE CHAIN

There are many ways by which the objectives of technology deployment in the value chain can be achieved. Indeed, the appropriate technologies may vary from industry to industry, as well as from firm to firm. However, we can provide a framework to capture the diversity of technology alternatives available to a firm as it ponders its choice of technologies to be deployed in the value chain. The framework that we present is built on two key questions:

1. Is the choice hardware or software dominant?
2. Is the value activity to be conducted in-house or outsourced?

> Hardware versus software dominant. Recall that all process innovations have three elements: hardware, software, and evaluation information. Some alternatives are hardware dominant in the sense that the physically embodied technology component is the major aspect of the particular innovation; a software-dominant innovation has a heavy emphasis on organizational arrangements within an organization. To keep this distinction clear in this chapter, we use *technology dominant* and *organization dominant.*
>
> In-house versus external sources. Similarly, in-house versus outsourcing is another way of capturing the mode of implementation.

The framework to describe the technology alternatives is presented in Figure 12.8

As shown in the figure, the technology alternatives may be grouped into four broad categories: technology-dominant approaches conducted in-house; organization-dominant choices conducted in-house; technology-dominant choices conducted by outsiders; and organization-dominant choices conducted outside. Figure 12.8 also arrays the currently popular approaches to technology choices within the framework.

We need to emphasize two points with respect to the framework:

1. In any given situation, the firm may adopt a combination of these approaches to accomplish its objectives; and
2. Some of the approaches blur the boundaries between technology-dominant and organization-dominant approaches. For example, re-

FIGURE 12.8 A FRAMEWORK FOR TECHNOLOGY CHOICES

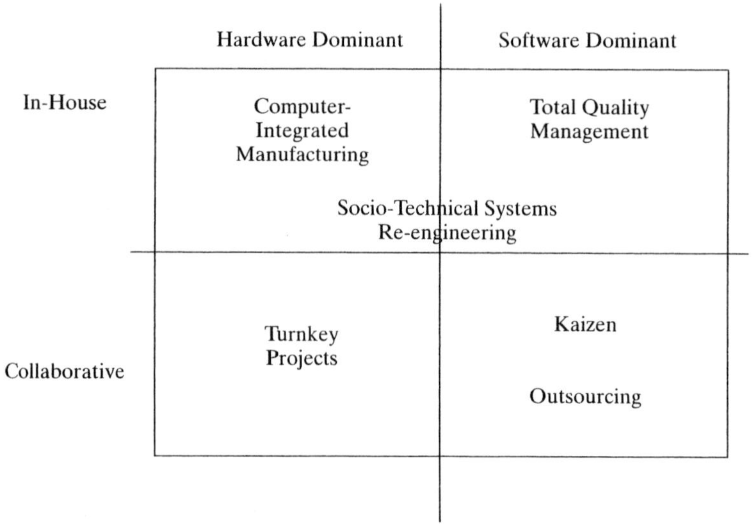

	Hardware Dominant	Software Dominant
In-House	Computer-Integrated Manufacturing	Total Quality Management
	Socio-Technical Systems Re-engineering	
Collaborative	Turnkey Projects	Kaizen Outsourcing

engineering often requires use of information technology architecture to accomplish its objectives.

We will sketch the major technology deployment approaches and then discuss the issue of implementation.

COMPUTER-INTEGRATED MANUFACTURING (CIM)

Recall the march of value chain configurations from craft production to mass customization. The traditional mass production factory was built around economies of scale and the natural life cycles of products. In other words, significant benefits could be gained by a plant through its size, by reducing investment cost per unit of installed capacity; through volume, by spreading fixed costs over a large number of units; and through time, by allowing learning and experience to be gained while waiting to reduce costs. These benefits came at a price: Mass markets need to be present; the demands can be predicted; and standardization should be possible. It was, however, recognized that once the product that the plant manufactured had reached maturity, the inflexible factory would in time then be faced with a rapidly aging product and falling markets.

Mass customization is made possible partly by the rise of new manufacturing technologies. The traditional trade-off between volume and variety and between costs and flexibility can be relaxed with these new flexible-manufacturing techniques. Computer-integrated manufacture (CIM) represents a family of technologies that helps to move manufacturing systems to higher levels of flexibility.

Figure 12.9 presents the family of technologies that are involved in computer-integrated manufacturing. The more prevalent of these are the MRP systems, JIT systems, and FMS systems, as well as computer-aided manufacturing (CAM).

FIGURE 12.9 COMPUTER-INTEGRATED MANUFACTURING

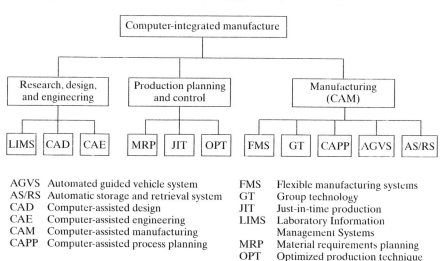

AGVS	Automated guided vehicle system	FMS Flexible manufacturing systems
AS/RS	Automatic storage and retrieval system	GT Group technology
CAD	Computer-assisted design	JIT Just-in-time production
CAE	Computer-assisted engineering	LIMS Laboratory Information
CAM	Computer-assisted manufacturing	Management Systems
CAPP	Computer-assisted process planning	MRP Material requirements planning
		OPT Optimized production technique

Source: From Jeremy Howells and Michelle Wood, *The Globalization of Production and Technology.* Commission of the European Communities. London: Belhaven Press, 1993. Reprinted by permission.

Materials resources planning (MRP). MRP systems appeared in the late 1960s for scheduling the purchase of raw materials, their use and flow in manufacturing systems in terms of inventory levels, and the output of final finished goods. They evolved into the MRP2 systems by incorporating additional features, such as capacity planning, cost accounting, and performance reporting.

Just in time (JIT). The essence of JIT is to buy parts when they are needed to go into production or assembly, with delivery of parts on the same day or even every hour. The system is geared toward providing major assemblies just in time to go into final end products at the proper assembly line workstation; subassemblies just in time to go into major assemblies; or parts just in time to go into subassemblies; and so on down to the level of the purchased part—and even beyond that into and toward the manufacturing stages in suppliers' plants.[3]

Flexible manufacturing systems (FMS). The origins of flexible manufacturing systems can be traced to the development of programmable automation, which involved the use of computers to guide the operations of one or more relatively unspecialized machines in accordance with preprogrammed instructions to produce an array of specified parts. The computer selects and transmits relevant instructions to the controls on each machine, specifying the sequence in which various tools are to be used and operations to be performed by each. As a result, the given array of equipment can produce a variety of parts in different volumes and sequences, with little loss of production time in shifting from one product to another without requiring skilled operators and with minimal need for manning.

Flexible manufacturing systems involve the combination of a given set of flexible/programmable machines into an integrated system controlled by a cell computer into either small-scale manufacturing cells or large clusters of "computer-integrated manufacture." In terms of manufacturing cells, machines are grouped in cells in such a way that each cell involves a set of machines required for the production of a family of parts and linked together into a group.[4]

Computer-assisted design (CAD), *manufacture* (CAM), and *engineering* (CAE). The impact of such systems as MRP, JIT, and FMS caused management to start collecting and analyzing data on how the actual manufacturing system operated in a clear and precise manner. Such systems also implied that the previously separate activities and functions needed to be seen in a more integrated fashion. The desire to integrate led to the adoption of optional, more generalized systems that sought to monitor and coordinate sets of technologies and crosscut production with other key functions of the firm. The most recently cited example of integration involves the merging of computer-aided manufacturing (CAM) and computer-aided design (CAD) from a CAD/CAM link. Up until recently, such CAD/CAM links have been one way—with the CAD module user acquiring the component geometry that has been built up on the CAD system, allowing the user of the CAM modular to design jigs or produce numerical control output without re-specifying the component geometry. Only more recently has there been full CAD/CAM integration involving two-way communications between the modules.[5]

The evolution toward integration of systems led to the emergence of computer integrated manufacture. Indeed, computer-integrated manufacture (CIM) is considered more to be a philosophy than a specific technology. Not all CIM systems will have all the various components; some will be redundant, and there will be significant variation in its overall format depending on the type of production involved. At its core, CIM involves providing the technology that integrates the diverse functions required for efficiently planned operation. However, although CIM represents an ideal, few firms operate systems anywhere approaching what might be called a CIM framework. In Box 12.1, we have illustrated how Honda has adopted systems close to computer-integrated manufacture.

BOX 12.1

HONDA

Properly implemented, CAD/CAM can drastically reduce the time required for planning, design, and production of a given product. This can be seen in the case of Honda, where CAD/CAE/CAM links form an integral part of the wider design and production system, which in turn forms part of the more general system of information and material flows within the company.

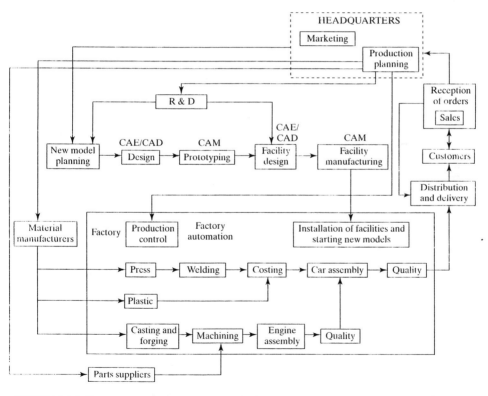

FIGURE 12.1.1 HONDA

Source: From Jeremy Howells and Michelle Wood, *The Globalization of Production and Technology*, Commission of the European Communities. London: Belhaven Press, 1993. Reprinted by permission.

Although firms implementing full-scale CIM are rare, in a recent study, dramatic changes have been discovered in a whole series of manufacturing criteria for firms implementing flexible manufacturing system technologies:

- Lead time is reduced on an average by 74 percent;
- Work in progress is reduced on average by 68 percent;
- Stock turnover increased on average by 350 percent; and
- Machine utilization increased on average by 63 percent.

Similar impressive results have been revealed by other studies investigating the impact of new manufacturing technologies.[6]

In contrast to computer-integrated manufacturing, which employs the use of information technologies and advanced technologies to speed the production process, organization-based approaches such as total quality management (TQM) focus on incremental improvements to improve the value chain activities.

TOTAL QUALITY MANAGEMENT

The total quality management (TQM) concept was originally developed by American consultants—primarily W. Edwards Deming, although others such as Joseph Duran contributed to further developments. During the last decade, many U.S. firms have experimented with total quality management approaches. This is partly due to the widespread success the Japanese firms enjoyed as a result of adopting Demming's philosophy. Although TQM approaches adopted in organizations vary to some degree, most of them advocate four basic principles:

- Intense focus on customer satisfaction;
- Accurate measurement of activities;
- Continuous improvement of products and processes; and
- Empowerment of people.

We referred to the total quality approaches to the conduct of research and development as well as QFD, in a new product development process. TQM originated in the manufacturing environment, initially as a way of enhancing the quality of the product and reducing defects. Indeed, Demming argued that improved quality means that cost decreases due to less re-work, fewer mistakes, fewer delays, and better use of time and materials. This leads to a chain reaction: Productivity increases, and better quality leads to higher market share. This, in turn, allows the company to raise prices, thereby increasing the company's profitability and allowing it to stay in business. Demming identified fourteen steps that should be part of any TQM program; these are summarized in Box 12.2.

Since the early 1980s, TQM practices have spread rapidly through U.S. industry. In Box 12.3, we have illustrated how Zytec Corporation has adopted TQM practices. As illustrated in the Zytec case, TQM focuses on changing corporate culture, which aligns the human, technological, and informational aspects of quality improvement with customer priorities.

There have been some impressive success stories of TQM programs. For example, in 1987, Motorola's semiconductor business was producing 6,000 defects per million parts; by 1992, this figure had been reduced to 40 per million, attributable to the adoption of TQM practices. Hitachi, Hewlett-Packard and Xerox, to name a few, have re-

BOX 12.2

DEMING'S PRINCIPLES

1. Create constancy of purpose toward improvement of product and service, with the aim of becoming competitive, staying in business, and providing jobs.

2. Adopt the new philosophy. We are in a new economic age. Western management must awaken to the challenge, learn its responsibilities, and take on leadership for change.

3. Cease dependence on inspection to achieve quality. Eliminate the need for inspection on a mass basis by building quality into the product in the first place.

4. End the practice of awarding business on the basis of price tag. Instead, minimize total cost.

5. Improve constantly and forever the system of production and service, to improve quality and productivity and thus constantly decrease costs.

6. Institute training on the job.

7. Institute leadership. The aim of leadership should be to help people, machines, and gadgets do a better job. Management leadership, as well as leadership of production workers, needs overhauling.

8. Drive out fear, so that everyone may work effectively for the company.

9. Break down barriers between departments. People in research, design, sales, and production must work as a team, to foresee problems in production and in use that may be encountered with the product or service.

10. Eliminate slogans, exhortations, and targets for the workforce asking for zero defects and new levels of productivity. Such exhortations only create adversarial relationships. The bulk of the causes of low quality and low productivity belong to the system and thus lie beyond the power of the workforce.

11. (a) Eliminate work standards on the factory floor; substitute leadership.
(b) Eliminate management by objective, management by numbers, and numerical goals; substitute leadership.

12. (a) Remove barriers that rob the hourly workers of their right to pride of workmanship. The responsibility of supervisors must be changed from sheer numbers to quality.
(b) Remove barriers that rob people in management and in engineering of their right to pride of workmanship.

13. Institute a vigorous program of education and self-improvement.

14. Put everybody in the company to work to accomplish the transformation. The transformation is everybody's job.

Source: Gabor, Andrea. *The Man Who Discovered Quality.* Copyright © 1990 by Andrea Gabor. Reprinted by permission of the *Times Books* division of Random House, Inc.

ported such success stories. However, despite such instances of spectacular success, TQM practices are not universally adopted. In 1992, for example, a study with American Quality Foundation found that only 20 percent of U.S. companies regularly review the consequences of quality performance, compared to 70 percent of Japanese companies. In another study of 500 American companies using TQM, Arthur D. Little found that only 26 percent believed that TQM was increasing their competitiveness; the study attributed this to the incomplete understanding of the TQM concept by many companies. Nonetheless, when properly implemented, TQM can give substantial benefits.

BOX 12.3

ZYTEC CORPORATION

Zytec was formed in 1984 when three Control Data Corporation executives arranged a leveraged buyout of the power supplies operation of Magnetic Peripherals, a Control Data subsidiary. Zytec's product sales of about $50 million in 1990 made it the fifth largest U.S. manufacturer of AC to DC power supplies, and repair sales of approximately $6 million made it the largest power supply repair company in North America. With approximately 700 employees, Zytec is about one-third the size of its largest competitor.

Zytec Corporation designs, manufactures, and repairs electronic power supplies for original equipment manufacturers (OEMs). Zytec's customers use these power supplies in a variety of products, including computers, hard-disk drives, telephone-switching equipment, and medical and testing equipment. Although there is a diverse range of potential customers, Zytec concentrates on high-volume power supplies for large electronics companies. Given its design capabilities, Zytec favors complex rather than simple power supplies. Zytec's 1993 product portfolio consisted of about 50 products, of which 2 accounted for about 40 percent of sales; the firm had about 15 customers, 2 of which were responsible for 60 percent of sales.

Responsiveness is a time- and customer-based concept. Given an understanding of a customer's requirements, Zytec can design a suitable product if one does not already exist. Poor quality in design or manufacture and/or an inability to respond to changes in market conditions will result in slow deliveries, lost sales, high material and finished goods inventories—and lost customers. With less time required to manufacture a product and the small batch sizes made possible by reduced setup or changeover times, customers do not have to accept long lead times. If one company cannot completely satisfy a customer's requirements, another firm will.

Disk drive manufacturers experienced this truth when Asian-designed and manufactured disk drives began appearing in North America in the mid-1980s. These drives were of better quality and lower cost than North American-built drives and nearly drove domestic manufacturers out of the market. This had a major impact on suppliers, including Zytec. Zytec's management realized that its own quality and cost problems were contributing to the disk drive makers' woes. Zytec was part of the problem, not an innocent victim.

These concerns were addressed in the total quality commitment program Zytec established in 1984 and extended in 1988. Zytec introduced new manufacturing concepts that included just-in-time (JIT) and total quality control (TQC).

Inventories at Zytec fell from about $17 million to $6 million between 1985 and 1986 and cycle times fell about 78 percent in mid-1986, actions that generated the cash for survival. "Plug and play" performance (trouble-free operation on receipt by the customer) increased from around 90 percent to 99.5 percent; manufacturing yields increased over 50 percent from 1988 to 1991.

What has enabled the firm to progress so rapidly is a four-step strategic quality planning process:

1. The first step is to collect data from customer feedback, formal and informal marketing research, and benchmarking, a process of ranking everything a firm does against the best in the world. This step ensures that no arbitrary strategic goals will be set.

2. The second step is the development of a long-range strategic plan (LRSP). Six cross-functional teams, each under the guidance of senior executives, develop plans, which are then reviewed and

Source: From Jeremy Howells and Michelle Wood, *The Globalization of Production and Technology,* Commission of the European Communities. London: Belhaven Press, 1993. Reprinted by permission.

critiqued by about 150 employees from all levels and functions in the firm. Suppliers and customers may also be invited to comment on the document, which is then refined and developed into a series of one-year corporate objectives.

3. The third step is the management by planning (MBP) process, in which each department sets its own annual improvement targets consistent with overall corporate objectives.

4. The fourth step is turning the long-range strategic objectives into financial plans.

The results of this process have been impressive: a 26 percent reduction in manufacturing cycle time, a 50 percent reduction in design cycle time, a 30 to 40 percent reduction in product costs, double-digit annual productivity growth in the period 1988 to 1991, and an increase to an average of more than 1 million hours between failures in a power supply. This has been achieved by, among other things, more attention to the design process and to suppliers.

All these gains can be attributed in large part to the corporate culture, which aligns the human, technological, and informational elements of quality improvement with customer priorities. The TQC process also integrates the business functions with each other as well as integrating suppliers and customers into a "seamless" organization.

Some approaches to value chain reconfiguration include technology as well as organization-related elements. We will deal with two of the more prominent approaches: (1) socio-technical systems approach and (2) re-engineering.

SOCIO-TECHNICAL SYSTEMS

The concept of socio-technical systems has largely been associated with the studies and consulting work done by the Tavistock Institute in England. The basic premise of the socio-technical systems approach is that to the extent the technology and organization (structure and social interaction of the workplace) are congruent, there will be greater productivity and enhanced organizational outcomes. One of the earliest Tavistock studies, in British coal mining, found that broadening both job scope and reintroducing a team approach to coal production, supplemented by incentives, significantly improved productivity morale and safety.[7] Another Tavistock project, this one in an Indian weaving mill, took the same direction in the case of semiautonomous work groups, with similar results.[8] In later experiments in Norway and Sweden, the creation of semi-autonomous work groups, which produced a final product, coupled with some other conditions, resulted in more job satisfaction and higher productivity and earnings.[9]

The socio-technical systems approach is one of the oldest in terms of transforming the value chain activities. Although the approach varies from setting to setting, all approaches involve three elements:

1. Self-governing work groups;
2. Redesign of work to conform to socio-technical requirements; and
3. Management system based on workplace democracy, training, and incentives.

In the United States, the most renowned of the socio-technical experiments was conducted in General Food's plant in Topeka. Box 12.4 describes the story of the Topeka plant, as it moved through several acquisitions.

SOCIO-TECHNICAL SYSTEMS IN A DOG FOOD FACTORY

The story dates back to 1966. One morning, in an isolated warehouse at a Gaines dog food plant in Kankakee, Illinois, a 20-year-old night-shift worker was found bound to a column with packaging tape. He was unhurt, but he couldn't get free. Once discovered, he was immediately cut down. The question was what to do next?

The workers who'd assaulted their colleague couldn't be punished because of union rules. And Lyman Ketchum and Ed Dulworth, the two senior managers in the plant, didn't *want* to punish them. Labor-management relations were already on the brink of explosion, in part a result of the unexpected success of Gainesburgers, which had pushed the decrepit facility to operate at three times its capacity.

Instead of "kicking ass and taking names" as some supervisors suggested, Ketchum and Dulworth opted for a more radical—and more productive—course: a socio-technical pilot project. The pair took their pitch for the workplace of the future to corporate management. "People have 'ego' needs," Dulworth argued. "They want self-esteem, a sense of accomplishment, autonomy, increasing knowledge and skill, and data on their performance."

Their idea: "Unlearn" every traditional practice and design a plant from scratch to capitalize on that aspect of human nature. What emerged was an experiment housed in a gleaming white silo-shaped plant on the Kansas prairie in Topeka. Sections of the plant painted in bright colors became natural centers where teams gravitated to compare notes—or to thrash out differences. There were no supervisors, only teams and team members who controlled plant operations. They hired new members, assigned shifts, set hours, and redesigned the placement of machinery. Everyone rotated through a wide variety of jobs. Significantly, they shared freely in information about the plant's finances and cash flow.

Without the overhead of middle managers, with an astonishingly low 2 percent absentee rate, and with a level of involvement bordering on ownership, the Topeka plant set performance records at General Foods. It became an example of the next-generation workplace: Curious executives and business reporters lined up for tours in such volumes that Dulworth began charging admission. But as the limelight shined brighter, GF worried about the glare. Corporate managers withdrew their support and declared the experiment "out of control." Ketchum and Dulworth were unceremoniously pushed out of the company. A new plant manager arrived with his marching orders: "Cut out this missionary nonsense." It was too late. The system had already taken on a life of its own. It seeped into the design of a new canned dog food plant next door.

In 1984, General Foods sold its pet food business to the Anderson Clayton conglomerate. In Topeka, the team structure persisted without management cultivation. By 1986, when Quaker Oats bought all of Anderson Clayton, the Gaines dog food plant was the crown jewel of the acquisition. But Quaker made no attempt to extend the Topeka system anywhere else in its organization.

Then in March 1995, when Heinz acquired Quaker, it looked as if the new owners might finally put the experiment to sleep. Heinz's initial reaction was to make the plant conform to its policies: Management shut down half the plant, eliminated the team system, suspended all the costly ongoing training that made the team system viable, and cut 150 jobs. But the team-based structure refused to roll over and play dead.

Source: Reprinted from Art Kleiner, "Management Fad Dog Food Factory" from the June/July 1996, issue of *Fast Company* magazine. All rights reserved. To subscribe, please call (800)688-1545.

Six months later, Heinz performed a public about-face to broadcast its faith in the Topeka system. Bill Goode, a vice president of human resources and quality for the company, says, "The system in Topeka has evolved to a much higher level than any of our other plants. We look at it as a model of where we'd like to go."

Training budgets are back in the 141-person plant; so are team meetings. Safety concerns belong to the shop floor once more. Pay-for-knowledge is intact, people still rotate jobs, and teams determine assignments. This old dog continues to teach management new tricks.

In contrast to the socio-technical systems approach, re-engineering employs the power of information technology to redesign the work place.

RE-ENGINEERING

In the opening vignette, we have illustrated how re-engineering was employed in one corporation. During the 1990s, re-engineering has been a vogue among large businesses in the United States, partly as a way of controlling costs. We will define re-engineering as follows:

> *Re-engineering* refers to the radical redesign of broad cross-functional business processes with the objective of order-of-magnitude performance gains, often with the aid of information technology.

Re-engineering is, indeed, in many ways a new synthesis of previously existing ideas.

1. The idea of managing and improving business processes comes primarily from the quality or continuous literature, described previously.
2. The second key feature of re-engineering is "clean sheet of paper" design of processes. Although firms may often disregard existing constraints in designing a new business process, such constraints must be considered during implementation, unless a new organizational unit is created. We saw that similar idea in the socio-technical systems approach as we discussed the story of the Topeka pet food factory of General Foods.
3. Unlike total quality management, however, re-engineering involves the use of information technology to enable new ways of working. This simply is a reflection of the fact that primarily IT-oriented management consultants created re-engineering synthesis.

In 1994, a survey of several North American and European companies found that re-engineering was quite prevalent, with 69 percent of North American and 75 percent of European companies respectively having at least one project under way.[10] The most popular processes to be re-engineered in North America were customer service, fulfillment manufacturing processes, and customer acquisition processes. In Europe, on the other hand, manufacturing processes were primarily the target for re-engineering.[11]

All the approaches discussed until now focus on changes in the value chain configuration inside a firm. However, increasingly approaches to modifying the value chain embrace relationships with external entities. In some cases, the value chain activities may be outsourced; in others, the focus may be on obtaining technology from outside. We focus on three different types of collaborative arrangements: (1) outsourcing, (2) supplier integration, and (3) turnkey projects.

OUTSOURCING

What will the business itself be and what will it obtain from its business partners? This is often referred to as the question of value constellation. The principle behind the design of value constellation is that a firm should not do any activity that other firms can do more effectively and efficiently. In other words, a firm should stick to its knitting or should do those activities that are within its sphere of core competence. Indeed, several innovative companies have attempted to build strong value constellation through judicious reliance on other firms.

- Marriott Host, a division of Marriott Corporation, operates cafeterias at airports and on highways. Instead of relying solely on its own recipes and brand names, Host has chosen to develop strategic alliances with national brand name leaders in selected fast-food segments. For example, Host operates Pizza Hut kiosks inside its own restaurants and has found that pizza sales under the partnership arrangement are significantly higher than when it operates with its own recipes and brand names.
- During the late 1970s, Marriott Corporation concluded that in the lodging business its dominating competencies were in hospitality management rather than in real estate management. This discovery led to the fundamental shift in the company's approach to allocation of its resources. As one element of its strategy, the company began to sell their real estate to investor syndicates while retaining a long-term contract for the management of the property.

Indeed there are no universal guidelines as to when a company should rely on partners. The optimum solution relies on the specifics of the particular situation and the results of a comparison of the capabilities of a firm and those of potential business partners. However, the outsourcing option is not entirely risk free. At least three types of risks are associated with relying on external partners: (1) nonperformance, (2) profit skimming, and (3) elimination.

1. *The risk of nonperformance.* The partner selected may fail to live up to its obligations either because of a competitive decline in its capabilities or because its priorities no longer include serving the firm. A business can guard against this risk in a number of ways, including developing alternative suppliers, maintaining a credible threat of backward integration, and becoming a part owner in the supplier by buying an equity stake.
2. *The risk of profit skimming.* The partners selected may skim most of the profits generated by the value constellation and leave a firm only marginally profitable. It is reported that IBM's PC business unit eventually fell into this trap when it decided to rely on Microsoft Corporation to provide the operating system and Intel Corporation to provide the microprocessor. To prevent the risk of profit skimming by its partners in a value constellation, a business unit can retain some critical nonsubstitutable activities, keep upgrading its competencies in these critical activities so that its dominant superiority prevents a decline in a partners' dependence on the business unit, or

acquire an equity stake in the business partners early in the game, before they become overly powerful.

3. *The risk of elimination.* Business partners may integrate forward and squeeze out the firm altogether. This risk is basically an extreme portion of the risk of profit skimming. The basic safeguards against both risks are the same.[12]

Outsourcing firms' value chain activities, however, requires attention to managing the value constellation. This is often referred to as external integration. External integration often decreases costs while increasing delivered value. For example:

- Companies such as Motorola and National Semiconductor make semiconductor chips and boards for industrial markets worldwide. Suppose that one of such a company's business units is charged with a mission to develop a market for the company's products in the automotive industry, such as an integrated circuit board for antilock braking systems (ABS). If the semi-conductor manufacturer is located in the United States and the auto manufacturer is in Germany, for the needed external integration of the value chain to occur, it may well be necessary for the semiconductor manufacturer to establish an ABS design center in close physical proximity to the auto manufacturer's design center in Germany.
- Electronic data interchange (EDI) is rapidly becoming an important means of integration between the buying departments of customers and the sales/distribution departments of sellers in a wide spectrum of industries ranging from consumer goods to pharmaceuticals.

There are a number of interrelated forces that may be seen to influence the trend towards outsourcing:

- That nature of global competition in particular industrial sectors has provided a force for change in supply activities, as have new manufacturing technology, practices such as JIT, and lean production efforts.
- Second, the arguments for focus on core competencies have led many firms to reconsider what materials and components they should produce themselves and what areas they should outsource.
- Finally, the need to gain flexibility has been a factor that has also been stressed in reasons for firms to increase their outsourcing.

There are other developments in supply chain relationships that are significantly reshaping the value activities of a company.

BUYER-SUPPLIER RELATIONSHIPS AND SUPPLY TIERS

During the last two decades, corporate supply strategies of firms have followed one of the two routes: single, "comakership" supply deals or multiple sources. The move toward single sourcing has been part of a wider process towards flexibility and quality improvements in manufacturing.

SINGLE SOURCING
This implies a longer term relationship and an emphasis on mutual cost effectiveness, including quality considerations. For Japanese companies, the desire is to have single-source suppliers who heavily depend on them, for example, having 60 percent of their

turnover being devoted to one customer.[13] There are three major benefits of single sourcing:

1. Product cost reduction to improve communication associated with close buyer/seller relationships, where mutual understanding establishes a basis for cooperative problem solving and the necessity for no adjustments to be made to parts and components, which occurs when changing from a part supplied by one vendor to the same part supplied by another vendor;

2. Lower price through reduction in vendor's order processing, sales, transportation, and material handling, and fewer re-works and repairs; and

3. Stability of supply through long-term agreements and shipments able to be undertaken with frequency and timeliness required by JIT.

However, single sourcing is expected to open up a firm to major risks associated with strikes, deceptions of the supplier's plant, and higher costs. As a result, there has been a move towards dual sourcing.

DUAL SOURCING

These programs have been seen as a compromise between single and multiple source procurement systems. During 1980 and 1981, General Electric introduced a dual source savings (DSS) program to reduce the number of single-sourced items by opening up as much as possible to competitive bidding. The program reportedly led to a reevaluation of the supplier network with new suppliers coming on board. The savings initially were small, but over time, suppliers became increasingly competitive, and sourcing changes became more frequent as first one supplier and then another reduced prices.[14]

Because suppliers are not all of equal importance to the purchasing firms, the differing strategies—single sourcing versus double sourcing—have led to different supplier configurations within firms. For major Japanese companies, clear tiers of suppliers and contractors can be identified, with only a relatively small number of primary contractors having direct contact with the lead manufacturer. For most North American and European companies, this hierarchical pattern is less structured, with the number of direct suppliers being very much larger than their Japanese counterparts.

In Japanese companies, supplier relationships play a key role in value constellation. In general, about 60 percent of the total value added or final products within the automobile sector are sourced from a limited number of direct suppliers who, in turn, are supplied by a larger number of smaller subcontractors and second-tier suppliers. The Japanese production chains are pyramidal, whereby 31 percent of subcontractors carry out work for only one customer, and almost 50 percent for two customers.[15] Japanese value constellation is, thus, of a unique nature, and suppliers often benefit from membership to the industrial *keiretsu* or corporate associations. Although there is a higher degree of outsourcing, this may well take place within the security of these corporate trading relations. Figure 12.10 displays both of the Japanese and European/U.S. models of supplier relationships. As can be seen in the figure, the different firms adopt different approaches to the value configurations.

TURNKEY PROJECTS

Unlike outsourcing arrangements or supplier networks, wherein a firm relies on external agents to carry out part of its value configuration, sometimes firms may build up

(a) Japanese Model

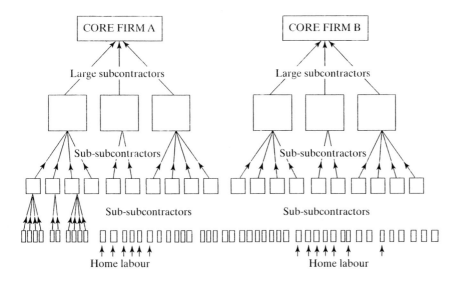

(b) European / U.S. Model

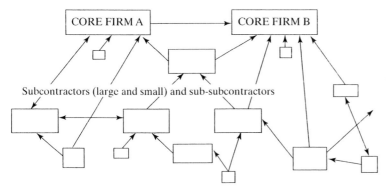

FIGURE 12.10 JAPANESE AND EUROPEAN SUPPLIER RELATIONSHIPS

Source: From Jeremy Howells and Michelle Wood, *The Globalization of Production and Technology,* Commission of the European Communities. London: Belhaven Press, 1993. Reprinted by permission.

their value chain activities in-house with technology assistance from outside agents. Turnkey projects have been one mechanism by which many of the developing countries build up their industrial base. For example, during the 1960s, as India was going through the early phases of its industrialization, it relied on firms in technically advanced Western countries to build up its steel and nuclear power plants. In a turnkey project, the supplier firm builds the entire value chain activity related to a particular segment of a firm's operations, trains the firm's workers, and in some cases, may even continue

TABLE 12.5   A Comparative Analysis of Approaches

Dimensions	TQM	Socio-Technical	Re-engineering
Approach	Software dominant	Software and hardware dominant	Software and hardware dominant
Objectives	Quality, customer responsiveness	Costs and human satisfaction	Costs, speed of execution
Implementation	Participative	Expert analysis	Top down
Human Focus	High	Work groups	Limited
Technology Focus	None	Manufacturing	Information technology
Nature of Change Process	Incremental	Redesign	Drastic
Settings Appropriate	Manufacturing	Manufacturing	Staff and middle management

managing operations of the project for a sustained period of time. Turnkey projects thus, have served as a method by which firms have brought advanced technology capability inside the firm from external sources. In chapter 9, we have illustrated how acquisitions licensing and consulting arrangements can also be employed by firms to bring in technological know-how from the outside.

In summary, there are a number of different approaches by which firms deploy technology in their value chain activities. It should be remembered, however, that a firm's choice of any or a combination of these approaches should be guided by the four factors: industry context, technology context, strategic context, and resources and capabilities of the firm. Further, some of these approaches invoke contradictory assumptions; therefore, simultaneous implementation of them may result in problems for an organization. For example, as currently practiced, TQM and re-engineering approaches differ in terms of the underlying managerial philosophy, attitudes towards people, and technology. In Table 12.5, we have summarized the differences among some of the major approaches. Finally, significant managerial attention is required during the implementation of all the approaches, a topic to which we now turn.

IMPLEMENTATION OF VALUE CHAIN RECONFIGURATION

Implementation of value chain reconfiguration takes place over an extended period of time. Many of the approaches that were listed in the previous section—TQM, reengineering, or external sourcing—have sometimes met with failure due to faulty implementation. Suffice to say, the implementation of value chain reconfiguration needs to be managed carefully in order for the firm to reap their intended benefits.

Implementation of value chain reconfigurations is indeed a more complex process than the execution of a well-laid out plan. The implementation process has three distinct characteristics of the process: (1) reinvention, (2) mutual adaptation, and (3) J-curve of implementation.

REINVENTION

The approach to software-dominant value chain reconfiguration such as TQM or re-engineering usually requires an organization or a major subunit within it to adopt a different way of operating. Sometimes, the practices are imported from outside through consultants (as in the case of re-engineering); in some cases, the practices may be transported from one part of the organization to the other (for example, from a research and development unit). Thus, it resembles a process of diffusion. Recall the concept of re-invention that we introduced in the chapter on diffusion. Reinvention referred to the process by which innovation is shaped by its users during the process of adoption. Reinvention is necessary, because any general approach to value chain reconfiguration needs to be tailored to the particular organizational circumstances for it to be implemented successfully. In other words, any approach to value chain reconfiguration needs to be customized to the particular circumstances facing a firm. This customization serves three major purposes:

1. To make the approach relevant to the organizational context;
2. To render it easy for the organizational members to understand the approach; and
3. To make it easy for the participants to operate under the new system.

However, for effective reinvention to ensue, the principle of mutual adaptation should be observed.

MUTUAL ADAPTATION

Unlike reinvention, which focused on the changes to technology or approach to the value chain reconfiguration induced by an adopting organization, mutual adaptation is the simultaneous adaptation of the organization to use the new technology or approach, along with the reinvention of the technology to conform to the adopting organization. Mutual adaptation requires that managers in charge of implementing the new technologies recognize and assume responsibility for both technical and organizational change. Rarely does any approach to value chain reconfiguration leave the existing organization untouched.[16]

J-CURVE OF IMPLEMENTATION

Implementation of any new technology or approach to value chain reconfiguration upsets the status quo. As a consequence, during the early phases of implementation, benefits of change are not readily apparent to many of the individuals who are involved in the transition. *J*-curve of implementation simply captures the idea: Things get worse before they get better. The *J*-curve is illustrated in Figure 12.11. As illustrated in the figure, firms have to invest in time, money, and personnel during the early stages of implementation; however, the benefits of these investments are likely to flow back to the organization only in the later phases of implementation.

In our earlier discussion of the technology deployment in value chains, it was noted that many of the approaches, such as TQM or re-engineering, that promised significant gains to the organization, were not successful due to faulty implementation. The three characteristics of implementation (reinvention, mutual adaptation, and the *J*-curve of

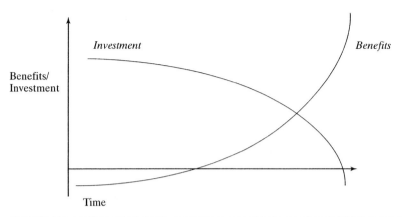

FIGURE 12.11 *J*-CURVE OF IMPLEMENTATION

implementation) suggest some guidelines that organizations need to follow in order fc the implementation of technology change to be successful. We enumerate six majc guidelines:

1. *Management commitment.* One of the most important conditions for implementation to be successful is management commitment in terms of resources and attention. Three specific goals need to be performed during implementation: sponsor, champion, and manager. It is the role of the sponsor to make resources available; a champion is needed to keep the need for change visible in the eyes of an organization; and the managerial role ensures that the implementation is on track and bottlenecks and problems are addressed and resolved. Without sponsorship, championship, and managerial stewardship of the change, most change programs are likely to fail.

2. *User involvement.* There are reasons for involving users in the development of a change process. First, the implementation implies some level of change in users' work, and the research on change suggests that people are more receptive when they contribute to its design. Second, involving users in the design of value chain activities results in superior designs because the users have specialized knowledge about the environment in which the changes will be utilized; that knowledge should be embodied in the change design.

3. *Organizational integration.* As pointed out in our discussion on mutual adaptation, a process of implementation should specifically allow for the individuals affected by the change to alter the technological approach by customizing it and to adjust the organization in the process of mutual adaptation. Indeed, in one study of 34 projects that developed software tools to enhance internal productivity in 4 large U.S.-based electronics firms, the researchers found that in addition to the quality and cost of technology and its initial compatibility with the user environment, that two managerial processes were more important in explaining different levels and types of successful implementation: user involvement and mutual adaptation.[17]

4. *Functional integration.* Almost all value chain reconfigurations have defects that spill over and beyond the individuals who are affected by the change.

The spillovers may include other units within a firm or, in some cases, entities outside the organization: suppliers and customers. For example, outsourcing the information systems in banks may affect its customers. Similarly, adoption of TQM in operations may affect marketing or research and development functions within the organization. Such effects need to be managed carefully.

5. *Investment in training.* For value chain reconfiguration to yield its full benefits, the individuals who are part of the value chain activity should have the requisite knowledge, attitudes, and skills. This suggests that a firm will have to commit to significant investment in training in the early phases of the implementation but may have to continue over an extended period of time depending on the magnitude of the change involved.

6. *Monitoring implementation.* Management stewardship of implementation is critical to its success. Here, implementation programs proceed without problems or bottlenecks. It requires managerial intervention to resolve the bottleneck and find solutions to incoming problems. This, in turn, implies that the implementation should be carefully monitored. Feedback mechanisms, both from within the firm and from outside the firm need to be instituted for ongoing stewardship of implementation.

In summary, technology deployment in value chain requires careful implementation.

INFLUENCE OF ENVIRONMENTAL TRENDS ON VALUE CHAINS

The three trends—time compression, technology integration, and globalization—have had significant influence on the value chain configurations of firms, as summarized in Figure 12.12.

FIGURE 12.12 INFLUENCE OF ENVIRONMENTAL TRENDS

Environmental Trend | *Impact on Value Chains*

Globalization → Global Switching

Time Compression → Use of Technology to Increase Speed

Technology Integration → Collaborative Approach: Outsourcing, Supplier Networks

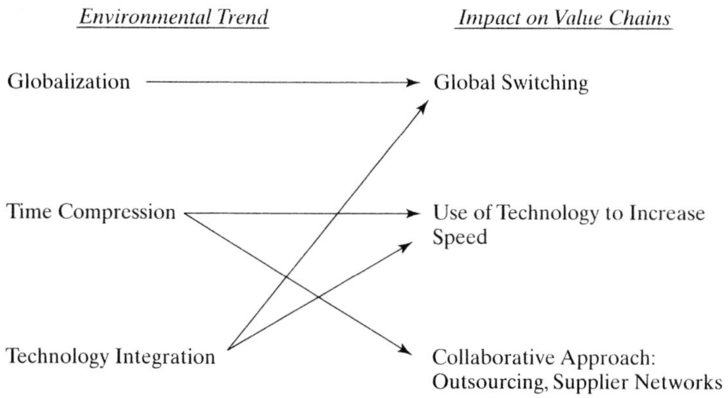

- Time compression has led industry clockspeeds, and in turn, this has induced firms to adopt advanced technologies, outsourcing, and other external arrangements.
- The potential for technology integration has resulted in adoption of external sources of technology into the value chains of corporations.
- Finally, value chains are being modified in the wake of globalization, a point to which we now turn.

GLOBALIZATION OF VALUE CHAINS

As the trend toward globalization has intensified, overseas facilities have become creasingly significant in terms of value chain activities, especially for multinational c porations. Indeed a number of major multinational companies have establis overseas centers that now act as headquarters or lead sites for particular division businesses. For example:

- A number of ICI businesses are controlled abroad, so local plants and establishments now take their lead from these overseas operations.
- DuPont has in 1991 moved its global headquarters for its agricultural products division to Geneva, Switzerland.
- IBM moved the headquarters of its worldwide communications systems from New York to London in 1991.
- Monsanto relocated the headquarters of Monsanto Refins from St. Louis to Brussels in 1992.
- Roche coordinates its worldwide R&D activities from the United States in a multiresearch center at Nutley, New Jersey, where some 350 scientists are located.[18]

Indeed, such changes bring about the need for effective coordination of value chain tivities across worldwide locations. One development that has facilitated the coordi tion function in an organization is the spread and use of global corporate comput communication networks. The availability of global, e-mail, and database systems; development of "computer-hyphenated" methods that allow designs to be transfer between sites; and the increasing use of videoconferencing all have supported more fective inter-site coordination. For example, within Nissan, CAD drawings can rapidly transferred between research, technical, and engineering units in Japan, United Kingdom, the United States, and Spain by using its NDC-MET and NICE-N computer network, shown in Figure 12.13. Glaxo, similarly, has a computer commu cation network linking its major research sites in the United Kingdom, United Sta Switzerland, and Italy, as shown in Figure 12.14.

Three further plans are developing with respect to the globalization of value ch activity: (1) global switching, (2) global focusing, and (3) global sourcing.

GLOBAL SWITCHING

Global switching refers to the practice by which companies coordinate their differ value chain activities in an integrated fashion on a global basis. Although the abilit "switch" geographically is best exemplified during new product development (see ch ter 11), switching can also occur within various value chain activities. For example,

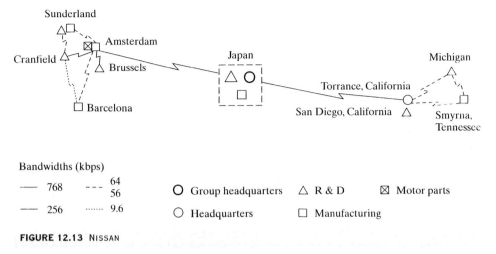

FIGURE 12.13 NISSAN

Source: From Jeremy Howells and Michelle Wood, *The Globalization of Production and Technology,* Commission of the European Communities. London: Belhaven Press, 1993. Reprinted by permission.

manufacture of certain products can be switched from one plant to another plant located on opposite sides of the world. This is often referred to as horizontal switching.

Horizontal switching refers to linkages and flows between overseas establishments, particularly as it relates to manufacturing. The phenomenon of global switching has been established since the mid-1950s. IBM is an example: The desire to escape possible nationalization meant that IBM in Europe in the 1960s and 1970s adopted the strategy of international horizontal switching, so as to make plants within individual European countries as unattractive as possible for nationalization. This created plants that would be highly integrated and dependent on overseas components/materials, thereby ensuring that they would not be able to survive on their own on a purely national basis.[19] In addition to political factors, other factors have also encouraged switching between manufacturing operations:

1. Lower manufacturing and labor costs of overseas production. In order to remain competitive, U.S. and European companies have moved large parts of their production offshore. For example, a U.K. clothing company, Dewhirst, cut costs by sourcing the first batch of an order from Asia but then made subsequent batches in its U.K. factories, which offer a speedier service by reducing delivery time.[20] The trend toward offshore production facilities due to cost advantages was an important factor in the spread of multinational manufacturing operations in the 1960s, 1970s and the 1980s. Inevitably, the spread of such facilities led to increased global switching.
2. Increase in international sourcing. Increasing international sourcing and standardization of components and materials between overseas sites producing similar products and product ranges have also led to global horizontal switching. This is particularly evident in electronics, where companies are involved in complex assignment problems associated with bundling a wide range of components that are manufactured or purchased from a whole range of plants worldwide and have been finally assembled in a particular location.

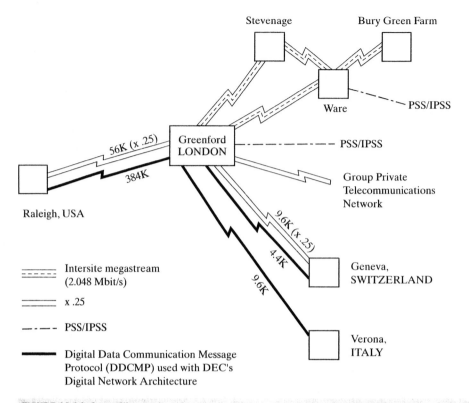

FIGURE 12.14 GLAXO WELLCOME

Source: From Jeremy Howells and Michelle Wood, *The Globalization of Production and Technology,* Com mission of the European Communities. London: Belhaven Press, 1993. Reprinted by permission.

Global switching refers to the ability of companies to coordinate their value chain ac tivities in an integrated fashion on a global scale. In the case of the new product deve opment process, this is often referred to as *vertical global switching,* because it involve in-depth functional linkages.

Traditionally, the new product development process was taken mainly on one sit or a set of closely interlinked sites within a national territory. However, increasing large multinationals have had the ability to switch such sequencing across nation boundaries. Thus, development may be undertaken in one country, initial productio scale-up in another, full production and related component production in another, an first market launch in a completely different country. Although there are significant cc ordination issues that crop up during the new product development process in vertic globalization, the switching provides considerable economic and technical benefits fo corporations. They are able to exploit the different technical manufacturing and ma keting skills of the various sites.

In Box 12.5, we have illustrated new product launches by Glaxo and Texas Instru ments based on the principle of vertical switching.

BOX 12.5

VERTICAL SWITCHING

The ability to switch geographically between sites in terms of functional sequencing is best seen in the case of new product development and commercialization. Consider two examples:

Glaxo. The product Salmeterol involved R&D at its site in Ware in the United Kingdom, followed by extensive clinical trials all over the world. The scale-up production for the active ingredients of the drug was transferred to Montrose in Scotland, which went into full-scale primary production. Another

primary production would be Singapore; both Montrose and Singapore would also supply secondary production and packaging operators in Evreux in France and Ware in the United Kingdom. The first market launch would be in the United Kingdom. This is sketched in Figure 12.5.1.

Texas Instruments. By 1993, TI had 60 manufacturing facilities worldwide in 18 countries. Consider an example quoted by the company. A chip might be designed in Europe or

FIGURE 12.5.1 GLAXO-WELLCOME

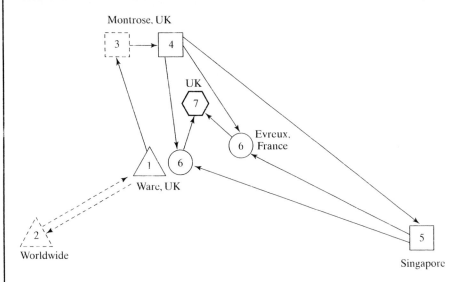

1–7 Numbering indicates sequence of events in the new product development and launch

△ Research and Development

◁ Clinical trials and product regulation

⌐⌐ Scale-up Primary Production

☐ Full-Scale Primary Production

○ Secondary Production

⬡ First market launch of product

Source: From Jeremy Howells and Michelle Wood, *The Globalization of Production and Technology,* Commission of the European Communities. London: Belhaven Press, 1993. Reprinted by permission.

Box 12.5 (*continued*)

Japan; then the chip specifications could be transferred by satellite to one of its major plants in Texas, where the components can be produced, and sent to Kuala Lumpur or one of the other plants in East Asia for final integration. This is shown schematically in the figure:

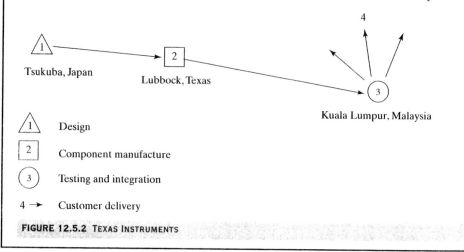

△1   Design

☐2   Component manufacture

◯3   Testing and integration

4 →   Customer delivery

FIGURE 12.5.2 Texas Instruments

GLOBAL FOCUSING

Global focusing refers to the concentration of value chain activities involved in a particular product, product group, or related technologies on a single or closely related set of sites in selected locations across the world. Whereas global switching focuses on functional specialization in different regions, global focusing tries to take advantage of product specialization within selected regions.

The main advantage of global focusing is its basic simplicity:

1. Problems of coordination are reduced by allowing cross-functional specialization to develop around a particular group or technology.
2. The facility may be located nearby or can use effective key local suppliers.
3. It can gain benefits from good linkages with location at or near to "lead innovative customers."

However, there are some disadvantages as well:

1. Focusing a particular unit on one product or technology exposes the firm to downturns or fluctuations in demand, which over the long term could lead to closure as the markets or technologies would warrant.
2. A firm reduces its flexibility in allocating spared productive capacity: This would lead to suboptimum allocation of the company's total resources.

GLOBAL SOURCING

As major corporations extend their global reach, they are also able to increase their geographical scope of materials and components sourcing. Global sourcing may offer several special benefits:

1. It may widen the number of potential best-practice suppliers that a company can utilize.

2. It may increase more competition between potential suppliers.

3. It can allow access to suppliers based in countries that have a lead in certain technologies or manufacturing practices for a particular component or product.

These need to be weighed against the advantages of local sourcing: easier cooperation and coordination with operations; a quicker response to the needs of production; effective use of local sources; and greater plant autonomy over material expenditure.

Indeed, most companies use a mix of global/local sourcing. A recent study of *Fortune 1000* firms found that nearly 60 percent employed a combined form of sourcing.[21] In Box 12.6, we have illustrated the Hewlett-Packard experience with global procurement strategy. In the coming decade, we can expect further changes in the practices of the firm as a trend toward globalization continues.

BOX 12.6

CORPORATE PROCUREMENT

Changing global conditions have led many large companies to rethink their procurement practices. Consider the following examples:

Hewlett-Packard. Although Hewlett-Packard has grown and established autonomous production divisions, recent years have also seen the creation of a corporate procurement and materials management group. The main responsibility of this group, which represents approximately 18 percent of corporate purchasing employment, is a support and guidance function (rather than directly involved in buying materials/inputs) for the individual, decentralized purchasing departments. In addition, the central group is required to develop worldwide forecasts for the total corporate component consumption; provide specialist support and guidance for "critically important materials" and high-value contracts; manage component/specification databases; monitor supplier performance on a company-wide basis and provide support to individual divisions for international procurement; and to provide leadership for the development of corporate procurement strategy (Lee, Dobler and Burt, 1991).

Similar practices are also instituted in other companies such as Shell, Nokia Data, Hoechst, and General Motors.

Shell. Within Shell, each operating company manages its own materials activities, with the bulk of their materials purchasing coming from local and "regional" sources. However, the increasing trend towards local purchasing by the operating companies with Shell created a need for a company-wide procurement coordinating operation. As a result, a Group Materials Unit was established in The Hague, supported by the other units in Houston and Tokyo. Group Materials, apart from providing a key coordination role, works on providing standards and specifications for materials purchased by the operating companies as well as providing advice on a wide range of supply issues including materials handling and inventory management. In order to gain more direct benefits from collective purchasing power and procurement expertise, Shell has also established commodity coordination groups to obtain value for money in the purchase of bulk materials.

Nokia Data. As part of Nokia Data's planned "multidomestic" growth strategy, procurement coordination has been placed within the responsibility of central management, though the actual purchasing falls within the remit of the local production management.

Source: From Jeremy Howells and Michelle Wood, *The Globalization of Production and Technology.* Commission of the European Communities. London: Belhaven Press, 1993. Reprinted by permission.

Box 12.6 (*continued*)

The aim here is to decentralize (operational) decision making in order to achieve "a strong country management voice in local activities" (Kashani and Howard, 1991).

Hoechst. Faced with fragmentation of the purchasing effort and lack of company-wide standards for materials/components, Hoechst is establishing European teams to target particular supply areas on a Europe-wide basis. One material is titanium oxide, which was used in 15 sites across Europe and was purchased on a highly decentralized basis. Other supply areas to receive attention include cars, packaging, scientific and computer equipment and key industrial equipment such as pumps and valves. The objective is to create scale benefits in purchasing by buying in much larger lots to gain a better price and to exploit international pricing differences for particular items. Although the purchasing is therefore aggregated and led by a Europe-wide team, the actual pur-

chasing function is decentralized to national procurement units that take responsibility for particular supply items. As part of this process, the company realized that it was purchasing equipment that varied in standard according to different national regulatory standards. As a result, the company is seeking to establish company-wide standards for the particular pieces of equipment it is purchasing. A key element in both these issues has been to establish company-wide information sharing in procurement to extend the knowledge base, in terms of sourcing and supply.

General Motors. Within General Motors, global sourcing of components for the whole company is recognized as a key route to reducing costs, especially in the very short term. Consolidation of material and component requirements through worldwide volume purchasing will provide General Motors with the purchasing power to reduce material input costs.

❖ CHAPTER SUMMARY

In this chapter, we have summarized the deployment of technology in the value chain of firms. The deployment is mostly triggered by business strategy considerations, but in some cases it may also be to build capabilities to deploy in the marketplace.

The characteristics of competitive domains determine where in the value chains the technology can be deployed in order to gain competitive advantage. The deployment is constrained or facilitated by the availability of specific technologies. Business strategy, low cost, or differentiation determines whether the firm should adopt a specific technology. The strategy should be specified in terms of specific objectives—efficiency, customer responsiveness, quality, or innovativeness. The deployment of technology requires inter-functional integration. Almost always, when new products are introduced, firms will have to adjust their value chains. The decision to deploy a specific technological approach should be based on four criteria: appropriateness in the light of objective, resource capabilities of the focal firm, cost-benefit analysis, and implementability.

There are four steps involved in the process of arriving at the choice of specific technologies to deploy in the value chains. Diagnosis includes assessment of the technological environment and the competitive domains, a firm's strategy, and the specific objectives of deployment. Next-feasible technological alternatives are analyzed for potential deployment. The alternatives are evaluated against the four decision criteria, and finally, the choice is implemented. Implementation is central to effective deployment.

Four major sets of alternatives are available to a firm for deployment in its value chain. These may be arrayed along two dimensions: technology versus organization dominant and internal versus external arrangement. In recent years, computer-integrated manufacturing, total quality management, socio-technical systems, re-engineering, outsourcing, building buyer-supplier relationships, and turnkey projects have been variously implemented in firms.

Three major forces are at work during implementation: reinvention, mutual adaptation, and the *J*-curve phenomenon. Factors that determine the success of implementation include management commitment, user involvement, organizational and functional integration, and investment in training and ongoing monitoring.

In recent years, the pressures of time compression, the potential for technology integration, and globalization have led to value chain reconfigurations. Globalization has led to firms adopting three different sets of strategies: global switching, global focusing, and global sourcing.

❖ NOTES

1. Nolan, Richard L., and Stoddard, Donna B. "Cigna Property and Casualty Reengineering (A)," Harvard Business School Case #9-196-059.

2. Hill, C. W. L. and Jones, G. R. *Strategic Management.* Boston, MA: Houghton Mifflin Company, 1995.

3. Goldhar, J. D. and Schlie, W. "Computer technology and international competition: Part I: Factory of the future," *Integrated Manufacturing Systems,* 1991, pp. 16–22; Schonberger, R. J. "The transfer of Japanese manufacturing management approaches to U.S. industry," *Academy of Management Review,* 1982b, Vol. 7, pp. 479–87.

4. Gold, B. "Perspectives on continuing advances in automation: Vast limitations and imaging potentials," *Technovation,* 1986, Vol. 4, pp. 153–162; Mital, A. "Economics of flexible assembly automation: Influence of production and market factors," in H. R. Parsaei and A. Mital. (eds.) *Economics of Advanced Manufacturing Systems.* London: Chapman and Hall, 1992, pp. 45–72; Haywood, B. and Beffant, J. "Organization and integration of production systems," in M. Warner, W. Wobbe, and B. Brodner (eds.) *New Technology and Manufacturing Management.* Chichester: Wiley, 1990, pp. 75–85.

5. This section has also benefited from Howells, J. and M. Wood. *The Globalization of Production and Technology.* Commission of the European Communities. London: Bel Haven Press, 1993.

6. Howells and Wood. ibid.

7. Trist, E. L., G. W. Higgin, H. Murray, and A. B. Pollock. *Organization Choice.* London: Tavistock, 1965.

8. Rice, A. K. "Productivity and social organization in an Indian weaving shed: An examination of some aspects of the socio-technical system of an experimental automatic loom shed," *Human Relations,* 1953, Vol. 6, pp. 297–329.

9. Doc, E. A. and Dhorsrud. "Socio-technical approach to job design and organization development," *Management International Review,* 1968, Vol. 8, pp. 120–131.

10. "State of reengineering executive summary." CFC Index. Cambridge, MA: 1994.

11. This section also benefited from Thomas Davenport's essay, "Business process engineering: Its past, present and possible future." Harvard Business School, North #9-196-082.

12. Anil, K. Gupta. "Business unit strategy: Managing the single business," in L. Fahey and R. Randall. (eds.) *The Portable MBA in Strategy.* New York: John Wiley and Sons. 1993, pp. 100–107.

13. Schonberger, R. J. *Japanese Manufacturing Techniques.* New York: The Free Press, 1982.

14. Schonberger, R. J. *World Class Manufacturing Casebook: Implementing JIT and TQC.* New York: The Free Press, 1987.

15. Drevor, M. and Christie, I. *Manufacturers and Suppliers in Britain and Japan: Competitiveness and Growth of Small Firms.* London: Policy Studies Institute, 1988.

16. Leonard-Barton, D. "Implementation as mutual adaptation of technology organization," *Research Policy,* 1988, Vol. 17, pp. 251–67.

17. Ibid.

18. Howells, Jeremy and Michelle Wood. *The Globalization of Production and Technology,* Commission of the European Communities. London: Bell Haven Press, 1993.

19. Blackbourn, A. "The special behavior of American firms in Western Europe," in

F.E.I. Hamilton. (ed.) *Special Perspectives on Industrial Organization and Decision Making.* London: Wiley, 1974, pp. 245–64.

20. Rawsthorn, A. "Still struggling to get out of a <>," *Financial Times,* May 2, 1991, p. 23.

21. Fearon, H. E. *Purchasing Organizational Relationships.* Dange, AZ: NAPM Inc., 198

PART
IV

ROLE OF GENERAL MANAGEMENT

In this section, our attention shifts to three crosscutting processes that are important in any domain of technology: organization, intellectual-property protection, and valuation and financing of technology ventures. Truly, these are the domains of general management.

In chapter 13, we will discuss the principles of organizing for R&D, new-product development, and value-chain reconfiguration. We will also stress the importance of integration across the three domains of technology strategy.

In chapter 14, we will focus on intellectual-property protection. Although intellectual property is protected by effective product-market strategies, firms employ legal strategies that add a layer of complexity to the protection of intellectual property. In this chapter, we will enumerate the basic ideas in legal protection.

Finally, in chapter 15, we will focus on the valuation and financing of technology projects and ventures. We will demonstrate the inadequacy of the more popular financial tools in the valuation of many technology projects. We will also discuss the role played by globalization in financing of technology ventures.

CHAPTER 13

ORGANIZING FOR INNOVATION

Among the first to start a corporate research library, General Electric Corporation founded its research and development center in 1900. In that year, GE hired Willis R. Whitney, then an assistant professor of chemistry at the Massachusetts Institute of Technology, to become the director of the world's first industrial research laboratory.

Why did GE create the center? At the turn of the century, GE's principle business of electric lighting was based on inventions of Edison. The electric bar was then made of high-resistance carbon filament; however, newer inventions had made it technically obsolete. So, General Electric wanted to remain competitive in advanced products. Hence, a central research laboratory.

Charles Steinmetz, who himself had made significant contributions to the theory of alternative currents, was the first to propose a research laboratory for GE. He had paid at least one visit to Cooper Hewitt's laboratory by mid-1900. Cooper Hewitt's work posed a major threat to General Electric. Steinmetz's perception of the threat it represented resulted in his making a formal proposal for a laboratory focused on fundamental research, mainly in the field of lighting. So on September 21, 1900, he wrote the wise president, Edwin W. Rice, head of General Electric's manufacturing and engineering. Steinmetz argued that a research laboratory needed to be instituted, a laboratory that was to be kept separate from day-to-day production responsibilities.

To their credit, two other GE technical leaders agreed with Steinmetz's proposal: an attorney, Albert G. Davis, and Elihu Thomson, then a consultant to GE. Spurred by their agreement, Edwin Rice secured the approval of GE's president, Charles Coffin. Both Rice and Davis then went to Boston to discuss the post of director with Whitney.

Whitney is not the first professional scientist to be employed in American industry, or even in General Electric. Nor was his laboratory the first established by that company or its predecessors. That honor must be reserved for Thomas Edison's Menlo Park. But Edison's focus was on invention. Whitney suffered the marks of pioneering attempts by American industry to employ sci-

in keeping GE a high-technology company. Indeed, GE proudly proclaims that over the years it has consistently led all of the companies in obtaining U.S. patents, becoming in 1979 the first firm in history to pass the 50,000 page patent milestone.[1]

General Electric was not the only company to have established a central scientific laboratory. Other famous corporate laboratories created in the early 20th century included the Bell Labs of AT&T, DuPont Laboratories, Dow's laboratory, GM's technical center, and many others. Indeed, during the late 1970s, Monsanto established a scientific laboratory in its move towards biotechnology; the first fruits of this laboratory were realized only in 1996.

Setting up central research laboratories is only one way of organizing for innovation. Indeed, firms use multiple organizational mechanisms to stimulate technological innovation. As markets and technology environment change, firms rely on different mechanisms for accomplishing and sustaining innovation. Thus, management is regularly faced with organizational questions regarding innovation. Indeed, the way innovative efforts are organized has a substantial impact on their effectiveness and efficiency. Inappropriate organizational mechanisms can hamper the unleashing of creative talent, increase the cost of output, and delay results. It can increase the risk of unwelcome surprises due to external developments. Most damagingly, as we summarized in our discussion of third generation principles, suboptimal organization can lead to poor communication and indeed, strategic failures.

The design of an organization for technology management tasks is a key implementation decision. In Figure 13.1, we have reproduced the steps involved in the formulation of technology strategy. As shown in the figure, once the technology appropriation and deployment projects are chosen, a firm has three sets of implementation-related decisions: mode of implementation, organizational strategies, and intellectual property strategies. Recall that we dealt with the mode of implementation in the chapters on

FIGURE 13.1 Steps in the Formulation of Technology Strategy

•Technology Intelligence
•Profiling Competitive Domains
•Identifying Profit Sites

ENVIRONMENTAL ASSESSMENT

•Technology Inventory   •Appropriation of Technology   •Mode of Implementation
•Firms' Competitive Position   •Deployment in Products   •Organizational Strategy
•Technology Requirements   •Deployment in Value Chains   •Intellectual Property Strategy

*COMPETITIVE POSITION
OF FIRM*

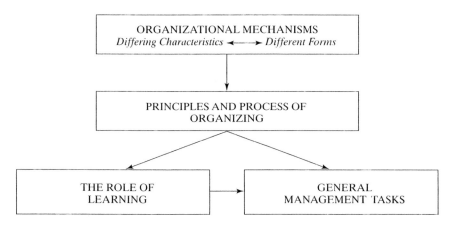

FIGURE 13.2 CHAPTER OVERVIEW

appropriation and deployment. In this chapter, we will deal with the organizational strategy. In the ensuing chapter, we will deal with intellectual property strategy.

In this chapter, we will focus on the methods by which firms organize for innovation. We will try to answer the following questions:

1. How is organizing for innovation different from organizing for other functions in business?
2. What are the organizational arrangements usually employed by firms to stimulate innovation?
3. How do firms sustain innovation in their organizations?
4. What are the key general management tasks involved in organizing for innovation?

The chapter overview is presented in Figure 13.2. The scheme of the chapter is as follows. First, we will describe how the organization design for innovation differs from the organization of operations and discuss the common organizational arrangements by which innovation is accomplished in organizations. Second, we will summarize the principles and process of designing an organization for technology management domains. Third, we will visit the role of learning, the cultural glue that helps organizations maintain high levels of innovation. Finally, we will focus on the key general management roles involved in organizing for innovation.

ORGANIZATIONAL MECHANISMS FOR INNOVATION

DIFFERENT CHARACTERISTICS OF ORGANIZATION DESIGNS FOR INNOVATION

In our discussion of appropriation and deployment of technology, it must have become clear to the reader that innovation—be it in research and development, new product development, or even changeover in value chain activity—is a nonroutine activity. Unlike

operations, the steps involved in innovation cannot be formalized or prespecified in de
tail in many cases, and there is a fair amount of uncertainty surrounding the task to b
performed during the course of implementation.

Arguably, the most significant conclusion emerging from three decades of researc
is that, because the task of innovation differs significantly from operations, the effectiv
organizational mechanisms for innovation are different from those useful for opera
tions. We will elaborate this theme in the two following sections: (1) differences betwee
research and development and operations and (2) differences between research an
development.

DIFFERENCES BETWEEN R&D AND OPERATIONS

Historically, the tasks of innovation within an organization were often associated wit
the R&D departments in a firm: The R&D departments were organized to create ir
novative products and processes, whereas operations sought predictability, reliabilit
and efficiency. One of the earliest insights in organizing for innovation was that the tas
for innovation and operations differed considerably along three dimensions: (1) natur
of feedback, (2) goal orientation, and (3) interpersonal orientation.

Nature of feedback. In traditional manufacturing environments, employees
performed more or less clearly defined tasks. The outcomes of their activities
were clearly visible to them, and the results of their efforts were available
within a short time span. Unlike manufacturing environments, the individuals
who were engaged in R&D activities performed tasks that were not clearly
specifiable. The feedback—outcomes of the activities performed by the
individuals—was ambiguous, at best. Further, there was significant delay in
the feedback, because the project might have taken several months or years.

Goal orientation. Because the tasks were clearly specified and the feedback was clear and quick, the appropriate goal orientation for operating environments was shorter: Individuals were likely to set relatively short-term
goals that served their purposes. In contrast, the appropriate time horizon in
a research and development department tended to be much longer term, because the nature of the path and the quality of the feedback were considerably ambiguous.

Interpersonal orientation. On this dimension, both manufacturing and
R&D departments resemble each other. The interpersonal orientation appropriate for employees working in these two departments tended to be impersonal. Whereas in the operating environments, individuals focused on
opinions, in the R&D departments, they focused on written information. For
the appropriate performance of activities in each of these departments, the
information needed to be objective. Hence, the interpersonal relationships in
most of these departments tend to be characterized by impersonality: based
on objective, quantifiable or verifiable information.[2]

These differences are summarized in Table 13.1. Just what do these differences im
ply for the organization of each of these departments? Two broad generalizations hav
emerged during the last two decades of research.

TABLE 13.1 Differences Between R&D and Operations

Dimension	R&D	Manufacturing	Sales
Formalization	Low Basic research Lowest	High	High Lower than manufacturing
Interpersonal Orientation	Moderate task and relationship Applied research Lower on task	High task orientation	High relationship orientation
Time Horizon	Long-term Basic research Longest	Short term	Short term Longer than manufacturing

1. The nature of the structure that is appropriate for the effective functioning of these two kinds of environments is different. Broadly, the structure should fit the uncertainty of the task performed by these environments. Hence, in the operating environment we should expect greater formality of structure, written policies, procedures, and regulations. However, such high levels of formality in organizational structure are inappropriate for R&D departments. Effective R&D departments are likely to be informal, with a limited number of written rules, procedures, and regulations, so as not to stifle creativity and innovation.

2. The leadership styles appropriate for these environments also are different. Whereas an authoritarian, command-and-control leader may be successful in the operating environment, this leadership style is likely to be dysfunctional in an R&D environment, where a participative leadership style is likely to be more effective.

In Box 13.1, we have showcased the landmark research study that honed in on these differences in structure and leadership styles appropriate for operating and R&D environments. Other studies have later confirmed many of these findings.

DIFFERENCES BETWEEN RESEARCH AND DEVELOPMENT

Not all innovation tasks are alike. In our discussion of appropriation of technology environment, we distinguished between three types of research: basic research, applied research, and development. Research—basic or applied—and development are associated with particular task environments in terms of their operational time horizon, degree of uncertainty, presence of commercial objectives, and degree of orientation in terms of the value of the research to the firm's current needs.[3] The major differences are displayed in Table 13.2. The characteristics and orientation of research and development activities will, in turn, influence the structure of these departments.

Typically, when firms begin to focus on basic or applied research, they tend to center around a research laboratory; development activity, on the other hand, can take place

BOX 13.1

THE CLASSIC RESEARCH
OF LAWRENCE AND LORSCH

Paul Lawrence and Jay Lorsch investigated the structural characteristics of organizations in three industries: six in plastics, two in containers, and two in food industries. In the plastics industry, the dominant competitive issue was the development of new products and processes. In the container business, the conditions were quite stable with limited innovation. In the food business, the markets were dynamic, but product innovations were incremental.

According to the researchers, each organization has four functional areas: marketing, manufacturing, applied research, and fundamental—basic—research. In our terminology, both fundamental and applied research fell under research and development. The researchers studied the differences among the departments along three major dimensions: formality of structure, interpersonal orientation, and time orientation.

- *Formality of structure.* Examining the organization charts and interviewing the managers in charge of the units, the researchers concluded that the manufacturing departments had the highest degree of structure, whereas fundamental research had the lowest. Sales and applied research departments fell in between the extremes, and predictably sales was higher on formality of structure.

- *Interpersonal orientation.* Using a standard paper and pencil test that measured a person's relationship and task orien-

tation, the researchers concluded that the production personnel were most task oriented and salespeople were most relationship oriented. Both fundamental and applied researchers fell between the extremes, with applied researchers scoring higher on relationship and fundamental researchers scoring higher on task orientation.

- *Time orientation.* The time orientation was measured by asking managers through a questionnaire how much of their time was devoted to activities that contributed to company profits in different future time periods. The primary orientation was evaluated to how quickly they received feedback. Both sales and manufacturing personnel reported that their activities would affect profits in the near future, usually in 1 month or less. Fundamental researchers were oriented toward much longer time horizons, often several years into the future. Applied researchers were also longer term oriented, although some aspects of their work were not so and, hence, they were classified as medium to longer term oriented.

The researchers concluded that the methods of management differed according to the departments; they also noted that general management would have to exert significant control to bring about unity of purpose among these diverse departments.

Source: Lawrence, Paul and J. Lorsch. *Organization and Environment.* Cambridge, MA: Harvard Business School Classics, 1966.

within an R&D department or with the help of product development teams. The more the focus of R&D is toward basic research, the firms begin to attract Ph.D.-level candidates who have in-depth and focus expertise in very narrow topics; when the focus is on development, firms tend to attract graduate-level employees who have broad and dispersed training. The goals, professional orientation, and work methods of these two types of individuals differ significantly:

TABLE 13.2   Differences Among Research and Development

Dimension	Research	Development
Structure	Well defined; clearly defined position	Ill defined, with overlapping responsibilities
Communications	Informal and casual	Meetings, formal systems
Work Method	Scientific and codified	Ad hoc and uncodified
Goals	New ideas	Profitable ideas
Time	Mostly internal	Externally imposed
Human Resources	Specialists, mostly Ph.D.s	Broad, mostly MBA level

- Scientists or doctoral-level employees would love to be world-renowned scientists. Their orientation is to develop new ideas as well as emphasize the quality of investigation. Their work methods are scientific and codified. The time pressure is internal—how long does it take? And the communication channels they rely on tend to be formal and fragile.
- Unlike these individuals, typical individuals in the development settings are more commercial minded: They may want to become a venture manager. They are much more oriented towards planning and research for big ideas that work, and they emphasize quantity of results. Finally, their work methods tend to be ad hoc and unsystematic. The time pressures are externally imposed—how long do we have? Finally, they tend to rely on formal systems and meetings for communication channels.

In summary, just as research and development broadly differ from operations in terms of appropriate structures, the focus of activity within research and development tends to have an influence on the appropriateness of staffing as well as structures developed by firms. These differences have prompted firms to adopt specific organizational arrangements for the execution of innovative tasks, a topic to which we now turn.

CONTEMPORARY MECHANISMS OF ORGANIZING FOR INNOVATION

Broadly, firms have employed three different organizational mechanisms for stimulating and sustaining innovation: (1) separate units for innovative activity, (2) project-based organization, and (3) new venture division. These different organizational elements have appeared in different industries and in different environmental conditions.

SEPARATE UNITS FOR INNOVATIVE ACTIVITY

The oldest mechanism for stimulating innovation within an organization, either through new products or processes, is the creation of an R&D department or a central research laboratory. Creating of such centers signals that a firm is committed to building technological capability in pursuit of competitive advantage. Specifically, such centers of innovative activity enable a firm to:

- Conduct focused near basic and applied research that is strategically aligned with the firm's efforts;

- Conduct higher and long lead-time research projects that are essential to a firm's strategic objectives;
- Establish a means to gather, synthesize, and transfer scientific and technical information from the scientific community;
- Create radically new process and product technologies that could be developed into new products and services; and
- Act as a window on science and technology developments that could pose a threat or opportunity for the firm.[4]

In a medium-sized firm with one or a few product lines, where the corporate organization is along functional lines, R&D departments are usually the mechanisms installeto stimulate innovation. We have, in our discussions of the differences between thR&D operations, illustrated how this department needs to be managed somewhat diferently from the ongoing operations of the company. In a medium-sized firm, the department focuses primarily on development and less on basic research.

Large firms, be they multidivisional or operating in high-technology industries such electronics or pharmaceuticals, occasionally start a central research unit to focus on basor near basic research efforts. Recall the GE case presented in the opening vignette. For eample, during the 1970s, Monsanto decided to enter biotechnology, then an industry in thvery early phases of development. Monsanto's vehicle for entry into the biotechnology setor was through the setting up of a corporate research and development facility in St. Loui

Given the focus on research, corporate research facilities usually support a criticmass of scientists over a relatively long period of time. Scientists and engineers who arattracted to corporate research facilities are not interested in the potential profitabilitof their work but are more intrigued by the scientific problem itself. As a consequencthey are likely to leave for a more stable internal environment, should they view theiprojects being frequently canceled due to lack of funding. In short, setting up a corporate innovative center requires a long-term commitment of substantial resources on thpart of the firms.

When does a company set up a corporate research center? Because these researccenters consume significant amounts of resources over an extended period of time, decision to set up the center should be anchored in sound economic reasons. We maidentify at least four major strategic reasons:

1. When firms seek leadership in product introductions (that is, they have early-to-market products), and they seek to use technical excellence as a basis for building competitive advantage;
2. When competitors have established their own corporate laboratories, thus signaling an era of technological change in the industry;
3. For conducting long-term product and process development, especially when various divisions are focused on shorter medium-term results; and
4. When there are economies of scale in consolidated research, whereby the various divisions share the common technologies.[5]

As we stated earlier, corporate R&D centers can be very expensive, because they require sustaining a critical mass of scientists for a fairly long period of time. Thus, it matake 7 to 20 years for the results to be realized from the establishment of a corporatresearch center.[6] Also if the scientific efforts are not coordinated, a research facility ca easily move away from the corporate goals, as illustrated in the case of Xerox's PARC facility, summarized in our discussion of technology appropriation.

PROJECT ORGANIZATION

When the focus of innovation is on creating new products or embedding new technologies in the value chain, they usually take the form of projects. Although projects can be initiated on an ad hoc basis, many organizations use project organizations to sustain innovation. Projects require team efforts, because they need to bring together technical talent from diverse disciplines (as in the case of building the space shuttle) or functions (as in the case of the cross-disciplinary teams in new product development processes).

Although it is important to keep technical creativity focused on business goals, the leadership should encourage technical excellence and creativity as a way of stimulating innovation during the performance of the project. This requires that the leader should provide both technical and managerial stewardship. Effective project leaders are technical personnel who have first demonstrated outstanding technical ability and then demonstrated managerial ability.[7]

There are two forms of permanent project organizations utilized by firms: (1) matrix organizations and (2) quasi-structure.

Matrix Organization   During the late 1950s and 1960s, the project organization called the *matrix structure* evolved within the aerospace industry, partly stimulated by the Department of Defense (DOD). Having been enormously impressed by the performance of the DOD project control system during the 1950s, DOD began to require that all defense contract proposals be accompanied by a similar project control system. A matrix more easily handles project control than a functional organization, because matrix managers can focus exclusively on project progress without worrying about developing technical skills. Because of the great technological requirements for completing major long-term aerospace projects, functional excellence could not be sacrificed. This meant that an organization that shared a dual focus had to be developed. Matrix organization was a natural response.

Matrix structures involved a dual authority structure. Here, the subunits are configured so that the employees within functional departments have two bosses: a functional boss and a project boss. Both bosses have traditional rights as supervisors to assign tasks, evaluate work, and influence the rewards and promotions their subordinates receive. In this way, matrix structures were a genuine structural innovation, because they departed from the rigid hierarchical vertical structures particularly seen in larger organizations until that time. Matrix structures are configured on typical organizational charts with dotted-line relationships, in which an engineer, for example, would report out of his or her functional engineering group to a project organization. "Dotted-line" relationships have become a shorthand for one's matrix boss, in addition to one's functional boss.

Matrix organizations have been used not merely in aerospace industries, but in other industries such as pharmaceuticals, insurance, law firms, hospitals, universities, and government agencies. Many of these later matrix forms were created for technology or product development or, in many cases, to manage perpetual change. In Figure 13.3, we have illustrated a matrix organization.

Quasi-structure   For many high-technology firms, where eternal innovation seems the price of survival, an organizational form recently termed *quasi-structure* has superseded

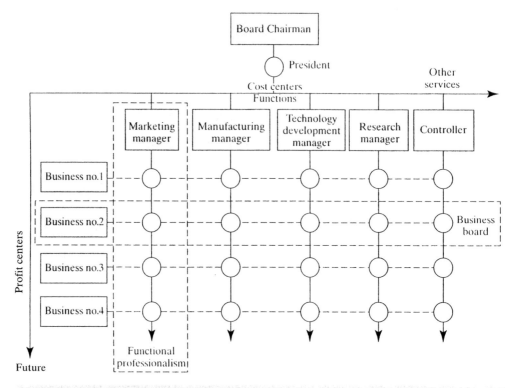

FIGURE 13.3 MATRIX ORGANIZATION

Source: Reprinted by permission of *Harvard Business Review* from "How the Multidimensional Structure Works at Dow-Corning," by William C. Coggin, January-February 1974. Copyright © 1974 by the President and Fellows of Harvard College; all rights reserved.

matrix structures. Firms such as Intel, National Semiconductor, Texas Instruments, Hewlett-Packard, and Motorola have discovered that matrix organizations (with the dual reporting relationships) often tend to create more problems than they solve. Hence, they have reverted to an organizational form with clear organizational reporting relationships. These firms maintain a formal structure as well as a quasi-formal structure. There are four major characteristics of quasi-structures:

1. Formal structure is actively used to guide the employees in firms, for delineating their responsibilities, defining the connections between positions and people, and in general, for ensuring that attention is allocated to appropriate tasks. This set of explicit reporting relationships maintains internal predictability in the midst of frequent product and manufacturing process changes.

2. However, formal structure was continually redefined; innovating organizations reorganize frequently, and employees have come to regard structural change as a part of life in these companies.

3. The process by which this reorganization is accomplished is substantially participative. Although the members of the top-management team may

sketch the major skeletal changes in the structure, the group and the division levels detail the reorganized structure jointly, thereby with lower level managers closer to the impacted groups.

4. In addition, these organizations employ quasi-formal structures, which consist of an extensive use of committees, task forces, teams, and dotted-line relationships. The quasi-formal structures resemble formal structure, because they are formally sanctioned by the organization and explicitly recognized as legitimate. However, they change with an even greater frequency than formal structure as problems are resolved or new problems appear. Also, these groups are relevant-based and problem-focused and transcend the formal structural boundaries that might otherwise impede problem solving.[8]

NEW VENTURE DIVISION

Radically new products sometimes coming out of R&D departments or central research units have no obvious organizational locations. To alleviate this problem, firms often create a new venture division (NVD). NVDs decouple the new ventures from the established spheres of business operations and seek to move their development to a place of some sufficiency. The NVD provides an internal-to-the-firm environment in which new business opportunities can be explored, incubated, turned into projects, and provided with the opportunity to demonstrate economic viability. At that point, they should presumably be more readily integrated into existing divisions or be established as new operating divisions of a firm.

Generally, NVDs are staffed and managed differently from the regular operating organization. NVDs allow more entrepreneurship and attract more risk-takers; the rewards are based on the success of the venture, not on predictable milestones as in an operating division. Table 13.3 summarizes these differences.

The three modes of organization—project organization, central research units, and new venture divisions—vary along a number of dimensions.

- In theory, project organization—be it traditional matrix or quasi-structure—attempts to accomplish efficiency and flexibility simultaneously. However, traditional matrix structure is difficult to manage given the dual authority structure and the lack of clarity of relationships within the structure. Thus, it may accomplish only satisfactory levels of customer focus and business integration.
- Quasi-structures, on the other hand, may accomplish greater customer focus and integration; however, they are difficult to implement, because they need to be supported by very strong cultures and long-standing history of practice in their respective firms.
- Unlike the project organization, central research units are less efficient and flexible; however, they are relatively easier to manage, given the clarity of relationship. However, significant managerial attention is required for the central research unit to develop a customer focus, as well as to be integrated with the business operations.
- Finally, the new venture departments achieve a high degree of customer focus and business integration; however, they are relatively less flexible than the other two forms: They can focus only on the markets for which they are conceived.

TABLE 13.3   Differences Between NVD and an Operating Division

Dimensions	NVD	Operating Division
Span of Control	Wide	Narrow
Job Descriptions	Loose	Detailed
Controls	Loose	Tight
Planning Frequency	Frequent	Infrequent
Planning Detail	Low	High
Time Frames	Long	Short
Performance Criteria	Innovation and risk-taking	Current profits
Compensation	Deferred	Current
Size of Reward	Large	Small

Source: Reprinted from "New Venture Units: Use Them Wisely to Manage Innovation," by Christopher Bar? *Sloan Management Review,* Summer 1998, vol. 29, no. 4, p. 39, by permission of publisher. Copyright 1988 b? Sloan Management Review Association. All rights reserved.

We will now discuss the key factors that a firm needs to consider in choosing organiz? tional mechanisms for stimulating innovation.

PRINCIPLES AND PROCESS OF ORGANIZING

The problem of organization during execution may be broadly broken into two: th? choice of organizational mechanism and the challenge of maintaining linkages acros? the organization.

THE CHOICE OF ORGANIZATIONAL MECHANISM

A number of alternative mechanisms are available to firms in their efforts to organiz? for innovation. Indeed, many large firms use multiple mechanisms to accomplish thei? objectives of innovation. Further, the same firm may rely on a different mix of mecha? nisms over time, as environmental conditions and strategic contexts change.

The choice of organizational mechanism at any point in time reflects a comple? trade-off that involves consideration of environmental, strategic, and economic factor? We will discuss four major factors: (1) environmental factors, (2) strategic contex? (3) economic considerations, and (4) factors related to globalization.

ENVIRONMENTAL FACTORS

Throughout the book, we have emphasized the role played by both market and technology related factors in the management of technology. These factors also determine, to a larg? extent, the appropriate organizational forms for stimulating innovation. For exampl? central research units have generally been used when the technology is in the relativel? early stages of development, and the rate of market development is relatively slow. I? contrast, new venture divisions are more applicable when the technologies in which th? firm is operating are relatively mature. The principle underlying the choice of organiza? tional mechanism can be stated simply:

> The organizational mechanism should be sensitive to the more salient of the two environmental sectors: market and technology.

Thus, when the technology sector is more salient, that is, technological developments lead to later market development, corporate research centers seem to be appropriate; when market development is the salient activity, especially in the case of mature technologies, new venture divisions can serve as appropriate organizational mechanisms. When both market and technology assume saliency, the traditional matrix may be appropriate, especially when the rate of change in the technology and market sectors is relatively moderate. Quasi-structures seem to have amassed in high-technology industries where, in addition to technology, the market dynamics have been relatively fast. Figure 13.4 summarizes our discussion of the relationships between environmental factors and organizational mechanisms.

STRATEGIC CONTEXT

Corporate strategy of a firm has a major influence in the overriding organizational framework that it adopts for its functioning. There are two ways in which corporate strategy influences the mechanisms for organizing for innovation:

1. Innovative activity is only one of the activities performed by a firm. Thus, it is profoundly influenced by the overall corporate structure of a firm, which in turn is shaped by the firm's corporate strategy. For example, the evolution of many firms into M-form (divisional structures) structures has led to restructuring of R&D in one of the two ways. First, it has led to the decentralization of R&D, with R&D being relocated within the various divisions; second, it has led to an elaboration of corporate research centers where it was necessary to have specialized research departments to mesh with the particular needs of different product divisions. Indeed, the process of diversification has led the organizational choice in the case of innovative activity to be much more complex, because diversification opened many possible avenues for competing on technology and, hence, of designing R&D structure and functioning.

2. The corporate strategy has a profound influence on the mix of research that a firm decides to carry out—basic, applied, or development. The kind of

FIGURE 13.4 CHOICE OF ORGANIZATIONAL MECHANISM

	MARKET SALIENCE		
	High	Medium	Low
High	Quasi-Structures Separate unit for innovative activity	Matrix Separate unit for innovative activity	Ad hoc project teams Separate unit for innovative activity
TECHNOLOGY SALIENCE **Medium**	NVD Separate unit for innovative activity	Matrix/NVD R&D units	Ad hoc teams
Low	Strategic business unit	Ad hoc teams	Ad hoc project teams

research not only determines how it is managed (see Table 13.2) but also where the innovative activity is performed. Thus, product development may be carried out in an operating division and basic research in a central facility. Process development may, in turn, be carried out in close proximity to the manufacturing centers of the firm.

ECONOMIC CONSIDERATIONS

Large multidivisional corporations, or large companies with multiple product line wrestle with the question of where they should locate their innovative activity: Shoul the activity be decentralized and located in the divisions, or centralized and located i a central research facility?

Centralization   Centralization often yields internal benefits in research:

- First, centralization takes advantage of economies of scale and scope, associated with large operations.
- Second, any center of science requires scientific instruments, facilities, and specialist staffs; the attended indivisibilities may be associated with the minimum research laboratory sizes.
- Third, central facilities usually result in good internal communication links with the R&D function.
- Fourth, researchers can pursue original ideas and not be involved in short-term operational problems.
- Fifth, some may be able to reduce the risk of competitor copying or leap-frogging in key research fields by protecting individual property.
- Sixth, the central research labs may be able to create a well-established network with universities, government, and other support agencies.[9]

However, these benefits of centralization need to be weighed against the benefits c decentralization.

Decentralization   In general, decentralization has the advantage of good external cou pling and communication linkages with other organizational functions:

- First, R&D is likely to be focused on the actual needs of the business and operational units.
- Second, informal communication between R&D and other corporate functions is likely to result from a decentralized structure.
- Third, the decentralized structure may allow a firm to tap into scarce pools of scientific and technical talent.
- Fourth, the decentralized research centers may enable competitive surveillance in specific localities, especially in overseas locations.
- Fifth, by establishing R&D units in selected regions, a firm may be able to tap into government aid and incentives.
- Finally, the R&D may be more responsive to various local market needs.

In recent years, developments in communication links (e-mail, videoconferencing, etc and the perception by many companies that innovation should be more commerciall oriented have caused the companies to consider a more decentralized pattern of inno vative activity. One arena in which this has become salient is the decision to locate in novative activity overseas, a topic to which we now turn.

ESTABLISHMENT OF OVERSEAS RESEARCH UNITS

Concurrent with the globalization of research and development activity, major multinational corporations have begun to locate research facilities abroad. Two primary reasons behind these moves are the ability to tap into pools of scientific and technical labor and the attraction of a low-cost research basis. For example, Hoechst's establishment of overseas R&D activities was the result of their desire to benefit from the balance of foreign chemists and pharmacologists as well as the need to be part of those communities at the forefront of pharmaceutical research.[10] Similarly, many U.S. multinationals located research in the United Kingdom partly because of its low cost as well as for other factors, such as acclaimed scientific reputation and similarity in cultural background.

The three ways in which R&D laboratories have been set up abroad are:

1. The direct establishment of a research facility on a site on its own or with existing corporate facilities;
2. Indirectly through the acquisition of an overseas company; and
3. As an evolutionary process associated with overseas manufacturing and other facilities.[11]

Although initially the need to recruit talent and to reduce the cost of R&D spurred firms to locate R&D overseas, increasingly the question of centralization versus decentralization has to be reopened, as research activities expand considerably overseas. There are several reasons that prompt coordination of activities across research sites or, in general, greater centralization: to avoid duplication and improve efficiency; to increase information and resource sharing to enable a wider research reach; or to allow research to be undertaken on a split or a multisite basis. Increasingly such coordination is accomplished by two means:

1. Cross-border teamwork. This involves the research staff located at two or three different countries working on the same project. For example, Ericsson's design teams based in Europe have worked over several design centers.
2. Use of information and communication technologies. The increasing use of shared databases, electronic mail, media conferencing and workstation technology has enabled companies to explore ways in which R&D can be undertaken between separate sites.[12]

Although the communication and information technologies are only being marginally taken up by companies in R&D, the use of these technologies is expected to offer considerable operational and strategic benefits to firms as they coordinate innovative activities across multiple locations.

MANAGING LINKAGES

In addition to the linkages at the strategic level, operating-level linkages among the three domains of technology activity—appropriation and deployment in products and processes—need to be established and managed for the fruits of technology strategy to lead to value creation. The linkages are crucial both for in-house activity and externally sourced activities.

IN-HOUSE ACTIVITY

As shown in Figure 13.5, two sets of linkage are especially important: (1) linkages b tween appropriation and deployment and (2) linkages between deployment in produc and processes:

> Linkage between appropriation and deployment. When a separate unit for innovative activity is created, as in the case of a central research unit, the fruits of innovation may be related to the core business of a firm to varying degrees. As the relatedness decreases, firms typically engender greater difficulty in transferring the results of innovation to the operating organization. As we have seen, NVD was one mechanism by which some *large* firms have coped with the challenge of linkage. The factors that determine the nature of the linkage are operating relatedness and the strategic importance of the product to the firm. A variety of mechanisms are available for the transfer of innovation to operations, as shown in Figure 13.6.
>
> Linkage between product development and manufacturing and commercialization. Even within current markets, when a firm plans to launch a new product, significant alterations in value chains may be needed for commercialization. In general, the more innovative a product, the more the need for different processes within manufacturing and marketing. Whereas incremental product innovations may require only marginal changes in the current manufacturing and marketing, innovative products may require major realignment of existing operations and marketing and, in some cases, development of processes separate from the ongoing operations.

EXTERNAL SOURCING

Even when external sourcing is employed, firms need to manage the linkages betwee various domains of technology management.

FIGURE 13.5 OPERATING LINKAGES

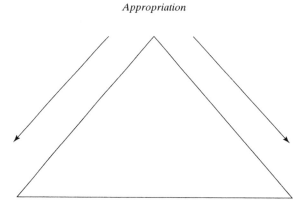

Appropriation

Deployment in Products ⟶ *Deployment in Value Chains*

Strategic Importance

	High	Medium	Low
High	Direct Integration	"Micro" New Ventures Department	Nurturing and Contracting
Operational Relatedness	New Product Department	NVD	Contracting
Low	Strategic Business Unit	Independent Business Unit	Spin-off

FIGURE 13.6 LINKAGES BETWEEN APPROPRIATION AND DEPLOYMENT

Source: From Burgelman and Sayles, "Organization Designs for Corporate Entrepreneurship." Copyright © 1984, by The Regents of the University of California. Reprinted from the *California Management Review,* Vol. 26, No. 3, p. 161. By permission of the Regents. All rights reserved.

- Critical to the acquisition of technological capabilities or new product ideas from outside is a clear understanding of technical characteristics of the acquisition, in addition to the commercial potential. For example, in the case of pharmaceutical companies that license drugs, the technical evaluation should constitute a major activity in the decision to license in a specific chemical or biological entity. Similarly, the operating organization should be readied to accept the innovation from outside.
- In the case of value chain deployment, ongoing monitoring is needed to minimize the risks of nonexecution, profit skimming, and the loss of intellectual property.

In summary, the organization design for implementation should focus on the organizational mechanism as well as the linkages to the operating organization. However, implementation involves human interfaces, and this necessitates attention to the softer side of the enterprise. Firms that have developed a culture of learning have an advantage in execution, even if appropriate structural mechanisms are in place.

CHARACTERISTICS OF CONTINUOUSLY INNOVATIVE ORGANIZATIONS

Consider the story of Microsoft, presented in Box 13.2. Although Microsoft has been the success story of the 1980s and the 1990s, there is no guarantee that Microsoft will have continued success. Nor is there any guarantee that Microsoft will be able to

---

BOX 13.2

MICROSOFT AND THE CHALLENGE
OF SUSTAINING INNOVATION

Microsoft is the world's undisputed leader in computer operating systems and software. Microsoft strategy from its founding to the present is a textbook example of superior understanding of economics and competitive drive of an evolving industry. In particular, by 1985, Bill Gates was correct in recognizing that the future would see a mass market for computers designed for personal use; software, not hardware, would offer the greatest opportunities for profit; and that the advantage would begin by setting the standards in operating systems and applications.

There is a fit between Microsoft strategies and the characteristics of the emerging PC industry. Bill Gates and his executives placed great importance on achieving dominance to make possible per-unit margins and high absolute R&D spending. Thus, Microsoft prices, markets, licenses, and supports products worldwide. It offers huge discounts on the assumption that it is far better to collect a small sum for each copy of the product if lower prices lead to exponential growth in the market. Over time, these and other tactics have given Microsoft overwhelming leads in such key markets as programming languages (BASIC), character-based operating systems (MS-DOS), graphical operating systems for the PC (Windows), and backstop application seats (Office). Selling millions of copies of Windows and Office also helped OLE (object linking and embedding) into a de facto standard for applications developers.

Microsoft's founders had the opportunities to create a favorable industry structure. The company has not been content to lead the structure but has cultivated it carefully. Clearly, Microsoft owes much of its success to developing an installed base of products and cus-

tomers, which has established its products as the industry standards. By being the standards provided, Microsoft maintains sales and profits in the short term, but more importantly it is able to generate new markets based on these standards.

Microsoft has established and taken advantage of connections between operating systems and applications. Furthermore, they bundled applications into suites of products such as Microsoft Office. This packaging created barriers and additional costs to customers who might want to purchase competing products. Microsoft has always employed successive pricing as part of its volume strategy to establish itself in mass markets. In addition, Microsoft has negotiated long-term contracts with hardware manufacturers to create barriers to other software providers. From 1988 until 1994, Microsoft employed "per-processor licensing" for operating systems. Rather than charging a license fee based upon the volume of the units actually shipped with MS-DOS, Microsoft offered PC manufacturers especially low royalty fees if they paid something for each computer they shipped, regardless of whether the hardware company bundled each machine with MS-DOS. This provided a strong disincentive for hardware manufacturers to bundle competing products and was an effective barrier to DR-DOS, IBM's OSx2, and IBM PC-DOS. Whatever the intent behind this practice, Microsoft products became so popular that hardware companies were reluctant to bundle any other software, and they usually wanted the volume discount. Their processing licensing is one of the practices Microsoft agreed to review as part of the 1994 consent decree with the U.S. Justice Department.

Source: From Laverty, K. J. "Lessons from Microsoft, A Model for Strategy and Leadership?" *Strategy and Leadership,* March/April 1996, Vol. 34, No. 2, pp. 44–48.

"Synch and stabilize" describes Microsoft's approach to product development. The entire product development process helps individual developers frequently synchronize their work with other members of the team and stabilize their products in increments as components evolve. Among the features of this process is that development and testing occur in parallel and that product specifications are permitted to evolve, rather than being fixed at the outset. These practices resemble concurrent engineering and incremental bills used in other firms. Microsoft uses lots of things. They adhere to the philosophy that small teams work best, but large complex projects require coordination among large groups of professionals. Microsoft has modularized projects so that the individual components of features can be the responsibility of small, relatively autonomous teams; very few but extremely rigid groups accomplish coordination across the teams. Interdependencies across teams are therefore reduced to a few critical points. With these exceptions, members of a team can function with energy and commitment of completely autonomous groups in a much smaller company.

If Microsoft is to continually grow and evolve, it must employ dynamic capabilities to build new core competence in areas beyond which it currently has expertise. However, the question really is unanswered: Can Microsoft sustain its advantages?

Indeed, Microsoft has its share of weaknesses and faces continued threats from the environment.

- For one, Microsoft has relied primarily on incremental innovations: Windows 95 still has some MS-DOS embedded within it.

- Second, continued growth will be a constant challenge, for there is always the danger of going beyond the ability of processes to coordinate. Bill Gates' dominant role in the company is a source of concern: There is a lack of obvious successors, although Bill Gates has indicated that he plans on another decade of leadership.

- Third, the company remains vulnerable to competition from more specialized firms that are better at inventing new technologies or introducing innovative products to new markets. These companies have included Intuit, with Quicken and personal finances software; Novell, with office networking; and Lotus, with notes for office grouping.

- Another threat to Microsoft lies in its ongoing problems with the U.S. Justice Department.

- Perhaps the greatest threat to Microsoft is that the part of technological development is leading them into areas where they will not be able to rely upon the advantages they have enjoyed in the past and at present. Microsoft must be able to continue to grow and evolve and to build new core competencies in areas that are, for now at least, up for grabs.

sustain the levels of innovation that it has achieved in the past. We have argued that technology is the engine of economic progress, both for nations and for organizations. That is in the generic sense; continual acquisition and deployment of technology (knowledge, attitudes, and skills) becomes the central characteristic of continuously innovative organizations.

In our discussion of innovation, we summarized the importance of structures that promote innovation. We also emphasized the role played by learning: learning from doing; learning from customers, suppliers, and other firms; and even learning from competitors through intelligence and imitation. This implies "culture," a soft side that needs to be developed along with formal strategies and structures within firms.

What are some of the cultural traits of innovative organizations? We may identify five cultural traits of such organizations:

1. *Enthusiasm for knowledge.* Perhaps the most important characteristic is the respect and encouragement for accumulation of knowledge as a legitimate undertaking. Both managers and people who are involved in the organization are curious: They are information seekers. They believe that perhaps the fundamentally most important skill is the ability to learn.

2. *Drive to stay ahead in knowledge.* This means staying knowledgeable about the latest developments in technology. This is not necessarily being first to commercialize technology. However, it reflects a commitment to stay ahead of capabilities. This drive to access the latest knowledge keeps people listening, another absolutely critical skill.

3. *Tight coupling of complimentary skill sets.* This refers to simultaneous attention to both developing deep reservoirs of knowledge and skill in special capabilities and having a plan to diminish the boundaries between disciplines. Tight coupling requires a respect for a knowledge basis other than one's own and enables flow of knowledge from research organizations into product development, whether the researchers reside inside a firm's laboratories or are outside entities such as thinktanks or national laboratories.

4. *Alteration in activities.* This reflects the comprehension of the fact that activities are never completely perfected. There is a continual reexamination of assumptions through experimentation and further divisions. There is a "try it and learn it" attitude to counteract the arrogance of excellence.

5. *Higher order teaming.* There is continual self-examination to discover insights within one activity that may be transferred to other activities within the firm. For example, firms often use project teams as mechanisms to generate higher level process learning.[13]

Continuously innovative organizations go through cycles of both incremental and evolutionary change. In recent years, General Electric and Hewlett-Packard have reformed themselves through continual refinement of their systems and structures. On the other hand, other organized firms such as Cabbott, IBM, or Intel have made evolutionary changes to reorient themselves to realities of the marketplace. Whether incremental or evolutionary, continuously innovative firms pay significant attention to replenishing their skills and capabilities. The soft side does not emerge naturally: It is the result of leadership.

ROLE OF LEADERSHIP

The decisions related to the technology strategy and the choice of organizational mechanisms for innovation are usually the domain of general management. The general management exercises leadership by building a culture of learning. Thus, the general management task involved in successful implementation of organizational mechanisms extends beyond the decisions related to the choice of organizational mechanisms. It includes, broadly, four additional tasks: (1) definition of purpose, (2) choice of leadership, (3) managing transition, and (4) resource allocation.

DEFINITION OF PURPOSE

Any organizational mechanism should be sustained by a clear definition of purpose. Because an organization has many alternatives to choose from at any given point in time, factions within an organization coalesce around their preferred alternative. However, organizational mechanisms can succeed only if they are sustained by a clear purpose. It is the collective responsibility of the general management to maintain the clarity of objectives behind the choice of specific organizational mechanisms.

CHOICE OF LEADERSHIP

One of the fundamental ways in which the general management of an organization expresses its will is through the selection of individuals to head the organizational mechanism for innovation, be it the research and development department, a project team, or a central research laboratory. In the domain of technology management, the individual selected for a leadership position should fulfill three conditions:

1. The individual should be able to deal with business as well as with technology-related issues;
2. The individual should have a stellar technical reputation so that he/she is credible to his/her subordinates; and
3. The person should have sufficient political acumen so that he/she can be credible among the general management so as to obtain sufficient funds to carry out important projects.

MANAGING TRANSITION

These organizational mechanisms are likely to change over time as the corporate strategies and the markets change. The general management role extends to managing the transition between one mix of organizational forms to another. Successful transitions do not occur overnight and require patience for successful implementation. It is important that general managers support the transitions through communication as well as their own behavior.

RESOURCE ALLOCATION

Finally, any organizational mechanism will succeed only to the extent that requisite resources are made available: people, time, and money. It is the general management's responsibility to ensure that sufficient resources flow to the organizational mechanism.

❖ CHAPTER SUMMARY

In this chapter, we summarized the critical issues involved in the choice of organizational form for implementing technology management. Organizational mechanisms for innovation differ from operations in the nature of feedback, goal orientation, and time frames. In general, R&D units deal with ambiguous feedback, ambiguous goals, and have long-term orientation. Further, the units that are research focused tend to have codified procedures and hire specialized PhDs; their time frames are internally imposed, and they bet on great ideas. Development units are driven by market pressures, hire generalist employees, and are focused on profitable ideas.

Firms have typically employed three organizational mechanisms for innovative activity. The first, a separate unit for research and development, may take the form of an R&D department, or central research unit. Second, they use project teams—either permanent, as in the case of a matrix, or ad hoc, as in quasi-structures. Finally, they ma employ a new venture division as a mechanism for transferring the fruits of researc to markets.

Environmental and strategic considerations enter the choice of the organization: mechanisms. In addition, firms always have to find a balance between centralization an decentralization of the innovative activity. They also have to manage the linkages b tween the innovative unit and the operating organization.

In addition to structural mechanisms, a culture of learning enables the full e: ploitation of innovation. The culture consists of enthusiasm for knowledge, drive to st ahead of knowledge, tight coupling of complementary skill sets, alteration in activitie and higher order learning. This has to be reinforced by leadership through clear defin tion of purpose, choice of leaders, managing transition, and resource allocation.

❖ NOTES

1. Wise, G. "A new role for professional scientists in industry: Industrial research at General Electric 1900–1916," *Technology and Culture,* Vol. 21, 1980, pp. 408–415; General Electric, "Descriptive material on the corporate research laboratories." 1980, Schenectady, New York.

2. Lawrence and Lorsch. *Organization and Environment.* Cambridge, MA: Harvard Business School Press, 1966.

3. Howells, J. R. "The location of research and development," *Regional Studies,* 1984, Vol. 18, pages 13–29.

4. Rosenbloom, R. S. and A. M. Cantrow. "The nurturing of corporate research," *Harvard Business Review,* January-February 1982.

5. Rosenbloom, R. S. and A. M. Cantrow. op. cit.

6. Rosenbloom, R. S. and A. M. Cantrow. op. cit.

7. McDonough, E. S., III, and R. M. Kinnunen. "Management control of new product development projects," *IEEE Transactions on Engineering Management,* 1984, Vol. EM-31 No. 1, pp. 18–21.

8. Schoonhoven, C. B. and M. Jelinek. "Dynamic tension in innovative high technology firms: Managing rapid technological chang through organizational structure," in Bon Glinow, M. and S. Mohrman. (eds.) *Manag ing Complexity in High Technology Organt zations,* London: Oxford University Press, 1990, pp. 90–118.

9. Howells, J. and M. Wood. *The Globalizatio of Production and Technology.* op. cit.

10. Dunning, J. H. *Multinationals, Technology and Competitiveness.* London: Unwin Hyman, 1988.

11. Behrman, J. N. and Fischer, W. A. *Overseas R&D Activities of Transnational Companie* Cambridge, MA: Oeigeschlager, Gunn & Hain, 1980.

12. Howells, J. R. "Going Global: The Use of ICD Networks in Research and Development." New Castle, England: University of New Castle Dyne, New Castle PICD Cent Working Paper Five, 1992.

13. Laverty, K. J. "Lessons from Microsoft, A Model for Strategy and Leadership?" *Strategy and Leadership,* March/April 199 Vol. 34, No. 2, pp. 44–48.

14. Leonard-Barton, D. *Wellsprings of Knowledge.* Boston, MA: Harvard Business Scho Press, 1995.

INTELLECTUAL PROPERTY STRATEGY

As the Intel architecture emerged as the dominant design in microprocessors, Intel decided to keep newer versions of the chip proprietary, prosecuting any firm that violated its intellectual property. In keeping with this decision, it filed a suit against NEC, claiming that NEC had violated the copyright on the microcode for its 8088 and 8086 microprocessors. The case was first tried in 1986, but it was retried on appeal by NEC in 1989, when Judge William Gray ruled that NEC had violated Intel's 8088 and 8086 microcode. The ruling meant that the microcode for the next generations of Intel microprocessors could be copyrighted. Further, the firms to which Intel had licensed (e.g., AMD) earlier versions of its microprocessors could not build later generations without new licenses.

Fighting NEC in court sent the message to the microchip community that Intel would use legal means to protect its intellectual property. Intel made this threat even more credible when it subsequently filed lawsuits against AMD and won. Thus, in 1990 Intel filed a lawsuit against AMD, alleging violation of its trademark when AMD used the numbers 386 in the naming of its part AM386. In 1991, Intel filed another lawsuit against AMD, claiming two transgressions: AMD had violated the copyright for its 386 microcode and for the control program in 386's PLA.

Despite Intel's success in defending its intellectual property, some firms entered the Intel microprocessor architecture market. AMD, Cyrix, NextGen, IBM, and Chips & Technologies, at one time or another, produced Intel-compatible microprocessors. Consequently, in addition to protecting its intellectual property, Intel had to seek other ways to protect its profits from these entrants. In 1985, it got out of the DRAM business to concentrate on microprocessors. With the focus on microprocessors, the firm was able to develop new generations of microprocessors with dramatically higher complexity and order of magnitude increase in performance.

What is of more significance is that Intel was able to introduce these more complex and better performing processors at a faster rate than it had the slimmer and slower earlier generations (see the table). For example, the P6 (Pentium Pro) would be introduced only 3 years after the Pentium and would be about twice as complex and twice as fast. This compared favorably with the 486, which was introduced 4 years after its predecessor, the 386. Some generations of microprocessors were introduced before sales of the earlier generation had peaked.

Intel's Rapid Introduction of New Generations of Microprocessors

Processor	Description	Number of Transistors	Design Start	Formal Introduction
286[†]	16-bit	130,000	1978	February 1982
386	32-bit	1.2 million	1982	October 1985
486	32-bit	1.2 million	1986	April 1989
Pentium	32-bit	3.1 million	1989	March 199.
Pentium Pro	64-bit	5.5 million	1990	March 1995
786	64-bit	8 million	1993	1997
886	64-bit	15 million[‡]	N/A	N/A
1286	N/A	1 billion[‡]	N/A	N/A

*Million instructions per second.

[†]This is actually the 80286, but usually just called the 286. The 80386 and 80486 are similarly abbreviated.

Intel has also been working hard to establish a brand name identity. Although the microprocessor has been responsible for most of the performance improvements in personal computers, this processor has been buried in the black box that is the personal computer and, with it, Intel's identity. That is, until 1991, when Intel went directly to end users, advertising heavily and promoting its Intel Inside logo in numerous technical and business magazines and on national television. It also promoted its logo by offering personal computer makers discounts on chips if they displayed the logo on the personal computers they sold.

The landmark ruling that microcode can be copyrighted practically prevents competitors from imitating Intel's designs. This makes it very difficult for competitors to design a microprocessor that can run all the software that PC users have accumulated over the years, and which only runs on an Intel architecture, of which its microcode is a critical part. Customer switching costs to another machine are high. Because microprocessor design is very complex, trying to circumvent the microcode makes the task of designing it even more formidable.[1]

A s illustrated in the story of Intel, firms undertake efforts to protect the value tha they derive from technology management activities. Appropriation of technology (its deployment in products and value chains involves knowledge assets that form th basis on which firms create value. Loss of that knowledge to competitors erodes th value that can be appropriated by the focal firm. When the competitive domains are a tractive, competitors have strong incentive to threaten a firm's position by appropria ing the firm's knowledge. If the focal firm does not protect against the loss of knowledg it is likely to dissipate all the benefits of its technology management activities.

In this chapter, we will outline the actions that firms take to protect the outputs of their knowledge management activities. Specifically, we will answer questions such as:

1. What is intellectual property, and what is intellectual property strategy?
2. What are the mechanisms by which firms protect their intellectual property?
3. How has globalization influenced the intellectual property strategy?

In Figure 14.1, we have reproduced the steps involved in formulating a technology strategy. As shown in the figure, intellectual property strategy supports a firm's management of technology in its various domains: appropriation, deployment in products, and value chains.

Firms protect their knowledge assets through technology- and market-related actions and through legal means. For example, Intel created newer products and undertook several actions in the marketplace, both individually and through collaborative arrangements. Indeed both technology- and market-related actions should be a centerpiece of the strategy for protecting knowledge assets. Thus, as we have underscored in this book, during the formulation of technology strategy, there should be significant interfaces between technology managers and business strategists.

In addition, a significant component of a firm's strategy for protecting knowledge assets involves the legal system. The crafting of intellectual property strategy should, thus, interface strategists and corporate attorneys. Since technology- and market-related actions have been extensively dealt with in the book, we will simply summarize them in terms of their role in intellectual property protection. In this chapter, we will highlight the central role played by legal strategies.

Figure 14.2 presents the chapter overview. First, we will define intellectual property. Second, we will focus on the generic means by which firms protect their intellectual property. Third, we will outline the technology- and market-related actions by which intellectual property is protected. Fourth, we will deal in greater detail with the legal system of intellectual property protection in the United States. Fifth, we will summarize the challenges created by globalization and the emerging remedies. We will conclude with managerial implications and a chapter summary.

FIGURE 14.1 STEPS IN THE FORMULATION OF TECHNOLOGY STRATEGY

•Technology Intelligence
•Profiling Competitive Domains
•Identifying Profit Sites

ENVIRONMENTAL ASSESSMENT

| *Strategic Diagnosis* | *Formulation of Technology Strategy* | *Crafting an Implementation Approach* | *Execution* |

•Technology Inventory   •Appropriation of Technology   •Mode of Implementation
•Firms' Competitive Position   •Deployment in Products   •Organizational Strategy
•Technology Requirements   •Deployment in Value Chains   •Intellectual Property Strategy

COMPETITIVE POSITION
OF FIRM

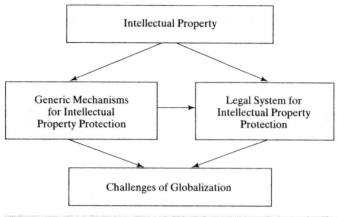

FIGURE 14.2 CHAPTER OVERVIEW

INTELLECTUAL PROPERTY

We have seen that the knowledge assets of a firm span the entire technology deve
ment continuum from tacit knowledge to the knowledge that is physically embodie
products and processes. These knowledge assets are often termed *intellectual capital*
though the major contributors to the intellectual capital are intangible, they ca
thought of in terms similar to the tangible assets of the firm. *Intellectual property* is
gal concept that refers to components of the intellectual capital that may be prote
under the law.

Just like physical assets, intellectual capital enables firms to derive profits fro
activities. For example, technical knowledge can be deployed in products to gain c
petitive advantage. Alternatively, knowledge of specific processes may enable a fir
reduce the cost of operations, thereby enhancing its profitability. Or, a firm may lic
its intellectual property to others and earn fees from the licensee. Finally, a firm can
its technology and profitably recoup the funds that it invested in the developmer
that technology.

Because intellectual capital is the key to competitive advantage and profitabili
a free-market economy, competitors will try to appropriate it for their own ends. A
may lose its intellectual property to its competitors in three ways:

1. *Imitation.* Imitation is a serious threat to any competitive advantage, be it
   based on intellectual capital or otherwise. Unless imitators face severe costs
   of imitation through retaliation, or legal action, they can benefit from the investments made by the innovators, without incurring the costs of innovation.
2. *Obsolescence.* Competitors can themselves engage in innovation and produce a superior product or service that acts as a substitute to a firm's products or services.
3. *Infringement or theft.* Competitors can infringe or worse, steal, a firm's
   knowledge assets. For example, when Kodak entered the instant camera

market in the 1980s, Polaroid filed a patent infringement suit against it, effectively driving Kodak out of the market. Industrial espionage also made headlines when Hitachi and Mitsubishi stole technological secrets from IBM.

The need for protection arises, therefore, in order for a firm to control its knowledge assets and thus maintain its advantage. The *intellectual property strategy* of a firm thus refers to the approach that it takes to seal its intellectual assets from the forces of imitation, obsolescence, or infringement and theft.

GENERIC MECHANISMS FOR INTELLECTUAL PROPERTY PROTECTION

Generally, a firm tries to protect its intellectual property in three ways:

1. A firm may undertake actions in the product market to prevent competitors from eroding its competitive position through imitation. For example, it may invest in advertising, develop a system of licensing with exclusive arrangements with the licensees, or shut out the distribution channels to potential imitators.
2. It may focus on continuous innovation to thwart imitation and obsolescence. Continuous innovation enables a firm to keep one step ahead of the competition by introducing, for example, a series of new products.
3. The firm may seek legal protection through patents, copyrights, trade secrets, or trademarks. When a firm seeks recourse in the legal system, it relies on the intellectual property system of a country to defend or protect its intellectual property from competitors.

Figure 14.3 summarizes the three major mechanisms of protection.

FIGURE 14.3 GENERIC MECHANISMS FOR INTELLECTUAL PROPERTY PROTECTION

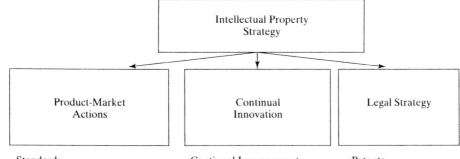

PRODUCT-MARKET ACTIONS

Strategic action in the product markets may thwart imitation and obsolescence.

IMITATION

For competitors to be able to imitate, four sets of requirements need to be met: (1) recognition, (2) diagnosis, (3) resources, and (4) incentives. These four requirements provide
arenas of action by a focal firm to thwart imitation:

1. *Recognition.* Competitors must be able to identify the intellectual capital
   that forms the basis of a firm's competitive advantage. Thus, a firm may take
   steps to prevent the leakage of information about specific intellectual capital to the marketplace. This information then becomes unavailable to competitors, thus preempting their recognition of the intellectual capital. For
   many process innovations, secrecy may be more effective than patents as a
   means of protecting the intellectual property.[2]
2. *Diagnosis.* The competitors must be able to figure out how the intellectual
   capital can be constructed. Why has Hewlett-Packard been successful in
   new product development? How can one replicate the things they do in order to imitate? For many would-be imitators, this is not a trivial problem.
   The more the sources of performance, the more difficult to replicate. In general, any capabilities that reside in the coordinated efforts of organizational
   members, or what we have labeled software-dominant innovations, are difficult to imitate.
3. *Resources.* The would-be imitators should have the requisite resources to
   replicate the intellectual capital. To the extent that a firm's technology or
   know-how is based on resources that are not easily accessible, the more difficult it is to imitate the knowledge.
4. *Costs and incentives.* The cost/benefit calculus must be such that the competitors see profit from imitation.

In addition to obscuring the information or basing the knowledge on hard-to-get assets,
a focal firm may try to preempt the resources being available to competitors or make
it costly for them to imitate. These actions are clearly visible to competitors. Actions
undertaken by a firm that are visible in the marketplace include:

- *Engaging in the battle for standards.* The battle for standards during the era
  of technology emergence is an important one for many firms. Once the standards are established, all firms need to conform to the standard for them to
  be viable competitors.
- *Erecting entry barriers.* Creation of entry barriers such as access to distribution outlets, thwarting test marketing efforts, or establishing significant brand
  recognition may enable a firm to prevent the loss of intellectual capital.
- *Limiting pricing.* A focal firm may forego some short-run profits by pricing
  the product or service below what can be borne by the market in order to
  discourage the competitors or to signal to them that the firm has definite
  cost advantage over them.
- *Making collaborative arrangements.* A network of firms may support each
  other for mutual benefit, each protecting its intellectual capital. Microsoft's

success against Apple, to some extent, is the result of building collaborative arrangements with independent software vendors, which made the Microsoft system de facto standard among the operating systems.

Table 14.1 summarizes these requirements and the generic mechanisms by which firms combat each competitor move.

OBSOLESCENCE

Strategic actions may also prevent the erosion of the intellectual capital through obsolescence. When a superior substitute emerges, a firm may decide to target specific market segments or find other uses or missions for its product so that it can continue to appropriate value from the intellectual capital that it owns. As we saw in our discussion of disruptive technologies (chapter 11), existing customers may find it difficult to change over to the new product, even if it is superior, because of the costs of switching. Introduction of products with additional features attractive to the customers or appropriate marketing actions such as pricing may preempt the customer migration to the new product.

CONTINUAL INNOVATION

A second way in which firms prevent the loss of intellectual capital is to seek to upgrade or replenish it through continual innovation. This may occur in several ways:

1. *Incremental innovation.* Because there is significant potential for improvement during major stages of the *S*-curve of innovation, firms may try to capture the requisite learning through continual improvement. This makes it more difficult for other imitating firms to catch up in product or process performance.
2. *Product cannibalization.* A firm may preempt its competitors through successive generations of superior products that cannibalize the firm's own products. Intel did this in microprocessing through successive generations of faster chips.
3. *Product platform and product family.* Competing from a product platform enables a firm to be cost-effective. The imitator will have to suffer a cost disadvantage and often becomes noncompetitive in terms of price and features.

TABLE 14.1 Requirements for Imitation and Isolating Mechanisms

Requirements for Imitation	*Isolating Mechanisms*
Identification	• *Obscure* superior performance
Diagnosis	• Rely upon multiple sources of competitive advantage to create *causal ambiguity*
Resource acquisition	• Base competitive advantage upon resources and capabilities that are *immobile* and *difficult to replicate*
Incentives for imitation	• *Deterrence*—signal aggressive intentions to imitators
	• *Preemption*—exploit all available investment opportunities

Source: Grant, Robert. *Contemporary Strategy Analysis.* Cambridge, MA: Basil Blackwell, 1991.

4. *Radical innovation.* Through significant investment in R&D, a firm may come out with a radical innovation based on a totally new technology to overtake its own product. Unlike cannibalization, the technology is fundamentally different from the one deployed in current products.

Neither product-market actions nor continual innovation address infringement or the by competing firms. Hence, in addition, a firm will have to protect itself against uneth cal and sometimes illegal actions of competitors. This requires a legal strategy, i.e., th privileges granted by the legal system. In the following section, we will focus on the le gal protection component of the intellectual property strategy. We will first summariz the U.S. intellectual property system and then discuss some of the challenges brougl about by the globalization of the technological environment.

U.S. INTELLECTUAL PROPERTY SYSTEM

The U.S. intellectual property system is designed to correct an inherent defect in th free-market system. In free-market economies such as the United States, competitio is cherished, because competitive effects are advantageous to the consumer and soc ety, at least at first glance. However, left to itself, free competition may dampen th motivation for investing money and resources in the development of intellectual prop erty, the basis of profitability for many firms. Why go to the expense when everyone els can just take a free ride on a firm's efforts when it is done? In such an environment, firm may logically conclude that it is better to simply wait for some other individual t develop new products or processes. Therefore, if firms are allowed to compete freel without regard to property rights, the net result may be that creativity is stifled to th detriment of social welfare. Only with property rights enforced by law would a firm b willing to undertake such efforts. This justification for property rights conforms to th philosophical teachings of John Locke: Put simply, people must be motivated to perforr labor, and the best way to encourage and reward it is through property protection.[3]

In the United States, there are four major forms of intellectual property protectior (1) patents, (2) trade secrets, (3) copyrights, and (4) trademarks. Table 14.2 summarize the distinctive features of each of these forms of intellectual property protection.

THE U.S. PATENT SYSTEM

The U.S. patent system is governed by the Patent Act, first established in 1790 althoug it has been amended on numerous occasions, thereafter. The Patent Act entitles a per son to a patent for an invention if that invention is novel, nonobvious, and a prope subject for protection. Patents are given to the creators of innovations or the origina tors of novel and nonobvious ornamental designs. The term for patent protection in th United States begins when a patent is granted and lasts for 17 years for a useful inver tion and 14 years for a design. The duration of a patent is intended to achieve a delicat balance, providing an inventor sufficient incentives to undertake the risks of develop ment while returning the invention as early as possible to the public domain, where fre competition can begin. During the life of the patent, the details of the inventions ar fully disclosed to the public for scrutiny, thus increasing the likelihood that competitiv

TABLE 14.2 U.S. Intellectual Property System

Form of Protection	What It Protects	Standards for Protection	Length of Protection
Patents			
—Utility	Inventions	Useful, novel, nonobvious	17 years after patent issues
—Designs	Designs	Ornamental novel, nonobvious	14 years after patent issues
Trade Secret	Information	Secret, valuable	Unlimited
Copyright	Expressions in tangible media	Original	Life of author plus 50 years
Trademark	Identifying symbols	Capable of distinguishing source of goods	Unlimited

Source: From Burgunder, Lee B. *Legal Aspects of Managing Technology.* Cincinnati, OH: South-Western Publishing Co., 1995, p. 9.

improvements will hit the market either immediately or on the expiration of protection (or sooner) if the invention is approved.

There are three tests to be met for a product or design to be patentable: (1) novelty, (2) nonobviousness, and (3) proper subject.

There are three tests of novelty. The first is that a person may not stake a claim to an invention that was publicly available before the person invented it. The second is that if two or more persons allege that they are entitled to patent rights in the United States for the same development, then priority will be given to the person deemed to have invented it first. The third guiding principle, based on the rapid disclosure of rationale of patents, is that there are reasons not to delay too long after the completion of an invention before filing for a patent.

The standards for nonobviousness require that an invention must be something more than that which would be obvious, in light of publicly available knowledge, to one who is skilled in the development field.

The proper subjects for patent protection vary between inventions and design. Insofar as inventions are concerned, the guiding principle is that all things made by human ingenuity are patentable, but naturally occurring things are not. The concept is at the center of the debate over the patentability of computer programs and biotechnology. In the case of design patent, product designs may be patented if they are primarily ornamental. In this regard, important questions are arising in the computer field, as for instance the patentability of screen displays.

In contrast to copyrights and trade secrets, an inventor must undertake an arduous examination and approval process to receive a patent application. The inventor initiates the process by filing a patent application with the Patent and Trademark Office (PTO). The most important components of the application are:

1. The description of the invention, which must be sufficient to enable one skilled in the art to practice it;

2. An illustration of the best part of carrying out the invention known to the inventor at the time of filing the application;
3. All information known to the inventor that may bear on the patentability of the invention, such as pertaining to its novelty or its obviousness; and
4. The precise aspects of the invention claimed for patent protection.

All information presented to the PTO is treated in confidence until a patent is granted at which time it becomes publicly available. Currently, it usually takes from 1½ to over 3 years for a patent to be issued, depending on the type of invention and its complexity

Once gained, the patent entitles the patent holder to take action against infringers of the patent. Infringers include those who would make, use, or sell the invention in the United States without permission. Thus, the pay-off from successful patent application is that the courts will enforce the right to exclude others from enjoying the fruits of one invention. It does this in two ways:

- By issuing an injunction that prohibits further infringement; and
- By ordering that compensation be paid for the infringing acts.

Compensation may include royalty for the sales made by the infringer, lost profits by the patent holder, and the interest lost due to the delay between the time of the lost profit and the time at which the payment was made by the infringer. In many cases of willful infringement, the compensation may include punitive awards and the patent holder's attorney fees. These amounts could be staggering; for example, Kodak was ordered to pay $909 million to Polaroid for its infringement of instant photography patents.[4]

THE U.S. COPYRIGHT SYSTEM

The U.S. copyright system is used to prevent others from copying creative expression that are fixed in tangible media, so that the authors will have sufficient incentives to share their talents. Items such as books, sculptures, movies, and paintings clearly may be protected by copyright. By the terms of the copyright statutes, one can obtain copyright protection for original works of authorship fixed in any tangible medium of expression

> Courts have interpreted originality to mean that the work must be original to the author. By that interpretation, a work is original to the extent that it manifests some personal creative effort. This is true even if the resultant work turns out to be exactly like one that is already existing and publicly distributed. The word *original,* therefore, normally does not present a problem for one contemplating copyright protection as long as the work encompasses at least some very minimal amount of personal creativity.
>
> The phrase *works of authorship* comprises a wide array of categories. One may receive copyright protection for works that are literary, musical, dramatic, or choreographic. All of the original works such as movies and sound recordings are also subject to copyright protections. In addition, pictures, graphics, and sculptures may be protected through copyright to the extent that they are not inseparable components of useful products.

Probably the most peculiar feature of copyright is that it protects only expression. This is an important dividing line between copyrights and patents. If one wants protection for a product idea, process, or system, then one must look to the patent system rather than copyright to receive protection. Copyright, on the other hand, never protects ideas; it covers only ways of expressing them.

Copyright owners may choose from a number of remedies:

1. **Court-ordered injunction.** Court orders may require the infringer to stop engaging the infringement activity.
2. **Actual damages.** Although hard to prove, the copyright owner may sue for actual damages and the infringer's profits.
3. **Attorney's fees and court costs.** If the registration was timely, the copyright owner may be eligible to receive attorney's fees and court costs.
4. **Criminal penalties.** It is a criminal offense to infringe a copyright willfully and for private gains.

TRADE SECRET PROTECTION

A third, very important, component of the intellectual property system is trade secret protection. Trade secret laws protect valuable information that is not publicly known and that is subject to measures to preserve its secrecy. Similar to patents and copyrights, the rationale for the protection is to stimulate the development of new inventions, techniques, and other creations, as well as to preserve high moral standards of corporate conduct. According to the Uniform Trade Secrets Act (UTSA), first devised in 1979, a trade secret holder is entitled to remedies when the trade secret has been misappropriated. According to the UTSA, there are three essential components to a trade secret.

The first concern is the type of information that may construe a trade secret. Trade secret protection may apply to engineering information, formulas, customer information and lists, sources of raw materials, manufacturing processes, design manuals, operating and pricing policies, marketing strategies, equipment and machinery, computer hardware and flow charts, and drawings and blueprints. Clearly, trade secret protection covers a much wider area of business interests than does patent protection, which is limited to use for processes, machines, and compositions.

The second aspect of a trade secret is that it must be economically valuable. The cost is not known or easily ascertained by those who might benefit from it. Thus, it is not enough to have the information; it must be valuable because it provides an advantage not directly available to those in the industry.

The third requirement for trade secret status is that the information be subject to reasonable measures to preserve its secrecy. Such a requirement implies that if one does not recognize the importance of secrecy to the value of information and, thus, does not take reasonable steps to maintain that value, then there is no reason to expect the law to come to the rescue.

The UTSA prohibits misappropriation of trade secrets. The key elements to misappropriation are whether:

- One acquired the trade secret by improper means,
- One handled the information in a way that breaches his/her duty to maintain secrecy, and
- There was sufficient awareness about the violation of trade secret rights.

High-technology companies have found trade secret protection to be an important com
ponent of their intellectual property strategy. The trade secret protection is especiall
valuable when it deals with the evolution of intellectual property through employee
The dispute between Apple Computer and its founder, Steve Jobs, made headlines whe
Jobs formed a new company called NeXT after leaving Apple. In that situation, whic
was finally settled, Apple alleged that Steve Jobs had improperly been using Apple re
sources and proprietary secrets to form the new company and its products.

The trade secret holder is entitled to three types of monetary remuneration fo
misappropriation:

1. The amount needed to compensate the trade secret holder for the losses
   due to misappropriation;
2. The illegal riches made by the misappropriator by virtue of unlawful use or
   disclosure; and
3. Criminal remedies, although this may vary from state to state in the
   United States.

TRADEMARK PROTECTION

The fourth, and final, major arm of the intellectual property system is trademark pro
tection. Trademarks provide legal exclusivity through property protection of identifi
cation symbols and characteristics. Unlike patents, trade secrets, and copyrights, th
goal of trademark policies is to combat unethical marketing practices, protect goodwi
and enhance distributional efficiency. Normally, to determine if a business behavio
amounts to unfair competition, three conditions are to be met:

1. The product or services of the first company must employ a symbol or
   device—a trademark—that consumers use to identify its source;
2. A competitor must use a symbol or device that is so similar that consumers
   might confuse it with that of the first company; and
3. The competitor must have adapted the symbol or device having known, or
   under circumstances that it should have known, about the prior use by the
   first company.

The most important remedy for unfair competition is usually an injunction, preventing th
competitor from using the identifying trademark. Trademark protection for high-technol
ogy goods is an integral part of the marketing and distribution strategy. With complex tech
nological products such as computers, it is not always possible to recognize the value c
superior components or processes until after the product is used for some time. Howeve
if the product carries an identifier exclusively associated with resources consistentl
known for high standards, then a consumer who desires that quality can easily find it. *In
tel inside* is a classic example of the assurances that a trademark can provide the consume

As in the case of patents, copyrights, or trade secrets, infringements of trademark
is associated with a set of remedies:

1. The most powerful remedy available is injunction, i.e., prohibition against
   the infringing use.
2. Trademark infringement may also lead to monetary relief, including the infringer's profits, actual damages suffered by the owner or trademark holder,
   and the costs of bringing suit.

TABLE 14.3   Remedies for Infringement

Form of Protection	Losses	Types of Damages Damages	Court Fees
Patents	Profits from lost sales Royalty on infringer's sales Price erosion and prejudgment interest	Treble damages if willful	Attorney's fees if willful
Trade Secrets	Profits from lost sales Unjust enrichment by the infringer	Double damages if willful	Attorney's fees if willful
Copyrights	Court-ordered injunction Infringer's profits	Statutory damages	Attorney's fees
Trademarks	Infringer's profits	Actual damages	Costs of bringing suit

3. Especially in the case of imported goods, the U.S. Customs Service may seize the infringing merchandise.

Patents, copyrights, trade secrets, and trademarks are the major components of the intellectual property system in the United States. Table 14.3 compares four legal mechanisms for intellectual property protection.

There are certainly other laws and statutes that protect most specific aspects of intellectual property in various high-technology contexts. The Semiconductor Chip Protection Act is a case in point. In addition, many high-technology industries such as computers, telecommunications, and biotechnology are specifically regulated by various government agencies.

Firms typically do not invoke the legal mechanisms as the only method of protection of their intellectual property. Most often, they use a combination of competitive strategy, continuous innovation, and legal mechanisms to protect intellectual property. In Box 14.1, we have illustrated the case of Sun Microsystems, in terms of how they use legal mechanisms to protect their products.

BOX 14.1

SUN MICROSYSTEMS

In 1987, when Sun Microsystems introduced the first workstation using its SPARC RISC technology, it also announced that it would license the technology to anyone who wanted it. It was literally giving away the technology it had developed, instead of using its intellectual property protection rights as a barrier to entry. It backed this promise in 1989 with the formation of SPARC International Inc., an independent corporation with responsibility for supporting any firm that wanted to produce Sun workstation clones.

Sources: 1) Ould, A. "SPARC Clone Market Is on the Rocks," *PC Week,* July 22, 1991; 2) *UNIX World,* October 1991; 3) Afuah, Allan. *Innovation Management,* 1998, New York: Oxford University Press.

Box 14.1 (*continued*)

The table gives the data about the market share of Sun relative to its competitors in the SPARC market. Sun has maintained a very high share of the SPARC market, in spite of cloners. To understand why, we need to look at what it did on the entire value chain:

1. Product-market actions. Although Sun allowed other firms to clone its workstation design, downstream along the value chain, it protected its brand name reputation and distribution channels. Some customers were not willing to forgo Sun's reputation and brand name for the expected lower prices of cloners (which turned out to be not very low, compared to Sun's). Sun also offered excellent service, which cloners could not. Cloners also found out that it was

not easy to convince Sun's distributors to carry their workstations, because Sun took advantage of the relationships that it had forged with its distribution channels and customers prior to licensing out its technology.

2. Continual innovation. Upstream in R&D, Sun was able to make advances that some cloners could not. Sun was often the first to introduce newer generations of workstations and did so more often than the cloners. Sun was also able to offer discounts to customers that cloners could not always match.

As seen from Sun's experience, firms usually take a variety of measures, sometimes in the product markets and sometimes through continual innovation.

TABLE 14.1.1

| | *Market Share Within SPARC Camp (%)* | | | |
	1989	*1990*	*1991*	*1992*
Sun	98.90	97.70	93.68	92.18
Tatung	0.00	0.75	1.39	1.67
Fujitsu	0.00	0.00	0.00	1.57
CompuAdd	0.00	0.00	0.00	1.07
Axil Workstation	0.00	0.00	0.00	0.85
DTK Computer	0.00	0.00	0.00	0.64
Aries Research	0.00	0.04	0.05	0.37
Solbourne	0.89	0.95	2.49	0.31
Opus Systems	0.00	0.36	1.00	0.21
Others*	0.21	0.21	0.39	1.13
Total	100.00	100.00	100.00	100.00

*Others include Matsushita, Solflower Computer, Integrix, Twinhead, CMS Computing, Mobius Computing, Vertos Technology, and Samo America.
Source: Data from IDC. Company reports.

THE CHALLENGES OF GLOBALIZATION

The globalization of the technological environment has brought complex challenges fc firms managing their intellectual property. According to one account, exports of inte lectual property assets from the United States have more than doubled during the pa;

8 years and now account for more than 25 percent of total U.S. exports.[5] By some estimates, the inadequate international protection for U.S. patents, trademarks, and copyrights cost the U.S. economy $18 billion in sales and 250,000 jobs every year. Further, the sales losses for the U.S. software industry alone were at over $9 billion, suggesting that software piracy is the norm in a host of countries.[6]

Deterrence of international pirating activities is usually accomplished through unilateral, bilateral, and multilateral means.

Unilateral steps. A unilateral action can be defined as an independent step by a country, such as the United States, to protect its citizens from following piracy activities. Largely, there are two sets of unilateral measurers in the United States: (1) the patent, copyright, and trademark laws and (2) customs service regulations to block the importation of goods violating U.S. intellectual property rights. Unilateral options are usually the easiest to implement but tend to be the least effective, especially for companies with widespread international marketing activities.

Bilateral agreements. Bilateral agreements are promises between two nations to conduct their policy affairs in certain ways. Bilateral agreements, such as the one between the United States and the Soviet Union in 1990, have successfully resulted in intellectual property reform overseas. Another bilateral tool used by the U.S. government to induce changes in intellectual property policies of foreign countries is based on Section 301, a provision of the U.S. Trade and Tariff Act. The section allows the U.S. trade representative, with the approval of the President, to take retaliatory actions against any foreign country that condones unreasonable or discriminatory trading practices that unduly burden U.S. trade or foreign investment. Bilateral agreements are, thus, an improvement over unilateral options, but they lead to a patchwork of varying international standards.

Multilateral methods. Multilateral approaches reach beyond bilateral agreements in that many countries together agree to conform to a policy framework. Currently, there are several important multilateral agreements pertaining separately to patents, copyrights, and trademarks. Table 14.4 shows a list of the most important multilateral agreements affecting the protection of intellectual property.

The international system of intellectual property protection is, thus, evolving through a combination of unilateral, bilateral, and multilateral arrangements. We now point out some of the key implications of globalization for the four forms of intellectual property protection widely used in the United States.

PATENT PROTECTION

The patent policies throughout the world, especially among the major developed countries, share a fair amount of commonality. For example, all require that an invention be new and nonobvious to be patentable. Countries, however, have different policies regarding subject matter, length of protection, interpretation of claims, requirements for novelty, confidentiality of applications, and priority between different inventors, to name just a few.

TABLE 14.4 Major International Multilateral Agreements

Form of Intellectual Property	Agreements
Patents	Paris Convention
	Patent Cooperation Treaty
	European Patent Convention
Copyrights	Berne Convention
	Universal Copyright Convention
Trademarks	Paris Convention
	Madrid Arrangement
	Madrid Protocol
Comprehensive	GATT
	Treaty of Rome and Maastricht Treaty
	NAFTA

Source: From Burgunder, Lee B. *Legal Aspects of Managing Technology.* Cincinnati, OH: South-Western Publishing Co., 1995, p. 26.

Substantially, two major differences between the patent policies of the Unite States and those of other nations may prove to be significant for a U.S. inventor. Onl three countries in the world—the United States, Jordan, and the Philippines—rely o the first-to-invent priority standard. All other nations use a first-to-file system. Secon there are significant differences in the way many other countries handle the issue c novelty. In the United States, there is a 1-year grace period for filing after certain trig gering events such as a sale or publication. Many other countries are not so lenien Some nations deny patent protection when triggering events occur within their borde at any time prior to filing. Japan is somewhat like this, although it has a 6-month perio for certain limited acts of the inventor, such as making a demonstration at a trade shov Other countries are even more stringent, barring patent rights if triggering events hav occurred anywhere in the world prior to filing.

In the patent arena, the most important multilateral accords are the Convention c the Union of Paris, for the protection of industrial property (Paris Convention); th Patent Cooperation Treaty; and the European Patent Convention. The members of th Paris Convention, totaling around 80 nations, have agreed that inventors from foreig signatory countries should be afforded the same rights under a member's patent law as enjoyed by the citizens of that member. Both the Patent Cooperation Treaty, signe by more than 55 countries, and the European Patent Convention, signed by 17 Euro pean nations, provide for certain procedural advantages in filing patent application in member nations. Under the European Patent Convention, an inventor seekin patent protection in Europe may file one application with the European Patent Offic (EPO), which will certainly examine the application under the terms of the conven tion. If the patent is granted, the patent rights are effective in all member countrie designated in the application. Under the Patent Cooperation Treaty, an inventor ca file an international application with an appropriate receiving office, designating th member country in which the patent is sought. Both the U.S. PTO and the EPO serv as receiving offices.

COPYRIGHT

International copyright policy is dominated by two multilateral arrangements: the Universal Copyright Convention and the Berne Convention. The fundamental principle of both copyright conventions is the same: Foreigners from signatory countries must be granted national treatment under the copyright laws of any other member country. Historically, the United States had shunned the Berne Convention. Indeed, its reluctance to alter its system of copyright protection caused the United States to create the alternative Universal Copyright Convention. According to the Universal Copyright Convention, participants must comply with certain formalities for protection, such as the copyright notice and possibly registration. An important tenet of the Berne Convention, however, is that the enjoyment and exercise of copyright shall not be subject to any formality. On October 31, 1988, the Berne Convention established itself as the dominant multilateral agreement when the United States became its 79th participant.

TRADEMARKS

The trademark laws vary considerably among various countries. Unlike in the United States, where priority is based on use (or intent to use), in most countries trademark rights are granted to the first person to file for registration. Further, in many countries the protection does not depend on use or even intent to use. Thus, in many countries the first to file their trademark registration obtains trademark rights, no matter whether that person has used or intends to use the mark within those markets.

Certain international developments now occurring should soon facilitate international trademark protection for high-technology companies with U.S. trademarks. For example, the United States is a member of the Patent Convention, which applies to trademarks as well as patents. A second multinational agreement is the Madrid Agreement, joined by 29 commercial nations (but not the United States), which facilitates the procedures for filing trademark applications in the signatory countries in a way similar to the Patent Cooperation Treaty. The third major multilateral trademark accord is the Madrid Protocol. The Madrid Protocol is a direct descendent of the Madrid Agreement but is expected to have wider appeal because it deals with certain objections that some nations, such as the United States, have had with the Madrid Agreement.

GRAY MARKETS

The challenges of intellectual property protection, created by the globalization of the technological environment, may be illustrated in the case of "gray markets." A gray market is developed when a foreign-manufactured good, bearing a valid U.S. trademark, is imported into the United States without the permission of the U.S. trademark code. There are four main ways in which a gray market is created.

1. A domestic U.S. trademark holder authorizes an independent foreign manufacturer to use its trademark, and the manufacturer agrees not to export to the United States. A gray market is created when the foreign manufacturer exports to the United States or when a third party purchaser exports to the United States.

2. An independent foreign manufacturing company sells the U.S. trademark rights to a domestic U.S. company. A gray market is created when the foreign manufacturer exports to the United States or a third-party purchaser exports to the United States.

3. A foreign manufacturing company is affiliated with a domestic U.S. company that owns the U.S. trademark rights. The foreign firm incorporates the U.S. subsidiary to distribute products to the United States, and the U.S. subsidiary owns the U.S. trademark rights. A gray market is created when the foreign manufacturer or third-party purchaser exports to the United States.

4. The domestic U.S. trademark owner establishes a foreign manufacturing subsidiary or a division. A gray market is created when a third-party producer exports to the United States.

The problem with the gray market is that an entity other than the firm is taking advantage of the firm's investments and promotions, distribution, and services within the United States without sharing in those costs. Their free riding could have a detrimental impact on the firm's goodwill, especially if there any differences in the product, such as with warranty terms. On the other hand, the firm did authorize the manufacture and sale of these goods with the trademark and exercised control of the manufacturing process. Thus, these goods are clearly different from counterfeit goods made by unscrupulous parties. The question is whether the sale of these products in the United States violates the firm's trademark rights, allowing it to either block the importation or to sue for infringement.

MANAGERIAL IMPLICATIONS

Protection of knowledge assets should be an important support activity in technology management.

1. All technology management activities should be insured against potential intellectual property loss.
2. Technology managers should look for ways to insure against the loss of intellectual property in product market actions, innovation, and legal mechanisms.
3. Thus, intellectual property protection should be worked out in conjunction with business managers as well as corporate attorneys.

❖ CHAPTER SUMMARY

Protection of the knowledge assets that constitute the basis of competitive advantage is a central support activity in management of technology. Intellectual property is a legal concept that provides legal protection from infringement of knowledge assets from an owner. The loss of knowledge assets may come about through imitation, obsolescence, infringement, and theft. Generically, firms protect against the loss of knowledge assets in three ways: through actions in the product markets, by continuous innovation, and through legal action.

Product-market actions protect against imitation and, sometimes, obsolescence. Imitation requires that the imitators identify the asset, figure out how to imitate, have the resources to do so, and have enough incentives to engage in imitation. The focal firm can keep information secret, anchor the competitive advantage in difficult-to-get resources, preempt acquisition of requisite resources, or make imitation less attractive through pricing and other actions.

Continual innovation may also counteract the pressures of imitation and obsolescence. This could be achieved through incremental innovation, product cannibalization, deploying the concept of product family, and radical innovation.

Four means of legal protection are available to firms: patents, copyrights, trade secrets, and trademarks. Patents protect product designs and processes; copyrights protect forms of expression; trade secrets protect migration of sensitive information to competitors; and trademarks protect brands and logos. In each of these cases, the courts allow for damages for infringement.

The international system of intellectual property protection is evolving through a combination of unilateral, bilateral, and multilateral arrangements. The patent policies throughout the world, especially among the major developed countries, share a fair amount of commonality. In the patent arena, the most important multilateral accords are the Convention of the Union of Paris, for the protection of industrial property (Paris Convention); the Patent Cooperation Treaty; and the European Patent Convention. International copyright policy is dominated by two multilateral arrangements: the Universal Copyright Convention and the Berne Convention. Finally, the trademark laws vary considerably among countries.

❖ NOTES

1. *Innovation Management* by Allan Afuah, copyright © 1997 by Oxford University Press, Inc. Used with permission of Oxford University Press.

2. Levin, R. C., A. K. Klevorick, R. R. Nelson, and S. G. Winter. "Appropriating the returns from industrial research and development," *Brookings Papers on Economic Activity* (1987): 3, pp. 793–796.

3. Hughes, J. "The Philosophy of Intellectual Property," *Georgetown Law Journal* (1988): pp. 330–339.

4. Polaroid Corp. v. Eastman Kodak Co., 16 U.S.P.Q. 2d (BNA) 1481 (D. Mass. 1990).

5. McCarroll, D. "Who's Bright Idea?" *Time*, June 10, 1997, p. 44.

6. "Software Pirates Wreak Worldwide Plundering," San Luis Obispo County Telegram-Tribune, June 10, 1993.

CHAPTER
15

PROJECT VALUATION AND FINANCING

After he wrecked his ultralight airplane, John Hunter had to make a decision to rebuild his plane, or to improve the design. Hunter saw an opportunity to enhance the structure and features of his plane. With that, Hunter turned his hobby of 15 years into a full-time job and hopefully a profitable company.

He spent almost 4 years reading and studying engineering books to gain the technical knowledge he needed to begin the redesign of his plane. Hunter found an engineering firm in Lawrence, Kansas, the DAR Corporation, which provided critical assistance and engineering expertise. The DAR Corporation owns cutting-edge engineering software that Hunter and his company, Dream-Wings, have relied heavily upon for the design and testing phase of the new ultralight aircraft.

"The state of Kansas provided many incentives for me to locate my company here," Hunter said on moving his family to Lawrence from Maryland. "Here, I am closer to the engineering expertise of the DAR Corporation, and people and resources from the aviation industry."

Hunter has experienced many challenges along the way. First, he is faced with producing a plane that is light, affordable, and stronger than those already on the market. But one of the biggest challenges Hunter has encountered is finding the funding to keep going.

"I have found that without adequate funding, everything takes longer and everything costs more," said Hunter.

Kansas Technology Enterprise Corporation (KTEC) has been able to assist Hunter with this problem. DreamWings has received $99,891 from the Applied Research Matching Fund. The company also has received funding from the Kansas Innovation Corporation (KIC), Lawrence, through their seed capital fund. DreamWings also has received technical assistance from KTEC's National Institute for Aviation Research in Wichita.

DreamWings recently displayed its design at the Oshkosh Air Show. According to Hunter, they received an overwhelming response from potential customers. "People would walk past our plane and do a double-take. It was as if we had magnets that were drawing people in."

So, what makes these planes so attractive? First, there is the sleek, eye-catching design, backed by the versatility and easy construction of the plane.

These planes are built with advanced technology, yet remain affordable. Hunter said their unique shapes don't just look beautiful, they provide great in-flight visibility and superior handling.

"I am surprised that no one else in the industry is doing this," Hunter said. "I had a potential customer tell me, 'finally, someone is taking ultralights into the twenty-first century.'"

DreamWings had its first planes ready to fly in a few short months, and the company started shipping the planes and filling orders in 1999.[1]

As illustrated in the vignette, John Hunter, the owner of DreamWings, had discovered a niche market in ultralight planes as a result of his hobby and experiences with small airplanes. He had developed sufficient technical knowledge, and he had assistance from DAR Corporation for designing and developing the aircraft. However, starting Dream-Wings was not easy. As Hunter himself points out, securing adequate financial resources to start the firm was a difficult task to accomplish. Fortunately for him, Hunter was able to get financing from Kansas Technology Enterprise Corporation (KTEC) and Kansas Innovation Corporation (KIC)—both quasi-government agencies. In addition, he was also able to get assistance *in kind* from DAR Corporation: cutting-edge engineering software that would otherwise have cost Mr. Hunter several thousands of dollars. Thus, different sources of financing enabled him to start DreamWings.

As underscored by Hunter's experience, financial considerations affect all technology decisions. We have emphasized throughout the book that creating value is a central objective of the management of technology. Investors will finance technology endeavors only when they are convinced that it is in their self-interest, i.e., when it provides an adequate return consistent with the risks of the endeavor.

The financial considerations involved in technology decisions are the focus of this chapter. These considerations are not confined to the realm of financing technology endeavors. As underscored in our discussion of technology strategy, value-based management is the cornerstone of management technology. Does the strategy create value for the customers? Is that value appropriable by the firm? Do the financial resources exist to implement the technology project? If not, can they be raised from external sources? The answers to these questions are significant not merely for start-ups, such as Dream-Wings, but also for large firms. For example, decisions about R&D projects involve the risk-return trade-off. Similarly, during the strategic planning phase of new product development, the potential value a new product is projected to create for a firm is a major criterion for authorizing development projects.

In this chapter, we will focus on the major financial questions involved in management of technology. For example,

1. How is the value of a technology project to be assessed?
2. How can one finance a technology start-up or project?
3. How do firms communicate with their investors regarding the attractiveness of a technology project?

Such questions occupy the center stage of discussion in the finance discipline. Historically, the answers to these questions have developed for low to moderate uncertainty

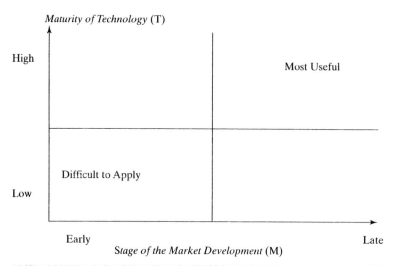

FIGURE 15.1 TRADITIONAL FINANCIAL TOOLS AND TECHNIQUES ARRAYED ON THE TECHNOLOGY-MARKET CHART

contexts. As shown in the T-Matrix in Figure 15.1, the financial techniques most fre quently employed in firms are well suited for mature technology contexts, with low lev els of uncertainty. Different techniques are needed for the contexts where the technologies involved are not mature and, therefore, introduce a high level of uncer tainty. Further, unlike market uncertainty, which most business firms understand rea sonably well, the technical uncertainties are rendered obscure because of the specialize jargon spoken by the scientists and technologists—a fact we highlighted during our dis cussion of technology intelligence.

In this chapter, we will discuss four interrelated financial issues involved in the man agement of technology. Figure 15.2 presents the chapter overview.

FIGURE 15.2 FINANCIAL CONSIDERATIONS: A CONCEPTUAL OVERVIEW

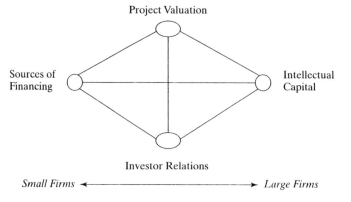

1. Project valuation will focus on the challenges involved in valuing (financially) a technology-related project. How do projects that involve technologies early in their life cycle differ from those projects that involve mature technologies? How do industry differences—the stages before the emergence of dominant design and the era of incremental evolution—get factored into the models of financial evaluation?
2. Intellectual capital will focus on assessing the value of intangible assets—knowledge—owned by a firm. For example, how does the capital market value intellectual capital, especially R&D? How much should an acquirer pay for a knowledge-intensive firm?
3. Financing will focus on obtaining the requisite monetary resources for projects. For example, which sources of financing are feasible for projects in differing stages of technology maturity? What has been the influence of the three environmental trends—globalization, technology integration, and time compression—on the sources of financing in recent years?
4. Market signaling refers to the attempts by firms to communicate with the capital markets. What kinds of information do investors value in the realm of technology? How is that information factored into their evaluation of the value of a firm?

The context of the four activities and, hence, the appropriateness of the financial techniques are different for start-ups such as DreamWings and large firms, many of which are publicly traded. For example, John Hunter's challenge was to persuade the quasi-government agencies such as KTEC or KIC to provide him with capital, whereas a large publicly traded firm like Hewlett-Packard may be able to raise the necessary finances for a technology project from internal operations. Similarly, Hewlett-Packard may choose to signal the initiation or completion of technology-related projects to their (public) capital markets, an issue that is of no relevance to DreamWings. Where appropriate, we will highlight the differences between start-ups and large firms in our discussion.

The scheme of the chapter is as follows. First, we will discuss the challenges of project valuation, anchoring our discussion in the concept of project life cycle. Second, we will summarize the research evidence pertaining to intellectual capital and the challenges involved in valuing the firms in knowledge-intensive industries. Third, we will highlight the challenges of financing, the generic sources of financial resources, and the financing activity in small and large firms. Fourth, we will summarize the role played by market signaling. Fifth, we will discuss the influence of environmental trends on financing. We will conclude with some managerial implications and a chapter summary.

PROJECT VALUATION

PROJECT LIFE CYCLE

All technology projects evolve over a number of stages, from initiation to completion to operations or commercialization, as has been discussed in chapter 2. By *life cycle of a project,* we mean all the activities sequenced over time from the beginning through operations or commercialization that need to be performed for the completion of th project. The exact specification of the stages of a project will depend on both the typ of project and the characteristics of industry. For example,

- In the aerospace industry, when large aircraft or space-related projects are undertaken, the stages of a project are often labeled as concept development, detailed definition, implementation, and launch and operations.
- In the pharmaceutical industry, these stages may be labeled as basic research done before filing a patent, preclinical studies that are done prior to an initial new drug application (IND) to the Food and Drug administration (FDA), and clinical trials involving human beings over three phases (Phases I, II, III)—trials that should be conducted to establish the safety, efficacy, and side effects if a firm is to satisfactorily file a new drug application.

When the technology is not mature, more time may have to be spent in the early stage of the project. However, when the project involves only incremental technology inno vation, or when the technology is mature, the early stages of a project may be short, an most of the project activities are likely to be confined to the execution and implemer tation of the project.

The concept of project life cycle is useful to illustrate three key ideas:

1. The funds required for completing the activities in a project will vary over time;
2. The risk-return trade-off in a project changes over its life cycle; and
3. Different project control mechanisms are needed over the course of the project.

FUNDS REQUIRED

The financial outlays required for completing the project vary in relative amounts ove the stages of project evolution. A typical pattern of financial outlays required in a pro ect over its various stages is portrayed in Figure 15.3. As shown in the figure, any pro

FIGURE 15.3 PROJECT LIFE CYCLE

Aerospace Industry: Concept Definition ⟶ Development ⟶ Building of the Air/Space Craft ⟶ Launch

Pharmaceutical: Basic Research/ ⟶ Phase I and Phase II ⟶ Phase III ⟶ Long-Term Phase IV
Industry: Preclinical

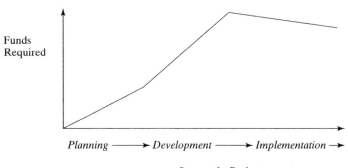

Planning ⟶ Development ⟶ Implementation ⟶

Stages of a Project

ect requires small financial outlays in the beginning, when the project is being planned or when its feasibility is being studied. After the planning stage, which may itself consist of several steps, the funds required for a particular project increase considerably. During the implementation stage, projects typically require a lot of manpower, physical assets, and materials; consequently, the funds required will generally be the highest. Once the project is completed and as it moves into either operations or commercialization, the funds for the project decline considerably. For example, in a major aerospace project, the early phases of concept definition and development may consume a few hundred million dollars; the implementation stage—when the aircraft or spacecraft is being built—will consume the most amount of dollars, usually in the range of billions. As the aircraft or spacecraft moves into operations, the funds required for the particular project decline considerably. Similarly, in a major drug development project, the funds required for Phases I and II are considerably lower than for Phase III.

RISK-RETURN TRADE-OFF

The uncertainties pertaining to a project decline over its life cycle. In the early stages, both the technical uncertainties pertaining to the feasibility of the project and the market uncertainties pertaining to the consumer acceptance of the project are relatively higher than during the later stages of the project. During the early (planning) phase, when the project is being planned or when its feasibility is being assessed, an important goal is to ensure that the firm anticipates most of the uncertainties so that it can make a judgment regarding the economic viability of the project. Thus, although this phase consumes the least amount of dollars, it is a very important phase, because it sets the stage for the ensuing economic performance of the project. As the project evolves, and as information is generated, the market estimates and the technical feasibility of the project become increasingly clearer. For example, in a major drug development effort, as the Phase I trials proceed, a firm may generate a more realistic picture of the market potential of the drug being developed. It is also possible that during Phase I trials the firm may gain information regarding the unfeasibility of the project, which may then lead to its termination.

CONTROL MECHANISMS

A further implication of the project life concept is the need to control the project execution and the funds allocated to it over time. Indeed, the funds allocated to a project during a particular period of time is an important mechanism of control that a firm can use to manage the project. Four important points can be made with respect to these control mechanisms.

1. Before any major project is launched, a firm should devote some financial resources to assess the feasibility and to plan the project.
2. During the feasibility assessment, a firm should take into account the total life cycle cost of the project, incorporating the best information it has available. By total life cycle cost, we refer to the total amount of funds that a firm will have to allocate over the entire life cycle of the project.
3. As a project evolves, as both technical and market-related uncertainties clear up, checkpoints should be established for periodic reviews of the project and the funds that are allocated to it.
4. Finally, during the evolution of the project, at several checkpoints a further economic assessment should be made. When a project generates information regarding its unfeasibility, then it should be shut down.

Projects lie at the heart of many technology management decisions. An understand
of the project life cycle concept is useful to appreciate the challenges in valuation a
financing the project.

PROJECT VALUATION

Valuation refers to those activities, tools, and techniques that are involved in determ
ing the economic worth of an activity. Valuation lies at the heart of economic analy
and strategic decision making. Over the years, a number of tools and techniques ha
been developed for valuation. Indeed, different groups of players ranging from vent
capitalists, bankers, chief financial officers, and strategy analysts to ordinary invest
participating in the stock market are interested in valuation techniques.

Project valuation refers to the activities involved in estimating the economic wo
of a project or a start-up. In the case of large firms such as Hewlett-Packard, projects
lated to the major activities in the management of technology—appropriation, and
ployment in new products or value chain—may be considered during the course of a ye

- Should we undertake an R&D project that examines the ergonomics of office organization?
- Should we introduce a new scanner in the market that incorporates voice
  recognition technology?
- Should we change the architecture of our IT?

Similar questions may also be important for investors in quasi-government agencies
they examine the feasibility of financing a start-up. The answers to these questions hir
on the assessment of the economic worth of the project.

Traditional project valuation tools, currently popular in many firms, are based
the economic concept of net present value. Net present value incorporates two comm
sense ideas to fix the value of a project:

1. The time value of money, that is, a dollar today is worth more than a dollar
   earned tomorrow.
2. Riskiness of a project, that is, the valuation of a project should take into account the inherent risk of the project under consideration.

The net present value method has typically been operationalized in firms by the d
counted cash flow (DCF) method. Box 15.1 summarizes the DCF method of proj
evaluation.

Historically, the discounted cash flow method was developed for valuing bonds a
stocks.[2] Later, firms adopted it to value internal projects. The method is applicable
valuation contexts where four crucial assumptions underpinning the net present val
concept are valid:

- First, the cash flow over an extended period of time can be forecast with a
  reasonable degree of confidence. This facilitates the application of the concept of time value of money.
- Second, there exists sufficient information regarding several projects from a
  firm's historical records or past experience from which the riskiness of the
  project under consideration can be assessed.

BOX 15.1

DISCOUNTED CASH FLOW

One method of performing these NPV analyses is to use the discounted cash flow (DCF) model represented by equation (1). Expected profits for each period t are discounted back to the present using the appropriate discount rate r, at each period for a specific duration T:

$$PV = \sum_{t=1}^{t=T} \frac{E(x_t)}{(1 + r_t)^t} \qquad (1)$$

The discounting reflects the fact that money has a higher value today than it does tomorrow. The discount rate, r, is the opportunity cost of capital for the project in question. It is the expected rate of return that could be earned from an investment of similar risk. It reflects the systematic risk that is specific to the project and is therefore undiversifiable.

This can be estimated using a model such as the capital asset pricing model (CAPM):

$$r_t = r_{ft} \beta_i (r_m - r_f) \qquad (2)$$

That is, the discount rate is equal to rf, the risk-free rate, such as the interest rate on treasury bills, plus a risk premium. This risk premium is equal to the systematic risk β_i of the project, and the excess return over the market return r_m. The (beta) of similar projects (within or outside the firm) is used. Often, however, the β of a specific project is difficult to measure, making it difficult to estimate the discount rate. Sometimes the discount rate is approximated with the weighted cost of capital (WACC)—a good approximation if the company's projects have similar betas.

- Third, the knowledge accumulation during the course of a project and the role of management are known with reasonable certainty, such that they can be factored into the earnings estimate as well as the riskiness of the project.
- Finally, DCF assumes that investments are reversible, and the decision to invest is a now or never decision.

A majority of large U.S. companies use net present value or internal rate of return in their formal capital budgeting systems. These systems have evolved to facilitate top managers in their decisions to separate good investments from bad. A typical large company has between 2,000 and 10,000 capital projects to evaluate each year. Many R&D managers discuss the results of discounted cash flow evaluations. This, however, may stifle innovation when the assumptions behind the method are not valid. In Box 15.2, we have summarized the major reasons why the traditional capital budgeting systems stifle innovation.

As portrayed in Figure 15.1, the assumptions underlying the discounted cash flow method are more or less valid in technology decisions where both the technology and the market are relatively mature. However, as also shown in the figure, when either technology or market is in the early stages of development, the assumptions behind the discounted cash flows are seriously violated. This may happen at certain points in (1) the technology life cycle and (2) industry evolution.

TECHNOLOGY LIFE CYCLE

The early stage of the technology life cycle, as illustrated by the S-curve of innovation, is the era of embryonic technologies, where the uncertainty surrounding the development of technology is quite high. At this stage, the technology-related projects have

---

BOX 15.2

HOW CAPITAL BUDGETING
DETERS INNOVATION

When a company fails to stay dominant in key markets, internal systems of resource allocation may be the cause. The decline often begins when financial managers impose strict controls on new capital spending. Operating and R&D managers soon realize that innovative products and processes are failing to clear the capital budgeting hurdles. The company then falls behind in technology and begins to lose market share.

A major reason is that discounted cash flow measures do not recognize the value of a wide range of competitive commitments. More importantly, these measures do not value commitments to innovate in advance of the competition. Specifically,

1. In many companies, high cash flows from existing products make the option to innovate look very unattractive. If the company evaluates new products case by case using standard DCF techniques, it will consistently postpone introductions.

2. A policy of cannibalization can outperform strict application of discounted cash flow techniques quarter-by-quarter. Such a policy discourages competitors from engaging in parallel R&D. This increases the value of existing products because the company now controls their date of obsolescence.

3. For almost any company with established products, early introduction of new products will appear to be a losing proposition at the time of the introduction. In contrast, over the whole product development cycle, early introduction is usually a sensible policy.

Capital budgeting systems fail in situations like these because they are inherently incremental. They support decisions that are sensible when viewed in isolation. Innovation generally demands a series of commitments spaced over time. These are precisely the sort of interrelated decisions that capital budgeting systems are least well equipped to handle.

Source: Baldwin, Carliss. "How Capital Budgeting Deters Innovation—and What to Do about It," *Research Technology Management,* November-December, 1991, pp. 39–45.

---

relatively no commonality with projects that a firm has undertaken in the past. In the context, several assumptions of the discounted cash flow method are not met:

1. There are no existing or past projects whose riskiness can be used as a proxy for estimating the riskiness of the innovation.
2. During the early stages of development of a technology, significant learning takes place, which reduces the riskiness of the innovation and enhances the efficiency of the manufacturing process.
3. Because of the importance of learning in the early stage of innovation, management plays a significant role, and this role is underplayed in the discounted cash flow methods.

Thus, DCF assumptions are violated during the early stage of a technology life cycle. However, in later stages of the life cycle, when the uncertainty and learning levels are considerably lower, DCF may be an appropriate tool for valuation of projects.

EVOLUTION OF COMPETITIVE DOMAINS

As underscored in our discussion of the dynamics triggered by technological change (refer to chapter 5), during the era of ferment, competitive domains undergo technological, market, and strategic turbulence. As a result, the uncertainty faced by a firm undertaking a technology project can be quite high. However, this has to be weighed against the risks involved in *not* pursuing a project, whereby a firm may be shut out of attractive segments of the market. During the later stages, that is, in the era of incremental change, many of the assumptions of the discounted cash flow method may be valid and, hence, this method may be quite applicable.

The discounted cash flow method often leads to dysfunctional consequences when used in the early stage of the technology life cycle or during the era of ferment. An example may illustrate this problem. Drug development projects in the pharmaceutical industry often take 10 to 15 years for successful completion. In a typically large pharmaceutical company like Merck, there will always be drug development projects in various stages of completion. Some projects may be in the exploratory stage; some others may be in Phase I or II; and a few others may be in the commercialization stage, when the firm is well on its way to capture the market for an approved drug. In other words, a firm will have a portfolio of projects in various stages of development. The discounted cash flow methods are appropriate for later stage projects. However, they impose an undue burden on the early stage projects, where the technology is not mature. This is so for several reasons. First, the riskiness of the early stage projects is relatively high; second, the earning streams from these projects, if successful, are a number of years away; third, and as a result, DCF methods typically favor later stage projects over early stage projects. This implies that, if DCF metrics are uniformly imposed on all projects, it is likely to lead to a situation where the firm will fund no early stage projects and will have no drug pipeline. Indeed, many progressive pharmaceutical firms augment traditional discounted flow methods with alternative approaches such as option pricing for valuing early stage projects. This is a topic to which we now turn.

OPTION PRICING MODELS

These models are replacing the traditional discounted cash flow methods in valuation of technology-related projects. Consider the following example from the machine tool industry:

> During the 1970s, some manufacturing firms invested in automatic and electronically controlled machine tools. Returns on the initial investments were reported as modest. However, microprocessor-based technologies arrived in the early 1980s, bringing about the opportunity for much more dramatic returns. Those firms that had previously invested in electronically controlled machine tools were able to migrate quickly and cheaply to the new technology. Because operators, maintenance personnel, and process engineers were already comfortable with electronic technology, it was relatively simple to retool existing machines in powerful microelectronics. Companies that had earlier deferred investment in electronically controlled machine tools quickly fell behind.[3]

As illustrated in the preceding story, technological innovations have two fundamental properties:

1. Past decisions that influence future technological options, and
2. An inherent uncertainty over future innovation opportunities.

Option pricing models in technology have evolved to take these two characteristics i account. Thus, a company facing an opportunity to invest in technology is holding so thing much like a financial call option: It has the right, but not the obligation, to buy asset (namely, the entitlement due to the stream of profits from the project) at a fut time of its choosing. When the company makes an irreversible investment (i.e., an penditure of funds), it "exercises," in effect, its call option.

So, the problem of how to exploit that investment opportunity can be summari thus: How does this company exercise the investment option? When a company ex cises its option by making an irreversible investment in technology, it effectively "kil the option. In other words, by deciding to go ahead with the expenditure, the compa gives up the possibility of waiting for new information that might affect the desirabi or timing of the investment. It cannot then disinvest, should market conditions chan adversely. That lost option value is an opportunity cost that must be included as par the cost of investment. In Box 15.3, we have illustrated an example of option pricin

BOX 15.3

OPTION PRICING

It is by now well recognized that real options are able to capture management's flexibility to adapt its future strategy in response to unexpected market developments. Similar to options on financial securities, these "real options" involve discretionary decisions or rights, with no obligation, to acquire or exchange the value of one asset for a specified value/price. Valuation of real options, such as the option to defer, expand, contract, abandon, switch use, or alter a capital investment or a contingent decision plan, has brought a revolution to modern corporate resource allocation.

Among the most important real options are those involving multistage decisions or compound growth options, that is, options whose exercise brings forth additional options as well as generating cash flows. Research and development projects are examples of investments that are likely to open the door to future opportunities. Traditional discounted cash flow (DCF) methods often ignore the value of this embedded flexibility. The traditional net present value (NPV) approach, for example, recommends ac-

cepting a project immediately if its NPV is greater than zero. It is, thus, more like a commitment to invest (that is, a futures contract, rather than a right or option). A passive application of NPV fails to consider the value of flexibility that management has when it undertakes a project to adapt and revise its decisions in the future as new information comes out. Traditional NPV makes implicit assumptions that management cannot react to deviations from the expected scenario of cash flows, presuming management's passive commitment to a certain operating strategy.

In the real world, however, the expected scenario of cash flows will likely not be realized when new information arrives and uncertainty in the marketplace gets resolved. Management may then have the flexibility to alter its operating strategy, based on the new information that emerged, in order to maximize its upside future potential or limit losses. Management's flexibility, for example to defer, contract, expand, or abandon its operating strategy, adds value to the NPV of expected

Source: Reprinted from *The Quarterly Review of Economics and Finance,* Volume 38, S. Panayi and L. Trigeorgis, "Multi-stage Real Options: The Cases of Information Technology Infrastructure and Band Expansion," pp. 675–692, Copyright 1998, with permission from Elsevier Science.

cash flows (based on initial management expectations). This calls for an expanded or strategic NPV criterion that reflects both the value components: the traditional NPV of expected cash flows and the option value of operating and strategic flexibility.

$$
\begin{array}{c}
\text{Expanded} \\
\text{(Strategic)} \\
\text{NPV}
\end{array}
=
\begin{array}{c}
\text{Traditional} \\
\text{NPV}
\end{array}
+
\begin{array}{c}
\text{Value of} \\
\text{option} \\
\text{flexibility}
\end{array}
$$

Many companies invest in the research and development of new products or technologies, for example, that may result in remote, contingent, and uncertain cash flows or in a wide range of applications at some future stage, but which may also have a high probability of failure. An R&D investment is a case of compound real option, leading to the exercise of follow-on discretionary investment opportunities at subsequent stages.

Such multistage investments can thus be viewed as (compound) call options, having as the underlying asset the project value (the present value of expected cash inflows from the completed and operating follow-on project), V1, with the exercise price being the necessary investment outlay. In the two-stage case, for example, today's investment (I1) in R&D or in in-formation technology infrastructure creates opportunities that will enable the firm to exercise a specific staged capital commitment in the technology investment and pay a small fee (I1) to acquire the right to make future commercialization investments, instead of ignoring the new technology (even in certain cases when it seems to have a negative NPV). If the technology is proven at future time t1 when new information arrives and future cash flow uncertainty is gradually resolved, management can decide to proceed with further installments on the staged capital commitment (if V2 > I2). But if the technology turns out to be unprofitable, management can decide not to make the follow-on investment (I2) and avoid further losses.

Research and development of a new technology can be viewed as a series of sequential decisions, with research as the first stage, followed up with decisions on technical construction and commercialization/implementation in subsequent stages (see the figure).

A. STAGE I: RESEARCH

First, management has to decide whether to engage in research for the discovery of a new product or technology. This often depends on

FIGURE 15.3.1 MULTI-STAGE DECISIONS (OPTIONS) EMBEDDED IN R&D IN VARIOUS STAGES

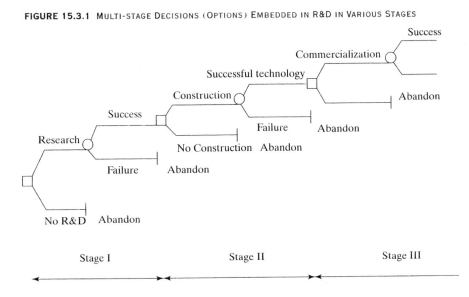

Box 15.3 (*continued*)

whether management finds such an investment of strategic import for the company's future growth. Indeed, success in many industries (for example, in high tech) demands a steady flow of new and innovative processes or products, yet research has become an increasingly costly and time-consuming undertaking. Naturally, better-informed decisions can be made after uncertainty gets resolved over time. That is why when management eventually decides to go ahead with an R&D investment, it often decides to finance it with a staged series of investment installments. An early investment gives the right to make further installments and proceed to subsequent stages, but only if things turn out favorably in each stage. If research fails to produce the new product or technology, the R&D project can stop at this phase. Meanwhile, even if the firm may not have discovered a new technology, it may still have gained significant knowledge that may be useful in some other areas.

B. STAGE II: TECHNICAL CONSTRUCTION/DEVELOPMENT

Once the research stage is proven to be a success, management may decide to start the technical construction resource and development phase. Technical construction requires considerable capital as well as human resources to be committed. Technical knowledge for the construction is not only difficult to find but also costly. Besides, new information that arrives may prove that such an investment is not profitable enough for the firm to justify its research and construction expenses. Management will eventually decide what is best for the firm according to the new information that arrives. If

these problems are surpassed and technical construction and subsequent commercialization are seen to be essential for the competitiveness of the firm, construction will commence.

The project in this phase is dominated by technical construction uncertainty. The technical feasibility of the technology needs to be ascertained. If the construction phase of the technology fails, management can abandon the project in order to avoid further losses. Of course, if technological construction is successful, management can go on to the next phase of implementation and commercialization.

C. STAGE III: IMPLEMENTATION/ COMMERCIALIZATION

The final stage is the implementation or commercialization of the new technology in the market. Management considers the possibilities that the new product or technology might be successfully launched in the marketplace. At this phase, the new product or technology typically faces competition from substitutes, and management has to make sure that it has properly anticipated competitive reaction and its impact on profit value before launching the product into the market. Success will largely depend on whether the resulting benefits for the firm can be kept proprietary or are diffused to the industry (shared with competition). If the implementation phase fails, the firm may still abandon the project and potentially sell the technology or its plant and equipment for salvage value.

The basic structure of multistage decision making is not unique to R&D. In fact, it is prevalent in many (if not most) strategic situations.

Option value has important implications for managers as they think about their investment decisions. For example, it is often highly desirable to delay an investment decision and wait for more information about market conditions or technological possibilities, even though a standard DCF analysis indicates that the investment is economical right now. On the other hand, as in the case of investment in electronically controlled machines, there may be situations in which uncertainty over future market conditions should prompt a company to speed certain investments. Such is the ca when investments create additional options that give a company the ability (although not the obligation) to do additional future investing. R&D could lead to pay patterns; for example, land purchases could lead to development of mineral resources. A company might also choose to speed investments that would yield information and thereby reduce uncertainty.[4]

What is the relationship between call options and innovation? As discussed in our chapter on innovation (chapter 3), the process of innovation usually consists of many steps, and the outcome of each is uncertain. Indeed, the innovation journey sometimes closes and sometimes opens opportunities that were not visible at the beginning. This is true for specific projects over the project life cycle. For example, during the process of developing a drug for allergy, a pharmaceutical firm may discover another use for the drug in a related area, or it might discover conversely that the drug will be effective in cases of only certain types of allergy and, thus, has restricted market potential. Indeed, it is not infrequent in drug development that, at the end of the earlier stages of drug development when some of the uncertainties are resolved, the pharmaceutical firm has a better idea as to whether it should continue or abandon the project. Investing in the earlier stages can, therefore, be viewed as buying a call option that gives the manager the right to invest in the second stage. Indeed, if the manager does not invest in the first stage, he or she does not have the ability to move on to the second stage, should the information generated in the first stage prove to be positive. Successful pharmaceutical firms such as Merck are employing options modeling in their drug development process. In Box 15.4, we have illustrated the story of Merck as portrayed by its chief financial officer, Judy Lewent.

BOX 15.4

FINANCIAL ENGINEERING AT MERCK

Merck & Co., Inc., invested over billions of dollars in R&D. The company spent much of the money on risky, long-term projects that are notoriously difficult to evaluate. The company is seldom, if ever, criticized for being shortsighted. Yet at Merck, it is the longest horizon, most strategic projects that receive the most intense and financially sophisticated analyses. In fact, Merck's finance function is active and influential with a highly quantitative, analytical orientation. Why doesn't all this analysis choke off long-term investing, as critics of modern finance theory say it should? In part, because Merck is a leader in building financial models of scientific and commercial processes and in

using those models to improve business decisions. Merck's models use probability distributions for numerous variables and come up with a range of possible outcomes that both stimulate discussion and facilitate decision making.

For example, Merck's Research Planning Model integrates economics, finance, statistics, and computer science to produce disciplined quantitative analyses of specific elements of Merck's business. These models provide Merck executives with information both about risks and returns and about financial performance for specific projects and activities.

In 1983, major drug development projects at Merck were not formally, prospectively

Source: Nichols, Nancy A. "Scientific Management at Merck," *Harvard Business Review,* January-February 1994, pp. 89–99.

Box 15.4 (*continued*)

evaluated as capital investments. They faced rigorous scientific scrutiny, to be sure, but comparatively little economic or financial scrutiny. Judy Lewent, then chief financial advisor to Merck's research division, sought to create two specific capabilities in a comprehensive Research Planning Model:

1. The ability to assess risk and return, project by project, prior to the commitment of significant funds; and

2. The ability to assess the contribution of the research laboratories to the health and performance of the entire corporation.

To build the Research Planning Model, Lewent and her staff used a technique known as *Monte Carlo simulation.* The model's inputs include scientific and therapeutic variables, capital expenditures, production and selling costs, product prices and quantities, and macro-

economic variables like interest, inflation, and exchange rates. For all these variables, the model uses ranges rather than point estimates, for example, "optimistic," "expected," and "pessimistic" values for a variable or actual probability distributions. The computer repeatedly draws values from permissible ranges and computes outcomes based on specified relationships between the variables and other parameters. In this way, the model synthesizes probability distributions for key output variables, such as annual nominal- and constant-dollar forecasts of revenues, cash flow, return on investment, and net present value. Hence, the output from the model is not merely a point forecast for, say, net present value, but a frequency distribution showing the probability that a project's NPV will exceed a certain level. Summary statistics, such as standard deviation per unit of time, can be computed from the synthesized distribution and then used in other analyses, such as an option analysis.

So, how does the option pricing method differ from the traditional discounted cash flow methods? In Table 15.1, we have highlighted the major differences between the two approaches. As shown in the table, the option pricing methods are much more appropriate when the uncertainties of technology and market preclude clear assessment of the risk, the earning streams, and the investments required in a project.

TABLE 15.1 Option Pricing Models Versus Discounted Cash Flow Method

	Option Pricing	*Discounted Cash Flow*
Nature of Decision	A series of irreversible acts	Reversible, or One shot
Major Decision Choices	Invest or delay for more information	Invest or not
Organizational Learning	Valued	Not valued
Context Appropriate for Use	High uncertainty	Low uncertainty
Illustrative Contexts	Radical innovation Era of ferment	Incremental innovation Industry maturity

INTELLECTUAL CAPITAL

Intellectual capital refers to the "knowledge assets" owned by a firm. Because technology includes tacit knowledge, i.e., knowledge that is not embodied as physical assets, in many high-technology firms, the intellectual capital may economically be far more significant than the physical assets. However, as we discussed in chapter 1, intellectual capital possesses characteristics that are markedly different from physical assets. For instance, many financial analysts have puzzled over the valuation of many of the Internet stocks, whose price/earnings multiples have been markedly high relative to their counterparts in the traditional sectors of the economy. The valuation of intellectual capital becomes an important concern not only of investors, but also of potential acquirers, that is, firms that are interested in buying a high-technology company. For example, how should they value the intellectual capital of the target firm, in addition to their physical assets?

Although intuitively appealing, the notion of intellectual capital raises significant challenges in its measurement and estimation. It is often difficult to answer the question: Does intellectual capital exist? Accounting treatments have historically focused on the valuation of capital goods and have not begun to address the issues of intellectual capital. Typically, tacit knowledge or knowledge assets owned by the firm are not reflected in its balance sheet; even R&D expenditures are expensed away. Indeed, if they exist, they are sometimes subsumed under the catch-all term *goodwill*. Indirect economic evidence, however, suggests that in many industries the intellectual capital may be the most important asset owned by a firm. In Box 15.5, we have presented a summary of research that provides indirect evidence of the intellectual capital owned by firms.

Where does the intellectual capital of a firm reside? At a very general level, we can say that the individuals within the firm collectively hold intellectual capital. To be more specific, intellectual capital resides in the value chain activities—both primary and secondary—performed by individuals in the firm. This link to the value chain is important for several reasons.

1. The primary value chain activity may be clearly explicated; therefore, the valuation of the intellectual capital embedded in primary activities is probably much easier than in the case of secondary activities. In many traditional industries (capital and consumer intensive), the primary value chain is economically the most significant and, hence, the existing tools of measuring intellectual capital (such as accounting treatments of goodwill) may be adequate.
2. In many secondary activities such as technology development, the experience gained by individuals by engaging in the relevant activities may provide the critical intellectual capital needed for the firm. These are much more difficult to explicate. For example, as people engage in new product development activity, they may carry over the knowledge gained through the experience in one project to another. If there are economies of learning, a firm may grow more efficient in their new product development efforts over time by employing the same people.

BOX 15.5

INTELLECTUAL CAPITAL AND R&D

How does one value the intellectual capital, especially that pertains to knowledge assets? During the last few years, two different approaches have emerged: (1) market valuation of R&D, and (2) nonfinancial indicators of R&D.

MARKET VALUATION OF R&D

There are two ways by which market valuation of R&D is achieved: purchased R&D and targeted-stock issues.

1. Purchased R&D
    Given the magnitude of corporate expenditures on R&D (over $150 billion in 1997) and the ever-increasing demand for technology, one would expect markets for R&D to develop. Of course, markets for patent rights and the licensing of R&D have long been in operation. But recent years have witnessed a relatively new development—a large number of corporate acquisitions in the software, pharmaceutical, biotech, and electronics industries in which R&D-in-process was by far the major asset acquired. This became evident due to an accounting requirement that acquiring companies estimate separately the fair market value of the acquired assets, including R&D-in-process. In a recent study of such acquisitions, Zhen Deng and Lev found that the fair market values of acquired R&D (yet-to-be-completed R&D projects) amounted, on average, to 75 percent *of the acquisition price.* Such acquisitions, numbering in the hundreds per year, are primarily trades in R&D and technology.
    The fair market values assigned by management to acquired R&D-in-process are generally based on the present value of estimated cash flows from projects under development. Those fair values are closely associated with stock prices of acquiring firms, which in turn lends some credibility to management estimates. Moreover, a recent study of Australian companies reported that revaluations of intangibles (a procedure allowed in Australia but not in the United States) are significantly associated with stock prices, suggesting once more that investors pay attention to managers' assessments of market values of R&D.

2. Targeted-stock issues
    In addition to acquisitions where R&D is the prime asset acquired, another manifestation of developing markets for R&D are the targeted stocks issued in recent years by high-tech companies such as Alza and Genzyme. In that still small number of cases, the value of the security is derived from a specific R&D program or pool of patents transferred by the patent company to the new entity, thus representing a further step in the progressive securitization of intangibles. In time, the prices observed in such markets will provide "comparables" or multiples for the purpose of intangibles and enterprise valuations.

NONFINANCIAL INDICATORS OF R&D VALUE

In search of reliable measures of R&D output, economists have experimented with various nonfinancial indicators, such as the number of patents registered by a company (patent counts), patent renewal and fee data, number of innovations, and citations of patents. Patent counts and the number of innovations emerging from a company's R&D program have

Source: From Baruch Lev, "R&D and Capital Markets," *Journal of Applied Corporate Finance,* 1999, Vol. 11, No. 4, pp. 21–35. Reprinted by permission.

been found to be associated with both the level of corporate investment in R&D and with firms' market values. Citations of firms' patents included in subsequent patent applications offer a more reliable measure of R&D value than the absolute number of patents, because such citations are an objective indicator of the impact of a firm's research activities on the subsequent development of science and technology.

Various studies have shown that patent citations capture important aspects of R&D value. For example:

- Trajtenberg (1990) reports a positive association between citation counts and consumer welfare measures for CAT scanners;

- Shane (1993), in examining 11 semiconductor companies, finds that patent counts weighed by citations contribute to the explanation of cross-sectional differences in Tobin's q measures (market value over replacement cost of assets); and

- Hall et al. (1998) report that citation-weighted patent counts are associated with firms' market values (after controlling for the firms' R&D capital).

In a direct test of the usefulness of patent citations to investors, Deng et al. (1999) and Hirschey et al. (1998) examine the ability of various measures derived from patent citations to predict subsequent stock returns and market-to-book (M/B) values in various R&D-intensive industries. The following three measures were all found to be significantly associated with future market-to-book values and stock returns of up to 3 years:

- The number of patents granted to the firm in a given year;

- The intensity of citations of a firm's patents in subsequent patents; and

- A "science linkage" measure that reflects the number of citations in a firm's patents (backward citations) of scientific papers and conferences (in contrast with citations of previous patents).

The science linkage indicator is of special interest, because it reflects the extent to which the firm engages in science-related or basic research as opposed to product development or process improvement.

Information about the nature of a company's R&D activities is generally not available in its financial statements. But, as the research suggests, nonfinancial indicators of R&D output such as number of patents, innovations, and trademarks—and, in particular, measures based on patent citations—offer a promising set of measures for firm valuation and security analysis.

Why is intellectual capital important? We may cite several reasons:

- First, for managers, intellectual capital uniquely owned by a firm is an important basis for formulating an effective strategy, because it may open up unique opportunities to compete in the firm's markets.
- Second, intellectual capital also occasionally holds keys to improving operating efficiency.
- Third, in many knowledge-intensive industries, the market value of a firm often depends mostly on its intellectual capital, and the net cash flows of the organization should reflect the advantages offered by the unique intellectual capital.
- Finally, in concrete situations such as mergers and acquisitions, valuation of the intellectual property may be a significant challenge when an acquiring firm determines the fair market value of a target firm it is attempting to acquire.

In Box 15.6, we have illustrated the value paid for Excite by a firm in the industry information economy.

VALUATION OF AN INTERNET COMPANY, EXCITE

Dramatizing the extraordinary economics of the Internet, high-speed Internet provider At Home Corp. agreed in January 1999 to buy Excite Inc., one of the World Wide Web's busiest sites, for $7.5 billion in stock.

The deal and its price tag—more than double Excite's recent market valuation—are another sign of the frantic scramble for customer traffic and market share in the booming interactive arena. They also illustrate how the highflying stock of Internet companies has become a currency that outweighs conventional concerns such as sales and profits.

Management of both companies defended the transaction as a shrewd bet on the future of their evolving medium. Excite, which lags behind Yahoo! Inc. in traffic, nevertheless offers At Home access to a huge consumer following based on its search services, information content, electronic mail, and commerce. The two companies expect to offer a wide range of personalized services to consumers, promising advertisers detailed marketing information about those users.

Source: Republished with permission of Dow Jones & Company, from Kara Swisher, "Excite Purchase For $7.5 Billion In Stock Is Set," *The Wall Street Journal,* January 20, 1999, B1; permission conveyed through Copyright Clearance Center, Inc.

FINANCING

FUNDAMENTAL CHALLENGES IN FINANCING

Two fundamental challenges are involved in financing technology projects: adverse lection and moral hazard.

1. *Adverse selection* refers to a problem that can occur in two ways. First, only those firms who are not good at innovation will go to outside financing; second, firms go for outside financing because they know that the technology project is too much of a risk for them to use their own money and would rather use someone else's.

2. *Moral hazard* refers to the problem that can occur in a principal-agent relationship: The financier employs an agent or a manager to undertake the technology project, but the agent would rather be doing work that is best for him, which may not be the best thing for the financier.

Both adverse selection and moral hazards are problems generated by information certainty and asymmetry. Technology projects are fraught with uncertainty; therefo the person who proposes a technology project may not know enough about it to p vide the person who finances it with information that either needs. Moreover, the formation is likely to change as the technology project proceeds, and the manager of project learns more about what goes into the product and what the customers want. course, this provides the manager of the technology project an opportunity to hold b some of the information, or the manager may not be able to articulate accurately what she knows about the project. The information is asymmetric: The person who finances the project does not have the same information that the manager of the project has. Also, once having provided the funds, the financier has limited opportunities for monitoring the project or, in other words, prevents the manager from using the funds for a more risky venture that he himself would not have financed with his own money.

SOURCES OF FINANCING

In theory, there are three generic sources of financing available for technology-related projects: (1) private equity market, (2) funds generated from operations, and (3) collaborative arrangements.

PRIVATE EQUITY MARKET

This represents the external sources of financing a project. The organized private equity market typically consists of issuers of private equity, investors, and intermediaries:

- The issuers are largely firms that are not likely to be able to obtain financing in the debt or public equity market.
- Investors are largely organizations that have diversified investment portfolios and, therefore, can afford to invest part of their portfolios in very risky ventures. These include public and private pension funds, foundations, investment banks, insurance companies, and wealthy families and individuals.
- Intermediaries are the investors' limited partners. The intermediaries may be limited partnerships managed by independent partnership organizations or by affiliates of financial institutions. They may also be intermediaries such as small business investment companies (SBICs) and publicly traded investment companies.[5]

FUNDS FROM OPERATIONS

In the case of an ongoing firm, a second source of financing is the funds generated from its operations. Some of these funds may be ploughed back to fund economically attractive technology projects. However, funds from operations are not a source of financing for many companies even after they have been incorporated. Consider the case of Internet start-ups. For them, the funds from operations are several years away, and many of them are not profitable for long periods of time. In their case, major financial commitments will have to be made for significant periods of time before there is any prospect of generating funds from operations.

COLLABORATIVE ARRANGEMENTS

Collaborative arrangements represent a third form of financing where both the firm and its partner provide resources of various kinds for execution of a project: human capital, physical resources, and financial resources. These collaborative arrangements may assume several forms as enumerated in chapter 9.

The challenges of moral hazard and adverse selection are particularly acute in the case of start-up firms that have to look outside for financing their venture. However, in large corporations where the people who evaluate the projects and make the financing decisions are usually separate from those who are proposing the projects, the problems may still persist. We will discuss the start-ups and the large company issues separately.

FINANCING A START-UP

In our opening vignette, we illustrated the challenges faced by John Hunter, as he w
trying to finance his start-up enterprise. In many technology-based start-ups, the
certainty of success of a venture is indeed quite high. In addition, both the moral h
ard and adverse selection problems inhibit the flow of funds to the start-up.

For an entrepreneur interested in starting up a technology-based company, it is u
ful to think of the front start-up as evolving over stages. In Figure 15.4, we have p
vided a simple model of evolution of the stages of a start-up that correspond to t
development of technology and the life cycle of a project. As shown in the figure,
can identify six stages in the evolution of a start-up:

> Basic research, which in the case of a start-up may involve the entrepre-
> neur to test some aspects of the technology being developed.
> Applied research, which involves the incorporation of technology into a
> new product process or service.
> Commercialization, which includes all activities involved in moving the
> product into market—developing a business for the market, assessment, a
> business plan, and so on.
> Start-up, which involves embodying the activities in the form of a business.
> Rollout, when the firm starts manufacturing and marketing its products or
> services in selected target markets.
> Growth, which involves the growth in sales and continued investment in
> the manufacturing and marketing capabilities of the firm to enhance its sales.

As shown in Figure 15.4, the funds required for the operation of the start-up increa
over the various stages from basic research to growth. In this sense, this is similar to t
technology project life cycle we discussed earlier. Indeed, basic research activities befc
start-up of a new venture are usually undertaken by individuals in the laboratory, be
in a university setting, a government-funded research center, or corporate R&D un
The funds required for these activities are relatively minuscule compared to a full-blo
enterprise. Applied research may require the building of a prototype and, therefore, w
require additional amounts of money to buy the material and lease/acquire manufa
turing facilities for building the prototype. The commercialization stage requires t
building of a viable business plan and, therefore, requires estimates of the market p
tential, estimates of manufacturing capability and the administrative and workers' cc
involved in operating the venture. As shown in the figure, the amount of funds requir
during start-up, roll out, and the growth phases are significantly higher relative to t
previous stages.

Not all start-ups go through the initial stages in such a clear sequence. For examp
some of the Internet company start-ups do not require basic research, although th
need considerable applied research. These firms face a considerably dynamic enviro
ment and require frequent changes as they develop both their product and the busine
plan. By one estimate, in the case of Internet companies, it may take $250,000
$500,000 to get a viable business plan. Up to $10 million may be needed to get a wor
ing model, and even then the company will have to constantly keep pace with the en
ronment so as not to be overtaken by competitors.[6] Many of these companies are n
profitable for a long period of time, and for them, funds from operations are seve
years away.

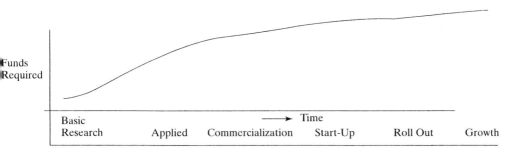

FIGURE 15.4 STAGES OF A HIGH TECHNOLOGY START-UP

Also as shown in the figure the activities during the various stages of a start-up are financed from different sources of funds.

- During the basic research and applied research phases of a start-up, the project is riddled with technical and commercial uncertainty, and as a result, an entrepreneur will find it very difficult to raise money through debt or from the private equity markets. During these stages, the activities are financed either by government sources such as an SBIR grant or through personal sources. Private placement memorandums and/or angels are also widely used in some of the second and even first stages of a start-up. In addition, if the person is working in a large firm, the corporate R&D resources are often utilized for the benefit of both basic and applied research.
- Government sources continue to play an important role in many start-ups during commercialization stages. Also, the entrepreneur may have access to facilities provided by investors, both private and public. Additionally, private placement may be another source of funds for the commercialization phase.
- During the later stages of the start-up, the entrepreneur may rely on venture capital funds, and when he or she is ready to move into the growth phase, the firm may have the opportunity of initiating a public offering or raising money through mergers and acquisitions with larger firms.

In our discussion of innovation networks, we noted that in the United States several regional networks are being developed with the assistance of state governments to foster innovation. State networks include not merely technology developers but also facilitators, such as the venture capital funds. Recall that two state government agencies—KTF and KIC—provided the initial financing for the start-up of DreamWings. Indeed, shown in the different sources of financing for a start-up, both government agencies a private corporations are assisting with financing of technology start-ups.

CHALLENGES FOR THE ENTREPRENEUR

Reliance on external sources of financing, be they government or private, opens up t potential for conflict between ownership and control. As external sources of finan ing are injected into the operations of the company, the outside shareholders m increasingly demand a voice in the running of the company. Sometimes, the objectiv of the private equity provider may diverge from the objectives of the entrepreneur; this case, conflicts between the two are highly likely. Thus, the choice of the specific p vate equity provider is an important issue to which the entrepreneur should pay atte tion. For example, many of the university-based biotechnology start-ups in the Midwe prefer equity providers that will allow the start-up to continue operating out of the Mi west. In other words, these start-ups look for equity providers who will not demand th the operations be moved to either the east or west coast—regions which have a great concentration of technical labor force in biotechnology.

VENTURE CAPITAL PROCESS

Because financing the technology project is flawed with adverse selection and mor hazard challenges, how should a venture capitalist or an equity provider evaluate t controls put forth by an entrepreneur?

The venture capital process involves an intense company scrutiny by the ventu capital providers of the business plan, management team and the request for funds. T steps involved in a particular venture capital process are enumerated in Table 15.2. T initial contact between the start-up and the venture capitalists may be initiated by ther of the two parties. Having decided to explore the start-up further, the venture cap talist will spend a significant amount of time examining the business potential of t

TABLE 15.2   Steps in Venture Capital Process

1. Introductory Visit
2. Business Plan Review
3. Due Diligence Check
   a. Founders
   b. Targeted Markets
4. Additional Visits
5. Negotiations
6. Draft Agreement
7. Legal Documents
8. Closing Date Set
9. Checks Deposited
10. Checks Cashed/Stocks Issued

Sources: Adapted from (1) Roure, J. B. and M. Maidique. "Linking Prefunding Factors and High-technology Venture Success"; Fast, N. "Pitfalls of Corporate Venturing," *Research Management,* March 1981, pp. 21–24.

start-up. This may include an initial visit, examination and analysis of the business plan presented by the start-up, and of course due diligence checks on the founders and the targeted market. This may be followed by additional visits by the venture capital providers and further checks on the various aspects of the business plan. It is only after this initial screening that negotiations will begin in earnest between the two parties; when the negotiations are successful, an agreement is reached on the terms of the venture capital provisions. Of course, venture capital includes legal documents as well as transfer of funds from the venture capital to the start-up.

Just what do the venture capitalists look for during their initial scrutiny of the business plan and management team? We can identify four major sets of factors that lead to a start-up successfully negotiating with venture capital:

1. *Nature of the management team within the start-up.* The venture capitalist typically looks for an experienced and complete management team that has successfully worked together. By complete, it is meant that the management team has all the necessary expertise that is required to operate the start-up successfully.
2. *Nature of the market.* The venture capitalist usually prefers start-ups with aggressive intentions in the market. This can take two forms: a high-growth segment, where the company can play an important role and expect a higher market share; or a target market with no strong competitors and with a limited number of potential customers that is large by incapacity. The venture capitalists usually do not like to fund start-ups with "me-too" products.
3. *Nature of the product.* The start-up should be offering a product with significant performance improvements.
4. *Technology development.* Because the venture capital funds in the early stages flow into technology development, the start-up should have a well-articulated defensible technology plan consistent with its market needs.[7]

Suffice to say, the venture capitalist tries to attenuate the adverse selection and moral hazard problems through initial scrutiny, terms of agreement, and monitoring mechanisms that are placed in the continual evaluation of the start-up.

In summary, raising the necessary funds for a start-up is a significant challenge faced by many entrepreneurs, as evidenced by the case of DreamWorks. Indeed, the entrepreneurs will have to look for different sources of funding at different stages of the start-up. Infusion of venture capital funds into the start-up will require the entrepreneur to accommodate the interest of the capital providers.

FINANCIAL PROJECTS IN LARGE FIRMS

The challenges of financing a technology project in a large firm are different from those for a start-up in three major ways:

1. The technology development projects are carried out in several different parts of the organization: central research laboratory, corporate R&D unit, and divisional R&D department.
2. Each unit will have a portfolio of projects as opposed to a single project, as we described in our discussion of modern-day projects.

3. The raising of finances for the firm from outside is usually mounted from the finance department, rather than from the technology groups. The decisions about debt, raising equity in public markets, and negotiations with strategic alliance partners will usually involve the representatives from the finance department, who have the expertise in valuation of projects, and financing related issues.

Invariably, the financing of technology projects in large firms is tied up with its budgeting process. In our discussion of project evaluation, we have underscored the tendencies of the typical budgeting process to drive out innovation. Indeed, the emergence of option pricing models is a response to the need to protect innovation from the dysfunctional pressures of the typical budgeting processes. Nonetheless, the responsibility for maintaining the innovativeness of a firm, to a large extent, will hinge on the success of technology managers in influencing the flow of funds to appropriate technology projects.

MARKET SIGNALING

Market signaling refers to the process by which managers communicate various aspects of the firm and its performance to outside investors, primarily in public markets. In matters pertaining to technology, signaling becomes a major mechanism by which managers can provide credible, economically relevant information to outside investors in determining the value of the firm and the projects the firm is undertaking. This is so for two reasons:

1. The time lag between the investment in technology and the realization of the benefits is generally unknown and often long, increasing the uncertainty about the value.
2. The managers inside the firm typically are likely to know more about the technology projects they are undertaking than outside investors.

Regulations governing the disclosure of technology are confined to R&D expenditure, and therefore much of the signaling is within the discretion of the managers.

Available evidence suggests that investors value positively information obtained during signaling, even though it is not mandated by regulations:

- New product announcements by firms typically enhance the value of the firm by 3 percent, thus suggesting that investors welcome those announcements.
- When information is available, investors distinguish projects in different stages of the R&D process, such as initiation and commercialization, rewarding in particular maturing R&D projects that are close to commercialization.
- In announcement of strategic alliances, it is typically the firm that brings technology to the table that gains in terms of the capital market responses.

It was widely believed in the 1980s and the early 1990s that investors were obsessed with quarterly earnings. As a result of this belief, many U.S. managers routinely sacrificed the long-term profitable growth of their firms by curtailing investments such as R&D with long payouts but focused instead on the projects that yielded immediate payoffs.

However, the evidence indicates specifically that capital markets consider appropriate investments in technology to be a significant value-increasing activity. Thus, for example, a number of event studies register a significantly positive investor reaction to corporate announcements of new technology initiatives, particularly to firms belonging to the high technology sector operating on the cutting edge of technology. Evidence of investors' positive reaction to R&D increases, despite the negative effect of such increases on their short-term earnings, largely dispel the allegations of investor myopia with respect to R&D.

INFLUENCE OF ENVIRONMENTAL TRENDS

The three environmental trends—globalization, time compression, and technology innovation—are influencing the sources of financing used for technology projects. Refer to Figure 15.5. In reference to the sources of financing a technology project, private equity markets are increasingly becoming global, and flows of funds transcend national boundaries. As a result of time compression, the capital providers are increasingly impatient; this has, in turn, increased the move towards collaborative arrangements as a mechanism of financing and executing technology projects. Finally, the potential for technology integration is putting divisions together within a large company to find methods of collaborating, as well as a heightened interest in collaborative arrangements with outsiders for speedy execution of the projects.

Perhaps, the most dramatic development over the past two decades has been the global growth of venture capital. Prior to 1980, venture capital was virtually nonexistent outside the United States. By 1990, the global venture capital market had grown to over $80 billion. In 1988, Europe and the United Kingdom exceeded, for the first time ever, the total amount of capital raised by venture capital funds in the United States ($4.1 billion versus $2.95 billion). Even more astonishing in 1989, $6.28 billion of new capital flowed into Europe in venture capital pools, while U.S. commitments continued to decline. Further, the total venture capital pool in Europe was rapidly approaching the size of the U.S. pool: $34.8 billion versus $33.4 billion. Canada, Australia, and a host of other countries in Asia, South America, and Africa have created substantial venture

FIGURE 15.5 ENVIRONMENTAL TRENDS AND FINANCIAL CONSIDERATIONS

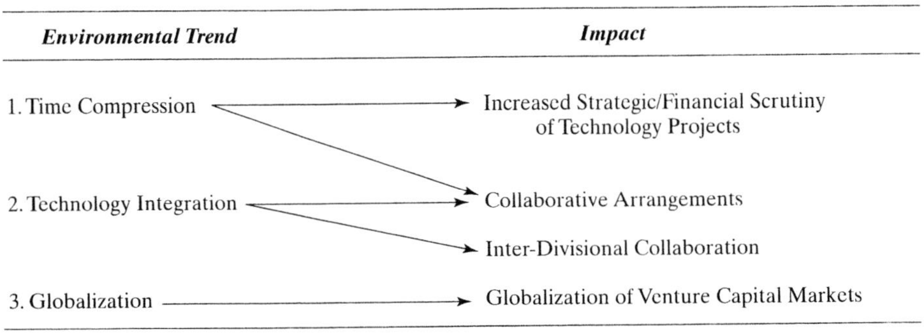

Environmental Trend	*Impact*
1. Time Compression	Increased Strategic/Financial Scrutiny of Technology Projects
2. Technology Integration	Collaborative Arrangements
	Inter-Divisional Collaboration
3. Globalization	Globalization of Venture Capital Markets

capital industries. The former Soviets have great interest in how American ventu
capital industry works.[8] Thus, in recent years the entrepreneurs have had the potent
of accessing global venture capital funds.

MANAGERIAL IMPLICATIONS

Technology managers have a significant role in the financial aspects of technology ma
agement. We can discuss the role that should played by the technology managers at tw
levels: (1) project and (2) the chief technology officer.

PROJECT LEVEL

The success in obtaining funds for a specific project within a firm often depends on tw
separate individuals: champion and sponsor.

> The *project champion* is an individual who makes a decisive contribution
> to the project by actively and enthusiastically promoting its progress through
> critical stages.
> The *project sponsor* refers to an individual, often a senior executive, in en-
> suring adequate funds and resources flow to the project and the organiza-
> tional barriers preventing the accomplishment of the project are removed
> during execution.

Different individuals may play these roles in different firms.

- In a small firm, the technological entrepreneur plays the dual role of sponsor and champion.
- In a medium-sized single industry firm, however, different individuals typically play the role of the champion and sponsor.
- In a large firm, the sponsor is away from technical details of the project but
  plays the role of a catalyst or devil's advocate. He or she expects that techni-
  cians will develop the best solutions to technical problems. However, the
  sponsor typically intervenes in ensuring the flow of funds to the project and
  making sure that the barriers to the execution of a project are removed.
- In still larger, diversified corporations, the process changes further. Here,
  in addition to product champions a number of project sponsors emerge. A
  single sponsor cannot deal with the complexities of very different businesses
  which the firm has diversified.

An illustration of these roles is provided in Box 15.7 from the experience of Pilkingto
Brothers. In Table 15.3, we have sketched the differences in the roles of champion an
sponsor in different types of organizations.[9]

CHIEF TECHNOLOGY OFFICER

Many corporations have a portfolio of projects for technology appropriation or deplo
ment in new products. Because the details of the projects usually evolve over time, th
funding for technology projects is mixed with the annual or periodic budgeting cycl

<table>
<tr><td colspan="2" align="center">**BOX 15.7**</td></tr>
</table>

PILKINGTON BROTHERS

In the development of the float glass process at Pilkington Brothers, an integrated British glass manufacturer, the technological championing was performed by Alister Pilkington, a distant relative of the founding family. Alister conceived a radically new way of making plate glass one evening while he was washing the family dishes. Developing the process was a big financial gamble for the Pilkington Brothers. However, Harry Pilkington, Chairman of the Board, absorbed the risk of the young Alister's innovation and made it possible for the company later to reap $250 million in licensing fees from its competitors. The Pilkington story is a classic example of the sponsor and the champion working in unison—the simplest entrepreneurial network.

Source: From Maidrique, M. A. "Entrepreneurs, Champions, and Technological Innovation," *Sloan Management Review,* pp. 51–76.

performed in an organization. During the annual budgeting cycle, in which the finance department plays a significant role, the chief technology officer becomes the primary champion of the technology portfolio. To effectively execute this role, the CTO will need to maintain communication on an ongoing basis with the finance department regarding the emerging details of the various projects, as well as the portfolio of technology projects under consideration by the firm. In this process, the CTO becomes the arbiter of the objectives of the corporation during the technology portfolio decisions.

Although there are many ways of maintaining communication between the technology sector and the finance sector, one of the innovations to emerge in the last decade is the concept of a *technical walk-through.* In the opening vignette in chapter 1, we illustrated how Marty Kaplan, Sprint's CTO pioneered technical walk through in his organization. A technical walk-through is a process where the originator of the technology project presents his or her case to the finance group and everyone else who is involved.

TABLE 15.3   Role of Project Champion and Sponsor

Type of Firm	*Champion*	*Sponsor*
1. Small Firm	← Entrepreneur →	
2. Medium-Sized Single Industry Firm	Scientists/ Marketing	R&D Manager CTO or CEO
3. Large Firm	Scientists/ Marketing	A senior manager, usually removed from technical details
4. Diversified Firm		
a. Divisional-Level Projects	Scientists/ Marketing	Many sponsors depending on the number of divisions
b. Inter-Divisional Projects	Corporate R&D Group Presidents	Senior level managers including CEO

Usually orchestrated by the CTO, a technical walk-through facilitates communicati
between technology managers and financial analysts.

❖ CHAPTER SUMMARY

Financial considerations are important in management of technology. Investors v
finance technology endeavors only when they are convinced that it is in their se
interest. Four major financial considerations are project valuation, intellectual capi
financing, and market signaling.

All technology projects evolve over a number of stages, from initiation to comp
tion to operations or commercialization. By life cycle of a project, we mean all the
tivities sequenced over time from the beginning till operations or commercializati
that need to be performed for the completion of the project. The funds required fo
project are small in the beginning during the planning phase and are highest during
implementation stage. Project valuation refers to the activities involved in estimat
the economic worth of a project or a start-up.

A majority of large U.S. companies use net present value or internal rate of ret
in their formal capital budgeting systems. The assumptions underlying the discount
cash flow method are more or less valid in technology decisions where both the te
nology and the market are relatively mature. However, when either technology or
market is in the early stages of development, the assumptions behind the discount
cash flows are seriously violated. As a result, many progressive firms augment tra
tional discounted flow methods with alternative approaches, such as option pricing
valuing early stage projects.

Because technology includes tacit knowledge, i.e., knowledge that is not embod
as physical assets, in many high-technology firms the intellectual capital may econor
cally be far more significant than the physical assets. Although intuitively appeali
the notion of intellectual capital raises significant challenges in its measurement a
estimation.

Two fundamental challenges are involved in financing technology projects: adve
selection and moral hazard. The challenges of moral hazard and adverse selection
particularly acute in the case of start-up firms that have to look outside for financ
their venture. As a result, the activities during the various stages of a start-up are
nanced from different sources of funds. As external sources of financing are injec
into the operations of the company, the outside shareholders may increasingly dema
a voice in the running of the company. Sometimes, the objectives of the private equ
provider may diverge from the objectives of the entrepreneur; in this case, the confli
between the two are highly likely. The venture capital process involves an intense co
pany scrutiny by the venture capital providers of the business plan, management tea
and the request for funds. The venture capitalist tries to attenuate the adverse select
and moral hazard problems through initial scrutiny, terms of agreement, and monit
ing mechanisms that are placed in the continual evaluation of the start-up.

The financing of technology projects in large firms is tied with the budget
process. Nonetheless, the responsibility for maintaining the innovativeness of a firm
a large extent, will hinge on the success of technology managers in influencing the fl
of funds to appropriate projects. In matters pertaining to technology, signaling becon
a major mechanism by which managers in large firms can provide credible, econor

cally relevant information to outside investors in determining the value of the firm and the projects the firm is undertaking.

The three environmental trends—globalization, time compression, and technology innovation—are influencing the sources of financing used for technology projects. Perhaps the most dramatic development over the past 2 decades has been the global growth of venture capital.

❖ NOTES

1. "Company taking ultralight planes into the 21st century," *KTECnology,* September/October 1998, Issue 28, p. 5. Reprinted by permission.

2. Brealey, R. A. and S. C. Myers. *Principals of Corporate Finance.* New York: McGraw Hill, 1995.

3. Kaplan, Robert. "Must CIM be justified by faith alone?" *Harvard Business Review,* Vol. 64 (1986), pp. 87–93, as paraphrased in Grenadienr, Stephen R. and Allen M Weiss. "Investment in Technological Innovations: An Option Pricing Approach," April 19, 1995.

4. Dixit, Avinash K. and Robert M. Pindyck. "The Options Approach to Capital Investment," *Harvard Business Review,* May/June 1995, pp. 105–130.

5. Fenn, G. W., N. Liang, and S. Prowse. "The Economics of Private Equity," Board of Governors of the Federal Reserve System, Washington, D.C., 1995

6. Pinches, George. Private Communication, June 16, 1999.

7. Roure, J. B. and M. A. Maidique. "Linking Prefunding Factors and High Technology Ventures Success: An Exploratory Study," in Burgelman, Robert, and Maidique, M.A. *Strategic Management of Technology and Innovation,* Chicago: Irwin, 1988.

8. Bygrave, W. D. and J. A. Timmons. *Venture Capital at the Crossroads.* Boston, MA: Harvard Business School Press, 1992, p. 44.

9. Maidique, Modesto A. "Entrepreneur's, Champions, and Technological Innovation," *Sloan Management Review,* Winter 1980, pp. 59–76.